THE ROMAN BATHS AND
MACELLUM AT WROXETER

Excavations by Graham Webster
1955–85

THE ROMAN BATHS AND *MACELLUM* AT WROXETER

Excavations by Graham Webster
1955–85

compiled and edited by Peter Ellis

with contributions by
F W Anderson, Justine Bayley, Gillian Braithwaite,
Richard Brickstock, John Casey, HEM Cool, Geoffrey Dannell,
Margaret Darling, Brenda Dickinson, Peter Ellis, Jane Evans, Jane Faiers,
Kay Hartley, Martin Henig, Michael Heyworth, Helen Hughes,
Nigel Jeffries, Barry Knight, Glenys Lloyd-Morgan, Fiona Macalister,
Donald Mackreth, Simon Mays, Beverly Meddens, Graham Morgan,
Quita Mould, Barbara Noddle, Grace Simpson, Andrew Smith,
Jane Timby, Graham Webster, Roger White, and David Williams

illustrations by
Heather Bird, Diana Bonakis, Mark Breedon,
Nigel Dodds, and Donald Mackreth

ENGLISH HERITAGE

2000

ARCHAEOLOGICAL REPORT 9

THE ROMAN BATHS AND *MACELLUM* AT WROXETER

Excavations by Graham Webster
1955–85

compiled and edited by Peter Ellis

with contributions by
F W Anderson, Justine Bayley, Gillian Braithwaite,
Richard Brickstock, John Casey, HEM Cool, Geoffrey Dannell,
Margaret Darling, Brenda Dickinson, Peter Ellis, Jane Evans, Jane Faiers,
Kay Hartley, Martin Henig, Michael Heyworth, Helen Hughes,
Nigel Jeffries, Barry Knight, Glenys Lloyd-Morgan, Fiona Macalister,
Donald Mackreth, Simon Mays, Beverly Meddens, Graham Morgan,
Quita Mould, Barbara Noddle, Grace Simpson, Andrew Smith,
Jane Timby, Graham Webster, Roger White, and David Williams

illustrations by
Heather Bird, Diana Bonakis, Mark Breedon,
Nigel Dodds, and Donald Mackreth

ENGLISH HERITAGE
2000
ARCHAEOLOGICAL REPORT 9

Copyright © English Heritage 2000

First published 2000 by
English Heritage, 23 Savile Row, London W1X 1AB

Printed by Snoeck-Ducaju & Zoon, Ghent

ISBN 1 85074 606 0
Product code XC10849

Editor: Blaise Vyner
Layout design: Multiplex Techniques Ltd
Print Production Manager: Richard Jones, Publications and Design, English Heritage
Brought to press by Dr Karen Dorn
and Andrew McLaren, Publications and Design, English Heritage

Contents

Illustrations

Tables

Acknowledgements

Dr Graham Webster's acknowledgements in the military volume apply to the excavations as a whole. The grateful thanks recorded there to all the volunteers, excavators, and supervisors who worked on the Training School excavations over so many years are repeated here.

The Society of Antiquaries are gratefully thanked for permission to reproduce the drawing from George Fox's notebooks. Jane Timby would like to thank Sally Exon, James Dinn, and Michael Faiers for working on and supplying computer data.

With regard to his report on the *insula* buildings, Donald Mackreth is grateful to Peter Ellis, Roger White, Christine Mackreth, Graham Webster, and John Peter Wild for their valuable comments. With regard to his brooch report, Donald Mackreth is grateful to Mr B Bennison of Rowley's House Museum for sending him the High Ercall brooch similar to no 26.

Peter Ellis would like to thank Dr Graham Webster for his help with many aspects of this report. Thanks are due to Donald Mackreth, Jane Timby, and Roger White for discussions and correspondence on many details; to Cameron Moffett and Jennifer Hall for their initial post-excavation work, and help with the finds; to Heather Bird for the site illustrations, and for replanning certain areas; to Dr Sara Lunt and Glynis Edwards for facilitating access to the finds; to Graham Norrie for the preparation of the photographs; to all the specialist contributors for their comments; to the report editor, Blaise Vyner; to Dr Ellen McAdam, Dr Karen Dorn and English Heritage Publications and Design staff; and to colleagues at Birmingham University Field Archaeology Unit. Paul Bidwell usefully commented on the text and John Wacher is also thanked for his comments. Gill Andrews, the project monitor for English Heritage, played an essential part in the success of the project from the initial assessment stages through to completion.

Summary

The Roman town of Wroxeter is sited on the east bank of the River Severn in Shropshire. The area occupied by the town has remained a green field site since the end of its Roman and sub-Roman occupation. Archaeological excavations began in the nineteenth century and have been largely concentrated on *insula* 5 where the baths, the baths basilical hall, and *macellum* were sited, and where a large block of masonry, the Old Work, survives. This report describes the results from excavations undertaken between 1955 and 1985 on the southern part of the *insula*, the site of the baths and *macellum*, and includes an edition of the nineteenth-century excavations compiled from a number of different sources. The excavations also revealed well-preserved remains of a Roman fortress lying beneath the town; this evidence is described in a separate volume.

Timber-framed buildings were constructed *c* AD 90 based on the footings of a military building. These fronted Watling Street, the main thoroughfare through the early town, and may have been shops with dwelling quarters to their rear. The buildings were replaced once in the same position and work seems to have started on a further renewal on a slightly different frontage but was not completed.

The *insula* was then given over to public buildings. The work is assumed to have been carried out in tandem with the construction of the forum on an adjacent *insula* which was dedicated AD 129/30. However the evidence suggests that the buildings were not completed until a generation later. The main building on the site, the baths, ran south from the basilical hall. The *frigidarium* was divided from the *tepidarium* by two small rooms, perhaps used for applying oil to the bathers, with the *caldarium* beyond. Two rooms on either side of the baths housed *laconica*. The main walls of *tepidarium* and *caldarium* were doubled in width by the construction of an additional wall after building work had started. The layout of barrel-vaulted roofs can be restored. At a date in the later third century a second *caldarium* was added to the baths connected via the western *laconicum* which was converted into a *tepidarium*. The *praefurnia* of the side suites were abandoned and rebuilt. After the baths fell into disuse, the *frigidarium* continued in use into the post-Roman period, becoming in all probability a church which was later, in the medieval and post-medieval periods, used for farm storage, the reason for the survival of the Old Work. To its north, post-Roman use of the basilical hall area is described in a separate volume.

In the baths *palaestra*, a *natatio* was originally built but abandoned early in the third century and infilled with rubbish including butchered animal bone waste from the *macellum*. The *palaestra* was subsequently the site of the additional *caldarium*, but a porticoed walkway was maintained and allowed continued access from the *macellum* and street to the basilical hall. The area on the other side of the baths was regularly resurfaced throughout the Roman period; water supply features were incorporated in its courtyards.

On the Watling Street frontage a range of buildings comprised a *macellum* separated by an access corridor from two large rooms presumably used for offices and perhaps later for *tabernae*. A latrine was built to their rear. The excavations examined the *macellum* and the latrine. The main drain for the baths ran beneath the range and there was some evidence that originally the *macellum* was not part of the plan. However it was built at the same time as the drain which ran beneath its east side and serviced a small latrine in a corner of the building. The *macellum* was a rectangular structure with a central courtyard and portico, and with shops on three sides. The floor surfaces, as with others in the west range, had been raised by 1m above the street levels. At the end of the third century the courtyard porticos were refloored and the stylobate sleeper walls reconstructed. Similar flooring in the main latrine and in the baths indicates an *insula*-wide campaign of repair which may have included the building of the added *caldarium*.

Street porticos located on the west and south side of the *insula* were examined in detail. The initial building campaign raised their levels but no evidence of the treatment of the surfaces was found. In the first half of the third century, a number of pits were dug into the porticos and filled with animal bone waste similar to that found in the infilled *natatio*. Later in the century the porticos were floored with a compact gravel surface, and this was maintained and refurbished through to the later fourth century. Heavily worn areas then indicate a change in use of the porticos with some evidence of structures beneath the roof. The portico stylobate sleeper wall was robbed and the roof presumably removed at a date after that indicated by late fourth-century coins. Subsequently the area alongside Watling Street remained in use with paths running towards the *macellum* doorways and the corridor through to the baths. The porticos were thus the site of markets and market stalls from the earliest civilian buildings until after the end of the Roman period. The published excavations in the basilical hall have demonstrated a long and important sequence of post-Roman activity to which this evidence can be added.

Finds from the excavations derive mainly from the initial building campaign although there are significant third-century groups of pottery from the portico pits and the infilled *natatio*, in addition to the animal bone assemblages which indicate the specialised butchery undertaken in the *macellum* and the nearby porticos.

Although explored and cleared in the nineteenth century the excavations of the baths and *macellum* allow the construction sequence to be unravelled and later developments to be examined in detail particularly in the porticos. Civilian baths in Britain that can be examined as a whole are rare. The *macellum* too is a rarity in the Province and there have been few detailed excavations of *macellum* sites in the Empire. The building can be seen as the focus of a street market which functioned through at least three centuries.

Résumé

La ville romaine de Wroxeter est située sur la rive Est du fleuve Severn en Shropshire. L'espace occupé par la ville est resté un site agreste depuis la fin de son occupation romaine et post-romaine. Les fouilles archéologiques commencèrent au dix-neuvième siècle et furent concentrées essentiellement sur l'*insula* 5 où se trouvaient les thermes, la salle basilicale des thermes, et le *macellum*, où survit encore un grand bloc de maçonnerie, appelé aujourd'hui "the Old Work". Ce rapport décrit les résultats de fouilles entreprises entre 1955 et 1985 sur la partie Sud de l'*insula*, le site des thermes et du *macellum*. Il y est inclut aussi une édition des fouilles du dix-neuvième siècle compilée à partir de plusieurs sources différentes. Les fouilles révélèrent aussi les vestiges bien conservés d'une forteresse romaine enterrée sous la ville, dont les détails peuvent être trouvés dans un volume séparé.

Des bâtiments en bois d'oeuvre furent construits vers 90 apr. J.-C. utilisant la base d'un bâtiment militaire. Ceux-ci donnaient sur la fameuse route appelée "Watling Street", qui était le passage principal à travers la ville initiale. Ces bâtiments étaient peut-être des magasins, avec des quartiers d'habitation à l'arrière. Les bâtiments furent remplacés une fois dans leur même position et d'autres travaux de renouvellement semblent avoir été commencés sur une façade légèrement différente mais ils ne furent pas complétés.

L'insula fut alors affectée aux bâtiments publics. Il semblerait que les travaux aient été accomplis en tandem avec la construction du forum sur un îlot adjacent consacré en 129/ 30 apr. J.-C.. Cependant les évidences suggèrent que les bâtiments ne furent pas complétés avant la prochaine génération. Le bâtiment principal sur le site- les thermes, courait au Sud de la salle basilicale. Le *frigidarium* était séparé du *tepidarium* par deux petites pièces, qui étaient utilisées peut-être pour l'application de l'huile aux baigneurs, avec le *caldarium* au-delà. Deux pièces de part et d'autre des bains hébergeaient les *laconica*. Les murs principaux des *tepidarium* et *caldarium* étaient doublés en largeur par la construction d'un mur supplémentaire, bâti après que les travaux aient été commencés. L'agencement de toits à voûtes en berceau peut être restaurés. Plus tard à la fin du troisième siècle, un second *caldarium* fut ajouté aux thermes relié par le *laconicum* occidental, lui-même converti en tepidarium. Les *praefurnia* des salles adjacentes furent abandonnées et rebâties. Après que les thermes tombèrent en désuétude, le *frigidarium* continua d'opérer jusqu'après la période romaine, devenant selon toute probabilité une église qui fut elle-même par la suite, à l'époque médiévale et post-médiévale, employées pour l'entreposage de ferme. Cette utilisation de l'édifice à travers le temps a ainsi permis la survie du "Old Work". Au Nord de ce dernier, l'utilisation du site de la salle basilicale après la période romaine est décrite dans un volume séparé.

Dans la palestre, un *natatio* avait été bâti à l'origine mais il fut abandonné tôt durant le troisième siècle et remblayé avec des ordures parmi lesquelles des déchets d'os d'animaux de boucherie provenant du *macellum*. La palestre, devint depuis le site du *caldarium* supplémentaire, mais un passage-portique fut gardé, permittant ainsi de continuer l'accès à partir du *macellum* ou de la rue vers la salle basilicale. La suface de l'autre côté des thermes fut régulièrement refaite à travers la période romaine et des systèmes d'approvisionnement d'eau furent incorporés dans leurs cours.

Donnant sur la voie principale- la "Watling Street", une rangée de bâtiments comprenait un *macellum* séparé de deux grandes pièces par un couloir d'accès. Ces pièces étaient probablement utilisées comme bureaux et peut-être ultérieurement comme *tabernae*. Des latrines furent bâties à l'arrière. Les fouilles examinèrent le *macellum* et les latrines. L'égout principal pour les thermes courait au-dessous de la rangée de bâtiments et il semblerait qu'à l'origine le *macellum* n'ait pas fait partie du plan. Cependant il fut bâti en même temps que l'égout qui courait au-dessous de son côté Est, desservant des petites latrines dans un coin du bâtiment. Le *macellum* était un édifice rectangulaire avec une cour centrale et un portique, ainsi que des magasins sur trois côtés. Ses sols, ainsi que ceux d'autres bâtiments dans la rangée Ouest, avaient été élevés d'1 m. au-dessus de ceux de la ville primitive. À la fin du troisième siècle les sols des portiques de la cour furent refaits et les solins en muret des stylobates reconstruits. Des sols similaires dans les latrines principales et dans les thermes indiquent une campagne de réparation à travers toute l'*insula*, qui peut-être incluait aussi le bâtiment rajouté du *caldarium*.

Les portiques de la rue situés sur les côtés Sud et Ouest de l'*insula* furent examinés en détail. La campagne initiale de construction éleva leurs niveaux mais aucunes évidences du traitement des sols ne furent retrouvées. Pendant la première moitié du troisième siècle, des fosses furent creusées dans les portiques et remblayées avec des déchets d'os d'animaux similaires à ceux trouvés dans le *natatio* rebouché. Par la suite au même siècle, on fit les sols des portiques avec du gravier compacté, et ceux-ci furent entretenus et remis à neuf jusqu'à la fin du quatrième siècle. Des endroits énormément usés indiquent alors un changement d'utilisation des portiques, comme certaines évidences de structures au-dessous du toit. Le solin en muret des stylobates du portique fut pillé et le toit probablement enlevé. Des monnaies du quatrième siècle tardif indiquèrent la dates de ces changements. Ultérieurement l'espace le long de "Watling Street" resta utilisé avec des allées menant aux portes du *macellum* et au couloir qui conduisait aux thermes. Ainsi les portiques furent le site d'un marché et d'éventaires dès l'apparition des premiers bâtiments civils jusqu'après la fin de la période romaine. La publication des fouilles de la salle basilicale a démontré une suite importante et longue d'activités post-romaines auxquelles ces évidences peuvent être rajoutées.

Les matériaux trouvés sur les fouilles proviennent principalement de la campagne de construction initiale. Toutefois il existe d'importants groupes de poterie du troisième siècle trouvés dans les fosses du portique et dans le remblai du *natatio*. De plus les assemblages d'os d'animaux indiquent la boucherie spécialisée entreprise dans le *macellum* et les portiques proches.

Bien qu'explorées et dégagées au dix-neuvième siècle les fouilles des thermes et du *macellum* permirent de révéler la succession de construction et d'examiner en détail les développements ultérieurs, particulièrement dans les portiques. Les thermes publiques en Grande Bretagne qui peuvent être examinés en entiers sont rares. Dans la Province, le *macellum* aussi est une rareté en lui-même et il existe peu de fouilles détaillées de sites de *macellum* dans l'Empire. L'édifice peut être vu comme le centre d'un marché qui fonctionna pendant au moins trois siècles.

Traduction: Agnés Shepherd

Zusammenfassung

Die römische Stadt Wroxeter liegt am Ostufer des Flusses Severn in Shropshire. Das von der Stadt eingenommene Gebiet ist seit dem Ende der römischen und subrömischen Besiedlung ein grünes Feld geblieben. Archäologische Ausgrabungen begannen im 19. Jahrhundert und haben sich größtenteils auf die Insula 5 konzentriert, wo sich die Thermen, die Basilika der Thermen und das *Macellum* befanden, und wo ein großer Block Mauerwerk, das 'Alte Werk' (Old Work), erhalten blieb. Dieser Bericht beschreibt die Ergebnisse von Ausgrabungen, die zwischen 1955 und 1985 im südlichen Teil der *Insula*, dem Bereich der Thermen und des *Macellums* durchgeführt wurden; die Ausgrabungsergebnisse aus dem 19. Jahrhundert, die aus unterschiedlichen Quellen zusammengetragen wurden, werden mitvorgelegt. Die von den Ausgrabungen ebenfalls freigelegten gut erhaltenen Überreste einer römischen Festung unterhalb der Stadt werden in einem separaten Band beschrieben.

Etwa im Jahr 90 n. Chr. wurden auf den Sockeln eines militärischen Gebäudes Fachwerkgebäude errichtet. Diese lagen mit der Vorderseite der Watling Street zugewandt, dem Hauptdurchgangsweg durch die frühe Stadt, und mögen Läden mit dahinterliegenden Unterkünften gewesen sein. Die Gebäude wurden in derselben Lage einmal erneuert, und Arbeiten an einer weiteren Erneuerung, mit einer etwas anderen Straßenfront, scheinen begonnen worden zu sein, wurden aber nicht vollendet.

Später wurde die *Insula* einer Nutzung durch öffentliche Gebäude zugefürt. Die Arbeiten wurden vermutlich parallel zum Bau des 129/30 n. Chr.

eingeweihten Forums in der angrenzenden *Insula* durchgeführt. Die Befunde lassen jedoch vermuten, daß die Gebäude erst eine Generation später vollendet wurden. Das Hauptgebäude an diesem Platz waren die Thermen, die sich südlich der Basilika erstreckten. Das *Frigidarium* war vom *Tepidarium* durch zwei kleine Räume getrennt, die vielleicht zum Einölen der Badenden genutzt wurden; das *Caldarium* schloß sich an sie an. Zwei Räume auf beiden Seiten der Thermen beherbergten *Laconica*. Nach Baubeginn wurden die Hauptwände von *Tepidarium* und *Caldarium* durch die Errichtung einer zusätzlichen Wand in ihrer Breite verdoppelt. Die Anordnung des Tonnengewölbes läßt sich rekonstruieren. Zu einem bestimmten Zeitpunkt während des späten dritten Jahrhunderts wurde ein zweites *Caldarium* zu den Thermen hinzugefügt und mit ihnen durch das westliche *Laconicum* verbunden, das in ein *Tepidarium* umgewandelt wurde. Die *Praefurnia* der Seitenräume wurden aufgegeben und neu gebaut. Nachdem die Thermen unbrauchbar geworden waren, wurde das *Frigidarium* bis in nachrömische Zeit weitergenutzt und zwar aller Wahrscheinlichkeit nach als Kirche, die später, in mittelalterlichen und nachmittelalterlichen Perioden als Speicher einer Farm diente–wodurch das Alte Werk erhalten blieb. Die nachrömische Nutzung des sich nördlich anschließenden Gebietes der Basilika wird in einem separaten Band beschrieben.

In der *Palaestra* der Thermen war ursprünglich eine *Natatio* gebaut worden, doch wurde sie früh im dritten Jahrhundert aufgegeben und mit Abfall zugefüllt, worunter sich auch Knochenreste geschlachteter Tiere aus dem *Macellum* befanden. Die *Palaestra* war später die Stelle des zusätzlichen *Caldariums*, aber ein beibehaltener Säulengang erlaubte weiterhin Zugang zur Basilika vom *Macellum* und der Straße. Das Gebiet auf der anderen Seite der Thermen wurde in römischer Zeit regelmässig neu belegt; in die dortigen Höfe wurden Wasserversorgungselemente eingebaut.

Eine Gebäudereihe entlang der Watling Street enthielt ein *Macellum*, das durch einen Zugangskorridor von zwei großen Räumen getrennt war, die vermutlich als Büros und vielleicht später als *Tabernae* genutzt wurden. Nach hinten hin schloß sich eine Latrine an. Die Ausgrabungen untersuchten das *Macellum* und die Latrine. Die Hauptkanalisation der Thermen verlief unter dieser Gebäudereihe und es gibt einige Anhaltspunkte dafür, daß das *Macellum* ursprünglich nicht Teil des Gesamtplanes war. Es wurde jedoch zur gleichen Zeit gebaut wie die Kanalisation, die unter seiner Ostseite verlief und eine kleine Latrine in einer Ecke des Gebäudes bediente. Das *Macellum* war ein rechteckiges Gebäude mit einem zentralen Hof und Säulengang sowie mit Läden an drei Seiten. Die Bodenniveaus waren–wie dies auch mit anderen in der Westreihe geschehen war–um 1 m über diejenigen der frühen Stadt angehoben worden. Am Ende des dritten Jahrhunderts wurden die Säulengänge im Hof mit neuen Fußböden versehen und die Stylobatmauern erneuert. Ähnliche Fußböden in der Hauptlatrine und in den Thermen zeugen von einer die gesamte *Insula* umfassende Reparaturkampagne, die auch den Bau des zusätzlichen *Caldariums* miteingeschlossen haben mag.

Die Säulengänge zur Straße hin, die an der westlichen und südlichen Seite der *Insula* lagen, wurden im Detail untersucht. Während der ersten Baukampagne wurden ihre Niveaus angehoben, doch Hinweise auf die Behandlung der Oberflächen wurden nicht gefunden. In der ersten Häfte des dritten Jahrhunderts wurde in den Säulengängen eine Anzahl von Gruben eingetieft und mit Tierknochenabfall gefüllt, das dem in der zugefüllten *Natatio* gefundenen ähnelt. Später im gleichen

Jahrhundert wurden die Böden der Säulengänge mit einer kompakten Kiesoberfläche versehen, die bis in das späte vierte Jahrhundert instandgehalten wurde. Danach weisen stark abgenutzte Gebiete auf einen Wandel des Gebrauchs der Säulengänge hin, und es gibt Hinweise auf Strukturen unter dem Dach. Zu einem späteren Zeitpunkt, der durch Münzen des späten vierten Jahrhunderts definiert ist, wurden die Stylobatmauer des Säulengangs geraubt sowie vermutlich das Dach entfernt. Das Gebiet entlang Watling Street blieb anschließend in Gebrauch und auf die Eingänge des *Macellums* und den Korridor, der zu den Thermen führte, verliefen Wege hin. Die Säulengänge waren somit von der Zeit der frühesten zivilen Gebäude bis nach dem Ende der römischen Zeit ein Platz für Märkte und Marktstände. Die publizierten Ausgrabungen in der Basilika haben eine lange und wichtige Abfolge nachrömischer Aktivität nachgewiesen, zu der diese Befunde hinzugefügt werden können.

Funde von den Ausgrabungen stammen hauptsächlich aus der ersten Baukampagne, obwohl es wichtige Gruppen von Keramikfunden des dritten Jahrhunderts aus den Gruben der Säulengänge und dem zugefüllten *Natatio* gibt sowie die Tierknochenkollektionen, die nahelegen, daß im *Macellum* und in den benachbarten Säulengängen spezialisiertes Schlachten vonstatten ging.

Obwohl das Gebiet im 19. Jahrhundert sondiert und freigeräumt wurde, erlauben es die Ausgrabungen der Thermen und des *Macellums* die Bauabfolge zu entwirren und spätere Entwicklungen im Detail zu untersuchen, vor allem in den Säulengängen. Zivile Thermen, die als ganze untersucht werden können, sind selten in Großbritannien. Auch das *Macellum* ist eine Seltenheit in der Provinz, und es gibt nur wenige detaillierte Ausgrabungen von *Macellum*-Fundplätzen im Römischen Reich. Das Gebäude kann als Zentrum eines Straßenmarktes betrachtet werden, der über mindestens drei Jahrhunderte hinweg in Betrieb war.

Übersetzung: Cornelius Holtorf

1 Introduction

by Peter Ellis and Roger White

Background to the excavations

The site

Viroconium was the *civitas* capital of the *Cornovii* (Cunliffe 1991, 188; Webster 1991), and one of the more important Roman towns in Britain judging by the size of its forum and, later, the area enclosed by ramparts (Wacher 1995; Millett 1990, fig 59). The town was sited on the east bank of the River Severn (Figs 1.1 and 1.2). The drift geology is fluvio-glacial sands and gravels with pockets of Mercia Mudstone (Keuper Marl) overlying Bridgnorth (Triassic) sandstone (Soil Survey of England and Wales 1:50,000 map for Shrewsbury). Only sand deposits were encountered in the excavations. Two major Roman routes crossed the Severn at Wroxeter, Watling Street running east-west from the Midlands to Central Wales (Margary 1973, 1h and 64), while a north-south route (Margary 6a and 6b) ran down the Welsh Marches from Chester to Caerleon.

There are a number of topographical factors that suggest the location of the town was of importance before the advent of the Roman army. Landscape analysis suggests a pre-Roman field layout with roads focused on a river crossing (Bassett 1990). Aerial photography indicates numerous enclosed farmsteads in the area, thought to be Iron Age in origin (Whimster 1989; Ellis *et al* 1994);and their numbers in the area around Wroxeter indicate a concentration of population and perhaps a pre-Roman focus. The Wrekin hillfort to the east represents a central Cornovian place, and the link between The Wrekin and Wroxeter is emphasised by the transfer of the name from one to the other. Excavation evidence is hampered by the probable non-use of pottery in the area in the Iron Age. However, a ditch-marked enclosure and other ditches have been found predating the legionary fortress (Webster forthcoming). The main enclosure seems likely to be military but the slight ditches may be earlier. All this evidence indicates that Wroxeter was sited in the tribal heartland of the *Cornovii* and suggests the possibility of a pre-existing Iron Age focus yet to be discovered. The layout of the later town *insulae* suggests that the areas of *insulae* 8 and 15 were the focus of a pre-existing settlement sited on the river. Landscape evidence suggests that the original river crossing was at the bend in the Severn west of *insula* 8 as indicated by early road alignments (Bassett 1990, fig 19a).

The immediate precursor of the town was a legionary fortress whose layout had a continuing influence on the plan of *insulae* and streets of the town (Webster 1988b; forthcoming). Its position is known or can be securely predicted as a result of excavation and air photography. The site chosen was on ground sloping gently down towards the Severn.

The evidence suggests that alliances were made with the *Cornovii*, and that conquest by force was not a factor in this area (Cunliffe 1991, 202; Millett 1990, 51; Ellis *et al* 1994, 109), although recent finds of *pilae* on the Wrekin could support the latter explanation (White and Webster 1994). Air photography has demonstrated other military sites, marching camps, and forts, in the plain of the Severn, and these may indicate a concentration of Roman forces prior to the invasion of the

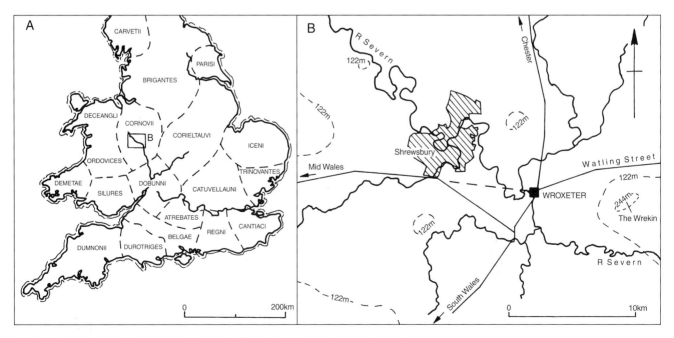

Fig 1.1 Location of Wroxeter, A in south Britain, B in region; scales as shown

1

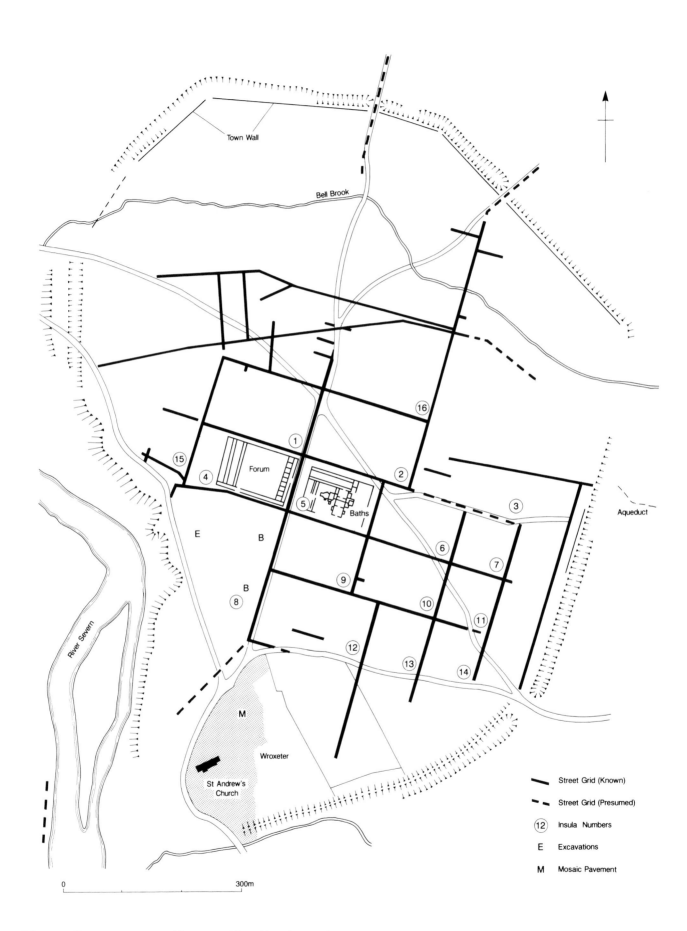

Fig 1.2 The Roman town with street grid and insula *numbers*

Welsh uplands, which lie within sight to the west. The military presence may also be connected with the lead mines of west Shropshire; the mining resources of Britain representing a factor in the Roman conquest.

Air photography has suggested the location of a civilian settlement outside the fortress and this may have remained after the departure of *Legio XX* to its new base at Chester and provided the impetus for the development of the town. The town was enclosed by an earthwork rampart in the second half of the second century or later and the circuit was enlarged in the third to include the valley of the Bell Brook to the north. The forum of the town was dedicated to Hadrian in AD 129 or 130. Its buildings fronting on the main street, Watling St, were destroyed by fire in the second century, and although then rebuilt, apparently went out of use in the later third century (Atkinson 1942). The baths *insula*, the subject of this report, lay on the opposite side of the street.

Insula 5

Insula 5 at Wroxeter was one of a pair known to have been devoted to the public buildings of the Roman town, the forum on *insula* 4 and the baths on *insula* 5 (Fig 1.2). In the following report the *insula* 5 buildings and areas have been numbered (Fig 2.7). The main baths or the second-century baths refers to the north-south running block of *frigidarium*, *tepidarium* and *caldarium*, Rooms 3, 4, 5, and 6, and its lateral Rooms, 8 and 10, in the centre of the *insula*. The basilical hall refers to the exercise hall to its north, Room 1, with which the baths formed a single unit. The standing section of the south wall of the basilical hall and north wall of the *frigidarium* has been known for many years as the Old Work. The basilical hall area is referred to as the *Palaestra* in the report on the excavations undertaken there (Barker *et al* 1997), but this term is not used here. To its south on the west side of the main baths is an added *caldarium* and *praefurnium*, Rooms 12 and 13, built in the third century. This is referred to as the added *caldarium*. On the west side of the *insula* facing the forum across Watling Street was a range of buildings referred to here as the west range. These comprised two Rooms, 17 and 18, with a latrine, Room 20, to the rear divided by a corridor – the baths corridor, 21 – from an enclosed market to the south, 22, referred to here as the *macellum*.

Between the west range and the main baths was the baths *palaestra*, 15, with a small *natatio* or swimming pool, 14. This was later encroached on by the added *caldarium* and the pool was infilled. This area is called the baths courtyard to avoid confusion with the *Palaestra* of the companion volume on the basilical hall. A portico ran on the west, 15W, and north, 15N, sides of the baths courtyard; the courtyard portico. The swimming pool has been referred to as the *piscina* in interim reports, but is here named a *natatio* following the definition proposed by Nielsen (1993, I, 154). East of the main baths was an area, 16, which has been only

partially explored but which is presumed to have been open. In the basilical hall volume this is named the baths precinct and this has been retained in this report. The function of the area may have been as a further exercise yard or *palaestra*, or as a service yard. Finally the *insula* was surrounded by covered walkways on its north, west and south sides and these are referred to as the porticos, and numbered 23N, 23W, and 23S.

The standing buildings and their restoration

Building stone used in the Roman town comprised a red sandstone from the Keele Beds of the Upper Coal measures, a buff sandstone and a grey coarse stone of Hoar Edge Grit, part of the Ordovician system, and a grey-white freestone occasionally with a purple tinge, of Big Flint Rock of the Middle Coal Measures. Large blocks and carved work used a grey or brown-grey sandstone, also Big Flint Rock. A dark coloured carbonaceous limestone, a pale pinkish-white limestone possibly from the Llanymynech hills, and a green-grey micaceous flagstone possibly from Corvedale were used for mosaics and roofing slates. Of these stones the common building stone, Hoar Edge Grit and Keele Beds stone, both occur south of Wroxeter at Hoar Edge and Acton Burnell, 12km and 7km from Wroxeter respectively, while the Big Flint Rock stone used for architectural details would have come from east of Wroxeter in the Ketley area, 15km from Wroxeter. Sources for the principal building stones used at Wroxeter were all sited near Roman roads (Cantrill 1931; White and Ixer 1997).

Photographs of the nineteenth-century excavations show the extent of survival of standing masonry and the loss since they were first unearthed. Apart from the structural analyses outlined below, no comprehensive detailed study of the surviving structures has been made. Much of the stonework has been reinstated over many years and the records made (by the Ministry of Public Buildings and Works and the later Department of the Environment) were inadequate. No proper plan of the *insula* existed until 1990 when an EDM 1:100 plan, the basis of the illustrations in this report, was prepared by Birmingham University Field Archaeology Unit. This, however, records reinstated work.

Some structural work has been undertaken. A detailed study of the *macellum* was made by Donald Mackreth in 1980 (archive E 1.1), and an interpretative study has been published of the Old Work (Webster and Woodfield 1966). Plans of some of the walls were made during the excavations by Webster and Barker, and a photographic survey was made during the 1988/9 excavations.

Consolidation began before the start of the 1955–85 excavations, and the two operations ran in tandem for much of the sixties. Unfortunately, it was not always the case that excavation preceded consolidation

4

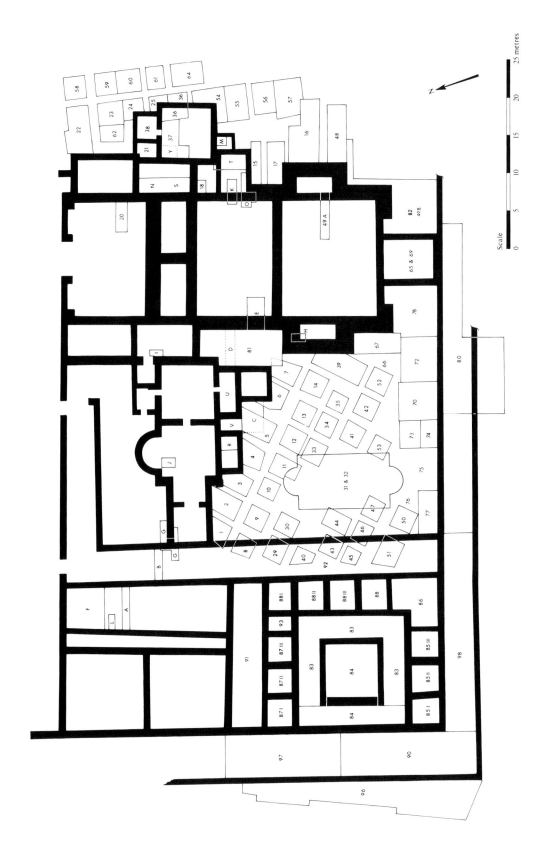

Fig 1.3 Location of 1955–85 excavation boxes; 1:500

of the above-ground remains. Examination of the remains today allows some record to be drawn up of how much was rebuilt. Establishing what has been reconstructed is hampered by the fact that all the walls have been pointed in modern mortar. However, it is possible to suggest rebuilt walls by the replacement of ancient bonding tiles with modern copies. When the latter have been identified at ground level, it has been assumed that the wall has been completely rebuilt, but other walls which did not have bonding courses at foundation level may only have been taken down as far as the first bonding course. In the south walls of Rooms 8 and 10, it seems that the one or two modern tiles visible may have been inserted without rebuilding the wall as the original Roman tile course does not extend through the whole wall.

The amount of rebuilding was considerable and although some genuine butt joins and other features have been retained, others appear to be inaccurate. Totally rebuilt walls, listed from west to east, comprise walls 19/20A; 20A/15W; the east-west walls in the *macellum* east range and that at the north entrance of the *macellum*; 15W/13; 12/9; 9/9C; 9/9B; 9A and B/15; 15/3A; 9/8; part of 3/4B; and finally the flues in 11B. Other possibly rebuilt or refaced walls comprise 18/19; the north and west ranges of the *macellum*; 12A/15; and 10/24.

Previous excavations

The excavations by Thomas Wright in 1859 and 1860 focused on the large upstanding piece of masonry, the Old Work, in Near Old Works field. Much of the activity was limited to the baths, which was almost completely cleared while the basilical hall was only trenched. This year-long campaign was followed up in 1867 by a limited excavation directed by Henry Johnson on the latrine area, Rooms 20A and B. Excavations in 1894 and 1896 by George Fox were

limited to the *frigidarium* Room 3 and its cold plunge pools.

The only record of the work carried out by John Morris and Francis Jackson in 1930–31 is provided in two brief notes by Morris (1932–4). Three areas were excavated: Rooms 17 and 18 and the area to the north of the western baths suite and south of the basilical hall including the latrine.

Further excavation was undertaken by Kathleen Kenyon in 1936 and 1937, occupying a five week period in 1936 and seven in 1937, and was focused on the baths although three trenches were also cut across the defences (Kenyon 1938, 175–6). Work on the baths was concentrated on two areas, Room 5 and the eastern baths suite, and the basilical hall. The results of work on the latter are discussed elsewhere (Barker *et al* 1997, Chapter 2). Kenyon's fundamental point, that the basilical hall and baths suite were two separate buildings only joined together at a later stage, was quite wrong. Other interpretations in her report can now be modified in the light of the recent excavations.

Of particular importance in the understanding of *insula* 5 are the excavations by Thomas Wright. In Chapter 6 the various texts have been run together in an ordered sequence using the original words so far as possible and accompanied by original illustrations, in an edited version with a commentary by Donald Mackreth.

The excavations reported on here covered much of the southern part of the *insula* (Fig 1.3). They were accompanied between 1960 and 1985 by excavation of the basilical hall and the baths precinct to its east (Barker *et al* 1997). In 1988 and 1989 the baths *frigidarium*, and its lateral alcoves, the added *caldarium*, and the latrine area were excavated down to *in situ* Roman levels by Michael Corbishley and Roger White (Fig 1.4). This work was undertaken preparatory to the laying of surfaces for the public. The results have been

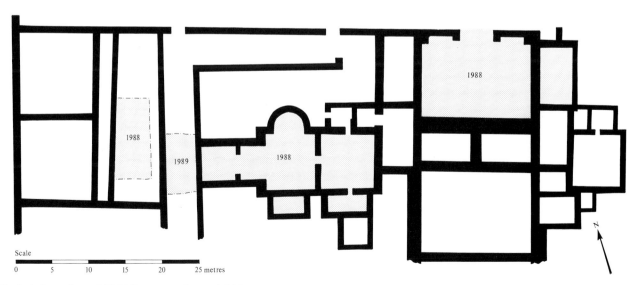

Scale
0   5   10   15   20   25 metres

Fig 1.4 Location of 1988/9 excavations; 1:500

included in this report. The plans of the uppermost surviving surfaces have been presented here together with the earlier excavation results from the 1955–85 campaign, and the detailed descriptions have been incorporated in the text.

The 1955–85 excavations

Aims and personnel

Excavations were undertaken at Wroxeter under the direction of Graham Webster in a 31 year campaign of summer seasons between 1955 and 1985 (Fig 1.3). The work was undertaken principally by volunteers taking part in a University of Birmingham Extramural Department summer school, generally run as two consecutive sessions of a fortnight each. Some clearance of the spoil heaps of earlier excavators and some archaeological excavation was also undertaken in the earlier years by prisoners. From the 1970s a paid group of supervisors was employed.

The aim of the excavations was to excavate a sample area of the stratigraphy in the centre of the town in order to understand the history of the development of the town from the archaeological sequence. In the event the success of the excavations was outstanding, with a section of the military fortress excavated comprising the west defences and part of the *porta praetoria*, the *via sagularis*, and parts of two centurial blocks (Webster 1988b). Above these levels an extensive area of the early civilian occupation levels was recorded. The public buildings on the *insula* were examined in detail and areas of late occupation were also studied. The excavation evidence was accompanied by the recovery of large quantities of artefacts and ecofacts allowing the material culture of the fortress and town to be reconstructed and evaluated in great detail.

The sequence of excavations

Excavations began in 1955 with four small exploratory trenches, trench A in the latrines, 20B, C to the south of the added *caldarium*, 12B, and D and E on either side of the west wall of the *tepidarium*, 5 (Figs 1.3 and 2.7; Table 1.1). The next year saw further trenches, F and L, in the latrine area, 20A and B, trench J in Room 12, trenches B in the baths courtyard west corridor, 15W, and G in Room 13, and four trenches in the main baths, H in the *caldarium* (6), M in Room 11C, and N/S in Room 10. In 1957 small scale excavations were undertaken in the east lateral suites, trenches K, O, and T in Room 5A, and Y in Room 11, and trench I was excavated in Room 8. South of the added *caldarium*, trench R was excavated in Room 12B, trench U in Room 9C, and trench V in the space between the two. In the same year ten boxes were opened in the baths courtyard and three to the east of the main baths in the baths precinct.

Table 1.1 Sequence of excavated boxes, 1955–85

	porticos	west range	courtyard	baths	baths precinct
1955		A	C D	E	
1956		F L	B G	H J M N/S	
1957		R U V	I K O T Y 1–7 12–14	15–17	
1958			2 4–12 14	20	16 17
1959			8 9 12 31 33	21 36 37	22–25
1960			9 29 34 35 39	21 36–8	16
1961			29 42–5 47	37	16 49
1962			35 39–41 45 46 52 53	37	
1963			6 12 34 44 50 51	37 48	55–61
1964			63	37 38	49 54–7 59–62
1965			4 6 13 63 66	65	22 49 54 55–7 59 60 64 66
1966			2 4 6 7 39 41 47 66		49 54 56 57
1967			1 2 9 10 30 32 41 44	65 69	49
1968			41 50 52 66 70	69	49
1969	80		50 70 72–8		49
1970	80		70 72 78 81		49
1971		83			49 82
1972	80	83 86			49
1973	80 90	83–87			
1974		84–87			
1975	90	83–88 93	92		
1976	80	83–88			49
1977	80 96–7	84–5 91			
1978	80 90 97–8	83–4 91			
1979	80 97–8	83–4 91			
1980	80 97–8	83–4			
1981	80 90 97–8	84 91			
1982	80 90 97–8	84 87 91			
1983	90 97–8	84 91			
1984	90 97–8	84 87 91			
1985	90 97–8	91			

The courtyard area was excavated over the next 14 years. From 1957–63 this took place by means of boxes and from 1964–70 by an open area excavation with the baulks removed from between the earlier boxes. The area in the angle of Rooms 5, 8, and 9, first examined in 1955, was reopened in 1975.

The baths precinct excavations continued from 1957 to 1966 with a succession of boxes running obliquely to the east of the main baths. The *praefurnium* dump of the main baths was first excavated in 1961 and then in consecutive years from 1964 to 1972 with a final season in 1976. Excavations continued in the east lateral suites of the main baths in Rooms 11, 11A and 11B, which were cleared to their floor levels with one deeper-cut excavation in Room 11. Excavations were also undertaken in the *frigidarium* in 1958 and in the *praefurnium*, Room 8, between 1965 and 1968. In the south portico, excavations in Box 80 south of the baths courtyard were undertaken intermittently from 1969 to 1982. The courtyard excavations were carried down to the subsoil surface. In the baths precinct, excavation was not taken below the second-century levels except in a few areas where military features were sampled. In both areas the box baulks were removed some time after the excavations of the individual boxes, and the record of features from the baulks was deficient.

The focus of excavation changed in 1971 from the courtyard, baths, and baths precinct, to the *macellum* and the street porticos on its west and south. The second-century structure was retained, but excavation was carried down beneath its floor levels to the natural surface. In the porticos similar deep excavation was undertaken though less completely. The final excavation season was undertaken in 1985.

Methods

Until the mid-60s excavation was by the box method advocated by Wheeler (Table 1.1). Two areas, the courtyard and the baths's precinct were excavated by a grid of boxes. In 1964 and 1965 in both areas the baulks were removed and the excavations opened out to area excavations. The baths precinct area was not further excavated. Excavations in the *macellum* and the porticos was undertaken within the confines of the standing structure.

The recording method was by site notebooks for each box. The records were made by the students with summaries or discussion texts by the supervisors. Disturbed upper layers were recorded as +, followed by numbered contexts starting at 1 for each box. Generally the record provides a brief description of the context and its relationship with others. The notebooks also contain a detailed additional account of the finds from each layer, generally with a spot date for pottery.

In 1974 a system of recording features in a unique number sequence on *pro forma* was introduced. From then on records were made of features as excavated and, in addition, written up retrospectively in the same format. The site notebooks, section drawings and plans from the 1955–1974 excavations were all annotated with the new feature numbers.

Illustrations changed from imperial to metric when the excavation shifted from the courtyard and baths precinct to the *macellum*. The pre-1970 excavation boxes were illustrated by 1″ to1′ section drawings (1:12). Plans were provided in the site notebooks at 1″ or ½″ to 1′ (1:12 or 1:24). Overall plans were at 1/4″ to 1′ (1:48). After 1970, sections were drawn at 1:10 and plans at 1:20, with some variations. Running sections were drawn across the courtyard and the baths precinct, although the baulk sections were not drawn when the boxes were united to an area excavation. Two running sections were maintained in the *macellum* (S27 and S28), and one in the corridor to the north (S30). Their upper levels start at the third-century levels. A long section in the south portico details the second and third-century horizons (S29). There are some gaps on the main running sections principally due to the collapse of sections before they were drawn, when they were left over the winter.

Levels were not generally taken but on five occasions key points were levelled to a site datum and thence to OD. The levels shown on the illustrated sections are all estimated using this data and the detailed levelling values recorded in 1988–9. Planning was by triangulation and by offsets from base lines.

On occasions difficulties were encountered with backfilling and reopening the excavations between seasons. This was generally undertaken by unsupervised Ministry of Works staff. The excavation records particularly pinpoint two areas where archaeology was destroyed, one at the west end of the baths corridor and the other in Box 85 in Rooms 22.10–12.

Finds

The excavation recording system was strongly oriented to the finds. Finds data were entered with each context entry in the site notebooks. Spot dating of pottery was undertaken from the outset and the dating evidence was added to each context.

The collection strategies differed according to the different categories of finds. Small finds and coins were all collected and entered in a small finds book where they were given an individual number. Some items were subsequently discarded. Glass was kept from all contexts. From the mid-1970s onward, animal bone was retained from stratified contexts. All Romano-British pottery was collected but some, principally from the overburden layers, was subsequently discarded. Medieval and post-medieval pottery was not retained, but its presence was recorded in the site notebooks. Only complete examples of brick and tile or diagnostic pieces or fragments with graffiti were retained over most of the excavation period, although a greater quantity was collected from the later years, particularly from the porticos. Mortar, *opus signinum*, cement, and plaster were retained where they occurred in large fragments or were deemed potentially diagnostic. Collection became more complete in the later years from the porticos.

Storage and conservation strategies were overwhelmed in some cases by the quantities found. As a result some material was left unmarked and cannot now be provenanced. Some mixing has occurred between finds from 1955–1985 and those from Kathleen Kenyon's excavations on the *insula*, and in *insula* 9 (Kenyon 1981).

Interim reports

Reports on the excavations have appeared regularly in *The Journal for Roman Studies* and in *Britannia* in the 'Roman Britain in 19xx' sections. The results were also reported in more detail in 24 reports presented in the *West Midlands Archaeological News Sheet*, and in annual accounts prepared in the form of A4 sheets available to volunteers and others. A considered summary of the military and early civilian sequence was published soon after the end of the excavations (Webster 1988b), and in shorter form later (Webster 1990), while the second-century building sequence has been recently discussed (Webster 1993).

Post-excavation projects

Post-excavation work on the excavations has been undertaken in two campaigns. In the first (from 1985–1990) the excavation data was reassembled on context *pro forma* with cross references to illustrations. Most of the imperial drawings were redrawn to metric scale by eye and the metric drawings traced in ink. Photographs were collated and listed. Matrices following the Harris method were prepared for all the boxes except those in the baths precinct. The site features and contexts were phased to four groups – military, early civil, main construction, and post main construction (the latter three corresponding to Periods 1, 2, and 3 in this volume).

The present volume results from a second post-excavation campaign undertaken between 1991 and 1995. This was initiated by a MAP 2 assessment (English Heritage 1991). A report was produced outlining the excavation results, the research aims for further work, the potential for study of the finds categories, a proposed programme of work, and a report synopsis (Ellis 1991; 1992).

The excavation research aims (Archive F4) fell into three groups. The first focused on elucidating the function, development, and significance of the *insula* 5 structures, with particular attention drawn to the early civil and post-Roman potential. The second concentrated on maximising the socio-economic data. The possibility of identifying material directly associated with the use of the baths and *macellum*, of identifying status, of pinpointing economic change through time, of comparing material with evidence from Wroxeter's hinterland, and finally of reviewing the Wroxeter evidence in comparison with other towns were all particularly noted. Finally the research aims intended to assess the results and to state whether the finds assemblages might be typical of baths or *macella* and so be used predictively. Successes and failures in attaining the research aims are discussed in a project review (Archive F5).

Key groups of stratigraphically important contexts were defined (Table 1.2). These formed the focus for specialist contributions and are headed KG in the tables and lists. It was hoped that dating or functional evidence might be available from all the key groups but in some cases none was forthcoming.

Post-excavation work on the stratigraphy provided a phased database for contexts and features (Archive B7). The phasing was divided into four Periods, 1–4. Period 1, the early civilian town, was subdivided into three phases, 1.1, 1.2, and 1.3. For Periods 2–4, the site was divided into five areas. From west to east these were the porticos (P), the west range (WR), the baths courtyard (C), the baths (B), and the baths precinct (BP). Each was phased separately. Periods 2 and 3 were thus divided into sub-phases dependent on area.

Table 1.2 Key groups: area and overall phases in brackets

1	Building 5 (1.3)
2	Construction trench of portico sleeper wall F4030 (P 2.1: 2.2)
3	Construction trench of second portico sleeper walls (P 2.2: 2.4)
4	Unused construction trenches under *macellum* (WR 2.1: 2.1)
5	Initial *macellum* construction trenches (WR 2.1, P 2.1, C 2.1: 2.1)
6	Inspection pits in *macellum*, corridor, and baths (WR 2.2, C 2.1, BP 2.1: 2.3)
7	Secondary *macellum* construction trenches (WR 2.2: 2.4)
8	Baths construction trenches and floors (B 2.1, C 2.1, BP 2.1: 2.1)
9	Construction trenches of additional baths wall (C 2.1, B 2.2, BP 2.1: 2.2)
10	Construction trench of south courtyard wall (P 2.2, C 2.2: 2.4)
11	Construction trench of courtyard sleeper wall F2135 (C 2.3: 2.5)
12	Construction trench of courtyard sleeper wall F2136 (C 2.4: 2.6)
13	The *natatio* (C 2.4: 2.6)
14	*Natatio* infill (C 3.1: 3.1)
15	Construction features Rooms 12 and 13 (C 3.2, B 3.2: 3.3)
16	Initial portico pits (P 3.1: 3.1)
17	Secondary portico pits (P 3.2: 3.1)
18	*Praefurnium* dump from Room 7 (BP 2.3: 2.6)
19	Baths precinct initial waterpipe trenches (BP 3.1: 3.1)
20	Baths precinct secondary waterpipe trenches (BP 3.2: 3.3)
21	*Macellum* herringbone floor (WR 3.1: 3.3)
22	Construction trenches of Rooms 9C and 12B (C 3.2, B 3.2: 3.3)
23	*Praefurnium* dump from Room 13 (C 3.2: 3.3)
24	*Praefurnium* dump from Room 9D (C 3.2: 3.3)
25	Late levels street portico (P 3.4A and B, P 3.5, P3.6: 3.5)
26	Construction trenches of Room 9D (C3.2, B 3.2: 3.3)
27	Construction trenches of latrine (WR 2.1, C 2.1: 2.1)
28	Construction trenches of Room 5A (B 3.1, BP 3.1: 3.1)
29	Construction trenches of Room 11C (B 3.2, BP 3.2: 3.3)

P portico, WR west range, C courtyard, B baths, BP baths precinct

Thus P 2.2 referred to Period 2, phase 2 in the porticos, BP 3.1 to Period 3, phase 1 in the baths precinct. The stratigraphic periodisations by areas have been grouped into an overall scheme which represents a best fit of the evidence but cannot be proven because the walls of the buildings separate the various blocks of stratigraphy. The area phases, the main periodisation, and the stratigraphic position of the key groups are tabulated (Table 1.3).

The illustrations are based on the 1:100 plan of the site undertaken in 1990. This was enlarged to 1:50 and the excavation plans, reduced from 1:10 and 1:20 or 1:12 and 1:24, to 1:50, were then superimposed. As would be expected some adjustment of site drawings and overall plan to achieve a match has been necessary in some instances. Where contradictions were not resolvable the areas in question have been replanned.

The common use of descriptions for the different locations has been referred to above. In addition the following should be noted. The excavation trenches are referred to throughout as boxes, and the five areas outlined above as areas. The contexts are shown as the box

Table 1.3 Correlation of overall and area phasing

period	phase	portico	west range	courtyard	baths	baths precinct	key groups
1	1						
	2			1.1, 1.2, 1.3 overall			
	3						1
2	1	P 2.1	WR2.1	C2.1	B2.1	BP2.1	4 5 8 27
	2		WR2.2		B2.2		2 9
	3						6
	4	P2.2		C2.2		BP2.2	3 7 10
	5	P2.3	WR2.3	C2.3			11
	6			C2.4		BP2.3	12 13 18
3	1	P3.1		C3.1	B3.1	BP3.1	14 16 17 19
		P3.2					28
	2	P3.3					
	3		WR3.1	C3.2	B3.2	BP3.2	15 20–24 26 29
	4			C3.3			
	5	P3.4A	WR3.2		B3.3	BP3.3	25
		P3.4B					
	6	P3.5	WR3.3	C3.4	B3.4	BP3.4	
	7	P3.6					
4		P4	WR4	C4	B4	BP4	

divided from the context number, thus 80/161 is context 161 in box 80. A new numbering system for the rooms in the baths complex has been established to supersede the separate but incomplete numberings already used by Kenyon (1938) and by Webster (Fig 2.7).

Although the assessment report identified the finds categories, it was not until the report had been drawn up and the project was under way that the long task of preparing a finds inventory and grouping and re-boxing finds was undertaken. Furthermore some finds reports, especially the animal bone report, had been undertaken using a phasing based on the four groups noted above. The phasing was particularly complete for the south portico and much of the animal bone reported on here derives from there.

Only a small proportion of the small finds are reported on here. The report is based on the items drawn by Diana Bonakis each year. These were selected on the basis of their intrinsic interest in illuminating aspects of the site or of Romano-British life. For this report, finds possibly associated with the *macellum* have been examined in detail. The glass report is complete, but others are based on key groups only. A handful of coins were found after the coin report was completed, and these have been excluded. The painted wall and ceiling plaster from the *caldarium* has already been described (Davey and Ling 1982, 200). Painted plaster from the *macellum* was noted during the study of the mortars by Graham Morgan and no pieces indicated intricate designs. However a full study of the painted plaster remains to be undertaken. A report by Gerald Brodribb on selected items amongst the brick and tile collection is available in the archive (Archive E14). A large collection of material remains to be studied.

There is therefore a large collection of artefacts and ecofacts which have not been examined and remain for students in the future. It should be noted that a large body of finds data, most in the form of completed reports, exists unpublished from the Barker excavations. The potential for further work on the *insula* 5 finds is great.

The strategy for finds publication

Finds reports from the 1955–85 excavations are divided between this volume and the fortress excavation volume (Webster fothcoming) with military finds generally appearing in the military volume and post-military finds in this volume, but there are exceptions. For the military volume, finds that could be readily identified as having been used in the fortress, the coins, small finds, brooches, intaglii, and vessel glass, were presented regardless of their stratigraphic position. For the other categories of finds only the stratified material was presented and residual military material thus appears in this volume. Some reports could not be divided and there is therefore some repetition of finds data between the two volumes. The coin catalogue appears here while the pre-AD 90 coins are also repeated in the first volume. Some pots are illustrated both in stratified groups and in the form series and occur in both volumes.

A number of finds reports were in preparation or had been completed when the preparation of this volume for publication began in 1991. While some finds work concentrated on the key groups, for other categories, generally those where work was already in hand in 1991, it proved possible to look at all the finds. The vessel and window glass, glass objects, brooches, intaglii, stone objects, and metalworking evidence dealt with all the recovered stratified finds. For other categories a selective approach was adopted. The small finds report only deals in detail with material from three of the key groups (KG 16, 17, 21) although a general selection of objects is described and illustrated, and items of religious significance are dealt with fully. The pottery also deals principally with material from the key groups. However, earlier work (especially Darling 1976 and Faiers 1990), which also included a report on the *natatio* infill and a catalogue of much of the third and fourth-century pottery, both by Graham Webster, allowed the approach to be considerably widened. Animal bone reports cover all of the *natatio* infill (KG 14) and a 50% sample of the portico pits (KG 16, 17). Unstratified material has generally not been analysed and reported on, with the exception of the brooches, intaglii, and vessel glass, and some of the small finds selected for illustration.

Archive

The excavation archive records and finds are housed at the English Heritage Historic Properties store at Atcham, Shropshire. Access should be arranged through the Historic Properties section of English Heritage. The paper archive is stored under the following headings: A, Field and post-excavation illustrations; B, Site records; C, Finds records 1955–91; D, Photographs; E, 1992–5 Post-excavation archive; F, Miscellaneous; together with a detailed index, F7. A few finds are on display at the site museum and at Rowley's House Museum, Shrewsbury.

The 1988–89 excavations

The results of excavation in 1988–89 are incorporated in this report. These excavations, directed by Mike Corbishley and Roger White, were undertaken prior to the gravelling of Rooms 3, 3B, 9, 9C, 12A, 12B, 12C, 13, 15W and 20, as part of the process of site reinstatement (Fig 1.4). The areas examined had previously been grassed and required some consolidation prior to gravelling. The extent of survival of stratified levels was unknown and the de-turfing was therefore undertaken by archaeologists. The latest Romano-British surfaces were uncovered and recorded, but no archaeological deposits were removed. A report has been prepared by Roger White and forms part of the archive. The main findings and descriptions have been incorporated in the text below where relevant. The archive is internally indexed and cross-referenced. It is held under the heading B6 with the 1955–85 archive.

Presentation

The following report presents the excavation results in Chapter 2 under separate headings for the early civil period (Period 1); the construction of the public buildings (Period 2); their subsequent use, development, and decay (Period 3); and finally for the modern period (Period 4). For Periods 2, 3, and 4 the data are presented by area, while at the end of Periods 2 and 3 a suggested overall phasing is discussed. In all the sections the

exposition of the results of excavation, the dating evidence and the discussion are kept separate. In Chapter 3 a discussion of the function of the second-century and later buildings and an illustrated restoration is presented, followed by a structural description of the *macellum* and a suggested building sequence. Chapter 4 outlines the finds evidence by means of a series of specialist contributions on the artefacts and ecofacts. Chapter 5 presents a discussion and a chronological summary. Chapter 6 contains the edited reworking of the nineteenth-century excavation reports by Donald Mackreth.

The figures and tables are numbered consecutively for each chapter with the chapter number as a prefix. The conventions used on the illustrated sections are shown on Fig 1.5. Figures 2.8, 2.9, 2.19 and 2.45 locate the main sections across buildings but the captions for section figures also note where the section locations are shown. The courtyard section (Fig 2.39; S31) is located on Fig 2.31. Text references to sections are as Fig 00, S00. Feature profiles are not numbered. Half tone photographs are numbered in consecutively with the graphics.

Key

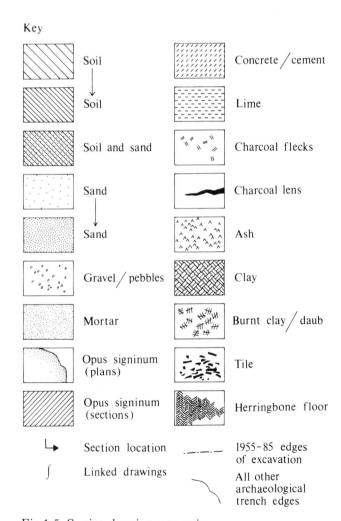

Fig 1.5 Section drawing conventions

2 The excavation evidence
by Peter Ellis

Period 1: the early town AD 90–130

Introduction

During the later stages of excavation there were difficulties in disentangling late military and early post-military structures. The difficulties are reflected in the site notebooks and in the interim reports following the end of the excavations. A report in 1988 corresponds with the account presented here (Webster 1988b, fig 6.15), but a later report in 1990 presents a very much reduced number of features for the early civil period (Webster 1990, fig 9). The military volume represents the final interpretation (Webster forthcoming), and argues for a sequence of four phases, 7i–7iv, of military buildings following the levelling of the rampart, the infilling of the fortress ditch, and the abandonment of the *via sagularis*. These are based on a stone building, Building A/B.

From the perspective of this report, and following the structural analysis for it, some elements of military phases 7i–7iv seem doubtful. The remaining elements of the early town after phase 7iv seem incomprehensible by themselves (Webster 1990, fig 3), and the suggested late military and early civilian features coincide in such specific areas as to suggest they are connected. Dating evidence not to hand when the military report was completed tends to place some phase 7 features later. The evidence suggests that all the ephemeral evidence of timber buildings represents structures added to a timber building based on the footings of a military stone building (A/B), and that with the exception of a clearly defined and well-floored veranda to its east which would have been associated with the stone building before its demolition, all belong to a post-military phase. This interpretation is particularly supported by the fact that these buildings, other than the structure replacing Building A/B, either overlie the slighted rampart or block the military *via sagularis*. In this report the evidence is therefore recast to present a somewhat different picture from that in the military report, and a number of features are thus presented in both volumes. These are: F281, F867, F919, F938 (Building 1); F195 and F1079 (Building 2); and F382, F509, F520, F665, F666, F715, F803, and F1079 (Building 3).

The military legacy

The abandoned fortress site still retained the *via sagularis* of the fortress as a surface feature, even though in its last military stage this had comprised areas of haphazard gravelling rather than a maintained surface. The rampart had been removed and the ditch carefully infilled. The abandonment of the rampart *ascensus* in Phase 5 may indicate that this occurred at the end of the first military occupation rather than at the final departure of the military (Webster forthcoming). To the west of the road was the site of a demolished stone building (Webster forthcoming: Building A/B; Fig 2.1: Room1.10; Fig 2.2: Room 3.7), and the stub of its footings would still have been visible (Figs 2.4: S2; 2.5; 2.38: S27, F262, F512, and F513). East of the road had been a large timber store building on three sides of an open yard, marked by robbing trenches. A number of rubbish pits represented the last clearance phase, and the whole area was covered by a general horizon of compacted soil and demolition material, some of it burnt. Only in the vicinity of the former Building A/B, where its stone rubble lay, was there any difference in the composition of this horizon.

Phase 1

Building 1

Buildings 1 and 2 were represented by a layout of similarly-sized rooms running along the street frontage, and by two ranges of rooms extending to their east (Fig 2.1). The numbers on plan represent the Building numbers followed by the room numbers; 3.2 is Room 2 in Building 3. The Building 1 walls along the street were sill beam trenches, F823, F825, F867, and F973. The trenches were all 0.15m wide with varying depths, none more than 0.05m. The junction of the three northern trenches with the internal walls between Rooms 1, 2, and 3 was marked by square postholes, F824, F1047, and F1045, set on sandstone slabs at a similar depth of between 0.31 and 0.35m. The posthole sizes suggested squared uprights of 0.15m square for F824, 0.16m square for F1047, and 0.19m square for F1045. Other rectangular postholes unconnected with interior walls were recorded on the west front of the building, one midway along the west wall of Room 3, and another, F822, measuring 0.14 by 0.09m, on the west wall of Room 1, perhaps marking a doorway. Another possible doorway was seen in the west wall of Room 2, F825, where it came to an apparent end short of the corner of the room.

In places, lines of flat stones, F814, F981, and F4088, interrupted wall trench F973 marking the west side of Rooms 4 and 5 (Fig 2.58: S50). The relationship of these two groups of stone with the sill beam trenches was not clear. They were tentatively recorded as predating the trenches but may instead have been secondary, perhaps a consolidation of the frontage at entry thresholds. The red sandstone blocks shared similarities with the stonework of the military building A/B and may have been reused from it. There was no evidence for a continuation of the street frontage line south of Room 5.

The sill beam trenches on the frontage were integral with palisade trenches containing slight uprights forming the interior walls. The wall between Rooms 1 and 2, F830, was the best surviving example of these palisade trenches (Fig 2.3; Webster 1988b, fig 6.14). The trench, approximately 0.3m wide and 0.3m deep, was filled with clay in which the marks of a number of stake uprights could be seen. These averaged 0.08m in diameter and some were set on stones, possibly of the same origin as those along the west side of the building, placed at the base of the trench. The bottom 0.11m of the wall itself survived as a stub of hard clay and daub on either side of the stake placements, demonstrating a wall width of 0.16m. The four remaining party walls between Rooms 2 and 3, 3 and 4, 4 and 5, and on the south side of Room 5, were similarly of palisade trench construction but were less well recorded. Wall F1043 between Rooms 2 and 3, had been replaced by a sill beam trench in Phase 2, but the shadow of uprights was recorded at the base of the trench (Fig 2.4: S3). The walls between Rooms 3 and 4, F994, and the south wall of Room 5, F919, were not excavated, and were seen only as stakehole lines in plan, while the wall between Rooms 4 and 5, F938, was only noted in a section.

Wall F830 between Rooms 1 and 2 was traced further east than the others. The eastern palisade trench, F565 (Fig 2.4), joined a similar north-south trench, F4086. No setting for a structural upright was found at the junction. A more westerly rear wall was found in Room 3 marked by a short surviving length of palisade trench, F956, of similar dimensions to F830. No evidence of the east walls of Rooms 4, 5, and 6 on this line was found, and they may have been removed by the cutting of later pits.

Walls are aligned on Building A/B from the fortress, and its footings must have been reused (Fig 2.1: Room 1.10). The north wall of Room 3 and the south wall of Room 5 run towards its corners. A Phase 2 trench, F509, at the north-west corner may have masked an earlier wall line. The southern wall, F919 and F281, continued in Phase 2. Rooms 2 and 3 were floored with clay, overlain in the latter by a floor of coarse orange sand and trample. Room 4 was floored with sandy gravel. A number of stakeholes were noted in Room 2.

To the rear of Rooms 1 and 2 were further building trenches. A main east-west wall line F592 had been built over by a later wall line (Fig 2.1) and some evidence may have been lost (Fig 2.4: S1, S2). Its sill beam trench was of less uniform depth than those to the west, perhaps reflecting the military levels beneath. It had sloping sides in places, possibly the result of a later removal of timbers. To the west a short length of sill beam trench, F701, continued its line. To the east the trench was not recorded on the further side of a later cut which may have removed its return to the north and south. The irregularity of wall lines here may be seen as a product of the stone demolition levels of the military building A/B into which the wall trenches were cut. On the south side of F592 a short length of sill beam trench, F738, was found, cut by Phase 2 features. This was aligned with a posthole, F782, 0.06m square, set in F592, and the same line was continued northward, after a gap, by a short length of sill beam trench, F811. The gap was marked at the south end of F811 by a rectangular posthole F809, 0.7m by 0.5m, with an associated post pit, F808, 0.17m deep. Three metres to the west another length of sill beam trench, F4087, formed a further division. Thus three possible rooms, none wider than 3m, lay on the north side of F592 between the rear wall of Room 2 and the presumed back wall of the building. It is possible that F811 was an interior feature of a larger room, rather than a wall line, especially since a visually identical clay floor was found on either side. On the south side of F592, F738 indicates further rooms with the area to the east of F738 floored with clay on which were trampled spreads of dirty sand.

No Period 1 floor was found in Room 1.10. Section 2 (Fig 2.4) shows F592 cut from a level above the top of the retained wall footing, and Section 1 (Fig 2.4) shows that this was the level of the floor of Room 1.11 and later of Room 3.8. Excavation inside Building A/B located an upper military floor level of clay (Fig 2.4: S5, layer 3). If this had been reused in Period 1 it would thus have lain 0.2m or so below the floor levels to the north. Since there is a slope southward this would have been a possibility. However there is a slight indication of a sand floor at a higher level (Fig 2.4: S5, layer 1). This was not noted during excavation, and appears to overrun the top of the wall stub F262 suggesting that it is not associated. However, the remains of sill beams set on the wall stubs of Building A/B may not have been distinguishable in excavation from the floor.

Building 2

The west and north wall trenches of Room 1, F1063 and F2006, were for sill beams (Figs 2.1; 2.38: S29). No evidence was seen of any northward continuation of the west wall of the room, suggesting that this was the north-west corner of the building. At the junction a substantial posthole, packed with stone and with a large fragment of tile, was clearly a structural member. Both walls contained evidence of other, slighter, postholes. These may be an indication of earlier palisade trenches, or of later refurbishment, but cannot easily be parallelled by other building methods used. Similar trenches with widely-spaced postholes were found in Phase 2, but these were clay-filled trenches whereas F2006 and F1063 had clearly held timbers. The trenches were wider at 0.22m that those recorded for Building 1, although this may represent disturbance from robbing. The south side of the room was suggested by a short length of sill beam trench, F1088, 0.16m wide, and a further room was suggested to the south by the continuation of F1063. The room was apparently divided at a later date by a sill beam trench, F1062, which overran the west wall line, a posthole, F1069, marking the junction. Two large stones were found in the base of the trench and these had presumably supported and levelled the sill beam.

To the east a group of wall lines was recorded which may be associated. Sill beam trenches F995 and F837 continued the line of F1088 eastward. Irregularities here may be excavation planning errors. To the north were indications of a palisade trench, F1079, F195, and F4089, running from the south-west corner of Room 1.10 set on the former Building A/B (Fig 2.4: S4). To the west was a succession of clay and gravel floors (Fig 2.4: S4, layers 1–4). The characteristic upturn of the floors at the wall line indicates that reflooring was to counteract subsidence and wear.

This eastern group may be associated with the trenches on the west frontage, or alternatively, it is possible that they represent elements of a separate building, distinct from Building 2, and perhaps fronting a street to the south.

Coins of Claudius and Nero (cat nos 24, 67, and 86) were found. A pipeclay figurine was found in F994 (Fig 4.12, 139). Vessel glass comprised a mid-Flavian cup (38), two fragments from prismatic bottles (80 and 87) and two from cylindrical bottles (90 and 92), of which no 90 would have been out of use early in the second century, and other fragments (16, 22, 26, 29, 36, 37, 49, 50, 52, 61, 62, 66, and 70). A glass counter was also found (no 62). Only five of these objects came from rooms on the street frontage and four of these were from footings trenches. The remainder came from the rear of Room 2.2, including two of the coins, and from Room 2.3, while only three items came from the eastern part of Building 1. Pottery is considered under Phase 3.

Phase 2

Building 3

Rebuildings of Building 1 and 2 are numbered Buildings 3 and 4 (Fig 2.2). In Building 3, the wall between Rooms 1 and 2 was a rebuilding of that between first phase Rooms 2 and 3, this time in the form of a shallow sill beam trench, F969 (Fig 2.4: S3). To the west the latter abutted the retained Phase 1 wall F867, the junction marked by a posthole, F971, slighter and less deeply set than its predecessor F1047, measuring 0.14 by 0.08 by 0.12m deep. The wall was followed east to where, as F509, it terminated at the north-east corner of Room 3.7, the former Room 1.10 set within the footings of Building A/B, cutting through its demolition layers (Fig 2.4: S4). A posthole, F520, was set in F509, and the trench may have been a clay-filled base for timber framing, and thus different to F969 and perhaps earlier. There was another indication of a wall in Room 1 which is discussed below.

Fig 2.3 Building 1 wall F830 between Rooms 1.1 and 1.2; view east

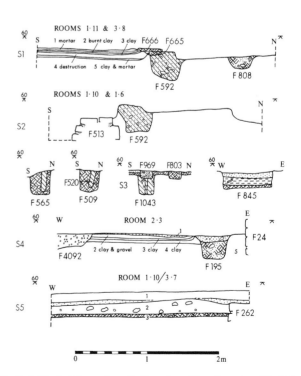

Fig 2.4 Period 1, sections 1–5 and profiles, location Fig 2.1; 1:50

The uprights of the Phase 1 wall F830 had been sawn off level with the Phase 2 ground level, and this may have occurred at the outset of Phase 2 since none of the other Phase 1 palisade trench walls were retained into Phase 2. The north and south walls of Room 3, F870 and F1085, replaced those of its predecessor, Phase 1 Room 4, on slightly different lines to the north and south of the original wall lines. The west walls, however, remained unchanged from Phase 1. A clay floor had been laid in Room 1 and sand floors in Rooms 2 and 3 (Fig 2.4: S3).

To the rear, the Phase 1 east-west wall, F592, was cut by a slighter trench, F665, slightly off its line to the south (Fig 2.4: S1). The trench continued the line marked by the wall between Rooms 1 and 2, running adjacent to the north wall of the former Building A/B. It presumably contained a slight sill beam. A single wall, F352, ran to the north, and from its junction with F665 westward the line of the latter was continued by a clay-filled trench F382. These walls were different in character to F665 and may have been additions. Both were based on clay-packed trenches and retained evidence both of rectangular upright placements in F352 and F382, and of timbers having been set on the clay base between the uprights. Wall F352 served to form two rooms, 5 and 6, both provided with clay floors, the floor in 3.5 sealing the Phase 1 features. On the east side of Room 5 was an area of clay mixed with pebbles, F667, set against the east wall, the base for an internal room feature. To the south of the east-west wall line, and joining it at right angles, were two further walls, F746 and F715, the latter cutting the Phase 1 floor, both of which appeared in the short lengths excavated to be sill beam trenches. Trench F715 partitioned two further rooms, Rooms 8 and 9, both with clay floors. A well-marked area of trampled clay, F666, set into F665 may have marked the threshold of a doorway between Rooms 5 and 8. This may have been a repetition of a doorway from Phase 1 since its east side coincides with the line marked by F738 in Phase 1. The latter was however sealed beneath the floor of Room 8. The demolition layers here contained white painted wall plaster, perhaps from the building, although similar material was found in the demolition layers of Building A/B.

Returning to Room 1, a soiled clay layer over the floor of the room respected a rectilinear pit, F845. The pit was 0.17m deep, and had vertical, plank-lined sides to east and west, and a sloping north side also plank-lined (Figs 2.2; 2.4). This may have been a storage pit, or, despite its shallow depth, a latrine pit as was suggested by its fill of dirty sand and clay. Nearby was an east-west sill beam trench, F803, also cutting the floor of the room (Fig 2.4: S3). It measured 0.17m wide by 0.05m deep and was contemporary with a floor of discontinuous clay patches which overlay the floor associated with F845. This group of features – wall line, floors, and pit – may be later than Building 3.

Building 4

The east part of Building 4 was the best preserved of the Period 1 structures. The west frontage was presumably retained from Phase 1 although the east-west wall, F1062, was not. The rear wall of the building was found and a succession of rooms to the west, principally marked by sill beam trenches. The walls of the two easternmost rooms, 8 and 9, were, however, treated differently and these may have been an addition. The eastern limit of the building was marked by a ditch, F952 (Fig 2.38: S29).

Room 2 was floored with pebbles while to its east the floor of Room 5 was of *opus signinum*. In the south-east corner of the room was a sandstone and tile footing, F979, set on the floor. Further east, patchy spreads of gravel were recorded in Rooms 6 and 8. The party wall between Rooms 8 and 9, F940/F941, was set on stones (Webster 1988b, fig 6.16). These were a heterogeneous collection with some set on a flat tile base as well as three pitched stones of millstone grit. The east wall, F943, also contained stone and tile set in a trench. The west wall of Room 9, F947, resembled other sill beam trenches and had no indication of stone footings. Room 9 contained the remains of an oven, F868, set away from the west wall. This was built of a variety of tiles with *tubulatio*, *imbrex*, and *tegula* in the base course. Over this was a heavily burnt area and a further tile structure above. The floor of the room was of clay.

Seven coins were found, none later than Claudius (cat nos 23, 37, 48, 58, 62, 82, and 730). All came from Building 4. Small finds included a toggle possibly from textile working from Building 4 (Fig 4.16, 174). Vessel glass comprised fragments from a cast cup (Fig 4.37, 2), a beaker (13), a bowl (40), a jug (41), an unguent bottle (43), and other bottles (83–86, 91, 93), as well as body pieces from vessels (12, 19, 23, 24, 30, 34, 35, 47, 53, 56–9, 63–5, 69, 73, and 76). The group dated from the later first to the mid-second century. A melon bead (no 1) and counter (43) were also found, both from Building 3. A fragment of *tegula* was noted. Most of the glass came from Building 4, with eight items from the street frontage rooms and only four from the rear of Building 3. The pottery is considered under Phase 3.

Phase 3

Building 5

The final evidence of buildings comprised a small number of sill beam trenches (Fig 2.5). The Phase 2 sill beam trenches on the street frontage were buried beneath layers of sandy silt with trodden and burnt surfaces. Amongst them were spreads of red sandstone and some tile fragments. Cut into these layers in the northern part of the excavated area, were three sill beam trenches, F846, F832, and F864. At the north end of F846 the trench widened into a posthole, F850,

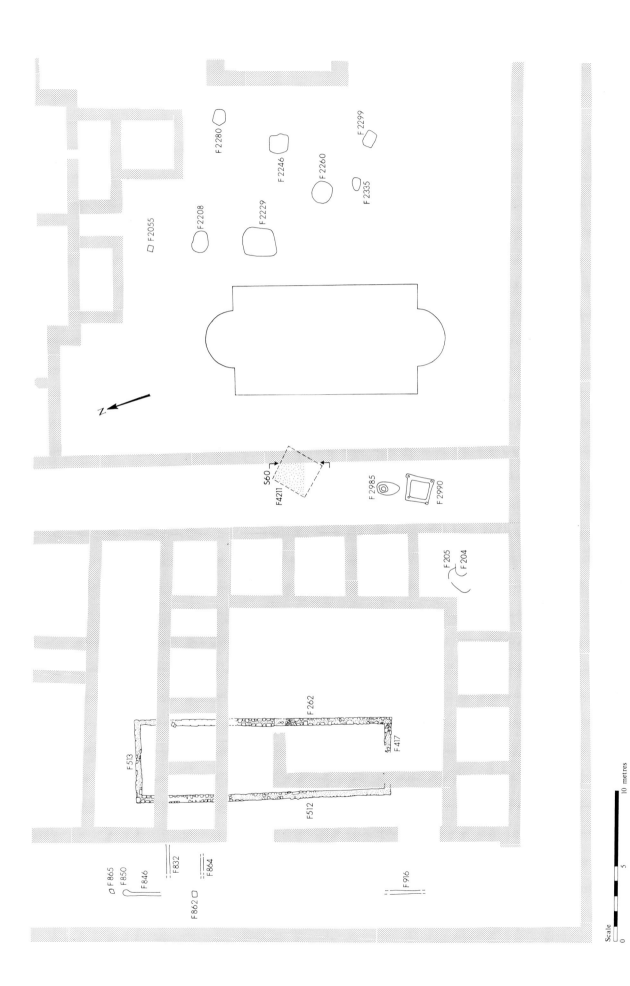

Fig 2.5 Period 1, phase 3; Building 5 and Period 1 pits; 1:250

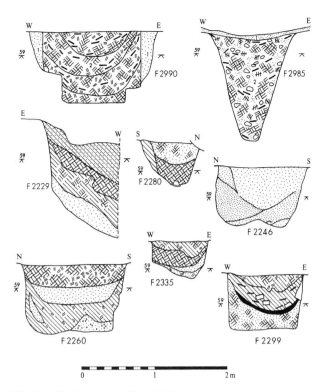

Fig 2.6 Period 1, profiles; 1:50

and a second posthole, F865 lay further north on the wall line. A third posthole, F862, to the south, was also on the line of the slot. A further isolated section of trench, F916, was found to the south. This was less clearly stratigraphically separate from the Period 1 evidence, but it lay on the line of F846 not on the west frontage line of the earlier Period 1 buildings. In addition a number of heavily burnt areas, possibly hearths, were found at this horizon, and two shallow soil-filled cuttings. It is assumed that Room 1.10/3.7 reusing Building A/B was retained and that the sill beams represent a rebuilding of rooms to its west.

To the rear of the street frontage buildings was a plank-lined latrine pit, F2990 (Fig 2.6). The pit cut military barrack block features and the military demolition horizon. It was about 1.3m square and 1.1m deep. Its sides were lined with grey clay about 0.1m thick with a timber facing suggested by fragments of wood and charcoal set both vertically and horizontally. The shadow of an upright 0.4m long set at the foot of the south side was recorded. At the north-east and south-east corners were two well-marked postholes. A less definite one was recorded in the north-west corner, while the south-west corner was disturbed. Four posts seem likely at the corners perhaps supporting a floor across the pit.

In the lower layers filling the pit, organic material resembling coprolites was noted. The pit fill matrix was of the material recorded over the whole site as military demolition material. The fill included tile fragments, one triangular piece with mortar adhering, and one recognisable tegula, as well as fragments of concrete, plaster, mortar, and sandstone and water worn stones. The

infilling was sealed beneath a layer of dark clay containing charcoal and daub. Some evidence of sandy floors were noted nearby, particularly F4211 (Fig 2.70: S60).

A number of pits were distinguished from the numerous examples from the military clearance phase by their stratigraphic position. All these suggested post-military pits cut through the military demolition horizon, and four cut the robbing trenches of a military store building, the latest military structure in this area. The pits were in two groups. The western group comprised two intercutting pits F204 and F205 which had been truncated by later features. The eastern group numbered eight features of which one, F2055, was perhaps a posthole, while the remainder were clearly pits. The backfills differed (Fig 2.6). F2246 for example was entirely filled with sand, while F2229 had lower fills of soil, sand, and clay and an upper fill of dark soil. F2260 was another pit with a soil fill, in this case at its base. F2280 and F2335 had predominantly clay fills, and F2299 a band of burnt charcoal.

Over Building 4 there had been a wholesale removal of structures and spread of demolition debris (Fig 2.38: S29, layer 21). Beneath the latter were indications that the buildings had been carefully dismantled. Many of the sill beam trenches contained demolition material and the beams themselves must have been removed as was suggested by possible crowbar marks in the trench marking the north wall of Room 4.5. The absence of tiles may indicate roofs of shingles or thatch, but may also suggest that tiled roofs were stripped for reuse. Plaster and wattle and daub fragments indicated the composition and surface treatment of walls.

To the north, a pit, F600, and an oven-like scoop were found within Building 3 beneath its demolition layer. Pit F600 (Fig 2.2), in the area of Room 3.5, was filled with clay, loam, and charcoal, and the possible oven in the area of Room 3.2, with heavily burnt clay. Both may date from after the abandonment of the building but before its levelling, since they are difficult to set in the context of the building itself. Much of the demolition layer had been burnt and presumably this represented spread bonfires from remains of the buildings which could not be reused. However, much remained unburnt, including sections of wattle with bark intact. These levels were in places covered in soil layers.

Nine coins were found, the two latest dating to Vespasian (cat nos 47, 56, 65, 69, 79, 101, 108, 703, and 732). A coin of Claudius was found in F916, and of Vespasian on floor F4211. Amongst the small finds, military items (Figs 4.6, 5; 4.7, 27), a needle from textile working from pit F2260 (Fig 4.16, 160), and a lid (Fig 4.23, 237) are illustrated. A brooch dated to AD 50–150 was found (Fig 4.35, 35). The vessel glass collection was predominantly first-century but included second-century pieces such as an unguent bottle (45). Some glass came from the pits to the east, F204 (cat no 14), F205 (17 and 67), F2287 (4, 9, 11, 78, and 88), and F2990 (4.37, 39; 3, 7, 33, 39, 46, and 48). Two melon

beads (cat nos 2 and 3) and a counter (44) in glass, and
two honestones (cat nos 1 and 2) were also found. Of
the latter, no 2 (Fig 4.48) came from Kent and was of
the same type as those suggested to have been for sale in
the forum portico in the second century (Atkinson 1942,
129). The animal bone collection included some fragments with specialist butchery marks.

Pottery from Period 1 contained highly fragmented
material and much of the material may be residual
from the military period. Samian indicated residuality
of c 70%. The few pieces of samian dated possibly later
than AD 90, other than those dated simply Flavian,
comprised a vessel dated to AD 75–95 in Phase 1.2,
and three vessels in Phase 1.3, one dated AD 80–100,
one late Flavian, and one, a central Gaulish piece,
Trajanic, as well as a Flavian/Trajanic stamp from pit
F2990 (no 184). An Antonine central Gaulish sherd in
F862, Phase 1.3, must be intrusive. Samian of Period
1 date occurred in later contexts and also occurred in a
handful of military contexts, mostly the overall demolition and levelling horizon (Webster forthcoming).
Samian from the pits was of military date and included
a proportion of pre-Flavian material, indicating that
pottery from them was largely residual. An amphora
stamp of AD 50–100 and a mortaria stamp of AD
70–100 were found, the latter in F2990. A later date
was indicated by the presence, in a few Phase 3 contexts not included in the tables (pers comm Margaret
Darling), of Black Burnished Ware pottery from
Dorset (BB1), which evidence from elsewhere suggests
started to arrive in the north of Britain c AD 120 but
may have arrived at Wroxeter earlier.

The dating evidence suggests activity in the period
AD 90–120 but cannot be defined more sharply to
assign dates to any of the three phases. The coarse pottery from Period 1 contexts was indistinguishable from
the military pottery, while the diagnostic pieces such as
samian were predominantly of military date. The glass
collection from Period 1, however, could be distinguished from the military period collection, but, again,
no sharper definition was possible. The almost complete
absence of Trajanic samian might suggest a break in
occupation. However, Trajanic samian and coins are
present in later contexts.

Period 1 building types and plans

The majority of walls were marked by trench lines in
which sill beams had been set, occasionally on stones
placed in the base of the trench. A rarely encountered
variation of this type had stone-filled trenches onto
which sill beams would have been placed at a level
above the contemporary ground level. A second wall
construction method was witnessed by post trenches in
which lines of small post or stakeholes were set, occasionally on padstones. A third building type was represented by a clay-filled trench interrupted by more
widely spaced rectangular sectioned uprights. There
were indications that short horizontal beams had been

placed on the clay packing between the uprights, and
would have lain above the ground level. Material in the
demolition deposits showed the walls of both types of
building to have been of wattle and daub, with nails
indicating timber framing. The absence of tiles suggested shingle or thatch roofs.

Different building methods were used in different
phases. Post and sill beam trenches were used in Phase
1, while sill beam and clay-filled trenches were used in
Phase 2. The rotting of ground-set timbers seems to
have influenced their replacement in the latest additions to the rear of Buildings 3 and 4 by wall techniques
which set the base plates above the ground.

The Period 1 record was not complete. Insufficient
time affected excavation in the area covering the southern end of the buildings on the street frontage. This
took place in the last season and was not fully completed. Some wall lines were recorded only as lines of
small postholes, although more careful excavation further north had revealed the trenches into which they
had been set. This may account for the apparent gap
between the two suggested buildings. Where more time
had been available for excavation it was clear that some
of the sill beam trenches replaced deeper post trenches. Although not all sill beam trenches were checked
for earlier post trenches, it is possible that two-phase
walls were present in the majority of cases. However, it
seems that post trenches were never used for the street
frontage, where walls were set in sill beam trenches
from the outset.

Over-enthusiastic mechanical clearance of the area in
preparation for the 1980 season removed the possibility
of observing a stratigraphic link between Building 1
Rooms 2 and 6, and Building 3 Rooms 1 and 4. This
work was undertaken without archaeological supervision
and mistakenly cut into unrecorded Period 1 levels.

No complete room plans were recorded, although
many can be restored on the basis of elements of two,
three, or four sides. The best surviving wall lines were
recorded on the west frontage where they were cut into
ditch fills, and to the east where they were clearly visible
in the former intervallum road. In other areas the
demolition layers into which the structures were cut,
may have rendered the slight remains less visible. The
Period 1 deposits were generally compressed into layers averaging 0.3m deep. In contrast the constant
replacement of similar buildings elsewhere, necessitated by the method of construction, resulted in a considerable rise in the ground level, as at Verulamium Insula
XIV (Frere 1972, 5).

Some truncation of deposits may have occurred to
remove other evidence of the Phase 3 Building 5. This
seems to have been a complete rebuilding on a prepared ground surface, and with a frontage set in from
the earlier line, perhaps to accommodate a covered
walkway since no evidence of road gravels was found.
Either the great part of the evidence for this building
was lost in Period 2 building works, or the new building was unfinished.

18

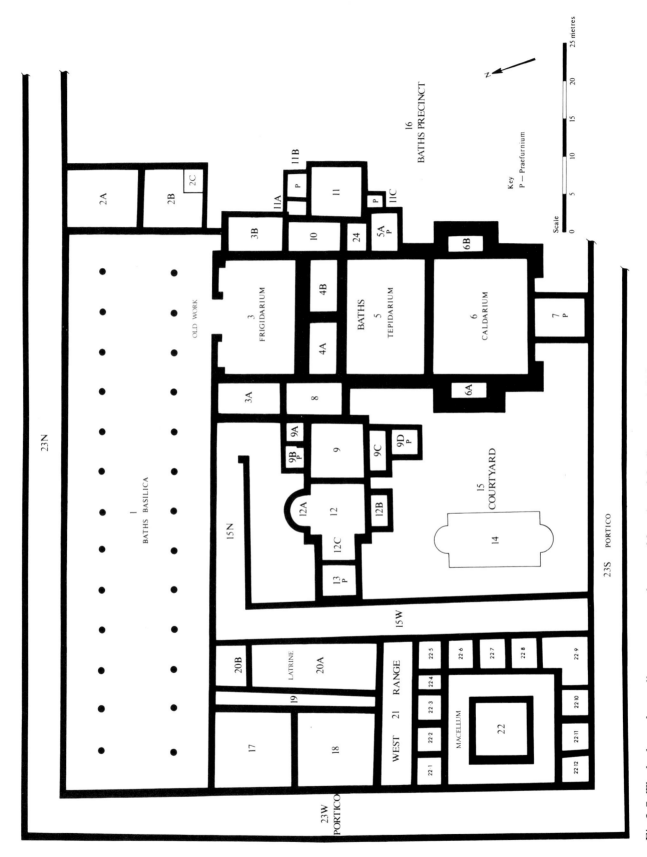

Fig 2.7 The baths and macellum, room numbers, and location of the five areas; 1:500

Period 1 buildings were carefully sought in the area east of Rooms 1.10 and 3.7 (Building A/B), south of Rooms 1.11 and 1.12, and north of Room 2.3 and Building 4, but none was found. The sections do not suggest any greater degree of truncation here than elsewhere (Fig 2.38). It seems likely that a courtyard area was maintained to the rear of Rooms 1.10 and 3.7, the former Building A/B.

Period 2: the second-century public buildings

Baths

Baths phase 1 (B 2.1)

Room and area numbers are shown on Fig 2.7. A number of small scale excavations was undertaken within the baths building (Figs 1.3 and 2.8). These comprised both cuttings into deposits *in situ* and areas cleared of demolition material.

The walls of Rooms 3A, 3B, 8, and 10 were butted on to the main baths block and were thus secondary. All the walls of the phase were of a red sandstone from the Keele Beds. There was evidence of early wall arrangements in Rooms 8 and 10 that was subsequently abandoned. Excavations there uncovered walls beneath the floors of the rooms, two of which also survived incorporated in later masonry (Fig 2.10: S6 and S8). In Room 10 a cutting was carried down against the outer face of the main baths wall beneath the base of the hypocaust. This located two well-built walls, F4009 and F4010, butted against the main wall (Fig 2.10: S5; Fig 2.11). The northern of the two walls lay on the line of the north wall of 11 and may have been the same.

The subsoil surface was sealed by a layer of daub and charcoal, 4, and by a layer of gravelly sand, 3 (Fig 2.10: S6). These were presumably military deposits and perhaps represent the infilling of pits. Layer 3 had been partially removed by a large cutting, F4154, to insert the two walls and the south wall of Room 10, F4011. The foundation trench, F4214, for the north wall, F4008, was cut from the north side of layer 3. Sandstone chippings, layer 2, represented debris from construction work on the new wall footings which were built freestanding. Dumps of sand, layer 1, had then brought the level up. The wall stubs were subsequently levelled off beneath the floor of Room 10, F4220.

In Room 8 the east-west running wall, F4066, between Room 9 and Rooms 9A and 9B, can be seen surviving in the fabric of the west wall, and it clearly continued eastward (Fig 2.10: S8). A small scale excavation beneath the floor of Room 8 confirmed this, by locating the wall footings, F4156, beneath the floor of the room (Fig 2.10: S7). Wall F4066 and its footings were bonded in at a low level to the west wall of Room 8, F4067, where it ran to the south, although a tile course in the east-west wall was not continued in the

north-south wall. Wall F4067 was set on a large red sandstone block and this line was continued beneath the T-junction of the walls by a large grey sandstone block, F4221, 1.1m long and 0.3m deep. This had been reused since a rebate could be seen on its upper northern edge. In contrast F4069, the west wall of Room 8 north of F4066, was clearly butted to F4066.

In the *frigidarium*, Room 2, a trench was cut on the east side of the room (Fig 2.12: S9). The floor of the room, F4024, comprised a succession of pitched purple sandstone and mortar layers, 1.2m deep, to take the concrete floor surface. Stones from the lowest course weighed between 14 and 23kg. The floor levels and make up were all set abutting the *frigidarium* wall. Mortar spillage on the pitched stones next to the wall suggested that this might be from wall construction above the floor level. The cut into natural, F4142, below the floor make up was a pit, presumably military; the floor deepened over the pit.

The floor was more fully recorded in 1988–9. This showed other archaeological trenches beside that of the 1955–85 campaign, but demonstrated that the original surface survived intact in places (Fig 2.8). The original floor was of *opus signinum*, set on mortar and overlying sandstone rubble. The surface had been worn through to the rubble in places and there had been considerable sinkage. Traces of the mosaics known in the niches of the Old Work were found, and it could be seen that the floor had been laid first and then the wall mosaics set in place. The tesserae were of micaceous flagstone, generally used for borders in the basilical hall.

A trench was cut on the west side of the *tepidarium*, Room 5 (Fig 2.12: S10; Fig 2.13). The footings of the west wall of the baths, F4213, were exposed at the base of a robber trench. The subfloor, F4125, was 0.81m deep and composed of two layers of pitched sandstone each with an overlying concrete layer. The lowest tile of the *pilae* stacks measured 0.3m square with 0.23m square tiles above. None of the original stacks survived complete but sections of the upper floor fallen between them showed that it was at least 0.15m thick, and may, from the evidence of photographs, have been as much as 0.3m thick. The *pilae* were recorded across the southern half of the room. They were set more or less at 0.6m intervals both north-south and east-west.

Two further trenches were cut across the east wall, F4003, and the subfloor. The floor here was almost 1m deep. The *pilae* had been destroyed in Period 3 alterations (Fig 2.12: S11–13). The wall widths varied in the two cuttings.

A similar hypocaust system was present in Room 6, the *caldarium*, where again a strong underfloor, F4136, was located in a cutting in the west alcove, Room 6A, with a layer of soot above (Fig 2.12: S14). The lowest part of F4136 was a layer of cobbles set in sand. Above this was pitched sandstone supporting an upper surface of concrete, giving a total floor depth of 1.27m.

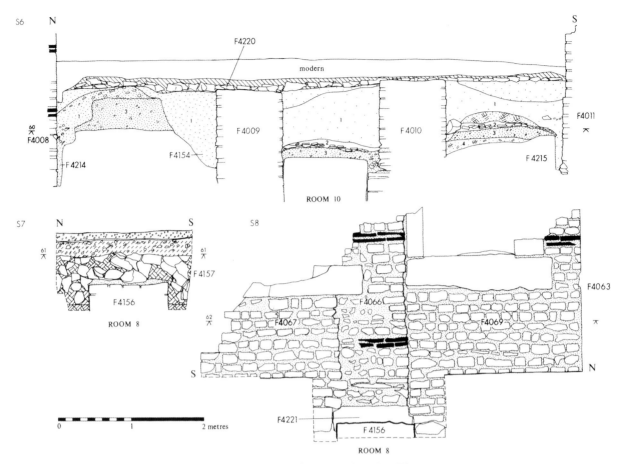

Fig 2.10 Unused and replaced walls in Rooms 8 and 10, sections 6-8, location Fig 2.8; 1:50

Fig 2.11 Room 10 unused walls; view south-west

The floor appeared to overlie the north wall of 6A, F4213. There was no evidence of *pilae* here. A trench on the east side of Room 6 was cut to the surface of the underfloor (Fig 2.12: S15). The *pilae* stacks of 0.18m square tiles were set on a larger tile about 0.29m square, slightly different sizes to those found in the *tepidarium*. One complete stack was found measuring 0.67m high. The tiles were bonded with clay. The suspended floor, F4141, was badly crushed and broken but fragments suggested a thickness of at least 0.23m with a tessellated surface patterned principally in grey and white but with some red tesserae.

The east and west walls of the *caldarium* continued across the face of the two lateral alcoves in both of which would have been *labra*. Two areas of suspended floor *in situ* were found in addition to F4141 seen in section. *Pilae* were not found in the southern part of the *caldarium*. Part of a pattern of octagons and roundels for the painted roof has been restored from plaster finds within the room (Davey and Ling 1982, 200). A fragment of red painted wall plaster was found on which a graffito had been scored. Possible fragments of tufa voussoirs were found and some tufa blocks were still bonded together with mortar and crushed tile. Fragments of box tile suggested *tubulatio* linings for the walls.

Beyond Room 6 was the principal furnace room with the walls of the *praefurnium* and boiler support against the *caldarium* south wall (Figs 2.8 and 2.51).

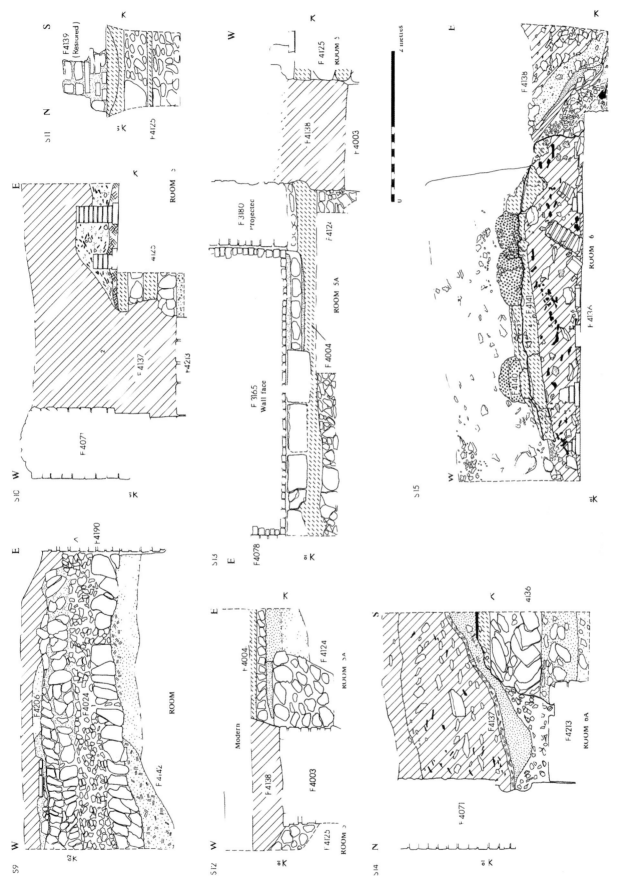

Fig 2.12 Sections 9-15 in Baths Rooms 3, 5, and 6, location Fig 2.8; 1:50

The south wall was earlier than the south courtyard wall which clasped it. A major entry from the street and a minor doorway to the baths precinct to the east is suggested by the surviving evidence. Excavations uncovered a succession of flue arrangements beneath the boiler supports in the north of the room, with superimposed re-buildings. In the south part of the room was dumped material from the final furnace clearance. This is described under Baths phase 3.3 below.

Clearance in Room 3B in 1988 located surviving floor levels on either side of an earlier archaeological trench. The floor was a simple white mosaic bedded on *opus signinum*. The floor did not extend to the walls but would have butted against a stone step on the west side and stone benches on the other sides. The bench on the east was set on mortar and had been faced with 0.17m thick stone slabs of which two survived. These had been faced with *opus signinum*. The step and benches had been renewed at some point as can be seen on the west wall where sandstone blocks and tiles had been set to form an edge to the mosaic.

Clearance in Rooms 11 and 11B revealed a primary arched opening for the *praefurnium* flue between the two rooms (Fig 2.14; 2.15: S17). In Room 11B the tiled flue walls, F4209 and F4210, had been rebuilt on many occasions. They ran through the arch into Room 11, forming a heat duct running towards the centre of the room although of the west wall only the mortar impressions survived (Fig 2.8). In Room 11B, steps, F3161 and F3162, ran down from a doorway, F3159, in its east wall, F3096 (Fig 2.15: S16 and 19). In later phases the doorway had been successively raised to conform with the levels outside and had been rebuilt in a final narrower form. The arrangement of flue and steps was mirrored in Room 9B on the west side.

The floor of Room 11 was of *opus signinum* set on a sandstone rubble base (Fig 2.15: S17, layer 7; S18, layer 2). Cement surfaces still survived on the side walls (Fig 2.16). The foundation trench for the north wall, F3164, had been backfilled with stone rubble (Fig 2.15: S18, layers 3 and 4; Fig 2.16). Although this fill differed from that in the foundation trench of F4009 in Room 10 to the west, the two walls follow the same line and are likely to be the same build as was the case in Room 8 in the west lateral suite.

Room 9 on the opposite side of the baths was cleared in 1988–9 (Fig 2.8). All that survived here was the concrete underfloor, although nineteenth-century photographs show a few *pilae in situ*. Very little of its surface survived. The concrete matrix contained cobbles, pebbles, and tile chips. The subfloor had been completely eroded in an area south of the *praefurnium* flue from 9B, exposing the mortar and rubble raft beneath.

Externally the baths walls were built with slight offsets. The foundation trenches were not examined, but those for Rooms 5 and 6 are likely to have been at least 2m deep, the depth of the footings of a later added wall around the outside of the rooms. Where the walls were buried by underfloor footings, as in the *tepidarium*, they were invariably found to have facing stones and struck mortar joints as could only have been the case with walls built free standing.

Fig 2.13   Room 5, west side: subfloor and pilae; *view north-east*

Fig 2.14 Room 11B, praefurnium *arch; view south-west*

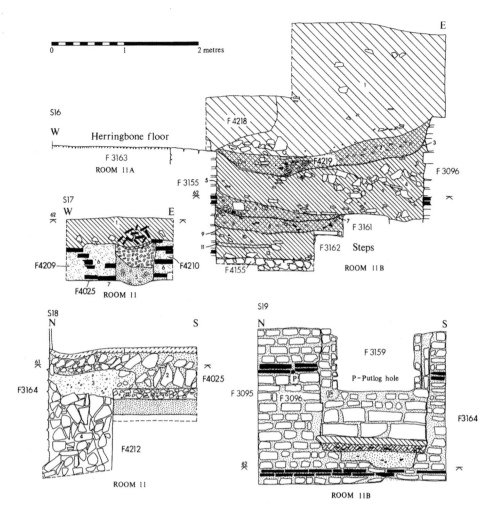

Fig 2.15 Sections 16-19 in Rooms 11 and 11B, location Fig 2.8; 1:50

To the east of 11B, a stack of six box flue tiles, the uppermost broken, had been placed vertically against the outside face of the footings in the foundation trench of the east wall (Figs 2.17; 2.41: S36). The lowest tile was set on a flat tile at the base of the trench. A similar tile stack was recorded on the exterior of the south wall of Room 11, again in its foundation trench (Figs 2.18; 2.41: S35). Four box tiles were recorded here, again starting at the base of the trench.

The early walls in Rooms 8 and 10 on either side of Room 4 indicate a primary arrangement of the lateral rooms which was subsequently superseded. Wall F4068 and its footing F4156 and wall F4009 represent an initial continuation of the north walls of Rooms 9 and 11 to abut the main baths block; masonry tusks on the latter indicating that they were planned from the beginning. They were presumably intended to form the north walls of Rooms 8 and 10 which would have left a corridor between them and the alcoves containing the *frigidarium* plunge baths, Rooms 3A and 3B. The bonding of F4066 with the wall between Rooms 8 and 9 was presumably replicated on the east side, giving two rooms in the lateral suites on either side. However, the corner entrances at the south-west and south-east of the *frigidarium* discussed by Donald Mackreth in Chapter 3, suggest that this layout was abandoned before completion.

The southern wall, F4010, in Room 10 is not easily understood. It is possible that the wall was intended as an additional foundation beneath the floor of the room across an earlier infilled feature. The floor found in Room 8 would have formed the base for *pilae* stacks with a suspended floor at the level of the threshold stones leading to Rooms 9 and 9B.

The vertical box tile stacks found to the south of Room 11 and east of Room 11B were both set within the wall foundation trenches and seem to be primary, neither section showing any evidence that they were inserted. The northern stack might be seen as a flue from the furnace Room 11B, but there was no evidence there or in Room 11C that they were connected with the interior of the rooms. The stacks may have been intended as a damp course arrangement. Externally applied *tubulatio* have been noted in London at the Lime Street bath house, although there the *tubulatio* were laid in horizontal courses (Frere 1984b, 309, pl XIXG). However the survival of only two vertically arranged stacks makes this unlikely. If the stacks were intended as drainage sumps, it might be expected that they would be secondary insertions rather than being apparently provided *ab initio*.

Fig 2.16 Room 11, junction of north and west walls, view north-west

Fig 2.17 Baths precinct, east wall of Room 11B, box tile stack; view south

A final possibility is that the tiles on end were used as a rough reckoner of the depth of the footings during the construction process.

Fig 2.18 Room 11C, box tile stack; view east

The quantity of pottery collected was small and was dated first-century with the exception of a carinated bowl of Flavian/Trajanic date.

Baths phase 2 (B 2.2)

An additional wall, F3180 and F4071, on the east and west side respectively, was provided surrounding Rooms 5 and 6 (Fig 2.8). The wall was of grey coloured Hoar Edge Grit stone in contrast to the earlier Keele Beds stone. Its foundation trench was examined in three cuttings on the west side (Fig 2.39: S30, F3244), a single cutting on the south side (Fig 2.51: S47, F4134), and three further cuttings on the east side (Fig 2.42: S37 and S38, F3181). It averaged over 2m deep and was cut from the initial Phase 1 construction levels in the courtyard and the baths precinct. On the west side of the *caldarium* it described a wide sweep in plan, running from the south-west corner of the alcove to the south-west corner of the baths (Fig 2.31). It was also followed northward in plan as far as Room 10 where it cut the foundation trench of the room. The trench was cut in a single process with no indications of lengths of trench opened at different stages.

On the east side the line of the additional wall was interrupted northward by a later building, Room 5A. It was not clear whether the south wall of 5A had cut through the additional wall. Excavations across the *tepidarium* footings into Room 5A sectioned uncoursed stone footings, F4124, 0.83m wide on the line of the additional wall (Fig 2.12: S12 and S13). Excavation was insufficient to clarify whether there was a foundation trench. A small cutting at the angle of the *tepidarium* and Room 10 revealed no evidence of the additional wall.

The additional wall was butted up against the wall of the *caldarium* and *tepidarium* (Fig 2.12: S10 and S14, F4071). Where the latter was subsequently robbed it was possible to see how close was the contact of the new outer wall by the impression of the offsets of the inner wall on the inside of the outer wall. A stone with a building inscription had been reused upside down at the south external angle of the alcove 6A. The inscription was similar to that on two other stones found in earlier excavations, one definitely and the other probably from Room 17 (Wright 1966, 218).

At some point in the life of the baths, but presumably relatively early, the Phase 1 walls beneath the floors of Rooms 8 and 10 were levelled. The north part of the west wall of Room 8 had been butted on to the east-west wall which remained as a wall stub (Fig 2.10: S8). The remains of the footings to the east had then been sealed in by the floor of the room, F4157. This was 0.8m deep and made of concrete set on a pitched purple sandstone base which ran up over the footings from deeper sections on either side (Fig 2.10: S7).

The east wall of Room 10 had likewise been extended northward to abut the south wall of Room 3B. Both east-west cross walls were levelled. Little remained of the floor here but a spread of purple sandstone beneath the modern surface suggested the survival of a make up layer similar to that in Room 8 (Fig 2.10: S6, F4220).

The function of the Room 5 and 6 additional wall seems likely to have been to provide additional support for a barrel vault over the *caldarium* and *tepidarium*. The later robbing of the primary wall around Rooms 5 and 6 (Baths Phase 3.4, below) denies the opportunity to demonstrate whether subsidence or cracking had occurred, although the latter was reported by the excavator (Webster 1991, 76). It must be suspected that none had taken place and that the additional wall was provided before the vault had been completed. The very great size of the additional wall trench, and its apparently continuous rather than sectional build, must suggest that no danger was foreseen of any bowing outward of the original walls. Had this been the case its insertion would have been a hazardous enterprise. It would seem most likely that the initial wall width was seen to be insufficient early in the campaign.

Although the surviving sections show that the additional wall continued to at least 1m above ground level, it may not have been carried up to eaves level. The evidence from Room 5A might suggest that the wall may have originally continued northward to the south wall of Room 10. Its later removal in Room 5A (Baths phase B 3.1, below) suggests that it was not built to roof level and that its function must therefore have been essentially to reinforce the foundations of the primary wall around Rooms 5 and 6. The evidence of F4124 from Room 5A could be interpreted as representing the rubble filled foundation trench of the original wall; the additional wall would therefore have terminated short of Room 10, again indicating additional footings rather than a wall to roof level.

Other additional walls around baths have been noted. At Caerleon a wall around the *caldarium* and *tepidarium* has very slight foundations and was not carried much more than 1.4m above the contemporary ground level (Zienkiewicz 1986, I, 220). A parallel was suggested with Vindonissa where a concrete apron was added around the *caldarium*, and in both cases a structural function was adduced, specifically to counteract outward bowing (Zienkiewicz 1986, I, 221 n1). The pattern of robbing at the Jewry walls baths, Leicester, also suggests an additional wall (Kenyon 1948).

There was no dating evidence for this phase from within the baths. From the foundation trench of the additional wall (KG 9) came a samian sherd dated to AD 100–150 and early second-century pottery.

West Range

West Range phase 1 (WR 2.1)

Excavations at the north end of the latrine re-examined an area previously excavated by Wright and Johnson (Fig 2.19; Chapter 6, section 4). A wall, F4038, was located dividing off a northern latrine room, running parallel to the basilical hall and 4.4m from it. The lower levels of the east wall of the latrine butted against F4038, although the upper sections of both walls were bonded (Fig 2.20: S20). The wall, of red sandstone facing stones from the Keele Beds and a mortar and rubble core, had been constructed at the same time as a floor footing, F4039, to its north, similar to those found in the baths. The floor was 0.9m deep and had been cut into the natural sand judging by its base level which was lower than the natural surface to the south (Fig 2.20: S20 and S21). It had been constructed of two layers of pitched sandstones divided by mortar beneath a layer of concrete (Fig 2.20: S21; Fig 2.21: S23). A circular mound, F4037, of mortar and stone, 0.3m high and about 1.5m in diameter, was located in the north-west corner of the floor.

To the north, sandstone footings, F4035, suggest the base of the baths drain known to run east to west along the south side of the basilical hall. To the west the wall and the floor both abutted a similar north-south running pitched sandstone foundation, F4036, beneath the west wall of the latrine (Fig 2.20: S20 and 21; Fig 2.21: S24), and this must represent surviving elements of a southward turn of the drain. The west side of the drain was not clearly located but was presumably formed by the west wall of the latrine.

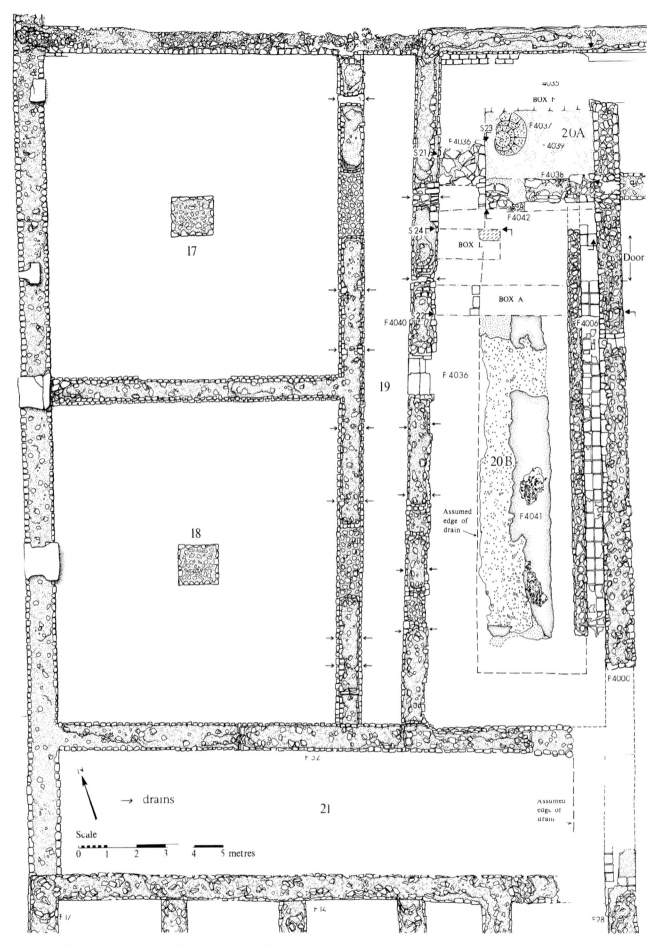

Fig 2.19 West range: latrine and ?tabernae; 1:125

In two of the sections, a regular east side of a single stone thickness was carried up 1.06m above the pitched stone (Fig 2.20: S21and S22). This was not present in a third cutting located between the first two (Fig 2.21: S24). Here the drain footing continued eastward to a minimum distance of 2.4m from the west wall of the latrine. A spread of concrete, F4042, may represent the remains of a lateral opening off the drain. Further evidence of a feature here was seen in a narrow cutting on the south side of wall F4038 which showed a wall running south (Fig 2.19). A small rectangular side drain may have led to the main drain in the north-west corner of Room 20B. The drain was seen to turn at the south end of the Room to run down the east side of the *macellum*. At the south-east corner of the latrine it was seen at a right-angled turn during a brief exposure during restoration work by Ministry workmen (Fig 2.22).

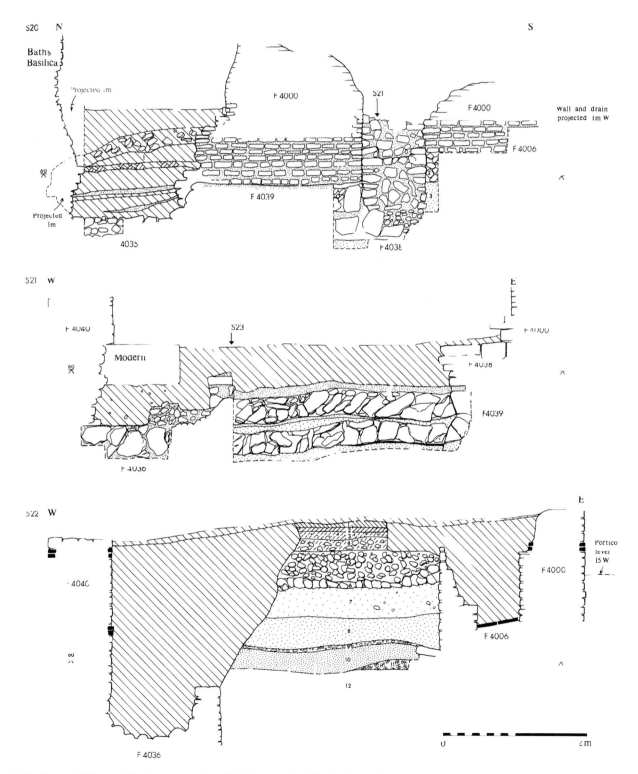

Fig 2.20 Room 20A and B, latrine sections 20-22, location Fig 2.19; 1:50

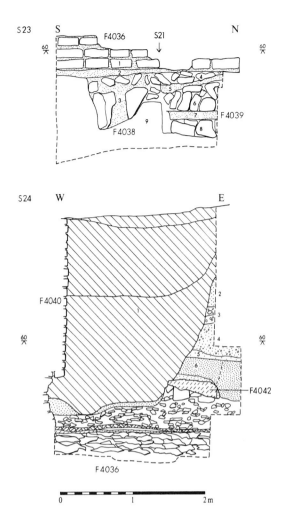

Fig 2.21 Room 20B, latrine sections 23-24, location Fig 2.19; 1:50

Fig 2.22 North wall of corridor 21, west side of drain; view north-west

Beneath the later *macellum*, two trenches were found running north-south. (Figs 2.23 and 2.24). The trenches, F355 and F364, were cut to a depth of 0.3m (Fig 2.38: S27; Fig 2.39: S30). They were separated by 3.5m and, although only a small part of the eastern one was located, seemed to run parallel down the centre of the range. Upcast from the trenches overlay the Period 1 and military destruction horizon. Trench F364 was seen to terminate with a rounded end, at a point 5m to the north of the *insula* perimeter. A posthole, F75, may have been associated.

The drain, F4085, continued beneath the east side of the *macellum*, and had been built as one with the *macellum* (Fig 2.9; Fig 2.25: S25). Three successive stages in the building of the interior walls of the east range have been isolated and these were clear in wall F27 (Fig 2.26; Archive E1.1). Despite the completeness of the robbing, it was possible to see that the east wall of the *macellum* formed the east side of the drain. This was particularly marked by an area of stone work built into the wall opposite the outlet from the *macellum*, presumably to obviate damage to the wall (Fig 2.27). The line of the drain across the south portico was marked by its eastern side, the drain itself having been extensively robbed (Fig 2.19; Fig 2.38: S29).

The *macellum* construction level comprised large blocks of red Keele Beds sandstone, sandstone chippings, and tile, as well as spreads of mortar and sand. An area of burning possibly marked a hearth. A spread of cobbles was also recorded, perhaps used as a hard-standing. Between the inner and outer rectangle of the primary *macellum* walls, where there were later dumps, it was not possible to distinguish a Phase 1 building level from subsequent construction debris described below. The same was true in the main access corridor north of the *macellum* (Fig 2.39: S30). The *macellum* construction sequence can be unravelled from the surviving walls (Fig 3.4; Chapter 3). In this phase it is assumed that the walls shown in Fig 3.4 stage 3 had been constructed.

The foundation trench, F4174, for the east wall of the latrine was sectioned (Fig 2.70: S56), and two sections of *macellum* foundation trench were partly emptied, one on the interior of the west wall at the south end, and the other on the south side of the internal south wall.

In the excavations in the latrine it seems likely that the footings found against the wall of the basilical hall represent the base of the main baths drain. This area had been explored by Henry Johnson in the nineteenth century, when the workmen found themselves in a drain, 2.74m below ground level, large enough to 'creep' into (Chapter 6, section 4.8). The south side of the drain would have been robbed out in the area examined but would have been marked only by a low wall between the drain, F4035, and the massive floor footing, F4039. The section across the suggested drain footing against the basilical hall wall shows a projection from the east which may represent the seating for a drain cover (Fig 2.20: S20).

The evidence on the west side of the latrine shows a similar feature and indicates that the main baths drain turned south. The raised east side and pitched base of F4036 must represent the surviving remains of footings which would have lain beneath a flagstone drain base.

The floor surface in Room 20A thus lay at the same level as the base of the drain as it turned a right angle southward at least 1.6m below the floor level of Room 20B. Its depth suggests that this was a lowered area intended to give access to the drain and there could

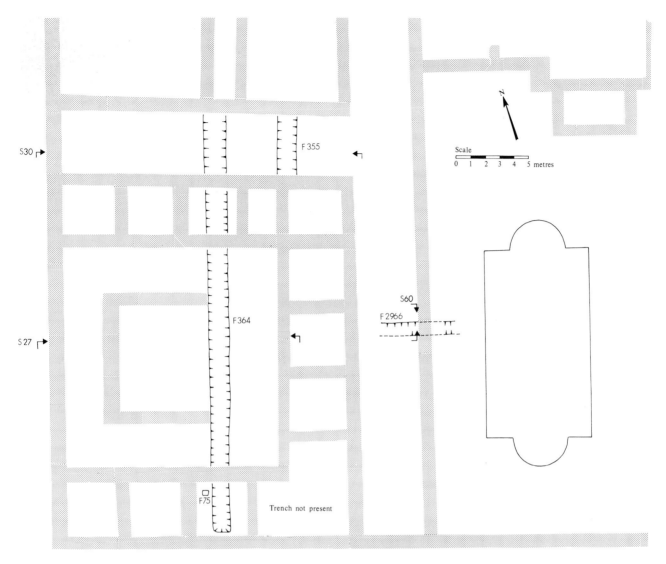

S30

F 355

Scale
0 1 2 3 4 5 metres

S60

F 2966

F 364

S 27

F 75

Trench not present

Trenches not present

Fig 2.23 West range and courtyard, Period 2.1 unused construction trenches; 1:250

well have been a timber floor above at the level of Room 20B which could then have been used by latrine attendants as suggested by Donald Mackreth (Chapter 3). The mortar area F4037 could conceivably have been the setting for a roof support.

The *macellum* walls F28 and F29 would have formed a corridor within which the drain could be built, in the same way as the south wall of the basilical hall and the sleeper wall of the north portico of the courtyard may have done.

The two apparently unused trenches beneath the *macellum* may have been marking out trenches for proposed buildings or simply have been mistakes. If the former then the western trench may have been intended for a southern continuation of the east wall of Rooms 17 and 18 indicating an original intention to have a west range the depth of Rooms 17 and 18 along the street frontage. This suggestion is enhanced by wall F4038 in the latrine. This predated the east wall of the latrine in its initial courses, and projected eastward would form an extension of the stylobate sleeper wall defining por-

tico 15N on the south side of the basilical hall. A similar conclusion would arise if the two trenches were seen as marking either side of a continuation of the main drain running directly south from the west side of the latrine. A third unused trench found in the courtyard may have been intended to mark a drain from the *natatio* (see below). However, these trenches may also be seen simply as errors. The western trench would have been a mistaken southward continuation of the east wall of Rooms 17 and 18, and the eastern trench a mistaken northward extension of the *macellum* internal wall.

Two coins, the latest of Trajan (AD 103–11) were found in *macellum* construction layers (cat nos 15 and 123). A military object (Fig 4.6, 4), a needle used for textile working (Fig 4.16, 168), a handle from an item of furniture (Fig 4.25, 254), and a melon bead fragment (cat no 10) were found. With the exception of a few first-century pieces, datable vessel glass was from pieces in use in the later first and the first half of the second centuries (Figs 4.37, 703; 4.42, 815; cat nos 668, 669, 680, 693, 694, 713, 749, 751–2, 756, 759, 766–8, 796,

Fig 2.24 West range, unused construction trench; view south-west

810, 814, 817, 828, 829, 837–9, 850, 858, 859, 866, and 872). Joining fragments from the same vessel were found in WR 2.1 and C 2.1 layers (678 and 892).

Pottery in the unused foundation trenches (KG 4) included a sherd of samian dated Hadrianic/Early Antonine, AD 130–50, and a fragment of a locally-made mortarium dated to AD 120–60, suggesting a date *c* AD 130. There was no dating evidence from excavations in the latrines (KG 27); the east latrine wall is dated to AD 120–50 from the courtyard excavations. Pottery from the foundation trenches of the *macellum* included BB1 sherds dated to later than AD 120 and two further mortaria fragments dated to AD 120–60 and 100–160. About two-thirds of the pottery from this phase was thought to be residual. The residual content and the small numbers of BB1 sherds suggested a *terminus post quem* of *c* AD 120.

West Range phase 2 (WR 2.2)

Within the interior walls of the *macellum*, the Phase 1 building levels and the two unused foundation trenches were sealed beneath a dump of sand (Fig 2.38: S27 and S28, layer 8). Layer 3 in the south-east room, 22.9, may also have been deposited (Fig 2.25: S25).

A number of pits were cut into these dumps (Figs 2.28 and 2.29). They comprised five set against the interior walls from within the central courtyard area,

F585 and F586 on the north side, F584 on the east (Fig 2.38: S27), and F577 and F578 on the south (Fig 2.38: S28, F577). All were rectangular in plan with uneroded vertical or steep sides. Their fills were of sand with tile and stone. On the south side of the courtyard, a further pit, F118, similar to those within the central area, was located on the interior of the building's south wall, cut from the Phase 1 level.

Within the intended main corridor between the street and the courtyard, four similar pits, F354, F375, F379, and F380, were dug against the south wall of Rooms 18, 19, and 20A, and two, F538 and F539, against the north wall of the *macellum*. These, too, were cut from the Phase 1 surface.

The fills of the pits within the *macellum*, and cut against the walls to the north, did not contain evidence of rubbish, and resembled the material through which they had been cut. The profiles and fills of the pits suggest that they were neatly opened and rapidly backfilled. These pits were identified as a special group and called 'inspection pits' by the excavators, and there seems little doubt that they were intended to gain an impression of the depth and nature of the wall footings. Apart from these similar pits, five other examples, three in the courtyard and three in the baths precinct, were also found.

If these similar pits were contemporary, then the ground level was initially raised, in the area examined, only in the interior rectangle of the *macellum*. Dumping

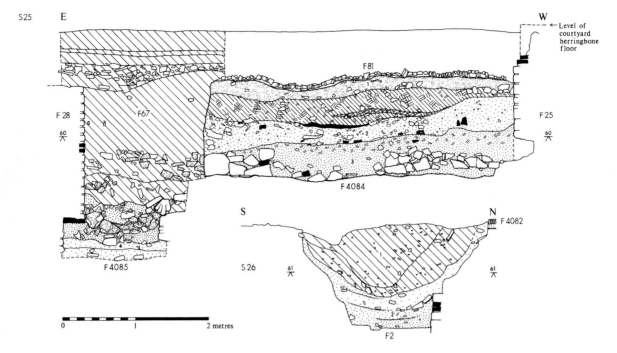

Fig 2.25 Macellum *drain sections 25–26, location Fig 2.9; 1:50*

Fig 2.26 Macellum *east range, wall F27; view north*

Fig 2.27 Macellum *east wall, F28, stonework opposite outlet; view east*

in the block to the north may have occurred now or later. A large hollow, F203, with evidence of burning, and a stakehole, F567, were found within the dumps, suggesting a pause in their deposition (Fig 2.28).

The portico sleeper walls within the *macellum* were constructed from the surface of the dumps. Their construction followed the deposition of a layer of mortar perhaps indicating an initial surface (Fig 2.38: S27 and 28, layer 7). Mixing platforms of white mortar or plaster attested construction work or plastering of completed walls. The sleeper walls were set on rubble footings with coursed stonework above. The material used was the Keele Beds sandstone of the first phase building campaign. The wall on the east side of the western walkway was carried across the face of the south walkway, and may have also crossed the north walkway. The wall came to a rough unfinished end here, and a trench was recorded crossing the walkway.

The trench may have been to insert the wall at a later date; perhaps it had been left incomplete to aid access. The wall may, however, have run originally across the walkway and then been robbed out.

Finds were in general few. A fragment of decorative chain (Fig 4.7, 41), a stone palette, and a fragment of a melon bead (cat no 11) were found, but no coins. One item of late first-century to early second-century vessel glass was datable amongst a small group (Fig 4.44, 735 and 736; cat nos 753, 757, 765, 778, 779, and 846). A glass counter (cat no 47) was found. Soil samples from the dump were analysed (Canti 1988).

From the sand dump, a mortarium fragment dated to AD 120–60 was the latest datable pottery, together with a small number of BB1 sherds. A sherd of Trajanic samian came from one of the corridor inspection pits. With this exception, there was no distinctively second-century pottery from the pits (KG 6).

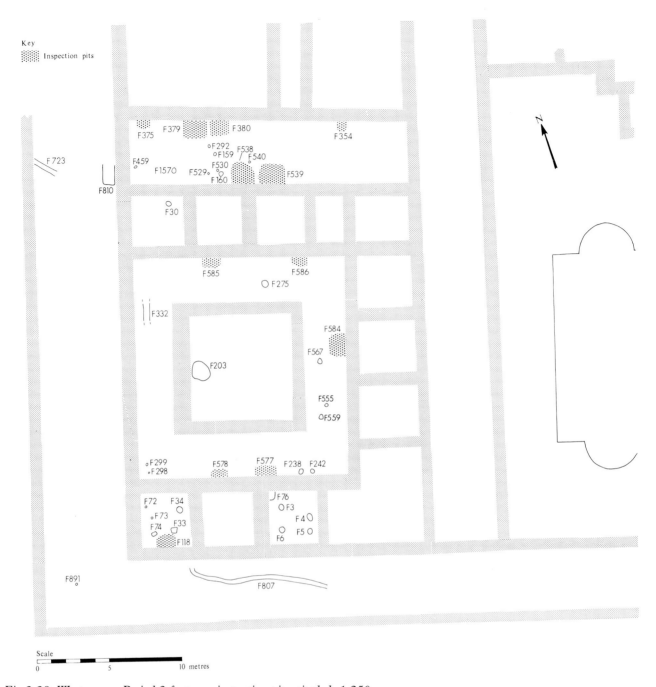

Fig 2.28 West range, Period 2 features, inspection pits stippled; 1:250

The latest samian from the foundation trenches of the *macellum* inner courtyard wall (KG 7) was Hadrianic/Early Antonine. Overall residuality was thought to be as high as 80%. A date similar to WR 2.1 was suggested.

West Range phase 3 (WR 2.3)

The Phase 2 dumps and pits within the *macellum* walls were sealed beneath a further deposit of sand (Fig 2.38: S27 and S28, layers 3 and 6). These sand dumps contained small fragments of tile and stone, and there were interleaved layers of burnt material and pockets of tile. At the south-west interior corner of the *macellum*, the dump comprised sandstone with tile fragments and

wall plaster, sealed beneath a further sand dump. A surface of sand with mortar and sandstone fragments here may represent all that survived of the second-century surface. At the upper level seven postholes were recorded, of which two, F555 and F559, were packed with tile (Fig 2.28). A trench, F332, was found just inside the northern entrance from the west. Spreads of mortar or possibly degraded grey stone chippings which break down to resemble mortar, were also seen on the surface of the dumps.

The Phase 3 surfaces in the walkways of the *macellum* were lost in subsequent re-flooring, but the central courtyard may have retained its original footing. This comprised a layer of rubble, F79, composed of rounded river cobbles set on a spread of soil and broken tile

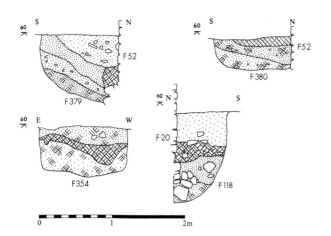

Fig 2.29 West range, inspection pit profiles; 1:50

(Fig 2.38: S27 and S28, layers 4 and 5; Fig 2.52). The relationship of the superstructure of the courtyard drain terminal with the footing was lost in later robbing. The ground level in the area between the outer and inner wall rectangles of the building was brought up to that of the *macellum* interior courtyard in one deposit. In the northern rooms red sandstone chippings were sealed beneath dumped sand. The make up layers in the eastern range of rooms had been removed together with the drain filling in nineteenth-century excavations. To the south, pit F118, was sealed beneath layers of sand containing red sandstone and *tegula* and *imbrex* tile fragments. On the upper surface of the dump were major spreads of construction debris comprising dumps of red sandstone with possible mortar mixing areas. Some grey sandstone blocks from Hoar Edge grits were noted in the rubble. In Room 22.9 a section of these dumps was recorded together with the main drain (Fig 2.25: S25, layers 1 and 2). The subsidiary drain would have been provided with stone facing, but this had been subsequently robbed. A number of postholes in Rooms 22.10 and 12 may represent settings for scaffolding posts as the building was completed (Fig 2.28).

The inspection pits in the corridor north of the *macellum* were sealed by layers of red sandstone rubble, some with tile. Hoar Edge Grit sandstone rubble was also found as well as tile, mortar, and white plaster. This debris was sealed beneath thick layers of sand and clay containing charcoal and tile. On the dump surface were rubble deposits and areas of broken tile and mortar. A scatter of used *opus spicatum* tiles and a *pila* brick was found as well as mortar spreads and a layer with tile, cobbles, stone, and tesserae. There were indications too of dirty trampled surface. Six postholes occurred at this level (Fig 2.28). These upper layers and the postholes were sealed beneath a gravel surface forming the first level within what was now the corridor through from the street to the baths courtyard. The material used to raise the level of the *macellum* and infilling the corridor cannot be linked to any contemporary groundwork within the *insula*, and

may have been brought in. The inner courtyard footing of cobbles may indicate the former presence of a heavy feature above.

Six coins were found, the latest dating to Vespasian (cat nos 4, 9, 27, 40, 43, and 106). A possibly military stud (Fig 4.7, 22), a finger ring (Fig 4.7, 33), a bracelet (Fig 4.8, 50), a toilet implement and counter (Fig 4.11, 121, 126), a statuette (Fig 4.12, 137), three styli and a seal box (Fig 4.13, 142, 143, 147, and 150), a weight (Fig 4.14, 154), a weaving tablet (Fig 4.16, 173), a lock and key (Fig 4.19, 185 and 202), a spatula (Fig 4.22, 231), a furniture fitting (Fig 4.25, 252), and two scrap fragments (Fig 4.29, 291 and 293) are illustrated small finds, and a fragment of wall veneer and a honestone (cat no 22) were also noted. Three brooches were found, two dating to AD 90–175 (Fig 4.32, 2, 4, and 10), and an intaglio thought to be not earlier than the last quarter of the second century and perhaps intrusive (Fig 4.36, 6). Vessel glass comprised early to mid second-century pieces as well as first-century fragments (Fig 4.37, 702; 4.40, 731; 4.43, 821; 4.44, 737 and 743; cat nos 666–7, 670–2, 674, 676, 679, 682–6, 688–92, 695–701, 712, 714–5, 717–9, 727, 738–9, 741, 746–8, 754–5, 758, 762–4, 769–70, 774–5, 777, 780–3, 786–8, 790–1, 795, 797–801, 803, 805–7, 813, 819, 823–5, 827, 830–1, 834–6, 840–1, 847, 849, 852, 854–5, 860–1, 864–5, 867–8, and 874). There were two intrusive fourth-century pieces, one from the corridor (Fig 4.46, 869), and one from Room 22.10 in the *macellum* (Fig 4.46, 742). Three glass counters and a stirring rod were also found (cat nos 48, 52, 63, and 67). Three crucibles from metalworking were collected (cat nos 3–5) and a fragment of a pottery bowl used to apply blue dye.

From the dumps, 29 sherds of Antonine and over 70 sherds of Hadrianic/Early Antonine samian (Fig 4.97, D13; stamp no 195), together with a large amount of BB1 allowed Faiers to suggest a *terminus post quem* of AD 160–70, although a mid second-century date could perhaps be more safely argued. The proportion of BB1 at 1:7.5 of the total and the quantity of residual material, calculated at 40%, indicate a difference between the Phase 2 and 3 assemblages. Two sherds of East Gaulish samian with dates running into the third century, and a sherd of Nene valley ware seem likely to be intrusive.

There were a number of pottery cross-fits between sherds in the *macellum* courtyard. There were also joins between the courtyard dumps and the dumps within the *macellum* rooms. Joins were also recorded from this group with sherds from the upper dumps in the porticos (P 2.3) and from the make up layers in the courtyard portico (C 2.3). Although a large proportion of the small finds and glass objects come from the corridor, the finds mark a sharp contrast between the two dumps in the *macellum*, with WR 2.2 dumps containing few finds of any category. The two dumps clearly derived from different sources.

Porticos

Portico phase 1 (P 2.1)

Foundation trenches for the *macellum* were cut from the Period 1 levels. On these surfaces in the west portico a spread of builders material was recorded outside the *macellum* entrance. The surfaces were heavily trampled. A pit, F810, had been cut against the west wall of the range of offices and *macellum* from the west side (Fig 2.28; Fig 2.58: S48). This was located at the entrance way to the corridor.

Construction of a stylobate sleeper wall earlier than the surviving example may have taken place in this phase. In Box 80, the eastern section excavated in the south portico, the sleeper wall was seen to have been of three successive builds with the earliest wall built of coursed stonework, the stones all of Keele Beds sandstone (Fig 2.65: S55, F4030). The wall came to a stepped end within the section examined. The surface of each exposed course was unmortared and it was clear that this was an unfinished rather than a demolished section. On the contemporary ground surface, layers of gravel and some evidence of rutting indicated that traffic entered the site at what was presumably an entrance way. This superseded sleeper wall was also recorded some 48m to the west in Box 98 where it was traced for 8.5m (Fig 2.9; Fig 2.58: S52). Its eastern end may mark the other side of a wide gap left open for construction traffic. These two stretches of wall in the south portico suggest that they were accompanied by an early sleeper wall for the west portico although there was no evidence of two phases in the later wall.

Four coins were found, all Claudian (cat nos 26, 32, 73, and 68). Military pendants (Fig 4.6, 13), toilet implements (Fig 4.11, 117 and 122), a seal box (Fig 4.13,152), a furniture fitting (Fig 4.25, 251), and a nail (Fig 4.26, 264) are illustrated small finds. Datable vessel glass was principally first-century with a few items in use up to the mid second century (cat nos 107–8, 116, 121, 125, 128, 133, 145, 220, 256, 290, 292, 311, 317, 319, 353–4, 367–8, 372, 418, 443, 445–6, 521, 526, 528, 533, 553, 556, 564, 592, and 612–3). A melon bead and two glass counter (cat nos 4, 51, and 66) were also found.

The latest pottery was samian of Hadrianic/Antonine date. Other material included BB1 and a local beaker copy, and suggested a date of AD 120 or 130. Pottery from this phase was highly fragmented with a residuality level calculated at 86%.

Portico phase 2 (P 2.2)

The sleeper wall in the west portico, F206, was built as one with a second sleeper wall in the south portico, F4031. The remains of a buttress were noted where they joined at the south-west corner of the *insula* (Fig 2.9). The south portico wall cut through and replaced the west part of the earlier wall F4030 (Fig 2.58: S52) but butted against the unfinished end of F4030 in Box 80 (Fig 2.65). Construction of the south wall of the courtyard, F3227, took place prior to dumping to raise the portico level and would presumably have been contemporary with the building of F4031 (Fig 2.60: S53).

On the west side of the *macellum* the written record suggests two phases of builder's activity separated by a levelling dump of sand. This is not represented in the sections which show a general dump of material (Fig 2.58: S48–S51 layer 18). The first phase was represented to the south by dumps of building material, F951, and of water-worn cobbles and red sandstone fragments lying on the Phase 1 surface. These can be seen at the west end of S29 (Fig 2.38, layers 18–20). Layers making up F951 included *imbrex*, *tegula*, *tubulatio*, and *opus spicatum* tile fragments, both Keele Beds and Hoar Edge Grit sandstone, although the former was predominant, mortar, nails, wall plaster fragments, and tesserae. An iron water pipe collar was found, as well as quantities of metallurgical waste.

There were other spreads of stone to the north of F951. These contained water-worn cobbles, a layer of Keele Beds sandstone chippings, and an area of mortar mixing. These were sealed beneath a sand dump, containing fragments of *opus spicatum* and *imbrex* tile, sandstone chippings, nails, and painted wall plaster.

On the resulting level was further evidence of building work. Opposite the entrance to the *macellum* was a succession of mortar mixing areas and spreads of wall plaster. These were made up of laminations of hard mortar and gravel aggregates, interleaved with a mixing area for plaster rendering. Further south similar mortar mixing areas were seen. These layers were covered in places by further spreads of sandstone in which Hoar Edge Grit stone was dominant over the Keele Beds stone.

These levels were sealed beneath a sandy grey layer (Fig 2.58: S48–S50, layer 17). This was seen in plan to be a spread of grey stone chippings, much degraded and forming a compact sandy horizon. Similar layers were seen in nineteenth-century excavations in Rooms 17 and 18 to the north. At the same level were two shallow gullies and seven postholes, one packed with red sandstone and tile.

These dumps were not replicated in the south portico apart from a dump of roof tiles (Fig 2.58: S52, F4221). A gully, F807, was traced for 7m (Fig 2.28). The dumps outside the west side of the *macellum* may represent material brought in, perhaps from the works on the west side of the street, simply to raise the level. However the presence of materials used in the *macellum*, particularly *opus spicatum* tiles and water-worn cobbles, suggests that this material was builders' spoil from construction of the *macellum*. Pottery was less fragmented than that from Phase 1 and the proportion of non-residual pottery was high at 70%. On the new surface was evidence of builders' levels, postholes, possibly from scaffolding, and dumps of roof tile, suggesting a second phase of work on the *macellum*.

Analysis of the *macellum* construction sequence (Fig 3.4; Chapter 3) suggests entry to the building works from the south, with the southern walls built later then the others. The breaks in the south stylobate sleeper walls and the absence of dumps in the south portico support this interpretation.

Four coins were found. Setting aside an intrusive fourth-century coin (cat no 558), the latest coin of three was of Trajan (cat no 120, with 94 and 111). Illustrated small finds comprise a toilet implement from F951 (Fig 4.11: 125), three furniture hinges (Fig 4.24, 242, 244, and 245), and a nail (Fig 4.26, 260). A first-century intaglio was found (Fig 4.36, 8). Three honestones were found (Fig 4.48, 4 and 5, cat no 6), two grooved examples from Kent coming from F951. Glass was of first-century date with some of later first to mid-second-century date (Fig 4.37, cat nos 112, 115, 127, 134, 136, 143B, 147, 159, 160, 191, 202, 222–4, 235, 289, 298, 315, 322, 329, 342–3, 346, 361–6, 395, 399, 403–6, 412–3, 416–7, 463, 488, 491, 501, 503, 520, 534–5, 542, 558–60, 585–6, and 633b), with a group from F951 (Fig 4.38, 287: cat nos 97, 111, 126, 137, 176, 217, 236, 307, 345, 410, 484, 494, 502, 505, 544, 590, and 591). A glass bead and counter were also found (cat nos 30 and 45). Three crucibles used for metalworking were in the dump F951 (cat nos 6–8). Three crucibles used for metalworking were in the dump F951 (cat nos 6–8).

Ten sherds of Antonine samian and fifteen of Hadrianic/early Antonine date were found (stamp no 121/2). The average sherd weight was nearly double that of P 2.1 reflecting the presence of dumped material as well as more shattered residual pottery (Fig 4.90). A BB1 dish (Fig 4.70, D3.14) in F951 at the base of the west portico dump can be dated early Antonine+. This together with the samian indicates a date *c* AD 150.

Portico phase 3 (P 2.3)

In the west portico a further deposit of sand raised the level to the first portico walkway floor, marked by a mortar and gravel surface (Fig 2.58: S48–50, layer 6). At this level the surviving steps into the *macellum* were sited (S49). The three entrance steps to the north door may indicate a similar arrangement at the south door, although only one stone survived there. The surface of the northern entrance stones was partly heavily worn and partly tooled (Fig 2.30), indicating the position of the next flight over the unworn area. The foot of the steps indicates the completed portico floor level, but no evidence of its composition was found. Some truncation may have occurred in places. A short length of trench, F723, was recorded cut into the portico fills and cut across the stylobate sleeper (Fig 2.28). Stones from the stylobate itself would have sealed the trench, and some upper sealing may be envisaged in the portico. The gully seems likely to have held a water pipe or drain.

On the south side of the *macellum* the Phase 2 gully, F807, and roof tile dump, F4221, were sealed beneath dumps of sand and clay (Fig 2.38: S29, layer 17; Fig 2.58: S52). Within this horizon were occasional discontinuities, with records of a stone and mortar layer and a sandy layer with tile, tesserae, stones, nails, and metallurgical waste incorporated. The layer also contained *opus spicatum* and *tegula* tile. At the south-west corner of the building, a posthole, F891, was recorded.

The dumping process in both west and south portico represented the final levelling to complete the walkways. The final floor may have been the upper level of the sand dumps themselves with stone steps to the *macellum*. As elsewhere the walkways were levelled up within existing walls. The gully, F723, at the top of the dumps seems to have been cut across the stylobate sleeper wall before the stylobate itself, and therefore the portico columns and roof were in place. The rooftile dump, F4221, which preceded the dumps in the south portico, must therefore have derived from roofing work on the *macellum* rather than the porticos.

Six coins were found of which one, dating to the later third-century, was intrusive (cat no 254). The remainder were all first-century (31, 38, 54, 71, and 93). A sculpture of a water nymph and her jug, thought to have derived from a fountain in the fortress was found (Webster 1988b, figs 6.18 and 19). A possibly military stud (Fig 4.7, 30), a toilet implement (Fig 4.11, 113), a weight (Fig 4.14, 153), a lock (Fig 4.19, 188), and a fragment of scrap (Fig 4.29, 287) are illustrated small finds. Two brooches, one dated AD 75–175 were found (Fig 4.33, 13 and 19). Datable glass was later-first to mid-second century (Figs 4.38, 286; 4.39, 275 and 278; 4.41, 532; cat nos 104–6, 109–10, 114, 117, 119, 138–9, 146, 149–50, 154, 156, 163, 193, 205, 214,

Fig 2.30 Macellum entrance steps, F4048; view south

218, 221, 243, 252, 257, 270, 272, 297, 299, 306, 310, 321, 325, 330, 339, 355, 357–8, 369, 371, 392, 400, 408, 423–4, 427, 438, 440, 450, 466–7, 472, 478, 499, 506, 515, 523–4, 554, 561, 563, 589, 596–7, 603, 610, 626–7, 629, 652, 654, and 657). Three glass beads were found (cat nos 5, 6, and 27), and a crucible used for metalworking (cat no 9). Human infant bones came from the south portico dumps beside the *macellum*.

A total of 28 sherds of Antonine samian included two stamps dated to AD 160–200 (nos 18 and 125). An amphora stamp of AD 150 was also found (cat no 3). Two sherds of Rhaetian mortaria were also of Antonine date. Amongst the Antonine samian, a Central Gaulish sherd dated to AD 170–200 may be intrusive as would be a few sherds of third-century pottery, one from a posthole and one probably associated with a third-century rebuilding of the south portico stylobate.

The distribution of finds demonstrates a difference between the dumps in Box 80 and those to the west, since out of all the items listed above only one coin, the scrap fragment, and two pieces of glass were found there. The Box 80 dumps were, however, more cut into by later pits.

Courtyard

Courtyard phase 1 (C 2.1)

On the west side of the courtyard area, a trench, F2966, similar to the unused foundation trenches found beneath the *macellum*, ran east-west (Fig 2.23). The trench was 1m wide and 0.3m deep and was traced in sections for over 6m (Fig 2.70: S60). There was no evidence of the trench 10m to the east where excavations would have located it again, nor beneath the *macellum* to the west.

The east wall of the drain and of the *macellum*, the south wall of Rooms 8 and 9, the additional wall round the baths Rooms 5 and 6, and the south wall of the courtyard were all cut from the Period 1 demolition level.

Piles of sandstone chippings and squared blocks, and sand and stone layers with tile and tesserae were found (Fig 2.39: S31 layer 17; Fig 2.71: S65, layers 15 and 16). Some of the sandstone layers were widespread, with particular concentrations in Boxes 13, 14, 34, 35, and 39, and mortar mixing areas were also noted there and in Boxes 53 and 67 (Fig 1.3). A dump of *imbrex* tile was found in Box 34, and an area of brick and wall plaster was found in Box 50. Three hearths were found in Box 9, of which one, F2050, was clay lined and the remainder were marked by areas of burning (Fig 2.31). Another hearth in Box 12 was constructed of tiles set in mortar. A short length of stone-filled trench, F2382, was also located.

Arrangements in the north of the courtyard are not known. However the evidence from the latrine excavations in Phase WR 1 had suggested that the sleeper wall for the portico here was built then to define an area for the baths main conduit along the face of the basilical hall.

The additional wall around the baths *caldarium* and *tepidarium* was set in a 2m deep trench F3244 (Fig 2.39: S31). The foundation trench swung out in a wide arc on the south-west side of 6A. At the north end it cut the foundation trench, F4014, for the south wall of Room 8 (Fig 2.31).

Of two coins (cat nos 100 and 117), the most recent dated to Trajan and came from F483 the *macellum* foundation trench. A lamp holder (Fig 4.23, 238) and a furniture fitting (Fig 4.25, 249) and fragments of wall veneer were found. Four brooches were found, one of Iron Age type, one first-century, one dating to AD 90–175, and one dating to AD 50–150 (Fig 4.32, 1 and 7; Fig 4.35, 36; no 42). The glass collection is not dated any later than the first quarter of the second century (Figs 4.38, 911; 4.39, 904; 4.41, 948, cat nos 877, 880, 885, 888, 890, 893, 894, 902, 906, 916, 926, 929, 933, 935–6, 943, 951, 954, 956, 964–5, 970, 972–3, and 981). Two glass beads, four counters (Fig 4.47, 54), and a funnel stem were found (cat nos 17, 28, 45–6, 49, 69). Pottery suggested a date of AD 120+. The latest samian was Trajanic, and only four sherds of BB1 were found. Residual pottery was calculated as over 86%. The trench for the west wall of the latrine (KG 27) contained a BB1 dish dated to AD 120–50, and the foundation trench for the additional baths wall (KG 9) contained a samian sherd dated to AD 100–150.

Courtyard phase 2 (C 2.2)

A pit, F2259, on the east of the courtyard area was a rectangular cut through the foundation trench to the face of the Room 5 and 6 additional wall, and carried 2.27m down to the base of the wall. Two similar pits, F4158 and F4159 were recorded against the face of the south wall of Room 9 (Fig 2.31: Fig 2.48: S41). These were deep unweathered cuttings with uniform backfills, resembling the inspection pits found in and around the *macellum*. The depth of F2259 was the same as the depth of the additional wall foundation trench, and pits F4158 and F4159 seemed too to be cut to the base of the footings of Room 9 at a depth of 1.5m.

The initial construction of the *natatio* in the south-west of the courtyard can be placed in Phase 2 and the structure may then have been built up through Phase 3 and completed in Phase 4. The *natatio* is described under Phase 4.

Although the south courtyard wall foundation trench was cut from C 2.1 levels, the *macellum* construction sequence showed that it postdated the east wall of the *macellum* (Chapter 3). A dump of sand was then deposited over the whole courtyard area sealing the Phase 1 building dumps, the Room 5 and 6 additional wall foundation trench and the pits, and butting up against the walls of the *natatio* and the south courtyard wall. Some of the detailed sections suggest that the material was a succession of dumps (Fig 2.70: S56 layer 11; S57 and S58 layer 18; Fig 2.71: S66, layer 10 and S61 layer 20). However, the main section, and

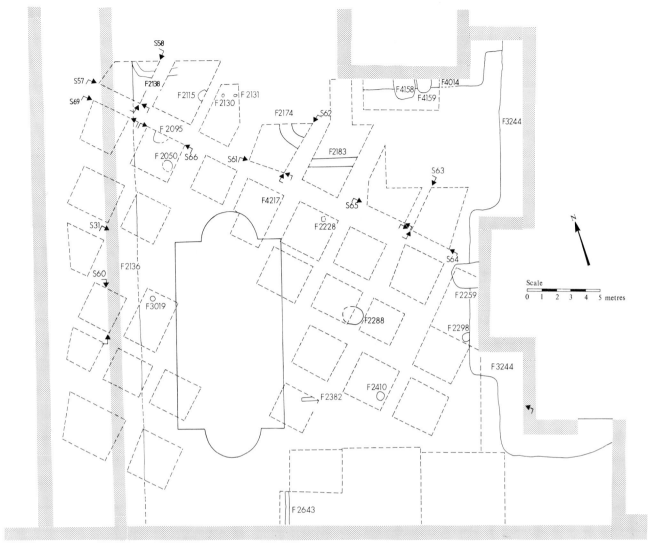

Fig 2.31 Period 2 courtyard features; 1:250

others amongst the detailed sections, show the material as deposited in a level horizon (Fig 2.39: S31, layer 16; Fig 2.70: S59, layers 21–23; Fig 2.71: S63, layers 12 and 13; S65, layer 12, and S66, layer 9).

Seven coins were found, all first-century except for an intrusive third-century coin (cat nos 11, 25, 35, 41, 61, 87, and 184). A ring (Fig 4.7, 32), a pin (Fig 4.10, 104), a shackle (Fig 4.19, 190), a jug handle (Fig 4.23, 236), the latter from F2274, are illustrated. A stone counter (cat no 50) came from F2255. Datable vessel glass was first century (cat nos 878, 884, 886, 887, 915, 917, 925, 928, 930, and 971). Two melon beads and a glass counter (cat nos 18, 19, and 57) were found.

Pottery was again overwhelmingly residual. Four Hadrianic/Antonine sherds of samian included one in the style of Cinnamus ii, AD 130–40 (Fig 4.98, D24). A few sherds of BB1 were noted. A samian stamp dated to AD 160–90 was found (no 146). A sherd of third-century pottery is likely to be intrusive. The *natatio* foundation trench (KG 13) contained two sherds of Flavian/Trajanic samian.

The origin of the dumped material may have been the excavation of the baths footings and spoil from the insertion of floors in the *tepidarium*, *caldarium*, and the lateral suites. This would have been a substantial quantity of material. The 2m depth of the additional wall foundation trench and its considerable width indicate the quantity from the foundation trenches. The depth of the walls may also be an indication of the excavation necessary to prepare the correct levels for the subfloor heating systems. The *tepidarium* and *caldarium* alone would have yielded 1000m³, and a further 600m³ might be estimated for the lateral suites. The considerable depth of the floors in the *frigidarium* and the north end of the latrine also suggest prior excavation. With the wall footing trenches, a total figure might have been near 3000m³. In addition some of the Phase C 2.2 material in the vicinity of the *natatio* may have derived from its shallow cut into the military levels below.

The uneven surface of Phase 1 and 2 suggests that this area was not available as an exercise yard until the termination of Phase 4, indicating that the *natatio* was seen as an integral part of the plan.

Courtyard phase 3 (C 2.3)

The sleeper wall, F2135, of the west portico of the courtyard was of coursed sandstone blocks set on rubble footings in a foundation trench, F4173, cut into the Phase 2 dumps (Fig 2.70: S56 and S59). On the west side, in 15W, the construction level for the wall was marked by mortar spreads and stone chippings at the level of the change from rubble footings to the coursed stonework (Fig 2.70: S56, layer 10 and S59, layer 19).

The level of the walkway in 15W between the sleeper wall and the east wall of the *macellum* and the east wall of the latrines was then raised with sand dumps (Fig 2.70: S56, layers 7–9 and S59, layers 15–18). At their upper level these had been sealed by deposits which contained tile and rubble, and sandstone chippings and mortar. A group of four postholes, a stakehole, and a linear trench, were recorded to the east of the latrine block. These features and the building debris were sealed beneath the initial portico walkway. This was formed of pebbles and small stones based on mixed levelling layers in places of ashy material and elsewhere of clay (Fig 2.70, S56, layers 5 and 6 and S59, layers 13 and 14).

In the courtyard, 15, east of the walkway, was a pit and a posthole. An area of burning was seen in section which suggested a hearth. This had been cut by one of the pits. These, although large in plan, were fairly shallow at 0.15m and 0.4m deep respectively. In the south-west corner of the area were dumps of burnt tile, charcoal, ashy soil, and burnt clay layers. A gully, F2138, was recorded for a short distance in the north-west corner of the excavated area (Fig 2.31; Fig 2.70: S58).

The construction process thus involved first the sleeper wall to a height of at least 0.5m, which then confined the subsequent dumps raising the level to that of the walkway. The top of F2135 lay at the level of the gravel surface, and was presumably finished with a course of ashlar forming both a base for the portico columns and a dwarf wall at the portico edge. An invariable feature of the wall sections was a robbing trench, F3030, on the interior of the wall in 15W, which may have served to remove evidence of a further line of sandstone blocks running along the interior face of the wall (Fig 2.70: S56, S57, and S59).

Four first-century coins were found (cat nos 19, 28, 29, and 57). Illustrated small finds comprise a pin (Fig 4.10, 98), a nail (Fig 4.26, 263), and a structural fitting (Fig 4.28, 281). Vessel glass dated to the mid-second century at the latest (Fig 4.37, 879 and 897; cat nos 876, 914, 931, 934, and 940). A glass counter was found (cat no 58). A pottery bowl used to contain Egyptian blue pigment was found in the courtyard portico.

In the 15W walkway dumps, a sherd of Antonine samian was the latest found. In addition there were 13 Hadrianic/early Antonine sherds (Fig 4.98, D25). The proportion of BB1 pottery had increased and the level of residual pottery was calculated as less than a half.

Joining sherds indicated that the walkway dump came from the same source as the Phase WR 2.3 dump in the *macellum* and the Phase P 2.3 dumps in the porticos. There were no datable sherds from the stylobate footing foundation trench. A date of *c* AD 140–50 is suggested.

Courtyard phase 4 (C2.4)

The Phase 2 dumps and Phase 3 features in the courtyard east of the portico were sealed by a levelling dump (Fig 2.39: S31, layer 14; Fig 2.70: S58, layer 17; Fig 2.71: S62, layer 19, and S66, layer 7).

The main feature of the courtyard was the *natatio* (Fig 2.32; Fig 2.39: S31). The base of the pool floor was a pitched stone foundation, 0.3m deep, partly of sandstone rubble and partly of river cobbles, sealed beneath a levelling layer, 0.15m deep, of mortar and stone. The walls for the pool had been set on this base. They were built of successive tile courses faced with stone, almost all of which had been removed in the later robbing (Fig 2.33). Parts of the two base courses survived at the north end of the pool with the courses above marked only by their impression in the *opus signinum* backing for the facing stones of the pool which had survived the robbing.

The floor of the *natatio* was formed of flagstones of fine-grained grey sandstone set in *opus signinum* (Figs 2.34 and 2.35). Some of the 0.06m thick flagstones survived, while the impression of others could be seen in places in the *opus signinum* base. The pool was 1.3m deep. No evidence survived of the treatment of the sides above the tile courses but a sandstone capping would be possible.

Similar stone to the slab floor was used as veneer on the pool sides attached to the *opus signinum* backing which would have acted additionally as a waterproofing course. Parts of the veneer and the *opus signinum* backing survived the later tile robbing in the north-east apse of the pool (Fig 2.36). The backing was 0.1m deep and the sandstone blocks thinner at 0.03m than those on the floor. Each had a rebate cut down either side to facilitate bonding. The apsidal ends to the pool suggest that curving steps allowed entry to the pool at either end, and these are assumed in the restoration (Fig 3.1).

The plan of the floor of the pool shows that the mortar impressions of the stone flags of the floor were mostly confined to the centre of the pool area and had a regular layout with no evidence of repairs and insertions (Fig 2.32). The mortar impressions in the south alcove of the pool differ, one set at an angle having had a straight side set against the curve of the end wall of the pool. The same irregularity is apparent in the position of the surviving flags. These were located at either end of the pool. At the north end the flags were less regularly laid and their orientation deviated from the orderly parallels of the central mortar impressions. However, they did continue the basic arrangement and were similarly sized. At the south end the layout was much more irregular and haphazard and parallelled that of the

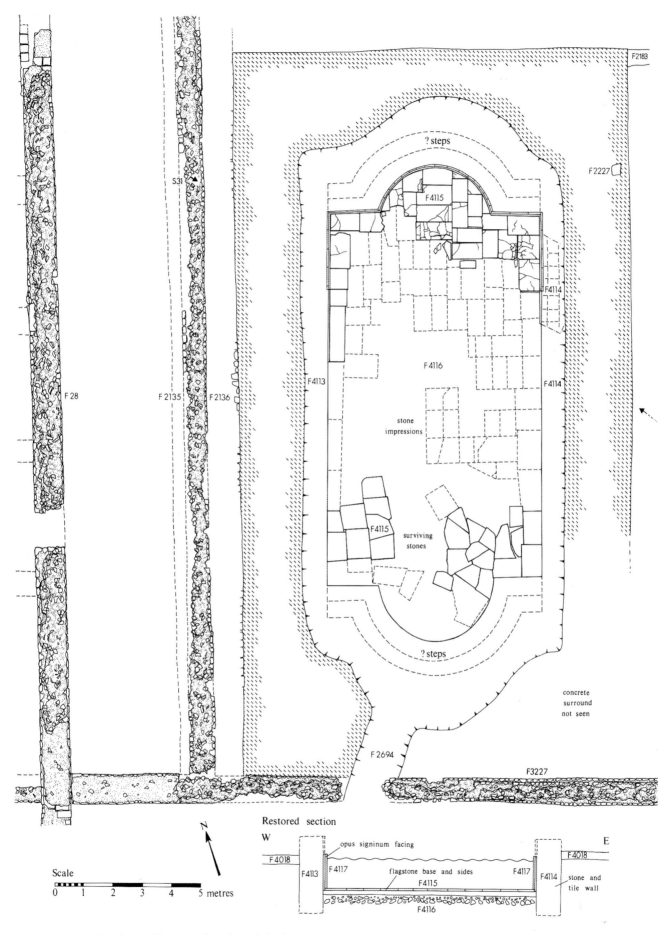

Fig 2.32 Natatio *plan with restored section; 1:125*

Fig 2.33 Natatio, *detail of flag floor and robbed east side, F4119; view west*

Fig 2.34 Natatio; *view south*

Fig 2.35 Natatio; *view east*

Fig 2.36 Natatio, *detail of northern end; view west*

mortar impressions in the same area. The irregular group of stones in the south-east part of the floor were of an inferior quality to the remainder.

Drainage was to the south. The drain had been robbed leaving a cut 1.8m deep and 0.9m wide. The sides were built within an outer facing of coursed blocks set on a random stone footing, within which part of a mortar and rubble core survived. This, it may be assumed, was the backing for a tile facing subsequently robbed together with the tile walls of the pool. Nothing remained of the drain base which was presumably of stone flags. If the coursed walling marked the drain base then a depth of 0.9m is indicated.

The *natatio* was presumably built up *pari passu* with the dumps rather than cut into them. The relationship between the completion of the *natatio* and the provision of the west portico walkway was not clearly established but presumably the courtyard completion followed that of the walkway.

If the flagstone impressions in the *natatio* and the flags themselves were a single building episode, then this would indicate that the floor was laid from north to south, limitations in the supply of slabs forcing the builders to use inferior stones of irregular shape at the

south end. Alternatively the flags at north and south might be seen as a relaying of broken pieces, perhaps as a result of the greater use of either end as entries to the pool. These flags may not have been robbed with the others because of their inferior quality or because they were sealed by an initial infilling.

On the courtyard side of the 15W portico sleeper wall, F2135, was a shallow footing, F2136, abutting the wall (Fig 2.39: S31; Fig 2.70: S56 and S57). This had been built in a foundation trench, F2144, cut from directly below the *natatio* concrete surround. Whatever was set on this added footing had been subsequently robbed. Possibilities are that it was a line of blocks forming a step down from the portico walkway to the level of the *natatio*, or, alternatively, the base of a gutter carrying off rain water from the portico roof, as was the case in the south portico (Figs 2.55; 2.63, F4165), and in the portico north of the basilical hall (Kenyon 1938, 183, pl 69; Webster and Daniels 1972). A third possibility is that, since no arrangements were recorded for water supply to the pool, it may have served in part to carry water to the *natatio*. The report on excavations in the north portico in 1930 and 1931 notes the presence of a gutter stone as well as the column placings (Morris 1932, ix).

The surface surrounding the *natatio* comprised a thick concrete floor, F4018, set on make up layers of large red sandstone blocks levelled off with sand (Fig 2.39: S31; Fig 2.70: S57 and S58; Fig 2.71: S61 and S62). A comparison of the levels shows that the surface sloped from east to west and from north to south. In one place the sandstone footing had been placed on a layer of chipped tiles, and a large sandstone block at least 0.3 by 0.25m was also found, both presumably debris from construction of the pool described above. A tile platform in Box 11, F4217, may have acted as the base of a feature (Figs 2.31 and 2.37). The concrete included further tile chips as well as tesserae. In one area on the north side it was possible to see a narrow void, F2020, against the face of the concrete resulting from wooden shuttering which had left its impression on the concrete face (Fig 2.71: S62). The north and east sides of the surface around the *natatio* were clear. Arrangements to the south were not recorded in the area excavation undertaken in the south part of the courtyard, but the surface may have continued as far as the south wall of the courtyard. On the west side the surround presumably abutted the step or gutter added in Phase 3 to the outer side of the portico sleeper wall. The relationship had been removed by later robbing although it was clear that the surface sealed the foundation trench of F2136. A second contemporary element on the courtyard side of the walkway was a step, of which part survived later

Fig 2.37 Courtyard, tiles F4217, natatio *surround F4018 to right; view east*

robbing. This was set on the line of the access corridor through from the street between the *macellum* and the office and latrine block to the north. The south side of the step coincided with the northern limit of the *natatio* surround (Fig 3.1).

The northern line of the surround was continued eastward as a rectangular sectioned trench, F2183, 0.6m wide by 0.2m deep (Figs 2.31 and 2.32). It cannot have been a long-lived feature, since it was buried beneath the surface of the courtyard beyond the surround, both of which must have formed a contemporary unit. The function of F2183 may have been simply as a marking out trench carried rather further than necessary, perhaps no more than the 2.5m distance recorded. F2183 may have been associated with F2174 a curving gully also sited at the north-east corner of the *natatio* surround (Fig 2.31; Fig 2.71: S62).

The surface, F4022, beyond the concrete surround represented the first level surface to be located in the courtyard (Fig 2.39: S31; Fig 2.71: S63–5, layer 11). In the northern half of the area examined, immediately east of the *natatio* surround, the surface was of concrete based on small sandstone blocks. Further east the sandstone base had been dispensed with and the concrete had been laid directly onto a sand surface. The concrete was recorded as having, like the main surround, tile fragments and mosaic cubes. A slight void between the two surfaces may indicate former shuttering. Further south the courtyard surface was less well represented, and although the sections show a levelled horizon, the surface itself had only survived as an intermittent mortar and sand horizon, with no evidence of rubble levelling beneath. In places a levelled clay surface may have acted as the courtyard base. Although less clearly marked the surface could be seen to continue as far as the Room 5 and 6 additional wall, sealing its foundation trench. Against the south wall of the courtyard the surface was again clear as a layer of mortar.

The excavated area covered roughly half of the baths courtyard, and it may thus be suggested that at least two thirds of the courtyard was covered in the hard concrete surface located in the northern part of the excavation. Why this surface was not present at the south end of the courtyard, and whether different surfaces were marked by any dividing feature is not clear.

A pin (Fig 4.9, 81) and a honestone were found (cat no 25). None of the glass was datable with the possible exception of a mid-first to mid-second-century fragment (Figs 4.42, 960; 4.46, 927; cat nos 896, 901a, 932 and 950). A pottery bowl used to contain haematite pigment was found.

Five Antonine samian sherds and a higher proportion of BB1 sherds overall suggested a date of AD 150+. A Hadrianic/early Antonine samian stamp was found (no 193). These sherds came from make up layers beneath the *natatio* surround. There was no dating evidence from the *natatio* itself.

Baths precinct

Baths precinct phase 1 (BP 2.1)

Excavations in the area east of the baths cut into military levels in Boxes 15, 16, 17, 48 and 49, uncovering evidence of beam slot trenches and pits sealed beneath an overall destruction horizon. Above this, mortar mixing areas and spreads of rubble, stone chippings, broken tile, brick, and tesserae marked builders areas east of the baths (Fig 2.40). The foundation trenches of the baths walls were sectioned in two places where tile stacks, already discussed above (Phase B 2.1), were located (Fig 2.41: S35 and S36).

The additional wall around Rooms 5 and 6 was set in a deep foundation trench. This was sectioned on the east and south sides, F3181 on the east (Fig 2.42: S37 and S38) and F4134 on the south (Fig 2.51: S47). Spoil from the trench was visible on the south side overlying the Period 1 building level (Fig 2.51: S47, layer 15). The wall seems likely to have continued to the south wall of Room 10 as discussed above (Phase B 2.1).

A particular concentration of building waste had substantially raised the ground level east of the junction of the baths and basilical hall. This comprised base layers of red sandstone, sealed by layers of sand, rubble, brick and tile, mortar, and tile chippings (Fig 2.41: S32 and S33, layer 15). The evidence suggested a similar sequence to the courtyard to the west with builders debris and the initial wall trenches followed by the additional wall around Rooms 5 and 6.

Two coins were found, one of which was fourth-century and intrusive and the other Republican (cat nos 2 and 683). A lock (Fig 4.19, 186), a fragment of furniture inlay (Fig 4.25, 256), and two melon beads (cat nos 22 and 23) were found. The small number of vessel glass fragments collected were undatable (cat nos 1012, 1025, 1045, and 1048). A crucible used for metalworking was found (cat no 2). Pottery was almost entirely of late first/early second-century date with no BB1. The exceptions were three Hadrianic/early Antonine samian sherds from beneath the *praefurnium* dump in Box 49.

Baths precinct phase 2 (BP 2.2)

A pit, F3179, was recorded on the east side of the baths cutting through the Room 5 and 6 additional wall foundation trench down to its footings (Fig 2.40; Fig 2.42: S37). A much smaller pit, F4133, was sectioned on the south side (Fig 2.51: S47), but this was also cut down against the wall footings, and both may represent further examples of inspection pits. Both were backfilled with clean sand.

To the south of the baths, on the east side of Room 7, a dump of sand sealed the Room 5 and 6 additional wall foundation trench and the pit F4133 (Fig 2.51: S47, layer 14). No distinction was apparent between the dump and the pit fill.

A surface of stone, F4148, sealing the Phase 1 layers, F3179, formed a courtyard level (Fig 2.41: S32, S33, and S36; Fig 2.42: S37 and S38). It faded out toward the east wall of 3B (Fig 2.41: S32), and towards 6B (Fig 2.42: S37). Elsewhere it sealed the baths foundation trenches (Fig 2.41: S36). There was no evidence of the surface east of Room 7.

To the north, a water supply conduit, F3101, was located cut through these layers (Fig 2.40; Fig 2.41: S32). The conduit was a solid stone structure with a slab stone base. It was 1.8m wide overall, the channel itself 1m wide, and 1.6m deep. The base was 0.2m deep as compared to the 0.4m thick sides. The drain fills had been completely emptied in the areas examined, and this seems most likely to have been undertaken during nineteenth-century investigations although not recorded. The upper part of the wall sides had been left untouched and these showed no indications of the springing for any arched cover, and flat stone slabs must have been used. The conduit was shown to have been built later than the baths building since its foundation trench cut through rubble and spoil layers which must have been associated with the building.

This was then sealed beneath a sand dump (Fig 2.41: S32, S33 and S36, layer 12). Some soil was present. The dump, which was confined to the northern area, was cut by a pit and a linear trench.

Two coins were found, the latest of Trajan (cat nos 51 and 114). A pin (Fig 4.9, 65), a needle for textile working (Fig 4.16, 162), and a spoon and a household utensil (Fig 4.22, 229 and 234) were found, the latter from F3169. A brooch dated to AD 90–175 was found (Fig 4.33, 17). Datable vessel glass fragments were in use between the mid first and mid second centuries (cat nos 1018, 1022, 1050, 1053, and 1065). A glass bead was found (Fig 4.47, 31).

Potsherd sizes were smaller than for Phase 1 indicating a greater degree of disturbance. Seventeen sherds of Antonine Central Gaulish samian included a stamp dated to AD 150–80 (no 39). BB1 sherds were early to mid-second century. A date of *c* AD 160 is suggested.

Baths precinct phase 3 (BP 2.3)

Above the sand layers in the northern excavated area and the F4148 horizon in the south were layers of mortar and deposits of spread brick and sand containing wall plaster. These layers were clear close to the walls of baths and thinning out to the east. They may represent external plastering of the baths undertaken at this stage. South of the baths there was also a clear horizon of mortar overlying layers of mortar, cement, and plaster (Fig 2.51: S47, layers 12 and 13).

The first of many layers of ash, burnt tile, and charcoal which were to form the *praefurnium* dump from Room 7 continuing into Period 3, was initially deposited onto the mortar and plaster layers south of Room 6 (Fig 2.51: S47, layer 11).

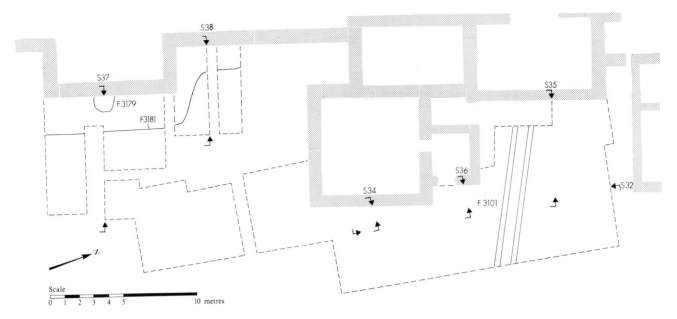

Fig 2.40 Baths precinct, Period 2; 1:250

A pin (Fig 4.9, 60) and a spatula (Fig 4.22, 233) are illustrated. One of the two vessel glass fragments was datable to the mid-first to the mid-second century (cat nos 1020 and 1061). Three samian sherds of Antonine date included a vessel possibly in the style of Paternus v dated to AD 155–95.

The overall Period 2 sequence

An overall construction sequence can be suggested (Fig 2.43). There are four pieces of evidence available to establish links between the sequences in the different areas. The first is the change of building stone, from red Keele Beds to grey Hoar Edge Grit sandstone. This change may imply the exhaustion of one quarry source and the subsequent exploitation of another or the choice of a more suitable stone for building purposes. A change of stone was linked with the stratigraphic sequence in excavations in *insula* 9 to the south of *insula* 5 by Kathleen Kenyon (1981). The baths Phase 1 walls are all in Keele Beds sandstone as are the latrines, the Rooms to the west and the lower parts of the *macellum*. Hoar Edge Grit stone appears with the Room 5 and 6 additional wall, and is used in secondary work in the upper part of the surviving *macellum* walls.

The second is the presence of the inspection pits. These suggest a need by builders to examine existing work. This would imply a halt in the construction campaign and the return to the site of a fresh team. The pits may therefore represent a single episode, and their stratigraphic position in different areas may be used to indicate a linkage. This linkage has already been presented in the west range, where the pits within the *macellum* were cut through a dump of material while those in the corridor to the north and in the Rooms to the south were not. From this it is assumed that the Phase 2 west range dump was limited to the interior of

the *macellum*. The other inspection pits occur at the primary Phase 1 building horizon and were noted in the courtyard where three were found, one against the Room 5 and 6 additional wall and two against Room 9, and in the baths precinct where two pits were found against the additional wall, one on the east and one on the south side. The pits against the additional wall indicate that this episode of reappraisal of the site followed the change of building stone source.

The third tool for linkage is the evidence of joining sherds. Cross-fits were found between sherds in the WR 2.3 dump in the *macellum*, the P 2.3 dump in the porticos, and the C 2.3 infilling down the baths courtyard portico. These serve to link the portico completion with the *macellum* completion and both with the provision of the courtyard walkway. This latter seems therefore to have been a discrete episode and the probability must be that it preceded final arrangements in the courtyard and the completion of the *natatio*. On the east side of the courtyard portico sleeper wall, the C 2.4 phase ended with the added gutter running down the face of the wall.

Finally the walls themselves demonstrate construction sequences from which it is possible to suggest relationships between the areas. Amongst the detailed evidence from the *macellum*, the secondary nature of the south wall of the courtyard in relation to the *macellum* can be demonstrated.

Given these linkages the following sequence can be suggested:

Phase 1

All the walls may have been set out with marking out trenches, a few of which were unused and thus indicate changes of plan. One change of plan may have been to build the *macellum* rather than to continue the one

44

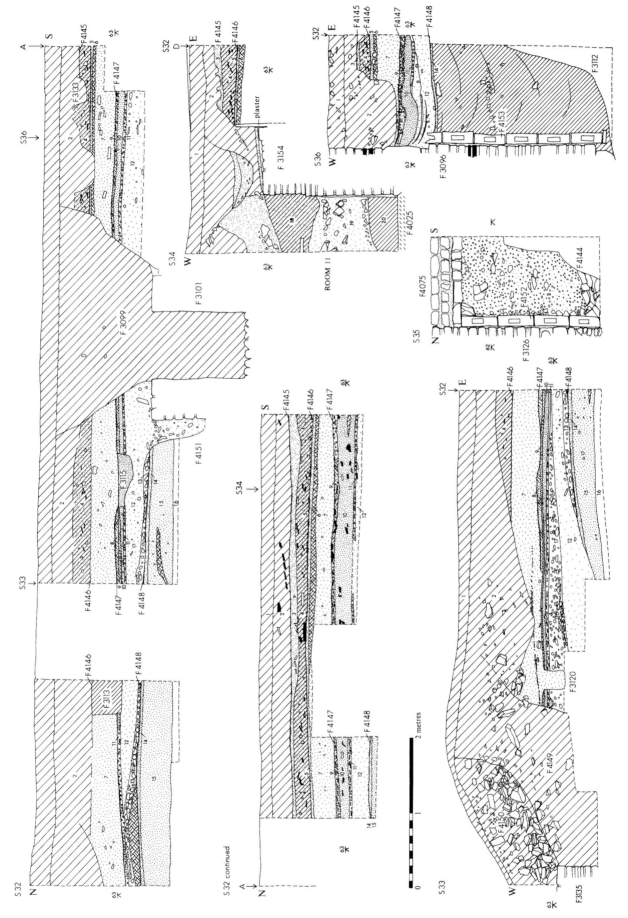

Fig 2.41 Baths precinct sections 32–36, location Fig 2.40; 1:50

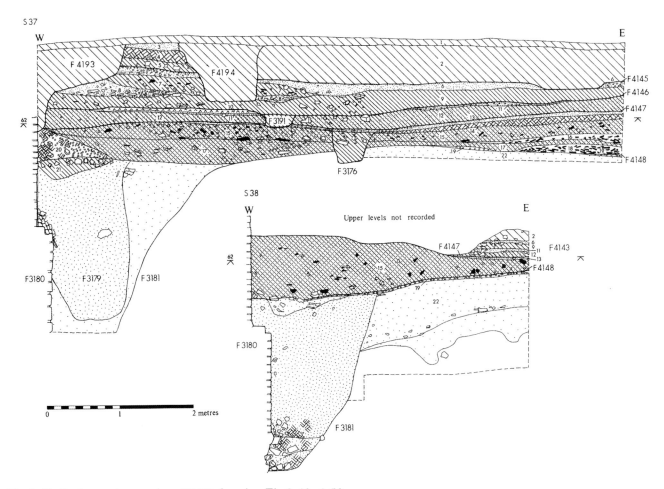

Fig 2.42 Baths precinct sections 37-38, location Fig 2.40; 1:50

block deep layout from the north. This is suggested by the two trenches apparently indicating a southward line for the drain, and is also supported by F4038, the east-west wall in the latrine, which may have originated as part of the sleeper wall for the 15N stylobate. A second change of plan is indicated by the slight trench to the west of the *natatio*, this may have been intended as the location of a drain. In the basilical hall a change of plan has been suggested at the east end where the Old Work indicates the addition of a section of wall to allow access from the baths precinct.

The building programme may have begun with the provision of the water supply and drainage system. The eastward turn at the south end of the latrine and the unity of the building of the drain with the *macellum* indicate that any earlier plan indicated by marking out trenches beneath the *macellum* was not long maintained. The unity of drain with the basilical hall south wall and the west wall of the latrine indicates a continuous building programme. The conduit in the baths precinct was, however, not primary. When the initial arrangements in the lateral suites, Rooms 8 and 10, were altered cannot be known. One of the abandoned walls was built to a height of 2m and this may have been a long-lived layout.

It seems likely that the main elements of the plan of the *insula* buildings were present by the end of the phase.

Phase 2

The Room 5 and 6 additional wall indicates a pause or dislocation in the building programme. The wall must have been the result of a major decision intended to strengthen the walls of the main barrel vaulted rooms. It is interesting to note the similarities between the Wroxeter baths and those at Chester. Perhaps Wroxeter was built to the Chester design but did not take account of the different geologies – rock lies beneath the Chester baths but sand at Wroxeter. A new stone source was used for the wall. Builders' access to the courtyard was from the south since a section of the stylobate sleeper was left unbuilt, and the south courtyard wall itself was not built until the *macellum* was complete. At the same time work was undertaken in the *macellum* with a dump of material within the building to raise its floor level.

Phase 3

The inspection pits may indicate a second pause and a return by a fresh team. The east range of the *macellum* above the main drain may have been completed. During any abandonment of the building project a market may well have continued on the west side of the *insula* where the porticos were eventually to be.

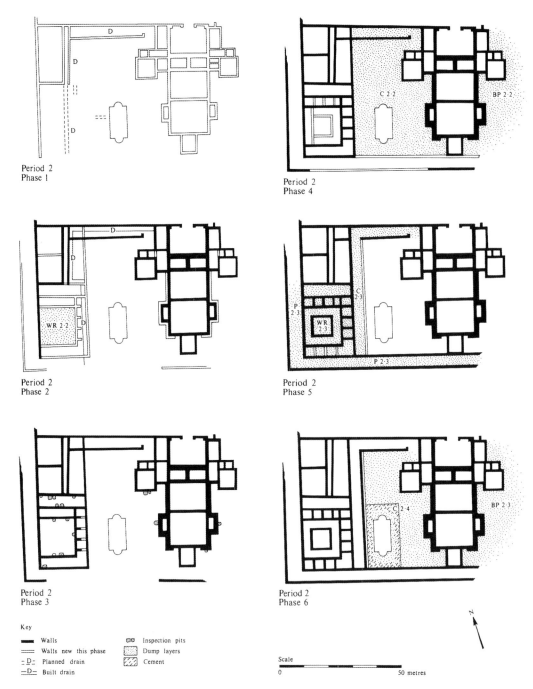

Fig 2.43 Period 2 sequence; 1:1500

Phase 4

The inspection pits may have led on directly to further work towards the completion of the buildings. In the *macellum* the interior courtyard walls were built and the north range completed. The initial dumps in the west portico may have been provided now. A particular concentration of building and metallurgical waste at the base of the west portico dump is dated *c* AD 150, suggesting its deposition late in the sequence. Some of the rubbish accumulated in the dumps may have been deposited from market stalls set up on the east side of Watling Street.

The courtyard south wall and the south portico stylobate sleeper walls were built. The courtyard dump was levelled across the area before the walkway sleeper

wall footing was built, and residual pottery suggests that this material was spoil from the building foundation trenches. The construction of the baths water supply in the baths precinct at this stage suggests that the provision of the water supply was secondary to the construction of the main drainage system.

Phase 5

The *macellum* south range of rooms may have been completed. Pottery cross-fits then suggest a single final dump in the *macellum*, in the porticos, and in the courtyard corridor which would have raised floors and walkways to their finished levels. This dump seems to have come from contemporary work elsewhere and is Antonine in date. The courtyard was thus provided with a covered walkway on its north and west side. The courtyard itself, however, remained incomplete with dumps partly surrounding the unfinished *natatio*.

Phase 6

A gutter was run down the east side of the courtyard portico sleeper wall. The *natatio* was then completed with its surround sealing Antonine pottery, and the surround may have been the last work undertaken. The baths precinct seems not to have been provided with its second recognisable courtyard surface until the next period, and the latest pottery from the second-century levels is dated to the end of the century.

There is some evidence from the east side that only now were the baths commissioned. Layers of plaster against its walls seal the Period 2 evidence in the baths precinct and were then sealed to the south of Room 6 by the first *praefurnium* dumps from Room 7. This can only be suggested since it is also possible that initial firing debris was taken through a doorway out to the street and deposited elsewhere.

Discussion of the dating evidence

The pottery and glass dating evidence is catalogued and discussed in the specialist reports below. The principal dating evidence for the area phases and key groups is tabulated (Tables 2.2 and 2.3). Dating the Period 2 sequence depends primarily on the pottery; the vessel glass evidence offering only a general date to the mid second century, and the coins being entirely residual. There are, however, a few coins and small finds offering dating evidence that suggests they were intrusive. The deposits with dating evidence were all dumps of material from the building campaign culminating in what are assumed to be the final surfaces on completion of the works. This final surface however was only clear and undisturbed in the courtyard. The *macellum* walkway floor, and perhaps its courtyard, was truncated by a later re-flooring. The portico surface was not sealed by any clear surface, while the baths precinct surface was in position before the end of the construction programme. The secure position of any of the crucial dating pieces can therefore always be argued.

There are pieces present which are dated into the later second or third century. The third and fourth-century coins found are presumed to be intrusive, the one in P 2.3 must have derived from a Period 3 third-century pit in the portico. The intaglio from WR 2.3 could have been introduced by the third-century repair of the *macellum* floor as would the fragments of third and fourth-century glass. Occasional pieces of third and fourth-century pottery would likewise be from later unrecognised intrusions.

Hadrianic or Hadrianic/early Antonine samian (the latter not necessarily implying an Antonine date – pers comm Brenda Dickinson) and the presence of BB1

suggest a date for the start of building works in the 120s or 130s. The Phase 1 groups across the different areas present a similar picture of residual, highly broken material together with a small quantity of Hadrianic pottery.

The links suggested by joining sherds focus attention on the P2.2 dump F951. This preceded a single contemporary dump in the porticos, west range, and courtyard, which would have had to have been in place for the *macellum* to be in use. Faiers suggests a mid-second century date for a BB1 vessel from F951 while Webster has argued for a pre-Antonine date (1993, 50). The presence of Antonine samian in layers associated with F951 would support the former date.

It is the length of the building programme and the date of its completion which requires the closest analysis and has the greatest implications for the construction of other second-century public buildings in the Province. While the baths themselves cannot be dated, the other buildings seem unlikely to have been in commission until the interior and exterior ground levels across the *insula* had been completed. Looking at the overall picture from the dumps, the evidence of the samian from across all the excavated areas points incontrovertibly to a continuation of the building programme into the Antonine period. A total of 94 sherds of Antonine samian from 58 vessels was found, including the four stamps discussed below, and two sherds of Antonine mortaria. Bearing in mind the longevity of samian as a well-curated tableware it must be seen as probable that deposition of the dumps would appreciably postdate their associated artefacts, and this suggestion can also be supported by the degree of abrasion, the brokenness of the pottery, and the accompanying presence of first and early-second century pottery in considerable quantities. The Antonine samian seems likely therefore to indicate a date later than the 140s.

Two of the stamps, both dated to AD 160–200 came from P 2.3 (nos 18 and 125), one, dated to AD 160–90 from C 2.2 (no 146), and one dated to AD 150–80 from BP 2.2 (no 39). Of the Antonine sherds, two from P 2.3 were dated to AD 160–95 and AD 170–200, and one from BP 2.3, was in the style of a potter dated AD 155–95. While these pieces might suggest dates well into the second half of the second century, the overall samian evidence suggests that vessels made before *c* AD 160 are dominant and types after AD 160 largely absent. Apart from the stamp from C 2.2, these later Antonine pieces were found in the uppermost Period 2 layers, and may therefore be intrusive.

In summary it may be suggested that the *insula* 5 buildings were begun in the 120s or 130s, either in tandem with the forum or following on from its completion, and were not finally completed until the middle of the century, as much as a generation after they were begun. A date of AD 160 or later can be argued on the basis of the stamps, but the nature of the Period 2 archaeology suggests it is safer to look at the general overall picture rather than at the particular evidence of one or two pieces offering later dates which may well have arrived in repairs or re-levellings unrecognised by the excavators.

Period 3: the third-century, fourth-century, and early post-Roman evidence

Baths

Baths phase 1 (B 3.1)

A room, 5A, was added to the east side of the *tepidarium* (Fig 2.8). The south and east walls of the room were set on large flat flagstones as much as 1.07m in length and 0.3m thick (Fig 2.12: S13; Fig 2.44). These rested on pitched sandstone footings levelled up with layers of sand, stone, and concrete. The walls were of sandstone blocks with double tile courses. The floor, F4004, was made up of the initial pitched sandstone and make up seen beneath the wall flagstones, overlain by further sandstone footings beneath a concrete floor, a total floor depth of 0.6m (Fig 2.12: S13). The concrete floor ran across the top of the footings, F4124,

interpreted in Phase B 2.1 as those of the additional wall around Rooms 5 and 6, and would have butted against the main north-south wall on the east side of the baths. The floor level was the same as that of the *tepidarium* subfloor, F4125. The north-east corner of the room abutted the south side of Room 11. The eastern section of the north wall was only traced for a short distance westward.

In the *tepidarium* the *pilae* had been replaced by a tile footing, F4139, positioned on the mid line of the new room to the east (Fig 2.12: S11).

Room 5A was an additional *praefurnium* added to Room 5, the second-century *tepidarium*, in order to increase heat there. The large footing in Room 5 must have been intended as support for a hot water bath at the level of the *suspensura* floor. The possible demolition of the additional wall between 5A and 5 would imply the building of an arch or other structural supports if the wall was originally built to eaves height.

Praefurnia added to *tepidaria* are known elsewhere in the northern Provinces in both military and civilian contexts (Nielsen 1993, 79, n41 for military baths, 83, n71 for civilian baths). Nielsen suggests that water in the pools heated from additional *praefurnia* was warm and that the *praefurnia* essentially served to provide additional heat in the hypocaust and *tubulatio*.

Fig 2.44 Room 5A; view east

A dead space, 24, would have been left to the north of 5A. No evidence was found for the drainage that must have been provided if the space was left open. The area may have been roofed and used as a room. Access would have been impossible from the baths or from Rooms 10 or 11, and could only have been from the new room, 5A. The construction of 5A was not directly dated. A water pipe trench in the baths precinct running directly towards it contained mid-third-century pottery (Fig 2.72, F3176).

Baths phase 2 (B 3.2)

Room 12, a *caldarium*, and Room 13, a *praefurnium*, were added to the west side of the main baths across the full width of the courtyard between the western portico and Room 9, the western *laconica* of the second-century baths. Two rooms, 9C and 9D, were added to the south side of the latter (Fig 2.45).

The north and south walls of Room 12 were butted on to the west side of Room 9, continuing the north and south wall lines of the latter westward. Massive ashlar blocks, F4052, were sited at the south-west corner of the room, and a robbing trench, F4051, in the north-west corner indicates a similar feature there. These corner blocks would have been matched on the east side. The north side of the room opened into a curved projecting apse, Room 12A, beyond the north wall, F4197. To the south the east and west wall footings of a rectangular alcove, 12B, were butted onto the south wall of Room 12, F4056, but the walls themselves, F2166 and F4057 were bonded with F4056. A third alcove, Room 13, on the west side was divided from Room 12 by wall F4054.

The north wall of Room 12, F4197, was traced across the face of the projecting apse. It was presumably taken no higher than the *suspensura* floor. The wall was set on a slight offset at the level of the foundation trench (Fig 2.46: S39). This was 1m wide and was packed with sandstone rubble, F4198. A second trench, in 12B, showed an offset on the south side of F4056, and a similar rubble-packed foundation trench, F4199 (Fig 2.46: S40).

A comparison of S40 (Fig 2.46) and S62 (Fig 2.71) situated to north and south of the south wall of 12B, F2175, shows that the level from which the foundation trenches for F4197 and F4056 was cut was almost 1m below the contemporary courtyard level. Further, there was no foundation trench on the north side of F2175 to match that to the south. The area of 12 and 12B, and presumably the whole area occupied by the new building must therefore have been dug out initially to a depth of around 1m.

The nature of the infilling was seen in Room 12. The foundation trench was sealed by a layer of clay and sand, layer 9, with a dump of stone chippings, layer 8, against the wall, presumably deriving from construction work. This in turn lay beneath a spread of sand, 7, on which was a second layer of chippings, 6, again sealed by a sand dump, 5. On this surface was the rubble make up, 3, for the subfloor, 2 (Fig 2.46: S39). Layer 1 was modern. A similar infilling of sand, layer 3, 4, and 5, was seen in 12B. These lay below a floor of closely-packed sandstone rubble, layer 2, with gravel, layer 1, above (Fig 2.46: S40).

The surviving upper surfaces of the subfloor in Room 12 were examined in 1988–9. In the centre of the room the floor was of concrete with pebble and tile inclusions, while to the south shattered *pilae* and one possibly *in situ pila* were found. The west wall of Room 9 had been knocked through and a pebble surface marked the gap, F4055, and spread out into Rooms 9 and 12. Two tiles were found which may have lined the opening. In the west alcove of the room, an east-west running flue had been cut in the floor. In Room 12B the floor found in the 1955–85 excavations had been removed by 1988–9.

The west end of Room 12 ran on into the *praefurnium*, Room 13. To the west the walls of 13 were butted against the footing, F2136, which had been added in Period 2 running along the east side of the courtyard sleeper wall (Fig 2.47). There was no evidence for the west wall of the room and the conclusion must be that it was set on F2136.

Clearance in 1988–9 showed that the western part of the floor of Room 13 had been removed by archaeological work. Part of this was represented by trenches excavated in the 1955–85 campaign, the remainder may have been undertaken in 1929. The eastern floor area survived sealed beneath a dark loam with smashed tiles and rubble.

The south walls of 12B and 13 were examined in cuttings on the south side (Fig 2.70: S58; Fig 2.71: S62). These showed wall footings of faced stones set in courses within deep foundation trenches. The wall of Room 13 was set on the footings with a slight offset.

A room, 9C, had been added on the south side of Room 9 (Fig 2.45). The same courtyard horizon cut by the foundation trench, F2117, of Room 12B was also cut by that for the additional room, F2182 (Fig 2.69). The room was built on timber and stone footings, its walls and wall footings abutting the south wall of Room 9 (Fig 2.48). The construction method involved lines of timber piles packed with stone rubble supporting beams set lengthways beneath the coursed stonework of the west, south, and east walls. The piles were rectangular-sectioned and had been driven just lower than the rubble packing (Fig 2.48: S41 and S43; Fig 2.49). The horizontal timbers were about 0.2m across and 0.25m deep; four, F4175–4178 were located on the west side, and three, F4179–4181 on the south. Three or four would have been provided on the east side. The walls were then constructed on the beams (Fig 2.48: S41–S43).

Room 9D further south was an addition to 9C, its walls, F4196 and F4079, sealing the foundation trench of 9C (Fig 2.45). The walls were of mortared stone set directly onto the Period 2 courtyard (Fig 2.71: S63, F2273).

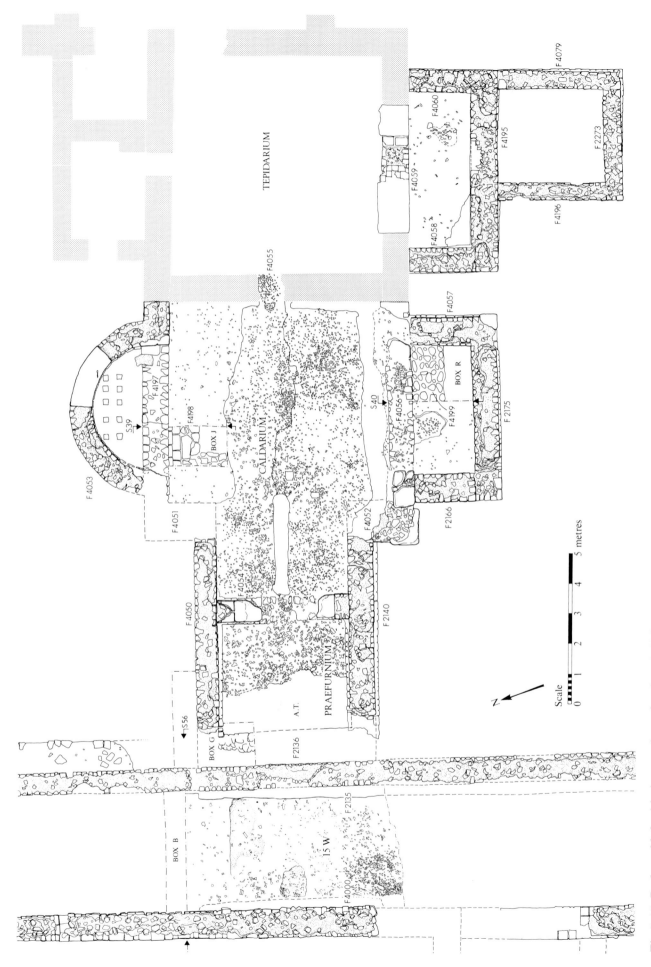

Fig 2.45 Baths, added caldarium *and* praefurniae; *1:125*

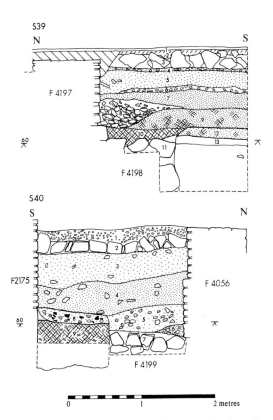

Fig 2.46 *Added* caldarium *sections 39-40, location Fig 2.45; 1:50*

Fig 2.47 *Courtyard portico and Room 13 west wall; view east*

This construction horizon was the same as that for 12, 12B, and 13, and 9D must have been their contemporary. An infant burial in a shallow grave, F2251, was recorded just to its south (Fig 2.69). A photograph taken in 1860 suggests a door opening to the east.

Photographs taken in 1860 (held by Shropshire Records and Research Unit, Shropshire Library Service, Shrewsbury) also show that the subfloor and *suspensura* floor levels of the added *caldarium*, Room 12, lay at the same level as those in Room 9 built in Period 2 Phase 1 while the baths floors to the east lay well below ground level (Fig 2.41: S34), the subfloor base of the added *caldarium* was set at the level of the exterior courtyard surface. It is clear that the fall in ground level to the west made the construction of a new *caldarium* there a far simpler operation in terms of equalizing floor levels throughout the baths complex than a position on the east side of the main baths.

The lower levels of the south wall of Room 9 had been opened leaving a ragged gap, F4059, below the level of its suspended floor. This would have been to accommodate a bath in 9C, Room 9 thus becoming a *tepidarium* with bath. Room 9D would have been a replacement to the *praefurnium* on the north side of Room 9, its off centre position is strange.

The use of timber in the footings of 9C may have been intended to counteract a section of ground thought to be weakened by pitting, although the only examples found were F4158 and F4159 from Phase C 2.2. It may be, alternatively, that the construction technique for 9C was selected in order to minimise the

depth of foundation trenches and hence possible damage to the existing buildings. In excavation the timber supports were shown as voids; the walls had thus stood successfully following decay of the timber foundations.

The west wall of Room 13 would have been based on F2136 cutting off the furnace room from the portico walkway. The stylobate columns presumably stayed in place with the west wall of the *praefurnium* less than a metre from them. Whatever function was fulfilled by the added footing F2136 would have been curtailed. Access to the baths and latrine was thus maintained from the *macellum* corridor. Dumps of *praefurnium* ash were found to the south of Room 13, but none had collected beneath the portico.

The need to establish solid surfaces on which to place the floors would have dictated the substantial groundworks prior to the new building. It is possible that the work indicates the existence of a Period 2 feature in the north part of the courtyard which would have been destroyed by the new buildings.

Arrangements to the south of the new building are discussed in detail below (C 3.2). However, it was clear that a new courtyard surface was laid after the *natatio* had been infilled.

Excavations in the *praefurnium* Room 11B on the east side of the baths showed that the furnace flue through to Room 11 had been rebuilt at successively higher levels within the original tile relieving arch in the wall between

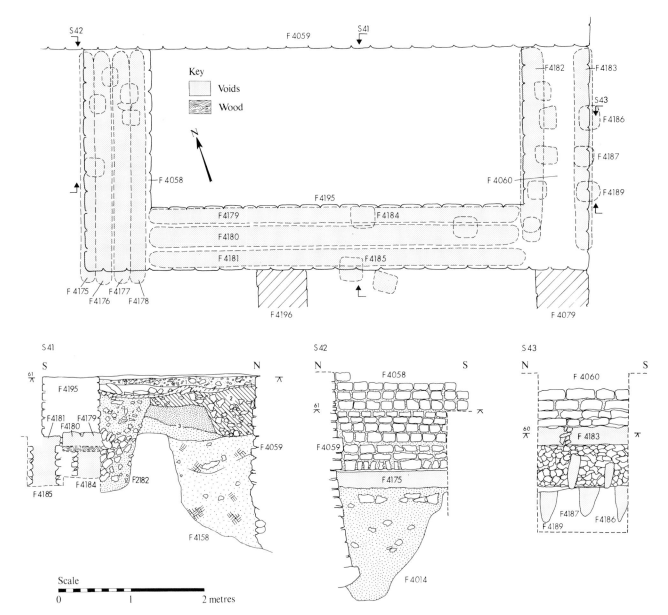

Fig 2.48 Room 9C plan and detail of footings sections 41-43; 1:50

11 and 11B (Fig 2.14). Part of the rakeout from the furnace was used to raise the floor level on which new flues were built. Successive floors of mortar were interleaved with ash and other debris (Fig 2.15: S16, layers 9 and 11). In the course of time the lower step, F3162, leading to the doorway to the east had become buried. At the same time the doorway itself had been raised to accommodate the raised level in the courtyard outside (Fig 2.15: S19). The level of the foot of the door would suggest a relationship with the external courtyard level F4147 of Phase BP 3.1 or F4146 of BP 3.2.

The *praefurnium* in 11B went out of use and was replaced by one to the south, and this may have replicated the addition of 9D to the east. A small room, 11C, was added in the angle formed by Room 5A and Room 11, its walls butting the walls of both rooms (Fig 2.18). Excavations in 1937 had revealed an arch cut through the south wall of Room 11 as a heating duct from an additional *praefurnium* in 11C (Kenyon 1938,

pl LXVIb). The north-east corner of the room was excavated below its floor level. The east wall, built of red sandstone, was set on a slight offset, its north end resting on the topmost of the four vertically-stacked box flue tiles from Phase B 2.1.

There is some evidence that Room 11B was reused for a different purpose subsequent to its use as a *praefurnium*. The room may have been infilled with 1m of rubble bringing its floor up to the level of 11A to the west (Fig 2.15: S16, layers 4–6). A new floor level may be represented by a crushed tile surface, layer 3, which later sank and had been cut by a possible pit, F4219. This suggested floor was not however noted in excavation. If accepted, it may indicate that there was now communication between Rooms 11A and 11B although 11A cannot have been used as a formal entry to the baths. Two grooves were cut down the north wall of the room. These were 0.25m wide and deep, and a height of 1.2m survives today. The

Fig 2.49 Room 9C; view north

addition of new door jambs, narrowing the eastern entrance, may have been undertaken at this time (Fig 2.15: S19).

An *opus spicatum* floor in Room 11A is taken to represent part of a major re-flooring throughout the *insula*. Its level was some 1.4m above the original floor in 11B but was at the same level as the suggested new floor (Fig 2.15: S16). The floor was not removed and has been consolidated on site (Fig 2.50).

There was no dating evidence from excavations within the added baths. The only datable find was a fragment of first-century vessel glass found beneath the floor (cat no 991). Pottery from the foundation trenches externally was also undiagnostic. It can be argued that the construction of the added baths would have been the impetus for, and have directly followed on from, the infilling of the *natatio* in the first half of the third century. A later date may be indicated by early fourth-century plaster from a vault found broken up and reused in the make up for a fifth-century floor in the basilical hall. The size of the vault indicated by the plaster fragments could not be matched by any roofs in the basilical hall area and it is possible that the material originated from Room 12.

Fragments of pottery bowls used for containing pigments of various colours were found in Room 11B, as well as an undiagnostic fragment of vessel glass.

Baths phase 3 (B 3.3)

Alterations in the *praefurnium*, Room 7, took place through from Phase B 2.2 to, presumably, B 3.3 (Fig 2.51: S44–46). As in Room 11B, successive flues had been rebuilt at a higher level based on renewed floors formed from sand mixed with burnt material from the furnace. The furnace base and flue had been replaced on at least three occasions. In the first, F4128, and third, F4126, the furnaces were similarly placed, while in the second phase, F4127, it had been built well to the south. The sequence of accompanying floors is not clear, but their greatly increased height above the original is marked by the furnace flues which ran from the furnace itself southward (Fig 2.51: S45). The north-south

Fig 2.50 Room 11A exterior entrance and herringbone floor; view south

and east-west sections are difficult to relate, and the former seems to have been partly cut down a nineteenth-century archaeological trench. Joining sherds were found between pottery in Room 7 and the *praefurnium* dump outside to the east.

There was an access from the *praefurnium* southward into the south street portico on the evidence of possible door jambs (Chapter 3). There would also have been an access eastward where the sections indicate the removal of a step on both sides of the east wall of Room 7. A footing, F4129, on the east side of the room was matched by a similar section of walling externally (Fig 2.51: S44).

Kathleen Kenyon suggested a late sequence in the use of Rooms 5A and 11C after both had been initially abandoned (Kenyon 1938, 190). She recorded that the partially lowered walls of 5A were sealed beneath a floor associated with a course of rebuilt wall, and this floor linked with a floor crossing the walls of 11C. There was no evidence for this sequence in the 1955–85 excavations.

The latest pottery from floor make up in Room 7, a Mancetter mortarium, was dated to the mid-third century. Other datable third-century sherds included BB1. The majority of the pottery was residual second century, as would be a coin of Lucilla, AD 164–9 (cat no 155). A bone pin of fourth-century date was found well sealed in

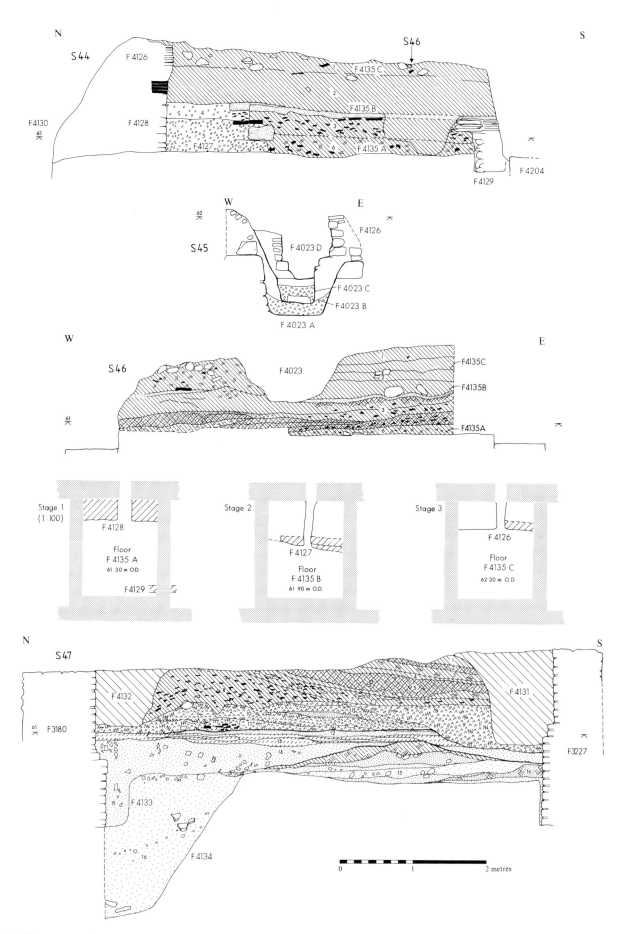

Fig 2.51 Room 7 sections 44–46, and Baths precinct section 47, location Fig 2.8; 1:50

the dumps within the room, and this may be the only finds evidence of use of the main baths through the fourth century (Fig 4.9, 69).

The centre two of the four doors between the *frigidarium* Room 3 and Rooms 4A and B were blocked. Excavations in the south-east corner of the *frigidarium* in 1988–9 exposed an area of patching, F4206, running to the doorway into Room 10 and the eastern door to Room 4B (Figs 2.8 and 3.1). The patching was micaceous flagstone tiles set on rubble which had been cut in to the original floor, and can be seen on the section from the 1955–85 trench (Fig 2.12: S9). Other areas of floor were identified where rubble had been packed into cuts in the original surface in an attempt to patch the floor. The process was parallelled in the basilical hall (Barker *et al* 1997). The implication of the repaired area leading to Room 10 and 4B is that the centre doors had already been blocked when the *frigidarium* floors were renovated at a date in the fifth century judging by that of similar repairs in the basilical hall.

Baths phase 4 (B 3.4)

The collapse and disuse of the baths is indicated particularly by the section cut in Room 6 (Fig 2.12: S15). The *pilae* stacks have been tilted and the *suspensura* floor above, F4141, broken and shifted. This suggests that the *suspensura* floor was broken through in order to remove *pilae* tiles. This occurred before the roof collapsed since large sections of the tufa and concrete roof, F4140, directly overlie the broken *suspensura* floor remains. The robbing trench for the east wall of Room 6 cuts through both *suspensura* and roof debris.

No such detail was obtained from the destruction levels elsewhere although the robbing of the main baths walls in Room 6 was parallelled in Room 5. These primary walls of the *caldarium* and *tepidarium* were removed to their foundation level. The outer added wall was not robbed to a similar depth, presumably because it lacked tile courses.

Room 11B was further infilled with rubble and soil (Fig 2.15: S16). In Room 11, a layer of soil on the floor, 20, was sealed by rubble, 19, and then by further soil deposits, 18 (Fig 2.41: S34). The rubble horizon may represent the broken *suspensura* floor, the tiles having been robbed more extensively than in Room 6. Elsewhere less robbing took place, the photographs from the 1860s indicating that *pilae* tiles survived well in Rooms 4A, 4B, 8, 9, and 12, while excavation showed lesser survival in Rooms 5 and 6. The *frigidarium* is presumed to have continued in use perhaps until the medieval period, explaining the survival of its north wall.

A coin dated to AD 244–7 (no 181) and a crucible used for metalworking (cat no 15) came from an occupation layer on the herringbone floor in Room 11A. Midlands fossil shell-tempered ware dated to the second half of the fourth century was found in the backfilling of Room 11.

West Range

West range phase 1 (WR 3.1)

The first third-century activity recorded in the west range of buildings may have been part of a major rebuilding programme; the archaeological evidence, however, was limited to new floors and to the repair or rebuilding of the inner courtyard sleeper wall of the *macellum* (Fig 2.9). This was demonstrated by a change in the stonework in the upper course which included tufa rock, mixed Hoar Edge Grit and Keele beds sandstone, and other building stones.

The covered walkways beneath the inner portico, and Room 22.9 at the south-east corner of the building were re-floored with herringbone tiles (Figs 2.9, 2.52, and 2.53). The new surface was carefully prepared. A base layer of sandstone, layer 2, supported a layer of concrete completed with a thin skim of *opus signinum*, layer 1 (Fig 2.38: S27 and S28). This was covered with a layer of crushed tile, and both formed the bedding for *opus spicatum* tiles set on a further layer of *opus signinum*. In the western walkway the tile surface, F4080, had suffered most from wear. However, displaced tiles and the underlying *opus signinum* floor were clear, as well as the rubble make up beneath. Layers of dark soil with charcoal (83/111, 84/48, and 84/49) also formed part of the make up and contained a number of metal and glass objects as well as quantities of pottery as will be noted in the catalogues (Fig 2.38: S27, layer 3). The floor bore signs of patching and repair, and had evidently had a long use.

In the north, east, and south walkways the floor survived better (Fig 2.9, F4081–F4083). A change in the layout occurred in the east corridor. Between a projection eastward of the north and south courtyard walls, tiles F4082 were set, running east-west rather than the north-south orientation prevailing elsewhere. The sharp change at the south-east corner may have marked a repair at the entrance to the latrine.

An *opus spicatum* floor at a lower level than in the courtyard walkways formed the floor of Room 22.9 (Fig 2.53). The floor here occurred on either side of the secondary drain running from the *macellum* courtyard to the main north-south drain. The tiles were set in mortar (Fig 2.25: S25, F81 on layer 1). There was no rubble or concrete base beneath, the mortar being set directly onto the Period 2 sand dumps.

Excavation failed to clarify the relationship of the boulder footing, F79, in the courtyard, with the newly built walls, and it is possible that the footing was added in this phase. Equally the primacy of rebuilt wall or *opus spicatum* floor could not be decided.

Excavations in the latrine, Room 20B, uncovered a skim of *opus signinum* set on concrete in turn based on a deep sandstone rubble base (Fig 2.20: S22, layers 2–6). *Opus spicatum* tiles were noted in the overburden together with roof tiles and demolition material, but none were found set on the floor. However, larger scale clearance of the same area in

Fig 2.52 Macellum *courtyard; view south*

1988–9 located an *in situ* area of *opus spicatum* flooring, and it would seem likely that the *opus signinum* floor uncovered in 1955 was in reality the base for *opus spicatum* tiles as in the *macellum*. In 1988/9 the sequence was seen to comprise a base layer of rubble sealed beneath *c* 0.3m of sand make up on which the *opus signinum* tile base was laid. Since this depth of rubble footing was not noted in the *macellum*, it is possible that these elements do not belong together, and that the rubble represents the base of an earlier floor.

The presence of *opus spicatum* tiles in Phase P 2.3 layers outside the *macellum* to the west suggests that a herringbone floor was an original feature of the *macellum*, and presumably of the walkways. A late third or early fourth-century replacement flooring seems to have been widespread through the public buildings. As noted above, Room 11A on the east side of the baths had an *opus spicatum* floor which lay directly beneath the demolition levels. Other herringbone floors were found in the basilical hall (Barker *et al* 1997), where they are dated to the earlier fourth century.

Four coins were found (cat nos 99, 126, 262, 321). Of the two dated to AD 270–3 one was sealed beneath the herringbone floor in the *macellum*, and the other came from the corridor to the north. Illustrated small finds are two chain fragments (Fig 4.7, 38 and 39), five pins (Fig 4.9, 63 and 67; Fig 4.10, 99, 100, and 110),

two toilet implements (Fig 4.11, 120 and 123), a textile working needle and pin (Fig 4.16, 163 and 169), two keys (Fig 4.19; 4.21, 197 and 198), a knife and handle (Figs 4.20, 210, 224), a spatula (Figs 4.22, 232), a furniture fragment, hinge, and mount (Figs 4.24, 241; 4.25, 246, and 250), a stud (Fig 4.26, 258), a hinge (Fig 4.26, 267), and scrap (Fig 4.29, 285). Two brooches dated to the second century were found (Fig 4.32, 5; Fig 4.35, 37). A honestone was found (cat no 23) and a fragment of wall veneer. All the small finds from these contexts have been the subject of analysis. Vessel glass was predominantly residual first and second century in date, but there were later second to third-century pieces and a fragment of typical fourth-century glass which could not date to earlier than the last quarter of the third century (Figs 4.38, 673 and 726; 4.39, 723; 4.40, 708; cat nos 664–5, 677, 707, 716, 725, 732–3, 760–1, 771, 776, 785, 804, 809, 811, 820, 826, 832–3, 842–5, 848, 862–3, and 870). A glass bead and counter (cat nos 13 and 53) and sherds of pottery vessels used to contain haematite and Egyptian blue pigments were found. Quantities of iron slag and furnace lining were also found.

The small finds analysis concluded that the finds represented rubbish in the floor make up. However it is possible that some of the material particularly the wall veneer, personal items, and furniture fragments were associated with the *macellum*.

Fig 2.53 Macellum *latrine, Room 22.9, herringbone floor; view west*

As noted above, dating evidence for the episode of re-flooring is provided by the coin of Tetricus II (AD 270–3, no 321). This was found in the rubble make up for the *macellum* walkway floor. The latest pottery included two early third-century samian sherds amongst quantities of residual second-century material, although the excavation records indicate the presence of unlocated late third-century sherds. A fragment of vessel glass diagnostically later third or early fourth century in date was also found securely sealed beneath the tile floor.

A similarity was noted between the material used to rebuild the upper courses of the *macellum* internal sleeper wall and the repair, F4166, of the upper course of the south portico sleeper wall (Fig 2.65: S55).

West range phase 2 (WR 3.2)

Long use following the *opus spicatum* floors of Phase WR 3.1 is witnessed by numerous repairs and re-levellings. A well-worn stone pathway leading from the northern entrance door into the interior is visible on photographs. The levels above the *opus spicatum* floors were disturbed. Many of the disturbances were recent, including drain trenches associated with the twentieth-century building sited here. A number of postholes seem likely also to be modern.

In the corridor a hearth of reused *pilae* brick and herringbone tile was sited towards its west end. Ash and cinders within the hearth and spread from it, were sealed beneath a patch of stone roof slates. These in turn formed the base of a gravel surface on which stone and herringbone tile fragments and bones were strewn. Further stone roofing tiles were sealed beneath an overburden of rubble.

A military stud fragment (Fig 4.7, 29) and a pin (Fig 4.10, 96) are illustrated from the small finds. There were no vessel glass fragments.

West range phase 3 (WR 3.3)

The drain beneath the east side of the *macellum* and the west side of the latrine was robbed of its sides and base (Fig 2.20: S21 and S22; Fig 2.21: S24; Fig 2.25: S25). The robbing trench, F67, left the mortar into which tiles had been keyed to make up the drain sides, but would have removed flagstone bases. The inner courtyard drain was also robbed of its tile sides and flagstone base, the impression of the latter remaining visible in their mortar settings (Fig 2.9; Fig 2.25: S26). The lower levels of both robbing trenches were filled with mortar and stone presumably waste from the robbing process; these layers lay beneath backfills of soil and rubble.

A deep pit, F87, not illustrated in plan but set in the centre of the corridor through from the street to the baths courtyard, was cut through the stone roof slates associated with the hearth (Fig 2.64). An uppermost level here, beneath the overburden, appeared to be a trodden surface. The pit was filled with layers of soil, tile and sand, 6, clay and sand, 5, beneath what may have been a sunk and compressed deposit of tiles, 4. This in turn was sealed by a further soil layer, 3, and tile dump, 2. The pit was levelled off with mortar and sand, 1, perhaps from a contemporary floor. The pit may have been a Romano-British feature. However there was no record of a sealing layer of stone tiles or rubble, and the pit could just as well belong to the modern period. Although its backfill contained solely Romano-British finds, the pit has been omitted from finds calculations.

Four coins were found, the latest of AD 364–78 (cat nos 173, 296, 465, and 610). Illustrated small finds are a bracelet (Fig 4.8, 45) and a fragment of scrap (Fig 4.29, 300). Vessel glass included a fourth-century fragment (cat nos 793, 871, and 875). A glass bead was found (Fig 4.47, 34).

Dating evidence from the drain robbing trench came from the four coins. Fourth-century pottery in the backfill of the Wright trench may indicate material redeposited from the robbing trenches.

Porticos

Porticos phase 1 (P 3.1)

The street porticos of the second-century public buildings were cut by a number of pits, some little more than large posthole size, and a gully (Fig 2.54). Some were linear trenches along the walls of the *macellum* and the courtyard boundary, while others were smaller and more randomly executed. These two groups have been placed in two Phases, P 3.1 and 3.2.

The possible P 3.1 group is composed of a number of long pits with straight parallel sides and rounded ends, cut close to the walls of the *macellum* and to the south wall of the courtyard. Only one, F855, was cut so as to expose footings. In the west portico, four pits, F579, F523, F602, and F736 from north to south, were cut close to the east wall, two were more centrally placed, F590, F597, and a smaller one, F572, was found against the outer sleeper wall. The area of the two *macellum* entries and of that to the corridor through to the baths courtyard was left undisturbed. Two features, F708 and F709, although included in this group, may instead represent a Period 2 entrance way feature.

In the south portico to the south of the *macellum*, the linear trenches listed from west to east were F800, F804, F801, F672, F766, F697, F790, F680, and, to the east of the drain, F974, F1012, and F1017. They were more randomly spaced, although there were again three long pits, F804, F801, and F766. F801 had been cut into by the semicircular pit, F855, alongside the *macellum* wall.

Further east in the south portico the pits seemed to have been dug as though constrained by some existing demarcation running down the middle of the porticos (Figs 2.56 and 2.57). On the north side F547, F486, and F417 were separated from a similar linear group respecting the portico sleeper wall, F561, F566, F518, and F564. Thus, despite repeated pit cutting, a ridge of undisturbed material was left as a central spine (Fig 2.60: S53). Again the southern group did not expose the sleeper wall footings.

Animal bone was present in most of the pits. Seven out of eight examined in detail contained large quantities of distinctive butchery waste which presumably derived from the specialist meat cuts provided at the *macellum*, although three were found in the eastern excavation in the south portico, well to the east of the *macellum*. The pit without a high degree of bone waste, F801, was poorly identified in the excavation.

A number of pit profiles are illustrated. In the west portico they comprise F602 and F736 (Fig 2.58: S50 and S51), and F572, F579, and F523 (Fig 2.59). In the south porticos illustrated pits are F804 and F855 (Fig 2.58: S52), F800, F672, F697, F680, and F974 (Fig 2.38: S29), and, further east, F564, F517, F518, and F486 (Fig 2.60: S53).

The two pits, F572 and F579 at the north end of the west portico are very slight but may have been deeper further north. The others present a similar profile and depth, cutting through the Period 2 portico make up layers down to, but not into, the Period 1 levels. The exceptions are F674 and F802 which are much shallower. The profile of F602 indicates that the pit's fill had sunk over a period of time, and that a gravel surface from the Phase P 3.3 floor had subsided into the pit. The profiles of the other pits suggest that the fills were densely packed. F804 in the south portico was surrounded by a number of small stakeholes as though some sort of marking out had occurred, or some protection of the pit edges. A small posthole, F890, at one corner may have been associated, although it appeared to have been cut by F804.

The interpretation of P 3.1 and the dating evidence is discussed with P 3.2 below.

Porticos phase 2 (P 3.2)

A second group saw a more dispersed layout and a more varied type of feature, ranging from pits similar to those in P 3.1 to smaller cuts some more similar to large postholes. In the west portico two pits, F599 and F631, were placed across the southern entrance to the *macellum*. The northern entrance was not pitted while F710 and F711 were set against the sleeper wall opposite the corridor entrance to the baths. Pits F623, F624, F626, F768, and F793 cut P 3.1 features, while F630 and F643 were situated at the corner. The south portico saw a particular cluster of intercutting pits, F634, F638, F651, F675, and F714 to the west of the main drain, two of which, F638 and F675, contained animal bone. The group was cut by a large trench, F678, with two further features,

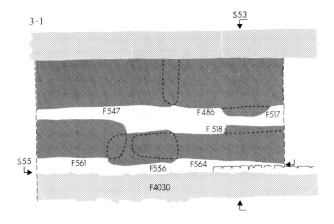

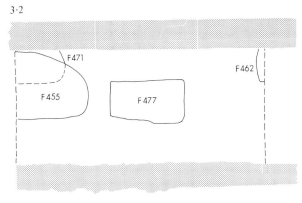

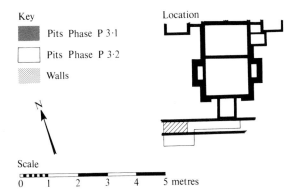

Key

■ Pits Phase P 3·1

□ Pits Phase P 3·2

▨ Walls

Location

Scale

0 1 2 3 4 5 metres

Fig 2.56 South portico, phase P 3.1 and 3.2 pits; 1:125

Fig 2.57 South portico P 3.1 pits, F564 and F486; view west

F760 and F679, to its north. To the west were four small features, F677, F682, F735, and F852. East of the drain were two pits, F1077 and F930. The latter was shown by finds evidence to be fourth century in date and to belong to later activity. Further east four pits, F471, F455, F477, and F462, again contained quantities of animal bone.

The illustrated profiles indicate the variety. In the west portico figured features are F626 and F768 (Fig 2.58: S51), F576, F599, F631, and F643 (Fig 2.59). In the south portico, from west to east, F735, F675, F697, F714, F760, F679, and F930 (Fig 2.38: S29). Further east F477 is shown (Fig 2.60). Of these many are shallow cuts, while F477, F599, F631, and F679 are similar to the P 3.1 group. The upper fill, layer 11, of F626 had subsided as had the fill of F477, as evidenced by the slope of the overlying subsequent gravel layers.

It is known from the forum porticos that stalls were maintained there at least in the second century, and the evidence from the baths *insula* porticos must be assessed in that light. The purpose of the P 3.1 and 3.2 pits seems to be predominantly for rubbish disposal, specifically for bone from meat joints. The majority of the pottery from the pits, in contrast, was not contemporary rubbish, so there were elements in the pit backfills deriving from the levels into which the pits were cut. One fragment of pottery joined with another from a WR 2.1 feature beneath the *macellum*. In addition some of the fills may have derived from subsequent levelling as is apparent in some of the sections. Pottery and other artefacts may therefore be from redeposited layers or be contemporary with the bone waste, or have arrived in later levelling.

The purpose of the pits which did not contain bone is unclear. F804 was thought to be a latrine trench on the basis of its green cessy fill. Others may have been the source of sand for mortar.

It was not possible to establish whether the pits were the result of a few episodes of pit digging or whether they represented the results of sporadic pit digging over a long period of time. If the former was the case then the episodes may have been linked with some refurbishment or repair process during which the normal regime in the porticos was abandoned for a while. However, even if the latter was the case then a total of nearly 60 pits dug over a period of perhaps half a century need not imply that there was no prohibition on rubbish being disposed of in this way.

With two exceptions, pits were not cut outside the two entrances to the *macellum*, suggesting that a permanent flooring had been placed there. This seems likely to have been an area of stone slabs which were robbed out in the next period (P 3.3). Their position outside the entrances is marked by the later robber trenches, F485 and F591 (Fig 2.61). The two exceptions F599 and F631 occur in the southern entrance way. The latter may be seen as falling just outside the suggested area of flooring. The former may therefore have been a feature from the next, P 3.3, phase.

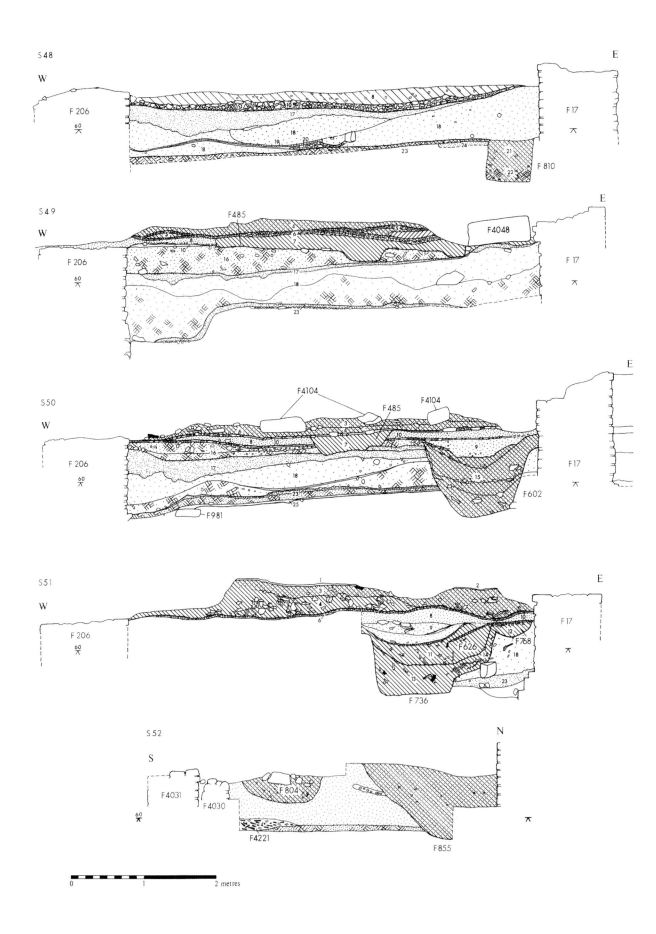

Fig 2.58 West portico, sections 48-51, south portico, section 52, location Fig 2.9; 1:50

Table 2.1 Finds from portico pits, KG 16 and 17

F455 (box 80, KG 17):	animal bone; bone pins; vessel glass (cat nos 258, 444, 546, and 611)
F462 (box 80, KG 17):	animal bone
F471 (box 80, KG 17):	animal bone; coin AD 141+ (cat no 146); pin
F477 (box 80, KG 17):	animal bone; coin AD 103-11 (cat no 119); nail; vessel glass (cat nos 192 and 581)
F486 (box 80, KG 16):	animal bone; military stud, two wallhooks, pottery counter, finger ring, two pins; vessel glass later second/early third century (cat nos 163, 183, 184, 492, 504, 531, 538, 569, and 570), window glass; pottery pre-AD 225
F523 (box 97, KG 16):	animal bone; fragment of silver, ring, scrap (Fig 4.29.296); crucible (cat no 11); vessel glass 638 ?fourth-century (cat nos 129, 167, 196, 266, 391, 393, 464, 549, and 638), window glass; pottery pre-AD 225
F547 (box 80, KG 16):	animal bone; pin, nail; vessel glass (cat nos 231, 379, 380, 381, and 571) pottery pre-AD 270
F556 (box 80, KG 16):	animal bone; vessel glass (cat no 350)
F561 (box 80, KG 16):	animal bone; needle, pin, brooch second-century (Fig 4.34.33); vessel glass (cat no 229), window glass; pottery pre-AD 225
F564 (box 80, KG 16):	animal bone; shale bracelet, two pins, wallhook, hinge (Fig 4.27.268), brooch AD 75-175 (Fig 4.34.30); vessel glass (cat nos 102, 230, and 313); pottery pre-AD 225
F572 (box 97, KG 16):	crucible (cat no 10); pottery pre-AD 225
F579 (box 97, KG 16):	mount, glass ring setting; vessel glass (cat nos 500 and 580); pottery pre-AD 270
F590 (box 90, KG 16):	vessel glass (cat no 312); bracelet (Fig 4.8.42); pottery pre-AD 270
F597 (box 90, KG 16):	animal bone; vessel glass (cat nos 314 and 451); pottery pre-AD 270
F599 (box 90, KG 17):	animal bone; vessel glass (cat nos 262, 527, 547, and 615); window glass
F602 (box 90, KG 16):	animal bone; coin AD 134-8 (cat no 132); two pins, shale bracelet, two collar ferrules, scrap, two wallhooks; hone (cat no 8); intaglio (Fig 4.36.1); vessel glass later second/early third century (cat nos 103, 113, 182, 185, 195, 452, 453, and 631), window glass; pottery into fourth century
F623 (box 90, KG 17):	finger ring, key, wallhook, water pipe collar, offcut
F624 (box 90, KG 17):	coin AD 134-8 (cat no 130)
F631 (box 90, KG 17):	animal bone; earring; two pins, scrap; vessel glass (cat nos 291, 323, 462, and 619)
F638 (box 98, KG 17):	animal bone; two tweezers, two pins (Fig 4.9.77 and 78), offcut, three wallhooks, lead fragment, bell (?religious function); vessel glass (cat nos 288, 293, 469, and 622)
F643 (box 90, KG 17):	animal bone; vessel glass (cat no 455)
F651 (box 98, KG 17):	animal bone
F672 (box 98, KG 16):	animal bone; coin AD 205 (cat no 171); third-century pins, oculist's stamp (Fig 4.30), needle (Fig 4.16.165), handle (Fig 4.21.223), stem, stud, water pipe collar; vessel glass later second/early third century (cat nos 186, 187, 194, 267, 284, and 471); window glass; pottery into fourth century
F675 (box 98, KG 17):	animal bone; third/fourth-century pin, wallhook, waste
F676 (box 90, KG 16):	vessel glass (cat nos 263 and 397)
F677 (box 98, KG 17):	animal bone; vessel glass (cat nos 268 and 269a)
F678 (box 98, KG 17):	animal bone; vessel glass (cat no 552), window glass
F679 (box 98, KG 17):	animal bone; wallhooks, brooch second-century (Fig 4.35.47); vessel glass (cat no 511)
F680 (box 98, KG 16):	animal bone; vessel glass (cat nos 132, 285, and 308)
F708 (box 90, KG 16):	loop; vessel glass (cat nos 101 and 265)
F709 (box 90, KG 16):	pin, brooch AD 100-175 (Fig 4.33.18)
F714 (box 98, KG 17):	animal bone; two pins (Fig 4.9.74), pottery counter, stylus, vessel glass (cat no 473)
F736 (box 90, KG 16):	animal bone; coin third-century (cat no 716); shale tray, five pins, earring, finger ring, two combs, four wall hooks, nails, offcuts; vessel glass (cat nos 124, 351, 517, 582, and 618); window glass; pottery pre-AD 270
F766 (box 98, KG 16):	animal bone; wallhook; vessel glass (cat nos 474 and 514); pottery pre-AD 225
F800 (box 98, KG 16):	animal bone; coin AD 155-6 (cat no 143); two needles (Fig 4.16.166), three pins, wallhook, nail, stone ring setting, bone ring, brooch AD 150-250 (Fig 4.34.31); vessel glass (cat nos 135, 168, 177, 178, 180, 237, 244, 276, 296, 328, 409, 411, 442, 498, 525, 543, and 587), window glass; pottery pre-AD 270
F801 (box 98, KG 16):	animal bone; seal-box
F804 (box 98, KG 16):	animal bone; pin, brooch AD 150-225 (Fig 122.27); vessel glass later second/early third century (cat nos 165, 189, 246, and 247); pottery pre-AD 225
F852 (box 98, KG 17):	animal bone; wallhooks, ?rake tooth; vessel glass (cat nos 200, 428, 522, and 598)
F855 (box 98, KG 16):	animal bone; coin (cat no 60); four bone pins, finial knob, ?weight, T-staple, structural item, stylus, die (Fig 4.11.136); vessel glass (cat nos 245, 301, 356, 426, 432, and 555); pottery pre-AD 225
F930 (box 98, KG 17):	animal bone; coins AD103-11, 150-1, 161-80 (cat nos 122, 141, 154); third/fourth-century household shrine (Fig 4.31), earring, two pins, one fourth-century (Fig 4.10.102), box hinge (Fig 4.24.243); vessel glass fourth-century (cat nos 100, 208, 250, 431, 434, 435, 600); pottery third/fourth century
F974 (box 98, KG 16):	animal bone; figurine (Fig 4.12.140), vessel glass (cat no 253)
F1012 (box 98, KG 16):	crucible (cat no 12)
F1017 (box 98, KG 16):	?steelyard arm, stem, two needles, pin (Fig 4.10.97), wallhook, nail, crucible (cat no 7); vessel glass (cat nos 294, 305, 334, 439, 475, 545, and 604) and counter (cat no 65); honestone (Fig 4.48.7); pottery pre-AD 225
F1077 (box 98, KG 17):	pottery

The finds evidence is tabulated (Table 2.1). The pottery evidence from the Phase 3.1 and 3.2 pits suggests three phases of deposition all in the third century. The phases do not accord with the suggested groups outlined above. The pottery may have entered the pits in backfilling over the primary fills, or in levelling material, and may therefore give a more complicated dating picture. However, F930 was clearly shown to be a late feature apart from its pottery contents which were dated to the late third century or later and included a sherd, perhaps intrusive, of Midlands fossil shell-tempered ware. The pottery dating evidence suggests the others all belong to the first half of the third century, perhaps into the first decades of the second half century.

Eight coins were found. From P 3.1 pits came coins of Antoninus Pius (AD 155–6) in F800 and of Caracalla (AD 205) in F672. From P 3.2 pits came a coin of Antoninus Pius in F930. Hadrianic and

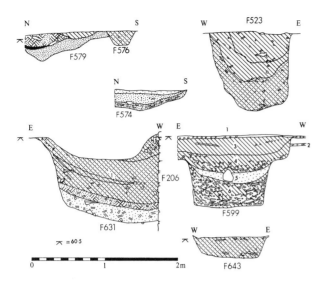

Fig 2.59 West portico, pit profiles, phases P 3.1 and P 3.2; 1:50

pre-Hadrianic coins were also found. Significant dating evidence came from F523 which contained a fragment of possible fourth-century glass, F672, third-century bone pins, F675, third- or fourth-century bone pins, and F930, a fourth-century lead shrine. Fragments of crucibles from metalworking were found in F523, F572, F1012, and F1017.

Similar pits were found in the north portico by Kathleen Kenyon, some of which were re-examined during the basilical hall excavations (Barker *et al* 1997).

Porticos phase 3 (P 3.3)

The pit cutting of P 3.1 terminated with the provision of a gravel surface in the porticos, followed by make up layers and re-gravelling where subsidence occurred

over pits, and then by a final gravel surface (illustrated on Figs 2.9 and 2.63). The two main floorings were composed of beds of sand, soil, and crushed stone with the gravel surface above set within a hard concrete-like mortar (Fig 2.58: S48–S51, layers 6 and 10; Fig 2.60: S53; S54, layers 7–9). Where sinkage had occurred into the earlier pits the additional gravel floors and broken sections of the initial floor occurred as fragmentary surfaces (Fig 2.58: S50 and S51). A particular feature of the surfaces was that, because of the weight of traffic and use, they had detached themselves in places from the walls against which they were butted, leaving shallow gully-like features between their edges and the walls. This relationship had been lost through later activity against the *macellum* and south courtyard walls but was clear along the west portico sleeper wall (Fig 2.9). This feature of the floors was also noted in the north portico (Barker *et al* 1997).

Arrangements at the two *macellum* entries were altered during this phase. The final gravel surface sealed two shallow but extensive soil-filled areas outside the entrances, F485 and F951, which may indicate the robbing of flagstones similar to those surviving at the entrances (Figs 2.61 and 2.67; Fig 2.58: S49 and S50). A sandstone base with a cut socket, F525, was located north of the northern entrance (Figs 2.9 and 2.61). It postdated the first gravel surface and was sealed by the last surface. It may represent evidence of a roof support but seems more likely to have been robbed from the entrance flooring and abandoned nearby. A second sandstone base was found near the south door but was not laid flat.

A number of posthole and trench features were recorded. These were confined to the northern excavated part of the west portico (Figs 2.61 and 2.62), and to the eastern excavated part of the south portico (Fig 2.63).

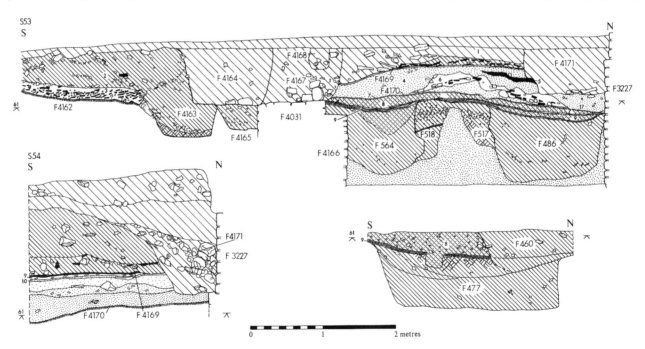

Fig 2.60 South portico, sections 53–54 and F477 profile, location Fig 2.63; 1:50

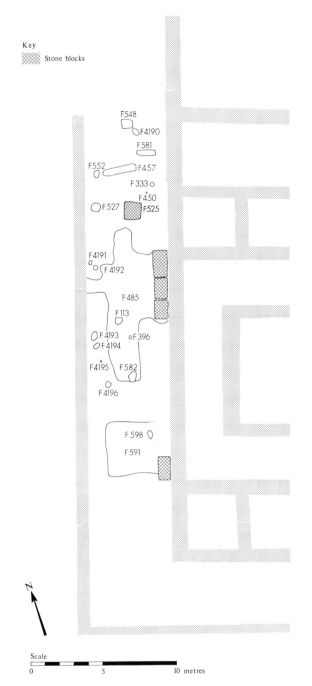

Key
░░ Stone blocks

F548
F4190
F581
F552   F457
F333
F450
F527   F525
F4191
F4192
F485
F113
F4193   F396
F4194
F4195   F582
F4196

F598
F591

N

Scale
0   5   10 metres

Fig 2.61 West portico, phase P 3.3 features; 1:250

Fig 2.62 West portico, phase P 3.3; view south

All cut through gravel horizons and were again sealed by the final gravel surface. In the west portico, two shallow trenches, F457 and F581, were located at the entrance to the corridor through to the baths, just north of F525 (Fig 2.64). Sixteen postholes or stakeholes, of which the profiles of F582 and F598 are illustrated (Fig 2.64), were apparently randomly spaced, with eight at the three entrance ways. In the south portico a linear trench, F300, was found, and three postholes or pits possibly placed in a line, F480, F460, and F475, the latter replaced by F465 (Fig 2.63).

To the south of the *macellum* the P 3.3 lower gravel surface lay at the level of the uppermost layers drawn on Sections 29 (Fig 2.38) and 52 (Fig 2.58); the section record starting directly after the last gravel surface had

been removed. East of the drain however the gravel surface lay at a lower level with a surviving fragment of the upper gravel surface sealing F930 at around the level of the first surface to the west (Fig 2.38: S29, layer 4). Thus although the portico walkway would have risen overall from west to east, there was nevertheless a step down eastward from the east wall of the main drain.

In the eastern excavation in the south portico, the sleeper wall footing had been repaired using a range of different stones, amongst which was tufa from bath vaults (Fig 2.65: S55, F4166). The similarity between F4166 and the rebuilt *macellum* courtyard wall has been noted above. The repair had been undertaken before the gravel surfaces had been lain (Fig 2.60: S53). Subsidence of the gravel surfaces emphasised the central spine uncut by pits and fragments of concreted gravel were found in the pits, suggesting a highly uneven surface at times.

These distinctive and strong floor surfaces mark a change from earlier portico use. Whatever the function of the features found it is clear that the whole portico area was regularly available for repair and refurbishment of its surfaces intermittently from the last P 3.2 pit cutting, through to the P 3.4 activity.

Eighteen coins were found, the latest from the west portico dated to AD 327–8, and from the south portico to AD 341–6 from Box 80 to the east, and to AD

64

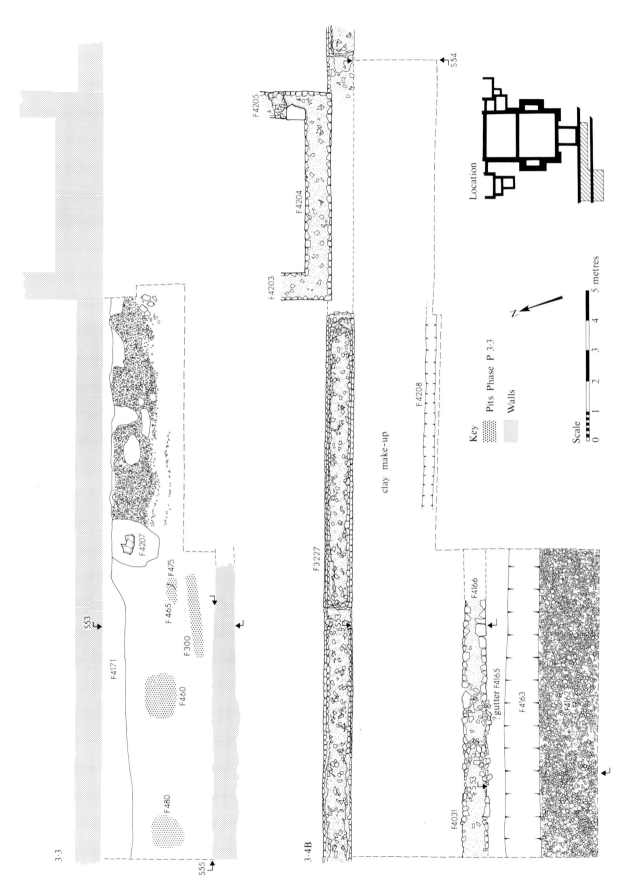

Fig 2.63 South portico, phase P 3.3 (above) and 3.4B (below); 1:125

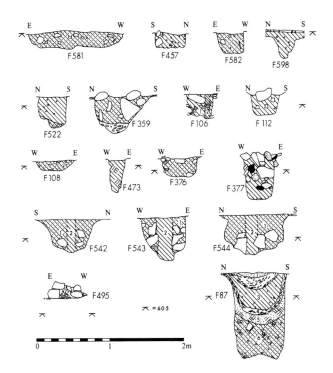

Fig 2.64 West portico, phases P 3.3, P 3.4A, and P 3.6 profiles, and West Range pit F87; 1:50

330–1 from Box 98 beside the *macellum* (cat nos 12, 113, 149, 159, 161, 168, 170, 179, 178, 183, 207, 240, 252, 286, 347, 396, 399, and 422). The latest gravel surface in the south portico is also given a *terminus post quem* by the fourth-century finds in pit F930 from P 3.2. Illustrated small finds comprise a possibly military stud (Fig 4.7, 21), a bracelet (Fig 4.8, 58), a pin (Fig 4.9, 84), a toilet implement and a counter (Fig 4.11, 114 and 131), a seal box (Fig 4.13, 151),

two nails (Fig 4.26, 262 and 265), a structural fitting (Fig 4.28, 277), and an item of scrap (Fig 4.29, 292). Seven brooches were found (Fig 4.32, 6 and 8; Fig 4.33, 22; Fig 4.34, 28 and 32; Fig 4.35, 45 and 41), an intaglio (Fig 4.36, 4), a stone palette, and two hon-estones (Fig 4.48, 10, cat no 9). Vessel glass was largely residual but included four fragments of fourth-century material all from the west portico and some third-century glass (Figs 4.39, 273; 4.40, 277; 4.41, 508; 4.43, 530; 4.44, 283 and 4.46, 199, cat nos 95–6, 98–9, 118, 122, 131, 140, 142, 143a, 152–3, 157, 171–4, 179, 181, 188, 190, 198, 212, 215, 225, 232–4, 238, 248–9, 251, 259–61, 264, 269b, 271, 282, 295, 303, 309, 326, 331–2, 335, 344, 348–9, 359, 370, 378, 386–90, 394, 398, 401–2, 407, 425, 429–30, 433, 436, 447–9, 456–61, 465, 470, 479, 486, 487, 489, 495, 497, 510b, 513, 540, 541, 548, 551, 557, 562, 568, 574–6, 578–9, 583–4, 593, 599, 601, 605, 614, 616–7, 621, 628, 633, and 643). Glass beads, part of a prismatic bottle, and a setting were also found (cat nos 7, 70, and 71). A crucible used for metalworking was recovered (cat no 13).

Pottery from the foundation trench of the renewed sleeper wall, F4031, in the eastern excavated area of the south portico contained later third-century pottery. This wall and the *macellum* courtyard wall may be from the same building campaign as was suggested by their similar builds. Posthole F582 west of the *macellum* and an unlocated posthole in this stratigraphic position contained Midlands fossil shell-tempered ware from the second half of the fourth century, but this may be intrusive material.

The evidence from the P3.1 and P3.2 pits suggests that the first gravel surface was laid in the second half of the third century, and that from the coins and glass

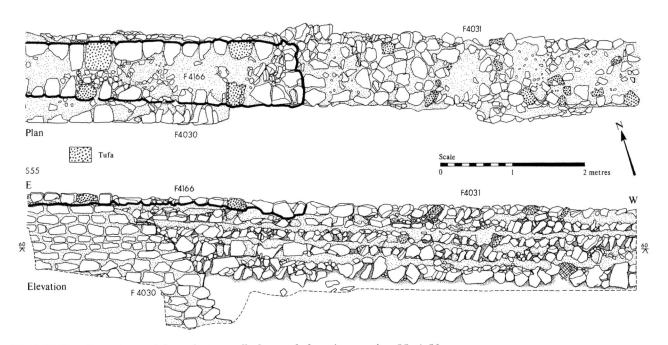

Fig 2.65 South portico, stylobate sleeper wall plan and elevation, section 55; 1:50

suggests that the final gravel surface was laid in the first half of the fourth century. The latest coin, of AD 341–6, was from posthole F460 in Box 80 which may perhaps have been cut through the gravel.

Porticos phase 4A (P 3.4A)

The west portico and the south portico west of the main drain exiting from beneath the *macellum*, were now treated differently from the south portico east of the main drain, and the two areas are differentiated, the western area described as Phase P 3.4A and the south portico east of the drain as Phase P 3.4B.

Above the gravel surfaces of P 3.3 was inconclusive evidence of stone spreads and beam trench marked structures laid out within the area of the porticos (Fig 2.55). These were confined to the area south of the north entrance to the *macellum*. To the north of the entrance the final P 3.3 gravel surface remained in use and was cut through by postholes.

One possible structure lay between the north and south entrances to the *macellum*, marked on the north side by postholes F336, F376, and F377, or perhaps by postholes F112 and F439. The south side was marked by three stone-packed postholes, F542–F544, with the marks of postpipes (Fig 2.64). Within this possible structure was an area of heavily worn rounded cobbles and sandstones, F4104. South of the southern entrance a second structure may have been marked by beam trenches, with F4105 directly south of the entrance and F4108 8m to the south. Again areas of worn stone, F4106 and F4107 were apparent (Fig 2.66). In the south portico, a third trench, F593, may mark a third and perhaps the most convincing structure. The trench was cut into the upper gravel surface of P 3.3, and to its west and south were compacted stone surfaces.

Alternatively the postholes, with the exception of F542–F544, may be seen as impermanent and random settings, parallelled by the postholes further north, two of which, F109 and F110, occurred outside the *macellum* entrance. In this case postholes F542–F544 may be interpreted as roof supports or scaffolding settings for repair of the roof. Outside the south entrance was a

Fig 2.66 West portico, phase P 3.4A F4106; view north-west

slight wall of two thicknesses of stone, F495, and this may have been a support for a timber boardwalk at the entrance (Fig 2.55). Trench F4105 may have served the same purpose. F4108 further south may be a drainage rather than a structural feature. Of the apparently randomly placed postholes, F106, F108, F359, F473, and F522 are illustrated (Fig 2.64).

Whatever the interpretation of the postholes, the areas of heavily worn boulders can be seen as marking significant areas, perhaps market stalls, or representing patching in the portico, again perhaps where heavy wear from market activities might occur, or, alternatively, as surviving sections of more widespread stone layers. They were heavily worn and seem therefore more likely not to have lain within structures. By contrast the area to the east of F593, which may have been enclosed, retained the portico surface from Phase P 3.3.

Twenty two coins were found, the latest being a group from the AD 360s and 370s (cat nos 138, 142, 166, 185, 203, 210, 250, 255, 274, 295, 318, 320, 438, 501, 503, 511, 546, 586, 588, 603, 604, and 640). A pin (Fig 4.10, 109) and a key (Fig 4.19, 192) are illustrated from the small finds. A honestone was found (cat no 11). Two of the vessel glass fragments were fourth-century in date (Fig 4.45, 162; cat nos 168, 203–4, 239, 241–2, 327, 338, 347, 420, 422, 468, 490, 550, 577, and 595). A melon bead (cat no 8) and a crucible used for metalworking (cat no 14) were also found.

The possible structural slot F593 contained a coin of AD 353+ and one of the three postholes F542–4 a coin of AD 367–73. Midlands fossil shell-tempered ware from the second half of the fourth century was found in wall F495, and in a number of contexts.

Porticos phase 4B (P 3.4B)

In the eastern area excavated, the remains of a tiled hearth, F4207, was found on the gravel surface with burnt material nearby (Fig 2.63). Further east the gravel surface had been worn away in patches.

These surfaces were then sealed by successive dumps of sand and soil interspersed by dumps of building rubble, bringing up the portico surface by 0.3m to a new level, F4169 (Fig 2.60: S53 and S54). On the new surface a trench, F4208, suggested the position of a structure (Fig 2.63). The uppermost level was particularly marked by areas of burning.

Seven coins were found, the latest one, of AD 375–8, was the only fourth-century coin (cat nos 105, 140, 167, 256, 352, 645, 725). Two pins (Fig 4.9, 66 and 86), a stylus (Fig 4.13, 145), a file (Fig 4.15, 156), and a key (Fig 4.19, 194) are illustrated from the small finds. Two honestones and three counters made from grey stone roofing slates were found (cat nos 12, 13, 34–6). Two fourth-century fragments were found amongst the vessel glass (Figs 4.40, 302, and 318; 4.41, 481; 4.46, 207; cat nos 210–11, 227–8, 341, 374–6, 437, 537, 565–7, and 658). The dump did not contain Midlands fossil shell-tempered ware and it is possible, disregarding the latest coin, to see it as redeposited from an earlier dump of material. Deposition, however, seems to have occurred in the later fourth century.

Porticos phase 5 (P 3.5)

In the west portico the stylobate was removed allowing the top of the sleeper wall to form part of an overall surface in places (Fig 2.55). To its west a robbing trench, F91, marked the former position of a drain running down the outside of the stylobate sleeper wall, as was the case in the street on the north side of the *insula* (Webster and Daniels 1972).

In the eastern excavated area in the south portico, the last Phase 4B level, F4169, was sealed by a layer of stone roofing slates (Fig 2.60: S53). This was itself sealed beneath rubble and destruction deposits of dark soil containing much building debris including slate, stone and ceramic rooftiles with *tegula* and *imbrex* recorded, as well as sandstone blocks, *pilae*, and painted plaster. There were many finds including a large mill stone. These rubble layers were then cut by a robbing trench, F4167, following the top of the portico sleeper wall (Fig 2.60: S53).

Fifty five coins were found, the latest of AD 388–95 (cat nos 156, 162, 201, 204, 224, 243, 246, 248, 301, 328, 332, 334, 370, 372, 378, 386, 413–4, 424, 452, 475–6, 479, 490, 497, 513, 515, 521, 524, 527, 544, 547, 549, 556, 559, 573, 576–7, 592, 597, 608, 618, 620, 635, 641, 653, 665–6, 669, 678, 685, 698, 714, 723, and 728). Illustrated small finds comprise a gouge (Fig 4.15, 157), a key (Fig 4.19, 193), a knife (Fig 4.20, 218), a furniture hinge (Fig 4.25, 248), a structural hinge and ring (Figs 4.27, 271; 4.28, 275), and scrap (Fig 4.29, 288). A honestone was found (cat no 14). Of the vessel glass two items were identifiably fourth-century (Figs 4.39, 279; 4.46, 333; cat nos 141, 197, 226, 274, 281, 337, 352, 373, 383, 493, 507,536, 572, 653, and 659). A *tegula* was recorded. Analyses of soils from two P 3.5 contexts and one from P 3.4B were made in 1972 by N Bridgewater (Archive E18).

Layers filling the robbing trench on the outside of the sleeper wall at the south end of the west corridor produced numerous coins ranging from the later third to the later fourth century. Midlands fossil shell-tempered ware from the second half of the fourth century was found in F91 and in F4167.

Porticos phase 6 (P 3.6)

In the west portico, a new level of stone rubble in which possible pathways could be seen, was laid out across the portico sleeper wall (Figs 2.55, 2.67, and 2.68). The line of the sleeper wall would only have been visible over part of its length. In the former portico area, the division marked by the posthole line and trench at the south entrance was sealed by further gravel and soil layers as were the other P 3.4A features. Areas of worn stone, F4098, F4099, F4100, F4101, and F4103 were spread across the former portico sleeper wall and stylobate. In the south-west of the excavated area, the edge of the road was represented by an area of smaller stones, F4102. The areas of stone were surrounded by mortar and soil. Some of the mortar pieces were quite large,

Fig 2.67 West portico, phase P 3.6; view north

Fig 2.68 West portico, phase P 3.6; view south

and could have been formed initially by being broken off reused stone. In the former portico area were possible surfaces (Fig 2.58: S51, layer 1).

The stone spreads were thought to form platforms similar to those from Period 4A. However the pattern formed by them is more suggestive of pathways leading to the *macellum* and corridor entrances. F4098 opposite the corridor entrance masked the underlying sleeper wall. It may have led both to the corridor and, diagonally, to the north *macellum* entrance. F4099 seemed to approach the northern entrance, again at an angle, this time from the south. Finally F4100 and F4101 appeared to be laid out to form paths to the southern *macellum* entrance, with the southern path, F4101, running across F91. This latter, although shown on Figure 2.55, had been infilled in Phase 3.5. These paths and the surrounding areas were sealed beneath dark soil layers which spread over the portico area, the sleeper wall, and the road surface. In the southern portico by the *macellum*, layers of grey roofing slates were sealed by further dark soil layers.

West of the *macellum*, therefore, activity continued following the destruction of the stylobate, and thus of the portico roof, and extended beyond the portico walkway into the street. The *macellum* seems to have remained in use judging by the maintained pathway to it.

A large number of coins (196) was found, the latest of Arcadius and the House of Theodosius (388–402). They are too many to list here but can be isolated from the catalogue. Illustrated small finds comprise military equipment (Fig 4.6, 7, 12, 14, and 19; Fig 4.7, 23), bracelets (Fig 4.8, 43, 44, and 55), toilet implements (Fig 4.11, 119 and 124), a textile working needle (Fig 4.16, 167) a lock strap and two keys (Fig 4.19, 189, 195, and 204), a knife (Fig 4.20, 214), a handle (Fig 4.21, 228), a structural hinge and fittings (Fig 4.28, 273, 276, and 278), and fragments of scrap (Fig 4.29, 295, 299, and 301). Datable vessel glass was fourth century (Figs 4.44, 144; 4.45, 634; 4.46, 651; cat nos 148, 151, 155, 240, 320, 384–5, 421, 485, 539, 573, 594, 635, 637, 646–8, 650, 655, and 661–2). Glass beads and counters were found (Fig 4.47, 38–40; cat nos 9, 32–3, 46, and 60). Of great interest was a fragment of window glass of a type which has been dated elsewhere to the seventh or eighth century AD, but which may have an earlier date, perhaps in the immediately post-Roman centuries. The pottery from these horizons contained Midlands fossil shell-tempered ware dated to the later fourth-century.

The dating evidence therefore suggests that P 3.4A and 3.4B can be placed in the second half of the fourth century, since the last P 3.3 gravel surface sealed a coin of AD 341. Given the solid consistency of this flooring a long lifespan for it can be suggested; indeed the first P 3.3 gravel surface lasted almost a century. The make up layers used for the P 3.4B dumps contained earlier residual finds.

Phase P 3.5 can be dated by coins to later than the end of the fourth century. But by this time the dating evidence of coins and pottery may be of little use. The

P 3.5 dating evidence suggests that all of the coins and pottery of P 3.6 were residual. How long use of the *macellum* and the area to its west continued will not be indicated by the end of coin loss and the sequence must belong after the formal end of the diocese. The evidence is considered further in Chapter 5.

Courtyard

Courtyard phase 1 (C 3.1)

The *natatio* provided in the last stage of the second-century building campaign, was abandoned and infilled (Fig 2.39: S31). The flagstone floor, F4115, had been partly robbed, and stones left at either end may indicate that robbing occurred after some infilling had taken place (Fig 2.32). In places the base fill was of black soil layers with charcoal containing tile. These were sealed beneath an overall deposit of mortar (Fig 2.39: 531, layer 10) containing rubble and crushed red tile. In one deposit the tile was seen to have been burnt and was accompanied by a deposit of ashy material. The overlying infilling was of ash layers, dark loamy clay, and tile and rubble. These were interleaved with sandy lenses as though the clay had originally been rubbish material and the sand a succession of sealing spreads. However the sand layers also contained sandstone blocks, and may have been further demolition material. The whole deposit, judging by the sections taken across the pool, was carefully placed and settled. The lower layers lay horizontally with no evidence of subsidence, the upper layers sloped slightly toward the centre. A pit, F4120, was seen in section cut from the upper infill (Fig 2.39: S31).

The infill contained a large amount of animal bone butchery waste similar to the material found in the portico pits. Pottery comprised large sherds with unworn breaks and both deposits are suggested to have been primary dumps of rubbish rather than redeposited material. There was also a substantial component of building debris in the lower dump layers. This may have come from structural features associated with the *natatio* which were dumped into the pool. The rubbish layers may have come from different sources, the butchery waste from the *macellum* and the pottery perhaps from the basilical hall.

There was no real indication of an overall surface re-establishing use of the courtyard. To the north, a layer similar to the upper deposit was recorded overlying the *natatio* surround (Fig 2.70: S57, layers 14 and 15; Fig 2.71: S61 and S62). It is possible that the courtyard surface was of trodden earth. There was no trodden surface apparent across the infilled *natatio*. Its walls were later robbed out (see C 3.4), and it may be that they survived above the ground level through most of Period 3.

Similar disuse and abandonment of open air pools are known elsewhere in the northern Provinces. As well as Wroxeter, Nielsen notes the infilling of *natationes* not long after construction at the Womens Baths at Augusta Raurica, both pools at Aventicum, and at Coriovallum (Nielsen 1993, 82, n62). She suggests that this infilling and the absence of *natationes* from later baths in the north, can be explained by the unsuitability of the northern climate. At Caerleon in contrast the *natatio* was subject to a number of changes and was only abandoned when the baths went out of use (Zienkiewicz 1986, I, 255); however this sequence occurred in a military context. It may be that it was particularly the winter conditions that made open air pools difficult to maintain, rather than general climatic conditions.

Two coins and a coin mould were found (cat nos 127, 147, and 734). The latest coin was of AD 141+, and the coin mould was for *asses* of Marcus Aurelius (AD 140–4). A key (Fig 4.19, 201) is illustrated from the small finds. Vessel glass was of mid-first to mid-second-century date but included a mid-third-century piece. A possible fourth-century fragment would be intrusive (Figs 4.38, 891; 4.40, 899; 4.41, 955; 4.43, 967 and 968; 4.44, 907, 908, 922; 4.45, 982; cat nos

909, 910, 912, 920a, 920b, 921, 938–9, 946–7, 949, 953, 957–8, 962, 966, 969, 975, and 982). The pottery offered the best dating evidence, the large collection suggesting a date of AD 210–30.

Courtyard phase 2 (C 3.2)

Excavations to the south of the added *caldarium* showed that little activity had intervened between the infilling of the *natatio* and the new construction. The footings of Room 13, F2140, were set on a rubble base wider than the footings above in a 1.07m deep foundation trench, F2137 (Fig 2.69; Fig 2.70: S58). The trench was cut from the same level as that occupied by the *natatio* surround, and had been sealed by a layer of sand, layer 16, which abutted the wall. Above this a layer of mixed soil and stone, 15, and a layer of sand, brought the level up to an offset marking the start of the wall proper. The layer of sand marked a courtyard surface, F4021, which was patchily present elsewhere against the new building (Fig 2.71: S62 and S65), but was not seen further

Fig 2.69 Courtyard, Period 3; 1:250

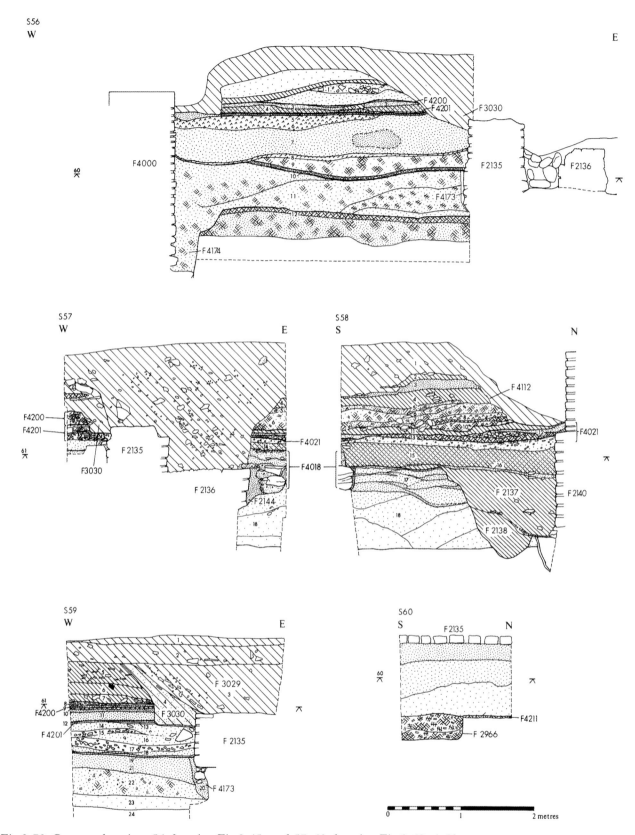

Fig 2.70 Courtyard sections 56, location Fig 2.45, and 57–60, location Fig 2.69; 1:50

south (Fig 2.39: S31). Construction debris, part of layer 13 (Fig 2.70: S58), was found on the surface of F4021.

The south wall of 12B was set in a trench, F2117, cut from slightly above the Period 2 *natatio* surround (Fig 2.71: S62). Excavations within the added

caldarium showed that this trench represented the south side of a deep cutting preparatory to building Rooms 12 and 13. The new courtyard surface, F4021, had been set on layer 14, overlying the Period 2 surface F4018. The two sections show a slightly different level from which the foundation trenches

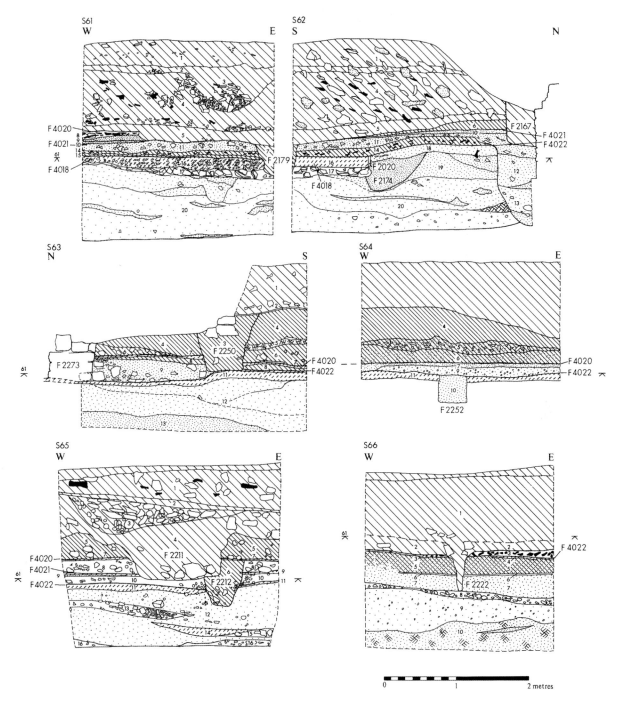

Fig 2.71 Courtyard sections 61–66, location Fig 2.69; 1:50

were cut, but both show the same surface, F4021, from which the new building was completed.

Spoil from the *praefurnium*, Room 13, was deposited as a dump, F4112, onto F4021 throughout the period of use of the added baths (Fig 2.69; Fig 2.70: S57 and S58, layers 2–10). A layer of soil, 11, overlay F4021, and underlay the dump. This latter comprised layers of burnt red clay, charcoal, ash, and rubble, 10, burnt clay, 9, ash and charcoal, 8, burnt clay, sand and charcoal, 5–7, soil and burnt debris, 4, compacted burnt material, 3, with rubble and soil, 2, at the uppermost surviving point. A second dump was recorded in the notebooks on the east side of Room 9D. Layer 5 on S63 (Fig 2.71), may represent part of it.

The level of the courtyard had now been raised to that of the courtyard walkway and to the surviving top of its sleeper wall (Fig 2.70: S57 and S58). There would no longer have been a step down from the portico to the courtyard.

Further east, F4021 was formed by layers of crushed brick and tile, presumably deriving from the construction of the added baths. This gave way the further the layer was from the new building, to a sand and stone horizon, or to tiles in soil. About 10m south of the added baths building the Roman levels had been truncated by later activity.

Despite the truncation, in one of the box excavations it was possible to see that a water pipe, F2092, had run across the courtyard between the added *caldarium* and the *macellum* (Fig 2.69). The trench was also marked by stakeholes (Fig 2.71: S66, F2222) cut in to the Period 2 levels, but the surface from which it was cut had been lost. A lining of tiles was recorded and three iron pipe collars were found *in situ*. This trench must have preceded the *praefurnium* dump and may have predated the added *caldarium*. Another pipe trench, F2252, was seen for a short distance running east-west from the main baths (Fig 2.69). The trench cut the Period 2 surface and predated the C 3.3 surface (Fig 2.71: S64). Pipe trench F2092 may have provided water to the *macellum*, and F2252 to Room 6A.

A number of features were recorded in the vicinity of the added baths which may be associated with the construction of the building (Fig 2.69). A particular group of postholes lay to the south of Room 12B comprising F2084, F2154, F2156, F2158, F2168, F2170, F2171 and F2172. One of these, F2170, lay at the north end of a trench, F2173. The edge of a gully, F2157, was also noted. South of Room 9D was an infant burial set in a shallow grave, F2251, and surrounded by stones; a posthole F2253 was recorded nearby. Other postholes were recorded, F2267, F2269, F2529, with an associated burnt area, F2330, in the centre of the courtyard, and F2698 and F2700 in the south-west corner.

A single first-century coin was found (cat no 66). Illustrated small finds comprise a military stud (Fig 4.7, 28), a pin (Fig 4.10, 91), and a punch (Fig 4.15, 155). A honestone was found (cat no 26). The datable vessel glass was limited to first and second-century material (cat nos 883, 913, and 942).

There was no diagnostic pottery from the added *caldarium* and *praefurnium* foundation trenches.

Courtyard phase 3 (C 3.3)

A second courtyard surface, F4020, survived in the area directly south of the new *caldarium*. The surface was very intermittent but was formed of sand and cement with, in places, tile (Fig 2.71: S61, S63–S65). A third water pipe trench, F2212, this time running between the added *caldarium* and the southern end of the main baths, was sealed by F4020 (Fig 2.69; Fig 2.71: S65). A posthole F2444 lay on the trench line to its south. The dump of furnace material, F4112, continued to build up on the south side of Room 13. It was not affected by the post-Roman truncation so clear elsewhere (Fig 2.70: S57 and 58).

The water pipe, F2212, may be associated with those in the baths precinct, F3191 and F3201, running towards the south end of the baths. It may be that it replaced an earlier pipe to be associated with F2252 from C 3.2.

Four coins were found, the latest of AD 268–70 (cat nos 50, 180, 214, and 715). A toilet implement (Fig 4.11, 115), a seal box lid (Fig 4.13, 149), and a hoe (Fig 4.17, 175) are illustrated from the small finds. A honestone was found (cat no 27). Of four fragments of vessel glass one was fourth-century (Figs 4.44, 919; 4.45, 983; cat nos 882 and 895).

There was no pottery from the *praefurnium* dumps of Room 13 later than the mid-third century. This seems unlikely to date the disuse of the added baths which presumably continued in use well into the fourth century. Midlands fossil shell-tempered ware from the second half of the fourth century was found in a courtyard context.

Courtyard phase 4 (C 3.4)

Evidence for later use of the courtyard area was much truncated. Nevertheless some indications can be seen on sections S63, 64, and 65 (Fig 2.71). These include dumps of soil and two apparent features, F2211 and F2250, the latter possibly a wall footing. These may however belong to Period 4. The long section across the courtyard (Fig 2.39: S31) shows an overall soil horizon overlying F4020. An upper surface, F4019, can be traced beneath more disturbed material. This is marked by a mortar surface (layer 5) which rises on a bank of material comprising a spread of tiles and some stone deposited against the wall of the baths.

Surface F4019 marks the level from which the *natatio* sides were robbed. Trenches F4118 and F4119 represent the removal of the sides, and a similar robbing process occurred for the drain (Fig 2.39, 531). There only the drain facing and base had been removed, but robbing of the *natatio* sides was almost complete. As suggested above, although the *natatio* had been sealed in the early third century, upper stones surviving through the third and fourth centuries may have indicated its position. Two possible postholes, F2318 and F2333, cut the robbed infill.

Six coins were found, five of which were from the mid-fourth century, the latest being of AD 364–75 (cat nos 136, 415, 493, 498, 5578, and 594). Illustrated small finds are two bracelets (Fig 4.8, 51 and 57), shears (Fig 4.17, 178), and scrap (Fig 4.29, 297). Four fragments of vessel glass included a fourth-century piece (Fig 4.45, 984; cat nos 976 and 978). Posthole F2318 and one context yielded Midlands fossil shell-tempered ware from the second half of the fourth century.

Baths precinct

Baths precinct phase 1 (BP 3.1)

To the east of Rooms 3B and 11, the second-century levels were raised by a deposit of sand forming the base make up for an overall spread of brick and tile chippings forming a hard-packed trampled courtyard surface, F4147 (Fig 2.41: S32, S33, and S36). This alternated in places with a horizon of mortar. Outside Room 3B the sections (S32 and S33) indicate a succession of surfaces. Further south more mixed layers of soil, stone, and mortar formed the make up, but the trampled courtyard surface was again clear (Fig 2.42: S37). Against the outer wall of Room 5, the underlying material was very deep (Fig 2.42: S38, layer 15).

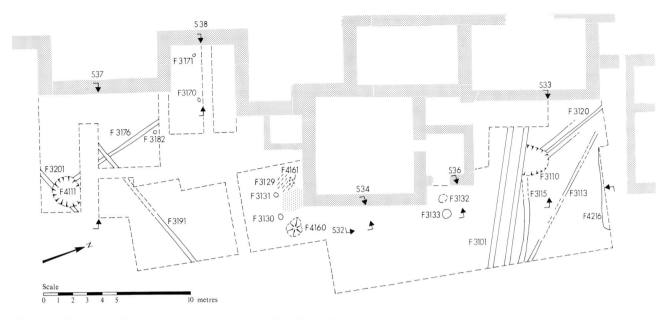

Fig 2.72 Baths precinct, Period 3, phases 3.2 and 3.3; 1:250

From this surface a number of water pipe trenches had been cut (Fig 2.72). In the northern area two were recorded; one to the east, F3115 (Fig 2.41, S32), running parallel with the BP 2.1 water conduit, and the second, F3120 (Fig 2.41: S33), running north-west from the conduit towards an entry into Room 2B located in the basilical hall excavations (Barker *et al* 1997). The linear trenches contained iron collars surviving at regular intervals. These would have bound sections of wooden water pipes which subsequently decayed. Where these water pipes would have met coincided with a Phase 4 robbing pit, F3110, on the north side of the water conduit, suggesting the later removal of a tile or stone feature at the connection. To the south was further evidence for water pipes similarly marked by trenches and iron collars. The main pipe, F3201, ran from the east to the southern *praefurnium*, Room 7. Only a short section of the trench was located. Remains of a second pipe were also recorded running north towards Room 5A, set in a flat based and vertical sided trench, F3176 (Fig 2.42: S37). Again, where the two pipes would have joined was a large robbing pit indicating a stone or tile water management feature. F3176 was not picked up in Section 38. A posthole, F3182, was recorded.

Directly to the east of the *praefurnium* in Room 7 a large dump of furnace material had been initiated in Phase BP 2.2 (Fig 2.51: S47). It comprised successive layers of ash, rubble and tiles, layers 9–11, large dumps of fire-cracked tiles, 7 and 8, mixed soil and burning spreads, 1, 3, 4, and 6 interleaved with layers of burnt clay, 5 and 2. The dump was found throughout the whole of Box 49B (Fig 1.3) and still continued eastward. Pottery sherds conjoined with sherds found in the floors of Room 7. The dump continued through BP 3.2. A second *praefurnium* dump, F4143, rested directly on F4147 (Fig 2.42: S38). The dump would

have been associated with Room 5A, and was formed of ash, tile, burnt sandy material, and brick.

The courtyard and its associated water pipe trenches represent the first evidence of a well-prepared surface east of the baths. The conduit was presumably retained but would now have been buried beneath the courtyard. The two robbing pits at the junctions of water pipes may indicate the former presence of a structure from which supplies could be controlled and diverted when required. It is also possible that water was pumped from here to cisterns in the baths, although this would perhaps be more likely nearer to the cisterns from which the *praefurnium* furnaces were fed.

Two coins were found, the latest of AD 253–8 (cat nos 187, 729). A military fitting (Fig 4.6, 16) a finger ring (Fig 4.7, 34), six pins (Fig 4.9, 59, 64, 70, 75, and 80; Fig 4.10, 90), a pierced tooth (Fig 4.12, 141), a weaving tablet (Fig 4.16, 172), a hoe (Fig 4.17, 176), a bone object (Fig 4.18, 184), and a stud (Fig 4.26, 257) are illustrated from the small finds. The only datable vessel glass was of the later second to mid third century (Fig 4.43, 1059; cat nos 1010, 1013, 1029, 1035–6, 1052, 1062, 1066–8, and 1071b). A glass counter was found (cat no 59). An intrusive post-medieval pewter object was found in the *praefurnium* dump (SF 1319, AML 788066).

Pottery from the water pipe trenches indicates a mid-third-century date. A sherd of Midlands fossil shell-tempered ware from F3176 is likely to be intrusive. The pottery dating evidence from the *praefurnium* dump in the baths precinct is also not later than the third century and this has been taken to suggest that the *caldarium* went out of use then. However there is no evidence that the material found represented the latest waste. As floor levels were raised and the mound to the east increased, spoil may well have been removed elsewhere through the entry from the south portico.

Baths precinct phase 2 (BP 3.2)

A further dumped deposit raised the baths precinct courtyard and terminated in a trodden surface, F4146, of intermittent spreads of clay and mortar with brick and gravel. In the northern area the make up layer was of sand (Fig 2.41: S32, S33, and S36, layer 7). There, F4146 was represented by a clay base to a mortared surface (S32, S34 and S36), while elsewhere the surface was not visible in section (S33). In the southern area the make up for F4146 was a mixed deposit and the surface itself was of sand and stone (Fig 2.42: S37). Outside Rooms 5A and 11C the surface was not present, instead the Phase BP 3.1 *praefurnium* dump, F4143, continued. Further water pipe trenches were cut from this level (Fig 2.72). To the north a trench, F3113, marked by a straight-sided flat-based cutting, and with iron pipe collars at regular intervals, ran directly from the east toward the entry into Room 1 noted for the BP 3.1 arrangements. In the southern area to the east of the *tepidarium* and *caldarium* the BP 3.1 pipe trench, F3201, was repeated some 4m to the north. The new pipe trench F3191 ran from the east toward the *caldarium* furnace Room 7, or perhaps to the *caldarium* alcove 6B (Fig 2.73; Fig 2.42: S37).

Spreads of tile and mortar or plaster, F3129, together with a group of stakeholes, F4161, a dump of building debris, F4160, and two postholes, F3130 and F3131, were found at the south-east corner of Room 11. Other postholes, F3132 and F3133 to the east of Room 11B, and F3170 and F3171 south of Room 5A, were found at this horizon.

It is possible that the BP 3.2 layouts of water supply supplemented rather than replaced the BP 3.1 arrangements, since there was no evidence of the earlier

Fig 2.73 Baths precinct, drain F3191, view north-east

trenches having been cut or dislocated, and their iron collars remained *in situ*. However it must be suspected that the use of a wooden pipe in the ground could not have been long without maintenance and replacement, for which there was no evidence in BP 3.2 nor any possibility of its being undertaken following the re-levelling of the yard. The features outside Room 11 indicate building works there.

Thirteen coins were found, the latest dated AD 273+ (cat nos 85, 109, 121, 124, 125, 134, 137, 144, 145, 309, 707, 709, and 710). Illustrated small finds comprise a military buckle tongue (Fig 4.6, 11), seven pins (Fig 4.9, 61, 71, 73, 79, and 89; Fig 4.10, 94 and 103), a toilet implement (Fig 4.11, 118), a stylus (Fig 4.13, 144), a handle (Fig 4.21, 220), a household utensil (Fig 4.23, 240), furniture inlay (Fig 4.25, 255), a structural fitting (Fig 4.28, 282), and scrap (Fig 4.29, 294 and 298). Three second-century brooches were found (Figs 4.33, 21; 4.35, 38 and 46), and three intaglii (Fig 4.36, 7, 9, and 10). Two stone discs made from roof tiles and a spindlewhorl were found (cat nos 52, 53, and 57). The latest piece of datable vessel glass was of the later second to mid-third century (Figs 4.37, 1002; 4.39, 1015; 4.40, 1004; 4.41, 1047 and 1049; 4.44, 1026; cat nos 999, 1003, 1006, 1017, 1021, 1024, 1030, 1033–4, 1037–44, 1046, 1055, 1058, 1064, 1069–71a, and 1075). Four glass beads were found (Fig 4.47, 35; cat nos 24–6).

Pottery from the water pipe trenches suggested a third-century date.

Baths precinct phase 3 (BP 3.3)

The courtyard level continued to be raised as evidenced by levelling layers of sand and soil make up and by trodden areas of compacted gravel and stone, F4145. The make up over F4146 was mixed material (Fig 2.41: S32–4, layer 4; Fig 2.42: S37, layer 9). The new surface was best represented in section to the south (Fig 2.42). To the north the layer had been truncated in places, although its possible horizon was still suggested by the make up layers. There was no evidence of further pipe trenches.

Six coins were found the latest of AD 348–50 (cat nos 95, 116, 128, 200, 329, and 484). Of the small finds a military stud (Fig 4.7, 26), a bracelet (Fig 4.8, 47), two pins (Fig 4.9, 85; Fig 4.10, 107), a textile working needle (Fig 4.16, 164), a strap (Fig 4.17, 179), a hipposandal (Fig 4.18, 182), a stud (Fig 4.26, 259), and a structural object (Fig 4.28, 283) are illustrated. An intaglio (Fig 4.36, 3) and a stone counter were found (cat no 54). Datable vessel glass was of the later second to third century (Figs 4.40, 1007; 4.44, 1027; 4.46, 1001; cat nos 1023, 1054, and 1063). A glass counter was found (cat no 51).

Midlands fossil shell-tempered ware from the second half of the fourth-century was recovered from four courtyard contexts.

Baths precinct phase 4 (BP 3.4)

Tile robbing of the water conduit and removal of its base flagstones was undertaken. The stratigraphic context could not be determined since the trenches had been reopened in Period 4, but the robbing must be seen in the same context as that occurring elsewhere on the *insula* after the baths had gone out of use but when the basilical hall was the focus of important reuse (Barker *et al* 1997).

In places there were dumps of material and a large hollow was noted in the south-east of the area excavated. These may be the result of Romano-British activity. On the drawn sections evidence of this is confined to layers 3, 4, and 5, at the west end of S37 (Fig 2.42). This may be the remains of spoil from stone robbing.

A single vessel glass fragment, of fourth-century date, was found (Fig 4.46, 1073).

The overall Period 3 sequence

The main features of the suggested sequence are illustrated (Fig 2.74) and selected dating evidence for phases and key groups is tabulated (Tables 2.2 and 2.3). As with the Period 2 evidence, linkages have to be hypothesised between different parts of the *insula* to suggest what might be contemporary and what might be earlier or later in the sequence. One link may be the animal bone deposits in the portico pits and in the *natatio* infilling. Pottery from the infilling and from the pits suggests a broadly similar date although not a similar source since the *natatio* pottery was less broken and seemed a primary deposit. The second is the herringbone floors found in the basilical hall, Room 11A, the latrine, and the *macellum*. The provision of these may have accompanied the building of the added *caldarium*. The new *praefurnia* in 9C and 11C may also be linked, both replacing *praefurnia* built at the same time and perhaps going out of commission at the same time. In addition the repaired *macellum* courtyard wall resembled the repaired portico stylobate wall, F4031, and may be contemporary. A third link may be the water pipe trenches. That to Room 5A was superseded by pipes possibly running round the baths into the courtyard. A fourth and final link may be between the abandonment of Room 11B as a *praefurnium*, the re-flooring of 11A, and the baths precinct Phase 1 courtyard.

Phase 1

Pit cutting in the porticos and infilling with butchers' waste from the *macellum* or from booths in the portico itself, occurred in the first half of the third century. At about the same time it was decided to abandon the *natatio* and this was infilled with rubble and a similar animal bone assemblage. A new *praefurnium*, Room 5A, was added on the east of the baths. A solid courtyard surface in the baths precinct together with a number of pipe trenches appear to be contemporary since one trench runs toward Room 5A. The *praefurnium* dump from Room 5A rested directly on the new surface.

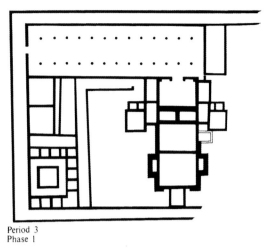

Period 3
Phase 1

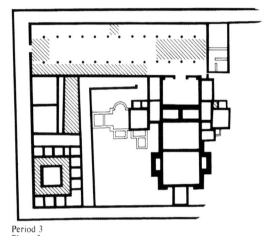

Period 3
Phase 3

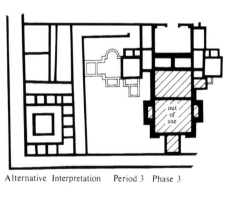

Alternative Interpretation   Period 3   Phase 3

Key

▬ Walls
═ Walls new this phase
▨ Herringbone tile floor
▨ Out of use

Scale
0   50 metres

Fig 2.74 Period 3 sequence; 1:1500

Phase 2

The porticos were surfaced with a hard gravel floor around the middle of the third century and this was retained through Phases 3 and 4. The floor surface sank into the earlier pits and was resurfaced from time to time. Sinkages were levelled up. Outside the

Table 2.2 Principal dating evidence from the finds (intrusive material in square brackets)

period	dating evidence
1.1	pre-AD 90 pottery and coins
1.2	later first to mid second-century glass; samian AD 75-95
1.3	brooch AD 50-150; early second-century vessel glass; late Flavian and Trajanic samian, BB1 pottery
P 2.1	coins of Claudius; mid-first to mid-second century glass; AD 130 pottery, Hadrianic/Antonine samian
P 2.2	coin of Domitian, [coin of Valentinian]; later first to mid second-century glass; Antonine samian
P 2.3	coins of Claudius [coin of Tetricus II]; brooch AD 75-175; later first to mid second-century glass; amphora AD 150, Antonine samian and two stamps of AD 160-200
WR 2.1	coin of Trajan; later first to mid second-century vessel glass; mortaria AD 120-160, samian AD 130-150
WR 2.2	early second-century vessel glass; mortarium AD 120-160; Antonine samian
WR 2.3	coin of Vespasian; intaglio last quarter second century; brooches AD 90-175; SF late first/early second century (cat 33); early to mid second-century vessel glass, [fourth-century glass]; Antonine samian
C 2.1	coin of Trajan; brooches AD 90-175 and 50-150; early second-century vessel glass; pottery AD 120
C 2.2	coin of Nero, [coin of Gallienus]; [SF third/fourth century cat 104]; first-century vessel glass; samian stamp AD 160-190
C 2.3	early second-century vessel glass; Antonine samian
C 2.4	mid first to mid second-century vessel glass; Antonine samian
BP 2.1	[coin of AD 375]; Hadrianic/early Antonine samian
BP 2.2	coin of Trajan; brooch AD 90-175; later first to mid second-century vessel glass; samian stamp AD 150-180, Antonine samian
BP 2.3	SF pre AD 200 (cat 60); mid first to mid second-century vessel glass; Antonine samian
P 3.1	latest coins AD 205 and third-century; intaglio AD 150, brooches AD 150-225 and 150-250; SF later Roman (cat 42); later second and early third-century glass; third-century pottery
P 3.2	latest coin AD 161-80; brooches AD 80-200 and second-century; second-century glass and fourth-century fragment (from F930); third-century glass and [fourth-century] pottery
P 3.3	latest coin AD 341-46; fourth-century vessel glass; later third-century and [later fourth-century] pottery
P 3.4A	latest coin AD 375; fourth-century vessel glass; later fourth-century pottery
P 3.4B	latest coin AD 375-8; fourth-century vessel glass
P 3.5	latest coin AD 388-402; fourth-century vessel glass; later fourth-century pottery
P 3.6	latest coin AD 388-402; fourth-century vessel glass; coloured window glass ?sub-Roman; SF fourth-century (cat nos 12 and 55); later fourth-century pottery
WR 3.1	coin of Tetricus II; brooch AD 80-200; SF pre AD 200 (cat 67); fragments second/third century glass, one AD 275 +; second-century pottery
WR 3.3	latest coin AD 365-78; fourth-century vessel glass; fourth-century pottery
C 3.1	Marcus Aurelius coin mould; pottery AD 210-230; mid third-century vessel glass, [fourth-century vessel glass]
C 3.3	third-century coins; fourth-century vessel glass; later fourth-century pottery
C 3.4	latest coin AD 364-75; fourth-century vessel glass; later fourth-century pottery
B 3.3	mid third-century pottery
B 3.4	later fourth-century pottery
BP 3.1	SFs pre AD 200 (cat 59 and 64) and ?fourth-century (cat 70); later second to mid third-century vessel glass
BP 3.2	latest coin AD 273+; SFs fourth-century (cat 77, 2, and 89); later second to mid third-century vessel glass
BP 3.3	latest coin AD 348-50; SFs third/fourth-century (cat 85, 107); later second to third-century vessel glass; later fourth-century pottery
BP 3.4	later fourth-century glass

P portico, WR west range, C courtyard, B baths, BP baths precinct

macellum entrances for the first part of the phase, the surfaces were apparently formed of stone blocks.

Phase 3

A major campaign of new building and refurbishment was undertaken around the end of the third century or the beginning of the fourth. This involved the building of Rooms 12 and 13 across the courtyard, and Rooms 9C and D. New herringbone floors were constructed throughout the *insula*, in the *macellum*, the latrine, Room 11A, and in the basilical hall. The *macellum* courtyard sleeper walls were rebuilt and the south portico stylobate sleeper wall. *Praefurnium* 11B for Room 11 was replaced by a new *praefurnium*, Room 11C. In the porticos the Phase 2 surfaces were cut by postholes and gullies associated with repair works and then resurfaced. There was intermittent evidence that the courtyard had been resurfaced and clearer evidence of a new courtyard in the baths precinct. This was associated with further

water pipes, one leading round the south of the baths and perhaps to be linked with the water pipes in the courtyard.

Phase 4

The porticos were again resurfaced around the middle of the fourth century in a hard gravel floor similar to that used in Phases 2 and 3, levelling up over the sunken fills of the Phase 1 pits. The paved entrance to the *macellum* was removed, its position infilled with soil and then sealed beneath the final gravel surface. A final surface was laid in the baths precinct.

Phase 5

Possible booths were set up under the west portico. The south portico was resurfaced at a higher level made up by dumped sand. The baths may have gone out of use, but the *frigidarium*, Room 10, and presumably Room 11A were retained.

Table 2.3 Principal dating evidence for the key groups (intrusive material in square brackets)

key group	dating evidence
1	–
2	–
3	–
4	samian AD 130-150, mortarium 120-160
5	early second-century glass
6	early second-century glass; mortaria AD 100-160 and 120–160
7	samian Hadrianic/early Antonine
8	early second-century vessel glass
9	first-century vessel glass; [SF 234 fourth-century]; samian AD 100-150
10	–
11	–
12	–
13	mid first to mid second-century vessel glass
14	see Table 2.2: C 3.1
15	second-century and [late fourth-century] pottery
16	see Table 2.2: P 3.1
17	see Table 2.2: C 3.2
18	coin of AD 164-9; [SF fourth-century (cat 69)]; first-century vessel glass; third-century pottery
19	mid third-century and [late fourth-century] pottery
20	first-century vessel glass; third-century pottery
21	early second-century glass; late second to early third-century pottery; coin Tetricus II
22	second-century pottery
23	mid third-century pottery
24	–
25	see Table 2.2: P 3.4A and B 3.5, 3.6
26	–
27	samian AD 120-150
28	–
29	–

Phase 6

The porticos went out of use and their stylobate walls were removed leaving the sleeper wall tops as part of surfaces outside the *insula* buildings and walls. Tiles were recovered from the drain walls, from the *natatio* walls, and from the original, inner, walls of the *tepidarium* and *caldarium*, Rooms 5 and 6.

Phase 7

The *macellum* continued in use with paths maintained running to its doors from the west. Excavations in the north of the *insula* revealed a long sequence of use of the basilical hall area. The *frigidarium* continued in use and later may have been converted into a church; burials were found in the nineteenth century on its south and west side. Buildings found in the north of the baths precinct (Barker *et al* 1997) were not parallelled in the south.

Discussion of the dating evidence

The dating evidence from the later Roman period depends on the occurrence of occasional coins, pottery, glass, and other artefacts amongst large quantities of overwhelmingly residual material. The later third-century coin found beneath the renewed *macellum* floor

is an example. This was accompanied by a few fragments of glass of a similar date. The pottery from the infilling of the *natatio* was the only large contemporary group found in the excavations, and indicated a clear early third-century date. The portico sequence is reasonably well dated first by pottery from the pits and subsequently by coins incorporated in the succeeding surfaces.

In contrast the added *caldarium* remains essentially undated. It can be argued to be contemporary with the infilling of the *natatio* or, instead, to be part of the general refurbishment of the *insula* buildings dated to the later third century by the *macellum* evidence. The addition of Room 5A and changes within the baths also remain undated.

The sequences in the courtyard and baths precinct may be dated by the latest coins and pottery. In the courtyard the C 3.1 infilling of the *natatio*, dated AD 210-30, was succeeded by C 3.2 which lacked dating evidence, and C 3.3 with a fourth-century date suggested by pottery and glass. In the baths precinct BP 3.1 and 3.2 were dated to the third century by coins, pottery, and glass, and BP 3.3 to the later fourth century by coins and pottery.

Turning to the dating evidence for the end of use of the baths, little assistance is given by the finds. None of the *praefurnium* dumps offered any evidence for fourth-century deposition with the exception of a bone pin found inside Room 7 well sealed in material spread across the initial floor which raised its level. Yet the widespread re-flooring across the *insula c* AD 300 must indicate that use of the baths continued into the fourth century. Although late fourth-century pottery was found in the courtyard and baths precinct areas, this material need not be associated with continuing use of the baths in view of the evidence for post-fourth-century use of the *insula* deriving from the basilical hall excavations.

Period 4: medieval and modern

Baths

The north wall of the *frigidarium* survives today as the Old Work. It is thought likely that the *frigidarium* itself was retained and the building may well have stood into the medieval period as has been discussed in the context of the basilical hall excavations (Barker *et al* 1997). The presence of grain, reported by Wright (Chapter 6, 2.15), suggests later use possibly as a barn in the medieval or post-medieval period.

The location of modern excavations in rooms 3, 3B, 12 and 13, was revealed in the 1988-9 excavations. A trench in 6 was reopened in 1955-85.

West Range

The *macellum* walls were trenched by Thomas Wright sufficiently to expose the plan. A pit, F87, in the corridor may be a modern feature. It was 1.4m deep and seems unlikely to have been dug when the corridor was in use. The *macellum* was the site of the curator's bungalow in the twentieth century. Service trenches on the east and south, cutting through the herringbone tile floor are associated.

Porticos

In places the portico sleeper wall and the courtyard south wall were trenched by excavators. Modern material was found directly above the dark earth of P 3.6. A number of pits were found in the south portico south of the baths. These were recent and were presumably dug between 1939 and 1945.

Courtyard

A deep disturbed overburden in the courtyard area predated the nineteenth-century excavations. This was suggested to be the result of medieval ploughing. Thomas Wright excavated an east-west trench across the courtyard, and a north-south trench in the *natatio*. Both were clear on the sections (for the *natatio* trench see Fig 2.39: S31, F4121).

3 The structural evidence

by Donald Mackreth

The plan, use, and appearance of *insula* 5

The following text looks first at the initial plan, dealing first with the parts shown in black on Fig 3.1 and the additions which are hatched, and then reviews in detail the basis of the restoration drawings (Figs 3.2 and 3.3). The terms used follow Nielsen's and Yegül's definitions (Nielsen 1990, I, 3–4; Yegül 1992, 487–494). Specific walls are referred to by the main spaces on each side, eg 1/15N, 8/3A etc, rather than by the excavation feature numbers. The plan and sections are based on a 1:200 reduction of the 1990 EDM survey.

Unused and abandoned elements of the initial plan

Both Thomas Wright and Kathleen Kenyon thought that the south aisle of the basilical hall could never have been roofed and that there were therefore two separate buildings, Kenyon also disregarding George Fox's arguments over a doorway in the middle of the Old Work (Kenyon 1938, 151–85). However, the structural element necessary for roofing the south aisle is still visible, and Barker's excavations revealed Fox's entrance into the baths from the hall and the spacing of the columns in the hall.

All arguments in favour of an earlier public building converted into baths have failed to stand up to scrutiny. Of those elements of the baths' plan thought by Graham Webster, following Kathleen Kenyon, to indicate an earlier forum, the secondary nature of the two walls found below the finished basement floor level in Room 10 is indicated by the presence of toothing stones in wall 4/10 (Webster 1975, fig 22). Similar toothing stones were used in the construction sequence in the *macellum*. As 3–6 could hardly not have been intended to be a baths suite *ab initio*, these walls, and the constructionally awkward 9/9A and B, should be seen as aborted parts of a baths' scheme.

On the face of things, there was to have been a major wall line from 9/9A across 4A and B to 11/11A. That the various lengths do not make a straight line is because they were laid out after the east and west walls of 3–6, and each stretch of wall served a different functional area. Full height walls were thus initially planned to form the south sides of corridors running from Room 3 to the lobbies 9A and 11A leading out of the building to 15 and 16. Access from either 8 or 10 to the lobbies could have been through a door in these additional walls, rather than via 3. But the same ends would be served by eliminating these walls and one can only assume that this kind of thinking took place, larger heated rooms being preferred.

The wall across the north end of 4A and 4B suggests that the south side of the *frigidarium*, Room 3, was originally intended to be treated in the same way as its north wall, the Old Work. In architectural terms, it might be expected that the south side of 3 would have been provided with three blind arches to match those on the north. The *frigidarium* of the Early Baths seems to have had the same set of features (Mackreth 1987, fig 58), but that example had disappeared long before. Like wall 3/4A and B, the Old Work is of double thickness below the floor (Kenyon 1938, pl 61c); the impression given by the conserved remains of there having been two walls is almost certainly false. It would seem that the south side was intended to be similarly treated, but an oddity in the plan and a feature of the existing wall demonstrates that the change must have taken place before the bedding course of large stones was laid. The plan oddity is that the layout of 3A and 3B in relation to 3 is not symmetrical. The dog-leg in the east end of the Old Work displaces 3B, and its south wall was accordingly adjusted southwards with the result that, while the door into 8 lies neatly in wall 3/8, the door into 10 had to be cut through the corner. If wall 3/4 had lain on the south part of its free-built foundation, this visual awkwardness could have been accommodated by running the east arch over to wall 3/10.

A primary concern would have been water supply and waste water disposal. The building sequence in the *macellum* shows that the main drains were begun at once, and this would have been so elsewhere. A major drain entered 3 from the east and would have formed a connection with that running from the north-east corner of 4A. To the west there is a break in the wall 1/15 immediately west of 3A with traces of a very large stone, possibly a lintel, low down. The lower structure of wall 1/15N shows that it ran thereafter along the south side of the basilical hall. Thence the drain ran down the west and south side of the latrine across the entrance way and down the east side of the *macellum*.

The longer of the two unused wall foundations found beneath the *macellum* is parallel with the main west wall, runs right down to wall 22/23S, and seems to spring from the south wall of 1 at the point where wall 17/19 begins. It should be seen as an error at worst, or as marking a range containing rooms like 17 and 18. The other wall is a continuation to the north of the west wall of the east range in the *macellum*, and marks one side of the drain's construction zone; this seems best understood as the product of a mistake.

The initial plan

The plan of the chief elements was prefigured in the legionary baths at Chester (Petch 1978, 23: plan). At Chester, applying the rule of symmetry to the baths, three rooms become apparent. The *frigidarium* has a *piscina* at each end, the *tepidarium* seems to have had a 'full-width' *exedra* on the east, and probably had one on the west as well, and the *caldarium* can be reconstructed with an extension east and west. Two walls run south from the west end of the basilical hall. The more westerly has either a return to the west or, more probably, a wall running west from it and if the north-south wall is continued to the boundary, a range about 18m wide inside can be projected, almost the same width as the west range at Wroxeter. A range of some kind fronting a principal street is almost a necessity, looking at fortress plans elsewhere (eg Webster 1985, figs 34–36, 38b).

Both plans occupy rectangular blocks; both have a basilical hall running along the north side with a main entrance at the west end; both have a main baths suite with the three main rooms running south from the east end of the hall; both have an area suitable for use as a *palaestra* between the main suite and a line of buildings lining the main road to the west. The proximity of a functioning set of baths of proven usefulness, coupled with the expertise to design and advise, if not build, explains the source and similarity.

Both baths belong to Nielsen's 'axial half-symmetric row type' (Nielsen 1990, II, 20). An extension to the basilical hall, or moving the baths half-way along its length, and a demonstrable repeat of the *palaestra*, would have made the plan a member of the fully symmetric row type (*ibid*, I, 67–70).

The Baths, Rooms 1–11

Rooms 8–11 at 168.3m^2, are much smaller than 5 and 6 at 392.7m^2, suggesting that the majority of bathers would have used Rooms 3–6, leaving a minority to use the dry heat suites before bathing. The basic routine, although there was no hard and fast rule (Yegül 1992, 33–9), consisted of undressing, followed by optional exercise, being oiled, moving through the *tepidarium*, to the *caldarium*, in which there was an *alveus* or hot water bath, and a supply of cold water, probably at Wroxeter in the *exedrae*, 6A and B. Returning back towards the *frigidarium*, the bather would be scraped before taking a plunge, then being dried, oiled again and perfumed, and dressed to return home for dinner.

Although major baths throughout the empire frequently had a succession of heated rooms, the three suites at Wroxeter form a relatively simple layout. The basilical hall, 1, is the chief promenade and entrance, while 2 at the east end should have served as the *apodyterium*, and probably also as a store-cum-shop for towels, soap and oil. Rooms 3, 5, and 6 form the chief suite, the first being fitted with *piscinae*, with seats around their sides, and the last with *exedrae* and an *alveus*.

Rooms 4A and B were divided by a wall, the evidence for which shows in the centre of the south face of 3/4 as a very shallow stub rising from a clear change in the major stone levelling course on which all the

chief walls of the range are bedded. The wall was later removed, since Wright found the remains of a hypocaust in 4 running through its line.

The function of the two rooms may have been connected with the process of applying and scraping off oil. Only at Piazza Armerina is there definite evidence for what might have been an *unctorium*. The small room there between *frigidarium* and *tepidarium* has a mosaic showing a man being oiled (Wilson 1983, 22, fig 1.10; Nielsen 1990, II, fig 40). As being anointed was a necessary beginning and a desirable ending to bathing, 4A and B may have served both purposes, the room at Piazza Armerina being suited for both. Yegül suggests that the representation of two pairs of sandals in mosaic, one with wishes for a good bath, the other hoping that the bather has had one, might be a sign of the direction of circulation (Yegül 1992, 38). A mosaic at Timgad (Nielsen 1990, II, fig 46) points to a clockwise rotation there, and this might have been a universal custom. Room 4B would then have been for the first application of oil and 4A for final toiletries. The west part of 5 may also have been where scraping and massaging could also have operated. However, the general lack of space should show that not many were massaged and that the use of oil was a rather perfunctory affair for most. The suggested door positions would allow people to by-pass those engaged in being oiled and massaged. The position of the primary doors in wall 3/4 is based on the wear on the major stone bedding course. The doors into 5 and 6 are placed in line with these, although there is actually no evidence for them.

Although water could be poured over bathers in the *caldarium*, the man with the bucket on the mosaic in the *unctorium* at Piazza Armerina suggests that the bather was sluiced down after scraping. The drain in 4A, the proposed exit room, may have been to accommodate this.

The similar areas of Rooms 8, 4A, 4B, and 10, respectively 31.365m^2, 32.66m^2, 32.2m^2 and 26.74m^2, may have had something in common. The smaller size of 10 is due to the fact that the east lateral suite is only three-quarters the size of the west one. If, as suggested above, the lateral suites were used by those exercising before bathing, they may have preferred being oiled in a warm room than in a cold one (Yegül 1992, 38–9), hence 8 and 10 may have been both *tepidaria* and *unctoria*. The Wroxeter layout has *laconica* in the lateral suites with dual-purpose heated ante-chambers, and the main suite also has the essential two heated rooms, but the *caldarium* should have been fitted with *labra* or basins in *exedrae* and an *alveus* at the south end. Rooms 4A and B were ante-rooms and need not have had doors communicating with 8 and 10, and doors are not shown. It is assumed that 5, like 8 and 10, was only indirectly heated and that there was no water supply to either 9 or 11. The relative sizes of 5 and 6, 155m^2 against 237.65m^2, or basically 2:3, shows which room was expected to contain the greater number. The *tepidarium* would have been more used by those returning from the *caldarium* than proceeding towards it.

In the *caldarium*, the *alveus* would have been fitted over the hottest part, next to the *praefurnium*, and there was evidence for north-south linear supports here. Plans which allow the size and siting of *alvei* to be very closely estimated (Nielsen 1990, II *passim*; Yegül 1992, *passim*) show that a wall as long as the south one in 6, *c* 15.4m, would not have had one running the whole length without more *praefurnia*. At Wroxeter there should thus have been only one *alveus*. Most fall in the range of 21–24m² with 28–29m² as a maximum (Nielsen 1990, II). An *alveus* in 6, was therefore probably about 3.25m wide by 7.4m long. The final stoke-hole in 7 was markedly off centre to the east. The intention may have been to create some kind of current through the bath.

The supply and disposal of water has received almost less attention than any other aspect of baths' sites (DeLaine 1988, 24). At Wroxeter, water would almost certainly have come from a *castellum aquae* on high ground somewhere north-east of the *insula*. No matter how slight the head, the water would have been under some pressure and pipes would have been the best way to convey it to the places where it was to be used. No reservoir or header tank (cf Nielsen 1990, II, fig 23) was provided at Wroxeter. The *alveus* in the *caldarium* would have taken a long time to heat using the hypocaust alone, and a *testudo* or kettle arrangement would have been used, if not a mixture of both (Bidwell 1979, fig 8; Nielsen 1990 II, fig 14). The crowns of the arches over the *praefurnia* in 9 and 11 are too low to house *testudines*; they were a structural device to allow the cheeks and immediate cover of the *praefurnium* to be repaired and replaced without injuring the actual structure of the building (Yegül 1992, figs 461–2, 464–5; Nielsen 1990 II, figs 24–5). Water disposal from the *alveus* and *piscinae* would have been via pipes to the main sewers.

Exercise yards and pool, 14–16

The relationship of the principal open area, 15, and its porticos, 15W and 15N, with the surrounding elements is complex. Area 15 may have been a *palaestra*, but it was also a place of resort, as the public entrance, 21, from the main street shows, the entrance also allowing access to the public latrines, 20, and there was evidence for a step over the gutter down to the open area of 15. Two doors from 1 into 15N emphasise the close integration of the area into the overall plan. Room 9A leads from 15 to a heated room, 8, which allows access to the *laconicum*, 9, or the main suite. Room 8 becomes even more an ante-chamber and this may reinforce its suggested role as an *unctorium*.

The *natatio*, 14, had steps across the full width at each end; the previously suggested *exedrae* covered with part domes are therefore withdrawn (Mackreth 1987, fig 61).

If 9A represented the connection between the *palaestra* and the baths, 11A may have served a similar purpose indicating that part of 16 had served as a *palaestra* on the east side. There is no evidence that there had not been a *natatio* in 16 as well as in 15, except where Kenyon's section was cut just south of 5A (Kenyon 1938, pl 69). The smaller size of 10–11 in relationship to 8–9 may point to 16 having been for more serious athletic pursuits. The herringbone flooring in 9A and 11A was a later third-century addition and thus what had been intended in the second-century design, was still a prime consideration then. This also implies that the elimination of the *natatio* is not to be equated with the abandonment of 15 as a *palaestra*.

West range and porticos, 17–23

These have more to do with traffic in the streets than with the baths. The basilical hall relates to both, and its siting and the position of its doors indicates the direction from which most people were expected to come. The greater width of the west portico reflects the importance of Watling Street with the forum opposite. The west range itself is divided into almost equal parts by the corridor 21 giving access to the latrines. The only door to the latter was in 15W, a bank of seats over the drain at the south end would have prevented any entry here. There may have been a door from 21 into the *macellum* designed to allow people approaching through 15 to get in easily.

The latrines, 20A, are separated from 17–18 by 19. Rain shed from the roofs of 17, 18, and 20A and B into 19 passed through an opening into the main drain.

Wright's interpretation of 17 and 18 as workshops was based on evidence that was sealed under the make-up for the floors and belongs to earlier periods. Room 17 is 10.7 by 10m (107m²), and Room 18 is 10.5 by 9.5m (99.75m²). They are very prominently sited: directly opposite the entrance to the forum which has proportionately the smallest amount of accommodation of any in the country. The forum rooms are confined to the front range perhaps because side rooms were impracticable. Rooms 17 and 18 and indeed the *macellum* may have been supplied to serve the functions usually accommodated in the front and side ranges of the forum. The rooms may have been meeting rooms for guilds, public offices, including weights and measures (de Ruyt 1983, 320–322), market halls in which extra stalls could be set up, or possibly *tabernae*. The doors are shown as being much narrower than in earlier plans. The notches in the ends of the bedding stones were almost certainly to key in the adjacent stones, and traces of this technique can be seen in wall 3/4.

The doors of the *macellum*, 22, opened into the portico 23, although there may have been a way in from 21. Leaving Room 22.4 aside, in the three ranges, Rooms 22.2, 7, and 11 are small, somewhere between 9.5m² and 12.52m² with one markedly smaller. All opened off the courtyard, except for that in the north-east corner. The largest room, 22.9, had its floor at a lower level and was entered from the walkway by steps and the best interpretation is that this had been a latrine. As 20A was clearly for the general public, the smaller one could only have fulfilled a special need. The Wroxeter *macellum* belongs to a select class in which latrines were fitted: Gigthis, Perge, and Puteoli where two corners have them (de Ruyt 1983, 315).

Later periods

The chief addition is Room 12 with its adjuncts 12A–C and 13, its *praefurnium*. The structure clearly butts the west wall of 9. The west wall of 13 ran along the top of the gutter footing of 15W, so closing the *praefurnium* off from the portico and blocking the gutter arrangement. The *palaestra* was thus still usable, even if the *natatio* had gone. Room 9C was an addition to Room 9. The restored responds in the opening from 9 were built when it was thought that 9C was of the same date as 9 itself, before excavation demonstrated otherwise. Room 9D was a new *praefurnium* for 9, replacing 9B on the north side. The early hypocaust in 9 was replaced by one matching the height of that in 12 whose *pilae* were 3′ 10″ high (1.17m) suggesting that the alterations to 9 were done at the same time that 12 was built. The vault of 9 was almost certainly replaced and probably matched that over 12. The form of the building would suit a quadripartite system, but the props afforded by the *exedrae* 12A–C could suit a domed roof.

The original hypocausts in 5 and 6 were much lower, Wright noting the difference when compared with the systems he found in 9 and 12 (Chapter 6, 2.10). This may represent the difference between Vitruvius' recommendations (Morgan 1960) for the height of *pilae* in public baths, 2Rft, (V.X.2) in the time of Augustus, and late Roman practice, 3Rft, as represented by Faventinus (Plommer 1973, 15, 62–5). The early photographs showing 4 also show that the hypocaust there was not as tall as those in 9–12, but the height of the hypocausts in 8 and 4 may have more to do with function and door threshold levels than with date. A nineteenth-century photograph shows the doorway between 8 and 9A with a masonry blocking which had been plastered. If this suite was still used as baths, then there was no longer direct access to a *palaestra* and this might suit late-Roman bathing habits.

Room 5A was a *praefurnium* attached to 5 with the remains of an extended flue inside the room. The side walls of 5A butted the casing wall which had been removed where it crossed 5A. The north wall of 5A began to run across to 5, but was almost completely robbed; the space to the north, 24, may have been tacitly abandoned, or there may have been access from 5A. East of 5A lies another *praefurnium*, 11C, butting both 5A and 11 and which obviously replaced 11B. A new wall was built across the collapsed arch of 11B. In the main baths, the wall dividing 4A from 4B was removed, the floor dug out and a hypocaust inserted. Wright's photographs show the lines of *pilae* lying across the line of the wall and running up to the face of the wall projecting from under wall 3/4. His plan, on the other hand, shows the supports for the *suspensura* running up

to the south face of 3/4, which is a mistake. Wright's description shows that the drain in the erstwhile 4A was still needed. Wall 4/5 appears on plans in its conserved form, very wide and completely artificial in character. At the least, a series of flues to allow heat from 5 to enter 4 must have been inserted. Equally nothing is known of wall 5/6, both having been destroyed to below the basement floors here.

The closing down of 9B and 11B and their replacement by 9C–D and 11C is neat enough to put together as products of a single scheme. If so, 5A and the alterations in 5, and probably 4, had come into being already, and were perhaps contemporary. If 6 had passed out of use, this would create a new *tepidarium* and *caldarium*, the extended flue in 5 running under a new *alveus*. The wide foundation of 4/5 and the robbed 5/6 would both have needed rebuilding, as the first needed flues to heat the new *tepidarium* and the second would need to have these eliminated. The opportunity may also have been taken to replace the vaults over 4 and 5 rather than patch where wall 4A/4B had been and line the whole with flues. The result may have been two new east-west vaults.

If the *caldarium*, Room 6, was retained, then the conversion of 5 into a *caldarium* may be equated with that of 9 into another with an *alveus*. The system in Rooms 5 and 6 was thus altered to have two *alvei*. Room 12 with its *alveus*, may have been added at the same time as 9C to form another double *alveus* suite. The lack of any major change in the east lateral suite, save for the switching of the *praefurnium* from north to south, suggests that there was still a need for a small dry heat suite, and perhaps for a *palaestra* to the east.

On the other hand, if 6 was abandoned, the main suite, being reduced to 4 and 5, would comprise an area of 224m², while the west suite was increased to an area of 186m², the east suite remaining the same size at 72m². The total area would then have been 482m² of heated room and 713m² including the *frigidarium*. Therefore, the loss of 6, but the addition of 4 and 12 resulted in no significant reduction in the capacity of the baths.

The last change in use for the baths is speculative. The Old Work has no obvious damage, other than the removal of large stones from the entrance and the adjacent structures, save for a hole in the east end. Its size and high position, if repeated in a symmetrical structure, would look remarkably like a window in a chapel or church pre-dating the thirteenth century, or even perhaps the foundation of Wroxeter church. The burials found by Wright would then have a context, and the Old Work a reason for having survived the destruction of all its neighbours.

Towards a reconstruction

The overall sequence of construction would have started with the baths suites since these required the greatest degree of 'know-how'. The basilical hall was a repetition of standard structural elements whose scale alone would place it early in the overall scheme. The last parts to be roofed would be the street-side porticos after the scaffolding had gone. The *macellum* was possibly the last major building to receive attention.

The sections on Figs 3.2 and 3.3 show how the site was adapted to fit the fall in levels from east to west. There is also a fall from north to south. The east-west lines show how the main baths suite is, in effect, a retaining element to accommodate the marked fall 16 to 15. There is generally a step up into buildings, hence the raised levels through 15W and 20, with an adjustment through the unused 19 to 17–18 which is, of course, floored in relation to 23W. The floors of the *macellum* form a raised platform and the cut-and-fill principle was one of the means by which soil displaced from levelling and foundation digging was disposed of.

An over-riding set of proportions must have governed the plan of the *insula*. The use of columns in porticos and in the basilical hall presupposes the application of some rules and the known spacing in one and the deducible spacing in the other may indicate what they were. There is evidence for the diameter of the columns used in the porticos, and for the probable form of the capitals in the basilical hall. It is assumed in calculating the intercolumniation that the columns would have been spaced an equal distance apart.

The porticos

In the north portico, the columns were centred at 2.95m, plus or minus 0.01m, or 10 Roman feet, showing that the known Roman foot (Rft) of 0.296m (Jones 1989, 37) was the one used here as opposed to 0.332m (Walthew 1978, 335). The size of the plinths of the bases was also marked out on the stylobate and these were 0.65m square. The remains of one base show that the order used was probably a kind of Roman Doric with a double torus, a type not described by Vitruvius but evidenced elsewhere. The top was too damaged for the base diameter of the shaft to be measured. However, published examples from the forum excavations give ratios between the shaft diameter at the bottom (D) to the diameter of the lower torus of the base proper of 1:1.317, 1:1.229, and 1:1$\frac{1}{3}$ (Atkinson 1942, fig 24A.7, 8, and 9 respectively). Equating these to simple ratios, 1:1$\frac{1}{3}$ and 1:1$\frac{1}{4}$, bases 1 and 3 are 1.22% and 2.05% out from the first, while base 2 is 1.68% away from the second. The first and third bases come from the forum east portico.

Using the ratio of 1:1$\frac{1}{3}$ and the distance of 0.65m between the marks on the stylobate, D becomes 0.4875m, or 1.65 Rft. The marks themselves merely indicate where the column was to be centred, which means that the actual D could be less, possibly 1.5 Rft or 0.4425m, 10% away. Examples of column shafting found in the basilical hall excavations measure 0.45m and 0.48m, and of bases across the torus 0.65m (Barker *et al* 1997, fig 332). Vitruvius recommends the reduction in the diameter of the shaft at its top of $\frac{1}{6}$D

for a column under 15 Rft high (III, III, 12). This would be 0.37m diameter and may be compared with the two examples from the basilical hall excavations of 0.39m and 0.34m from the upper part of a column and from a capital (Barker *et al* 1997, fig 332).

The intercolumniation would therefore be 10 Rft minus D, 8.5 Rft. The width of the north portico from the wall of the basilical hall to the outer face of the stylobate was 5.24m or 17.7 Rft, just under 3% from 17.75 Rft, and taking $\frac{1}{2}$D away from that gives 17 Rft which is twice 8.5, a simple 1:2 ratio. This ratio was not consistently used, presumably because the distance of the centre-line of the architrave and hence the wall-plate for the half trusses of the portico roofing, from the wall was presumably more important for the contractor than the aesthetics of proportions.

Although no stylobate survives in the west or south portico, the distance from the back wall to the centre of the sleeper walls can be used as approximations: 23W = *c* 6m, 23S = *c* 4.3m. For Vitruvius, the width of the portico should be twice as wide as the height of the column but this would suggest three different column heights, and three different values for D. The evidence suggests that this was not the case.

In 23W the distance between the centres of the north and south sleeper walls is close to 83.7m which gives 282.77 Rft. If the intercolumniation here was 10 Rft centre to centre the end columns would have to be moved towards the centre by 1.385 Rft, or 0.41m. However, using the value for D derived from 23N, the total length of the portico between the centres of the end columns equals 188.5D. This requires an odd number of bays whose spacing has to be xD plus $\frac{1}{2}$D. The equivalent spacing of columns in 23N was 6.667D. Adjusting that to 6.5D and dividing it into 188.5D, we get exactly 29 bays at 9.75 Rft centre to centre. Using a standard column all round would get rid of difficulties in roofing lines at the corners. Using the approximate widths given above for 23W and 23S minus $\frac{1}{2}$D as was done for 23N, and with H as 7.5D, the primitive ratios are 1:1.735 and 1:1.225. Adjusting these to 1:1.75 and 1:1.25, the widths to the centres of the respective sleeper walls come to 6.0495m and 4.3845m, both of which fit very comfortably.

If this system applies to the street-side porticos, then it should work in the internal porticos, 15W and 15N. Portico 15W is 46.7m or 157.7 Rft from the centre of the sleeper wall of 15N to the south boundary wall, and the width measured from the back wall to the stylobate centre line is 4.6m or 15.54 Rft, a ratio of 1:10.15. For 15N the figures are 19.25m (65.03 Rft) and 4.4m (14.86 Rft) which gives no simple ratio. Apart from the near 1:10 in 15W, no immediate ratios appear. However, a D of 1.5 Rft in 15W produces 16 bays of 9 Rft 10 Rins, and a ratio of width to height of 1:1$\frac{1}{3}$, and in 15N, 6 bays of 10 Rft 10 Rins with a width to height ratio of 1:1.25. A pilaster on the south wall of 15W, as there seems to have been in the baths basilica, would accommodate the excess of $\frac{1}{2}$D.

The conclusion is that a simple system of non-Vitruvian proportions was probably used, that the spacing of the columns along the stylobates was capable of being varied, but the height of the column derived from Vitruvius' recommendations for Doric, remained a constant.

The roof pitch in Figures 3.2 and 3.3 has been fixed on the assumption that the initial building at least was roofed in *imbrices* and *tegulae*. Tiles found in the porticos had been mortared in place without nails, suggesting that the portico roof was a dead weight and could not have had a steep pitch.

The basilical hall

The dimensions of the supports for the columns recorded on the southern sleeper wall show that there had been 14 bays of about 5.24m, or 17.75 Rft, the same as the width of the north portico from the back wall to the outer face of the stylobate. Six Rft is the only reasonable whole number for the spacing and this gives a D of 2.98 Rft suggesting that 3 was the intended measurement. The layout of the columns presupposes a half one at each end forming a pilaster or respond. Although the east and west walls do not survive at these points, the restricted destruction at the west end of the south row, and probably also of the north row, suggests that large blocks of stone forming the pilaster had been bedded into the walls there. The intercolumniation, therefore, was intended to be 5D or 15 Rft.

The best preserved section of column from the baths basilica site is complete and has a diameter of 3 Rft, and this is used for D in the following discussion. The aisles are plainly close to half the width of the nave: 4.9m and 5m to 10m, measuring from the side walls to the centre line of the colonnades. If the width is measured to the face of the column, the aisles would have been 16.55 Rft minus $\frac{1}{2}$D of 3 Rft which is close to the intercolumniation of 5D. The nave then becomes 30 Rft. According to Vitruvius the aisles should be as wide as the height of the columns and one third the width of the nave (V.I.5).

The evidence from Roman Britain is that the order used in grand halls such as this was Corinthian. Vitruvius gives elaborate rules for arriving at the height of a Corinthian column in temples (IV.I.1: III.V.1–5: III.III.6–10). In the basilical hall the intercolumniation was greater than 3D, and Vitruvius' rule of H = 8D might have applied, with an increase because of the added height of a Corinthian capital. The Ionic capital is to be half of 1 $\frac{1}{18}$D =$\frac{19}{36}$D, thus the Corinthian would be about 8.5D. Jones (1989, 42) has detected the use in practice of a module of 1/18th of height in Corinthian columns and the following general rules: height of shaft (h) = $\frac{5}{6}$ H; D is commonly H/10 or h/8; H, D and h should be whole numbers with h 5 Rft less than H (*ibid*, fig 4); and, finally, heights of base or capital added together are 1 $\frac{2}{3}$D (*ibid*, 47). Therefore, if D = 3 Rft, the base and capital will be 5 Rft together,

and H would be 30 Rft (H/10 or h/8 + 5 Rft, where h is 25 Rft), or the width of the nave, or twice that of the aisle.

The architectural fragments from the public areas of Wroxeter include a high proportion of unfinished Corinthian capitals amongst which is one of the stones forming the base of the porch for Building x. This was the upper stone and would have had the abacus and volutes at the top with the curling over of the row of leaves beneath that at the bottom. It is possible that the whole of the basilical hall was equipped with these, ready to be carved when money was available.

In estimating the height of the nave, Vitruvius says that, as in fora, the upper storey of a basilica should be three quarters the height of the lower (V.I.3,5). This includes the entablature and he says that Corinthian should have either a Doric or an Ionic one (IV.I.1). The ancient world obviously favoured the latter. Following his rules for columns between 25 and 30 feet in height (III.V.8–12), his entablature is very close to 2 $\frac{1}{6}$D. Jones (1989) did not deal with entablatures, but using his uniform series of examples, the average height is remarkably close to 2 $\frac{1}{3}$D, and this is used here to give 7 Rft. Therefore, the whole order would have been 37 Rft high. Three-quarters of that gives the height for the clerestory of 27.75 Rft and hence 64.75 Rft or 19.166m for the whole. The drawing shows an uncompromisingly tall building and a lower clerestory would seem to be a more comfortable proposition, but no reduction can be calculated from the data.

The basilical hall was built on a slope, which means that the roof should have sloped down from east to west. For a trabeate structure, this poses a problem over how this was accommodated, as any slope in the architrave would tend to impart a thrust. For there to be a dead weight on the columns, the architrave or, more properly, the top surface and the bearing faces on the underside, have to be level. A taper in the timberwork of the architrave would provide a level top and would probably have been visually undetectable. The roof trusses would have been set up vertically, but the ceiling of the nave may have presented more of a problem, unless tapering firrings had been used.

The dogleg in the south-east corner of the basilical hall only makes sense if there had been a minor door to the open area to the east. Although no trace of one survived, there was evidence that a pipe had run through the wall here (Barker *et al* 1997), a good sign that a door had actually existed. Excavations by Philip Barker located a door on the north side towards the east end, a door in 1/2A north of the pilaster, and a step outside the door into 23W.

Baths

The simple proportions of the initial plan point to a deliberate scheme. The primary western lateral suite is 96.34m^2, a third greater than the 71.92m^2 of the eastern one, and 24.55% of the main suite which might suggest that, at one stage, the two lateral suites were to be the same size and, combined, were to be half the areas of 5 and 6.

Vitruvius discusses proportions in *atria* (VI.III.3), *tablinia* (VI.III.5), and dining rooms (VI.III.8), but not in baths. Whatever care was taken over places in which columns were to be used, the lack of right angles in major parts of the plan of the baths *insula* imposes constraints on close analysis.

Assuming that 3 was at first designed to have a repeat of the blind arches on the south side, its measurements would have been close to 50 Rft by 40 Rft, a primitive ratio of 1:1¼. Room 5 has a ratio of 1:1½ and 6 returns to 1:1¼ but the measurements are not in multiples of 5 or 10 Rft which may suggest the ratios arrived at are false, perhaps because walls 4/5 and 5/6 were resited. Elsewhere, Room 11 is 1:1 allowing for bad setting out, but 9 clearly has no simple ratio. Room 20 might have been intended to be 75 Rft long, but the width increase rules out further analysis. Rooms 17 and 18 were perhaps planned to be the same size with a ratio of 1:1, but their layout is too poor to show this. However, the *macellum* court measures 48.99 Rft in both directions, and the walkways north, south, and east are all 11.15 Rft wide to the centre of the sleeper wall.

Establishing the appearance of the baths is assisted by the Old Work itself. A previous study was based on the south elevation alone (Webster and Woodfield 1966) and assumed that no roofing rested on the north edge. The end elevations show the extrados of a relieving arch and the marks left by giant stones lining the openings. The radius of the extrados is such that there could have been only two openings into each piscina. The profile through the scar of the east wall of 3 shows that the large stones had been laid 'Escomb fashion' (Taylor and Taylor 1965, 11).

The blind arches of the Old Work would have supplied the necessary support for a vault over 3. As the aisle of 1 was taller, this would have been an independent structure. The differing widths of the blind arches could not have supported quadripartite vaulting and there had almost certainly been a barrel vault. If in masonry without a timber structure above for a pitched roof, this would have been a fire-proof buffer between the baths and the basilical hall. Pentice roofs over the *piscinae* would leave plenty of room for windows in the walls of 3 above. In the sections and elevations it is assumed that the height of the surface over the blind arches marks the level from which all the vaults in the baths sprang. Fox recovered a fragment of a painted vault from 3 with a diameter between 15.87 Rft and 31.8 Rft (Fig 6.11). This could not have come from a vault in 3 itself, but the soffit of the central blind arch of 1/3 is a possible source. A parallel smaller east-west running vault over Rooms 4A and B would allow windows in each end.

The additional wall around 5 and 6 must have been provided to prop a structure and give a better seating for a vault. The way in which it runs round both *exedrae* of 6 suggests that it was a lateral thrust which was feared and thus that there was a north-south vault. Fragments of tufa in the rubble filling 5 and 6 show that this was the chief vaulting material. A tufa vault would exert much less thrust than ordinary stone, especially if it was provided with flues (Zienkiewicz 1986, 325, fig 107.3). The erection of one or two half rings perhaps raised fears that the walls supporting them were likely to be unstable and led to the added wall. Each *exedra* would have had a window in it and the end walls of the vault would have provided a large area for windows to light 5 and 6, the latter picking up any afternoon sun.

Although the *caldarium* dimensions of 15.3m and 13.6m do not indicate which way the vault ran, the *exedrae* are not central in their walls, and this would have been an architectural solecism unless they lay in side walls where they would provide support. Their displacement to the north was almost certainly due to the presence of an *alveus*, which, if symmetry was an aim, would have been about 11 Rft wide, in accord with the dimensions suggested earlier.

The *praefurnium*, 7, is shown with a complete roof and a gable tall enough to vent the space above the portico. The evidence thought to indicate a door in the east wall (Mackreth 1987, fig 60) rested on part of a large stone block at the south end, but it would seem more likely that this belonged to the framing of a large entrance in the south wall to accommodate the replacing of the various kettles and other metalwork. The walling here is missing, even though the portico rear wall survives immediately east and west.

The pattern of doors shown in the lateral suites can be seen on site today. Those into 8–9 and 10–11, being in the corners of the rooms, may actually show the preferred position rather than be the result of the ordering of the rooms. The doors into 8 and 10 and into 4A and B were lined in large stone blocks and this should have applied to all those in the primary plan.

The *palaestra* and public entrance

The *natatio* had thick foundations at each end and the remains of tilework and a difference in surface 2–3 Rft wide along the inner side showed that each end was fitted with at least two steps. Porticos 15W and 15N provided covered access to 20 from the street and the hall. There was a step to the doorway into 20, and the eastern doorway in the corridor 21 was framed in large blocks of stone one of which left the impression of its dressing on the east side of the entrance. Other sites of similar size to Wroxeter with an independent entrance into the palaestra comprise the Baths of Neptune and the Forum Baths at Ostia (Meiggs 1960, 410–411, figs 28–29); the Stabian Baths, Phase VII, and the Forum and Central Baths at Pompeii (Nielsen 1990 II, figs 75, 78, and 79); the baths at St Bertrand de Comminges (Guyon *et al* 1991, fig 1); and at Kempten (Nielsen 1990, fig 171).

The West Range

The latrines and 17–18 would have had straightforward double-pitched roofs based on trusses. The roofing arrangements over the corridor 21 are shown as continuations of the portico roofs on either side to two ridges with a trap between shedding into 19. The great span of 17 and 18 accounts for the blocks of masonry in the centre which would have supported the roof by carrying cross-members under the centres of the trusses. The north-south span of 17 and 18 is wider than the basilical hall, but even so, the size of the central supports seems a little out of proportion, assuming that there was only an ordinary offset at floor level. The whole of the front wall was bedded on a major stone course which almost certainly ran through to the north-west corner of the *macellum*; any evidence here was not recorded before conservation. There seem to have been great stone-framed entrances probably incorporating central piers which could have carried the west end of east-west arches across both 17 and 18. In 18 the central part of the east wall is broken down to a low level and a respond formed of large stone blocks may once have been here. Arches, or compound beams, could have supported beams and joists suggesting a first floor but the location of access to one is unknown.

The main entrances to the *macellum* were two stone-framed doors in the west wall which were approached by two steps in the portico itself. At least one other was probably needed before the walkway was gained. The columned court, 22A, had shops round three sides, a latrine in one corner and 22D in the other corner with no direct entrance from the court. But if 22F formed a corridor to 21, access to 22D was possible and here there could have been a staircase to an upper floor.

In the central court there were spaces on each corner and the centre of each side of the sleeper wall for a large stone block, save in the south-east corner where the robber trench for the drain to the small latrines had broken through the sleeper wall. The tops of the sleepers showed that they had been rebuilt between these stone settings and there was evidence that the centre of the threshold had had its stone block replaced by brickwork. The settings indicate columns and Wright found part of a Corinthian capital lying in the court (Fig 6.23). The top diameter of the shaft was 0.51m, and the measurement from the top of the necking ring to the top of the fragment is 0.38m. Assuming that the rest of the capital was no more than twice that, the whole height would have been 0.76m, or 2.57 Rft. The top diameter is 1.72 Rft and, had D been 2 Rft, the reduction is one part in eight, a not unreasonable amount bearing in mind Vitruvius' ratios for reduction (V.III.12). The capital height seems a lot. Using the rules deduced by Jones that two and two thirds D represented the combined heights of base and capital (Jones 1989, fig 4), and with D = 2 Rft and the mini-

mum for the base, $\frac{1}{2}$D, the capital would be 2.4 Rft high, or 2 Rins lower than the estimate for Wright's fragment. Such a Corinthian column should have been 20 Rft tall with an entablature of $2\frac{1}{3}$ D or 4 Rft 8 Rins high. In terms of the width of 22A, taking $\frac{1}{2}$D off the 11.15 Rft width, the ratio is close to 2:1, column to width.

If the capital derived from the portico, then, using the suggested standard portico column, H = 11.25 Rft which is close to the 11.15 Rft width of 22A. However, this would not be the case if $\frac{1}{2}$D is taken away, which means that we have returned to what seems to have happened in 23N.

The restoration study shows an upper floor in the *macellum*. The ground floor column of *c* 11.25 Rft has an entablature of *c* 3.5 Rft, with the upper order a quarter less, giving a total height to the top of 25 Rft 10 Rins, or 7.64m, all of which is more manageable than the 12.77m required by a 2 Rft diameter Corinthian column.

This exercise has proceeded from fairly general principles, which seem to have yielded simple proportions in the basilical hall and the north portico, and which can also be applied to 23W, 23S, 15W, and 15N, to an attempt to apply the same principles to other areas.

The *macellum* construction sequence

The surviving wall evidence allows a constructional sequence to be suggested (Fig 3.4). The final plan and which parts were started first are clear, but there are also traces of a structural sequence for some minor elements. However, there is no great certainty, and it should be understood that work probably continued on different parts of the building at the same time.

The actual construction was dictated, presumably, originally by three needs: firstly, to deal with all the major low level difficulties. In the *macellum* this was the main drain running beneath the east range of rooms. Secondly, the need to define the site and create retaining walls for the planned dump material. This was required so that the floor levels of the building would not only be above the external porticos, but also the west palaestral portico as well. Thirdly, the need to allow the introduction of men and building materials into the whole building complex in as efficient a manner as possible.

The north corridor could not have served as a main access into the interior of the *insula* for construction purposes, since the west wall of the *insula* was begun before the north and south walls of the corridor, and the drain would have been a major obstacle. It seems most reasonable to suppose that the materials for the baths themselves were brought on to the site either from the south or the east as these parts of the plan are unencumbered by anything other than precinct walls and, on the south, by the external portico. As far as the

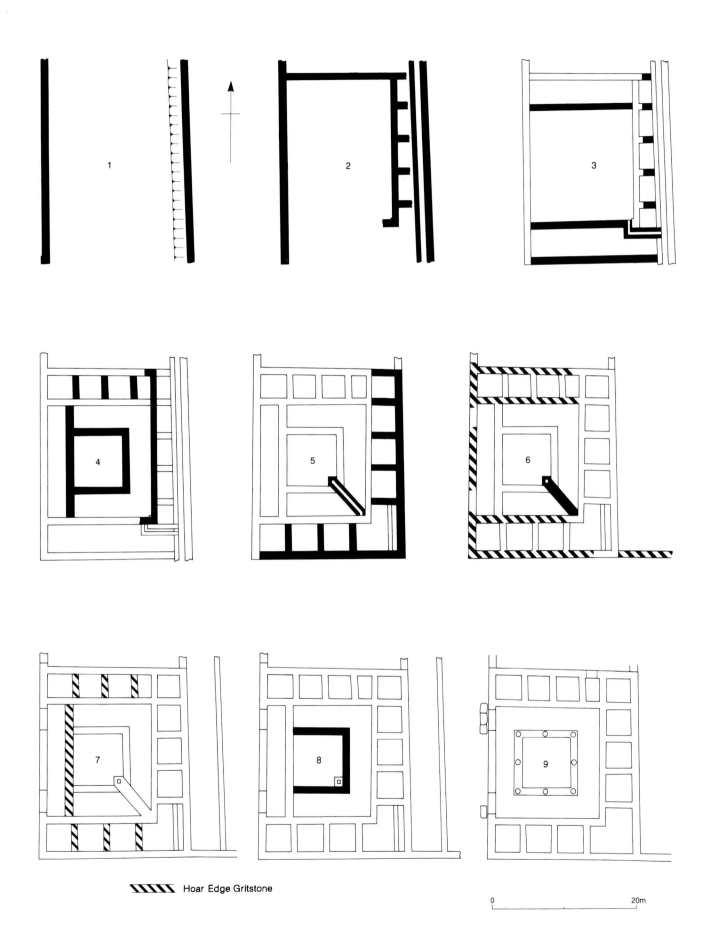

Hoar Edge Gritstone

0 20m

Fig 3.4 Macellum *construction sequence*

macellum is concerned, it is tempting to see the north end of the building as always having been in advance of the south so that essential materials could be brought in without too much difficulty. However, once the main south wall had been started (Fig 3.4), it may be presumed that the normal difficulties came into operation unless openings were left for construction gangs, but filled in such a manner that their former existence could not be detected, unlike the opening in the sleeper wall of the colonnade for the south external portico. Once the dumps for the planned floor surfaces were in place, the position altered and there was direct evidence for building works both in the north corridor and in the courtyard.

Detailed examination of the walls shows that the use of red sandstone from the Keele beds preceded the use of grey Hoar Edge grit stone. It is also assumed that, while the order of events may not have been staged precisely as presented, Fig 3.4 represents them as concisely as possible without crowding the general sequence of construction which the remains themselves suggest.

Stage 1 (Fig 3.4, 1)

The east and west walls of the *macellum*, F17 and F28, would have been accorded a similar priority (Figs 2.7 and 2.9). The first is a major boundary and is tied into the structures further north which may have been started by the time the *macellum* had been begun. Hence the main west wall, F17, was run through early and as a site limit. A pilaster at the south end marks not only a possible architectural treatment of the facade, but also the turn of the *insula*. The lowest stage of its construction is earlier than F14, F15, F20, or F22. The north wall of the *macellum*, F14, which returns as F29, also postdates F28, the main east wall. The first stage of the wall was the laying of foundations and the first red sandstone courses.

The main east wall, F28, could well have been put in early as a site boundary, but it was also to be the side of a major drain. While the west wall need not have been carried much above the first red sandstone phase until there was a need to begin to bond in other walls, the east wall had to start from a lower level and the completion of the drain conditioned much of the other work in the *macellum*. The first stages of the east wall consisted of digging the construction trench of the drain and the foundation trench of the wall, then the laying of the wall and drain foundation across the width of the trench so that the bottom of the drain was tied into the wall. The presence of putlog holes at this low level – they were later sealed by the sand make-up under the west palaestral portico floor – shows that the wall construction proceeded well in advance of the building of other well-faced walls.

It is not known what material formed the bottom of the drain itself, but the remains of brick in the wall suggest a double thickness of brick across the drain with a third course to mark the face of the wall. Once the west

side of the drain had been started, the construction of the drain would have proceeded apace to the top, with the other works being run in as and when they were needed (Fig 3.4, 1–5).

Stage 2 (Fig 3.4, 2)

The next earliest wall was F29 with a return at the north end to form the north side of the *macellum*, F14. A return west at the south end would have been made to mark the north limit of the south range. However, it was the main drain and the need to provide adequate support for the range above which must have influenced its early introduction and the construction of its first stage with the lower parts of the partition walls in the east range. These were run out to the west edge of the drain's construction trench, the courses stepping back progressively to the west wall. The return at the south end was continued west for a sufficient distance to mark the gap through which the minor drain, F4084, was to pass and to provide a base for its support when the time came.

The west portico sleeper wall would have been built at this stage. It returned along the line of the south portico for *c* 10m (F4030).

Stage 3 (Fig 3.4, 3)

The work on the main drain probably proceded from north to south and F29 was probably built from the north. Therefore, the south wall of the north range, F15, could have been started before all the first stage work on F29 had been completed. The north-west return provided marker stones for the partition walls of the north range. Also the character of the lower section of the south wall matches that of the north wall and is similarly provided with markers for the partition walls there. By the time that the sidewalls of the north range were ready to be tied in to the main west wall, the second red sandstone stage had already been begun. The north wall of the south range, F22, is shown as being built at this stage for the sake of convenience; it would have been as soon as possible and seems to have been built after the side walls of the north range. Inside the south range, the minor drain, F4084, was being constructed from its planned position where it crossed F22 up to the main drain which had reached such a height that the rest of the lower part of the partition walls could be completed.

Make up would have been dumped at this stage in the courtyard area and in the portico to the west. The major mortar mixing platforms in both areas may have been to prepare plaster for rendering walls already rising through the second floor, if not already at roof level.

The dumping was followed by a hiatus in the building programme suggested by the 'inspection pits' cut against the walls of the building (Fig 2.28). These were cut from the initial building level above the military and Period 1 destruction deposits except in the central courtyard where the pits cut through both the first make up and the mortar and plaster mixing deposits.

Stage 4 (Fig 3.4, 4)

In the north range, the red sandstone stage of the partition walls was being inserted and carefully finished to match the levels of the side walls. It seems likely, on general grounds, that the lower part of the partition walls was completed before the addition of the grey sandstone, yet the unused grey sandstone markers for the easternmost of these walls would seem to imply that the partition walls were only inserted when the grey sandstone had been added to both the side walls. This seems anomalous because, at first sight, it seems improbable that the red sandstone part would have been so carefully levelled off with the top of the same material in the side walls so that the grey sandstone could be made to match in depth the same material in the side walls. It may be noted that five courses of grey sandstone in the north wall is the equivalent of four courses of the same material in the south wall and partitions, which should mean that the north wall had been completed at this level first.

In the east range, the second stage of F29 was built and the drain and east wall, F28, brought up to capping level. In the south large dumps of make-up were placed.

In the central courtyard, work may have begun now on the sleeper walls of the ambulatory. Although there was no particular need to put in the sleeper walls and colonnades here until most of the basic structural building had been finished, the colonnade on the ground floor could have been placed so that floors on an upper storey could be run through both rooms and access areas. For the convenience of showing details on the plan, particularly to accommodate the minor drain, the work is shown commencing at this stage. The foundations were set in trenches cut through the initial make-up deposits. The foundations do not penetrate the early civil or military deposits in any real sense and this alone is a guarantee that there was no intention to impose any major loading on the walls here.

By now supplies of red sandstone were running low and it had been necessary to use rough material in the partition walls of the north range and a certain amount of minor stone pieces was crushed to form a dressing for the foundations of the central courtyard. Presumably stone for architectural detailing was now arriving specifically for the *macellum* as the levels of the building were approaching the point when the bases for important features had to be inserted. For instance, the west wall, F17, had reached the level on which the north and south entrances were to be placed as well as the entrance to the north corridor and the door for 17 and 18 further north. However, it is possible that the complete stone run needed for these had already been placed, as well as the west door threshold for the north corridor, as it was almost certainly part of the same large stone course.

Stage 5 (Fig 3.4, 5)

The last major work in red sandstone was now completed. It consisted of the running up of the east wall, F28, and the capping of the main drain, after which the partition walls were made up to a level from which they could be built without any reference to anything other than the general needs of the building above floor level. Along with this, the south wall, F20, was carried up to the surviving brick coursing, but with some admixture of grey sandstone which was now present on the site and was quite possibly being used north of the *macellum*. The partition walls in the south range were inserted into the Stage 4 dumps here, and finished off to match the top level of the red sandstone in the north wall. Inside the central courtyard the minor drain was also completed to at least the collection point, which may not have been built until the south and east courtyard walls had been finished: the drain robbers' trench removed all the evidence. The major stonework of the entrance at the east end of the north corridor was set in place.

Stage 6 (Fig 3.4, 6)

Now grey sandstone became the major constructional material. The large stone bases and at least the lower part of the jambs for the two entrances into the *macellum* through the west wall and possibly that into the north corridor if it had not been set already, were placed at this stage. The partition walls of the north and south ranges were taken up to their respective brick courses. From now on it is impossible to follow the construction of the major part of the *macellum* as next to nothing survives above this level. However, it should be pointed out that the columns with their architraves and entablature need not have been put in position until the structure was either level with an upper floor or higher still as it should have been easier to manoeuvre these elements into place from above than from the ground alone.

The minor drain in the central area was completed and capped in readiness for the sleeper walls and their superstructure round the courtyard. The capping of the drain may have been in tile; the drain is small and the only major structural problem would have been the point loading of the column at the south-east corner of the courtyard. Arguments for the reconstruction of the superstructure place a door over the point where the drain enters Room 22.9. A stone may have been used to bridge the drain at this point, although the basis for the original column run would almost certainly have been of large stones, any one of which could have spanned the drain without any difficulty. The size of the major drain in the east range was much wider and stone may have been used for capping throughout. However in the rooms north of the presumed latrine in 22.9, there is a distinct possibility that wooden floors had been used and so there would have been next to no loadings on the drain and large bricks used instead.

There was no evidence for the support of any capping in the surviving work of the east wall of the *macellum* and the possibility that none was placed as a wooden floor system would prevent any undue accident from happening. The unfinished drain in *insula* 4 issuing from the south-west corner of the forum court and running across the south portico and the one running away north and under the street there both show that large stones were used where areas were frequented.

The rear wall, F3227, of the south external portico where it runs away from the *macellum* was only added after F28 had risen to its full surviving height. As F3227 is in grey sandstone, it should not have been built before the stage represented by Fig 3.4, 6, but would have been finished by the time the *macellum* had reached the level at which the roofing could be bonded in. Initial dumping in the courtyard may have followed the construction of F3227. The south portico sleeper wall would also have been built at this stage.

Stage 7 (Fig 3.4, 7)

The partition walls in the north and south ranges were completed to what may be presumed to have been the intended floor level within. Work, at the levels being considered, continued on the courtyard. The west wall was completed up to a brick course which may have been a bedding for large blocks of stone, including the supports for the plinths for the columns. The three remaining courtyard walls were carried to an unknown level, but probably the one on which the presumed stone blocks for the original column supports were placed which may have rested on a brick course, but all this has been lost in the rebuild.

The major make-up deposits inside the rooms of the *macellum* were put in. These were never filled as high as the ambulatory was to be and the absence of any finished surface over the scaffold holes is the strongest evidence that the floors were to be of wood. Secondary make-up dumps were also added in the courtyard to complete the floor levels there. These consisted of large water-worn boulders, F79, set on compacted sand and gravel. The boulders ran up to the sides of the court without interruption. These could belong to the rebuilding as they were neatly bordered by the rebuilt parts of the sleeper walls, except along the west side. They were disturbed in the south-east corner by the drain robber trench which itself implies that the drain still survived after the boulders were placed. In other words, the drain was probably functioning after the rebuilding, but how it was fed is unclear as no clear sign was found for any other special surfacing in this area.

The surfaces in the ambulatory were subsequently replaced but the first floors would have lain at the same level. The same would be true of the central courtyard area if the foundation there is thought to belong to the *c* AD 300 rebuilding. There would have been considerable run-off from the roofs round it and guttering would be desirable. However no evidence of this survived.

The street porticos, the corridor to the north of the *macellum*, and the west ambulatory of the *palaestrum* were also raised to their completed levels at this stage.

Stage 8 (Fig 3.4, 8)

The external porticos would have been the last structures built. Few Roman buildings furnished at one time with external porticos survive in a good enough state for us to see how the roofs of these joined the main structure. The Temple of Janus at Autun and the circular temple at Perigueux are both well known for the state of their preservation and for having, by common consent, external porticos the evidence for which survives in the form of sleeper walls and holes in the main walls of the surviving building. It seems likely that, in these two buildings, the timberwork was inserted into previously prepared positions, and this may have applied at Wroxeter to the roofing of the porticos overlooking both streets and courtyard where these were backed by major structural elements such as the basilical hall and the *macellum*.

4 The finds

The Roman coins

By Richard Brickstock and John Casey

Reference to 'Period' in the following discussion is in relation to the currency divisions used in the histograms (Figs 4.1–4.4), which follow the methodology laid out in Casey (1994) and not to the structural periods described in the main text of the excavation report.

Introduction

The coins from these excavations extend in date from issues of the Dobunni to the end of the fourth century and tend to display the well-established period patterning which is characteristic of urban coin assemblages from Roman Britain (Casey 1994). The coins from the military fortress are catalogued here as well as those from the later civilian site. It has proved impossible to divorce the coinage from the military phases from consideration in this discussion, since there is an inextricable relationship between the coins of the military phase and the first structural phase following the fortress.

Period 1

Despite all structural contexts being post-military a good deal of coinage is present which derives either from disturbed military contexts or has entered the currency pool of Viroconium through the one-time presence of soldiers. Thus there is a certain degree of unreality in any attempt to define civilian and military in the earliest phases of civil life through the medium of the recovered coinage. This is especially true in the present case where the volume of pseudo-Claudian copper coinage of Period 1, normally closely associated

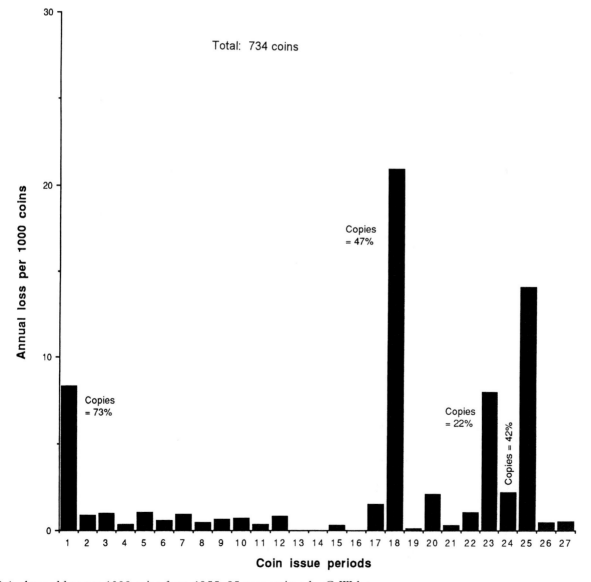

Fig 4.1 Annual loss per 1000 coins from 1955–85 excavations by G Webster

91

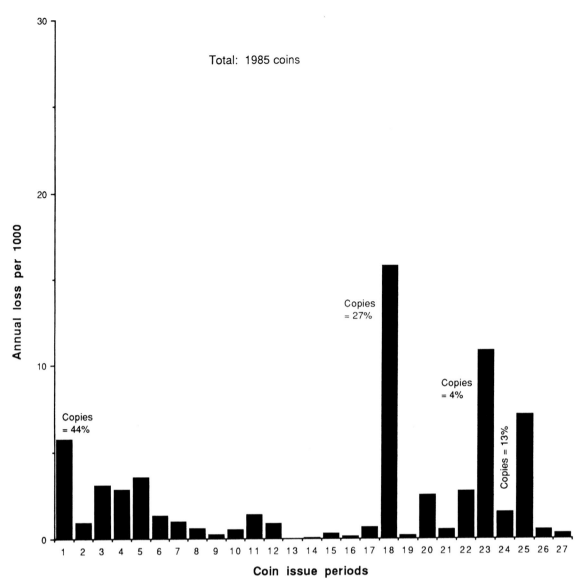

Fig 4.2 Annual loss per 1000 coins from Wroxeter sites other than Insula *5*

with the Julio-Claudian army, dominates the first-century coin pattern to a marked degree (Fig 4.1). Comparison with the pattern of Period 1 coinage from Wroxeter sites except *Insula* 5 (Fig 4.2) with that from Wroxeter sites as a whole (Fig 4.3) demonstrates the extent to which localised deeper archaeological sondage, and the erection of buildings with deep and substantial foundations, has increased the presence of Period 1 coins on the baths and *macellum* site. This is in marked contrast, for instance, with the coinage from the adjacent baths basilica excavations where pseudo-Claudian coinage (Fig 4.4) is poorly represented, demonstrating the derivation of the coins on this site from significantly later deposits than those under consideration here (Barker *et al* 1997). A further degree of uncertainty as to the economic significance of these coins is introduced by the fact that pseudo-Claudian coins remained in circulation in army contexts for many years after they ceased to be produced. The presence of such coins in the Coventina's Well votive deposit, at Carrawburgh on Hadrian's Wall, shows that

these coins were in circulation until at least the middle of the second century (Allason-Jones and MacKay 1985). The Wroxeter deposits present two aspects of residuality; physical in the sense of redeposit, and economic in the sense of persistence in the currency pool.

The pseudo-Claudian coinage

The analysis of the pseudo-Claudian coins does not include a group of 47 from the excavations which came to light after the report was finished. Scanning of this group does not suggest alterations to the conclusions below.

As has been observed a component of the earliest coinage in Roman Britain consists of copies of the copper and *orichalcum asses* and *dupondii* of Claudius. The context for this wave of imitation is well documented. Senatorial condemnation of the emperor Gaius (Caligula) extended to the melting down of his coinage. That this was effective may be judged by the scarcity of coin in his name carried to Britain by the invading

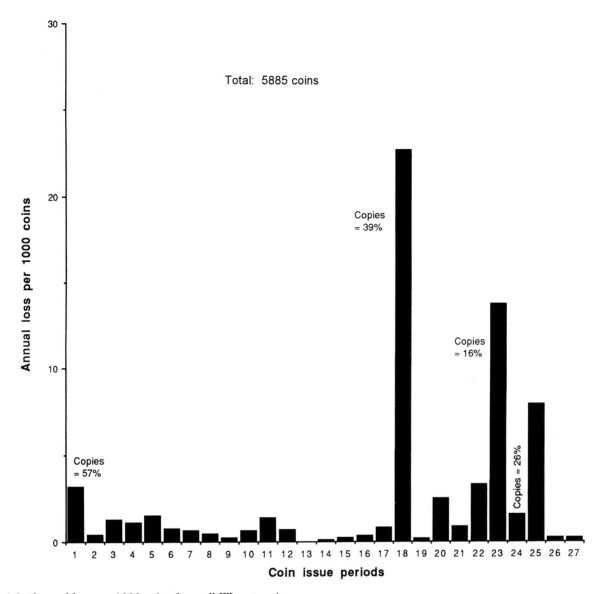

Fig 4.3 Annual loss per 1000 coins from all Wroxeter sites

armies of Claudius. An exception was made in the case of the condemned emperor's issues in the name of his grandfather, Agrippa, and his father, Germanicus, which are found in conquest period contexts, including Wroxeter (coins 16–22). For reasons that are not understood, the coin shortage created by the senatorial decision was exacerbated by Claudius whose base metal coinage dating after *c* AD 43, bearing the title *Pater Patriae*, is very scarce indeed. In Germany worn currency, which had been withdrawn from use, was recirculated. Coins had countermarks struck upon them to revalidate their use; these countermarks often re-value very worn coins to a lower denominational value. A *sestertius* of Claudius in the present catalogue (coin 31) bears a countermark PROB(avit), revalidating its use in the reign of Nero. Hence the invasion army was virtually bereft of small denomination currency. Untroubled by the impact of this situation on the emerging economy of the north-western provinces, the imperial authorities issued no base metal coinage at all for the first ten years of the reign of Nero (AD 54–64).

Throughout these two decades of monetary deprivation, copies of the last extant official coin of Claudius circulated throughout the military and passed into the civil sphere. The bulk of these copies comprise imitations, of varying degrees of fidelity, of the *asses* of Claudius with the reverse type of Minerva bearing a shield and flourishing a spear. Claudian copies are normally graded into four categories of deviation from the prototype (Sutherland 1935; Boon 1988; Kenyon 1987):

Grade 1 These are very close approximations of official issues, legends are correct and portraiture and reverse type are skilfully executed in a style distinctively at variance with the products of the imperial die cutters. Weights often fall below the *c* 11g of official issues, varying from full weight to *c* 8.5g.

Grade 2 Copies of this grade represent a further deviation from the stylistic fluency of official issues, and may themselves be copies of Grade 1 coins. Flans are often smaller in diameter than the dies struck on them,

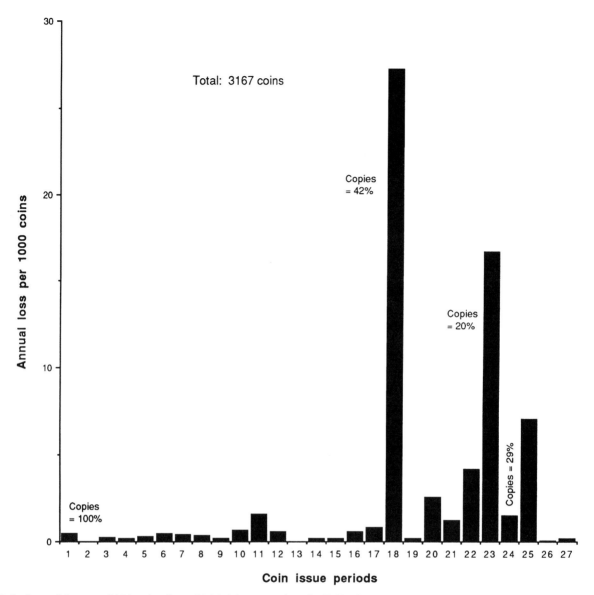

Fig 4.4 Annual loss per 1000 coins from 1966–90 excavations by P Barker

as a result legends are missing from the flan. When present, legends are epigraphically correct. Weights are, on average, lower than the prototype, clustering around the lowest weight of Grade I copies.

Grade 3 Copies in this category represent a deviation from the prototype which is characterized by crude execution of portrait and reverse type, both being rendered in a schematic manner. Weights are normally below the lowest range of Grade 2 copies, falling to 5.5g and less.

Grade 4 Essentially a sub-type of Grade 3, this version of the Claudian coinage is struck from dies which produced a reversal of either, or both, the obverse or reverse designs.

Within these categories there is a good deal of overlap in weights and flan sizes, and the attribution to specific grade in these cases is a subjective matter depending, in the end, on an aesthetic judgement.

Dating the appearance of the various grades of copy is assisted by the appearance of the coins in military

sites which can be associated with the advance of the Roman army from the south-east to the north and west. Thus a degree of horizontal stratigraphy is created by the activity of the army itself. At Colchester 76% of the Claudian copies are of Grade 2 and 14% are in the lowest category, indicative of the receipt by the site of a preponderance of copies early in the cycle of production (Kenyon 1987). By contrast, Usk, an undoubted Neronian site with a suggested foundation date of *c* AD 58 and an effective abandonment in the mid-60s (Boon 1982; Manning 1981), has 68% of its pseudo-Claudian coinage in the lowest categories of copies and 26% in Grade 2.

In the Wroxeter assemblage the bulk of the copies is heavily weighted towards the latter end of the production cycle in the Neronian period and is comparable to the picture derived from Usk:

Grade 1	19%
Grade 2	19%
Grade 3/4	62%

Periods 2–12

Relative to the coin deposition picture from Wroxeter as a whole (Fig 4.3) the present assemblage demonstrates something of a strength in the coinage of Nero, probably reflecting the military context of the site at this time, and a marked fall off of late Flavian issues (Period 4 = Domitian) which is not reflected in the coinage of Wroxeter as a whole. Thereafter the coin finds down to Period 12 (Severus Alexander) conform very closely to the spread normally associated with major urban sites in Britain, and are consonant with the overall numismatic history of the town visible in the 'all site' histogram. There is the normal transition from a largely base metal currency to one increasingly dependent on the *denarius* from the later second century. This probably represents a general rise in prices in Britain at about this time.

An unusual cluster of *sestertii* of Commodus is present (Period 9), the normal pattern being a very sharp falling off of *aes* coinage from the middle of the reign of Marcus Aurelius; this normal pattern is reflected in the overall coinage of Wroxeter. The coins of Commodus are all from different contexts but may still represent a scattered hoard rather than representing a genuine diffused element in the Wroxeter coin pool.

Of the Severan silver (Periods 10–12) a very high proportion, 78%, is of genuine coins; a similarly high figure can be derived from the larger baths-basilica assemblage – 83%. This contrasts with deposits of these periods on military sites where up to 90% of the coin consists of plated or cast counterfeits.

Periods 13–17

As is normal in Britain there is virtually no coin for the period between AD 235 and the accession of Valerian in AD 253. This twenty years saw a rapid, but not catastrophic, decline in the weight and purity of the silver coinage. The absence both of silver and base metal coins is a fact in all British site lists. An explanation for the absence of the *sestertius* and its fractions, may be sought in the wide availability of coin issued by Trajan, Hadrian, and Antoninus Pius, whose coins dominate in third-century assemblages and which were still available for overstriking by Postumus (AD 260–68) in his attempted restoration of the traditional denominational structure (Bastien 1967). In the light of these factors the dating of features to the mid-third century may well depend on the presence of worn, or very worn, second-century coins. Of the base metal coins of the relevant second-century emperors the wear pattern is as follows with the relevant coins from the baths-basilica in brackets:

	UW	SW	W	VW	EW
Trajan	–	2 (5)	2 (2)	– (5)	3 (5)
Hadrian	– (4)	3 (4)	1 (4)	– (4)	2 (3)
Antoninus Pius	–	– (6)	4 (9)	6 (7)	4 (3)

Of these coins 50% show very significant wear characteristics – ie are 'very worn' or 'extremely worn' – suggesting long circulation and vigorous economic use before deposition. If we add the 'worn' category to this total, over 70% of the coins are suggestive of an extended circulatory history. It is in this context that copies of second and third century *aes* coinage, represented by the forger's mould discussed below, should be viewed.

Periods 18–21

All sites at Wroxeter conform to the normal pattern of coin finds which characterise sites in Britain, whether military, urban, rural or religious. The pattern is a product of the violent fluctuations in the value of individual coins and their supply by the state, following the demise of the traditional currency system of the western provinces. By the reign of Valerian (AD 253–60) the 2–*denarius* piece, now virtually the only coin issued in bulk, had been reduced to 35% of the intrinsic value of the comparable denomination in the Severan period. This itself was a reduction of more than 35% from the standard of silver enjoyed under the early Antonines. The sole reign of Gallienus (AD 260–68) saw the disintegration of the empire into three parts, the north-western provinces constituting the Gallic Empire, and the eastern falling under the control of Palmyra. All attempted to keep their currency uniform in order to prevent outflows of precious metal resources to rival regimes. Period 18 represents the fall of the monetary standard from 0.5g of silver in the double *denarius* to a mere 0.1g, sufficient to give an appearance of silver on issues which did not survive in circulation. Period 19 saw a reform of the coinage with the issue of a 4–*denarius* coin. Enhanced denominational value coupled with a failure to supply this coinage to the north western provinces, results in very low deposition and recovery rates for material of this period. Shortfall in supply led to an epidemic of copying of the coinage of the Gallic Empire, and the 47% of copies presented in Period 18 certainly saw circulation as the normal small change coinage of Period 19 and should be acknowledged as such in any chronological discussion of this period. The characteristically high value graphed for the Period 18 coinage reflects two factors, the amount of low value coin in circulation, and its effective demonetization when large quantities of the new denomination coinage was introduced to Britain by the usurper Carausius, whose coinage is, as normal, relatively abundant (Period 20).

Periods 21–27

The recovery of Britain following the defeat of Allectus (AD 293–96) coincided with the introduction of sweeping monetary reforms by Diocletian and Maximian. In terms of site finds the most important innovation was the introduction of a 10–*denarius* coin which formed the main element of the transactional currency. This denomination is rarely found outside hoards, and such specimens as are present normally consist of issues from the end of the period, by which time the coin had halved from the weight of *c* 10g at which it had been introduced.

An overview of the fourth-century coin from the present excavation, the baths-basilica and the city as a whole, indicates that Wroxeter, or at least the areas that have been excavated, experienced a deficit in coin use. Compared with other fourth-century urban coin lists, Wroxeter has relatively low rates of coin loss in the period when Constantinian economic policies, which resulted in a systematic decline in the intrinsic value of the coinage, normally produce numerical values nearly as large as those of the Gallic Empire coinage of Period 18. This observation has particular relevance to the baths and *macellum* site where values for Period 23 are only about 50% of those for the city as a whole. The great majority of the coins derived from the porticos outside the *macellum* and may thus represent a different type of economic activity to that in the baths basilica. Of these coins, 22% are copies which can be ascribed to the years AD 341–6, when a localised supply problem created a shortage of small change in Britain and northern Gaul. By contrast, the adjacent baths-basilica site has approximately twice as many coins of Period 23, relative to other fourth-century issues, as the market area; though the former may be derived from transposed levelling deposits rather than being representative of coin use in the building itself.

The coin reforms of AD 348 are reflected in the declining recovery values represented by Period 24. Characteristic of this period is the large proportion of copies created to offset a shortfall of small change caused by the demonetization of coin of preceding periods by the rescript of Constantius II issued in AD 354 (Codex Theodosianus, 9.23.1: Phaar 1952). At Wroxeter as a whole, the proportion of copies is somewhat lower than usual (Brickstock and Casey 1997), but copies are present, however, both as site finds, and in a hoard from the baths basilica site (Brickstock 1992), demonstrating that a similar need for additional small denomination coinage was experienced at Wroxeter.

An interesting contrast between the two sites occurs in Period 25, covering the reigns of Valentinian, Valens, and Gratian. The market area may have experienced a genuine recovery of economic activity, since the Valentinianic coinage is better represented than the commonest Constantinian, though it should be noted that even the poorest specimen of the latter was of greater intrinsic value than the former; the Constantinian coin containing some element of silver, whilst the Valentinianic coinage was unalloyed copper. However, the proportion of Valentinianic coin from the baths-basilica is half that found in the southern baths and *macellum* area. In effect there is an exact reversal between the sites; double the values of Valentinianic to Constantinian in the market, the reverse in the baths-basilica area. Note should be taken of the caveat, above, about the origin of the baths-basilica coins before cross context deductions are made.

The volume of Valentinianic coin in the market area is within the pattern of the majority of urban sites. On the other hand the overall volume of this coinage at Wroxeter falls short of other town assemblages, in which Valentinianic coinage approximates to relative values of 75% of the Constantinian coinage of Period 23. The phenomenon of under-representation of Period 25 was discussed by Alison Ravetz in her pioneer work on coinage in Roman Britain (Ravetz 1964) where she concluded that some sites had benefited from such an influx of coinage in the first half of the fourth century that further supplies only represented a topping up of an existing currency pool. This view cannot now be maintained, not least because much of the earlier fourth-century coinage is seen to be located in contexts no longer accessible in the later period. Further, hoard evidence does not suggest that any significant quantity of coinage produced in the first half of the fourth century was normally available in the second half of the century. More pertinent is the hoard, numismatic, and contextual evidence of the effect of the law which demonetized the pre-AD 354 coinage (Brickstock 1987).

Periods 26–27

The last decades of formal Roman administration in Britain are characterised by a marked fall-off in coin finds. This site evidence is not to be confused with a run down in the economy of the diocese since finds of hoards of precious metal coins of this period, in both gold and silver, suggest the contrary (Archer 1979; Bland and Johns 1993). At Wroxeter the very last coinage, the issues of small bronzes dating to the years 388–402, though small in number, appear to fall into a pattern which is more clearly visible in the coinage of the same period in north Wales: coin issues dating to after the recovery of the West following the revolt of Eugenius (392–4) are not found. A link with the de-militarisation of Wales by Arbogastes, the *magister militum* of Eugenius, has been invoked to account for this situation (Casey 1991). The inclusion of Wroxeter in a zone encompassing north Wales and the west Midlands which was not supplied with the latest coinage to reach Britain may be postulated.

Attention should also be drawn to a coin published by Thomas Wright, which may have come from somewhere in the *insula* comprising the baths and *macellum*, which is the latest Roman coin known from a Roman-British archaeological context. The coin, mis-attributed by Wright to Valentinian I, is a small copper issue of Valentinian III (AD 425–55) dating to *c* AD 435 (Casey 1974). The circulation of this coinage is largely confined to Italy and North Africa. Here the excavations at Carthage revealed that this issue constituted the largest single element of the non-Vandalic coinage in the fifth century (Humphrey 1976 *et seq*). The possibility of importation from a source such as Carthage cannot be discounted in the light of the presence of the importation of Mediterranean ceramics into the west of Britain in the post-Roman period (Thomas 1981).

The 'Dobunnic' coins

Two specimens of the coinage (coins 10 and 11) conventionally attributed to the Dobunni were produced by the present excavation to add to the small total of such coins recorded from Wroxeter. Recent discussion of the coinage of the Dobunni raises the question of whether all of the coinage attributed to this tribe is correctly ascribed; the neutral term 'Western coinage' is advocated to describe this material (Haselgrove forthcoming). The 'Western coinage' from Wroxeter comprises issues of Mack Class B, C, G-I and in the name of Corio; the present specimens are of Mack Class B and C. The dating of this material is disputed but a bracket of the last two decades of the first century BC to *c* AD 40 encompasses all of the coins at Wroxeter. The context for the presence of such coins has been considered by Haselgrove who discusses the association of Celtic coinage with early Roman miliitary sites, especially in the case of the Kingsholm site at Gloucester, concluding that such coins were freely used by the army as a component of their currency. The early date of the Class C coins is not so much a reflection of an early date of deposition so much as the persistence in circulation of the commonest, ie largest volume, coins in the tribal repertoire. The problem of the relationship between base silver native coins and the Roman *denarius* and its subordinate *aes* fractions is less easy to solve. The essential point about Haselgrove's analysis is that it points to the fact that the presence of native coinage does not necessarily constitute *prima facie* evidence for an underlying native settlement.

Contextual discussion

There is only one situation in which adjacent contexts offer any opportunity to contribute a spatial/temporal analysis of the coin deposits. The excavation disclosed that the western and southern porticos of the *insula* outside the *macellum*, had been intensively used in the fourth century. The accumulation of coins from these contexts (Boxes 80, 90, 97, and 98) in P 3.4A points to an end of this activity shortly before the end of the Valentinianic period. The low tally of Valentinianic coppers, which had a circulation life to at least the end of the century, if not into the first decade of the following, must be regarded as significant. The individual specimens of this period are generally poorly dated but analysis of the issues of the mint of Arles (Constantia) indicates that coins dating to AD 374–5 are present. At this mint, the last mintmark for issues in which

Valentinian I (died 17 November 375) is present with Valens and Gratian is marked P CON; this mark is also the first employed on the coinage of the new imperial college of Valens, Gratian, and Valentinian II (accession date 22 November 375). Though Valentinian II is not found in the portico context, specimens of the P CON issue of Gratian are found, and these are the latest coins from P 3.4A. This phase extends therefore, on the coin evidence, to shortly before the end of Period 25. By contrast, the coinage from P 3.6 contexts outside the porticos (Box 96) points to a later date for this activity. Not only is the proportion of Valentinian coinage higher relative to the composition of the deposit as a whole, which suggests that, as might be expected, they achieved their maximum penetration of the coin pool some time in the following coin period, but coins dating to the last decade of the century are present (coins 696, 698, 699, and 701).

The coin mould

(with a note by Justine Bayley)

That copying coins was endemic at certain periods when official currency was lacking has already been dicussed in the context of pseudo-Claudian coins, the coinage of the Gallic Empire, and the supply of currency after AD 354; mention has also been made of an hiatus in petty currency in the years *c* AD 341–6. These episodes created a money of necessity which achieved if not official toleration at least indifference. More problematic are other instances where counterfeiting, rather than copying, was prevalent. Notoriously the *denarii* of the Severan period were counterfeited (Boon 1988; Peter 1990). Though Wroxeter appears to have escaped the worst of this phenomenon as far as recorded examples is concerned there is, in fact, a mould for producing these coins from the baths-basilica site (Brickstock and Casey 1997).

An intriguing, but minor, episode of counterfeiting is represented at Wroxeter by the presence of the obverse half of a bi-valve clay mould designed to produce a cast copy of an *as* of Marcus Aurelius, Caesar (Fig 4.5, no 734). Cast copies of the fractional coinage, in the form

Fig 4.5 Coin mould for asses *of Marcus Aurelius, cat no 734; scale as shown*

of *sestertii*, were first noted as occurring on the Rhine-Danube frontier in legionary fortresses and auxiliary forts and from this fact they were dubbed '*limes falsa*' ie 'frontier fakes'. Further research demonstrated that similar coins, but mainly *asses* rather than *sestertii*, were to be found in Britain (Boon 1965). The casts encompass copies of issues dating from the Antonine period through to the middle of the third century, the latter a period notorious for the absence of imperial base metal coinage in British site finds and hoards, though not necessarily so in some mainland Continental provinces. That early coins form part of the suite of material to be copied, derives from the absence of later official *exempla* and the fact, as noted above, that second-century fractional currency freely circulated for more than a century. *Limes falsa* are characterized by being smaller than their prototypes, a factor resulting from shrinkage of the cast and subsequent trimming of the edges, of thin fabric, and produced from an alloy with a high lead content (Boon 1988). The raison d'etre for the cast copies is more difficult to establish than the date of their production. Certainly in Britain they may have been produced to supplement meagre numbers of offical *asses* but their rarity hardly justifies a claim that they fulfilled this function to a significant degree. This is in contrast with the prolific emissions of pseudo-Claudian coins in an early crisis of currency supply.

Almost concurrently with the production of base metal copies was that of cast counterfeits of *denarii*. The bulk of these derive from Severan prototypes, and, for this reason, archaeologists normally attribute them to the reign of Septimius Severus, thus compounding the problem of assigning dates in third-century contexts. But on numismatic grounds alone, there are later coins muled with earlier, and the production of these casts, and the associated plated counterfeits, is almost certainly a product of the crisis which struck the coinage in the years after AD 238 with the reintroduction of the double *denarius*, itself a significant debasement of any two extant single *denarii*. The decline of this coin, both in weight and alloy, to a point in *c* AD 250 where new double *denarii* were struck on surviving *denarii*, provides a context in which the counterfeiting of what must have been coins of premium value would make sense within the criminal economy. By no stretch of the imagination, however, could the copying of derelict brass coins be seen in the same economic light. Unless, for reasons which cannot now be ascertained, a temporary demand for *asses* for a passing, but important, daily transaction created a need. Such transitory fluctuations in demand for specific denominations are normally associated with price changes for commodities such as the standard loaf or a specific quantity of something like oil, which are purchased on a daily basis in the market. No such easy solution can be advocated in the present case since the bulk of the *limes falsa* derive from military contexts where such commodities would be provided for the troops and paid for by direct deduction from pay.

Technical details of the mould are provided by Dr Justine Bayley of the Ancient Monuments Laboratory who comments:

> The clay of which it (ie the mould) is made is reduced fired and contains moderate amounts of semi-rounded quartz grains; there is also some indication of organic temper. The surface which bears the impression of the coin is rather finer textured than the other original surfaces, probably deliberately so to aid the quality of the casting. The mould is incomplete, only part of the valve surviving. There is no trace of the gate where the molten metal would have entered the mould but only about half of the circumference survives. There is, however, a slight groove running round the mould just outside the coin impression, presumably intended to mate with a ridge in the other valve giving correct register to the two halves. Sellwood (1976) illustrates a similar though better preserved clay mould which is double-sided, so he suggests a stack of mould pieces producing several coins at once. If the example from Wroxeter was used in a similar way it must have been the top or bottom piece as it only has an impression on one side.

> The mould fragment was x-rayed to see if any droplets of metal had been trapped in the cracks but none was found. The piece was also analysed by x-ray fluorescence to see if there were any slight traces of metal. The surface of the coin impression was compared to an area on the back of the mould and found to give signals for lead and zinc that were not detected from the back. This demonstrates that the mould has been used. However, the presence of small amounts of zinc and lead are not diagnostic, as their high vapour pressure means that they are almost universally detected in clay moulds whatever the composition of the alloy being cast.

On the grounds that the bulk of extant *limes falsa*, which are not *sestertii*, are *asses* we would expect the present mould to have been used for the production of the lesser denomination (ie *asses* rather than *dupondii*), the presence of zinc, a component of brass, notwithstanding.

Summary catalogue (coin number; issuer; type; date; reference; mint; context, phase)

A copy or counterfeit of a particular ruler/issuer is denoted thus 'CLAUDIUS II', and by c in the catalogue reference, thus c.of 261 = a copy of RIC 261. The use of the word 'of' indicates that a precise catalogue reference has been obtained; 'as' is used, for both official issues and copies, to denote an incompletely catalogued coin. Wear states are given in the archive catalogue and not, regrettably, in this shortened version.

Denominations

ANT   Antonianus
AS   As
AUREL   Aurelianus
DEN   Denarius (pl = plated)
DP   Dupondius
FOLL   'Follis'
SEST   Sestertius

Catalogues (catalogue numbers refer to RIC unless otherwise stated)

RIC   Mattingly et al 1926–84
BMC   Mattingly 1965–8
CK   Carson and Kent 1960
CR   Crawford 1974
E   Elmer 1941
HK   Hill and Kent 1960
MACK   Mack 1973
VA   Van Arsdell 1989

Mints

AM   Amiens
AQ   Aquileia
AR   Arles
CL   Cologne
CO   Colchester
CY   Cyzicus
LG   Lyons
LN   London
ME   Milan
NK   Nicomedia
RM   Rome
SS   Siscia
TC   Ticinum
TE   Thessalonica
TR   Trier

1   B.SCRIBONIUS; DEN; 154BC; CR201/1; RM; 50/13, M
2   L.TITURI L.F.SABINUS; DEN; 89BC; CR344/1c; RM; 22/19, BP 2.1
3   C PISO LF FRUGI; DEN; 67BC; CR408/16; 87/u/s, WR 4
4   MN CORDIUS RUFUS; DEN; 46BC; CR463/1a; RM; 83/ 530, WR 2.3
5   M.ANTONIUS; DEN; 32–31BC; CR544/24; 81/15, M
6   M.ANTONIUS; DEN; 32–31BC; CR544/31; 91/266, M
7   M.ANTONIUS; DEN; 32–31BC; CR544/8+; 39/20, M
8   M.ANTONIUS; DEN; 32BC; CR543/1; 70/68, M

9   LATE REPUBLIC/EARLY IMP; DEN; C1BC/AD; 83/506, WR 2.3
10   DOBUNNIC SILVER CLASS C; c 20BC-AD10; MACK378a, VA1045–1; 83/68, M
11   DOBUNNIC GOLD PLATED; AD30–60; MACK393, VA1035–1; 40/9, C 2.2
12   AUGUSTUS; DEN; 29–27BC; 264; 80/136, P 3.3
13   AUGUSTUS; AS; 15–10BC; 230; LG; 92/61, M
14   15 TIBERIUS; DEN; 36–37; 30; LG; 14 70/78, M; 15 85/63, WR 2.1
16–22   GAIUS; AS; 37–41; 58; RM; 16 80/245, M; 17 50/109, M; 18 80/191,M; 19 77/2, C 2.2; 20 98/192, M; 21 92/61, M; 22 80/189, M
23   'GAIUS'; AS; 41+; c.G2 as 58; 98/175, 1.2
24–6   CLAUDIUS I; DP; 41–50; 92; RM; 24 98/190, 1.1; 25 7/22, C 2.2; 26 80/181, P 2.1
27–8   CLAUDIUS I; DP; 41–50; 94; RM; 27 88/4, WR 2.3; 28 29/8, C 2.3
29   CLAUDIUS I; AS; 41–50; 95; RM; 45/3, C 2.3
30   CLAUDIUS I; AS; 41–50; 97; RM; 80/189, M
31   CLAUDIUS I; SEST; 41–50; 99; RM; 97/133, P 2.3
32–5   CLAUDIUS I; AS; 41–50; 100; RM; 32 80/179, P 2.1; 33 u/s; 34 48/u/s, BP 4; 35 29/16, C 2.2
36–8   CLAUDIUS I; AS; 41–50; 36 80/201, M; 37 98/168, 1.2; 38 98/87, P 2.3
39   CLAUDIUS I?; DP; 41–50; RM; 92/60, M
40–2   'CLAUDIUS I'; DP; 41+; c.G1 as 92; 40 87/100, WR 2.3; 41 12/27, C 2.2; 42 50/92, M
43   'CLAUDIUS I'; DP; 41+; c.G1 as 94; 85/224, WR 2.3
44   'CLAUDIUS I'; AS; 41+; c.G1 as 97; 84/399, M
45–6   'CLAUDIUS I'; AS; 41+; c.G1 as 100; 45 and 46 98/192, M
47   'CLAUDIUS I'; 41+; c.G1 as -; 98/178, 1.3
48   'CLAUDIUS I'; DP; 41+; c.G2 as 92; 98/152, 1.2
49   'CLAUDIUS I' MULE; DP; 41+; c.G2 as obv 94,rv 92; 85/65, M
50–4   'CLAUDIUS I'; AS; 41+; c.G2 as 100; 50 2/7, C 3.3; 51 22/13, BP   2.2; 52 80/191, M; 53 80/201, M; 54 98/52, P 2.3
55   'CLAUDIUS I'; DP; 41+; c.G3 as 92; 98/192, M
56   'CLAUDIUS I'; DP; 41+; c.G3 as 94; 90/198, 1.3
57–8   'CLAUDIUS I'; AS; 41+; c.G3 as 95; 57 45/3, C 2.3; 58 98/152, 1.2
59–66   'CLAUDIUS I'; AS; 41+; c.G3 as 100; 59 10/14, M; 60 98/100, F855, P 3.1; 61 50/11, C 2.2; 62 90/184, 1.2; 63 u/s; 64 u/s; 65 91/144, 1.3; 66 9/6, C 3.2

67   'CLAUDIUS I'; AS; 41+; c.G3 as -; 98/162, 1.1

68–80 'CLAUDIUS I'; AS; 41+; c.G4 as 100; 68 80/181, P 2.1; 69 98/178,1.3; 70 51/18, M; 71 98/138, P 2.3; 72 84/535, M; 73 80/181, P 2.1; 74 u/s; 75 9/22, M; 76 80/207, M; 77 u/s; 78 98/192, M; 79 98/178, 1.3; 80 42/7, M

81   'CLAUDIUS I'; AS; 41+; c.as; 80/191, M

82–3   'CLAUDIUS I'; 41+; c.as -; 82 98/156, 1.2; 83 98/211, M

84   'CLAUDIUS I'?; 41+; c.as -; 98/192, M

85   NERO; AS; 64–68; 58/4, BP 3.2

86   NERO; AS; 64–68; as 300; 91/164, 1.1

87   NERO; DP; c 64–67; as 375; 50/11, C 2.2

88   NERO; SEST; c 65; 389; LG; u/s

89   NERO; AS; c 65; 474; LG; 35/48, M

90   NERO; AS; c 66; as 542; LG; 78/15, M

91   NERO; AS; c 66–67; 543/5, 605; LG; 72/48, M

92   NERO; AS; c 66–67; 543/605; LG; 90/247, M

93   JULIO-CLAUDIAN; AS; C1st; 98/87, P 2.3

94   VESPASIAN; AS; 69–70; 399; LG; 90/177, P 2.2

95–6   VESPASIAN; AS; 69–78; 56/2, BP 3.3; 84/79, M

97   VESPASIAN; AS/DP; 69–79; 57/u/s, BP 4

98   VESPASIAN; DP; 70–79; as 541; RM; 57/u/s, BP 4

99   VESPASIAN; DP; 71–72; 475/740; 84/48, WR 3.1

100   VESPASIAN; AS; 71–79; as 494; 9/21, C 2.1

101   VESPASIAN; AS; 72–73; 528; RM; 91/158, 1.3

102   VESPASIAN; DP; 72–73; 743; LG; 87/114, M

103   VESPASIAN; AS; 72–78; as 528; 85/u/s, WR 4

104   VESPASIAN; AS; 73; 747; LG; 97/230, M

105   VESPASIAN; DEN; 74; 73–75; RM; 80/5, P 3.4B

106   VESPASIAN; DP; 77–78; 757c; LG; 91/94, WR 2.3

107–8 VESPASIAN; AS; 77–78; 763; LG; 107 81/15, M; 108 43/12, 1.3

109   DOMITIAN; DP; 84–96; RM; 59/5, BP 3.2

110   DOMITIAN; DP; 86; 326a; RM; 30/18, M

111   DOMITIAN; DEN; 89; 146; RM; 90/209, F951, P 2.2

112   DOMITIAN/HADRIAN?; AS; 81–117?; u/s

113   TRAJAN; SEST; 97–117; RM; 90/157, P 3.3

114   TRAJAN; AS; 98–101; as 392; RM; 36/23, BP 2.2

115–17 TRAJAN; DP; 98–117; RM; 115 41/u/s, C 4; 116 57/6, BP 3.3; 117 92/73, C 2.1

118   TRAJAN?; AS; 98–117; RM; 38/18, B 4

119–20 TRAJAN; SEST; 103–11; RM; 119 80/59, F477, P 3.2; 120 90/169. P2.2

121   TRAJAN; DEN; 103–11; 174; RM; 59/7, BP 3.2

122   TRAJAN; DEN; 103–11; 184; RM; 98/98, F930, P 3.2

123   TRAJAN; AS; 103–11; 536; RM; 83/536, WR 2.1

124   TRAJAN; DEN; 103–11; 99; RM; 59/4, BP 3.2

125   TRAJAN; DEN; 114–17; 317; RM; 58/5, BP 3.2

126   TRAJAN; DP; 114–17; BMC998; RM; 84/49, WR 3.1

127   'TRAJAN'?; DENpl; 97+; c.as -; 47/17, C 3.1

128–9 HADRIAN; SEST; 117–38; RM; 128 56/10, BP 3.3; 129 86/25, WR 4

130   HADRIAN; AS; 125–28; 669; RM; 90/94, F624, P 3.2

131   HADRIAN; AS; 125–38; as 654; RM; 61/u/s, BP 4

132   HADRIAN; SEST; 134–38; 790; RM; 90/100, F602, P 3.1

133   HADRIAN fragmented; DEN; 134–38; 299; RM; 38/21, B 4

134   HADRIAN?; AS; 117–38; RM; 59/5, BP 3.2

135   'HADRIAN'?; SEST; 132+?; 38/20, B 4

136   ANTONINUS PIUS; AS; 138–61; RM; 12/29, C 3.4

137   ANTONINUS PIUS; SEST; 139–61; RM; 58/2, BP 3.2

138   ANTONINUS PIUS; SEST; 139–61; as 534; RM; 98/20, P 3.4A

139   ANTONINUS PIUS; SEST; 139–61; as 746; RM; 38/7, B 4

140   ANTONINUS PIUS; SEST; 140–44; 651; RM; 80/4, P 3.4B

141   ANTONINUS PIUS; SEST; 150–51; 868; RM; 98/140, P 3.2

142   ANTONINUS PIUS; AS; 153–54; 924; RM; 98/20, P 3.4A

143   ANTONINUS PIUS; DP; 155–56; 950; RM; 90/205, P 3.1

144   FAUSTINA I; SEST; 138–41; Pius 1081; RM; 59/3, BP 3.2

145   FAUSTINA I, POSTH; SEST; 141+; Pius 1116; RM; 59/5, BP 3.2

146   FAUSTINA I, POSTH; DEN; 141+; Pius 361; RM; 80/100, P 3.2

147   FAUSTINA I, POSTH; DP/AS; 141+; as Pius 1161; RM; 47/17, C 3.1

148   FAUSTINA II; SEST; 145–75; RM; 16/u/s, BP 4

149   MARCUS AURELIUS; DP; 161; 798; RM; 97/25, P 3.3

150   MARCUS AURELIUS; SEST; 163–65; 861/888/898; RM; u/s

151   MARCUS AURELIUS; DP; 175–76; 1173; RM; 38/21, B 4

152 FAUSTINA II; DEN; 145–75; RM; 98/u/s,
P 4

153 FAUSTINA II; AS/DP; 161; Pius 1405c;
RM; u/s

154 FAUSTINA II; DEN; 161–80; Aurelius 677;
RM; 98/98, P 3.2

155 LUCILLA; SEST; 164–69; Aurelius – ; RM;
65/21, B 3.1

156 LUCILLA; SEST; 164–69; Aurelius 1736;
RM; 80/41, P 3.5

157 COMMODUS; SEST; 183; 354; RM;
49/u/s, BP 4

158 COMMODUS; SEST; 184–85; 440/52;
RM; 90/u/s, P 4

159 COMMODUS; SEST; 186–87; 513; RM;
97/25, P 3.3

160 COMMODUS; SEST; 186–87; 529; RM;
90/35, P 3.6

161 COMMODUS; DEN; 190–91; 227; RM;
97/25, P 3.3

162 SEPTIMIUS SEVERUS; DEN; 193–211;
80/21, P 3.5

163 SEPTIMIUS SEVERUS; DEN; 198–200;
122c; RM; 38/20, B 4

164 SEPTIMIUS SEVERUS; DEN; 200–01;
167a; RM; 90/48, P 3.4A

165 SEPTIMIUS SEVERUS; DEN; 204–07;
as 195; RM; 96/21, P 3.6

166 SEPTIMIUS SEVERUS; DEN; 207–10;
as 207; RM; 90/48, P 3.4A

167 JULIA DOMNA; DEN; 211–17; Caracalla
391; RM; 80/4, P 3.4B

168 'JULIA DOMNA'; DENpl; 196+; c.of
Severus 577; 90/73, P 3.3

169 'JULIA DOMNA'; DENpl; 196+; c.of
Severus 644; 98/12, P 4

170 'JULIA DOMNA'; DENpl; 196+; c.of
Severus 564; 98/93, P 3.3

171 CARACALLA; DEN; 205; 80b; RM; 98/40,
P 3.1

172 GETA; DEN; 198–212; 98/2, P 4

173 JULIA MAESA; DEN; 218–22; Elagabalus
271; 91/55, WR 3.3

174 SEVERUS ALEXANDER; DEN; 228–31;
226; RM; 57/u/s, BP 4

175 SEVERUS ALEXANDER; DEN; 233; 120;
RM; 38/5, BP 4

176 SEVERUS ALEXANDER ?plated; DEN;
223[+]; 32; RM; 22/2, BP 4

177 ORBIANA; DEN; 225; Sev.Alex. 319; 57/1,
BP 4

178 JULIA MAMAEA; DEN; 222–35; Sev.Alex.;
80/55, P 3.3

179 JULIA MAMAEA; DEN; 222–35; Sev.Alex.
343; RM; 98/93, P 3.3

180 'JULIA MAMAEA'; DENpl; 222+; c.as
Sev.Alex. 329; 2/7, C 3.3

181 PHILIP I; DEN; 244–47; 51; RM; 21/2,
B 3.4

182 VALERIAN; AS; 253–58; 86/30, WR 4

183 VALERIAN; ANT; 257; 106; ME; 97/67,
P 3.3

184 GALLIENUS, JOINT REIGN; ANT;
253–58; 77/2, C 2.2

185 GALLIENUS, JOINT REIGN; ANT;
253–58; 136; RM; 90/38, P 3.4A

186 GALLIENUS, JOINT REIGN; ANT;
256–57; 136; RM; 80/u/s, P 4

187 SALONINA, JOINT REIGN; ANT;
253–58; 35; RM; 49/165, BP 3.3

188 SALONINA, JOINT REIGN; ANT;
256–57; 31; RM; 98/2, P 4

189 GALLIENUS; ANT; 260–68; 90/u/s, P 4

190 GALLIENUS; ANT; 260–68; 157; RM; BP 4

191 GALLIENUS; ANT; 260–68; 159; RM;
98/8, P 3.6

192 GALLIENUS; ANT; 260–68; 163; RM;
58/u/s, BP 4

193–4 GALLIENUS; ANT; 260–68; 179; RM;
193 90/u/s, P 4; 194 90/17, P 3.6

195–6 GALLIENUS; ANT; 260–68; 181; RM;
195 90/u/s, P 4; 196 u/s

197 GALLIENUS; ANT; 260–68; 214; RM XI;
16/u/s, BP 4

198 GALLIENUS; ANT; 260–68; 214; RM;
98/12, P 4

199 GALLIENUS; ANT; 260–68; 245; RM;
86/21, WR 4

200 GALLIENUS; ANT; 260–68; 251; RM;
55/6, BP 3.3

201 GALLIENUS; ANT; 260–68; 256; RM;
80/39, P 3.5

202 GALLIENUS; ANT; 260–68; 280; RM;
90/41, P 3.6

203 GALLIENUS; ANT; 260–68; 280; RM;
97/18, P 3.4A

204 GALLIENUS; ANT; 260–68; 572; SS; 80/3,
P 3.5

205 'GALLIENUS'; ANT; 268+; c.as 236; 90/9,
P 3.6

206–7 SALONINA; ANT; 260–68; 24; RM;
206 39/u/s, C 4; 207 90/56, P 3.3

208–9 CLAUDIUS II; ANT; 268–70; 208 96/21,
P 3.6; 209 92/u/s, C 4

210 CLAUDIUS II; ANT; 268–70; 109/10; RM;
90/25, C 3.4A

211 CLAUDIUS II; ANT; 268–70; 110; RM;
96/21, P 3.6

212 CLAUDIUS II; ANT; 268–70; 54/5; RM;
u/s

213 CLAUDIUS II; ANT; 268–70; 80; RM;
96/21, P 3.6

214 CLAUDIUS II; ANT; 268–70; 91; RM;
35/1. C 3.3

215 CLAUDIUS II; ANT; 268–7O; 14/15; RM;
96/21, P 3.6

216 CLAUDIUS II?; ANT; 268–70?; as 27; u/s

217 'CLAUDIUS II'; ANT; 268+; c.as -; 9/u/s, C 4

218 'CLAUDIUS II'; ANT; 268+; c.of 16; 96/21, P 3.6

219–23 CLAUDIUS II,POSTH; ANT; 270; 261; 219 90/u/s, P 4; 220 98/17, P 4; 221 90/9, P 3.6; 222 90/17, P 3.6; 223 96/21, P 3.6

224–9 CLAUDIUS II,POSTH; ANT; 270; 266; 224 80/3, P 3.5; 225 83/u/s, WR 4; 226 49/u/s, BP 4; 227 96/21, P 3.6; 228 u/s; 229 60/5, BP 4

230 'CLAUDIUS II,POSTH'; ANT; 270+; c.as 261; 90/26, P 4

231–6 'CLAUDIUS II,POSTH'; ANT; 270+; c.of 261; 231 82/11, BP 4; 232 43/1, C 4; 233 96/21, P 3.6; 234 96/21, P 3.6; 235 u/s; 236 98/3, P 4

237 'CLAUDIUS II,POSTH'; ANT; 270+; c.of 266; 96/21, P 3.6

238 QUINTILLUS; ANT; 270; 20; RM; 49/68, BP 4

239 POSTUMUS; ANT; 260–68; 86/3, WR 4

240 POSTUMUS; ANT; 260–68; 318, E565; 90/157, P 3.3

241 POSTUMUS; ANT; 260–68; 328, E418; 82/10, BP 4

242 POSTUMUS; ANT; 260–68; 85, E301; 90/17, P 3.6

243–4 VICTORINUS; ANT; 268–69; as 40, E700; 243 80/46, P 3.5; 244 80/u/s, P 4

245–6 VICTORINUS; ANT; 269; 57, E741; 245 80/u/s, P 4; 246 80/3, P 3.5

247 VICTORINUS; ANT; 269–70; 75, E744; 84/u/s, WR 4

248 VICTORINUS; ANT; 270; 114, E683; 80/3, P 3.5

249 VICTORINUS; ANT; 270; 118, E682; 96/21, P 3.6

250 VICTORINUS; ANT; 270; as 118, E682; 90/45, P 3.4A

251 VICTORINUS/TETRICUS I; ANT; 268–73; 76/u/s, C 4

252–4 TETRICUS I; ANT; 270–72; 136, E764; 252 90/51, P 3.3; 253 38/46, B 4; 254 80/178, P 2.3

255 TETRICUS I; ANT; 270–72; 141, E765; 80/178, P 2.3

256 TETRICUS I; ANT; 270–72; as 136, E764; 80/16, P 3.4B

257–62 TETRICUS I; ANT; 270–73; 257 83/u/s, WR 4; 258 96/25, P 3.6; 259 90/u/s, P; 260 82/1, BP 4; 261 90/9, P 3.6; 262 91/22, WR 3.1

263 TETRICUS I; ANT; 270–73; 110–112, E-; 90/16, P 3.6

264 TETRICUS I; ANT; 270–73; 52, E-; 96/21, P 3.6

265 TETRICUS I; ANT; 270–73; 73, E-; 90/9, P 3.6

266 TETRICUS I; ANT; 270–73; 75var, E-; 90/49, P 3.6

267 TETRICUS I; ANT; 272; 90, E786; 56/1, BP 4

268 TETRICUS I; ANT; 273; 100, E771; 60/5, BP 4

269 TETRICUS I; ANT; 273; 100, E775; u/s

270 TETRICUS I; ANT; 273; 100/1, E771; 83/u/s, WR 4

271 TETRICUS I; ANT; 273; 121/3, E772; 83/u/s, WR 4

272 TETRICUS I; ANT; 273; 127, E788; 98/6, P 3.6

273 TETRICUS I; ANT; 273; 87, E787; 90/1, P 4

274 TETRICUS I; ANT; 273; 87/9, E787; 90/25, P 3.4A

275 TETRICUS I; ANT; 273; as 100, E771; 98/2, P 4

276 TETRICUS I; ANT; 273; as 79, E790; 49/u/s, BP 4

277 TETRICUS I; ANT; 273; as 88, E786/7; 80/2, P 4

278 TETRICUS I?; ANT; 270–73; 98/u/s, P 4

279 'TETRICUS I'; ANT; 273+; as 79/81, E790; 96/25, P 3.6

280 'TETRICUS I'; ANT; 273+; c.as 79/81, E790; 96/21, P 3.6

281 'TETRICUS I'; ANT; 273+; c.as 82/3, E-; 90/21, P 3.6

282–9 'TETRICUS I'; ANT; 273+; c.as -; 282 96/71, P 4; 283 96/21, P 3.6; 284 u/s; 285 u/s; 286 98/155, P 3.3; 287 96/21, P 3.6; 288 96/u/s, P4; 289 82/1, BP 4

290–7 'TETRICUS I'; ANT; 273+; c.as 100, E771; 290 86/u/s, WR 4; 291 90/35, P 3.6; 292 90/u/s, P 4; 293 90/19, P 3.6; 294 u/s; 295 97/41, P 3.4A; 296 91/55, WR 3.3; 297 96/21, P 3.6

298 'TETRICUS I'; ANT; 273+; c.as 108, E-; 82/6, BP 4

299 'TETRICUS I'; ANT; 273+; c.as 110, E-; 90/17, P 3.6

300–5 'TETRICUS I'; ANT; 273+; c.as 121, E772; 300 98/12, P 4; 301 90/5, P 3.5; 302 98/6, P 3.6; 303 u/s; 304 96/21, P 3.6; 305 98/6, P 3.6

306 'TETRICUS I'; ANT; 273+; c.as 140, E762; 98/u/s, P 4

307 'TETRICUS I'; ANT; 273+; c.as 145, E-; 84/u/s, WR 4

308 'TETRICUS I'; ANT; 273+; c.of -; 96/21, P 3.6

309 'TETRICUS I'; ANT; 273+; c.of 100, E771; 59/5, BP 3.2

310 'TETRICUS I'; ANT; 273+; c.of 100/1, E771; 82/1, BP 4

311 'TETRICUS I'; ANT; 273+; c.of 100/101, E771; 96/21, P 3.6

312 'TETRICUS I'; ANT; 273+; c.of 101, E771; 96/21, P 3.6

313 'TETRICUS I'; ANT; 273+; c.of 102, E-; 98/8, P 3.6

314 'TETRICUS I'; ANT; 273+; c.of 109, E-; 90/16, P 3.6

315 'TETRICUS I'; ANT; 273+; c.of 148, E788; u/s

316–17 TETRICUS II; ANT; 270–73; 316 90/u/s, P 4; 317 90/9, P 3.6

318 TETRICUS II; ANT; 270–73; 229, E-; 90/25, P 3.4A

319 TETRICUS II; ANT; 270–73; 254/8, E-; 98/12, P 4

320 TETRICUS II; ANT; 270–73; 255, E-; 90/25, P 3.4A

321 TETRICUS II; ANT; 270–73; 259, E777; 84/46, WR 3.1

322 TETRICUS II; ANT; 270–73; 264, E-; 96/21, P 3.6

323 TETRICUS II; ANT; 270–73; 270/4, E791/769; 90/21, P 3.6

324 TETRICUS II; ANT; 270–73; 272, E769; 90/9, P 3.6

325 TETRICUS II; ANT; 270–73; 272–74, E769; 98/12, P 4

326–7 TETRICUS II; ANT; 270–73; 272/4, E769; 326 96/21, P 3.6; 327 97/56, P 4

328 TETRICUS II; ANT; 270–73; as 267, E-; 80/3, P 3.5

329 TETRICUS II; ANT; 273; 270, E791; 54/1, BP 3.3

330 TETRICUS II?; ANT; 270–73; 96/21, P 3.6

331–5 'TETRICUS II'; ANT; 273+; c.as -; 331 86/21, WR 4; 332 80/39, P 3.5; 333 80/32, P 4; 334 90/5, P 3.5; 335 83/1, WR 4

336 'TETRICUS II'; ANT; 273+; c.as 248, E-; 96/21, P 3.6

337 'TETRICUS II'; ANT; 273+; c.as 265, E-; 60/7, BP 4

338–40 'TETRICUS II'; ANT; 273+; c.as 277, E-; 338 86/21, WR 4; 339 98/3, P 4; 340 98/u/s, P 4

341 'TETRICUS II'; ANT; 273+; c.as 280, E-; 96/71, P 4

342 'TETRICUS II'; ANT; 273+; c.of 232, E-; 82/1, BP 4

343 'TETRICUS II'; ANT; 273+; c.of 234, E-; 84/u/s, WR 4

344 'TETRICUS II'; ANT; 273+; c.of 254/8, E-; 82/1, BP 4

345 'TETRICUS II'; ANT; 273+; c.of 268, E-; 82/11, BP 4

346 'TETRICUS II'; ANT; 273+; c.of 280, E-; 96/21, P 3.6

347 RADIATE; ANT; 258–73; 80/55, P 3.3

348 RADIATE; ANT; 258–80; u/s

349 RADIATE?; ANT; C3rd?; 98/3, P 4

350–60 RADIATE COPY; ANT; 273+; c.as -; 350 49/u/s, BP 4; 351 84/12, WR 4; 352 80/7, P 3.4B; 353 82/4, BP 4; 354 96/21, P 3.6; 355 90/39, P4; 356 98/u/s, P 4; 357 u/s; 358 90/20, P 3.6; 359 96/22, P 3.6; 360 90/18, P 3.6

361 RADIATE COPY; ANT; 273+; 96/21, P 3.6

362–71 RADIATE COPY; ANT; 273+; c.as -; 362 90/19, P 3.6; 363 96/21, P 3.6; 364 96/21, P 3.6; 365 98/15, P 4; 366 96/21, P 3.6; 367 98/12, P 4; 368 82/11, BP 4; 369 84/12, WR 4; 370 90/5, P 3.5; 371 86/21, WR 4

372 RADIATE COPY; ANT; 273+; c.as Tetr.70, E784

373 RADIATE COPY; ANT; 273+; c.as Vict.78, E699; 48/u/s, BP 4

374 AURELIAN; AUREL; 273–75; 64; RM; 98/2, P 4

375 CARAUSIUS; AUREL; 286–90; 96/21, P 3/6

376–7 CARAUSIUS; AUREL; 286–90; 101; LN; 376 83/u/s, WR 4; 377 96/21, P 3.6

378 CARAUSIUS; AUREL; 286–90; 1047; 80/20, P 3.5

379 CARAUSIUS; AUREL; 286–90; 121; LN; 96/21, P 3.6

380 CARAUSIUS; AUREL; 286–90; 303; CO; 90/3, P 4

381 CARAUSIUS; AUREL; 286–90; 855; 90/33, P 3.6

382 CARAUSIUS; AUREL; 286–90; 883; 98/3, P 4

383 CARAUSIUS; AUREL; 286–90; 952; 90/33, P 3.6

384 CARAUSIUS; AUREL; 286–93; 82/10, BP 4

385 CARAUSIUS; AUREL; 286–93; 96/21, P 3.6

386 CARAUSIUS; AUREL; 290–93; 347; CO; 80/41, P 3.5

387 CARAUSIUS; AUREL; 290–93; 878/9; 90/17, P 3.6

388 'CARAUSIUS'; AUREL; 286+; 90/16, P 3.6

389 MAXIMIANUS; AUREL; 290–94; 5pt2 399; LG; 48/u/s, BP 4

390 MAXIMIANUS; FOLL; 298; 6LG32b; LG; u/s

391 LICINIUS I; FOLL; 316; 7TR120; TR B; u/s

392 CONSTANTINE I; FOLL; 316; 7TR105; TR; 82/1, BP 4

393 CONSTANTINE I; 318–19; 7TR209; TR S; 90/9, P 3.6

394 CONSTANTINE I; 320–21; 7LN185; LN P; 98/u/s, P 4

395 CONSTANTINE I; 321; as 7TR317; 91/u/s, WR 4

396 CONSTANTINE I; 327–28; 7TR504; TR P; 97/121, P 3.3

397 CONSTANTINE I; 330; 8CN22, HK1067; CN; 80/u/s, P 4

398 CONSTANTINE I; 330; 8CN22, HK1067; CN Z; 90/u/s, P 4

399 CONSTANTINE I; 330–31; 7LG247, HK190; LG P; 98/66, P 3.3

400 CONSTANTINE I; 330–31; 7TR529, HK58; TR P; 82/6, BP 4

401 CONSTANTINE I; 330–35; as 7TR522, HK51; u/s

402–3 CONSTANTINE I; 332; 7LG257, HK200; LG P; 402 10/u/s, C 4; 403 90/35, P 3.6

404–5 CONSTANTINE I; 332–33; 7TR542, HK65; TR P; 404 90/9, P 3.6; 405 90/33, P 3.6

406 ONSTANTINE I; 333–34; 7TR561, HK85; TR S; 96/22, P 3.6

407 CONSTANTINE I; 330–31; 7TR523, HK52; TR P; 90/21, P 3.6

408 CONSTANTINE I; 330–31; 7TR530, HK59; TR P; 31/u/s, C 4

409–10 CONSTANTINE I; 330–35; as 7TR523, HK52; 409 96/25, P 3.6; 410 90/14, P 3.6

411–12 CONSTANTINE I; 332–33; 7TR543, HK66; TR S; 411 96/21, P 3.6; 412 u/s

413 CONSTANTINE I; 335; 7AR393, HK397; AR S; 90/5, P 3.5

414 CONSTANTINE I; 330–31; 7LG236, HK180; LG P; 80/21, P 3.5

415 CONSTANTINE I; 330–31; 7TR525, HK53; TR S; 11/12, C 3.4

416 CONSTANTINE I; 330–31; 7TR526, HK54; TR; 98/2, P 4

417 CONSTANTINE I; 330–35; as 7TR518, HK48; 96/21, P 3.6

418 CONSTANTINE I; 334; 7AR381, HK384; AR P; 96/24, P 3.6

419 CONSTANTINE I; 335; 7LG271, HK222; LG S; 90/17, P 3.6

420 CONSTANTINE I; 335–37; 7TR590, HK92; TR S; 90/16, P 3.6

421–2 'CONSTANTINE I'; 341–46; c.as 7TR522, HK51; 421 90/9, P 3.6; 422 80/55, P 3.3

423–4 'CONSTANTINE I'; 341–46; c.of 7LG242, HK184; 90/9, P 3.6; 424 80/49, P 3.5

425 'CONSTANTINE I'; 341–46; c.of 7TR522, HK51; 90/9, P 3.6

426 'CONSTANTINE I'; 341–46; c.as 7TR449/ 523; u/s

427 'CONSTANTINE I'; 341–46; c.as 7TR520/ 523; 90/20, P 3.6

428–32 'CONSTANTINE I'; 341–46; c.as 7TR523, HK52; 428 97/u/s, P 4; 429 11/u/s, C 4; 430 u/s; 431 90/33, P 3.6; 432 92/u/s, C 4

433 'CONSTANTINE I'; 341–46; c.of 7LG241, HK185; 90/u/s, P 4

434 'CONSTANTINE I'; 341–46; c.of 7LG241, HK185; LG; 90/u/s, P 4

435–6 'CONSTANTINE I'; 341–46; c.as 7TR520, HK49; 435 90/17, P 3.6; 436 90/19, P 3.6

437 CONSTANTINE II,CAESAR; 323–24; 7LN283; LN; 82/1, BP 4

438 CONSTANTINE II,CAESAR; 323–24; 7TR433; TR; 90/48, P 3.4A

439 CONSTANTINE II,CAESAR; 323–24; 7TR441; TR S; 63/u/s, C 4

440 CONSTANTINE II,CAESAR; 323–24; as 7TR434; u/s

441 CONSTANTINE II,CAESAR; 332–33; 7TR539, HK63; TR S; 92/u/s, C 4

442 CONSTANTINE II,CAESAR; 333–34; 7TR566, HK81; TR P; 90/33, P 3.6

443 CONSTANTINE II,CAESAR; 330–31; 7LG244, HK187; LG; 90/9, P 3.6

444 CONSTANTINE II, CAESAR; 337; 7LG286, HK232; LG P; 72/u/s, C 4

445 'CONSTANTINE II,CAESAR'; 341–46; c.of 7LG238, HK181; u/s

446–7 'CONSTANTINE II,CAESAR'; 341–46; c.of 7TR520, HK49; 446 90/u/s, P 4; 447 82/1, BP 4

448 CONSTANTIUS II, CAESAR; 335–37; 7TR-, HK89; TR S; 90/u/s, P 4

449 CONSTANTIUS II, CAESAR; 335–37; 7TR592, HK94; TR P; 90/16, P 3.6

450 CONSTANTIUS II,CAESAR; 335–37; as 7TR592, HK94; 33/u/s, C 4

451 CONSTANTIUS II,CAESAR; 337; 7AR413, HK412; AR; 60/u/s, BP 4

452 CONSTANS,CAESAR; 335–37; as 7LG278, HK227; 90/5, P 3.5

453 CONSTANS,CAESAR; 335–37; as 7TR593, HK95; 83/u/s, WR 4

454 'CONSTANS/CS II,CAESAR'; 341–46; c.as 7TR558/560; 90/u/s, P 4

455 HELENA; 326; 7TR481; TR; 38/u/s, B 4

456 HELENA; 337–40; 8TR63, HK112; TR P; 90/17, P 3.6

457 HELENA; 337–41; as 8TR78, HK119; 90/9, P 3.6

458 THEODORA; 337–40; 8TR79, HK120; TR; 90/16, P 3.6

459–60 THEODORA; 337–41; as 8TR79, HK120; 459 90/9, P 3.6; 460 96/u/s, P 4

461 CONSTANTINE II; 337–40; 8LG14, HK247; TR; 80/u/s, P 4

462 CONSTANTINE II; 337–40; 8TR81, HK125; TR S; 60/u/s, BP 4

463 CONSTANS; 337–40; 8AR13, HK421; AR P; u/s

464 CONSTANS; 337–40; 8AR13, HK421; AR; 90/16, P 3.6

465 CONSTANS; 337–40; 8LG24, HK251 var; LG P; 91/55, WR 3.3

466 CONSTANS; 337–41; 8LG24/29, HK251/3; LG; 90/9, P 3.6

467–8 CONSTANS; 340–41; 8TR103, HK131; TR; 467 82/10, BP 4; 468 90/19, P 3.6

469 CONSTANS; 340–41; 8TR111, HK133; TR S, 90/u/s, P 4

470 CONSTANS; 340–41; 8TR111, HK133 var; TR P; 90/33, P 3.6

471 CONSTANS; 340–41; 8TR117, HK136; TR P; 98/6, P 3.6

472 CONSTANS; 337–40; 8RM16, HK592; RM; 90/u/s, P 4

473 CONSTANS; 346–48; 8LG40, HK257; LG P; 90/u/s, P 4

474–5 CONSTANS; 346–48; 8TR182, HK138; TR P; 474 6/u/s, C 4; 475 90/5, P 3.5

476 CONSTANS; 346–48; 8TR182var., HK137a; TR; 90/5, P 3.5

477 CONSTANS; 346–48; 8TR186, HK140a; TR S; 90/33, P 3.6

478 CONSTANS; 346–48; 8TR186, HK140a; TR; 90/33, P 3.6

479 CONSTANS; 346–48; 8TR195, HK148; TR T; 90/5, P 3.5

480 CONSTANS; 346–48; 8TR196, HK150; TR P; 82/11, BP 4

481 CONSTANS; 346–48; 8TR199, HK155; TR P; 82/u/s, BP 4

482 CONSTANS; 348–50; 8TR234, CK35; TR P; 23/2, BP 4

483 CONSTANS; 348–50; 8TR240, CK–; TR P; 45/u/s, C 4

484 CONSTANS; 348–50; 8TR243, CK46; TR S; 55/1, BP 3.3

485 'CONSTANS'; 346+; c.of 8TR185, HK140; 90/16, P 3.6

486 CONSTANTIUS II; 346–48; 8LG55, HK266; LG P; 90/35, P 3.6

487 CONSTANTIUS II; 346–48; 8TR194, HK146; TR T; 90/u/s, P 4

488 CONSTANTIUS II; 346–48; as 8TR181, HK137; 82.11, BP 4

489 CONSTANTIUS II; 348–50; 8TR222, CK30; TR S; 82/10, BP 4

490 CONSTANTIUS II; 353–54; as 8TR359, CK76; 90/5, P 3.5

491 CONSTANTIUS II; 354–55; 8AR266, CK457; AR S; 96/21, P 3.6

492 CONSTANTIUS II; 354–55; as 8AR266, CK457; 90/u/s, P 4

493 CONSTANTIUS II; 355–58; 8LG189, CK256; LG P; 11/12, C 3.4

494 CONSTANTIUS II; 355–58; 8LG197, CK259; LG P; 90/u/s, P 4

495 CONSTANTIUS II; 358–60; 8AR277, CK461; AR P; 90/u/s, P 4

496 'CONSTANTIUS II'; 341–46; c.as 8TR39, HK100; 6/u/s, C 4

497–503 'CONSTANTIUS II'; 353+; c.as 8TR359, CK76; 497 80/21, P 3.5; 498 11/12, C 3.4; 499 86/27, WR 4; 500 90/19, P 3.6; 501 90/45, P 3.4A; 502 96/23, P 3.6; 503 98/19, P 3.4A

504 CONSTANTIUS II/CONSTANS; 337–40; 8LG21/24, HK249/51; LG; 96/u/s, P 4

505 CONSTANTIUS II/CONSTANS; 346–48; 8LG38, HK256 var; LG P; 96/21, P 3.6

506 CONSTANTIUS II/CONSTANS; 346–48; as 8TR181, HK137; 90/18, P 3.6

507–8 HOUSE OF CONSTANTINE; 330–35; as 7TR518, HK48; 507 96/25, P 3.6; 508 83/u/s, WR 4

509 HOUSE OF CONSTANTINE; 332–33; 7TR537/540, HK60/4; TR; 91/1, WR 4

510 HOUSE OF CONSTANTINE; 335–41; as 7TR586, HK88; u/s

511–13 HOUSE OF CONSTANTINE; 335–41; as 7TR590, HK92; 511 90/25, P 3.4A; 512 90/17, P 3.6; 513 90/5, P 3.5

514 HOUSE OF CONSTANTINE; 335–41; as 7TR590, HK92; u/s

515 HOUSE OF CONSTANTINE; 335–41; as 8TR38, HK99; 90/5, P 3.5

516 HOUSE OF CONSTANTINE; 330–41; 84/u/s, WR 4

517 'HOUSE OF CONSTANTINE'; 341–46; c.as 7TR518, HK48; 90/16, P 3.6

518 MAGNENTIUS; 350–51; 8TR264, CK50; TR P; 90/41, P 3.6

519 MAGNENTIUS; 350–51; 8TR264, CK50; TR S; 90/u/s, P 4

520 'MAGNENTIUS'; 350+; c.as 8TR262, CK49; 8/u/s, C 4

521 'MAGNENTIUS'; 351+; c.as 8LG121, CK217; 90/5, P 3.5

522 JULIAN CAESAR; 355–68; 8AR268, CK–; AR T; 90/9, P 3.6

523 VALENTINIAN I; 364–67; CK281; LG S; 90/16, P 3.6

524 VALENTINIAN I; 364–67; CK284; LG S; 90/5, P 3.5

525 VALENTINIAN I; 364–67; CK287; LG II; 96/21, P 3.6

526 VALENTINIAN I; 364–67; CK484; AR S; 90/9, P 3.6

527 VALENTINIAN I; 364–67; CK487; AR II; 90/5, P 3.5

528 VALENTINIAN I; 364–67; CK84; TR P; 90/41, P 3.6

529 VALENTINIAN I; 364–75; CK1390/1; SS; u/s

530 VALENTINIAN I; 364–75; CK512; AR I; 90/u/s, P 4

531 VALENTINIAN I; 364–75; as CK78; 90/9, P 3.6

532 VALENTINIAN I; 364–75; as CK92; 90/41, P 3.6

533–4 VALENTINIAN I; 364–78; as CK275; 533 90/9, P 3.6; 534 90/u/s, P 4

535 VALENTINIAN I; 367–75; CK115; TR S; 90/u/s, P 4

536 VALENTINIAN I; 367–75; CK1390/1; SS; 90/33, P 3.6

537–8 VALENTINIAN I; 367–75; CK311; LG II; 537 90/39, P 4; 538 90/16, P 3.6

539 VALENTINIAN I; 367–75; CK317; LG II; 62/u/s, BP 4

540–1 VALENTINIAN I; 367–75; CK317; LG S; 540 90/u/s, P 4; 541 90/1, P 4

542   VALENTINIAN I; 367–75; CK338; LG S;
       84/47, WR 4
543   VALENTINIAN I; 367–75; CK506; AR S;
       90/9, P 3.6
544–5 VALENTINIAN I; 367–75; CK512; AR;
       544 90/5, P 3.5; 545 90/9, P 3.6
546   VALENTINIAN I; 367–75; CK512; AR III;
       90/59, P 3.4A
547   VALENTINIAN I; 367–75; CK519; AR III;
       80/41, P 3.5
548–50 VALENTINIAN I; 375; CK525; AR S; 548
       90/u/s, P 4; 549 90/5, P 3.5; 550 9 1 / 1 7 ,
       WR 4;
551   VALENTINIAN I; 375; CK525; AR; 91/17,
       WR 4
552   VALENTINIAN I; 375; CK525; AR S;
       91/u/s, WR 4
553   VALENTINIAN I; 364–67; CK481; AR II;
       90/33, P 3.6
554   VALENTINIAN I; 364–67; CK481; AR III;
       49/u/s, BP 4
555   VALENTINIAN I; 364–75; CK1361; SS 3;
       90/u/s, P 4
556   VALENTINIAN I; 364–75; as CK281; AR
       I; 90/5, P 3.5
557   VALENTINIAN I; 364–75; as CK527;
       12/26, C 3.4
558   VALENTINIAN I; 364–75; as CK86;
       90/169, P 2.2
559–61 VALENTINIAN I; 364–75; as CK96; 559
       90/5, P 3.5; 560 90/35, P 3.6; 90/u/s,   P 4
562   VALENTINIAN I; 367–75; CK1020/26;
       AQ; 90/12, P 3.6
563   VALENTINIAN I; 367–75; CK1393/4; SS;
       90/35, P 3.6
564   VALENTINIAN I; 367–75; CK501; AR P;
       96/21, P 3.6
565   VALENTINIAN I; 367–75; CK508; AR;
       90/9, P 3.6
566   VALENTINIAN I; 367–75; CK515/522;
       AR II; 21/u/s, B 4
567   VALENTINIAN I; 367–75; CK521; AR I;
       90/u/s, P 4
568   VALENTINIAN I; 367–75; CK522; AR III;
       33/u/s, C 4
569   VALENTINIAN I; 375; CK1041; AQ P;
       80/u/s, P 4
570   VALENTINIAN I; 375; CK527; AR P;
       84/9, WR 4
571–4 VALENTINIAN I; 375; CK527; AR S; 571
       10/u/s, C 4; 572 90/33, P 3.6; 573 90/5,
       P 3.5; 574 90/9, P 3.6
575   VALENTINIAN I; 375; CK724; RM P;
       96/21, P 3.6
576   VALENS; 364–67; CK970; AQ; 90/5, P 3.5
577   VALENS; 364–67; CK997; AQ; 90/5, P 3.5
578   VALENS; 364–75; as CK282; – II; 96/21, P 3.6
579   VALENS; 364–75; as CK480; AR; 90/19,
       P 3.6

580–1 VALENS; 364–78; as CK480; – II; 580
       96/21, P 3.6; 581 90/14, P 3.6
582–3 VALENS; 364–78; as CK526; 582 96/21,
       P 3.6; 583 90/u/s, P 4
584   VALENS; 364–78; as CK93; 37/u/s, B 4
585   VALENS; 367–75; CK1029; AQ S; 90/19,
       P 3.6
586   VALENS; 367–75; CK513; AR II; 90/7,
       P 3.4A
587   VALENS; 367–75; CK519; AR I; 90/9,
       P 3.6
588   VALENS; 367–75; CK520; AR; 90/7,
       P 3.4A
589–90 VALENS; 375; CK526; AR P; 589 33/u/s,
       C 4; 590 90/16, P 3.6
591   VALENS; 375; CK526; AR S; 90/35, P 3.6
592   VALENS; 375; CK526; AR; 90/5, P 3.5
593   VALENS; 375; CK526; AR P; 90/39, P 4
594   VALENS; 364–67; CK283; LG I; 11/12,
       C 3.4
595   VALENS; 364–67; CK285; LG P; 90/9,
       P 3.6
596   VALENS; 364–67; CK483; AR; 92/u/s, C 4
597   VALENS; 364–67; CK87; TR T; 90/5, P 3.5
598   VALENS; 364–67; CK972; AQ P; 90/u/s, P 4
599   VALENS; 364–75; CK322; LG P; 90/9,
       P 3.6
600   VALENS; 364–75; as CK280; LG II; 82/10,
       BP 4
601   VALENS; 364–78; as CK276; 90/9, P 3.6
602   VALENS; 364–78; as CK280; 97/u/s, P 4
603   VALENS; 364–78; as CK514; 90/24, P 3.4A
604–6 VALENS; 364–78; as CK82; 604 97/62.
       P 3.4A; 605 96/21, P 3.6; 606 90/1, P 4
607–10 VALENS; 364–78; as CK97; 607 90/19,
       P 3.6; 608 90/5, P 3.5; 609 90/9, P 3.6; 610
       91/55, WR 3.3
611   VALENS; 367–75; CK110; TR P; u/s
612   VALENS; 367–75; CK1417var; SS; 90/u/s,
       P 4
613   VALENS; 367–75; CK1427/9; SS; 90/39, P 4
614   VALENS; 367–75; CK309; LG I; 90/14,
       P 3.6
615   VALENS; 367–75; CK312; LG; 80/u/s, P 4
616–17 VALENS; 367–75; CK319; LG P; 616
       90/19, P 3.6; 617 90/39, P 4
618   VALENS; 367–75; CK340; LG P; 80/39,
       P 3.5
619   VALENS; 367–75; CK504; AR S; 90/39, P 4
620   VALENS; 367–75; CK514; AR II; 80/39,
       P 3.5
621   VALENS; 367–75; CK516; AR II; 96/22,
       P 3.6
622   VALENS; 367–75; CK516; AR; 90/9, P 3.6
623   VALENS; 367–75; CK519; AR I; 90/19,
       P 3.6
624   VALENS; 367–75; CK523; AR; 90/19, P 3.6
625   VALENS; 367–75; CK725; RM P; 90/20,
       P 3.6

626 VALENS; 367–75; CK725; RM T; 90/9, P 3.6
627 VALENS; 367–75; CK97; TR P; 90/33, P 3.6
628 VALENS; 367–78; as CK96; 90/20, P 3.6
629 VALENS; 367–78; as CK97; 96/21, P 3.6
630 VALENS; 375; CK527; AR S; 90/19, P 3.6
631–4 VALENS; 375; CK528; AR T; 631 u/s; 632 84/47, WR 4; 633 90/9, P 3.6; 634 90/17, P 3.6
635–7 VALENS; 375; CK528; AR P; 635 90/5, P 3.5; 636 90/9, P 3.4; 637 96/21, P 3.6
638–9 VALENS; 375; CK528; AR T; 638 96/21, P 3.6; 639 90/9, P 3.6
640 VALENS; 375; CK528; AR S; 90/25, P 3.4A
641 VALENS; 375; CK528; AR; 90/5, P 3.5
642–3 VALENS; 375; CK528; AR S; 642 90/20, P 3.6; 643 90/u/s, P 4
644 VALENS; 375–78; CK365; LG; 98/2, P 4
645 VALENS; 375–78; CK537; AR S; 80/16, P 3.4B
646 VALENS; 375–78; CK725; RM; 90/u/s, P 4
647 VALENS; 364–78; 92/u/s, C 4
648 VALENTINIAN/VALENS; 367–75; CK1424/7; SS; 96/u/s, P 4
649 GRATIAN; 367–75; CK331; LG S; 82/10, BP 4
650 GRATIAN; 367–75; CK335; LG S; 96/21, P 3.6
651 GRATIAN; 367–75; CK1392; SS; 88/3; Wr 4
652 GRATIAN; 367–75; CK1431 var; SS -; 90/19, P 3.6
653 GRATIAN; 367–75; CK345; LG P; 90/5, P 3.5
654 GRATIAN; 367–75; CK304; LG I; 90/20, P 3.6
655 GRATIAN; 367–75; CK349; LG P; 90/9, P 3.6
656 GRATIAN; 375; CK533; AR P; 96/25, P 3.6
657 GRATIAN; 375; CK726; RM T; 90/9, P 3.6
658 GRATIAN; 367–75; CK517/523a; AR III; u/s
659 GRATIAN; 367–75; as CK529; AR; 90/19, P 3.6
660 GRATIAN; 367–75; CK503/29; AR; 82/1, BP 4
661 GRATIAN; 367–75; CK505; AR; 90/u/s, P 4
662 GRATIAN; 367–75; as CK503; AR; 98/2, P 4
663–4 GRATIAN; 367–75; as CK529; AR; 663 90/19, P 3.6; 664 47/14, C 4
665 GRATIAN; 375; CK523a; AR II; 90/5, P 3.5
666–7 GRATIAN; 375; CK529; AR T; 666 90/5, P 3.5; 667 90/39, P 4
668 GRATIAN; 375; CK529; AR S; 90/19, P 3.6
669–70 GRATIAN; 375; CK529; AR; 669 90/5, P 3.5; 670 90/9, P 3.6
671 GRATIAN; 375; CK529; AR T; 90/33, P 3.6

672 GRATIAN; 375; CK529; AR S; 90/49, P 3.6
673–4 GRATIAN; 375; CK529; AR; 673 96/u/s, P 4; 674 96/21, P 3.6
675–80 GRATIAN; 375; CK529; AR T; 675 90/9, P 3.6; 676 90/33, P 3.6; 677 91/1, WR 4; 678 90/5, P 3.5; 679 98/u/s, P 4; 680 90/u/s, P 4
681 GRATIAN; 375; CK529; AR; 90/u/s, P 4
682 GRATIAN; 375; CK529; AR P; 90/u/s, P 4
683 GRATIAN; 375; CK529; AR; 17/46, BP 2.1
684 GRATIAN; 378–83; CK371; LG S; 47/25, C 4
685 GRATIAN; 378–83; CK378; LG S; 90/5, P 3.5
686 HOUSE OF VALENTINIAN; 364–78; as CK525; 90/9, P 3.6
687 HOUSE OF VALENTINIAN; 364–78; as CK92; 96/21, P 3.6
688 HOUSE OF VALENTINIAN; 367–78; as CK279; – III; 90/19, P 3.6
689–90 HOUSE OF VALENTINIAN; 364–78; as CK96; 689 96/21, P 3.6; 690 90/9, P 3.6
691 HOUSE OF VALENTINIAN; 367–75; CK514/16; AR II; 96/21, P 3.6
692 HOUSE OF VALENTINIAN; 367–78; as CK82; 98/2, P 4
693 HOUSE OF VALENTINIAN; 364–78; CK-; 96/u/s, P 4
694 MAGNUS MAXIMUS; 383–87; CK379; LG; 96/21, P 3.6
695 FLAVIUS VICTOR; 387–88; CK561; AR T; 98/2, P 4
696 VALENTINIAN II; 388–92; CK562; AR; 90/9, P 3.6
697 VALENTINIAN II; 388–92; CK562; AR P; 90/u/s, P 4
698 ARCADIUS; 388–95; as CK164; 90/5, P 3.5
699 THEODOSIUS I; 388–95; as CK163; 90/9, P 3.6
700 HOUSE OF THEODOSIUS; 383–87; as CK782; 90/u/s, P 4
701 HOUSE OF THEODOSIUS; 388–95; as CK162; 90/9, P 3.6
702 ILLEGIBLE; AS; C1st; 62/u/s, BP 4
703 ILLEGIBLE; C1st; 98/235, 1.3
704 ILLEGIBLE; AS?; C1/2nd; 73/27, M
705 ILLEGIBLE; C1/2nd; 33/u/s, C 4
706 ILLEGIBLE; C1/2nd; 90/18, P 3.6
707 ILLEGIBLE; C1/2nd?; 59/8, BP 3.2
708 ILLEGIBLE; ST/DP; C2nd; 4/u/s, C 4
709–10 ILLEGIBLE; DP?; C2nd?; 709 60/21, BP 3.2; 710 58/3, BP 3.2
711 ILLEGIBLE; AS?; C2nd?; 38/35, B 4
712 ILLEGIBLE; SEST; C2, late; 38/20, B 4
713 ILLEGIBLE; AS; C2/3rd; 60/u/s, BP 4
714 ILLEGIBLE; C3rd; 90/5, P 3.5
715–16 ILLEGIBLE; DENpl; C3rd; 715 2/7, P 3.3; 716 90/128, F736, P 3.1
717 ILLEGIBLE; C3rd?; 8/u/s, C 4
718–19 ILLEGIBLE; C3/4th; 718 62/u/s, BP 4; 719 u/s

720–2   ILLEGIBLE; C4th; 720 90/u/s, P 4; 721
         90/u/s, P 4; 722 96/21, P 3.6
723–4   ILLEGIBLE; C4th?; 723 90/5, P 3.5; 724
         98/3, P 4
725–32   ILLEGIBLE; 725 80/5, P 3.4B; 726 72/48,
         M; 727 72/48, M; 728 80/3, P 3.5; 729
         49/119, BP 3.1; 730 98/212, 1.2; 731 98/2,
         P 4; 732 98/178, 1.3
733   ILLEGIBLE AE; 98/2, P 4
734   OBVERSE COIN MOULD; AS; 140+; as
         1234b; 47/17, C 3.1

The small finds

by Quita Mould, with contributions by Graham Webster and Glenys Lloyd-Morgan

Summary

by Quita Mould

Introduction

This summary of the small finds recovered from the Webster excavations in *insula* 5 is based on a catalogue of small finds compiled by Graham Webster. These items were selected as being of intrinsic interest during the 31 years of excavation and were drawn by Diana Bonakis in a continuing programme of illustration during that time. For this report the illustrations and catalogue have been arranged by functional category and the individual descriptions updated by the author in the light of radiography and conservation. The latter was carried out by the Conservation Section of the Ancient Monuments Laboratory. Details of the items of religious significance have been provided by Glenys Lloyd-Morgan.

The summary incorporates information gained from a rapid appraisal of all the small finds based on the original small finds notebooks, which contain preliminary identifications of the objects made when they were first recovered, together with radiographs and conservation records, where available. On the basis of this assessment it was decided to report fully on small finds from period WR 3.1 in the *macellum* and from the portico pits of P 3.1 and P 3.2, and these reports follow this general summary. It was hoped that examination of these two groups would establish whether the small finds had been used and discarded in or near the *macellum*, or whether they derived from a wider pattern of use and loss.

The term bone is used to describe items of bone, antler or ivory; no individual material identification has been carried out.

Limitations of the summary

The small finds register for the excavations contains 6366 individual entries and the 303 objects illustrated here may not necessarily be a true reflection of the range and proportions of the items recovered, however, they do provide some idea of the variety and quality of the material found. In the current programme of work it has not been possible for all the small finds to be examined, and, until the total assemblage has been scanned, no valid quantification nor distributions can be attempted. The work which has been undertaken, however, leaves no doubt that additional categories of object will be identified when the total assemblage is examined. The necessary analysis must follow at a later date when resources allow. The scope of the following report is, therefore, limited.

Military equipment (Figs 4.6–7, 1–31)

The tip of a spearhead (Fig 4.6, 1) and an arrowhead (Fig 4.6, 2) along with a number of military fittings such as broken fastenings, hinge plates, buckles and studs, were recovered. Mike Bishop has drawn attention to the likely presence of the military in the towns of Roman Britain during the second and third centuries (Bishop 1989, 26) and while some of the fragmentary remains of military fittings, like those for *lorica segmentata* (Fig 4.6, 3–6), are residual survivors from earlier activity, others such as the fragment of scrolled fitting (Fig 4.6, 18) are comparable with military fittings from the German and Raetian frontiers and can be added to those already cited by Bishop (*ibid*). Vaned arrowheads with long sockets have been found in third-century contexts at Corbridge and Caerleon (Bishop and Coulston 1993, 139), however, the possibility exists that the arrowhead (Fig 4.6, 2) is post-Roman as an intrusive sherd of pottery was found in the same context. Later military activity in the fourth century may be suggested by the Dominate buckle (Fig 4.6, 12) of cast leaded brass, comparable with one from Catterick (Bishop and Coulston 1993, fig 126, 2), although these may have been part of the military style regalia (*cingulum militiae*) worn by civil servants at that time. A copper alloy nail cleaner (Fig 4.11, 115), found in an early fourth-century context, bears a resemblance to the 'Tortworth' type strap ends used on narrow belts of late Roman date, although lacking the opposing cusps or swellings which are commonly found at the neck of the type. A number of other objects such as the crescentic fitting (Fig 4.7, 20) comparable with an unstratified one from Richborough (Cunliffe 1968, pl XLV111, 223, 105) and another from Gorhambury found in a fourth-century context (Neal *et al* 1990, fig 125, 171), together with the phallic and dolphin-shaped studs (Fig 4.7, 22–3), occur in military contexts at other sites and are likely to have a military association.

Personal decorative items (Figs 4.7–10, 32–111)

Brooches, intaglios, and glass beads are discussed elsewhere. Fragments possibly from brooches (Fig 4.29, 297–301), including wire probably from brooch springs, featured amongst the scrap items recovered.

Ear-rings of copper alloy (Fig 4.7, 37) and finger-rings of silver, jet, and copper alloy were found.

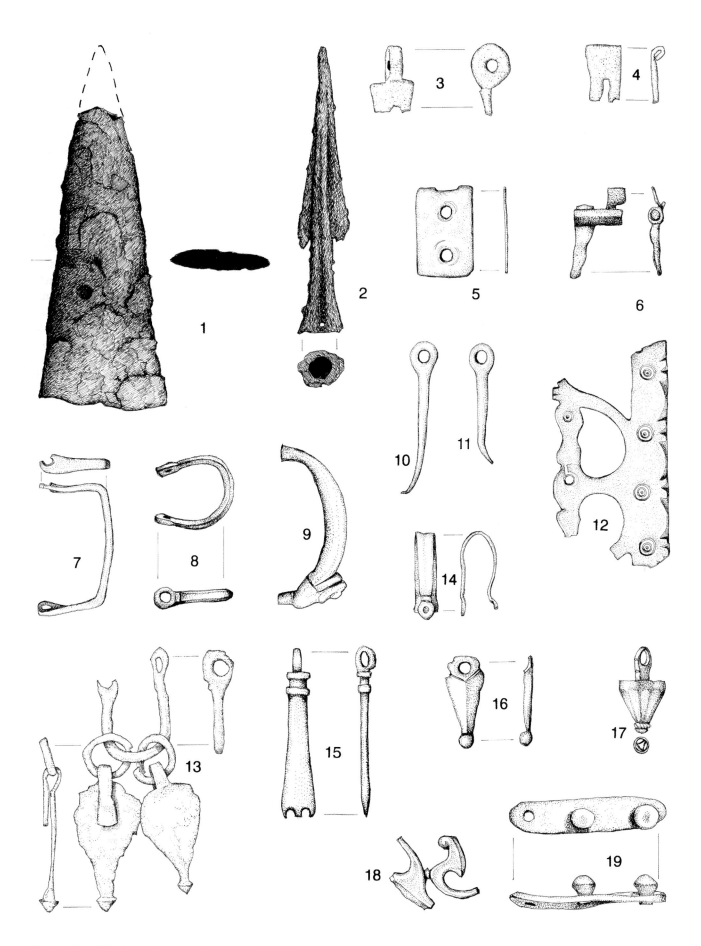

Fig 4.6 Small finds: military equipment; scale 1:1

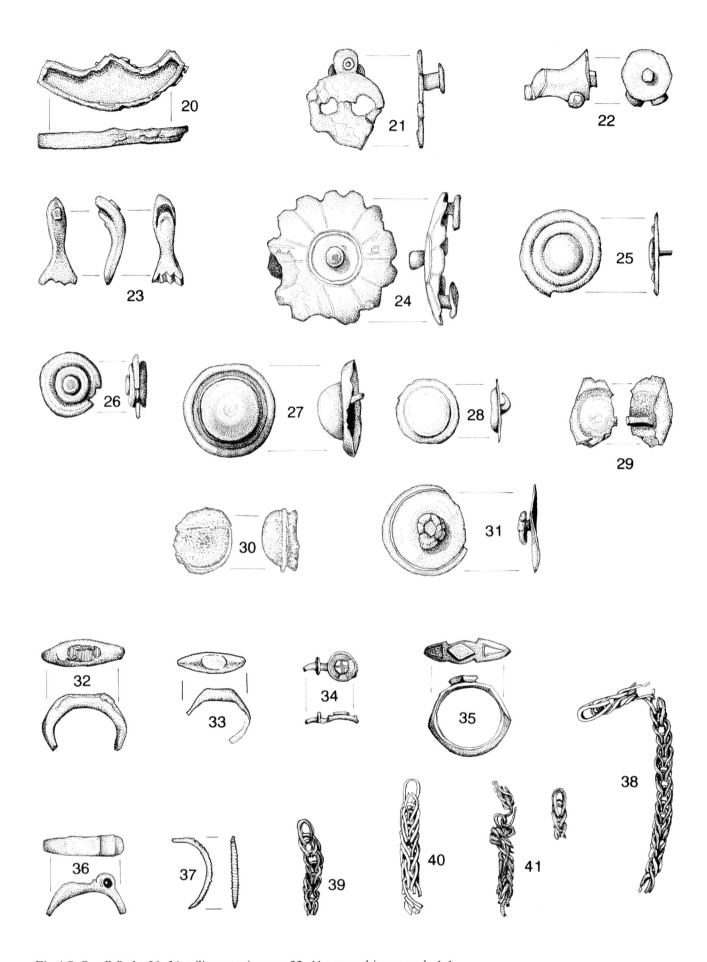

Fig 4.7 Small finds: 20–31 military equipment, 32–41 personal items; scale 1:1

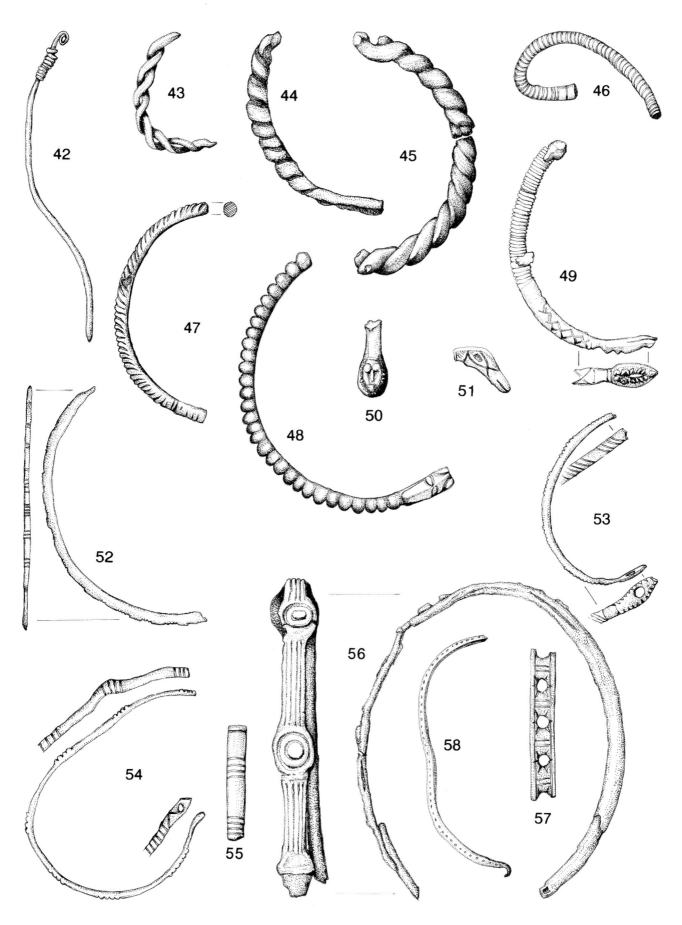

Fig 4.8 Small finds: bracelets; scale 1:1

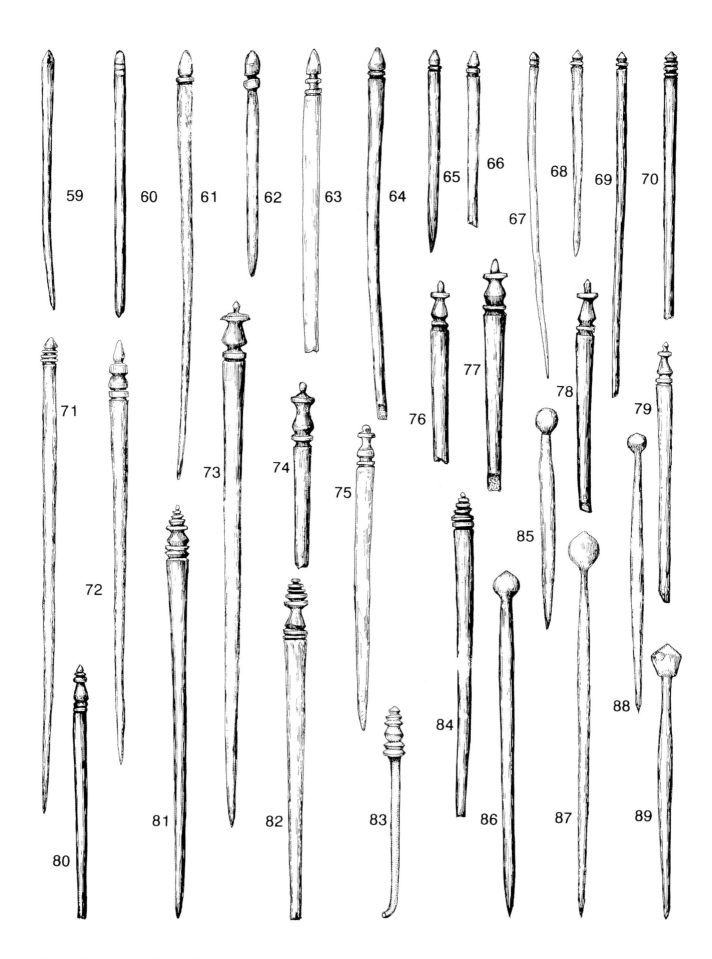

Fig 4.9 Small finds: pins; scale 1:1

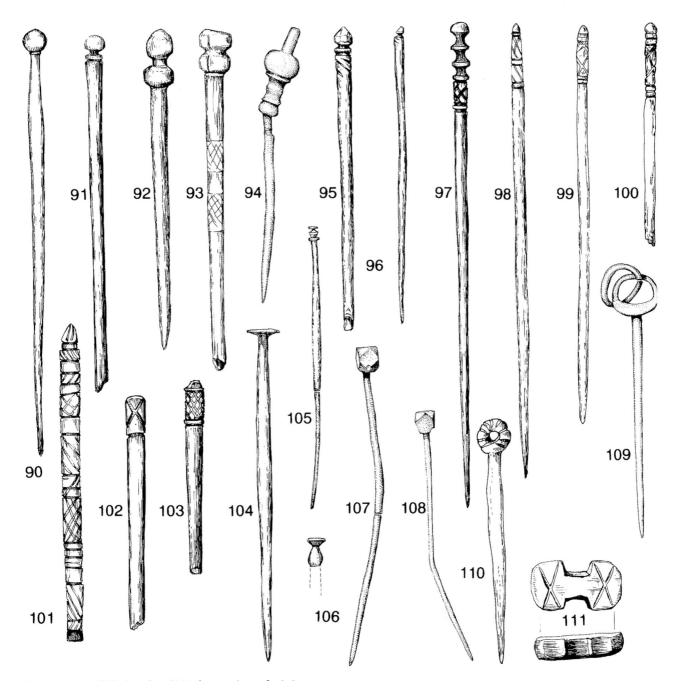

Fig 4.10 Small finds: pins (111 fastener); scale 1:1

Finger-rings of copper alloy included examples with oval bezels filled with enamel (Fig 4.7, 32–3), the shape of the hoop putting them within Henig's type III (1974a, 47, fig 1.55–6) dated to the second half of the first and the early-second century. The ring with lozenge-shaped raised bezel and faceted shoulders (Fig 4.7, 35) is of type VIII, characteristic of the third century (*ibid*, 49). An example with a round bezel with elaborate enamelled decoration and decorative moulding on the shoulder (Fig 4.7, 34) is comparable with a ring from Colchester (Crummy 1983, no 1781). A fragment of ring (Fig 4.7, 36) is most unusual in being described as having a stone set horizontally in one side of the hoop, regrettably it has not been examined by the author. Lengths of copper alloy double loop-in-loop chain were used for a variety of jewellery (Fig 4.7,

38–41), and also for other purposes such as suspending scale pans. Beads of glass and jet were common, and an emerald and lapis lazuli were also recorded.

Copper alloy and shale bracelets were commonly found. The cable-twisted bracelets (Fig 4.8, 43–45) are the most common Roman form. The single strand with adjustable fastening (Fig 4.8, 42) is a common form of late-Roman date. The ribbed bracelets (Fig 4.8, 46–47) imitate cable twisting. The heavily ribbed bracelet (Fig 4.8, 48) is beautifully executed in the celtic tradition with a horse head terminal. Bracelets with snakes head terminals were popular during the late third and fourth century, however, the illustrated examples (Fig 4.8, 49–50) are moulded with a flat underside comparable with the silver examples from Castlethorpe believed to date no later than the mid-second century (Cool 1979, 168).

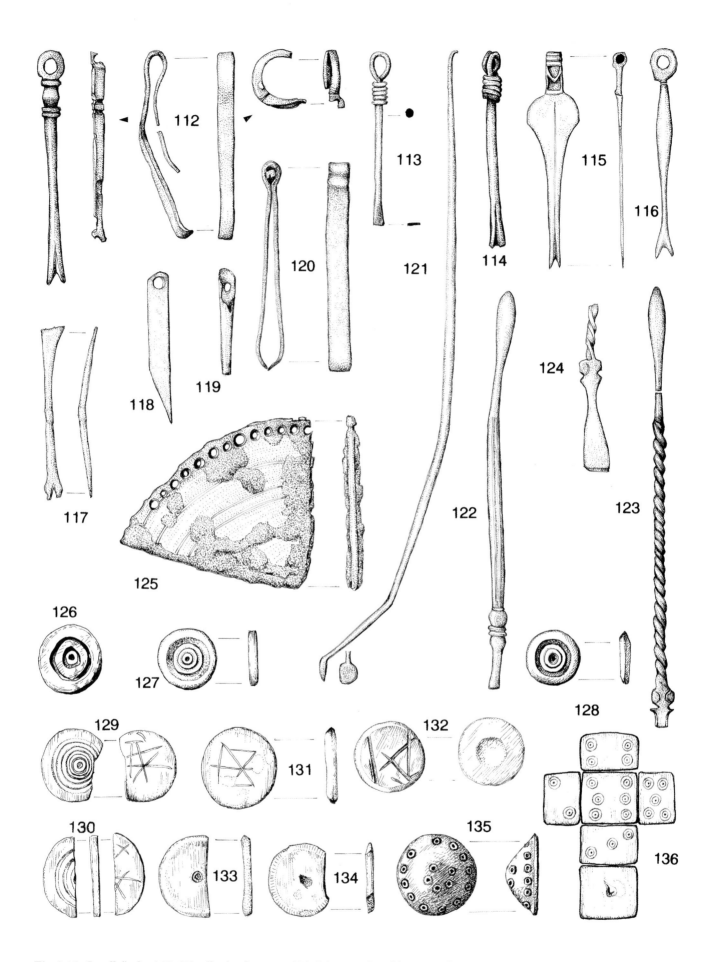

Fig 4.11 Small finds: 112–25 toilet implements, 126–36 recreational items; scale 1:1

The cable-twisted bracelet comprising strands of copper alloy and iron is less common, an example from Colchester, associated with early second-century pottery (May 1930, 276) had a coin of Nero threaded on it.

The fourth-century light bangles (Fig 4.8, 52–5, 57–8) included crenellated bracelets decorated with alternating panels of plain and incised linear decoration (Fig 4.8, 52–4). The ornament with one half decorated with roundels, the other plain, is of unusual form (Fig 4.8, 56) and may not be a bracelet.

A large number of hair pins were found, chiefly in bone with some copper alloy (Figs 4.9, 83, 4.10, 107–9), and jet. A number of the bone pins had been repointed being sufficiently prized to be mended for reuse. Pin types represented include Crummy (1983, 19–25) type 1 with a plain head (Fig 4.9, 59) and type 2 with transverse grooves beneath a conical head (Fig 4.9, 60–7) which have a proposed terminal date of c AD 200 (ibid, 21). In a number of examples the pin head is more pronounced and the grooves deepen to produce distinct reels of type 5 (Fig 4.9, 68–72) of fourth-century date. The faceted shank of this type is, however, missing. A variant with a distinctive finial knop and baluster moulding between reels (Fig 4.9, 73–82) can be paralleled at Fishbourne from period 3 occupation c AD 100–280 (Cunliffe 1971, fig 68.21). Some pins were further ornamented at the top of the stem by oblique incised grooves (Fig 4.10, 95–6), and this is taken further by adding a panel or panels of incised lattice decoration (Fig 4.10, 93, 97–103), taken to extreme by no 101.

Spherical-headed pins of type 3 (Fig 4.9, 85–9), flat-headed pins with bead and reel decoration below (Fig 4.10, 104–6) of type 6 (Crummy 1983, 24–5), and faceted, cuboid-headed copper alloy pins (Fig 4.10, 107–8) of type 4 are of third and fourth-century date.

The copper alloy projecting ring-headed pin (Fig 4.10, 109) articulates with a ring suggesting it to be a dress fastening pin, one of a pair originally joined by a chain (Cool 1990, 165, group 17). The crude example in bone (Fig 4.10, 110) which has been repointed appears to be a hair pin.

Pig fibula pins (Fig 4.16, 169) regarded as dress fastening pins have a long history which can be traced back to the pre-Roman Iron Age. The possibility exists that they are for textile working, and they are discussed under this heading below.

Toilet implements (Fig 4.11, 112–125)

Toilet implements were common finds and included mirror fragments (Fig 4.11, 125), a strigil, nail cleaners (Fig 4.11, 113–118), tweezers (Fig 4.11, 120), cosmetic spoons (Fig 4.11, 121) and probes (Fig 4.11, 122–4), polished stone mixing palettes, and bone hair combs. A chatelaine was found comprising tweezers and nail cleaners attached to a suspension loop (Fig 4.11, 112). One object (Fig 4.11, 119) may be a toilet implement, the stem is not broken but is bevelled into a blunt tip, possibly the result of reuse of a broken needle for textile working. It resembles a medieval or post-medieval lace tag and its occurrence in an uppermost layer of late-Roman date makes this a possibility. The long-handled toilet spoon (Fig 4.11, 121) was used to extract cosmetics from long-necked flasks; Merrifield (1965, 188) has suggested they may have been used to push back the nail cuticles but the length of handle would make it rather unwieldy. The bone spatulas (Fig 4.22, 231–4) may have been used as cosmetic spoons or surgeon's curettes. The spoon-probes (cyathiscomeles) (Fig 4.11, 122–124) may have had a medical rather than a purely cosmetic function. A broken oculist's stamp (Fig 4.30) was found in the P 3.1 pit F672 in the portico, indicating the preparation and likely sale of eye ointments (collyria).

The blades (Fig 4.20, 209–210) with ring terminals and decorated bone-handle plates, probably used as razors, are types found in first and early second-century contexts in Britain and Germany (Manning 1985, 111–2).

Recreational objects (Fig 4.11, 126–136)

Leisure activities are represented by a stone gaming board, bone dice (Fig 4.11, 136) and gaming counters of bone (Fig 4.11, 126–135), stone and glass. Bone gaming counters of Crummy's (1983, 91) type 1 plain (Fig 4.11, 131–3), type 2 with concentric grooves (Fig 4.11, 126–130), frequently with graffito on one face (Fig 4.11, 129–132), and type 4 with a notched rim (Fig 4.11, 134), were recovered. While convex counters like Fig 4.11, 135 with ring and dot decoration are known from late Roman contexts, they are more frequently post-Roman in date (MacGregor 1985, 133). A 'buzz-bone' (Fig 4.16.174) has been grouped with the textile working equipment below.

Items of religious significance (Fig 4.12, 137–141)

A small portable lead shrine containing a figurine of Venus (Fig 4.31) is comparable with another found in a barrack block at Wallsend Roman Fort (Segedunum) which contained a male figure, likely to be Mercury, and is dated to the fourth century (Allason-Jones 1984, 231–2). The fragments of broken pipeclay figurines (Fig 4.12, 137–40) come from household shrines. They are from the Allier region and are of late first and second-century date occurring residually in later contexts. Copper alloy bells which may have been used in religious ceremony were also found. Amulets recovered included a carved rams horn of Baltic amber and pierced animal teeth (Fig 4.12, 141).

Writing equipment (Fig 4.13, 142–152)

Writing equipment in the form of seal boxes with decorated lids (Fig 4.31, 149–152) and a large quantity of

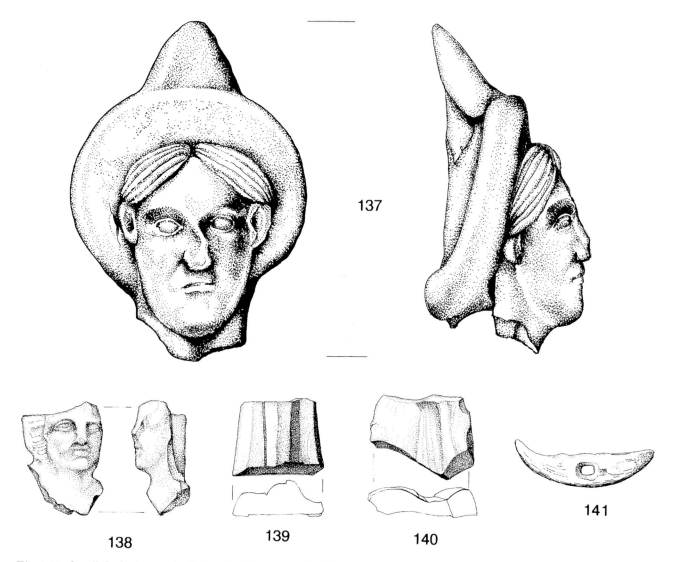

Fig 4.12 Small finds: items of religious significance; scale 1:1

styli were found. The styli were made in iron (Fig 4.13, 142–146), copper alloy (Fig 4.13, 147) and bone (Fig 4.13, 148). The iron styli varied from plain examples (Fig 4.13, 142) of Manning type 1 (1985, 85) to those with the stems decorated with mouldings (Fig 4.13, 146) or bands of non-ferrous metal inlay (Fig 4.13, 145) of Manning's type 4 (*ibid*).

Weights and measures (Fig 4.13, 153–154)

Lead (Fig 4.13, 153–54) and copper alloy weights with a lead core were recovered, and the broken arm from a steelyard was also recognised. It has been suggested that a length of bone and a copper alloy strip (Fig 4.29, 291) which display what appear to be a series of graduated marks may be tallies, however, tallies are more likely to have been made in wood which is easily carved. The copper alloy strip is more likely to be an offcut; the inscribed marks being simple tool marks. The bone tally may be broken from a comb side plate, the nicks being the result of cutting the individual teeth; unfortunately this item has not been examined by the author. Graffiti have been reported on three bone counters from the

excavations over the years (Wright 1964, 179, no 9; *ibid* 1968, 210, nos 32 and 34).

Craft tools (Figs 4.15–16, 155–174)

A relatively small collection of craft tools was recognised including tools for working in wood, metal, and possibly stone, leather, and textiles. Chisels, punches (Fig 4.15, 155), awls (Fig 4.15, 158), a possible gouge (Fig 4.15, 157), and a scraper (Fig 4.15, 159) are illustrated; of note is the relatively rare find of the saw tooth-setting file (Fig 4.15, 156).

Crucibles used for melting silver and copper alloy, along with scrap metal and the debris from such metal-working were recovered. Offcuts and trimmings of copper alloy sheet (Fig 4.29, 286–7, 289, 291) and what appear to be miscastings (Fig 4.29, 296) occurred, along with items likely to be scrap awaiting recycling (Fig 4.29, 285, 288 etc). A partly-made copper alloy spoon and partly-made wire have been recognised suggesting that spoons and possibly jewellery were made in the town, along with a copper alloy domed-headed nail or rivet (Fig 4.26, 263) still attached to the shank by

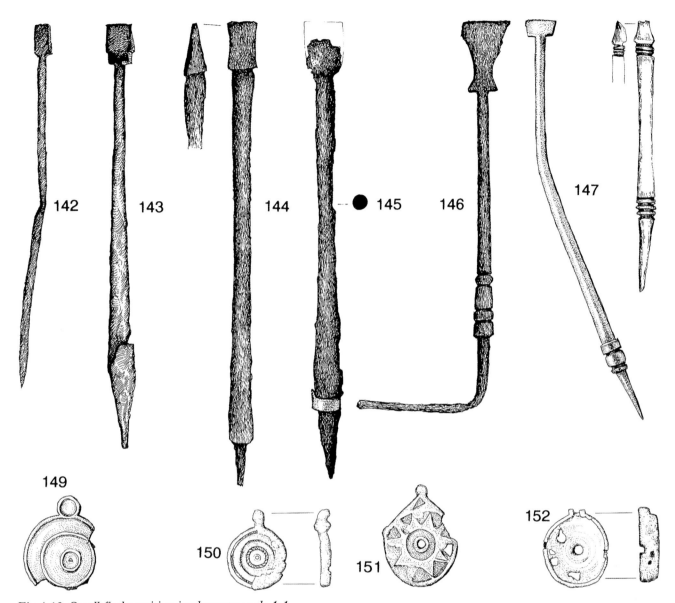

Fig 4.13 Small finds: writing implements; scale 1:1

which it was gripped during its manufacture, the impression of the jaws of the pliers by which it was held being clearly visible. A partly-made bone spoon along with probable bone handle and hinge unit rough-outs (Fig 4.25, 247) and sawn antler tines indicate a local bone and antler working industry. Small broken worked bone fragments (Fig 4.29, 302–3) recovered probably represent pieces broken or rejected during the manufacturing process. The more unusual shaped knives (eg Fig 4.20, 212) and the many whetstones may have been used in the working of bone and antler.

The presence and significance of the coin mould is discussed elsewhere (Brickstock and Casey, this volume).

Textile working is well represented (Fig 4.16, 160–74). A selection of needles of copper alloy and bone were found of Crummy's types 1, 2 and 3 (1983, 65–7). Types 1 (Fig 4.16, 160–3) and 2 (Fig 4.16, 164–6) were current throughout the Roman period, type 3 of copper alloy with the eye set within a groove (Fig 4.16, 167) appears to be a later Roman type. A tapering fragment of rolled sheet with a pierced head (Fig 4.11, 119) may represent another needle type with a flattened head found at South Shields (Allason-Jones and Miket 1984, 3.495, where others from Richborough and earlier excavations at Wroxeter are quoted). Similarly, there is nothing to prevent the crude 'pig fibula' pin (Fig 4.16, 169) from being used as a needle or a knitting pin rather than the dress pin which is often suggested (MacGregor 1985, 121–2).

Spindle whorls of pottery (Fig 4.16, 170), stone (Fig 4.16, 171), and possibly lead were found. The illustrated centrally-pierced lead weight (Fig 4.14, 153) could equally well be a spindle whorl. Bone weaving tablets of triangular (Fig 4.16, 173) and rectangular shape (Fig 4.16, 172) were used in sets for weaving braid (for a description of their use and a gazetteer see Wild 1970, 73–4, 140–1). The bone toggle (Fig 4.16, 174), a long bone with a central circular perforation, is of a type variously interpreted as a bobbin for winding yarn or possibly a toy 'buzz bone' (MacGregor 1985, 102–3, fig 59). These are becoming increasingly common finds on military sites, several being found on sites along Hadrian's Wall (Casey *et al* 1993, 204 for discussion and parallels).

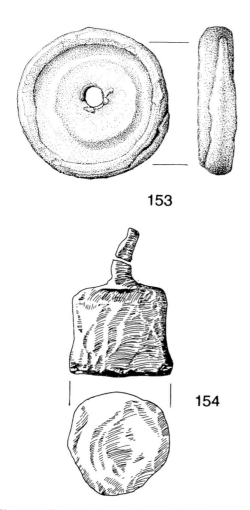

153

154

Fig 4.14 Small finds: weights; scale 1:1

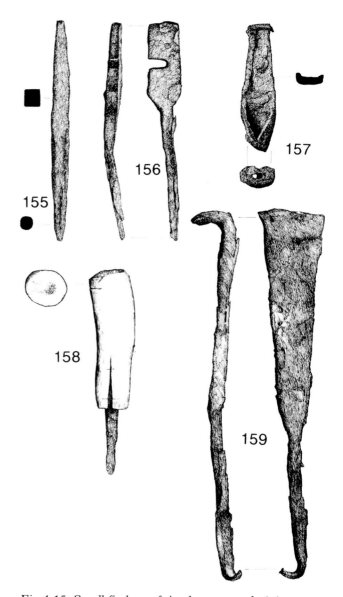

Fig 4.15 Small finds: craft implements; scale 1:1

Agricultural tools (Fig 4.17, 175–179)

Agricultural tools recognised include a possible plough ard tip, spade shoes, sickle, and a rake tooth (Fig 4.17, 177) from a hay-rake. A socketed hoe (Fig 4.17, 175) was found and it is likely that the fragmentary blade (Fig 4.17, 176) is also a hoe. Shears (Fig 4.17, 178) served a general purpose function like scissors and could have been used in the manufacture of textiles amongst other things (see above).

The forked implement (Fig 4.17, 179) is an unusual find. Forked objects of smaller size have been found at Segontium (Casey *et al* 1993, fig 10.17, 351) and recovered recently at Stanwick, Northants (pers comm Angela Wardle). The *vallus*, a harvesting machine described by Pliny and Palladius and depicted on a number of Gallo-Roman monumental stones (Rees 1981, 25) is known to have had a number of teeth which stripped the ears of corn from the stalk. The object is sufficiently robust to have performed such a function. The *vallus* was used on the large estates in Gaul, however, and so far there is no evidence that it was used in Britain.

Transport (Fig 4.18, 180–184)

Transport is attested by cart fittings, bridle fittings and hipposandals. The spatulate-headed linchpin (Fig 4.18,

183) is unusual in having the head loop curling upward to form the ring rather than simply turned over. Bridle fittings include a crudely perforated piece of bone or antler (Fig 4.18, 184) which may be a broken cheek piece for a leather bit, comparable with examples from Colchester (Crummy 1983, 105–6). The hipposandals (Fig 4.18, 180–82) were probably used as temporary horseshoes (for a discussion of their function see Manning 1985, 63). The vast majority come from towns whose metalled roads would cause excessive wear to the hooves unless some protection was given. Hipposandals of type 2 (Fig 4.18, 180–81) are the most commonly found in Britain, type 4 (Fig 4.18, 182) with rings attached to the wings less common.

Locks and keys (Fig 4.19, 185–206)

Lock furniture was well represented including lock plates and cases of copper alloy (Fig 4.19, 185) and iron (Fig 4.19, 186) and pieces from locking mechanisms (Fig 4.19, 187–9). The copper alloy lock plate (Fig 4.19,

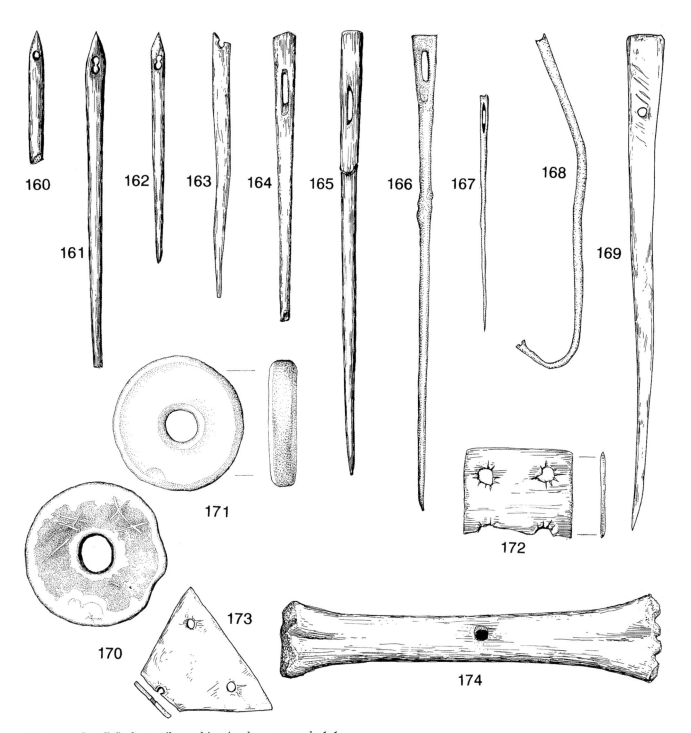

Fig 4.16 Small finds: textile working implements; scale 1:1

195) fronted a mechanism opening with a tumbler-lock slide-key. To these should be added the shackle with an integral lock (Fig 4.19, 190), more commonly shackles were closed with a padlock and chain.

A wide range of iron keys for opening padlocks (Fig 4.19, 205), tumbler (Fig 4.19, 191–203), and lever locks was found (Fig 4.19, 204). The simple key form (Fig 4.19, 193) was commonly made in wood, as seen at Vindolanda, or bone (Allason Jones and Miket 1984, 38, fig 2.22). Tumbler-lock lift-keys included T-shaped lift-keys (Fig 4.19, 191–2), the latter with three teeth of the original four remaining similar to another from Fishbourne (Cunliffe 1971, II, 131, fig

58.26), and a variety of L-shaped lift keys (Fig 4.19, 194–200) with a maximum of four teeth. The handles ranged from the plain (Fig 4.19, 198–9) to those with decorated handles and ring terminals (Fig 4.19, 194–6). Slide-keys (Fig 4.19, 201–3) are represented by examples with straight bits (Manning 1985 type 2, 93, fig 25.7). The lever-lock key (Fig 4.19, 204) opened the most complex locking mechanism. The trilobate copper alloy key handle (Fig 4.19, 206) is commonly found in military contexts and dated to post AD 150 (Fabricus 1894 et seq, 8, Taf 12, 51. Copper alloy finger rings with integral keys for small casket locks were also noted.

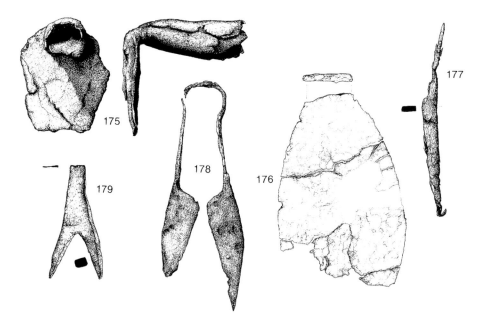

Fig 4.17 Small finds: agricultural implements; scale 1:2

Domestic utensils (Figs 4.20–4.23, 207–240)

A range of objects associated with food preparation, serving and storage was recovered.

Querns and stone rubbers to grind grain were found along with a variety of knives and whetstones to sharpen them. A quern of millstone grit came from the northeast of England, the majority of the whetstones which have been identified are made from stone which could be collected locally.

The cleaver (Fig 4.20, 207) was probably used to butcher meat. The wooden handle with its copper alloy hilt plate, possible leather washer and iron end plate suggests that the knife (Fig 4.20, 208) may be of post-Roman date, although it was not found associated with any other later material. If Roman, the narrow blade is likely to have had a specific function as had the razors (Fig 4.20, 209–10) mentioned earlier. The knives with centrally-placed tangs (Fig 4.20, 213–8) are common Roman forms likely to represent general purpose knives.

A number of bone (Fig 4.21, 220–5) and copper alloy handles (Fig 4.21, 226–8) were recovered several of which are likely to have been used on knives (Fig 4.21, 220–2, 224, 226). The ornate terminal (Fig 4.21, 227) may be a handle or a furniture finial, the cylinder (Fig 4.21, 228) with incised decoration may also be a handle fragment comparable with the larger lead-filled example from Caister-on-Sea (Darling and Gurney 1993, fig 99.698).

Spoons of copper alloy and bone were found, and there is some evidence to suggest that they were being manufactured in the town. Round-bowled spoons like the decorated one illustrated (Fig 4.22, 229) date from the later first and earlier second century. The shape of the oval bowl of the spoon with a decorated handle (Fig 4.22, 230) is similar to that on spoons from Caister-on-Sea (Darling and Gurney 1993, 92, fig

64.342–5), a common fourth-century type. Bone spatulas with pointed handles (Fig 4.22, 231–4) made from *fibula*, probably pig, are likely to have been used as simple spoons or possibly surgeons' currettes or sounds, they appear a little too wide to be used to extract and mix cosmetics. They are comparable with examples from the Roman fort at South Shields (Allason-Jones 1984, 2.111, 2.112), the grooved example (Fig 4.22, 234) being similar to one from grave 25 at Butt Road, Colchester, dated between *c* AD 320 and *c* AD 450 (Crummy 1983, 172, fig 210.4756).

A fragment of shale tray was noted. Shale trays rectangular or circular in shape usually dating to the late first and early second century were probably used as trenchers on which food was cut (Crummy 1983, 69). Copper alloy vessels are attested by a flagon lid and handle (Fig 4.23, 235) and small fragments of rim and handle (Fig 4.23, 236). The discs of copper alloy (Fig 4.23, 237), pot and stone are likely to be simple lids.

Pottery lamps and lamp holders of pottery, iron, copper alloy (Fig 4.23, 238) and lead were found. The spirally-twisted iron handle (Fig 4.23, 240) may come from a lamp or pot hanger, the terminal is broken but appears comparable with a flesh hook from Tokenhouse Yard, London (Manning 1985, 38, pl 51). The large iron hook (Fig 4.23, 239) may also be a pot hanger but its weight suggests a likely structural function.

Furniture (Figs 4.24–4.27, 241–266, 269–272)

A range of furniture fittings was recovered. The copper alloy finial probably comes from a folding stool (Fig 4.24, 241). An unusual bone hinge (Fig 4.24, 242) and the more commonly found cylindrical hinge units (Figs 4.24, 243–5, 4.25, 246–7) are from boxes or furniture doors. Iron loop hinges (Fig 4.27, 269–70) combining a pierced strap and a split spiked loop and hasp strap (Fig 4.27, 271) were used on the lids of chests or large

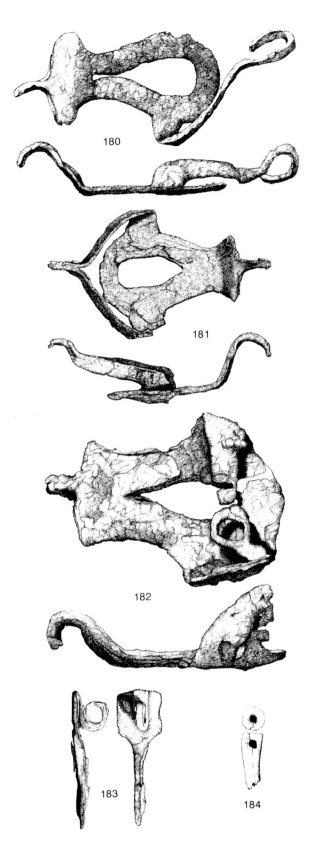

Fig 4.18 Small finds: transport; 1:3

boxes, the hinge strap with its hasp (Fig 4.25, 248) and fragments of decorative strapping of copper alloy (Fig 4.25, 249–50) were used on smaller examples. Furniture handles were held by small copper alloy split-spiked loops (Fig 4.25, 251–3). A handle (Fig 4.25, 254) with

bird beak terminal is from furniture, as it appears too large to be a carrying handle from a helmet. A variety of dome-headed nails (Fig 4.26, 258–63) and flat-headed studs (Fig 4.26, 264–6) of copper alloy and bone were used on domestic fittings and upholstery. The crudely executed lion head stud (Fig 4.26, 257) comes from a box. The lozenge-shaped bone inlay (Fig 4.25, 255–6) were used to decorate boxes along with inlay of mother of pearl. The position of the ring and dot decoration on the edge of one inlay (Fig 4.25, 255) is unexpected, suggesting it was used on the outer edge.

Structural fittings (Figs 4.27, 267; 4.28, 273–284)

Building materials recovered included stone veneers, painted plaster and mouldings, tesserae, and structural ironwork. Structural ironwork included hinge straps from drop hinges (Fig 4.27, 267) used on doors, and loop hinges (Fig 4.27, 268) used on vertically-mounted shutters or chests (Manning 1985, 126).

The large figure-of-eight chain links (Fig 4.28, 274) could have had a variety of functions, as would the ring articulating with a broken split-spiked loop (Fig 4.28, 275) and the ring-headed pins (Fig 4.28, 276–7) found. Cramps (Fig 4.28, 281) for wood, wallhooks (Fig 4.28, 278–9) and a large quantity of timber nails (Fig 4.28, 282–3) were also recovered.

Catalogue of the illustrated small finds

by Quita Mould and Graham Webster,
with a contribution by Glenys Lloyd-Morgan

Military equipment (Figs 4.6–4.7)

1   Iron tip of a spearhead; 49/+, BP 4 (SF 976, AML 787563)

2   Iron barbed arrowhead with pronounced midrib and round socket, possibly medieval; 60/1, F 3116, BP 4 (SF 570, AML 786298)

3   Copper alloy unusually solid ring terminal of a cuirass fastener (Ulbert 1969, Taf 34, nos 45–52); unprovenanced

4   Copper alloy small hinge fragment from a military cuirass (Ulbert 1969, Taf 34, nos 20–44); 84/137, WR 2.1 (SF 4599, AML 811134)

5   Copper alloy broken cuirass hinge plate with two rivet holes from *lorica segmentata*; 91/117, 1.3 (SF 5178, AML 830320)

6   Copper alloy hinge fragment from *lorica segmentata*; 97/25, P 3.3 (SF 3884, AML 787772)

7   Copper alloy small rectangular buckle with pierced terminals for separate pin bar; 96/21, P 3.6, KG 25 (SF 4147, AML 785858)

8   Copper alloy small semi-circular buckle (Ulbert 1969, Taf 26, nos 6–10); 82/4, BP 4 (SF 1989, AML 787704)

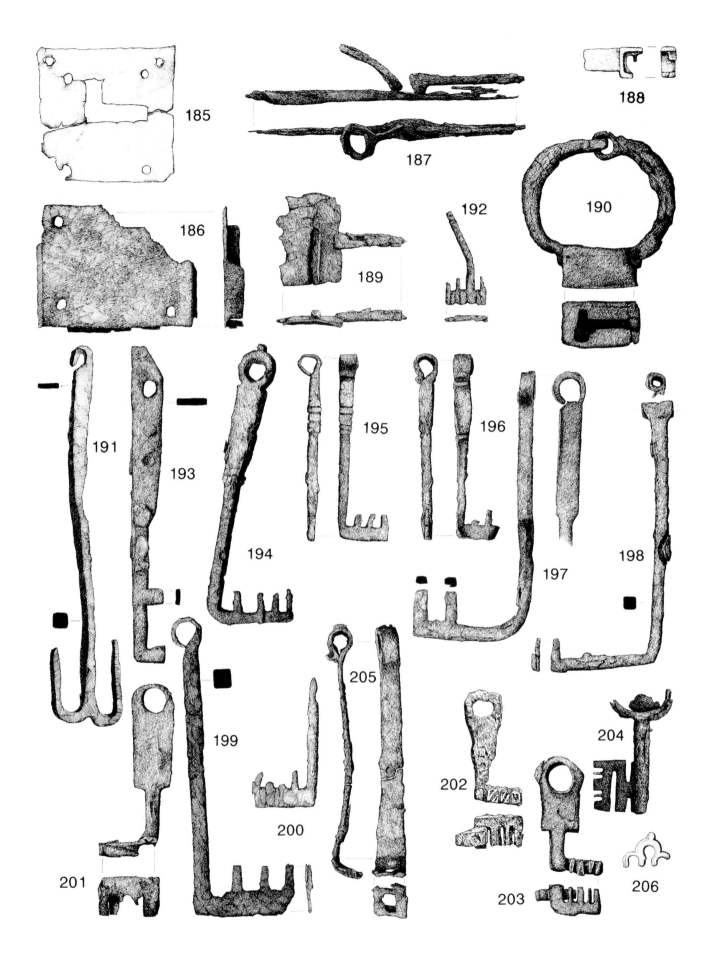

Fig 4.19 Small finds: locks and keys; scale 1:1

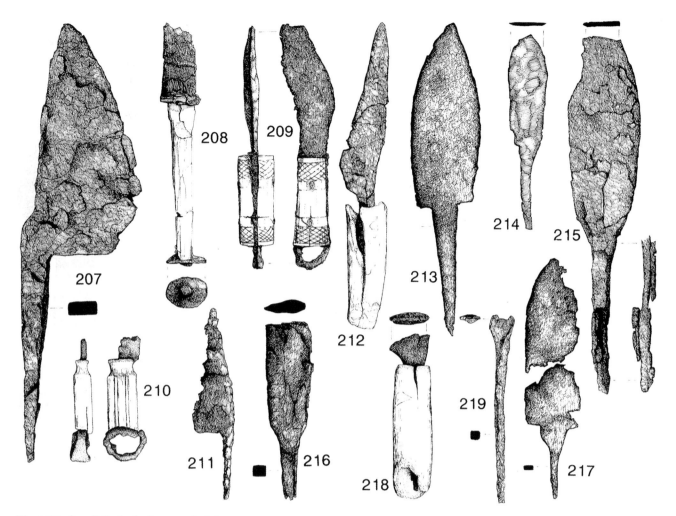

Fig 4.20 Small finds: knives; scale 1:1

9   Copper alloy buckle fragment with decoration at the junction of the frame and pin bar; 91/56, F87, WR 4 (SF 3701, AML 787780)
10   Copper alloy buckle tongue; 7/+, C 4
11   Copper alloy buckle tongue; 61/3, BP 3.2 (SF 684, AML 787687)
12   Copper alloy Dominate belt fitting with ring and dot and crude zoomorphic decoration (Bishop and Coulston 1993, fig 126.2); 90/17, P 3.6, KG 25 (SF 3521, AML 767034)
13   Copper alloy two pendants with knobbed finials, attached by rings to a U-shaped suspension loop with pierced terminals (Ulbert 1969, Taf 26, nos 6–10 and Taf 36, nos 9–10); 97/148, P 2.1 (SF 5529, AML 835975)
14   Copper alloy clip with pierced terminal, probably military (Ulbert 1969, Taf 35, nos 1 and 2); 96/21, P 3.6, KG 25 (SF 3717, AML 787789)
15   Copper alloy apron mount with pair of moulded collars at the neck; 38/21, BP 4 (SF 1007, AML 787047)
16   Copper alloy pierced fitting with a knobbed terminal, possibly military; 22/54, BP 3.1 (SF 1093, AML 801884)

17   Copper alloy cast cone-shaped pendant or fastener with faceted sides, probably military; 91/17, WR 4 (SF 3035, AML 786887)
18   Copper alloy scrolled mount fragment (Oldenstein 1976, Taf 6); 80/6, P 4 (SF 1660, AML 725723)
19   Copper alloy strip with two of the three dome-headed rivets remaining, possibly military; 90/33, P 3.6, KG 25 (SF 3882, AML 787783)
20   Copper alloy lunate-shaped object, hollowed out probably for decorative inlay (Cunliffe 1968, 105, pl XLVIII.223); 33/2, C 4 (SF 303, AML 786981)
21   Copper alloy broken openwork stud; 90/84, P 3.3 (SF 4642, AML 811150)
22   Copper alloy phallic-shaped stud (Frere 1972, fig 38.103–10); 83/533, WR 2.3 (SF 4424, AML 811082)
23   Copper alloy dolphin stud (Crummy 1983, fig 122.3223); 90/9, P 3.6, KG 25 (SF 3474, AML 786839)
24   Copper alloy rosette stud with two flat-headed rivets (Bushe-Fox 1932, pl XII.39); 64/+, BP 4 (SF 1040, AML 786990)

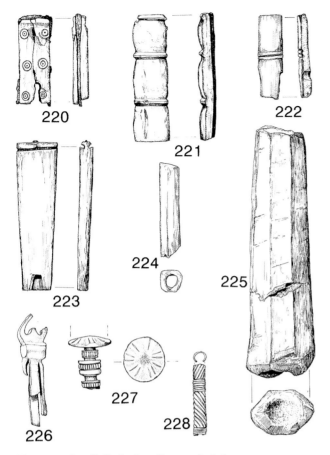

Fig 4.21 Small finds: handles; scale 1:1

25 Copper alloy circular stud with concentric decoration; 38/5, BP 4 (SF 899, AML 787042)

26 Copper alloy circular stud with concentric decoration, lead adhering to the back; 49/63, F3226, BP 3.3 (SF 1576, AML 725748)

27 Copper alloy round dome-headed stud; 91/108, 1.3 (SF 4512, AML 811112)

28 Copper alloy dome-headed stud with small flange and short curved shank (Ulbert 1969, Taf 29, nos 15–18); 81/51, C 3.2 (SF 1758, AML 786758)

29 Copper alloy stud fragment; 84/49, WR 3.2 (SF 3386, AML 760289)

30 Copper alloy domed stud head; 90/188, P 2.3 (SF 5989, AML 844190)

31 Copper alloy circular stud with a shank and washer; 87/+, WR 4 (SF 3135, AML 786784)

Finger rings, earrings, and chains (Fig 4.7)

32 Copper alloy finger ring with oval bezel containing traces of enamel; 53/4, C 2.2 (SF 776, AML 786753)

33 Copper alloy finger ring with oval bezel; 91/94, WR 2.3 (SF 3969, AML 785840)

34 Copper alloy finger ring with circular bezel with enamelled decoration comprising a blue central cross surrounded by two opaque white and one red/orange field (Stead 1980, fig 63.27); 56/18, BP 3.1 (SF 729, AML 787304)

35 Copper alloy finger ring with triangular decoration to either side of the lozenge-shaped bezel; 98/+, P 4 (SF 4304, AML 793472)

36 Copper alloy ring with a small black stone set horizontally into a projection; 83/+, WR 4 (SF 1987, AML 787188)

37 Copper alloy earring decorated with a series of shallow incised lines, Allason-Jones type 2e (Allason-Jones 1989a, 4); 91/9, WR 4 (SF 2121, AML 787744)

38 Copper alloy double loop-in loop chain; 84/49, WR 3.1 (SF 3390, AML 760290)

39 Copper alloy as 38 above; 84/49, WR 3.1 (SF 3363, AML 760285)

40 Copper alloy as 38 above; 50/+, C 4

41 Copper alloy as 38 above; 84/170, WR 2.2 (SF 3784, AML 787781)

Bracelets (Fig 4.8)

42 Copper alloy single strand wire bracelet originally with an expanding fastening; 90/97, F565, P 3.1, KG 16 (SF 4760, AML 821678)

43 Copper alloy fragment of two strand spirally-twisted cable bracelet; 90/12, P 3.6, KG 25 (SF 3098, AML 786819)

44 Copper alloy fragment of spirally-twisted cable bracelet; 90/33, P 3.6, KG 25 (SF 3867, AML 787763)

45 Copper alloy fragment of heavy two strand spirally-twisted bracelet; 91/55, WR 3.3 (SF 3525, AML 767035)

46 Copper alloy fragment of single strand bracelet grooved to resemble spiral-twisting; 65/+, B 4 (SF 1103, AML 786857)

47 Copper alloy bracelet with oblique incised decoration imitating spiral-twisting; 49/63, F3226, BP 3.3 (SF 1577, AML 786989)

48 Copper alloy cast bracelet with deeply ribbed upper face and flat back with celtic style horses head terminal; 48/1, F3194, BP 4 (SF 474, AML 787035)

49 Copper alloy bracelet with ribbed decoration and snakes head terminal; 59/+, BP 4 (SF 1024, AML 786993)

50 Copper alloy snakes head bracelet terminal with beaded border; 83/117, WR 2.3 (SF 4357, AML 793492)

51 Copper alloy decorative zoomorphic terminal, probably from a bracelet; C/3, C 3.4 (AML 786900)

52 Copper alloy crenellated bracelet with grooved lower panels (Crummy 1983, no 1659 from grave deposit *c* AD 320–450); 62/+, BP 4 (SF 880, AML 786743)

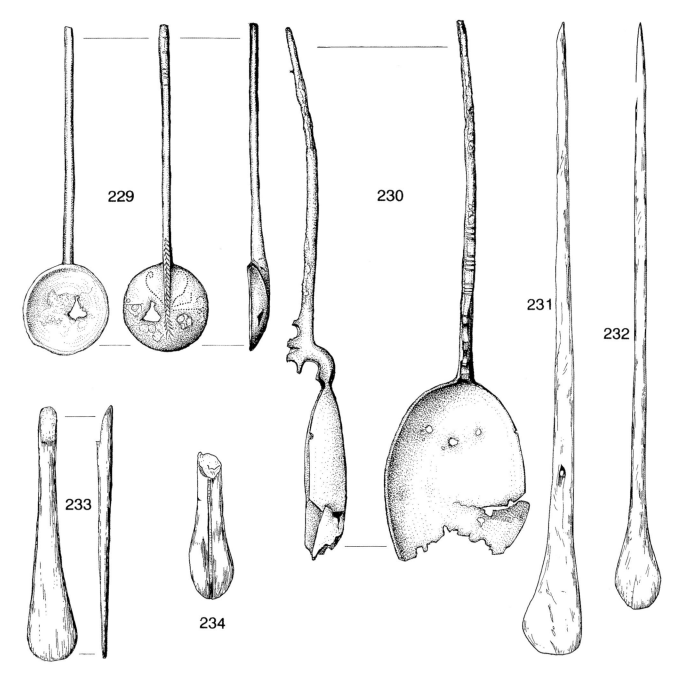

Fig 4.22 Small finds: household implements; scale 1:1

53   Copper alloy bracelet with pierced terminal, decorated with panels of oblique grooves; 31/+, C 4 (SF 270, AML 786986)

54   Copper alloy bracelet with pierced terminal, decorated with alternating plain and ridged bands; 90/+, P 4 (SF 3250, AML 786795)

55   Copper alloy strip bracelet fragment decorated with alternating plain and grooved panels; 90/16, P 3.6, KG 25 (SF 3655, AML 787792)

56   Copper alloy bracelet with one side decorated with four roundels with concentric circles and linear decoration between, the other side is plain with a round section; 90/71, P 3.3 (SF 4493, AML 811107)

57   Copper alloy strip bracelet fragment with raised edges and circular holes with six marks radiating from each, between paired grooves, probably a bracelet fragment (Blockley et al 1995, fig 435.384); 44/25 F3142, C 3.4 (SF 1297, AML 787188)

58   Copper alloy bracelet with hook and eye fastening decorated with punched dots; 90/+, P4 (SF 3660, AML 787791)

Pins (Figs 4.9–4.10)

59   Bone pin with plain, pointed head, Crummy type 1 (Crummy 1983, 20); 56/33, BP 3.1 (SF 1037, AML 786564)

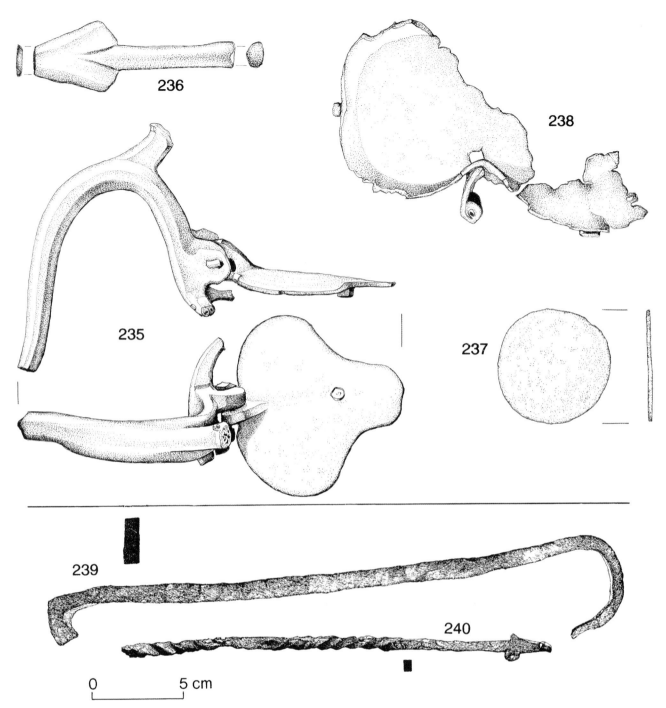

Fig 4.23 Small finds: household implements; scale 235–8, 1:1; 239–40, 1:2

60   Bone pin, tip missing, simple head with triple grooves beneath, Crummy type 2 (Crummy 1983, 21); 16/58, BP 2.3 (SF 78, AML 786593)

61   Bone pin with conical head with double groove below, type 2; 58/5, BP 3.2 (SF 656, AML 801491)

62   Bone pin, repointed, crude example as 61 above; 83/+, WR 4 (SF 2083, AML 786483)

63   Bone pin, broken stem, with triple grooves widely spaced; 86/24, WR 3.1 (SF 2194, AML 801505)

64   Bone pin, tip missing, as 61; 56/34, BP 3.1 (SF 970, AML 787383)

65   Bone pin, repointed, as 61; 25/30 BP 2.2 (SF 1100, AML 786566)

66   Bone pin, broken stem, as 61; 80/50, P 3.4B, KG 25 (SF 3567, AML 786520)

67   Bone pin, as 61; 84/49, WR 3.1 (SF 3314, AML 786487)

68   Bone pin, repointed, as 61, crisply carved; 22/+, BP 4 (SF 866, AML 801473)

69   Bone pin, tip missing, as 68; 65/28, C 3.1, KG 18 (SF 1320, AML 786631)

70   Bone pin, tip missing, quadruple grooved crisply carved; 16/31, BP 3.1, F3177, KG 19

71   Bone pin, as 70; 22/37, BP 3.2 (SF 885, AML 801475)

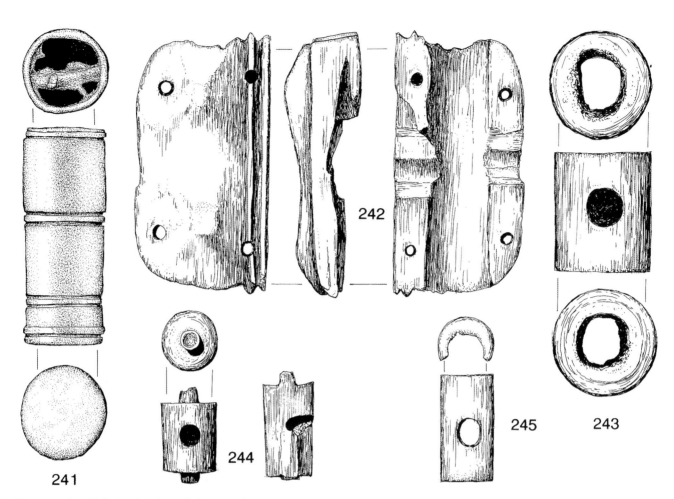

Fig 4.24 Small finds: furniture fittings; scale 1:1

72 Bone pin, quadruple grooved forming a triple reel and bead head; 63/+, C 4 (SF 1022, AML 786512)

73 Bone pin, head with bead or baluster between two reels with finial knop; 59/5, BP 3.2 (SF 598, AML 786542)

74 Bone pin, broken stem, as 73; 98/53, F714, P 3.2, KG 17 (SF 5270, AML 830249)

75 Bone pin, repointed, as 73; 22/23, BP 3.1 (SF 817, AML 787976)

76 Bone pin, broken stem, as 73; 98/145, F1017, P 3.1 KG 16 (SF 6033, AML 844454)

77 Bone pin, broken stem, as 73; 98/28, F638, P 3.2, KG 17 (SF 4948, AML 814700)

78 Bone pin, broken stem, as 73; 98/28, F638, P 3.2, KG 17 (SF 5265, AML 830248)

79 Bone pin, broken stem, as 73; 58/5, BP 3.2 (SF 637, AML 787598)

80 Bone pin, broken stem, head comprising bead between double reels with finial knop; 48/18, BP 3.1 (SF 513, AML 786604)

81 Bone pin with head with double reel, bead, four small reels and finial knop; 47/19, F4018, C 2.4 (SF 1225, AML 787330)

82 Bone pin, tip broken, as 81; 68/1, from *insula* 5 (SF 1374, AML 787346)

83 Copper alloy pin with an elaborate bead and reel moulded head and broken point, comparable with 82; 33/+, C 4 (SF 241, AML 786937)

84 Bone pin, point missing, head with five reels and finial knop; 80/59, F477, P 3.3 (SF 3879)

85 Bone pin with repointed, swollen stem and spherical head, Crummy type 3 (Crummy 1983, 21–22); 55/6, BP 3.3 (SF 852, AML 801485)

86 Bone pin as 85; 80/3, P 3.4B, KG 25 (SF 1658, AML 786477)

87 Bone pin with narrow neck as 85; 38/1, B 4 (SF 356, AML 786584)

88 Bone pin, swollen stem as 85; 38/44, B 4

89 Bone pin with swollen stem and spherical head with pointed top; 58/2, BP 3.2 (SF 806, AML 786548)

90 Bone pin, slightly swollen stem, spherical head with reel below; 22/58, BP 3.1 (SF 1047, AML 787982)

91 Bone pin, broken stem, reel and spherical bead head; 67/5, C 3.2 (SF 1153, AML 786567)

92 Bone pin, repointed, with spherical head with second sphere below separated by a short neck; 22/+, BP 4 (SF 882, AML 787978)

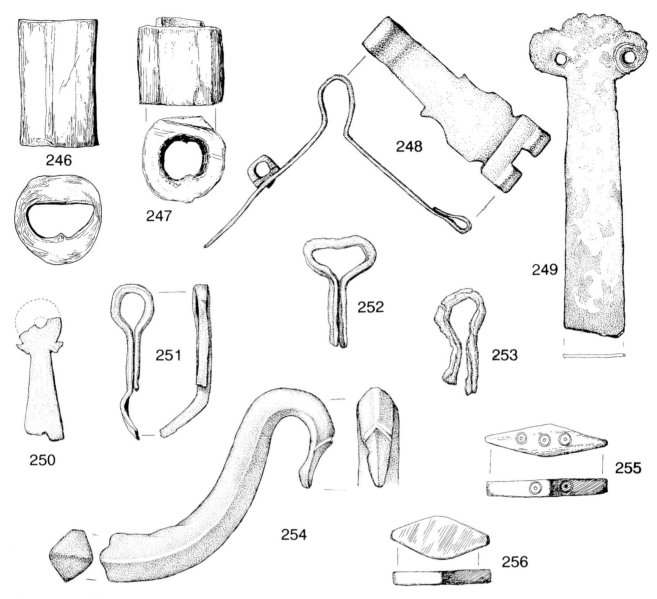

Fig 4.25 Small finds: furniture fittings; scale 1:1

93   Bone pin with double spherical head with two bands of incised lattice decoration half way down the broken stem; 87/1, WR 4 (SF 3281, AML 786513)

94   Copper alloy pin with spherical head with long finial and decorative mouldings below, possibly a decorative finial with fixing pin; 59/8, BP 3.2 (SF 713, AML 786983)

95   Bone pin, tip broken, reel and bead head with oblique grooves below; from *insula* 5 (SF 1382, AML 801496)

96   Bone pin, with small bead head with oblique grooves below; 91/20, WR 3.2 (SF 3083, AML 801507)

97   Bone pin with four well defined reels and spherical bead head, incised lattice decoration between lower reels; 88IV/3, WR 4 (SF 3823, AML 787958)

98   Bone pin with small conical head with three double grooves separated by bands of incised lattice decoration; 40/4, C 2.3 (SF 488, AML 787345)

99   Bone pin, head with two triple grooves with incised lattice decoration between; 84/49, WR 3.1 (SF 3378, AML 786508)

100   Bone pin, broken stem, as 99 above, carving better defined; 84/49, WR 3.1 (SF 3318, AML 786486)

101   Bone pin with knurled, conical head, broken stem covered by series of plain, incised lattice and obliquely grooved panels; 72/+, C 4 (SF 1285, AML 786543)

102   Bone pin, broken stem, head defined by a single groove and simple lattice decoration; 98/140, F930, P 3.2, KG 17 (SF 5889, AML 844440)

103   Bone pin, broken stem, head with lattice decoration between double grooves; 58/5, BP 3.2 (SF 646, AML 786547)

104   Bone pin, slightly swollen stem and flat, round head, Crummy type 6 (Crummy 1983, 24–5); 63/2, C 2.2 (SF 1151, AML 786602)

105   Bone pin with fine, slightly swollen stem and small reel, bead, flat reel head; 38/20, B 4 (SF 453, AML 786629)

106   Bone pin head with flat reel head and bead below remaining; F/4, WR 4

107   Copper alloy pin with faceted cuboid head, Crummy type 4, Cool group 15 (Crummy 1983, 22–3; Cool 1990, 164–5); 64/1, BP 3.3 (SF 1072, AML 787197)

108   Copper alloy pin as 107 above; 84/12, WR 4 (SF 2098, AML 787746)

109   Copper alloy pin with projecting ring head articulating with chain link, Cool group 17 (Cool 1990, 165); 90/25, P 3.4A, KG 25 (SF 3635, AML 786871)

110   Bone pin, repointed, centrally pierced circular head decorated with radiating grooves; 84/48, WR 3.1 (SF 3393, AML 786507)

Fasteners (Fig 4.10)

111   Bone toggle terminals decorated with an incised cross; 55/+, BP 4 (SF 1159, AML 787347)

Toilet implements (Fig 4.11)

112   Copper alloy chatelaine comprising two nail cleaners, simple tweezers and a broken suspension loop; 38/23, BP 4 (SF 459, AML 681674)

113   Copper alloy toilet implement with wire wound neck and a broken terminal; 90/87, P 2.3 (SF 5115, AML 830291)

114   Copper alloy nail cleaner with wire wound neck; 90/51, P 3.3 (SF 4317, AML 793476)

115   Copper alloy nail cleaner with cast, decorated neck; 17/21, C 3.3 (SF 11, AML 725760)

116   Copper alloy simple nail cleaner with bifurcated terminal; 5/15, C 2.1

117   Copper alloy implement probably a nail cleaner; 80/181, P 2.1 (SF 4835, AML 821698)

118   Copper alloy implement with pierced head and pointed terminal, probably a simple nail cleaner; 60/20, BP 3.2 (SF 950, AML 786948)

119   Copper alloy implement of rolled sheet with pierced head and tapering bevelled terminal; 90/31, P 3.6, KG 25 (SF 3833, AML 787784)

120   Copper alloy simple pair of narrow-armed tweezers; 84/49, WR 3.1 (SF 3152, AML 760273)

121   Copper alloy long-handled toilet spoon; 91/92, WR 2.3 (SF 4253, AML 793462)

122   Copper alloy medical or cosmetic probe with faceted stem, broken before the spatulate end (Cunliffe 1968, pl XLIII); 97/144, F810, P 2.1 (SF 5648, AML 836003)

123   Copper alloy medical or cosmetic probe with twisted stem broken before the spoon (Atkinson 1942, pl 50); 84/49, WR 3.1 (SF 3402, AML 786814)

124   Copper alloy flat, spatulate terminal of a cosmetic spoon with a twisted handle; 90/33, P 3.6, KG 25 (SF 3968, AML 785821)

125   Speculum; Glenys Lloyd-Morgan writes: Fragment of a Roman mirror disc with a penannular ring of countersunk holes. Only the non-reflective side has been drawn with *c* four turned concentric circles. The handle, now lost, would have had either a baluster-shaped grip, or, less commonly, an elongated loop handle. Compare the example from the cemetery at Whitchurch, Salop (Musty *et al* 1973). A not uncommon type found in Britain and other Roman provinces (Lloyd-Morgan 1981, 49–54, Group K). To date *c* 301 whole or fragmentary examples have been recorded from Europe, with a further 25, or possibly more, in British public and private collections; 90/204, F951, P 2.2 (SF 5922, AML 843157)

Recreational objects (Fig 4.11)

126   Bone counter crudely decorated with concentric circles on one face; 84/52, WR 2.3 (SF 3272, AML 786496)

127   Bone counter decorated with concentric circles on one face; E/4, B 4

128   Bone small counter with deeply incised concentric circles on one face; 90/125, P 3.3 (SF 5185, AML 830240)

129   Bone counter with concentric decoration on one face and graffito on the other; from *insula* 5 (SF 1372, AML 786558)

130   Bone half a counter, one side decorated with concentric circles, the other with graffito; 60/23, BP 4 (SF 1060)

131   Bone flat counter with graffito on one face; 98/21, P 3.3 (SF 4869, AML 814691)

132   Bone counter with graffito on one face, the other is dished; from *insula* 5 (SF 1392, AML 801499)

133   Bone half a counter with two small concentric circles at the centre; 60/22, F3116, BP 4 (SF 1033, AML 786574)

134   Bone counter with decorative markings round the edge; 16/39, BP 4 (SF 16)

135   Bone conical counter decorated with ring and dot motif; 31/+, C 4 (SF 228, AML 801480)

136   Bone die with numerals marked by double ring and dot motifs, opposite sides add up to seven; 98/101, F933, P 3.1, KG 16 (SF 5755, AML 844429)

Objects with religious significance
(Fig 4.12)

by Glenys Lloyd-Morgan

137   White pipeclay, head and neck only of a female figurine, with a headdress similar to those found on representations of the Rhineland Mother Goddesses. A central triangular section projects from just behind the headdress, and in line with the central parting, perhaps intended as part of a diadem; 86/23, WR 2.3 (SF 2169, AML 788096)

138   White pipeclay, fragment of Venus statuette with face and part of one ringlet on the right side of face and upper part of neck (Rouvier-Jeanlin 1972, type I Venus, 92, inv no 7291, and 111, no 74, inv no 28012); 22/2, BP 4 (SF 257, AML 786640)

139   Pipeclay fragment from a ?figurine. The fragment has what appears to be stylised folded draperies, with the back almost flat in cross-section; 97/208, F994, 1.1 (SF 5812, AML 844425)

140   Pipeclay fragment of the upper section of a ?female figurine with the upper section of the chest and bosom partially covered by a suggestion of light draperies; 98/139, F 974, P 3.1 (SF 6214)

141   Animal tooth pierced for suspension from a necklet or bracelet (Down and Rule 1971, 113, fig 5.17; Champion 1995, 415; Ross 1995, 440, 423; MacGregor 1985, 105, fig 61r); 22/54, BP 3.1 (SF 1108, AML 786482)

Three other pipeclay figurines and a pottery face have also been noted (not illustrated):

a) Fragment of orange clay pottery face applique, right hand side only, had been applied to the upper portion of a pot or jar now detached and incomplete; WB + (SF 1813)

b) Pipeclay fragment of a seated dog. Complete figures of this type show the dog upright and alert with bulging eyes and ears pricked forward, and wearing a collar with pendant. The fragment includes the collar, and the join of the right front leg to the chest is clear (Rouvier-Jeanlin 1972, 3435, nos 1051–61; La Baume 1964, 259, fig 245); 16/64, BP 3.1 (SF 54)

c) Pipeclay fragment showing the lower abdominal area, with navel indicated. Probably from a Venus statuette; 59/5, BP 3.2 (SF 686, AML 788114)

d) Pipeclay fragment of figurine of a female deity, most probably Venus, being the front section only from the shoulders to the pubic region, with the left arm by her side, and the right hand touching a lock of hair by the right ear (Rouvier-Jeanlin 1972, 110, pl 70.28012); 83/530, WR 2.3 (SF 4431, AML 8111176)

Writing equipment (Fig 4.13)

142   Iron simple stylus Manning type 1 (Manning 1985, 85); 91/92, WR 2.3 (SF 4271, AML 793512)

143   Iron stylus with shouldered eraser, shouldered stem and short point, Manning type 3; 91/502, F538, WR 2.3, KG 6 (SF 4311, AML 793521)

144   Iron stylus with short point and decorative mouldings at the shoulder visible in radiograph, Manning type 4; 58/3, BP 3.2 (SF 629, AML 787126)

145   Iron stylus with simple eraser, shoulder with inlaid copper alloy band and short point, Manning type 4; 80/51, P 3.4B, KG 25 (SF 2138, AML 786232)

146   Iron stylus with waisted eraser and decorative mouldings at the shoulder above the long point, Manning type 4; from *insula* 5 (SF 1396, AML 786318)

147   Copper alloy stylus with decorative mouldings above the short point, Manning type 4; 91/33, F124, WR 2.3 (SF 3918, AML 785819)

148   Bone stylus with point and broken eraser, neck and shoulder with grooved decoration; 22/2, BP 4

149   Copper alloy seal box lid with concentric decoration and central millefiori enamel of red, blue and white; 57/8, C 3.3 (SF 617, AML 725756)

150   Copper alloy seal box lid with concentric decoration; 91/94, WR 2.3 (SF 4451, AML 811091)

151   Copper alloy seal box lid probably originally decorated with enamel; 97/25, P 3.3 (SF 3998, AML 785864)

152   Copper alloy circular seal box base; 97/148, P 2.1 (SF 5659, AML 836007)

Weights and measures (Fig 4.14)

153   Lead circular weight, centrally pierced, with a slightly flanged edge; 98/52, P 2.3 (SF 5386, AML 835828)

154   Lead cylindrical weight of four and a half unciae with broken iron suspension loop; 91/94, WR 2.3 (SF 4004, AML 785534)

Craft tools (Fig 4.15)

155   Iron punch with square sectioned tang and round sectioned point; 10/2, C 3.2 (SF 73, AML 681653)

156   Iron saw-sharpening file with central tang, sloping shoulders and notched, broken, blade to set the teeth (Gaitzsch 1980, Taf 60, 295); 80/40, P 3.4B, KG 25 (SF 2075, AML 725624)

157   Iron gouge of rectangular section with burred head, blade is broken but appears to be a gouge or possibly a hollow punch; 80/3, P 3.5, KG 25 (SF 1899, AML 787156)

158   Iron awl of square section with slight shoulder seated in a crude bone handle; 49/+, BP 4 (SF 860, AML 725631)

159   Iron scraper with tapering shouldered blade and square sectioned tang with minerally preserved wood from the handle; 55/+, BP 4 (SF 1161, AML 786283)

Textile working (Fig 4.16)

160   Bone needle, broken, with pointed head and circular eye, Crummy type 1 (Crummy 1983, 65); 14/42, F2260, 1.3 (SF 1295, AML 787343)

161   Bone needle, point missing, pointed head with figure-of-eight shaped eye, Crummy type 1; 90/101, F599, P 3.2, KG 17 (SF 4907, AML 814696)

162   Bone short needle stained green, with pointed head and figure-of-eight shaped eye, Crummy type 1; 25/30, BP 2.2 (SF 1098, AML 786484)

163   Bone needle, head broken across the round eye; 84/49, WR 3.1 (SF 3158, AML 786500)

164   Bone needle with spatulate head and rectangular eye, Crummy type 2 (Crummy 1983, 65); 23/6, BP 3.3 (SF 263, AML 801476)

165   Bone needle with spatulate head and rectangular eye, Crummy type 2; 98/40, F672, P 3.1, KG 16 (SF 5009, AML 814709)

166   Copper alloy needle with flat head and rectangular eye, Crummy type 2; 90/205, F800, P 3.1 (SF 5871, AML 843145)

167   Copper alloy needle with eye set within a groove, Crummy type 3 (Crummy 1983, 67); 90/33, P 3.6, KG 25 (SF 3904, AML 785816)

168   Copper alloy needle stem broken across the eye; 84/137, WR 2.1 (SF 4667, AML 821642)

169   Bone 'pig fibula pin' with spatulate head and small round eye, possibly a needle; 84/49, WR 3.1 (SF 3410, AML 786501)

170   Pottery spindle whorl made of a fragment from a plain samian sherd with several scratch marks of irregular crosses; 98/107, P 4 (SF 5776, AML 844424)

171   Stone spindle whorl; 98/201, P 3.2 (SF 6218, AML 855534)

172   Bone square weaving tablet with four holes, broken; 62/7, BP 3.1 (SF 886, AML 786541)

173   Bone triangular weaving tablet with a thread hole and corner partly cut away; 84/154, WR 2.3 (SF 3715, AML 787959)

174   Bone toggle centrally pierced; 98/119, 1.2 (SF 5962, AML 844448)

Agricultural implements (Fig 4.17)

175   Iron hoe with sloping shouldered blade and open socket with minerally preserved wood from the handle; 92/1, C 3.3 (SF 3000, AML 786359)

176   Iron hoe with flat, oval-shaped blade and cranked tang (not drawn) with minerally preserved wood from the handle; 57/38, BP 3.1 (SF 1111, AML 681663)

177   Iron rake tooth with tang continuing the line of the back of the narrow, rectangular blade; 80/+, P 4 (SF 3668, AML 787532)

178   Iron shears with straight-edged blades, curving backs and looped spring; 44/25, F3142, C 3.4 (SF 1196, AML 725602)

179   Iron forked implement comprising a flat-sectioned strap branching into a thickened Y-shaped terminal ; 57/2, BP 3.3 (SF 586, AML 681652)

Items associated with transport (Fig 4.18)

180   Iron hipposandal with wing extending into the toe loop, Manning type 2 (Manning 1985, fig 16.65); unprovenanced (AML 725632)

181   Iron hipposandal with broken toe loop, Manning type 2; 48/+, BP 4 (SF 480, AML 725611)

182   Iron hipposandal with an oval opening in the sole plate and short side wings, one with a ring, Manning type 4 (Manning 1985, fig 16.65–6); 56/10, BP 3.3 (SF 1008, AML 786326)

183   Iron linchpin with spatulate head with rolled loop, Manning type 2b (Manning 1985, fig 20); unprovenanced (SF 1133, AML 681666)

184   Bone sawn with pierced hole in one side, possibly a cheekpiece for a leather bit (Crummy 1983, fig 109.2538); 16/47, BP 3.1 (SF 1223, AML 787341)

Locks and keys (Fig 4.19)

185   Copper alloy square lock plate with L-shaped keyhole for tumbler-lock slide key, nail hole at each corner (Crummy 1983, fig 135.4128); 83/524, F549, WR 2.3 (SF 4476, AML 811103)

186 Iron lock case nailed at each corner; 22/19, BP 2.1 (SF 407, AML 786235)

187 Iron bolt from a barb-spring padlock; unprovenanced

188 Copper alloy fragment of lock bolt; 90/179, P 2.3 (SF 5921, AML 843156)

189 Iron tanged strap fragment, pierced by two holes one with a strip lying above it, possibly from a sliding bolt for a fixed lock (Manning 1985, p 95, pl 42); 90/33, P 3.6, KG 25 (SF 3877, AML 787520)

190 Iron double-linked shackle with rectangular padlock; 12/27, C 2.2 (SF 81, 787127)

191 Iron T-shaped lift-key with small terminal hook (Manning 1985, fig 25.1), from *insula* 5 (SF 1412, AML 681660)

192 Iron T-shaped lift-key bit with two teeth on one side and one remaining on the other; 90/24, P 3.4A, KG 25 (SF 3636, AML 767026)

193 Iron simple lift-key with pierced strap handle and stem with two teeth on the same plane; 80/49, P 3.5, KG 25 (SF 3550, AML 767025)

194 Iron L-shaped lift-key with ring terminal with finial, decorative mouldings at junction of handle and stem and four teeth; 80/40, P 3.4B, KG 25 (SF 2067, AML 725622)

195 Iron L-shaped lift-key with three teeth and decorative mouldings at the neck; 90/17, P 3.6, KG 25

196 Iron L-shaped lift-key with scrolled loop terminal, decorative mouldings at the junction of handle and stem, and three-toothed bit; unprovenanced

197 Iron L-shaped lift-key with loop terminal and two-toothed bit; 84/49, WR 3.1 (SF 3398, AML 760270)

198 Iron L-shaped lift-key with rolled loop terminal and remains of four teeth visible in radiograph; 84/49, WR 3.1 (SF 3161, AML 760258)

199 Iron L-shaped lift-key with looped ring terminal and three teeth; 70/5, C 4 (SF 1486, AML 787107)

200 Iron L-shaped lift-key bit with four teeth; 85/+, WR 4 (AML 786291)

201 Iron L-shaped slide-key with wide handle with pierced terminal; 16/43, C 3.1 (SF 52, AML 681658)

202 Iron slide-key with pierced bow, strap handle and straight bit with five teeth; 91/94, WR 2.3 (SF 3971, AML 785494)

203 Iron slide-key with pierced bow, rectangular handle and bit with four teeth; unprovenanced (SF 3235, AML 760263)

204 Iron lever-lock key with piped stem and slits in the outer edge of the bit, Manning type 9 (Manning 1985, fig 25); 96/21, P 3.6, KG 25 (SF 4125, AML 785511)

205 Iron barb-spring padlock key with scrolled loop terminal, strap handle and pierced bit; 92/+, C 4 (SF 2156, AML 786354)

206 Copper alloy broken trefoil key handle; 83/+, WR 4 (SF 2053, AML 787678)

Knives (Fig 4.20)

207 Iron cleaver with rectangular-sectioned tang stepped where it joins the straight back, and convex edge rising to meet the back at the tip, Manning type 2 variant (Manning 1985, 122); 90/+, P 4 (SF 3271, AML 786288)

208 Iron knife with broken blade and tang set within a wooden handle with a copper alloy hilt plate and an iron end plate. Minerally replaced leather probably from a leather washer is present at the junction of the blade and handle; 91/11, F87, WR 4 (SF 2199, AML 801445)

209 Iron knife with broken down-turning blade and strap handle with ring terminal rivetted to paired bone handle plates with incised lattice decoration, Manning type 7b (Manning 1985, 112); from *insula* 5

210 Iron knife with fluted bone handle, ring terminal and broken blade; 86/24, WR 3.1 (SF 2178, AML 760271)

211 Iron knife with tang set on line with convex back which drops to meet the broken edge at the long pointed tip; 10/+, C 4 (SF 23, AML 681651)

212 Iron knife with tang embedded in crude bone handle. The narrow blade has a straight back and edge meeting at a long pointed tip; 24/+, BP 4 (SF 805, AML 787574)

213 Iron knife with centrally-placed tang and gently convex curving back and edge, Manning type 15 (Manning 1985, 115); 63/+, C 4 (SF 1068, AML 787140)

214 Iron knife with central tang, straight back and worn edge, Manning type 15; 90/21, P 3.6, KG 25 (SF 4133, AML 785471)

215 Iron knife with centrally-placed tang, straight shoulder, convex curving back meeting the edge at the upward pointing tip, Manning type 15; unprovenanced (SF 1179, AML 725601)

216 Iron knife with centrally-placed tang, sloping shoulders and straight back and edge, broken before the tip; 90/+, P 4

217 Iron knife with centrally-placed tang and straight back and edge meeting at a pointed tip; 9/+, C 4 (SF 302, AML 786369)

218 Iron knife with broken blade and centrally-placed tang set in a bone handle; 80/3, P 3.5, KG 25 (SF 1867, AML 787108)

219 Iron square-sectioned tang broken before the blade; 70/5, C 4 (SF 1491, AML 725627)

Handles (Fig 4.21)

220 Iron knife handle with paired bone handle plates decorated with double ring and dot motifs; 59/8, BP 3.2 (SF 736, AML 681694)

221 Bone handle with three lines of heavy ridge and groove decoration (Allason-Jones and Miket 1984, 2.54–57); 11/+, C 4 (SF 146, AML 786470)

222 Bone handle fragment with ridge and groove decoration; WB 55/+, BP 4 (SF 1163, AML 787315)

223 Bone flat-sectioned handle with grooved border around the terminal with central iron pin and notched base; 98/40, F672, P 3.1, KG 16 (SF 5031, AML 814711)

224 Bone simple cylindrical faceted handle; 83/111, WR 3.1 (SF 4025, AML 785756)

225 Bone roughly shaped tapering handle with lightly scratched Greek letter phi visible; unprovenanced

226 Copper alloy knife handle with delta-shaped terminal with angular collar and remains of four strips to enclose the organic handle; 84/12, WR 4 (SF 1996, AML 787720)

227 Copper alloy ornate finial with a circular terminal with a series of decorative mouldings below, possibly a handle; 88/3, WR 4 (SF 1833, AML 725737)

228 Copper alloy tubular fitting decorated with panels of oblique and parallel grooves, possibly a handle (Cool 1993, fig 99.698); 96/25, P 3.6, KG 25 (SF 3835, AML 78778)

Household utensils (Figs 4.22–4.23)

229 Copper alloy small spoon, tinned and decorated on the underside of the circular bowl and handle; 49/150, BP 2.2 (SF 2074, AML 725747)

230 Copper alloy spoon with decorated handle offset from the oval bowl; unprovenanced (SF 1178, AML 787695)

231 Bone *spatula* with long pointed stem handle, naturally occurring hole present at the neck; 84/52, WR 2.3 (SF 3157, AML 786522)

232 Bone *spatula* with pointed stem; 84/49, WR 3.1 (SF 3374, AML 786533)

233 Bone *spatula* with broken stem; 16/82, BP 2.3 (SF 203, AML 786632)

234 Bone spatulate terminal with a central groove (Crummy 1983, no 4756); 17/43, F3169, BP 2.2, KG 9 (SF 87, AML 787926)

235 Copper alloy handle fragment and hinged, trefoil-shaped lid for a spouted jug; 49/+, BP 4 (SF 898, AML 786988)

236 Copper alloy part of a jug handle; 7/21 F2274, C 2.2 (SF 19, AML 725776)

237 Copper alloy flat, circular lid; 98/178, 1.3 (SF 6329, AML 855746)

238 Copper alloy fragmentary open lamp holder; 92/18, C 2.1 (SF 3184, AML 786874)

239 Iron large hook with rectangular section, possibly a suspension hook or pot hanger; 60/18, BP 3.2 (SF 911, AML 786238)

240 Iron handle spirally twisted in opposing directions along its length with pointed terminal with paired decorative scrolls; 80/2, P 4 (SF 1642, AML 786377)

Furniture fittings (Figs 4.24–4.25)

241 Copper alloy tubular finial with grooved decoration probably for a folding stool; 91/23, WR 3.1 (SF 3479, AML 767030)

242 Bone leaf hinge with four rivet holes and semi-circular seating for a central pin; 90/204, F951, P 2.2 (SF 5890, AML 844441)

243 Bone cylindrical hinge unit with circular peg hole; 98/140, F930, P 3.2, KG 17 (SF 5891, AML 844442)

244 Bone two hinge units with peg holes and central pin; 90/204, F951, P 2.2 (SF 5780, AML 844431)

245 Bone hinge unit with peg hole; 90/204, F951, P 2.2 (SF 5901, AML 844443)

246 Bone hinge unit spacer with a D-shaped hole; 84/49, WR 3.1 (SF 3361, AML 786504)

247 Bone roughly worked hinge unit, possibly a rough-out or offcut; 65/+, C 4 (SF 1058, AML 786606)

248 Copper alloy decorative hinge strap and hasp box fitting; 80/3, P 3.5, KG 25 (SF 1889, AML 787200)

249 Copper alloy strip binding with broken trefoil terminal with two rivet holes; 92/18, C 2.1 (SF 3230, AML 786782)

250 Copper alloy mount with round, pierced terminal; 83/508, WR 3.1 (SF 4264, AML 793465)

251 Copper alloy split-spiked loop; 80/181, P 2.1 (SF 4850, AML 821703)

252 Copper alloy split-spiked loop; 85/224, WR 2.3 (SF 3143, AML 786854)

253 Copper alloy split-spiked loop; 98/35, F651, P 3.2, KG 17 (SF 4933, AML 821731)

254 Copper alloy half of a well made drop handle with an elegant bird beak terminal; 85/63, WR 2.1 (SF 3266, AML 786884)

255 Bone lozenge-shaped inlay decorated with ring and dot motifs on front face and, surprisingly, also on the sides; 58/8, BP 3.2 (SF 794, AML 786556)

256 Bone lozenge-shaped inlay, undecorated; 60/24, BP 2.1 (SF 1084, AML 801495)

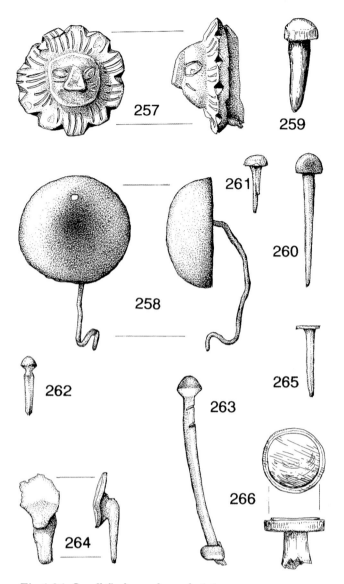

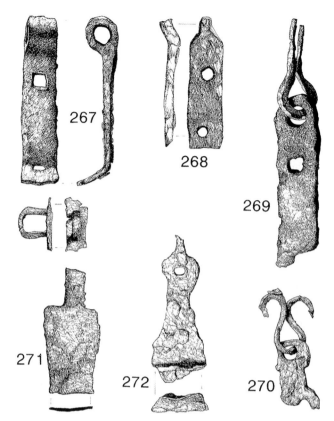

Fig 4.27 Small finds: hinges; scale 1:2

265   Copper alloy small flat-headed nail or tack; 90/82, F591, P 3.3 (SF 4742, AML 821670)
266   Bone stud with circular head and thick, broken shank; 38/2, B 4 (SF 363, AML 786598)

Fig 4.26 Small finds: studs; scale 1:1

Hinges (Fig 4.27)

267   Iron nailed drop-hinge strap with a circular head loop; 91/30, WR 3.1 (SF 3176, AML 760260)
268   Iron nailed loop-hinge strap with sloping shoulders, broken before the looped head; 80/124, F466, P 3.1, KG 16 (SF 4276, AML 793516)
269   Iron simple nailed hinge strap articulating with a split-spiked loop; 90/9, P 3.6, KG 25 (SF 3058, AML 786252)
270   Iron double-S hook articulating with the pierced head of a nailed strap, now broken; unprovenanced (AML 787109)
271   Iron shouldered strap with hasp on the projecting neck; 80/49, P 3.5, KG 25 (SF 3562, AML 786271)
272   Iron nailed hinge strap with decorative terminal, articulating with fragment of second strap; unprovenanced (AML 786339)

Studs and nails (Fig 4.26)

257   Copper alloy crude lion head stud for decorating a box or piece of furniture; 56/37, BP 3.1 (SF 1050, AML 786980)
258   Copper alloy large dome-headed stud; 84/49, WR 3.1 (SF 3376, AML 760288)
259   Bone stud with domed head and short thick stem; 56/6, BP 3.3 (SF 626, AML 786540)
260   Copper alloy nail with domed head; 90/168, P 2.2 (SF 5413, AML 835933)
261   Copper alloy small domed-headed nail; 98/28, F638, P 3.2, KG 17 (SF 4919, AML 821726)
262   Copper alloy small domed-headed nail; 90/56, P 3.3 (SF 4457, AML 811093)
263   Copper alloy partly-made domed-headed nail with tool marks present on the shank below the head; 29/8, C 2.3 (SF 413, AML 787203)
264   Copper alloy round flat-headed nail with a clenched shank; 80/179, P 2.1 (SF 4706, AML 821657)

Structural fittings (Fig 4.28)

273   Iron curving fragment of strap with nail hole at the point of fracture; 90/47, P 3.6, KG 25 (SF 4201, AML 785489)

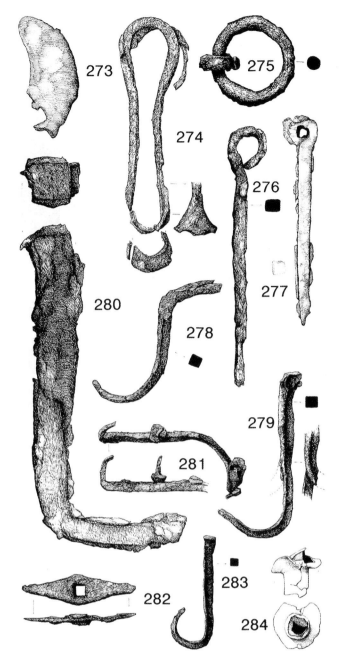

279   Iron wallhook as 278 with broken shank; 90/6, P 3.6, KG 25 (SF 2185, AML 786251)

280   Iron large square-sectioned angled shank; 49/+, BP 4 (SF 977, AML 786240)

281   Iron curving cleat with upstanding arms, two hobnails present in the encrustation appear unassociated with the object in radiograph; 92/2, C 2.3 (SF 2133, AML 787503)

282   Iron lozenge-shaped nail rove with central angular hole; 58/9, BP 3.2 (SF 829, AML 725620)

283   Iron curved nail shank, broken head; 60/3, BP 3.3 (SF 910, AML 786294)

284   Lead flanged cylinder fragment, possibly a pipe junction; 84/12, WR 4 (SF 2123, AML 786408)

Scrap (Fig 4.29)

285   Copper alloy two rectangular sheet fragments; 84/48, WR 3.1 (SF 3141, AML 786777)

286   Copper alloy triangular offcut of rectangular section; 83/+, WR 4 (SF 2041, AML 787715)

287   Copper alloy twisted strip of offcut sheet; 80/156, P 2.3 (SF 4830, AML 821696)

288   Copper alloy two fragments of repoussé decorated sheet; 80/3, P 3.5, KG 25 (SF 1818, AML 787880)

289   Copper alloy strip fragment decorated with a double line of repoussé dots; 83/+, WR 4 (SF 2016, AML 787700)

290   Lead offcut strip decorated with series of raised dots; 90/+, C 4 (SF 3520, AML 786405)

291   Copper alloy strip with groups of linear marks present likely to be tool marks; 91/92, WR 2.3 (SF 4079, AML 785839)

292   Copper alloy strip fitting rivetted at one end; 97/121, P 3.3 (SF 5153, AML 830304)

293   Copper alloy round-sectioned rod with a straight cut and an irregular end, possibly a handle as 236 above; 85/125 WR 2.3 (SF 3598, AML 786880)

294   Copper alloy as 293 with a hooked end, other broken; 59/8, BP 3.2 (SF 740, AML 786827)

295   Iron bar with square cross section; 90/34, P 3.6, KG 25 (SF 3869, AML 787517)

296   Copper alloy fragment of broken ring with opposing ?decorative terminals, appears to be a poor casting; 97/101, F523, P 3.1, KG 16 (SF 5343, AML 830398)

297   Copper alloy curved fragment with medial ridge, possibly a brooch fragment; 12/29, F2226, C 3.4 (SF 125, AML 787688)

Fig 4.28 Small finds: structural items; scale 1:2

274   Iron two articulating, long, waisted chain links; unprovenanced (SF 1182, AML 786281)

275   Iron ring articulating with head of split-spiked loop; 80/3, P 3.5, KG 25 (SF 1909, AML 786352)

276   Iron ring-headed pin with square-sectioned shank or possibly a handle with a looped terminal; 90/21, P 3.6, KG 25 (SF 3462, AML 786226)

277   Iron ring-headed pin with square-sectioned shank; 80/59 F477, P 3.3 (SF 3881, AML 786312)

278   Iron square-sectioned wallhook; 80/6, P 4 (SF 1674, AML 725607)

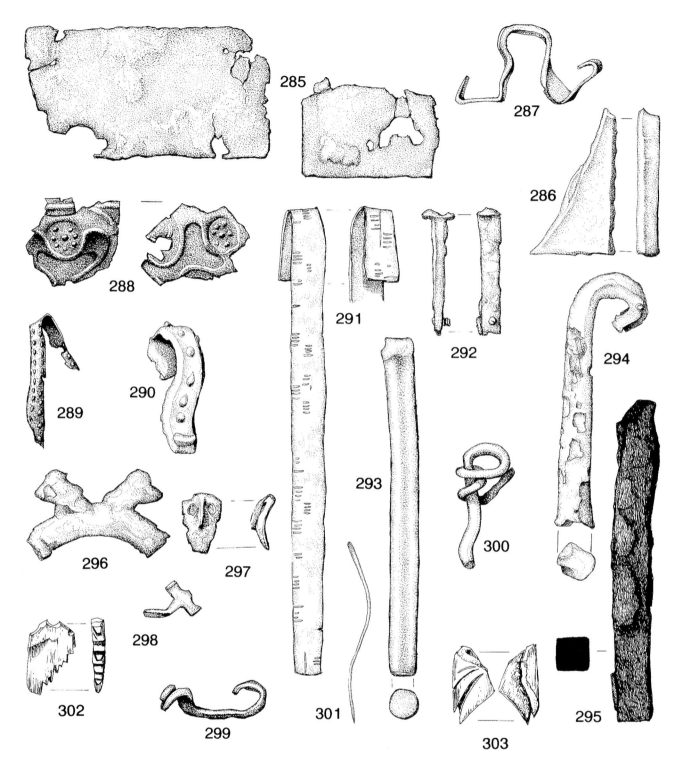

Fig 4.29 Small finds: scrap; scale 1:1

298   Copper alloy cruciform fragment of broken fitting, possibly a brooch; 59/8, BP 3.2 (SF 986, AML 786744)

299   Copper alloy fragment of twisted wire probably a brooch spring; 90/17, P 3.6, KG 25 (SF 3220, AML 786797)

300   Copper alloy twisted wire of varying thickness; 91/55, WR 3.3 (SF 3580, AML 786739)

301   Copper alloy fine stem, possibly a brooch pin, does not appear broken, may be a partly-made item; 90/16, P 3.6, KG 25 (SF 3322, AML 786762)

302   Bone carved fragment with a serrated edge, probably a discarded rough-out; 35/+, C 4 (SF 542, AML 786550)

303   Bone small broken fragment with carved grooves; 91/56, F87, WR 4 (SF 3744, AML 786554)

Small finds from the portico pits

by Quita Mould, with a contribution by
Glenys Lloyd-Morgan

Introduction

A total of 153 small finds was found in the P 3.1 and P 3.2 portico pits from key groups 16 and 17, two thirds of the finds (101 objects) occurring in KG 16 (Table 2.1). Eleven were not available for study, and information regarding these objects has been derived from previous documentation where available. The SF numbers shown in brackets are the site small find numbers. An item closely resembling an illustrated piece is referenced in the form 'as Fig 00.0'. Material referred to as shale in the text has not been formally identified and may be of either shale or jet.

The pottery evidence from the portico pits suggests they were filled during the first two thirds of the third century. The small finds recovered cannot be dated so precisely, generally spanning a range of approximately two centuries. The evidence for residuality in the pits provided by some pieces is parallelled by the pottery and glass evidence, and gives some indication of the nature of the deposits.

Dating

Nineteen pits from P 3.1, KG 16, contained small finds. Of these, ten contained bone hair pins of Crummy's type 1 (as Fig 4.9, 59) and 2 (as Fig 4.9, 60–71), or needles of Crummy type 1 (as Fig 4.16, 160–3) thought to date before 200 AD (Crummy 1983, 20–21 and 65). F736 also contained a copper alloy finger ring of Henig's type III (Henig 1974, 47) and a fragment of decorated shale tray likely to date to the first or second century (Crummy 1983, 69). Two of the pits (F564 and F602) containing the earlier Roman pins, also contained fragments of shale bracelets commonly found in third or fourth-century contexts, however, being plain they too may be residual from earlier deposits. One pit (F486) also contained a copper alloy pin with a glass head of Cool's group 14 (Cool 1990, 164). Regrettably the pin was not available for examination so that the method of attachment of the glass head to the metal stem is unknown, with the result that the proposed dating of mid-second century to the fourth century cannot be further refined. Only one pit (F672) contained five type 3 bone hair pins (as Fig 4.9, 85–9; Crummy 1983, 21–22) which could be dated to the third century, and in this case the finds were not accompanied by earlier material.

Eleven pits from P 3.2, KG 17, contained small finds. Of these, six contained potentially datable finds. Four pits (F455, F477, F631, and F714) contained personal decorative items dating no later than the end of the second century AD, again suggesting residuality. Only two pits (F675 and F930) contained small finds which date to the third or fourth century: a type 6 bone hair pin (as Fig 4.10, 104–6; Crummy 1983, 24–5) and a household shrine of lead (Fig 4.31) respectively. Pit F930 also contained a bone hair pin with simple lattice decoration (Fig 4.10, 102) likely to be of later Roman date.

The nature of the finds

The quantity of small finds recovered from the individual pits or from separate areas was insufficient to allow for statistical analysis but general trends could be observed. Very few small finds were recovered from pits in the northern excavated half of the west portico (Box 97) but the area was notable for having two crucibles (SF 4524 in F572 and SF 5175, AML 830409, in F523) associated with silver melting, however, no other manufacturing debris was recorded from this area. The small finds from the southern half of the west portico (Box 90) and from the south portico (Boxes 80 and 98) did not appear to differ significantly (Table 4.1). Fewer small finds were recovered from Box 80 than from 90 and 98, and a more limited range of functional types were represented, but this would appear to be proportional to the number of small finds recovered. The small finds suggest that the main focus of activity was the corner of the south and west porticoes. Activity seems to have declined in Box 80 in the south portico and Box 90 at the south end of the west portico in the later period (3.2), but appears to have been continuous in Box 98 directly south of the *macellum*.

Approximately a quarter of the finds from the pits were personal decorative items. If broken bone stems, likely to be hair pins, are included, this rises to 45% for P 3.1 and 33% for P 3.2 (Table 4.1). The occurrence of structural finds was relatively low, accounting for 26% of the finds from P 3.1 and 38% in P 3.2. The comparatively high incidence of wallhooks (as Fig 4.28, 278–9) was noticeable, with 18 items forming around 12% of the total assemblage. They occurred

Table 4.1 Small finds: functional categories from portico pits, P 3.1 and 3.2

category	box 80		box 90		box 98	
	3.1	*3.2*	*3.1*	*3.2*	*3.1*	*3.2*
jewellery	7	4	10	2	12	6
(broken pin stems)	6	1	5	2	6	2
toilet implements	–	–	1	1	–	1
writing	–	–	–	–	2	1
weights/measures	1	–	–	–	2	1
religion	–	–	–	–	–	2
tools	1	–	2	–	3	?1
manufacturing	1	–	2	3	1	2
domestic	1	1	4	–	3	1
structural	5	2	13	2	9	15
other	–	1	3	–	2	–
total	22	9	40	10	40	32

principally in Box 90 during P 3.1 and 98 in P 3.2. The wallhooks may have been used to hang and display goods for sale in the market. Eleven were found complete suggesting either that they had not been used, or, more likely, that they had been deposited still attached to timbers into which they had been hammered. If the latter was the case, the pits may have contained fragments of the wooden structure of the individual stalls or booths, perhaps disposed of when they were refurbished.

The slight evidence for writing and weights and measures may possibly be associated with commercial activity at the *macellum*, occurring chiefly in Box 98. However, of these items, two pottery counters (SF 4284, AML 793585, from F486 in Box 80 and SF 5287, AML 830223, from F714 in Box 98) may be gaming pieces and represent a leisure activity rather than commerce. The small quantity recovered could as easily derive from the environs of the bath house as the market place, as could an oculist's stamp (SF 4973). Tools recovered were bone needles with the exception of a possible broken rake tooth from F852 (SF 5618, AML 835778, P 3.2). The needles, like the jewellery and toilet implements found, could readily fit into a bath house or a domestic setting. The lead shrine containing the figure of Venus (Fig 4.31) is a household shrine, again, likely to have been used in a domestic context originally.

A maximum of 29% of the finds was complete and being principally small decorative items are likely to be the result of casual loss. As suggested above, the few complete items of structural ironwork recovered suggest that old timbers were disposed of. The majority of the finds were broken and probably represent the deliberate deposition of collected rubbish. The small finds, therefore, appear not to represent the rubbish exclusively from the *macellum* or the stalls under the portico, but rather general rubbish gathered from a wider area which may have included the market and the baths.

Summary of pit contents

West portico, north end (Box 97)

Six small finds were found from P 3.1. A crucible used for melting silver (SF 5175, AML 830409), a fragment of silver (unseen) and a plain copper alloy ring were found in pit F523. A second crucible (SF 4524) associated with silver melting was found in F572. A copper alloy mount and a glass ring setting (also unseen) were found in F579. No small finds were recovered from P 3.2 contexts.

West portico, south end, Box 90

Forty small finds were recovered from P 3.1, occurring principally in two pits, F602 and F736 (Table 4.2). Ten small finds were potentially dateable. Pit F602 contained two hair pins of type 2 (SF 4750, AM: 814683, and SF 4943, AML 814698) likely to date

Table 4.2 Small finds: from Box 90, P 3.1 and 3.2

	copper alloy		iron		bone		stone shale/ pot (*)	
	3.1	3.2	3.1	3.2	3.1	3.2	3.1	3.2
earring	1	1	–	–	–	–	–	–
pin	–	–	–	–	6	–	–	–
pin/needle stem	1	–	–	–	5	2	–	–
finger ring	1	1	–	–	–	–	–	–
bracelet	–	–	–	–	–	–	1	–
intaglio	–	–	–	–	–	–	1	–
stud	1	–	–	–	–	–	–	–
comb	–	–	–	–	1	1	–	–
ferrule	2	–	–	–	–	–	–	–
tray	–	–	–	–	–	–	1	–
spindlewhorl	–	–	–	–	–	–	*1	–
whetstone	–	–	–	–	–	–	1	–
strip	–	–	3	–	–	–	–	–
sheet, offcut	1	2	–	–	–	–	–	–
split–spiked loop	–	–	1	–	–	–	–	–
wallhook	–	–	5	1	–	–	–	–
T-staple	–	–	1	–	–	–	–	–
nail, type Ib	–	–	3	–	–	–	–	–
shank	–	–	2	–	–	–	–	–
waterpipe collar	–	–	–	1	–	–	–	–
worked frag	–	–	–	–	–	1	–	–
waste	1	–	–	–	–	–	–	–
total	8	4	15	2	12	4	5	0

before 200 AD, a fragment of shale bracelet (SF 4849, AML 814284), and an intaglio (Fig 4.36, 1). Two small copper alloy collar ferrules (SF 4781, AML 821688, and SF 4924, AML 821727) were found which may come from small knives, tools, or possibly brushes. An elongated grey pebble (SF 4792, AML 821626) of slightly micaceous sandstone of local provenance may have been used as a hone. A small quantity of copper alloy waste and a sheet offcut are manufacturing debris. Structural ironwork comprised two broken shanks likely to be wallhooks. Pit F736 contained twenty-four objects. Datable finds included a fragment of decorated shale tray (SF 5147, AML 830401) likely to be of first or second-century date and four bone hair pins of Crummy's type 2 and a single variant with a bead and reel head with a finial knop all dating before *c* 200 AD. The majority were personal decorative items. The copper alloy earring (SF 5202, AML 830331) of type 1 (Allason-Jones 1989a, 2) is of a type occurring throughout the Roman period. The copper alloy finger ring with an oval bezel (SF 5499, AML 835708) is of Henig's type III dated to the second half of the first and the early second century (Henig 1974, 47). In addition a bone 'tally' (SF 5306, AML 830255) was recorded, but is unfortunately not available for study. The identification seems unlikely to the author and its possible identification as the side plate of a bone comb is suggested. Structural ironwork was represented by four wallhooks and a small quantity of timber nails. A split-spiked loop and a broken bone pin stem were found separately (F708 and F709 respectively).

Ten small finds were found in P 3.2 occurring in two pits F623 and F631. F623 contained a copper alloy finger-ring key (SF 4757, AML 821676) comparable with another found *in situ* in the lock of a casket burial (G69) from the cemetery at Butt Road, Colchester (Crummy 1983, 85–88, 2195) dated *c* AD 320–450. Structural fittings such as a broken wallhook and waterpipe collar and a piece of offcut copper alloy sheet were also found. F631 contained a copper alloy earring of twisted wire (SF 5166, AML 830315), likely to be a type 9 or type 12 (Allason-Jones 1989a, 8–10) suggesting a first or second-century date, and therefore the presence of residual material. The feature also contained two broken bone hair pin stems, a partly-worked bone fragment and a copper alloy sheet offcut. A bone comb (SF 5340, AML 830258) is also recorded as coming from the context but regrettably was not available for study.

The majority of the small finds were broken, the small number of complete objects such as the small copper alloy finger ring (SF 5499), the earrings (SF 5166 and SF 5202) and stud (5303) are likely to represent casual losses.

South portico, east end, Box 98

A total of 40 small finds were found in eight pits from P 3.1 (Table 4.3). F672 contained five bone hair pins of type 3 (as Figs 97–8.85–90; Crummy 1983, 21–22) which date no earlier than *c* AD 200, three of which had been repointed. Of particular interest was the

Table 4.3 Small finds: from Box 98, P 3.1 and 3.2

	copper alloy		iron		bone		lead/ stone pot (*)	
	3.1	3.2	3.1	3.2	3.1	3.2	3.1	3.2
earring	–	1	–	–	–	–	–	–
pin	–	–	–	–	10	5	–	–
pin/needle stem	2	–	–	–	5	2	–	–
needle	–	–	–	–	3	–	–	–
finger ring setting	–	–	–	–	–	–	1	–
ring	–	–	–	–	1	–	–	–
stud	1	–	–	–	–	–	–	–
tweezers	–	1	–	–	–	–	–	–
oculist's stamp	–	–	–	–	–	–	1	–
weight/finial	1	–	–	–	–	–	–	–
knobbed stem	1	–	–	–	–	–	–	–
counter	–	–	–	–	–	–	–	*1
handle	–	–	–	–	1	–	–	–
hinge unit	–	–	–	–	1	1	–	–
seal box	1	–	–	–	–	–	–	–
stylus	–	1	–	–	1	–	–	–
bell	–	1	–	–	–	–	–	–
shrine	–	–	–	–	–	–	–	1
strip	–	–	1	–	–	–	–	–
sheet, offcut	–	1	–	–	–	–	–	–
wallhook	–	–	3	6	–	–	–	–
T-staple	–	–	1	–	–	–	–	–
nail, type Ib	–	–	1	7	–	–	–	–
shank	–	–	3	2	–	–	–	–
waterpipe collar	–	–	1	–	–	–	–	–
seating	–	–	–	–	–	–	–	1
waste	–	1	–	–	–	–	–	–
total	6	6	10	15	22	8	2	3

occurrence of an oculist's stamp (Fig 4.30, SF 4973). The object was reported in *Britannia*, (Hassall and Tomlin 1982, 419), and the details are repeated here. The fragment of green ?schist tapers to a blunt and broken point with one of the four long sides of the object formed by an edge broken in antiquity suggesting that it may have been an offcut from a larger block used by an engraver for practice rather than an actual stamp. Two of the faces on opposite long sides have been inscribed retrograde Q LVCILLANV[. and PENECILAD[. which can be read as Q (...) Lucillianus and penecil(le) ad or 'salve for...'. The disease is not mentioned on a number of similar stamps and is assumed to be *lippitudo* an inflammation or watering of the eye. Stone stamps, used to impress blocks of eye ointment (*collyria*), are frequently found to date from the second or third century (Boon 1983, 4). The recovery of the oculist's stamp adds further weight to the likelihood of Wroxeter being a centre for the treatment of eye disorders as suggested by the recovery of the quantity of *ex votos* plaster eyes and two pairs of eyes in gold sheet from the excavations in the baths basilica (Pretty 1997, 212). A bone handle (Fig 4.21, 223), fragments of copper alloy stem and stud, along with fragments of water pipe collar were also found. Two bone needles (SF 5446, AML 835887) of type 1 (Crummy 1983, 65), three pins (SF 5449, SF 5685, and SF 5873) of type 2 (*ibid*, 21), an iron wallhook, and a broken nail shank were found in F800. A stone setting for a ring (SF 5463, AML 835909) and a broken ring of bone (SF 5684, AML 836016) were also recorded from this context but were not available for study. A bone pin of type 1 (SF 5761) another of type 2 (SF 5538), and two broken pin stems came from F855, along with a cast finial knob of copper alloy (SF 5740, AML 836028), possibly a weight, and a small quantity of structural ironwork including a T-staple (SF 5744, AML 844540). A bone stylus (SF 5622) from the same context was unfortunately unseen. A knobbed copper stem (SF 6044, AML 844214) possibly the end of a steelyard arm was found in F1017 with a bone needle (SF 6023, AML 844453) of type 1, a broken bone pin or needle stem, a wallhook, and a type 1b timber nail (Manning 1985, 134). A complete wallhook (SF 5309) occurred in F766. A lozenge-shaped enamelled seal box (SF 5432, AML 835940) of second or third-century date was found in F801, the individual lozenge-shaped fields were blue with a central field of yellow. Similar seal-boxes have been found at earlier excavations at Wroxeter (Bushe-Fox 1916, pl.XVIII.25) and Old Penrith (Mould 1991, fig 100, 723). A thick pin stem of bone (SF 5722, AML 835906) likely to be a rough-out was found in F804.

A minimum of twelve objects recovered from P 3.1 were complete and being principally small decorative items are likely to be the result of casual loss.

Thirty-two small finds were found in six pits in P 3.2, of which a minimum of eleven were complete.

Fig 4.30 Oculist's stamp; scale 2:1

The outstanding find from Box 98 must be the household shrine of lead (SF 5815) containing a figure of Venus (see below) dated, by comparison with a similar shrine from Wallsend and the door from a third example from Vindolanda, to the fourth century (Allason-Jones 1984, 232), and possibly imported. The shrine was found in F930 along with a broken copper alloy earring (SF 5888, AML 844428), a bone hair pin (Fig 4.10, 102) with lattice decoration, a broken stem, and a unit from a box hinge (Fig 4.24, 243). A pair of copper alloy tweezers (SF 4932, AML 821730, as Fig 4.11, 120), a bone pin (SF 5347, AML 830260) of type 2, a broken stem, and a piece of offcut copper alloy sheet were found in F638, along with three wallhooks and a small seating of lead. Of interest in light of the household shrine is the square bell (SF 5267, AML 830365) of copper alloy also from F638 which may have been used in religious ceremonies (cf Crummy 1992, 186–7, no 1663, fig 5.51). A complete bone hair pin of type 1 (SF 5286, AML 830250) dating to before AD 200, a broken bone stem, and a pottery counter (SF 5287, AML 830223) were found in F714 with a copper alloy stylus (SF 5288, AML 830376) with a waisted eraser and decorative moulding on the stem (Manning type 4, 1985, 85, fig 24). A pin of type 6 (SF 5079, AML 830235) dated to the third or fourth century, an iron wallhook and a fragment of copper alloy waste occurred in F675. Pits F679 and F852 contained a small quantity of structural ironwork including wallhooks and a large pointed shank possibly a broken rake tooth (SF 5618, AML 835778 from F852).

South portico, west end, Box 80
Twenty two small finds from P 3.1 occurred in four pits, F486, 547, 561, and 564, (Table 4.4). The bone hair pins recovered were of Crummy's type 2 (1983, 21) or a variant with a finial knop (as Fig 4.9, 73–79),

likely to date before AD 200. A copper alloy pin with a glass head (SF 4375, AML 811072) is of Cool's group 14 (Cool 1990, 164) which may date from the mid second to the fourth century.

Over half of the objects (a minimum of 12) were broken, and the assemblage appears to be rubbish disposal. Complete structural ironwork found such as the timber nails and wallhooks may have been disposed of with attached timbers. The relatively small quantity of small finds occurring in each pit and their likely date range suggests that the majority may be residual.

Pit F486 contained 10 small finds including a copper alloy stud with a milled edge (SF 4265, AML 793466) which is likely to be a military fitting comparable with an example from Old Penrith (Mould 1991, fig 95, 680). An iron cranked shank with pointed terminals (SF 4293, AML 793519) from the

Table 4.4 Small finds: from Box 80, P 3.1 and 3.2

	copper alloy		iron		bone		shale/ pot (*)	
	3.1	3.2	3.1	3.2	3.1	3.2	3.1	3.2
pin	1	–	–	–	4	4	–	–
pin/needle stem	1	–	–	–	5	1	–	–
needle	–	–	–	–	1	–	–	–
bracelet	–	–	–	–	–	–	1	–
ring	–	–	1	–	–	–	–	–
stud	1	1	–	–	–	–	–	–
counter	–	–	–	–	–	–	*1	–
strip	–	1	–	–	–	–	–	–
sheet, offcut	1	–	–	–	–	–	–	
wallhook	–	–	2	–	–	–	–	–
nail, type Ib	–	–	2	1	–	–	–	–
shank	–	–	–	1	–	–	–	–
shank, cranked	–	–	1	–	–	–	–	–
total	4	2	6	2	10	5	2	0

same pit is comparable with another from a Flavian-Trajanic context at Segontium (Allason-Jones 1993, fig 10.16, 342) where its use as a wallhook is suggested. A U-shaped wallhook (SF 4426, AML 810953) of common form (Manning 1985, 129) was also found, and a pottery counter (SF 4284, AML 793585). The remaining finds from this pit were personal decorative items including a possible finger ring of iron (SF 4256, AML 793505), a bone hair pin of type 2 (Crummy 1983, 2) and a copper alloy pin with a glass head.

Pit F564 contained 8 objects including a fragment of shale bracelet, a bone pin and broken stems, and a broken iron wallhook. Pit F561 contained a broken bone needle and hair pin, while pit F547 contained a broken bone pin stem and a timber nail.

Fig 4.31 Lead shrine; scale 2:1

Nine small finds were found in P 3.2, occurring in three pits (F455, F471, and F477). One bone pin of type 1 (SF 4017, AML 785743) and two of type 2 (SF 3964, AML 785748 and SF 5054, AML 830233) dating before AD 200 were found. Only two of the finds were complete; the bone pin (SF 4017) may have been a casual loss, while a timber nail with a curved shank (SF 3989, AML 785455) had been deliberately pulled from the timber before being discarded.

The Venus shrine
by Glenys Lloyd-Morgan

The recent discoveries of two lead shrines from Britain with representations of the deity is unusual and gives a rare opportunity of shedding light on the practice of private worship, in both military and civilian contexts. The first example was found in the Wallsend Roman fort (Allason Jones 1984, pl XI). The figure inside the shrine is male, and may well be Mercury with a probable fourth-century date.

This second shrine is closely related to the Wallsend shrine, though in this instance the standing figure is of a female deity, with her right hand touching her left breast, and her left hand over her pudenda (Fig 4.31). In both instances the shrines have the remains of one or more loops into which an extension of the sides of the individual doors were fitted. Three survive on the Wallsend shrine, with only one slightly bent but complete loop on the lower left hand side of the Wroxeter piece.

The figure of Venus, with her stylised curly locks is unmistakeable, and her identity can be confirmed by the small child, presumably Eros, holding up a circular hand mirror for his mother to inspect her appearance. The example can be parallelled by a fresco in the Bath of the seven sages at Ostia, with a marine Venus Anadyomene and Cupid/Eros holding up her mirror; two white pipeclay groups, one with Eros holding up a hand mirror (Rouvier-Jeanlin 1972, 49, no 225, and 49, 141); and a terracotta statuette of Venus with Eros holding up an open lidded mirror, from Myrina, now in the Louvre (MYR 46), amongst other examples known in bronze, pipeclay, and other valuable materials.

In both the Wallsend and the Wroxeter shrines the centre above the arch of the shrine appears to be ornamented with what might be described as an antefix with a stylised head, with only a very small amount of damage.

The Wroxeter piece shows, as has been noted above, Eros holding a mirror. On the other side of Venus, as close in to her right leg as possible, there is another figure which was originally wrongly assumed by the writer to be the rudder and globe of Fortuna (in *Britannia*, 16, 285). A closer inspection suggests that this is a small child, and could well be Anteros, the other son of Mars and Venus/Aphrodite, who was said by Hesiod to have been born out of chaos together with Tartarus and Gaia.

Although only two of the lead shrines from Britain have been found up to the present time, there is at least one other item which has the loops for the doors of the shrines. This piece is unfortunately unprovenanced and is now in the Romische-Germanische Zentral Museum, Mainz am Rhein (O.29720). It is not a shrine but a tiny convex glass mirror recessed into a raised ring which holds it in place.

Finally it is perhaps appropriate to note one further example of a group which includes Venus. This is a piece now in the British Museum (Bronze Catalogue no 829), dated first or second century AD which shows a pantheistic Venus leaning against a trellis scattered with a range of attributes, and including the two small boys Eros and Anteros, the former still holding up his mother's mirror.

Small finds from the *macellum*

by Quita Mould

Introduction

A total of 142 small finds of metal, bone and stone was recovered from the *macellum* deposits belonging to Period WR 3.1 (Table 4.5). Thirteen of the objects were not available for examination and their previous records have been used where necessary. Small find numbers are shown in brackets. Some of the items have been catalogued and illustrated.

Objects represented

The majority could be classified as being either possible military fittings, personal decorative items, toilet implements, textile working implements, domestic utensils and fittings, structural items, or manufacturing debris. A small number of fragmentary objects, five of iron and five of copper alloy, could not be securely allocated to any one particular functional category.

Five copper alloy military fittings were recovered. A buckle with acorn finials (SF 4334, AML 793484) is comparable with examples from military levels at Wroxeter (Fig 4.7, 36–9 and parallels; Webster 1998) and Hadrian's Wall (Bishop and Coulston 1993, fig 80.6). A ring of faceted section (SF 3362, AML 810009) is likely to come from a legionary scabbard while the small looped sheet fitting (SF 4314, AML 793474) may be a plume tube from a helmet or possibly a *lorica segmentata* fitting. A broken loop (SF 3614, AML 736738) and a dome-headed stud (Fig 4.7, 29) are also likely to be military fittings.

A minimum of 17 personal decorative items were represented. Two copper alloy penannular brooches (SF 3144, AML 801407, and 3409, AML 801408, not reported on by Donald Mackreth) and a humped pin of iron probably from a third example were found. A pair of copper alloy earrings (SF 3384, AML 786809) of Allason-Jones type 1 (1989a, 2), the most commonly found style, and a small tack (SF 3205, AML 786788) or

Table 4.5 Small finds: the WR 3.1 collection from the *macellum*

	copper alloy	iron	bone	lead	stone/pot (*)
buckle	1	–	–	–	–
ring, scabbard	1	–	–	–	–
loop	1	–	–	–	–
stud, military	1	–	–	–	–
brooch	2	–	–	–	–
brooch pin	–	1	–	–	–
earring	3	–	–	–	–
chain frag	2	–	–	–	–
pin	–	–	9	–	–
needle	–	–	3	–	–
pin/needle stem	1	–	5	–	–
pin, pig fibula	–	–	1	–	–
spatula	–	–	1	–	–
tweezers	1	–	–	–	–
nail cleaner	1	–	–	–	–
probe	3	–	–	–	–
probe stem	2	–	–	–	–
mirror frag	1	–	–	–	–
suspension loop	1	–	–	–	–
counter	1	–	1	–	–
key	–	3	–	–	–
blade frag	–	1	–	–	–
whetstone	–	–	–	–	1
handle	–	–	1	–	–
finial	1	–	–	–	–
washer	1	–	–	–	–
mount	1	–	–	–	–
hinge unit	–	–	1	–	–
lampholder	–	–	–	1	–
stud/nail, domed	4	–	–	–	–
stud, flat	8	–	–	–	–
nail, spherical	1	–	–	–	–
hinge strap	–	1	–	–	–
joiner's dog	–	1	–	–	–
cramp	–	1	–	–	–
nail, type Ib	–	20	–	–	–
nail shanks	1	7	–	–	*1
tessera	–	–	–	–	*1
veneer	–	–	–	–	1
marble slab	–	–	–	–	1
wire	1	–	–	–	–
sheet offcut	4	–	–	1	–
waste	15	1	–	–	–
ring	1	1	–	–	–
sheet frag	4	1	–	–	–
strap frag	–	1	–	–	–
strip frag	1	2	–	–	–
fragments	4	–	–	2	–
silver flan	1	–	–	–	–
metal	1	–	–	–	–
total	71	41	22	4	4

earring of type 16 (*ibid*, 12) were recovered. Fragments of double loop-in-loop chain from jewellery were also found (Fig 4.7, 38–9, SF 3363, AML 760285, and SF 3390, AML 760290). Nine hair pins of bone occurred (Figs 4.9, 67; 4.10, 96, 99, 100, and 110) and five broken stems which may have come from pins or needles. No complete copper alloy pins were found. A pig fibula pin (Fig 4.16, 169) may have been used as a dress fastening.

A selection of copper alloy toilet implements was found, nine in total, including tweezers (Fig 4.11, 120), a nail cleaner (SF 3140, AML 786776, similar to Fig 4.11, 114), a possible mirror fragment (SF 4263,

AML 793464) and cosmetic probes (Fig 4.11, 123 etc). A long-handled spatula of bone (Fig 4.22, 232) may have been used as a cosmetic spoon. A single bone gaming counter was also noted (SF 3955, AML 785758).

Textile working was represented by three bone needles (Fig 4.16, 163), the broken stems of bone and copper alloy may also have come from needles. The pig fibula pin (Fig 4.16, 169) could have been used as a needle or knitting pin.

A broken knife blade, a simple bone handle (Fig 4.21, 224) and a whetstone (SF 4369, AML 793581) of a locally occurring fine-grained sandstone, are likely to represent domestic utensils rather than craft tools. The bone spatula (Fig 4.22, 232), mentioned above, may have been used as a simple spoon. The pointed terminal of the handle may suggest its use in eating shellfish comparable with metal spoons as described by Martial (*Epigrams*, 16, 121). Three iron keys were found, two being lift keys (Fig 4.19, 197–8) the other a slide key (Fig 4.19, 203). Other domestic fittings included a lead lampholder (SF 3369, AML 786413), a furniture finial of copper alloy (Fig 4.24, 241) probably from a folding stool, a bone hinge unit (Fig 4.25, 246), copper alloy studs and nails (eg Fig 4.26, 258) from upholstery and a copper alloy box mount (Fig 4.25, 250).

An iron door hinge (Fig 4.27, 267) and a small range of structural ironwork were recovered. A ceramic tessera (SF 4338, AML 793588), stone veneer of black micaceous slate (SF 3507), and a marble slab (SF 4023) all derive from a well appointed building. A pot containing a blue substance identified as Egyptian Blue pigment was recovered which may have been used in wall painting.

Manufacturing debris from the working of copper alloy, iron, and lead was recovered. Evidence of copper alloy working included a small quantity of waste fragments (SF 3388, AML 786780, SF 3403, AML 760292, and SF 4060, AML 785806) including solidified molten droplets, sheet offcuts (eg SF 3407–8, AML 786823–4, and SF 4339, AML 793487), scrap (eg Fig 4.29, 285; SF 3232, AML 786851) and a short length of partly-made wire (SF 3387, AML 786807). A total of 121 lbs of slag and a small quantity of hearth lining from small scale iron smithing was found in WB 83/111. A small amount of evidence of lead working was also noted (SF 3406). In addition a possible coin flan of base silver was found (SF 4344, AML 793488).

Dating

Coins of Vespasian and Hadrian were found. The military belt buckle is also of first or second-century date (Bishop and Coulston 1993), while the sheet fitting (SF 4314), if a plume tube, is comparable with those on early Principate helmets. The other items such as the scabbard ring, stud, and loop cannot be closely dated. Similarly the two copper alloy penannular brooches

found. The example seen by Mackreth cannot be paralleled by an example dated later than AD 200. The second example with Fowler D4 style terminals is a long-lived type. The humped style of the iron pin is generally considered to be an 'earlier' feature.

The earrings recovered of type 16 (Allason-Jones 1989a, 12), possibly a small stud rather than specifically an earring, and the pair of type 1 earrings the most commonly found style of Roman earring, occurred throughout the period (*ibid*, 2).

The bone hair pins comprised an example of Crummy's type 1 and two examples of type 2 with another three pins of type 2 with additional lattice decoration. At Colchester the type 1 and 2 pins have an end date of *c* AD 200 (Crummy 1983, 20–1). No pins of later Roman date (types 3, 4, 5, or 6 of third and fourth-century date) were found in these contexts. The repointed ring-headed pin (Fig 4.10, 110) is roughly made and likely to be a local product. Ring-headed pins of bone are unusual; examples with ring heads in copper alloy include a small group possibly from a single workshop (Cool 1990, group 9, 160, figs 6 and 7). An example occurred in the Walbrook, London suggesting a production date by AD 125. A southern British distribution has been suggested for the type.

The bone counter (SF 3955) with concentric rings on one face is of Crummy's type 2 which she dates to the mid to late Roman period from evidence from the Culver Street and Gilberd School excavations at Colchester (Crummy 1992, 220).

The nature of the assemblage

The proportion of complete objects and obviously broken objects is similar, so that while complete objects like the bone pins (Figs 4.9, 67; 4.10, 96; 4.16, 169), nail cleaner, tweezers (Fig 4.11, 120), bone spatula (Fig 4.22, 232), iron keys (Fig 4.19, 197–8, 203), and copper alloy tacks and studs are probably the result of casual loss, the similar quantity of broken items such as the pin (Fig 4.10, 100), needle, pin/needle stems, probes (Fig 4.11, 123) and the gaming counter are likely to come from the deliberate disposal of rubbish, as is the structural ironwork and manufacturing debris recovered. This suggests that the assemblage is most likely to be the result of the disposal of rubbish deliberately cleared from an area. The relatively high proportion of personal decorative items and toilet implements might be expected in the vicinity of the bath house. The occurrence of needles and copper alloy working debris can similarly be accommodated; at Caerleon both sewing and the repairing and manufacture of jewellery are suggested from the finds recovered from the baths (Allason-Jones 1989b, 179). The ironworking slag, however, is likely to have been brought in from further afield, slag being a common component of deliberate makeup layers. As the few datable small finds recovered suggest a first and second-century date this favours the interpretation that they were incorporated residually into the floor makeup deposits of *c* AD 300 rather than representing earlier third-century activity such as losses in the *macellum*.

The Romano-British brooches

by Donald Mackreth

Introduction

All the brooches listed below are made from copper alloy, unless otherwise stated. There is no extended essay here, unlike the introduction to the report on the military period brooches (Mackreth forthcoming). There would have been some justification, if the brooches recovered from the basilical hall excavations directed by Philip Barker were to be published in the foreseeable future, but so much depends upon the reader's appreciation of the actual brooches that it is pointless to discuss in detail items which cannot be seen either on the page or in microfiche.

All brooches from the post-military assemblage which can be guaranteed to have been used only during the period when Wroxeter was a site under military control have been included in the report on the military period brooches. Brooches which could have occurred in such deposits, but whose date ranges are known to have run into later times are, in a sense, in limbo. However, there should have been few of these and, even in the case of nos 1 and 2, as the dating comments make clear, little damage will have been done, beyond the loss of an opportunity for providing more evidence for the beginning of their 'floruits'.

The publication of both this and the collection recovered from the basilical hall excavations, would have given a more representative view of what was available to the local populace. However, to point the student in the right direction, those which either significantly amplify, or have direct parallels in, the report below, are noted in their correct places. The few which do not have a direct mention are: four brooches obviously derived from military contexts including a late Colchester; three Colchester Derivatives, one of which should have been made in the south-west; a Headstud with enamelled wings; a Trumpet brooch in the form of a fly and a small enamelled disc-on-bow Trumpet; an iron brooch almost certainly from Free Germany (eg Böhme 1972, Tafln 22–23, 900–912); an unclassified brooch looking like an enamelled Rosette; and six fully developed Crossbows. An important element in the basilical hall collection absent from the Webster assemblage is that which illustrates what was in use and discarded at the end of the use of the overall site: the absence of late Crossbows or of demonstrably late Penannulars (the latter from the basilical hall excavations are listed below before no 34) is due to the bulk of the baths *insula* south of the basilical hall having been stripped effectively of its latest deposits by 1955 when excavations began. The only area which displayed

consistently late occupation commensurate with that found in the basilical hall area was the west portico, and even here there were no deep deposits of the 'dark earth' such as those which survived, in however a cut-about state, to the north.

The suggested dates and sources of the brooches have been tabulated (Table 4.6).

Colchester Derivatives (Figs 4.32 and 4.33)

Brooches 1, 3–10 and 12 have or had their springs held in the Polden Hill manner: an axis bar through the coils is mounted in pierced plates at the ends of the wings, the chord being held by a rearward-facing hook behind the head of the bow.

Table 4.6 Brooches: dating and sources

No	phase	approximate context date AD	brooch date	brooch source
1	C 2.1	130	first-century	Severn Valley
2	WR 2.3	160	first-century	Severn Valley
3	military	90	90–175	Severn Valley
4	WR 2.3	160	90–175	Severn Valley
5	WR 3.1	300	90–175	Severn Valley
6	P 3.3	260–360	90–175	Severn Valley
7	C 2.1	130	90–175	Severn Valley
8	P 3.3	260–360	90–175	Severn Valley
9	u/s		90–175	Severn Valley
10	WR 2.3	160	90–175	Severn Valley
11	u/s		90–175	Severn Valley
12	u/s		90–175	Severn Valley
13	P 2.3	160	first-century	?south-east
14	u/s		100–175	west midlands
15	u/s		100–175	west midlands
16	–		100	?
17	BP 2.2	150	90–175	east midlands
18	P 3.1	230	100–175	?
19	P 2.3	160	75–175	midlands
20	u/s		75–175	?
21	BP 3.2	fourth-century	75–175	?
22	P 3.3	260–360	75–175	south Pennines
23	military	90	75–175	?
24	u/s		75–175	?
25	–		80–200	?
26	u/s		80–200	southern England
27	P 3.1	230	150–225	Britain
28	P 3.3	260–360	150–225	continent
29	u/s		150–225	continent
30	P 3.1	230	75–175	southern England
31	P 3.1	230	150–250	continent
32	P 3.3	260–360	second-century	?
33	P 3.1	230	second-century	?
34	u/s		90–210	?
35	1.3	120	50–150	?
36	C 2.1	130	50–150	?
37	WR 3.1	300	80–200	?
38	BP 3.2	fourth-century	80–200	?
39	P 3.2	250	80–200	?
40	u/s		Iron Age origin	?
41	P 3.3	260–360	Iron Age origin	?
42	C 2.1	130	Iron Age origin	?
43	u/s		late-/post-Roman	?
45	P 3.3	260–360	90–175	Severn Valley
46	BP 3.2	fourth-century	second-century	?
47	P 3.2	250	second-century	?

P portico, WR west range, C courtyard, BP baths precinct

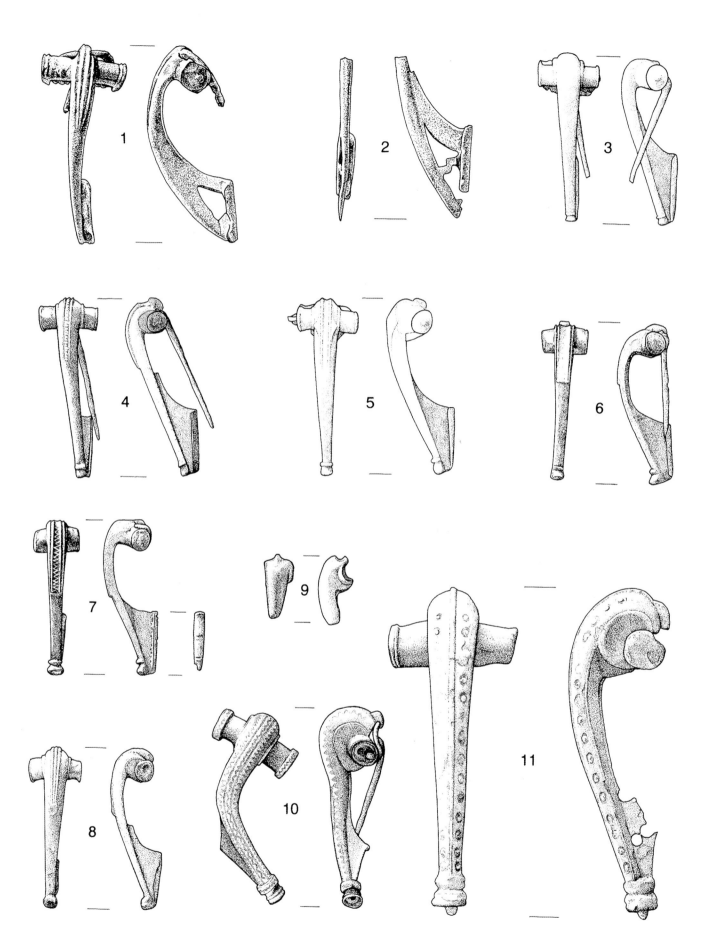

Fig 4.32 Brooches: Colchester derivatives; scale 1:1

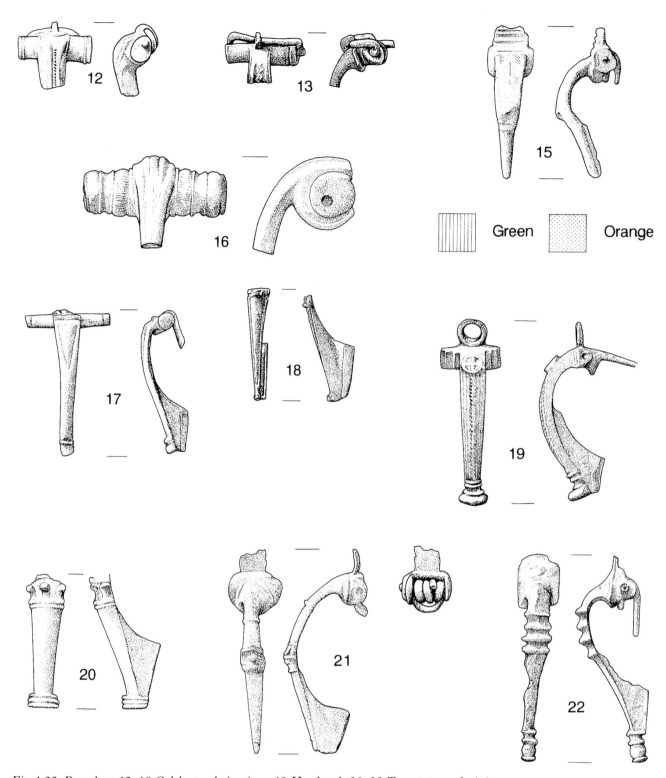

Fig 4.33 Brooches: 12–18 Colchester derivatives, 19 Headstud, 20–22 Trumpets; scale 1:1

Green   Orange

1   Each wing has a pair of prominent mouldings at its end. There is another pair running down the centre of the upper part of the bow. The catch-plate has a large piercing. 92/45, C 2.1 (SF 3510)

2   The head is lost. The plain bow tapers to a pointed foot. The catch-plate has a large triangular piercing divided by a dog-leg bar. 87/100, WR 2.3 (SF 5019)

Dated parallels are few, therefore typological considerations come into play. The chief of these is that piercings,

other than an occasional circular hole (eg basilical hall excavations, SF 339), are not a feature of full blown second-century brooches, and elaborate ones with dog-leg bars would normally not be expected late in the first century. Colchester Derivatives, whose catch-plate piercings are not the ordinary triangle or circle, have occurred in military contexts at Wroxeter (Mackreth forthcoming, nos 1 and 4). Although the head of no 2 is lost, the character of the piercing is enough to show that the brooch should be earlier than the general members of the group to which nos 3–12 belong. No 1 bears a family resemblance to nos 3–9, but its bow lacks the same kind of foot and the junction with the wings is like that found on Polden Hill brooches further south. All the limited dating evidence recorded by the writer for these is: Colchester, 49 – c AD 65 (Hawkes and Hull 1947, 311, pl 91.11); Nettleton, first century (Wedlake 1982, 123–25, fig 52.36A); Whitton, Glam, before AD 135 (Jarrett and Wrathmell 1981, 169, fig 69.10). This should include the normal residual factor. The dating begins well before that for the next group of brooches to be considered, but as two dated members of the next family have dog-leg bars in pierced catch-plates there is no simple argument: they come from Worcester and Wroxeter and are noted in the section dealing with dating. The first has no ornamental foot, but the second has one of the common form found on the type. Other examples with both, but without dating come from Saham Toney, Norfolk (Brown 1986, 27, fig 19.127), Richborough (Bushe-Fox 1949, 112, pl 27, 25), and Wall, Staffs (unpublished). In addition, the family has extreme cases like the highly elaborate catch-plate on a brooch from Polnaise, Scotland (Curle 1933, 336, fig 36.2–3). Piercings in the catch-plates of two brooches from Saalburg, although not well drawn, suggest that they could almost have been made by the same craftsman (Böhme 1970, 5, Abb.1, 4, 5). There is a strong possibility that these styles of catch-plate occur early in the series, possibly before AD 100.

As for the single large piercing in the catch-plate of no 1, none came from a securely stratified military context at Wroxeter. The dating for simple triangular holes is: Bagendon, c AD 50–60, definite prototype for next group (Clifford 1961, 173, fig 31.5); Camerton, AD 65–85 (Wedlake 1958, 218, fig 50.7); Verulamium, before the late first century, with foot (Lowther 1937, 37, fig 2.1), and AD 85–105 (Frere 1972, 114, fig 29.9); Wycomb, Glos, late first-early second century, with foot like those in next group (Rawes 1980, 17); Camerton, after AD 90, with foot (Wedlake 1958, 218, fig 50.8); Wroxeter, before c AD 150 (Bushe-Fox 1916, 23, pl 15.6). The dating again begins before that of the next group, but overlaps that, and the presence of definite feet, including the type of foot-knob found on brooches of the next family, shows that this is not the effect of residuality. Only one dated example of the 3–12 family with a triangular piecing has been recorded by the writer (see dating list after no 12) and only one undated example with the piercing and no foot ornament: Richborough (Cunliffe 1968, 80, pl 28.27). However weak these signs may be, there is a faint indication that the triangular piercing is also generally early in the series.

3 Each wing has a moulding at its end. The junction of the wings with the bow is masked on each side by a curved moulding rising from the wings. The bow is plain and tapers to a foot-knob with a

moulding across its top. 93/3, a military layer from the last *intervallum* road surface

4 Each wing has a ridge at its end. The junction of the bow with the wings is masked by curved plates rising from the wings. The upper bow has three ridges running down the centre, the middle one being beaded. The foot-knob has a moulding across its top. Two similar ones, only with a central ridge buried in the head, came from the basilical hall excavations (SFs 353 and 469). 84/201, WR 2.3 (SF 4680)

5 Similar to the previous example, on each side of the pair of ridges on the bow is a pair of curved lines which form a concave-sided lozenge across the bow. The rest of the brooch is a repeat of what has gone before. 86/24, WR 3.1 (SF 2179)

6 One wing has a trace of a moulding at its end. The upper bow has a bordering ridge set off from a wide central flute by a groove, the rest is like the previous examples. 90/56, P 3.3 (SF 4432)

7 The wings are plain. The upper bow has two mouldings down the middle separated by a broad flute having rocker-arm ornament along it. The lower bow is like the previous ones. The catch-plate return has three pairs of grooves. 3/20, C 2.1 (SF 116)

8 The wings are plain, their junction with the bow being masked by curved mouldings rising from the wings. The upper bow has three central ridges which converge on a small poorly-defined disc. The lower bow ends in a plain knob. 90/161, P 3.3 (SF 5436, AML 835943)

9 A fragment of a brooch of the same form as the last, but with a plain head. The wings are lost along with the lower bow with the catch-plate. 90/+, P 4 (SF 4196, AML 785815)

10 Each wing has a triple moulding at its end made up of wavy ridge between two plain ones, the spaces being filled with a silvery metal. The junction of the wings with the bow is masked by curved mouldings rising from the wings. The bow is humped over the wings. There is a sunken repeat of the ornament on the wings, complete with the metal filling, only the scalloped outer edges make the white metal form a series of cusps. The foot-knob has a ridge around its top and is divided by a short shank from the upper part which repeats the decoration on the wings. All this lies below the catch-plate and is dished beneath with a dimple in the middle. The catch-plate has a groove on the back defining the beginning of the return which has a triple moulding at its top. 83/512, WR 2/3 (SF 4360, AML 793493)

11 Each wing has a double moulding at its end and a curved moulding hiding the junction with the bow. A central ridge down the bow has, on each side, a series of small bosses rising from annular grooves. The foot-knob is worn leaving only slight traces of more than one moulding over a flute and

double mouldings under. There is a boss underneath. This brooch weighs 57.39g, more than six times heavier than the average.

Two brooches from the basilical hall excavations are not only related, but probably from the same manufacturer (SFs 152 and 263). 70/+, C 4 (SF 1301, AML 786910)

12   Each wing has a pair of mouldings at its end. The surviving head of the bow has a central sunken bead-row in its upper part. On each side is a ridge ending in a lobe at the top. Outside that is another which runs round the lobe to end in another lobe under that. There is a trace of an additional ridge at the fracture. A similar brooch was found in the basilical hall excavations (SF 132). Metal detector find.

All these belong to the chief Colchester Derivative family found in the western districts of England. It was made in great numbers somewhere in the central Severn Valley and traded extensively into Wales, the Cheshire plain and out to the east. It occurs sporadically over the rest of Roman Britain. A secondary workshop in the southern Pennines replaced the Polden Hill spring system with a hinged pin.

As Wroxeter lies in the heartland of the family, it is appropriate that a review of the dating evidence available to the writer should be given here: Croft Ambrey, *c* AD 75–160, four examples (Stanford 1974, 144, fig 67.2, 4, 5), one without foot but with a triangular piercing (*ibid*, 144, fig 67.1); Wroxeter, AD 80–120, with dog-leg bar in a pierced catch-plate (Bushe-Fox 1916, 23, pl 15.5); Derby, late first-early second century, two examples (Mackreth 1985, 283–5, fig 123.5; fig 124.10); Verulamium, AD 115–30 (Frere 1972, 114, fig 29.10); Worcester, probably before *c* AD 120, with divided piercing in the catchplate and no foot ornament (Mackreth 1992, 73, fig 37.1); Derby, *c* AD 120–50 (Mackreth 1985, 283–5, fig 124.8); Watercrook, AD 120–90, probably hinged (Potter 1979, 210, fig 84.11); Wall, Staffs, in rubbish dating at latest to Hadrianic-early Antonine times (Gould 1967, 17, fig 7.7); Caerleon, Hadrianic-Antonine (Brewer 1986, 170, fig 54.5); Derby, AD 150–75 (Mackreth 1985, 283–5, fig 123.6); Baldock, AD 150–80 (Stead and Rigby 1986, 113, fig 45.83); Shakenoak Farm, mid-second to mid-third century (Brodribb *et al* 1971, 118–19, fig 47.70); Whitton, Glam, ?before *c* AD 160 (Jarrett and Wrathmell 1981, 169, fig 69.12); Shakenoak Farm, before AD 180 (Brodribb *et al* 1968, 95, fig 27.7); Exeter, late second-early third (Mackreth 1991, 235, fig 101.20); Worcester, residual in early third-century dumps, three examples (Mackreth 1992, 73, fig 37.4, 5, and not illustrated), *c* AD 240–300 (*ibid*, 73–5, fig 37.6); Prestatyn, late third-early fourth century, hinged pin (Mackreth 1989a, 92, fig 37.10); Derby, late third-fourth century, with hinged pin (Mackreth 1985, 283–5, fig 125.11); Gloucester, late fourth century (Hassall and Rhodes 1975, 66, fig 26.1); Cirencester, AD 375–410/420, two examples (Mackreth 1986, 104, fig 77.1, 2).

The evidence is fairly clear: the type begins in the late first century and the incidence of those without feet and with piercings in their catchplates is in favour of these being in the earliest strand of the main type. Thereafter, the family develops and proliferates to about AD 175 at which point the dating becomes more diffuse, the dating of those after *c* AD 225 show that they must be residual. Of the five bridging AD 200, three are noted as being residual. Just as the evidence suggests which are early traits, hinged-pin specimens could all be after AD 125. The main type runs from *c* AD 75/85 to 175 by which time almost all had entered the ground, but there are enough to suggest that the type was to be seen for another twenty-five years.

13   The axis bar passes through a pierced lug behind the head of the bow, the chord being held in a crest on the head itself. Only the top survives, each wing having a groove at its end. The bow has another down each margin and the top of a panel in the centre which has a reserved wavy line down it. 98/87, P 2.3 (SF 5605, AML 835971)

14   A closely related brooch comes from the basilical hall excavations (SF 88). From excavation of street section north of the basilical hall (Webster and Daniels 1970, fig 4.3; SF 553).

15   The spring has an internal chord and is held in place by an axis bar running through the coils and the ends of a case with a rounded bottom and a squared top. On top are the remains of a cast-on loop on a pedestal. The top of the bow has a markedly curved profile and the section here has a rounded back and a flat front down which are three cells for enamel of which the only trace is of an orange. At the base of the cells is what seems to be a boss. The lower bow is narrower, possibly with a step on each side, and tapers towards the foot, now missing. Metal detector find

Had the spring-fixing system been a Polden Hill, it would have been relatively easy to have equated no 13 with some version of 14 or 15, more probably the latter. It is, however, a kind of hybrid: the mounting of the spring on lugs in the centre is reminiscent of the system using two holes in a single plate behind the head of the bow and found in south-eastern England. The reserved wavy line set in red enamel is found on three brooches from Wroxeter (Rowley's House Museum, X24, X26, X27), one is made in three pieces, has a Polden Hill spring system and a boss under the enamelled upper bow, relating it to no 14; the other two have a spring system like that of no 15 and an enamelled upper bow, as well as a feature under this, so linking all five together. All belong to the same general milieu, but the basic design is varied by being married to technical aspects drawn from different regions. The earliest ought to be the item made in three pieces and probably dating to before the close of the military site at Wroxeter. The other piece from Rowley's House Museum is not so easily disposed of, but the reserved wavy line is not to be expected on second-century brooches and this should carry no 13 with it. A point in favour of a first-century date for 13 is its hybrid spring fixing system, these are only to be expected in the first century.

The design of 14 is, without the boss, almost identical with one found in a family of brooches at home in south-west England (as an example from the basilical hall excavations), although examples can be found across southern England, but apparently not in the north. All have decoration, usually enamelled, on the upper bow, most having the mouldings at the base of that to be seen here. A sub-group of the family has more further down. Others have more elaborate mouldings at the bottom of the main panel, sometimes recalling the knop on the standard Trumpet (eg Nash-Williams 1930, 239, fig 2.2). Not all have sprung pins, but those that do are fitted with a crest as here, the others tend to have a tab cast on the head, often pierced to form a proper loop. Considering how the high proportion of those recorded by the writer come from Nor'Nour where they are undated (Hull 1967), the dating yielded by the rest is surprisingly consistent: Gadebridge Park, ?c AD 75–150 (Neal 1974, 125, fig 54.16); Chew, late first-second century (Rahtz and Greenfield 1977, fig 114.8); Caerleon, before c AD 125 (Wheeler and Wheeler 1928, 162, fig 13.4); Wroxeter, ?after AD 125 (Atkinson 1942, 205, fig 36.H40); Caerleon, c AD 130–80 (Wheeler and Wheeler 1928, 162, fig 13.13); Brockworth, Glos, before c AD 150 (Rawes 1981, 66, fig 7.3); Camerton, third century (Wedlake 1958, 221, fig 55.15A); Chew, late third-mid fourth century (Rahtz and Greenfield 1977, fig 114.10); Chichester, late fourth-early fifth century (Mackreth and Butcher 1981, 254–6, fig 10.1, 3).

The type appears to be essentially second century with a terminal date conforming with that of almost all British bow brooches: AD 150–75. Those which come from later contexts must be regarded as having been residual. In the specific case of no 14, its relationships are explored in the discussion of 13 and 15, but the median ornament on the lower bow coupled with the foot-knob and the plates on the sides of the head show it to be almost certainly a product of the same school represented by nos 3–12.

The remains of the cast-on loop and pedestal on no 14 point to the second century rather than the first. If the profile, the boss, the cast-on loop-and-pedestal and the spring system are taken as the chief features, the distribution centres on the West Midlands and runs up into Cumbria with a significant presence in the southern Pennines suggesting that it was an alternative design in the repertoire of those who produced the hinged-pin specimens of the family to which 3–12 belong. Examples, however, occur in a wider zone spreading into Gloucestershire and across into the eastern

Midlands. Very few, however, are found in the deep south-west, central southern or south-eastern England, East Anglia or up the east side of England north of the Wash. The limited dating evidence is: Derby, AD 115–40 (Mackreth 1985, 293–4, fig 128.33); Biglands, AD 125–180/197 (Potter 1979, 171, fig 11.16); east end of the Antonine Wall, c AD 140–160/165 (Robertson 1970, 223, fig 10.7). Three examples may not seem many, but they should serve to show that the basic design is second-century, but unlikely to be much later than c AD 175.

16 The wings have bead-and-reel mouldings, the reel nearest the bow being beaded. The bow is much slighter than the wings, is largely missing and has a sunken bead-row down the middle of the head. Unstratified (SF 1843)

The bead-and-reel moulding on the wings is only commonly found on the Rearhook and a few hinged brooches whose decorative repertoire derives mainly from that type. The Rearhook is specifically Icenian and hardly any survived the aftermath of the Boudiccan rebellion (Mackreth 1996). Hinged examples being, however, made mainly outside Icenian lands should have had a longer life, and there is no good evidence that pieces like the present one should be dated significantly after AD 100. Both 16 and 17 have hinged pins.

17 The axis bar for the pin was inserted into a slot in the back of the wings which was then closed round it. The pin is a piece of wire wound round the axis bar. Each wing has a rudimentary moulding at the end. The bow has a triangular boss on its head and a two-part foot-knob. 57/48, BP 2.2 (SF 1126)

The family to which 17 belongs employs a small range of motifs which are differently combined to great effect. The present example has the typical boss and foot, but the latter can be replaced by a fantail with dot-and-circle ornament. The upper bow may have a short beaded ridge which sometimes is combined with the fantail foot. The most extreme example is designed like the present specimen, but has a cross-moulding in the middle and a semicircular lug on each side just above that with a dot-and-circle stamp. The distribution recorded by the writer is distorted to some measure by the large-scale excavations at Verulamium as well as the general bias in the writer's collecting which possibly over emphasises Cambridgeshire and Northamptonshire. Even taking such factors into account, the centre of distribution is obviously Northamptonshire, Leicestershire and the northern end of Cambridgeshire. Thereafter, members of the family are to be found most commonly in the immediately peripheral counties. The numbers from Hertfordshire and also from Derby could point to an extension of their marketing. The single example from Wroxeter, and that means from all sites and Rowley's House Museum, must lie outside its normal area. A curious feature is that few of the pins on the type are properly hinged, most being formed by winding wire round the axis bar, as here. This suggests a relationship with what seems to be an early hybrid in which a bilateral spring is held between the increasingly thickened ends of the wings until the spring becomes so short that it seems that something like the present system must result. On typological grounds alone, the type should have originated in the first century. The recorded dating is: Bannaventa, late first-early second century (Dix and Taylor 1988, 334, fig 19.3); Weekley, late first century to *c* AD 175 (Jackson and Dix 1987, M76, fig 23.15); Verulamium, before *c* AD 150, two examples (Wheeler and Wheeler 1936, 206, fig 43.17, 18); Derby, Antonine (Mackreth 1985, 285, fig 125.12); Leicester, before AD 220 (Kenyon 1948, 249, fig 80.10); Derby, probably third-fourth century (Mackreth 1985, 285, fig 125.14), fourth century (*ibid*, 285, fig 125.13); Stantonbury, Beds, late fourth century (Marney and Mackreth 1987, 132, fig 41.14); Chichester, late fourth century or later (Down and Rule 1971, 83, fig 5.14.4). It is possible that the type, on this dating, could have begun in the late first century, but it is equally clear that it passed out of use before AD 200, if not AD 175. The break-down in the sequence of dating after the example from Leicester is enough to show at which point true residuality at least must start.

18 The bow was divided into two parts by a cross-groove and all above that is missing. The lower bow has groove down each side and tapers to a simple projecting foot. 90/140, F709, P 3.1, KG 16 (SF 5171, AML 830318)

Not enough really survives for a group to which this brooch could belong to be identified. Nothing suggests a first-century date and, like most British bow brooches, it probably had passed out of use by AD 175.

Headstud (Fig 4.33)

19 The axis bar for the hinged pin is housed in a half-round projection behind the wings. Each of which has three steps up to the bow. On the head is a cast-on loop, a stud below that with a reserved four-leaf motif in a circle of enamel and, under that, the bow has a groove down each side and two longitudinal cells for enamel with a series of reserved lozenges between. 98/52, P 2.3 (SF 5408, AML 835932)

This is a standard variety of Headstud, the stud having a simple cross or four-petalled motif or an annular groove. Its distribution is mainly in the Midlands, but runs into Lancashire and Yorkshire. The writer has

recorded none from further north and relatively few from the rest of southern England, although that may be due to biases in recording. The dating is sparse: Doncaster, AD 80–90 (Buckland and Magilton 1985, 88, fig 19.13); Nettleton, late first-early second century (Wedlake 1982, 128, fig 53.61); Worcester, residual in early to mid third-century deposits (Mackreth 1992, 75, fig 38.1). The type should, therefore, have begun in the later first century and have come to an end at least by AD 175 when most British bow brooches had passed out of use.

Trumpets (Fig 4.33)

20 The head and the trumpet are missing. The knop has a central moulding with three projections and a pair of narrow ones at the top of the lower bow. This has a central arris. The foot-knob is broad and made up of three mouldings. 70/5, C 4 (SF 1490)

21 The spring is housed like that in no 15. On the head is the stub of a tall pierced tab. The head-plate is round, the etiolated triangular-sectioned trumpet springing from a step. Half-way down the trumpet is a cross-moulding with a series of smaller ones just above. The simple petalled knob has a cross-moulding above and below. The lower bow is plain and has traces of two mouldings at the bottom. 58/10, BP 3.2 (SF 813)

22 The spring is mounted like that in the last brooch. The head-plate is tall, possibly once with a pierced tab or cast-on loop. The trumpet is short, narrow and rounded in front. The knop is made up of four cross-mouldings of almost equal size divided by broad flutes. The lower bow tapers to a cross-moulding under which is a fully moulded foot consisting of a wide moulding between two narrow ones. 80/59, F477, P 3.3 (SF 3853, AML 787762)

Other examples of Trumpets from the basilical hall excavations help to give a more rounded view of the type available in Wroxeter than the varieties here: SF 679 is a fine example of silver inlay in Celtic patterns (eg, Thompson 1963, *passim*); SF 314, a fragment only, weighing 27.76g, from a giant Trumpet which could not have weighed less than 60–70g, the multiple petalling recalls that on the Carmarthen brooch (Boon and Savory 1975) and the surviving top of the lower bow is moulded in relief in, again, Celtic patterns; SF 563, the collar from a loop-and-collar arrangement with a large petalled flower on its front, again reminiscent of the Carmarthen brooch (*ibid*); SF 193, an example whose petalled knop is only on the front of the bow like SF 881) which has a hinged pin.

A recent review of the general dating of Trumpets (Mackreth forthcoming) concluded that the overall *floruit* at best is from before *c* AD 75 to 150–75.

However, there are enough to suggest that the last survivors-in-use probably continued to 200, hardly any being seen after then. The remains of no 20 suggest that it is close to the standard petalled variety, but that the knop did not run all the way round the bow. No 21 is a little further removed in form, by having had a loop on a pedestal and in the way the spring is mounted. The present example lies at the northern end of the distribution which is very much south of Wroxeter, although examples from as far away as East Anglia are known. None is earlier than Hadrian. The knop of no 22 is distinctive and occurs most frequently in the southern Pennines with a tendency to occur more frequently immediately west and south-west of that region than in other immediately contiguous areas. One from Wroxeter was dated AD 110–30 (Bushe-Fox 1913, 26, fig 10.8) and another from Derby was AD 150–75 (Mackreth 1985, 291–3, fig 128.31).

Unclassified (Fig 4.34)

23 The spring is mounted on a tube which is held in pierced plates on either side of the plain circular head-plate. The tube implies a separate loop-and-collar arrangement. The bow is an extended trumpet, with a ridge round the top, running down to a pair of cross-ridges above a foot-knob made up of a boss with a ridge around the top. Mounted on the front of the bow is an excrescence consisting of a large bulbous extra moulding which runs from the top to about halfway down where it ends in a loop. The catch-plate has a groove across the top and bottom with another placed diagonally between. 10/11, military destruction layer (SF 809)

24 The spring and head-plate are a complete version of those on no 21. The trumpet head is a little rudimentary and runs down to a slight expansion on each side of the bow. Set vertically in the middle is a projecting plate with a profile having a concave surface at the base, another in the middle in which the top edge sweeps up so that a third is in effect in the corner. The foot is lost. 22/2, BP 4 (SF 305, AML 786898)

Both of these are marked by extraordinary excrescences on the front of the bow. Both are obviously related to the Trumpet type, but only 23 is a member of a group seemingly midway between an elaborate trunk folded back on itself (eg Camerton, Wedlake 1958, 224, fig 51.17) and the common form in which the trunk has been reduced to a kind of crest which may or may not have a hole through the lower lobe (eg Kirk 1949, 11, fig 3.4; Lee 1862, 62, pl 31.11). The writer has only recorded one possible parallel for 24 (Hattatt 1985, 112, fig 46.444) and only one of the whole group with a date: the example from Camerton above which came from a context of AD 150–200. However, the general type is unlikely to have a *floruit*

markedly different from that of the Trumpet type, even its origins may not be so early.

25 The pin was hinged. On the head is a cast-on loop. The head sweeps out to form wings each of which ends in a pair of mouldings. In the centre is a disc recessed for enamel and containing a reserved annulus. There is a small projection on each side. Above are two cross-mouldings and, below, four. The fantail foot has a groove along the borders and enamelling down the centre in a line of lozenges with infilling triangles. Two lozenges have traces of a red enamel. From excavation of street section north of the basilical hall (Webster and Daniels 1970; SF 563, AML 786897).

It is doubtful whether this design derived from any form of Trumpet as such, but what must typologically be one of the earliest examples has more of a trumpet head than the ruck (Butcher 1977, 64, fig 10.30). These apparently early ones have well shaped mouldings or bosses around the disc and a separately-made central stud. The fantail foot usually has enamelled triangular cells and some discs have cells which give them the appearance of being wheels (eg, Bushe-Fox 1914, 13, fig 4.3). Only the most general dating is available for this strand: Newstead, AD 80– *c* 200 (Curle 1911, 324, pl 86.24; Hartley 1972b, 54).

The common form is represented by the present example. Here, the incipient trumpet is replaced by surfaces which sweep out to become the front of the wings. The fantail foot sometimes has a reserved peltate design with a lozenge above (eg Hattatt 1987, 149–50, fig 49.990), or another celtic-style pattern (eg Sheppard 1907, 2, pl 27.4) and another version has three reserved pendants. The most extreme form for a whole brooch, however, is an example from South Uist (Lethbridge 1952, 182, fig 4.1) which is intermediate between the early ones and these. Dating is rare: Silchester, mid-second century (Boon 1969, 47, fig 6.8); Rudston, Yorks, ?second century (Stead 1980, 95, fig 61.14); Prestatyn, late third-early fourth century (Mackreth 1989a, 96–7, fig 39.21). In a small group, the disc is replaced by a rectangular panel, with rectangular cells for enamel. All of these save one have triangular cells on the foot, recalling the earlier style. The exception has a celtic-style design. None is dated, but, typologically, the foot designs point to an intermediate position between the main types discussed.

26 The spring was held between pierced lugs behind the head which has the stub of a cast-on loop on top. The trumpet head has four cells radiating out from the base. A deep glassy blue enamel survives in the outer cells. The knop of a Trumpet brooch is replaced here by an expansion with a prominent projecting, almost semi-circular, plate. The rest of the brooch is missing. Metal detector find

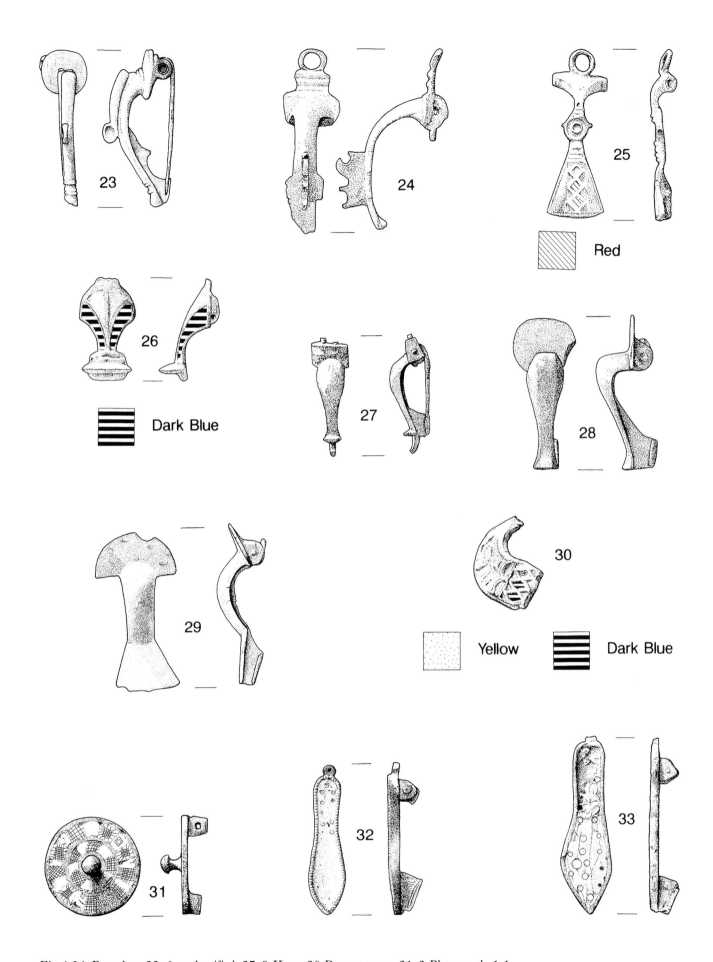

Fig 4.34 Brooches: 23–6 unclassified, 27–9 Knee, 30 Dragonesque, 31–3 Plate; scale 1:1

A brooch belonging to the same family, recognizably Almgren 101, only tricked out with applied silver wiring, came from the basilical hall excavation (SF 140). It is a member of a group (eg Bishop and Dore 1988, 161–163, fig 76.12) whose increasing numbers in Britain strongly suggest that it was made here and is locally represented by a fine well-preserved brooch from High Ercall, Salop.

It is surprising that Britain should have adopted a type more at home in Free Germany and military areas on the continent than inside the empire itself (Böhme 1972, Taf 21.849–864; Dollfus 1975; Feugère 1985; Haalebos 1986, fig 28.5–6; Jobst 1975; Kovrig 1937; Lerat 1956; Lerat 1957; Riha 1979): the British distribution is almost exclusively in southern England. One from Corbridge may have been imported from somewhere along the Danube (Haverfield 1911, 488, fig 4). While most examples had applied white metal applique, a few are enamelled, like the fragment here. White metal trim appears to be specifically British and, if the general date of the use of the technique is a guide, most British Almgren 101s will date between *c* AD 125 and the early third century. The dating of the brooches themselves is: Chichester, late first-mid/late second century (Mackreth 1989b, 188–9, not illustrated); Newstead, AD 80– *c* 200 (Curle 1911, 318, pl 85.2: Hartley 1972b, 54); Camerton, second century, probably Antonine (Wedlake 1958, 223, fig 52.16); Leicester, up to *c* AD 200 (Kenyon 1948, 251, fig 80.15). This seems to confirm the dating offered by the use of applied white metal. Enamelling is found on a wider range of designs, even though there are fewer examples overall (eg Hattatt 1985, 113, fig 47.447; Hattatt 1987, 142, fig 47.977, 978). However, the commonest pattern for the enamelled examples is the present one and the foot should be restored as a weak fantail with three prongs below and the field recessed for enamel in which reserved strips leave a cross with a dot in it in the middle. The only dated enamelled version is, luckily, of the same family as the present piece and comes from Dura Europos: AD 165–256 (Frisch and Toll 1949, 41, pl 9.2). As far as enamelling alone on brooches goes, none should be later than AD 225, even if as late as AD 200.

Knee (Fig 4.34)

27 The case for the spring has a flat rectangular front with the stubs of a cast-on loop on top. The bow is cabriole-shaped and has a long prong projecting from its base. The basilical hall excavations yielded three further examples of this British variety only with enamel or white metal trim: SFs 413, 87, and B102. 98/78, F 804, P 3.1, KG 16 (SF 5591, AML 835985)

28 The spring is mounted between two pierced lugs behind the circular head-plate. The bow is a faceted cabriole shape. 90/56, P 3.3 (SF 4456)

29 The spring is mounted like the last but behind a fan-shaped head. The bow is a simple arc joining the head-plate to the plain fantail foot. Metal detector find

The basilical hall excavations produced five examples of continental Knee brooches, including one with enamelled scrolls: SFs 219, 292, 413, 455, and 537. The first is almost certainly a British product: although it lacks the enamel or white metal trim found on the examples from the basilical hall excavations, the small size and generally slight character match. The other two brooches are continental. The overall dating of the Knee type in Britain has recently been reviewed and the conclusion was that its floruit was unequivocally in the second half of the second century and the early third. No 29 is only placed here because its upper part is very close to a variety of Knee brooch, but has yet to be established that the two can be equated even though the bows of brooches like 29 are frequently faceted like so many of those of continental Knee Brooches. The British dating is: Vindolanda, with mid third-century material (Bidwell 1985, 119, fig 39.7); Richborough, said to be third or fourth century (Bushe-Fox 1949, 118, pl 29.51). The roll-call of sites from which examples come is: Caerleon; Catterick, two examples; Corbridge, two examples; Ditchingham, Norfolk; Dorset; East Anglia; Housesteads; Lazonby, Cumbria; Leicester; Richborough, two published examples; South Shields; Staines, Middlesex; Vindolanda, two examples. The very strong military element here may mean that they were almost exclusively worn by soldiers.

Dragonesque (Fig 4.34)

30 All that survives is the centre and one neck of the familiar S-shape. The centre panel is enamelled in a central line of lozenges, containing a deepish blue, with infilling triangles. The surviving end has two long cells running away from the panel, each with a semicircle of what may be a yellow enamel next to that. 80/119, F466, P 3.1, KG 16 (SF 4406)

Commonly supposed to be a northern brooch because of the numbers found there, the type very probably originates in the south of England, the early ones being unenamelled and sometimes tinned or silvered. The matter of origin is not absolutely clear-cut as one from Wetwang shows (Hull and Hawkes 1987, 168, pl 50.2D): it could have been deposited before the Romans arrived in that part of the world. That it should be early is shown by the plate which is bowed, unlike the common form, but another iron example from Maiden Castle, even if found in a Late Roman context, should nevertheless be no later than the first century, and hardly later than AD 50–75 (Wheeler 1943, 262, fig 85.32). Collingwood published an unenamelled dragonesque from Braughing which he described as being the earliest form and as having been found associated with objects hardly later than the Claudian invasion (Collingwood, 1930, 53, fig 11a). The problem here is what he meant by associated. A plate form close to the main versions, but without enamel and with tinning or silvering, from Norfolk should not be second century (Hattatt 1985, 171, fig 70.609), but unenamelled ones are also found in the north: Traprain Law (Cree 1922, 251, fig.28,4).

Those made from wire have been omitted from the following discussion. The dating recorded by the writer is: Longthorpe, Cambs, Claudian-Neronian, unenamelled (Dannell and Wild 1987, 87, fig.21, 9); Old Winteringham, Neronian-early Flavian (Stead 1976, 198, fig 99.11); Newstead, AD 80– ?165 (Curle 1911, 320, pl 85.7), AD 80– *c* 200 (Curle 1933, 398, fig 1.2–3); Rudston, 90–110, unenamelled (Stead 1980, 95, fig 61.17); Milking Nook, ?Trajanic (Feachem 1951, 38, fig 2.H2; Daniels 1978, 168); Scole, Norfolk, two examples, Trajanic-mid-Antonine (Rogerson 1977, 133–134, fig 55.10, 11); Watercrook, *c* AD 110–40 (Potter 1979, 210–11, fig 84.14); Wroxeter, before *c* AD 130 (Bushe-Fox 1916, 24, pl 16.9); Rudston, AD 140–60, unenamelled (Stead 1980, 85, fig 61.16). The dating is relatively clear, the enamelled series begins apparently as early as the Flavian period and continues to no later than AD 175. In fact, the period AD 150–75 probably represents the time when survivors-in-use were entering the ground.

The distribution of the type is interesting. If Roman Britain is divided into zones, the following emerges: south of the Dee-Humber line, the writer has recorded 29 brooches; north of that line up to Hadrian's Wall, 39; from military sites on Hadrian's Wall and to the north, 10; from non-military sites in the same area, 12. The emphasis is on the second zone, but there are only 13 there, if Yorkshire is discounted. Most of the brooches from Yorkshire come from non-military sites, ten of them from caves, only eight coming from military sites, counting all those from York itself as such. If the distribution of the type amongst the civilian population is looked at, and it should be fairly safe to assume that finds from caves and ordinary rural sites in Yorkshire, and rural sites and towns south of there, represent this element in the population, the brooch type has its greatest currency in southern England running mainly up the eastern side into Yorkshire and leaving most of the West Midlands, the Marches and Wales outside. Ignoring the example from Richborough, 52 fall into this area, only 15 outside and south of Hadrian's wall and these include ten from military sites. In other words, it is the military which distort the impression of where such brooches are most frequently found and it should be obvious that, without the presence of the military in the north, it is unlikely that as many as 11 would have been found in Scotland, 6 coming from the extensive excavations on Traprain Law. If a main area for supply to the north of Roman Britain has to be looked for, the disproportionate number from Yorkshire suggests that it

was somewhere there. This is at variance with the conclusion reached by Feachem (1951, 34), but there has been a much greater incidence of excavation in the southern parts of Britain since then: when he wrote, the bias was towards military sites and, naturally, these lay mainly in the north.

Plate (Fig 4.34)

These three plate brooches are not truly representative of those which were available to the inhabitants of Wroxeter. The basilical hall excavations produced five British ones belonging to a large measure to the series which begins by having enamelling and white metal trim, and ends by being gilded and stamped, three more of less certain origin, one odd-shaped British brooch with white metal trim, a symmetrical enamelled brooch from the continent and one more which is basically unclassified, but related to part of the Plate series.

31 The pin was hinged. The circular plate has two annular recesses for enamel and millefiori, blocks of the latter being separated from each other by plain enamel. One millefiori cane was chequered in a deep sage green and yellow; another has a square made up of deep sage green with a yellow block in each corner, all within a pale blue border. In the centre is a stud reminiscent of a toad-stool. 90/205, F800, P 3.1, KG 16 (SF 5861)

Almost certainly imported from the continent, the writer has not yet identified any British brooches with separately-made studs. The chief decorative features is the use of millefiori and this is used either, as here, in a field of plain enamels, or is used as an overall pattern. In the dating list which follows, AM indicates all-over millefiori. Many brooches have no enamel or millefiori left and these have been excluded as there are no designs which were exclusively one or the other, or mixed. The dating is: Camelon, Flavian-Trajanic, or *c* AD 140–65 (Christison 1901, 405, pl A.3); Verulamium, AM, after Domitian (Wheeler and Wheeler 1936, 209, fig 45.36); Chichester, after early second century (Mackreth 1978, 287, fig 10,28, 54); Cramond, *c* AD 140–200 (Rae and Rae 1974, 193, fig 14.1); Wroxeter, AM, before middle of the second century (Bushe-Fox 1916, 25, pl 16.11); Colchester, probably AD 150–300 (Crummy 1983, 17, fig 14.81); Chichester, *c* AD 200 (Mackreth 1978, 288, fig 10.48,1); Tiefenthal, AM, first half of the third century (Exner 1939, 108, Taf 14.6.III.30); Colchester, *c* AD 250–300 (Crummy 1983, 18, fig 14.89); Nettleton, AM, with late fourth century coins (Wedlake 1982, 132, fig.55,76). The dating does not appear to indicate a closely defined period, but the following points can be made: definite date-ranges for contexts seem to come in about the middle of the second century and there is a relatively strong representation to the middle of the third. This contrasts with almost all brooches other than those which lead to the Crossbow and the British round or oval gilded and stamped Plate brooches.

32   In the shape of a sole of an item of footwear, there is a small tab at the heel. The borders of the plate are cross-cut, the centre being recessed for enamel now green in colour. At the heel end there are traces of circular dots representing hobnails. 90/125, P 3.3 (SF 5122, AML 830292)
33   The same as the last brooch, here the enamel may have been a pale turquoise with white hob-nails. 80/143, F561, P 3.1, KG 16 (SF 4416)

Although there are not great numbers of this, the most common brooch imitating an object, there is a high proportion of dated examples, more so if other imitations of objects are included. Although it is a small point, a group of soles have pointed toes (eg Hattatt 1987, 220, fig 68,1142), possibly reflecting a short-term fashion, somewhat like the famous Winklepicker. The sole should have been used in the first century, as plain ones with tinning are known. In the following list of dated brooches, all are soles of footwear unless another shape is specified: Augst, unenamelled, Neronian-early Flavian (Riha 1979, 200, Taf 66.1727); Verulamium, shield, AD 80–150 (Wheeler and Wheeler 1936, 209, fig 45.34); Chichester, late first to mid/late second century (Mackreth 1989b, 192, fig 26.2, 84); Quinton, Northants, unenamelled, AD 100–170 (Friendship-Taylor 1979, 28, 138, fig 63.478); Shakenoak Farm, second century (Brodribb et al 1973, 108, fig 53.179); Verulamium, AD 135–45 (Frere 1984a, 29, fig 9.50); Cramond, purse, c AD 140–200 (Rae and Rae 1974, 193, fig 14.2); Caerleon, repaired, AD 160–230 (Brewer 1986b, 172, fig 55.14); Augst, three dated examples, Hadrianic-early third century (Riha 1979, 203, Taf 68.1749–1756); Camerton, axe, AD 180–350 (Wedlake 1958, 232, fig.54,55); Dover, flagon, c AD 190–210, or ?later (Philp 1981, 150, fig 32.71); Nettleton, with late third-century coin (Wedlake 1982, 130, fig 54.71). Most examples are second century, but there is a suggestion that some persisted into the early third century.

Penannulars (Fig 4.35)

The basilical hall excavations produced an interesting clutch of Penannular brooches and those which are essentially parallel with the ones below are noted there. The remainder consist of four with rectangular-sectioned rings and folded back terminals (SFs 32, 131, 190, and 357). The first two have stamped rings, the second having stamps on the terminals as well; the third has a plain terminal and a series of nicks in both borders of the ring; the fourth has grouped ribbing like that on no 43, only with a saltire opposite the opening imitating the terminals. A fifth

brooch has a circular-sectioned fully ribbed ring with folded back pinched terminals and a sixth, in iron, is the same but with a plain ring and plain terminals. What is not represented in the present assemblage is a group of seven from the basilical hall excavations which has either castellated or plain raised terminals which were integral with the ring, five are in iron (SFs 11, 39, 56, 92, 185, 191, and 688). SF 185 has a pin half as long again as the diameter. The last two Penannulars from the other excavations are represented by their iron pins alone, the length of the first at least was twice the diameter of the ring (SFs 171 and 948).

34   The ring has a circular section. Each terminal is a crude disc with a cross-cut edge. The pin has a simple wrap-round and a slight hump in its profile. 22/4, BP 4 (SF 252, AML 801383)

The basilical hall excavations produced two more of these (SFs 45 and 446).

The dating of this type is: Newstead, two examples, AD 80– c 200 (Curle 1911, pl 88.12, 16; Hartley 1972b, 54); Chichester, ?late first-early second century (Down and Rule 1971, 81, fig 5.14, 302e); Mumrills, AD 140–160/165 (Macdonald and Curle 1929, 555, fig 115.7); Derby, ?mid-second century (Brassington 1980, 18, fig 8.c); Cappuck, AD 140– c 200 (Stevenson and Miller 1912, 46, 1911–1912, fig 11.2; Hartley 1972, 41); Leicester, ?c AD 130– 225 (Clay and Mellor 1985, 69, fig 38.7), early third century (Kenyon 1948, 252, fig 82.8); Old Winteringham, after AD 350 (Stead 1976, 201, fig 102.33), third or fourth century (ibid, 198, fig 100.20). Although the design may have begun in the first century, the dating is solidly second with a hint that it may have persisted into the third. Those from later contexts should have been residual.

35   The ring has a circular section. Each terminal consists of a pair of discs the outer one being cross-cut round its edge. Only the simple wrap-round of the pin survives. 97/156, 1.3 (SF 5534, AML 835977)
36   A repeat of the last, only with both discs cross-cut. The pin is like that of no 34. 78/4, C 2.1 (SF 1626)

There is one like 35 and 36 from the basilical hall excavations (SF 443), without cross-cutting which is probably not a prerequisite let alone an adequate basis for creating a new variety. The dating has been taken from similar two-reel brooches: Cirencester, AD 49–70/75 (McWhirr et al 1982, 92, fig 25.17); Leicester, AD 90–100 (Kenyon 1948, 252, fig 82.10); Newstead, AD 80– c 200 (Curle 1911, 320, pl 88.15: Hartley 1972b, 54); Baldock, AD 120–150 (Stead and Rigby 1986, 12, fig 49.157); Ravenglass, c AD 200–350/370 (Potter 1979, 69, fig 26.11).

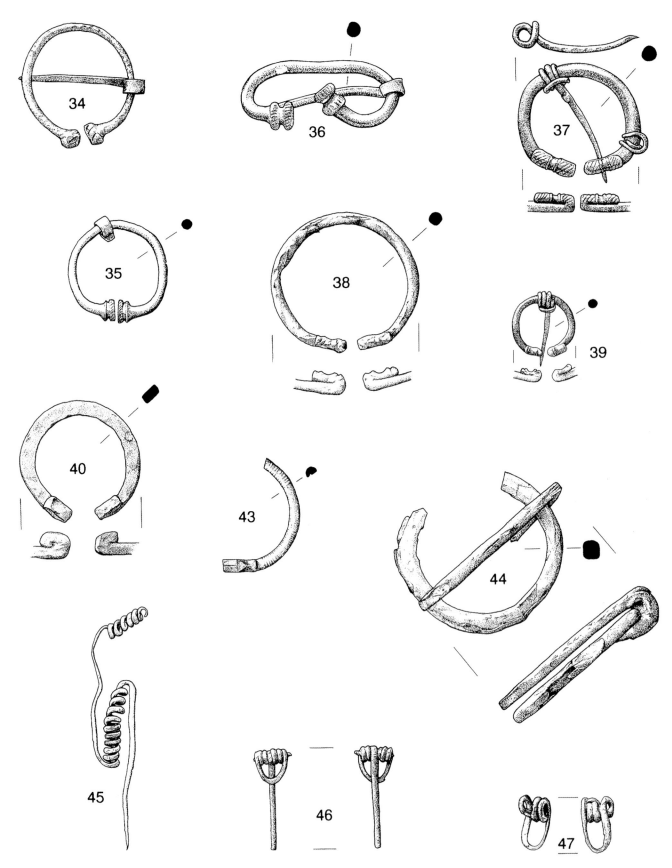

Fig 4.35 Brooches: 34–43 Penannular, 44–47 miscellaneous; scale 1:1

The date-range appears to run from the middle of the first century to, perhaps, the middle of the second, the example from Ravenglass should have been residual in its context.

37 The ring has a circular section. Each relatively long terminal is turned back along the surface of the ring. In the centre is a cross-flute with a narrow ridge on each side, and to either side of that

the terminal is diagonally ridged. The pin is a piece of wire wrapped round the ring simulating a three-coil-spring with an internal chord. There are the remains of another. 84/48, WR 3.1 (SF 3144, AML 801407)

38 Iron. The ring has a circular section. Each terminal is turned back along the surface of the ring and has a central wide cross-flute with a groove at each end. 59/8, BP 3.2 (SF 743, AML 801428)

39 A repeat of the last brooch, only much smaller and with a pin like that of no 37. 90/101, F599, P 3.2, KG 17 (SF 4879)

The basilical hall excavations produced only one brooch, in iron, which can be related to these three (SF 449). An almost exact parallel for no 37, including the remains of a second pin of the same form as the other, comes from Holt, Denbigh (Grimes 1930, 126, fig 54.3); a much less elaborate, but still exaggerated, design complete with the same style of pin comes from Prestatyn (see below). Despite the elaboration of the terminals on 37, there is little doubt that it is in essence of the same general design as the other two. The dating given here does not include the version in which the flute across the top is replaced by a curved chamfer on each side: Hod Hill, before AD 50 (Brailsford 1962, 13, fig 11.E17; Richmond 1968, 117–119); North Cerney, Glos, Claudian-Neronian (Mackreth 1988, 51, fig 24.26); Longthorpe, Cambs, c AD 43–60/65 (Frere and St Joseph 1974, 46, fig 24.13); Waddon Hill, Stoke Abbott, Dorset, c AD 50–60 (Webster 1981, 62, fig 25.11); Nettleton, probably first century (Wedlake 1982, 133, fig 55.84A); Prestatyn, AD 70s-160, two examples (Mackreth 1989a, 98, fig 40.26, 27); Monument 97, Orton Longueville, before AD 150/175 (Mackreth, forthcoming); Camerton, not before AD 150 (Wedlake 1958, 234, fig 54.64); Camerton, AD 150–200 (Wedlake 1958, 234, fig 54.63); Whitton, Glam, before AD 160 (Jarrett and Wrathmell 1981, 177, fig 71.29). There is a clutch in the middle of the first century, which might suggest that 38 and 39 at least could have derived from military levels, but there is a continuing strand running from the later first century into the latter part of the second. What is remarkable, and not to be entirely accounted for by the relatively small number of datings recorded by the writer, is that there is, apparently, none later than 200.

40 Iron. The ring has a thin rectangular section. One terminal is turned up and bent down to touch the ring at one end, the other is laid flat on the ring. 90/+, P 4 (SF 2159, AML 801443)

41 Iron. Not illustrated. The ring has an almost square section. The surviving terminal is like those of the last brooch. 90/161, P 3.3 (SF 5858)

42 Iron. Not illustrated. The ring has a square section. The terminals, as they have survived conservation, appear to be plain. There is what looks like a seam suggesting that the surviving squared-off appearance is the intended one. 92/45, P 2.1 (SF 3510)

The first two are examples of a clearly definable group, 42 is much less easy to deal with and is included here as it seems unlikely that an iron penannular would derive from unknown pre-existing Iron Age occupation here and even less likely that it would be from a military assemblage. The square ends of the brooch from Waulkmill listed in those with fully ribbed rings may be noted here. The terminals of the first two brooches are not failed attempts at coiling, but are examples of a definite group in its own right. The dated ones are: Verulamium, King Harry Lane cemetery, iron, O, early-mid first century, five examples (Stead and Rigby 1989, figs 114.146.3; 120.178.4; 156.327.2; 168.384.7; and 180.460.5); Weekley, Northants, iron, O, second quarter first century (Jackson and Dix 1987, M79, fig 24.25); Baldock, with two groups of ribbing (see 43), fourth century (Stead and Rigby 1986, 122, fig 49.155); Towcester, Northants, AD 350–375/400 (Brown and Woodfield 1983, 104, fig 35.4); Verulamium, fifth century (Frere 1984a, 31, fig 9.55); Lullingstone, iron, O, fourth century (Meates 1987, 102, fig 47.277); Morning Thorpe, Anglo-Saxon cemetery, iron, O, three examples (Green et al 1987, figs 394.F, 402.A, and 440.A); Sewerby, Anglo-Saxon cemetery, iron, O, two examples (Hirst 1985, 57, fig.38,2,3). Those marked with 'O' have round-sectioned rings, and all are iron. Three groups emerge: those which belong unequivocally to the British Iron Age, those with rectangular or square-sectioned rings which are uncompromisingly Late Roman, and those which come from Anglo-Saxon cemeteries and are, visually, indistinguishable from the first group.

If one looks at copper alloy brooches with round-sectioned rings and whose terminals behave in the same way, the result is: Portchester, AD 340–70 (Cunliffe 1975, 199, fig 109.7); Verulamium, AD 365–80 (Frere 1984a, 31, fig 9.56). There are remarkably few, but they bear out the generally late dates of those with rectangular or square-sectioned rings in either iron or copper alloy. The close connection between the iron examples with round-sectioned rings from the British Iron Age and Anglo-Saxon cemeteries cannot be because the Anglo-Saxons sought out the correct kind of site to plunder specifically iron items, it is because they belonged to a reflux Iron Age culture and should be assumed to have brought the style with them, but what does that do to the item from Lullingstone? There is a general opinion that Anglo-Saxons had no Penannular brooch tradition in their homelands (Dickinson 1982, 57), which ignores the detail that such brooches are found in continental cemeteries, but the jury can be said to be still out in that case. The answer, as indicated in the present discussion, may be that the indigenous natives were also wearing this style of penannular and that the actual style of ring can be ignored in favour of recognizing a specifically fourth-century type, and one which could well have run on into the fifth.

43   The ring has a D section. The curved upper surface shows signs of having groups of ribbing. The surviving terminal is cast-in with the ring and is zoomorphic. The ears are indicated by small triangular bosses, the forehead has a groove down it and the eyes are pointed interruptions of the chamfer which forms the snout and which sweeps out to make the mouth. Unstratified

Precise parallels for such brooches are hardly to be expected, but it is almost axiomatic that this style is late, the problem is to how to identify which elements are late and which are very late, probably leading on to what are 'dark age' brooches. In the following discussion, it is the style of the ring which is looked at and notes are made of other features: style of terminal and the presence of tubes at the ends of the pins, these being a characteristic of later brooches. The term 'integral' means that the terminal is not folded back along the top of the ring.

Full ribbing: Waulkmill, Aberdeenshire, silver, square cut ends to the ring (Coles 1904/5, 217, fig 14); Exeter, inverted frustum of a cone with basal moulding (Holbrook and Bidwell 1991, 240, fig 103.36); Ivy Chimneys, Witham, Essex, folded over, apparently undecorated, but the brooch was heavily stripped during conservation (to be published); Colchester, simple coil, tube, AD 350–450 (Crummy 1983, 18, fig.16, 103); Chichester, simple coil, mid fourth-early fifth century (Mackreth 1989b, 192); Ware, Herts, one and half coils ribbed on the surface with a median groove (unpublished); Cirencester, simple coil (unpublished); Botolph Bridge, Orton Longueville, Cambs, one and a half coils (private collection); Derby, one and a half coils, unstratified (Mackreth 1985, 32, fig 11.9); Axminster, Devon, broken coil, AD 225–mid fourth century (Silvester and Bidwell 1984, 49, fig 9.3); Great Horwood, Bucks, reel and flute, tube, with hoard *c* AD 350–425 (Waugh 1966, 64, fig 2.5); Lydney, faceted cube, ?proto tube, late Roman or later (Wheeler and Wheeler 1932, 79, fig 14.39; Group G, Dickinson 1982); Verulamium, ?folded over, ?proto-zoomorphic (Wheeler and Wheeler 1936, 210, fig 45.40); Halstock, Dorset, integral, ?proto-zoomorphic (unpublished); Norfolk, silver, integral, proto-zoomorphic (Hattatt 1987, 298, fig 9.1290); South Shields, integral, zoomorphic (Allason-Jones and Miket 1984, 110, 3.115); Traprain Law, integral, enamelled zoomorphic, tube (Kilbride-Jones 1980, 85, fig 20.1); Duston, Northants, integral, zoomorphic; Catterick, ?zoomorphic?, u/s with fourth-century pot (Kilbride-Jones 1980, 150, fig 52.14); Whitford Burrows, integral, zoomorphic (*ibid*, 148, fig 52.12);

South Shields, integral, zoomorphic, tube (*ibid*, 148, fig 52.10); Caernarvon, integral, zoomorphic (*ibid*, 150, fig 52.18); Nettleton, integral, zoomorphic, pseudo tube (Wedlake 1982, 135, fig 56.111); Caernarvon, integral, zoomorphic (Wheeler 1924, 137, fig.58,6); North Uist, integral, zoomorphic (Kilbride-Jones 1980, 150, fig 52.20); Tara, Meath, integral, zoomorphic (*ibid*, 150, fig 52.21); Caersws, integral, zoomorphic (Wheeler 1924, 138, fig 60); Feltwell, integral, zoomorphic, late fourth-early fifth century (Gurney 1986, 30, fig 22.2); Great Linford, almost exactly like the one from Feltwell, tube (Mynard and Zeepvat 1992, 148, fig 57.70); Birdoswald, integral, zoomorphic, pseudo-tube, after 383 (Kilbride-Jones 1980, 147, fig 52.2); Wilcote, integral, zoomorphic, tube, late fourth century (Brodribb *et al* 1973, 108, fig 109.180); Brancaster, integral, zoomorphic, fourth century (Hinchliffe and Green 1985, 42, fig 28.2); Mells, Som, integral, zoomorphic (St George Gray 1930, 81, fig 6.E17); Norfolk, integral, zoomorphic, tube (Hattatt 1985, 186, fig 75.656); Iwerne, ?integral, zoomorphic (Hawkes 1947, 55, fig 9.14); Lydney, folded over?, proto zoomorphic?, pseudo-tube (Wheeler and Wheeler 1932, 87–9, fig 14.37); Camerton, AD 150–200, ?integral, ?proto zoomorphic (Wedlake 1958, 232, fig 54.61); Ilchester, integral, ?proto zoomorphic, ?post fourth century (Leach 1982, 247, fig 117.29); Vindolanda, integral, corroded, tube 1.

Grouped ribbing: Cirencester, integral, waisted in plan (Corinium Museum, no number); Feltwell, integral, circular cell, topsoil (Gurney 1986, 15, fig 12.2); Barnsley Park, boss with basal moulding (Webster and Smith 1982, 142, fig 30.86); Hod Hill, boss with moulding and flat projecting face, ?before AD 50 (Brailsford 1962, 12, fig 11.E3; Richmond 1968, 117–19); Bicester, Oxon, simple coil (Hattatt 1987, 296, fig 96.1285); Lechlade, Glos, two coils (*ibid*, 296, fig 96.1282); Wakerley, Northants, one and a half coils, silver, Anglo-Saxon burial (Jackson and Ambrose 1978, 228, fig 65.1), and one with a full coil; Puckeridge, Skeleton Green, one and a half coils, AD 15–25 (Partridge 1981, fig 72.56); Baldock, folded over, but not flattened, fourth century (Stead and Rigby 1986, 122, fig 49.55); Portchester, integral, complex not zoomorphic, general layer (Cunliffe 1975, 199, fig 109.8); Dowkerbottom Cave, Settle, Yorks, integral, widening ends with diamond (Kilbride-Jones 1980, 148, fig 52.13); Baldock, integral, castellated, pseudo-tube, late fourth century (Stead and Rigby 1986, 122, fig 49.158); Barnsley Park, Glos, integral, zoomorphic, fourth century (Webster 1967); Milton Keynes, folded over, ?zoomorphic, early-mid fourth century (Marney and Mackreth 1987, 133, fig 41.18); Icklingham, integral, zoomorphic, (Kilbride-Jones 1980, 147, fig 52.6); Okstrow Brock, Birsay, Orkney, integral, proto-zoomorphic, pseudo-tube (*ibid*, 148, fig 52.8); South Shields, integral, zoomorphic, pseudo-tube (*ibid*, 148, fig 52.11); Witcombe, Glos, integral, zoomorphic (*ibid*, 147, fig 52.5); Woodeaton, Oxon, integral, zoomorphic, tube (*ibid*, 147, fig 52.4); Knowth, Meath, integral, zoomorphic (*ibid*, 147, fig 52.3); Canterbury, folded over, proto-zoomorphic (unpublished); Lydney, folded over, zoomorphic, (Wheeler and Wheeler 1932, 79, fig 14.38); Wroxeter, basilical hall excavations (SF 92).

As can be seen, dating is sparse. Amongst the fully ribbed rings, two with simple coils belong to the late fourth century and early fifth and one had a proper tube at the end of the pin (Colchester and Chichester), and another which may have had a simple coil is AD 225–mid fourth century (Axminster). Great Horwood produced an aberrant terminal, but was securely dated by the hoard with it. The largest of these brooches, those from Feltwell and Great Linford, had zoomorphic terminals and fall at best into the period late fourth century to perhaps the middle of the fifth century. Birdoswald produced a developed terminal and a pseudo-tube dating after AD 383. Of the rest, a fourth-century one comes from Brancaster, a late fourth-century one from Shakenoak Farm, Wilcote, and one from Ilchester may be after 400. There are two from Lydney which ought to be Late Roman, but the odd man out is the brooch from Camerton which should not really date to AD 150–200.

The partially ribbed brooches are even less well dated. Amongst the zoomorphic terminals, only the one from Milton Keynes has a date-range, AD 300–350, the Barnsley Park brooch is fourth-century, while the specimen from Lydney can only be assigned to the Late-Roman period. It is amongst the rest that something like a clear division in dating can be seen. The coil from Skeleton Green is AD 15–25 and the bossed terminal from Hod Hill is likely, but cannot be guaranteed, to have come from the Roman fort if not from the Iron Age site beneath. Thereafter, a castellated terminal is late fourth century (Baldock) and a simple coil comes from an Anglo-Saxon burial (Wakerley). The coiled terminal from Skeleton Green serves as a warning against making too many assertions. Perhaps the strongest claim to the zoomorphic terminal being late is the real lack of dated pieces, but the style of the junction of the pin with the ring is worth noting as well. If there is a typological development from simple wrap-rounds with grooves to splayed wrap-rounds with a pattern of grooves emerging to the final stage of the tube with its distinctive triple mouldings, then the dating of the middle stage may help to place the earliest time by which the last stage came into being. The Birdoswald brooch has a pseudo-tube and is later than 383 and the castellated terminal from Baldock also has one and is late fourth century. If this is a good sign, the tube as such stands a good chance of being at the earliest fifth century. The two dated ones amongst the fully ribbed rings date to AD 350–450 and 350–425 (Colchester, Great Horwood), there are none in the partially ribbed class.

As a postscript, two papers dealing with Migration/Early Medieval Penannulars may be cited. Dickinson's (1982) analysis of Group G penannulars shows that there may be no real distinction between fully ribbed rings or those ribbed in groups, except that the latter are more common. None illustrated by her has a tube ending to the pin, all are wrap-rounds, even if some show mouldings which were to develop into the full tube. However, as the bulk of G penannulars are apparently sixth century, there are perhaps some grounds for seeing some of the brooches mentioned in the discussion as being specifically fifth-century, but the writer would hesitate to nominate which designs can be safely regarded as such. Similarly, F3 penannulars found in Ireland show a clear relationship with Late Roman zoomorphic terminals, especially if the side view of the terminals is looked at (eg Newman 1989, figs 1.1 and 2; 2.1; and 4.1). Dating is hardly well established and the range of later sixth-early seventh century (*ibid*, 14) is really only a suggestion. This group has pins which run up to about three times the diameter of the ring and there are several which have tubular ends (*ibid*, figs 1.1 and 3.1). The final conclusion is hardly novel: features which were to become fairly popular elements in the design of 'Dark Age' brooches were in place by the end of the fourth century and the real disaster is our inability to follow them on through the fifth.

Object (Fig 4.35)

44 Iron. The remains of a large ring with a circular section. There is no evidence that there had been any terminals and the profile of the pin would suit a buckle pin rather than one for a penannular brooch. 91/+, WR 4 (SF 5395)

Fragments (Fig 4.35)

45 The almost complete spring and pin from a Colchester Derivative. As there are eleven coils in the complete half, there should have been 22 coils in all. 80/55, P 3.3 (SF 3944)

Only one type of brooch to the writer's knowledge would normally have in excess of 12–14 coils (eg Mackreth forthcoming).

46 Iron. The complete spring and most of the pin from the system used on nos 15, 21 and 22. The writer has not noted any in iron before: this may be a repair. 58/5, BP 3.2 (SF 675)

The brooch from which this came is unlikely to date earlier or later than the second century.

47 A damaged spring and chord from a system like that of the last, the same comment on dating applies here. 98/49, F679, P 3.2, KG 17 (SF 5091)

The Roman gems

by Martin Henig (Fig 4.36)

Note: in the catalogue the devices are described in impression. The shapes of stones are those shown in Henig 1974, fig 1.

1   Cornelian intaglio. Amber coloured stone with a few black inclusions. There is a chip on the top edge. The gem is oval in shape with a slightly convex upper side (Shape A5). Dim: 17 x 12 x 2mm. Device: Ceres stands to the front and faces right. She wears a chiton. In her left hand she holds a dish containing fruit or cakes; in her right hand she clasps two ears of corn. Ground line.

The type is a very common one. It is based on a statue of Ceres which balanced one of Bonus Eventus, possibly the work of Praxiteles (Henig 1974, 99–100; 1978, 77). Apart from examples published (Henig 1974, nos 259–74; 1978, additionally, nos App 135 and 136) a further twenty intaglios of the type, all cornelians, now come from the mid-second century jeweller's hoard from Snettisham, Norfolk, in the British Museum (Johns 1997, 87–8, nos 135–53, and 96, no 225). Two intaglios from Wroxeter (Henig 1974/1978, no 273), and one from Snettisham (Johns 1997, 87, no 135; Maaskant-Kleibrink 1992, 154, fig 7), may be singled out for their similar styles of cutting. Bearing the period assigned to the Snettisham cache in mind, a date of *c* AD 150 seems probable for this gem too. 90/100, F602, P 3.1, KG 16 (SF 4768)

2   Red Jasper intaglio. The gem is oval in shape with a flat upper face (Shape F1) but only the upper part survives. Dim: 10mm (originally 16mm) by 12mm by 2.25mm. Device: the youthful figure of Bonus Eventus stands in profile to the right. He wears a mantle or *chlamys* which hangs from his shoulders. In his left hand he holds two corn ears and in his right a bunch of grapes, partly lost through the break in the stone. Behind him is a tree. Published in Henig 1974/1978, no 197.

The type is represented by numerous gems (eg Krug 1981 no 297; Henig 1974/1978 no 189, where Bonus Eventus holds a dish instead of corn, and no 198; Sena Chiesa 1978, no 76 and Guiraud 1988, no 232, from Pouldergat, Finistère; no 233, from Castella, Lot-et-Garonne, as here but with no tree; Zienkiewicz 1986, 130–31, no 14, with a tree but with the corn ears in right hand and dish in left). This version may have been based on a statue by Euphranor. It dates to the second century AD. Context unknown and item not located in the archive but shown to the writer by the excavator *c*1970.

3   Cornelian intaglio. Uneven colour; chip on top edge. The gem is oval and has a very slightly convex upper face (Shape A4). Dim: very small, 8mm

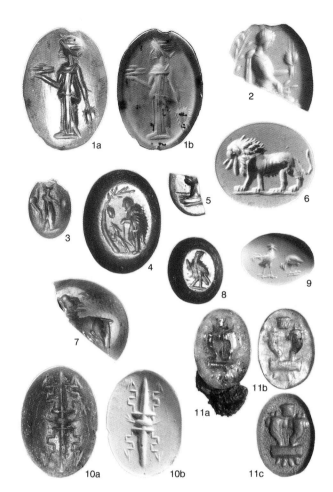

Fig 4.36 Intaglii: nos 2, 9, 10b and 11c are impressions, the remainder stones, nos 1 and 11 shown differently lit; scale 2:1

by 6mm by 2.5mm. Device: Fortuna or Abundantia stands to front and faces left. She wears a chiton. In her right hand she holds a patera; in her left hand a cornucopiae. Ground line. Very cursory work.

This too is a very common type (Henig 1974/1978, nos 328–36); also ten gems in the Snettisham cache (Johns 1997, 89–90, nos 157–66). It may date to the late second/early third century AD, corresponding with Maaskant-Kleibrink's *incoherent grooves style* (Maaskant-Kleibrink 1978, no 990). 56/28, BP 3.3 (SF 869)

4   Onyx intaglio. Oval stone with flat upper face and bevelled edge (Shape F4). Dim: 13.5mm by 11mm by 3mm. Device: the intaglio depicts an elderly countryman standing in profile to the right. He wears a thick goat- or sheep-skin coat and leans upon a stick. In front of him is his hound, leaping up at a bundle (containing game) which hangs from the tree. Ground line.

For type and style note a gem from Chester (Henig 1974/1978, no 498; see also Sena Chiesa 1966, nos 762 and 763, from Aquileia). There are a number of variants; sometimes the countryman watches goats as on gems from Hacheston, Suffolk, (Henig 1974/1978 no 500) and from Strageath (Frere and Wilkes 1989, 179, no 2). On an intaglio from the drain of the Fortress Baths at Caerleon, in a layer dated *c* AD 85–110, no animal is shown (Zienkiewicz 1986, 131, no 18), while an amethyst from the drain at Wroxeter leading from the forum and containing material down to *c* AD 160 portrays two herdsmen and two goats (Henig 1974/1978, no 497).

The type evokes plenty and prosperity and the mythical world in which the goatherd Faustuleus discovered the *Lupa Romana* suckling Romulus and Remus (see Maaskant-Kleibrink 1978, no 253). The gem should be dated to the Flavian/Trajanic period. 97/70, P 3.3 (SF 4228)

5   Cornelian intaglio. Oval stone with flat upper face (Shape F1). Only a fragment (about a quarter) remains. Dim: surviving height 6mm, thickness 2mm. Device: Draped bust in profile to the right. Only the chin, neck, and drapery around shoulders remain.

See Henig 1974/1978 nos 486, 487, for gems of about this size. It is not possible to tell whether a deity was intended (eg Zwierlein-Diehl 1979, no 1272, Apollo) or an emperor or private individual, and even the sex is uncertain. Unstratified from the excavations.

6   Yellow Jasper intaglio. Oval stone with flat upper face (Shape F1), small chip on side. Dim: 14mm by 11.25mm by 2mm. Device: A lion walks towards the right. In its jaws is the head of an animal. Ground line.

For the type on an intaglio see Henig 1974/1978 no 629 (onyx from Chesters fort). The most familiar example of the subject from Britain is a second-century mosaic from Verulamium where the lion carries the head of a stag (Toynbee 1964, 276–7, pl lxiii.b). Such symbols could have acted as *mementi mori* (see Henig 1977, 356).

The tawny coloured material of the gem is popular for renderings of lions and suggests an element of sympathetic magic. In the Lapidary of Socrates and Dionysios it is stated that a stone of the colour of a lion's pelt is a specific against the sting of a scorpion (Barb 1969, 305, n4; see Henig 1980, 331 for a gem of this colour showing a scorpion). It may have been regarded as possessing wider virtue in combatting malignant powers. For lions on yellow jaspers see Sena Chiesa 1966, nos 1153, 1154, 1156, 1160; Dimitrova-Milcheva 1981, nos 190, 192; Guiraud 1988, no 652 (from Épinal, Vosges); Zwierlein-Diehl 1991, no 1823; Spier 1992, no 387.

The gem is rather coarsely cut with the thick grooving associated with Maaskant-Kleinrink's *incoherent grooves style* (se 1978, no 1021) and I would prefer to date it no earlier than the last quarter of the second century. 84/57, WR 2.3 (SF 3258)

7   Orange cornelian intaglio. Gem of approximately circular form, slightly convex (Shape A5). It has been broken across and only about half of the stone remains. Dim: diam *c* 13mm, thickness 3.75mm. Device: a bovine stands with head raised in profile to the right.

For the type and style compare Maaskant-Kleibrink 1978, no 419; Guiraud 1988, no 680 (from Alésia, Côte-d'Or). This is Maaskant-Kleibrink's *flat bouterrolle style*, epitomised by the use of a broad drill, often on a round stone. The style and indeed the subject is entirely characteristic of Augustan glyptics (later first century BC). It should be noted that this is not the only old gem, perhaps an heirloom, from Wroxeter, as the military layers have yielded a Hellenistic intaglio showing Ptolemy XII *Auletes* and another Augustan gem depicting a lion. (On heirlooms upon gems from Britain see Henig 1991, esp figs 5 and 11.) 60/18, BP 3.2 (SF 1119)

8   Nicolo intaglio. Oval stone with flat upper face and bevelled edge (Shape F4). Small. Dimensions: 9mm by 8mm by 3.5mm. Device: An eagle stands to the right, its head turned to the left. Ground line.

The bird, neatly carved on a small stone, fills the field well and may be attributed to Maaskant-Kleibrink's *classicising style* (1978, 197). It was intended for quite a slender ring of a type characteristic of the first century AD. For eagles without attributes see Henig in Cunliffe 1988, 33, no 30, a *chalcedony* from the Bath cache and of Flavian date and Zwierlein-Diehl 1991, no 1930 (nicolo). Most had wreaths in their beaks. Another nicolo, Sena Chiesa 1966, no 1262, is nearest in size and style. The date of the gem could mean that it was residual from the military levels; the eagle had an especial significance to legionaries and is often shown on intaglios, standing between legionary standards (as Henig 1974/1978, nos 705–10). 90/211, P 2.2 (SF 5981)

9   Red Jasper intaglio. Oval with slightly convex upper face (Shape A1). Dim: 10mm by 7mm by 1.5mm. Device: Two cockerels; the victorious one on the left in profile to the right has its head raised and is crowing while the one on the right has its head lowered and is submissive. Ground lines. Published in Henig 1974/1978, no 682.

Compare two identical glass gems from Richborough (Henig 1974/1978, no 681) and from the basilical hall excavations at Wroxeter (Henig 1978, no App 185). In both of these the cock on the right holds a wreath in its beak. For other gems showing confronted cocks see Sena Chiesa 1966, no 134; Guiraud 1988, no 757 (Bavay, Nord), 758; Zwierlein-Diehl 1991, no 1949.

Apart from attesting the 'sport' of cock-fighting and the perhaps apotropaic nature of the cock both as a destroyer of vermin and a symbol of virility, the intaglio signifies success and victory. The gem is neatly cut in the *small grooves style* (see the red jasper showing a single cockerel, Maaskant-Kleibrink 1978, no 764).

Late first, or more probably second century AD, possibly Hadrianic. 59/10, F3114, BP 3.2 (SF 752). Item not located in the archive but shown to the writer by the excavator *c*. 1970.

10   Cornelian intaglio containing a few dark inclusions. Oval with convex upper face (Shape B5). Dimensions: 15mm by 11mm by 3mm. Device: A *fulmen* (thunderbolt), the attribute of Jupiter. Two short wings spring from the central boss, but the most distinctive features are the four lightning flashes, issuing from the projections flanking it, each conventionalised as a running key pattern terminating in an arrow head. Published in Henig 1974/1978 no 414.

An identical *fulmen* is depicted on the back face of a cornelian intaglio found at Thurleigh, Bedfordshire (inf Holly Duncan). This is likely to be a secondary cutting of a stone itself first engraved in the second century. Another example of this thunderbolt type is figured by Furtwängler (1986, no 8002), associated with the crescent and stars which symbolise the eternity of the heavens. For other representations of thunderbolts on gems see Henig 1974/1978 nos 415 (Westminster) and 416 (Lydney Park, Gloucestershire); Krug 1981, no 453; Zwierlein-Diehl 1991, no 2013.

The gem perhaps dates to the later second century AD. 58/4, BP 3.2 (SF 771)

11   Greenish, almost clear, glass intaglio. Ovoid with flat upper face and rounded sides). The device of the gem is moulded not engraved. It is set in the fragments of an iron ring of which one shoulder remains (Type Xb). Dim (of intaglio): 11 x 8 x 1.5mm. Device: Clasped hands holding a pair of cornucopiae. Between them is a small circular altar.

Compare another glass intaglio from the Cattlemarket site, Chichester, depicting two birds standing on altars and pecking from cornucopiae (Henig in Down 1989, 180, no 1). Note engraved intaglios: Henig 1974/1978, no App 36 (from Skeleton Green, Puckeridge, Herts, wine vessel instead of altar, three eagles perch on cornucopiae and crater); Sena Chiesa 1978, no 165, and Maaskant-Kleibrink 1978, no 729 (parrot on wine-vessel instead of altar); Zwierlein-Diehl 1991, no 2036 (no altar). The intaglio-type is typical of the first-century BC and first-century AD. The ring-form looks early third-century, so this may be quite a late impression. 38/35, B 4 (SF 463)

The Roman vessel glass
by H E M Cool

Introduction

Over 2,000 fragments of Roman vessel glass were found during the excavation of the baths and *macellum* at Wroxeter. The majority of this material is of first and second-century date, but third and fourth-century vessels are also represented. Table 4.7 shows the distribution of the glass between the different areas of the site. The two most prolific areas were the Porticos and the West Range reflecting the dumping that took place there during the building campaign. It is clear that much of the glass recovered does not directly reflect activity that took place on the site, but rather is rubbish derived from elsewhere in the town. The specialised nature of the occupation on the site is reflected in some parts of the assemblage, most notably in the number of bath flasks recovered.

Table 4.7 Vessel glass: fragments by colour and area of site

	period 1	portico	west range	courtyard	baths	baths precinct	total
pillar–moulded bowls	1	7	7	3	–	–	18
cast vessels	24	4	22	2	–	–	52
mould–blown vessel	2	11	–	–	–	–	13
polychrome–blown vessels	–	1	1	3	–	–	5
opaque blown vessels	1	1	–	–	–	–	2
'black' vessels	–	1	–	–	–	–	1
deep blue vessels	3	9	–	5	–	–	17
yellow/brown vessels	8	17	5	3	–	1	34
emerald green vessels	–	1	–	1	–	1	3
yellow/green vessels	5	6	7	5	1	1	25
pale green vessels	17	25	34	1	–	2	79
colourless vessels	8	269	30	6	2	22	337
blue/green vessels	53	494	142	100	6	39	834
blue/green bottles	34	280	126	43	–	32	515
late Roman green vessels	–	42	30	7	–	4	83
total	156	1168	404	179	9	102	2018

The material was catalogued according to the area of the site it was found on, and, within each site division, on the basis of manufacturing method first and colour of glass second. The catalogue is based on an earlier archive catalogue of all the vessel glass from Graham Webster's excavations prepared by Jennifer Price and the present author, but has been completely re-organised. The correlation of numbers from the two catalogues is available in archive. The catalogue is available in the archive (Archive E6) and a shortened version is presented below. The report was written in 1994.

The report starts with a brief typological overview of the entire assemblage organised chronologically. Following this there is a consideration of the assemblage from the point of view of function and status.

Typological overview

Claudian to mid-Flavian forms

A number of fragments from mid first-century vessels were found in post military contexts where they are clearly residual. These include polychrome (1 and 96) and strongly coloured (97–8, 876) monochrome pillar-moulded bowls, and cast strongly coloured bowls (100–1). There are also fragments from vessel types which go out of use slightly later in the mid to late Flavian period. Where these are found stratified in Period 1 early civilian contexts, it is just possible that they may represent contemporaneous deposition but again it is more likely that they represent residual material. Forms which fall into this category include a wide range of mould-blown vessels including ribbed bowls (3, 104), truncated conical beakers (108–10) and fragments from forms which cannot be closely identified (105–7). Other forms in this category include Hofheim cups and beakers (18–9, 38, 140–1, 270–2, 902, and

991), tubular unguent bottles with sheared rims (43, 309–11, and 916–7) and blue/green pillar-moulded bowls (98–9, 664–70, and 877–8). The last mentioned form was very common during the first century but virtually all examples had gone out of use by the end of the century. Some colours of glass ceased to be popular by the mid- to late Flavian period and this fact can also be used to judge whether a fragment is residual. Such colours include opaque blue (4), opaque white (112), deep blue (5–6, 883–7, and 114–121), emerald green (133, 890, and 999), dark yellow/brown (9, 11–2, 127–30, 675–7, and 998) as well as polychrome fragments with marvered decoration (111, 672, and 881–2). All the material in these three categories has already been discussed with the vessel glass found in military contexts (Cool and Price forthcoming), and no further discussion will be undertaken here.

Mid first to mid second-century tableware forms
(Figs 4.37–4.39)

The use of the casting technique to make glass vessels died out during the Flavian period. The last vessel types regularly made by this technique were a range of colourless bowls with everted rims and base rings (Grose 1991, 12; Cool and Price 1995, 27) represented in post-military contexts by the facet-cut example, 671, and the plain example, 102. Vessels of this type continued in use through the early second century and into the Antonine period as examples have been found on sites of that date at Cramond (Maxwell 1974, 198, fig 16.6–7) and Inveresk (Thomas 1988, fiche 2:B7, ill 49). By extension it is likely that rarer cast forms such as 2 and 879 and the undiagnostic cast colourless body fragments (103 and 880) are also of later first to mid second-century date. All of the cast colourless vessels from Wroxeter found

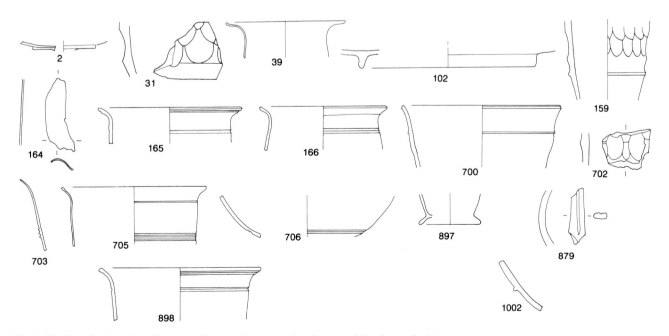

Fig 4.37 Vessel glass: late first to mid second-century beakers and bowls; scale 1:2

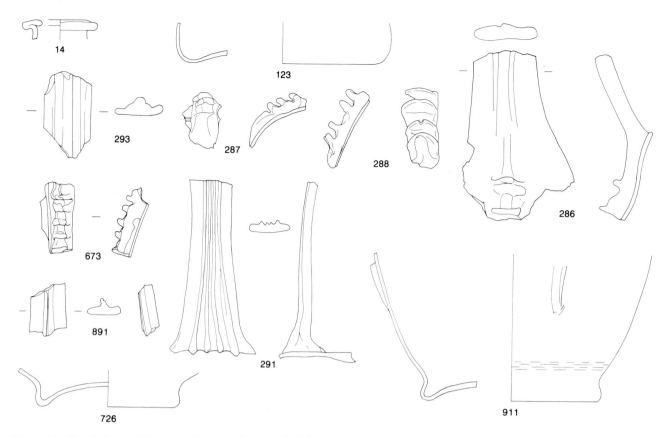

Fig 4.38 Vessel glass: globular and conical jugs; scale 1:2

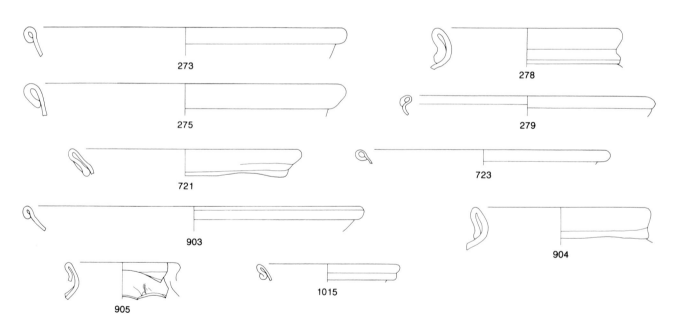

Fig 4.39 Vessel glass: tubular-rimmed bowls and collared jars; scale 1:2

during Graham Webster's excavations have been discussed in detail in the volume on the military occupation (Cool and Price forthcoming).

Facet-cut beakers with externally ground surfaces (Isings 1957, Form 21; Oliver 1984; Cool and Price 1995, 71) had come into use by the very early Flavian period at the latest, and are a common find on Flavian sites. It is becoming apparent, however, that a significant number were still in use in the middle of the

second century (Cool *et al* 1995, 1567). All of the facet-cut beakers found during Graham Webster's excavations at Wroxeter were discussed in the volume in connection with the military occupation, but many of those found in post military contexts (31, 159–60, 700–2, and 897) are as likely to have been associated with the civilian occupation as with the earlier military one. A similar date range may be suggested for the colourless beakers and cups where the exterior has been ground to leave ribs in relief (Cool and Price 1995, 73) represented here by 703 and 1002.

Another common Flavian form of drinking vessel that came into use during the mid first century is the indented beaker (Cool and Price 1995, 69). The only possible example from a post-military context is 164 which may have come from the variants with long narrow indentations (see for example Charlesworth 1959, 166, fig 22.1; Bushe-Fox 1932, 85, no 61, pl XV). A less common drinking vessel of this date is represented by 39 which is a thin-walled blue/green beaker with an out-turned fire-rounded rim. Beakers with fire-rounded rims have not often been found in first or early second-century contexts, as at that time cracked-off and ground rims were preferred. A very similar rim fragment was found at the Gilberd School, Colchester (Cool and Price 1995, 101, no 701) where vessel glass later than first century is rare, and the first to early second-century date of 39 cannot be doubted as it was found in a context dated to Period 1.3.

The commonest drinking vessel of the early to mid second century is the colourless wheel-cut beaker (Cool and Price 1995, 79). In this assemblage 165–68 705 and 898 all come from cylindrical examples. The body fragments 169–82 and the base fragments 704 and 1003 also come from this range of beakers but their precise variant cannot be identified. The body fragment 706 may come from the related and contemporary bowl form and have been similar to the shallow bowls found in a burial of probably Antonine date at Skeleton Green (Charlesworth 1981, fig 105.2a and 2b).

During this period the commonest tablewares other than drinking vessels are tubular-rimmed bowls (Isings Forms 44–5; Cool and Price 1995, 94), collared jars (Isings Form 67c; Cool and Price 1995, 106) and globular and conical jugs (Isings Forms 52 & 55; Cool and Price 1995, 120). With the exception of tubular-rimmed bowls which occur in earlier contexts, the forms first appeared during the late Neronian period and were widespread and numerous for the rest of the first century. Collared jars and globular jugs disappear during the early second century, but tubular-rimmed bowls and conical jugs continued in use into the middle of the second century. All three forms are represented at Wroxeter stratified in post-military contexts. Tubular-rimmed bowls are represented by 40, 273–6, 743, 903, and possibly by 279, 296, and 723; collared jars by 278, 721–2 904–5 and possibly 906; conical jugs by 123, 286, 673 and 1019; globular jugs by 291 and possibly 287, 342. 689, 726–7. Numbers 911–4 and possibly 1022 are lower body and base fragments that might come from either collared jars or globular jugs. The rim, neck and/or handle fragments 7–8, 14, 20, 41–2, 288–90, 297–9, 687–8, 725, 891–2, 896, 909–10, 915, 998, 1018, and 1020, and perhaps 293, 306 are also most likely to come from globular or conical jugs. One of these fragments, 287, appears to come from one of the less common variants of globular jugs. It is a lower handle attachment from a blue/green ribbed globular vessel

which may have been similar to the jug found with a pillar-moulded bowl at East Hall, Murston, Kent (Payne 1893, 40, pl IV no 1). Such pinched handle attachments are very common on the conical jug but appear to have been rare on the globular form.

Mid second to mid third-century tablewares
(Fig 4.40)

The commonest drinking vessel in use during this period is the colourless cylindrical cup with double ring base ring (Isings Form 85b; Cool and Price 1995, 82). These first appear c AD 160–70, become very common at the end of the second century and probably went out of use during the middle of the third century. The plain variant is represented at Wroxeter by 186–90, 709 and 1005. Numbers 183–4, 1004, and possibly 708 are examples of the trailed variant and it is possible that 185 and 707 are lower body fragments from similar trailed cups. Cylindrical cups were superseded during the second quarter of the third century by a colourless hemispherical cup with fire-rounded rim (ibid, 86), represented here by 899.

The most frequently found forms of jug during this period are funnel-mouthed jugs with ovoid globular or, less commonly, discoid bodies (Cool and Price 1995, 134). Spouted forms where the funnel mouth has either been pinched in or pulled up to form a spout often share similar body and handle forms and were contemporary (ibid, 131). It is often more difficult to identify the presence of such jugs in an assemblage compared with, for example, the presence of globular and conical jugs of Isings Forms 52 and 55. This is because the small fragments from the funnel-mouthed jugs tend to be less diagnostic than those from the globular and conical forms. Here 300 and 1007 are likely to have come from a funnel-mouthed jug as may have 318 though this might possibly be from a flask similar to that found in the Antonine fill of a sacred pool at Springhead, Kent (Penn 1960, fig 6.10). The spouted form is represented by 728.

The handle and body fragments 730–1 are worthy of special note. They come from small trailed jugs which probably belong to this range of funnel-mouthed jugs. They are unusual, however, in that the rod handles are attached at the junction of the neck and shoulder rather than further down the shoulder as is normal, and perhaps reflect a local workshop tradition. The handle and body junction of 302 is similar to 730–1 but insufficient of the body is preserved to show whether or not this too was a trailed jug.

Wheel-cut cylindrical bottles with folded rims made in good quality colourless glass (Cool and Price 1995, 200) developed in the later second century and were in use during the earlier part of the third century. In this assemblage the form is definitely represented by 205 and probably also by 209–10, 212 and 1010. Another vessel of this date may be represented by 277 which may come from a plate, a form which appears commonest at this time.

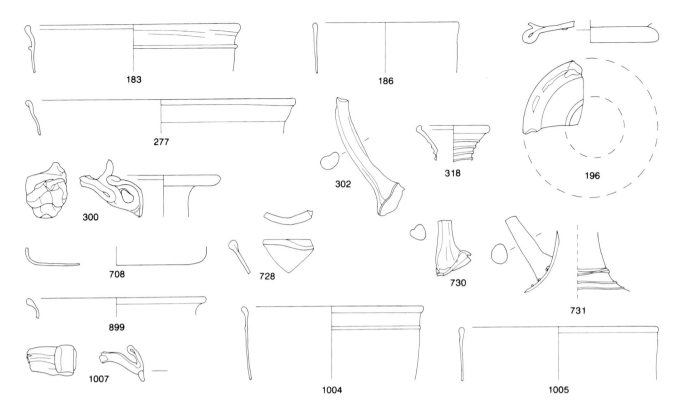

Fig 4.40 Vessel glass: mid second to mid third-century tablewares; scale 1:2

Later first to third-century containers
(Figs 4.41–4.44)

With the exception of unguent bottles, utilitarian container forms appear to have gone out of use during the third century. Unlike tablewares, most container forms do not appear to have been subject to changing fashion and many forms were long-lived. Thus they are not sensitive chronological indicators.

The commonest types of container found at Wroxeter, as at every other first and second-century site in Roman Britain, are blue/green prismatic and cylindrical bottles, 75–94, 481–631, 800–68, 945–81, 996–7, and 1048–71 (Isings Forms 50 and 51; Cool and Price 1995, 179). Square, hexagonal and cylindrical bottles become very common during the Flavian period. Cylindrical bottles went out of use early in the second century, whereas square and hexagonal bottles had a longer life with some square bottles still being in use in the early third century. Rectangular bottles (Isings Form 90; Cool and Price 1995, 185) appear to have been less common and in Britain most examples from dated contexts belong to the mid second century.

The prismatic bottles almost invariably have bases decorated with mouldings generally laid out with the aid of a compass, and one of the bases, 961, retains a faint cross from the original marking out of the mould. In the majority of cases the mouldings consist of one or more circular concentric circles with or without a central pellet. Most of the base fragments from Wroxeter come from bottles with circular mouldings. Number 968 comes from a probably square bottle with a base design of a diagonal cross in a circular moulding like that from Verulamium (Charlesworth 1966, fig 12). This is also a relatively common design. Number 967 is similar but has only one arm of the cross. It is possible that this central motif is the letter I, although such a pattern does not appear to be parallelled. Several of the other bases have patterns that are noteworthy either because the designs can be more closely dated or because they appear to be very unusual.

Number 530 comes from a small hexagonal bottle whose base is decorated with a pellet in each corner and probably a circular moulding centrally. This base pattern is known on similar small hexagonal bottles from York (Harden, 1962, 137, fig 88.H.34.c), Exeter (Charlesworth 1979, 227, fig 71.28), Colchester (Cool and Price 1995, no 2142, fig 11.8) and Neuville-le-Pollet, Seine Maritime (Sennequier 1985, 150, no 235). It seems likely that small hexagonal bottles with this pattern were being made in the later second century (Cool and Price 1995, 188).

The fragment 531 comes from the corner of a square bottle. The pattern consists of a circular moulding with a rod projecting into the corner. It is possible that the full design consisted of the letters AF inside a Q (Collingwood and Wright 1991, 105, nos 2419.75–81) and that the rod is the arm of the Q, though those are normally curved rather than straight as on 531. The AFQ bottles are likely to have been in use during the mid to late second century. One example was found in a pit dated to AD 160–70 at

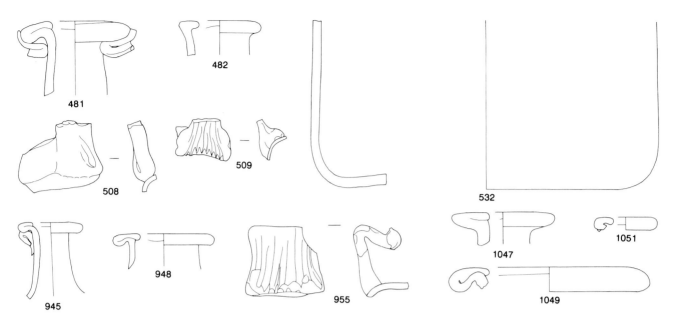

Fig 4.41 Vessel glass: blue/green bottle fragments; scale 1:2

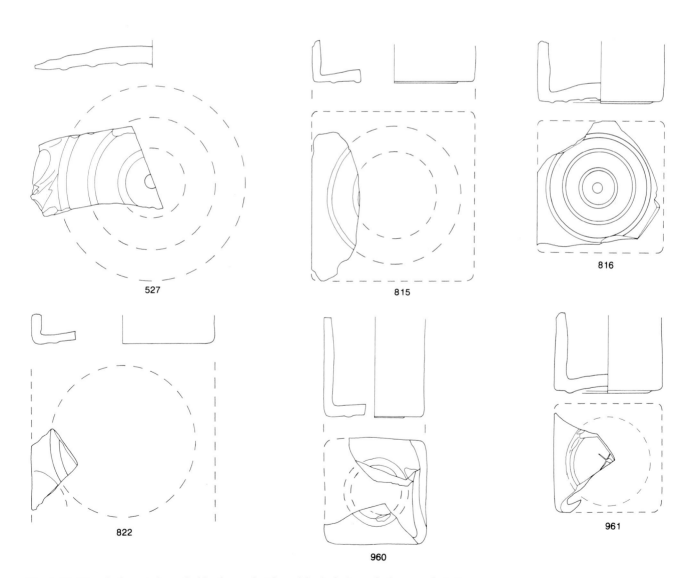

Fig 4.42 Vessel glass: prismatic blue/green bottles with circle base designs; scale 1:2

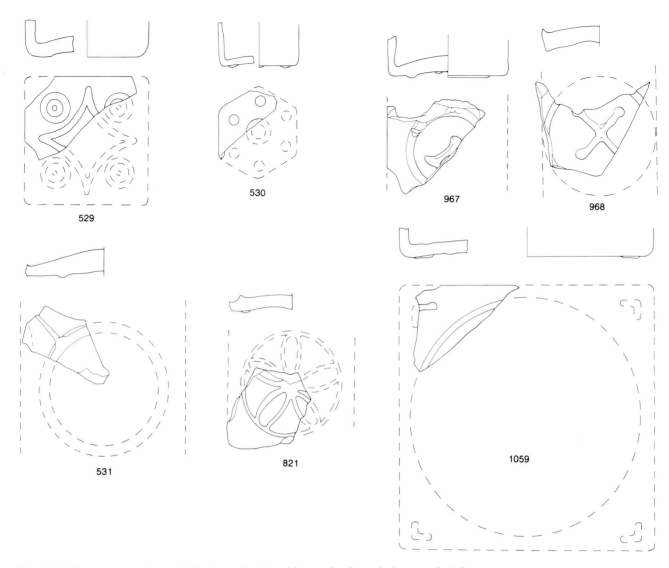

Fig 4.43 Vessel glass: prismatic blue/green bottles with complex base designs; scale 1:2

Felmongers, Harlow (Price 1987, 206, fig 4.35) and another with a hoard of metalwork found at Welshpool believed to have been deposited during the second half of the second century (Boon 1961, 31, fig 7.11).

The square bottle 529 has a concave-sided lozenge with a ring and pellet moulding in each corner. This design does not appear to be closely parallelled by bottles from British sites though a similar design with single pellets rather than ring and pellet corner mouldings is known from Aquileia (Calvi 1968, tav E, no 1)

Jars are a very long-lived form in use from the first to mid third centuries. The different rim finishes, however, do appear to have been popular at different times. Those with fire-rounded rims (Cool and Price 1995, 113) seem to have been in use mainly in the first and early second century. They are represented here by 122, 280–2, and 908. Examples with funnel mouths (285 and 724) appear to have been primarily in use during the second century (*ibid*, 112). The base fragment, 743, may also be from a funnel-mouthed jar decorated with indentations on the side similar to those found in a pit dated to *c* AD 160–70 at

Felmongers, Harlow (Price 1987, 205, fig 3.24–5). Using indented decoration on jars seems to have been restricted to those with funnel mouths. Jars with rolled-rim edges (Cool and Price 1995, 109) are not closely datable within the first to third-century period. They are represented in this assemblage by 144, 283–4, and 907.

Two conical unguent bottles (*ibid*, 161) are represented by 44 and 735. These were mainly in use during the later first century and earlier second century, though some were still in use in the later second century (Allen 1986, 104–5, fig 41.31). Discoid unguent bottles (Isings Form 82; Cool and Price 1995, 161 nos 1245–6) are commonest in the second century though they first appear during the later second century. One example (918) can be recognised with certainty, and fragments 45 and 312 are also likely to have come from similar unguent bottles

Bath flasks (Isings Form 61; Cool and Price 1995, 156) developed during the late Neronian period and became a vital accessory for a visit to the baths until at least the early third century. All of the examples found

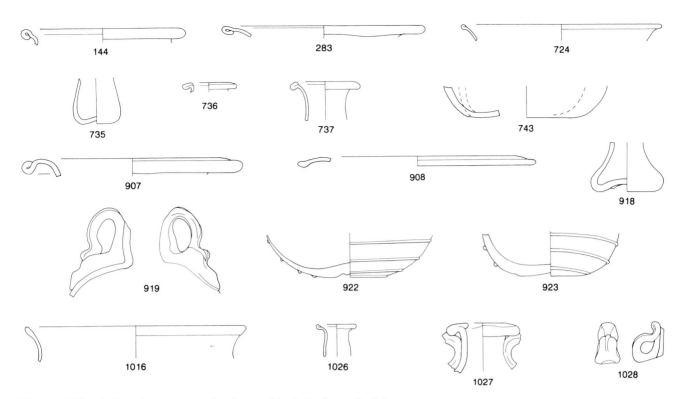

Fig 4.44 Vessel glass: jars, unguent bottles, and bath flasks; scale 1:2

during these excavations (919–23 and 1027–30) were blue/green and three (921–3) are decorated with spiral trails.

Later third to fourth-century tablewares
(Figs 4.45, 4.46)

For much of the second and third centuries the main colours used for vessels were blue/green and colourless glass with a small amount of pale green glass used primarily for flask and unguent bottle forms. In most cases the glass is of good quality with relatively small numbers of bubbles. Towards the end of the third century, however, a notable change comes over the glass used to make vessels. Colourless and blue/green glass became uncommon, and the preferred colour ranged from pale green-tinged colourless through light green to yellowish green. This glass is further distinguished from the earlier colourless and blue/green glass by the fact that it frequently contains many small bubbles. This very distinctive visual contrast to the earlier glass often allows late Roman glass to be recognised even when the form cannot be identified. This is reflected in the catalogues for the Wroxeter glass where fragments of this glass have been catalogued together under the heading greenish colourless bubbly glass (632–63, 869–75, 982–7, and 1072–5).

Most of the later Roman glass found at Wroxeter is made in this greenish colourless bubbly glass but there are also a few examples of late third to early fourth-century forms made in good quality colourless glass. These include two examples of cups with facet-cut designs arranged in geometric patterns (Cool and Price 1995, 77, no 415). Number 161 is an example of the commoner hemispherical form while 162 appears to have come from the rarer cylindrical form similar to an example found in York (Harden 1962, 136, fig 88.H.G. 210)

The commonest forms of fourth-century drinking vessels are hemispherical cups and conical beakers with cracked off rims (Isings Forms 96 and 106; Cool and Price 1995, 88). These probably came into use at the end of the third century and were used in large numbers throughout the fourth century and probably into the fifth century. In this assemblage conical beakers are represented by 634–6, 869–70, 982–3, and 1072, and hemispherical cups by 632–3. The rim fragments 637 and 871 could have come from either form. There is also one example, 710, of the less common variant of conical beaker decorated with rice grain facets. These often have patterns that are similar to the hemispherical cups with geometric patterns such as 161, as may be seen on an example from Grave 2253 at Krefeld Gellep dated to the first half of the fourth century (Pirling 1968, 34, Abb 1 no 1). It seems likely that conical beakers decorated in this way were only in use during the earlier part of the form's lifespan.

Hemispherical cups and conical beakers with fire-rounded rims in fourth-century glass, by contrast, do not start to appear until the middle of the fourth century (Cool and Price 1995, 92). They were in use during the second half of the fourth century and into the fifth century but were never as numerous as the forms with cracked-off rims. In this assemblage there is one example of a hemispherical cup with a fire rounded rim, 639, two fragments from conical beakers, 640–1, and two rim fragments that could come from either form, 642 and 985. Another form that appears to have been

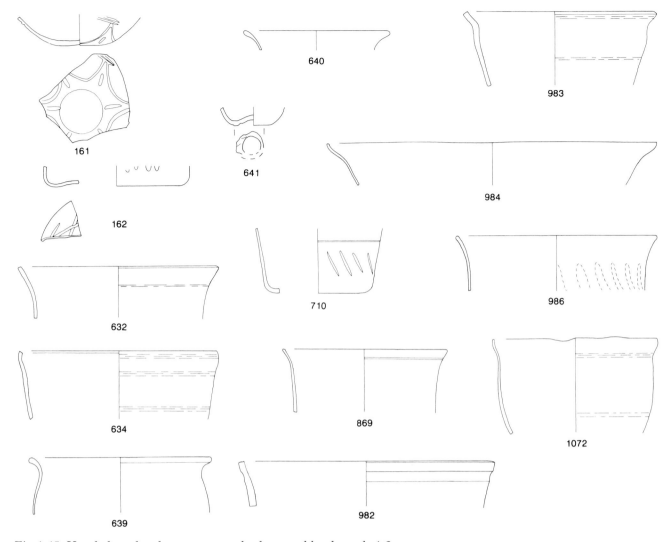

Fig 4.45 Vessel glass: fourth-century cups, beakers, and bowls; scale 1:2

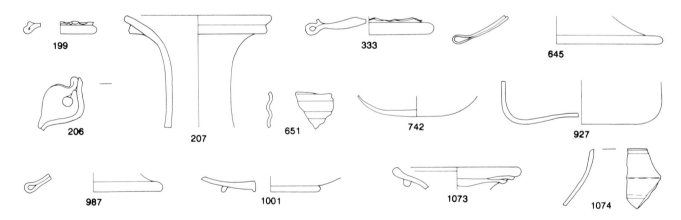

Fig 4.46 Vessel glass: fourth-century bottle, jug, and flasks, with miscellaneous base fragments; scale 1:2

commonest during the second half of the fourth century is the indented truncated conical bowl (Isings Form 117; Cool and Price 1995, 104). Numbers 636 and 984 may have come from bowls of this form.

One of the latest forms to be identified in this assemblage is the cylindrical bowl with fire-rounded rim and optic-blown decoration, represented here by 986. These appear to be absent from early to mid

fourth-century assemblages but have been found in late fourth-century ones. Several are present in the extensive dumps of the last third of the fourth century or later at Wellington Row, York (Site 1987.24, unpublished) and one lacking its rim was found in a pit at Dorchester-on-Thames dated to the end of the fourth century or early fifth century (Charlesworth 1984, 155, fig 39.18).

Many of the jug and bottle forms common during the fourth century have funnel mouths with a fire-rounded rim and thick trail below. The rim fragments 208, 643–4, 990, 1073 could have come from either jugs (Cool and Price 1995, 136 nos 1160–1) or cylindrical bottles (*ibid*, 201 nos 2245 and 2257). The base fragments 645–6 and 987 come from jugs and the rim fragment 208 from a bottle.

Two other fourth-century bottle forms are also represented. Frontinus bottles or barrel jugs (Isings Forms 89 and 128; Cool and Price 1995, 204) are a long-lived form with the one-handled form (Isings Form 89) known from late first or early second-century contexts and the two-handled form (Isings Form 128) appearing to be a fourth-century development which remained in use until late in the century. The examples from these excavations, 651–2, 874, clearly belong to the fourth century because of the glass they are made from. The dolphin-handled form of bottle (Isings Form 100b; Cool and Price 1995, 207) is represented by 206. This type of bottle was made in both a cylindrical and hexagonal form but insufficient of 206 is preserved to identify which variant it came from. Dolphin-handled bottles came into use during the later third century with most examples coming from fourth-century contexts. It appears that the cylindrical form went out of use during the mid fourth century, though the hexagonal form may have remained in use for a slightly longer period.

Catalogue of glass

The principles on which the catalogue is ordered are noted above. What follows is a summary of the full catalogue which is available in archive. It excludes undiagnostic body fragments which are indicated here by missing catalogue numbers. Measurements are only included where they relate to original rim or base diameter, handle sections etc. Bubbles are only noted here where they may be indicative of a late Roman date. Full details of bubble patterns, iridescence etc, together with full measurements and contextual details of the simply decorated and undiagnostic body fragments will be found in the full catalogue. Unless otherwise stated each entry refers to one fragment.

Some of the glass has already been catalogued and discussed in the volume considering the military occupation at Wroxeter (Cool and Price forthcoming). A concordance is provided below where appropriate giving the catalogue number in the military volume, the phase and the EVE value, although some of this data was not available when the military catalogue was prepared.

The following abbreviations are used PH – present height; RD – rim diameter; BD – base diameter. For prismatic bottles OCD is the diameter of the outer moulded circle and EW is the estimated width of the bottle. All measurements are in millimetres.

Period 1

Pillar moulded bowl
1   Military 4; 1.3; EVE 0.2

Cast
2   Military 55; 1.2; EVE 0.6

Mould blown
3   Military 59; 1.3; EVE 0.6

Strongly coloured
4   Military 90; 1.3

Yellow/brown
7   Military 104; 1.3; EVE 0.14
8   Jug, dark yellow/brown handle fragment; 91/117, 1.3; EVE 0.14
9   Ribbed body fragment

Yellow/Green
13   Military 112; 1.2; EVE 0.2
14   Jug/flask, rim bent out, up, in and flattened, cylindrical neck; 86/71, 1.3; PH 10, RD 40; EVE 0.14
15   Military 118; 1.3; EVE 0.14

Pale/Light Green
18   Military 123; 1.3; EVE 0.2
19   Military 124; 1.2; EVE 0.2
20   Jug, handle fragment with at least one prominent rib; 98/173, 1.3; EVE 0.14
21   Base fragment; side curving into low concave base; 97/156, 1.3

Colourless
31   Military 147; 1.3; EVE 0.4
32   Body fragment, convex-curved side, small self coloured blobs in low relief; 97/156, 1.3

Blue/Green
38   Military 178; 1.1; EVE 0.4
39   Military 184; 1.3; EVE 0.2
40   Tubular rimmed ?bowl, side curving through rounded carination to wide lower body. Terminals of two diagonal ribs dying out on carination; 98/124, 1.2; EVE 0.2
41   Jug, two joining fragments, angular ribbon handle with central rib; 90/184, 1.2; HS 30x6; EVE 0.14
42   Jug, straight handle with at least two rounded ribs; 90/184, 1.2; HS 15x5; EVE 0.14
43   Unguent bottle, complete, assymetrically outbent rim, edge sheared and rolled in in places, cylindrical neck; 98/130, 1.2; PH 28, RD 19x17, WT 0.5; EVE 0.14
44   Conical unguent bottle, straight side sloping out slightly to concave base; 91/85, 1.3; PH 25, BD *c* 20, WT 1.5; EVE 0.4

45   Discoid ?unguent bottle, lower body and base edge; 91/101, 1.3; EVE 0.2
46   Military 217; 1.3; EVE 0.2
47   Military 218; 1.2
75   Jar/bottle, folded and flattened rim fragment; 90/196, 1.3; RD 45; EVE 0.14
76   Prismatic bottle, base fragment, base design with at least two concentric circular mouldings; 97/201, 1.2; EVE 0.14
77   Prismatic bottle, description as 76, heat-affected; 97/179, 1.3; EVE 0.14
78   Square bottle, corner fragment of side and base; 63/10, 1.3; EVE 0.28
79–87   Prismatic bottles, sixteen body fragments; 85/134; 91/175, 1.1; 91/181; 98/97; 98/124; 98/144, 1.2; 91/106; 91/117; 97/156, 1.3
88–94   Cylindrical bottles, nine body fragments; 91/137; 98/148, 1.1; 91/181; 98/105 1.2; 63/15; 91/191, 1.3

Periods 2–4

Insula Porticos

Pillar Moulded Bowls
95   Military 3; P 3.3; EVE 0.4
96   Military 14; P 3.3; EVE 0.2
97   Military 15; P 2.2; EVE 0.2
98   Military 41; P 3.3; EVE 0.2
99   Military 41; P 3.3; EVE 0.2

Cast
100   Military 44; P 3.2, KG 17; EVE 0.2
101   Military 45; P 3.1, KG 16; EVE 0.2
102   Military 51; P 3.1, KG 16; EVE 0.4
103   Military 57; P 3.1, KG 16

Mould Blown
104   Military 60; P 2.3; EVE 0.4
105   Military 61; P 2.3; EVE 0.2
106   Military 72; P 2.3
107   Military 71; P 2.1
108   Military 74; P 2.1; EVE 0.4
109   Military 76; P 2.3; EVE 0.2
110   Military 78; P 2.3; EVE 0.2

Polychrome and strongly coloured
111   Military 81; P 2.2; EVE 0.14
112   Military 91; P 2.2
113   Very dark glass appearing black, body fragment, concave-sided; 90/100, 3.1 KG 16
114   Military 93; P 2.3; EVE 0.125
115   Military 97; P 2.2; EVE 0.14

Yellow/Brown
122   ?Jar, light yellow/brown, funnel mouth, rim edge fire-thickened, 90/170, P 3.3; PH 10, WT 2; EVE 0.17

123   Conical jug, light yellow/brown, some small bubbles, side sloping out to concave base, terminal of one rib in low relief, ring of wear on base; 90/157, P 3.3; PH 22, BD 110, WT 1.5; EVE 0.28

Yellow/Green
134   Military 115; P 2.2; EVE 0.14
135   Military 116; P 3.1, KG 16; EVE 0.14
136   Military 117; P 2.2; EVE 0.14
137   Ribbed body fragment

Pale/Light Green
140   Military 126; P 3.3; EVE 0.2
141   Military 127; P 3.5, KG 25; EVE 0.2
142   Beaker/?cup, straight-sided body fragment with two wheel-cut lines; 90/125, P 3.3
143A   Beaker/?cup, convex-curved body fragment with two wheel-cut lines; 97/121, P 3.3
143B   Beaker/?cup, convex-curved body fragment with abraded band; 97/179, 2.2
144   Jar, outbent rim, edge rolled out and down, mouth sloping in; 90/17, P 3.4, KG 25; PH 10, RD 90, WT 1.5; EVE 0.17
145   Jug/flask, cylindrical neck fragment; 80/179, P 2.1; EVE 0.14
146   Ribbed body fragment

Colourless
159   Military 142; P 2.2; EVE 0.4
160   Military 149; P; 2.2; EVE 0.2
161   Hemispherical facet-cut cup, convex-curved side sloping into base formed by circular facet, lower body decorated originally by row of six circular facets, parts of three remaining, lower parts of facets outlined with wheel-cut grooves forming a festoon pattern, parts of five of the original six remaining. The junctions of adjacent festoons marked by pairs of horizontal rice grain facets, one pair now remaining, vertical rice grain facets at edge of base below each junction, parts of all six remaining; 98/3, P 4; PH 14, BD 23, WT 2–4.5; EVE 0.4
162   Cylindrical facet-cut cup, vertical side curving into slightly concave base, tips of four rice grain or narrow oval facets on lower body. One rice grain facet on base parallel with edge, two crossed wheel-cut lines nearer centre; 98/20, P 3.4A, KG 25; PH 12, BD *c* 90, WT 1.5; EVE 0.2
163   Body fragment, slightly convex-curved side, one horizontal wheel-cut line. Fragment possibly broken at edge of facet; 80/117, P 3.1; KG 16
164   Military 157; P 2.3; EVE 0.2
165   Cylindrical beaker, curved rim, edge cracked off and ground, straight side. One wheel-cut line below rim edge, one broad wheel-cut line

on upper body; 98/81, P 3.1; KG 16; PH 18, RD *c* 80, WT 2; EVE 0.4

166 Cylindrical ?beaker, two fragments, curved rim, edge cracked off and ground. Straight side, one horizontal wheel-cut line below rim, two similar lines on upper body; 90/167, P 3.3; PH 25, RD 70, WT 1.5; EVE 0.4

167 Beaker, two joining fragments, curved rim, edge cracked off and ground, straight side; one wheel-cut line below rim edge; 97/72, P 3.1, KG 16; PH 18, RD 90, WT 1; EVE 0.2

168 Beaker, twenty seven body and two base fragments, straight side curving into shallow concave base, five wheel-cut lines on lower body; 90/205, P 3.1, KG 16; EVE 0.6

169–82 Twenty eight body fragments with wheel-cut lines

183 Cylindrical cup, slightly out-turned rim, edge fire-thickened, straight side. Horizontal trail on upper body; 80/130 P, 3.1, KG 16; PH 25, RD 115, WT 1.5; EVE 0.4

184 Cylindrical cup, three strain cracked rim and body fragments as 183; 80/129, P 3.1, KG 16; EVE 0.4

185 Cylindrical ?cup, flat lower body, curved trail; 90/100, P 3.1, KG 16; EVE 0.2

186 Cylindrical cup, vertical rim, edge fire-rounded, straight side; 98/40, P 3.1, KG 16; PH 27, RD 75, WT 1; EVE 0.4

187 Cylindrical cup, as 186; 98/40, F672, P 3.1, KG 16; PH 24, RD 90, WT 2; EVE 0.4

188 Cylindrical cup, as 186; 90/62, P 3.3; EVE 0.4

189 Cup, tubular pushed-in base ring, concave base broken at edge of trail on underside, side grozed; 98/81, P 3.1, KG 16; BD 50; EVE 0.4

190 Cup, part of circular trail on underside of concave base; 97/25, P 3.3; EVE 0.2

191 ?Beaker, slightly green-tinged body fragment with two wheel-cut lines; 90/177, P 2.2

192 ?Beaker, body fragment with one horizontal abraded band; 80/99, P 3.2, KG 17

193 Beaker/cup, two fragments, slightly green-tinged colourless, small bubbles. Out-turned rim, edge cracked off and ground, straight side sloping in, horizontal abraded band on upper body; 98/61, P 2.3; PH 12; EVE 0.2

194 Jug, edge of curved handle retaining one rib; 98/40, F672, P 3.1, KG 16; EVE 0.14

195 Jug, fragment from edge of ribbon handle; 90/100, F609, P 3.1, KG 16; EVE 0.14

196 ?Jug, tubular pushed-in base ring, concave base with narrow trail on underside, post technique scars on base ring, side broken; 97/100, F523, P 3.1, KG 16; BD 75; EVE 0.28

197 Jug/flask, slightly green-tinged colourless, Short, straight-sided ?neck, sloping out towards body and broken at junctions with rim and body; 80/3, P 3.5; EVE 0.14

198 Base, *c* twenty fragments, wide lower body, tubular pushed-in base ring, concave base thickening towards centre. Pontil scar with fragments of additional glass; 90/56, P 3.3; BD *c* 50 – 60

199 Base fragment, tubular pushed in base ring, concave base, side grozed; 97/51, P 3.3; BD 35

200–1 Two base fragments, as 199, side grozed; 98/88, P 3.2, KG 17; BD 45; 98/12, P 4

202 Base fragment, side curving into slightly concave base, trailed base ring; 90/179, P 2.2; PH 9, BD *c* 120, WT 2

203 Fragment with ?trailed base ring; 98/20, P 3.4A, KG 25

204 Three base fragments, convex-curved side, edge of concave base; 98/20, P 3.4A, KG 25

205 Bottle, two joining fragments, upper part of angular reeded handle with folded upper attachment retaining part of cylindrical neck; 97/52, P 2.3; EVE 0.14

206 Bottle, cylindrical neck; horizontal shoulder bending over to side, dolphin handle with perforation formed around tool. Trail attached to neck, trailed across shoulder, looped up to neck with small return trail; 98/+ P 4; height of handle 25; EVE 0.2

207 Bottle, two joining rim, two neck and *c* 50 strain cracked chips and fragments, some small bubbles, funnel mouth, rim edge fire rounded, cylindrical neck, thick trail below rim edge; 98/127, P 3.4B, KG 25; PH 60, RD 75; EVE 0.28

208 Bottle, small bubbles, distorted funnel mouth, rim edge fire-rounded, thick trail below rim edge; 98/140, P 3.2, KG 17; EVE 0.14

209 Bottle, 18 strain-cracked fragments from a reeded handle retaining parts of a folded upper handle attachment; 80/+, P 4; EVE 0.14

210 Bottle, six fragments from upper part of a reeded handle; 80/4, P 3.4B; EVE 0.14

211 ?Bottle, five strain-cracked fragments from a folded upper handle attachment; 80/5, P 3.4B

212 ?Bottle, two joining body fragments, cylindrical side curving over to shoulder, four horizontal wheel-cut lines on upper body; 98/90, P 3.3; EVE 0.14

213 ?Bottle, body fragment as 212, with two abraded bands; 98/12, P 4

214 Shoulder fragment probably from small cylindrical bottle; 97/133, P 2.3

215 Body fragment, part of V-shaped trail retaining small part of convex-curved side; 90/125, P 3.3

216–19 Five body fragments with trails

Blue/Green

270　　Military 169; P 2.3; EVE 0.4

271　　Military 175; P 3.3; EVE 0.4

272　　Military 177; P 2.3; EVE 0.2

273　　Tubular rimmed bowl, vertical rim, edge rolled out and down, straight side sloping in; 90/56, P 3.3; PH 14, RD 180, WT 2; EVE 0.4

274　　Tubular rimmed bowl, outbent rim, edge bent out and down; 80/3, P 3.5; PH 11, RD 180, WT 1.5; EVE 0.2

275　　Tubular rimmed bowl, as 273; 98/83, P 2.3; PH 16, RD 170, WT 2; EVE 0.2

276　　Tubular rimmed bowl, slightly outbent rim, edge bent out and down, body broken away at rim edge; 90/205, P 3.1, KG 16; RD 170; EVE 0.2

277　　Plate or ?bowl, rim edge rolled out and down, slightly convex-profiled upper body sloping in shallowly; 98/126, P 3.3; PH 11, RD 220, WT 1.5; EVE 0.4

278　　Collared jar, slightly outbent rim, thickened edge perhaps rolled in then bent out and down and tooled along bottom, side sloping out; 98/83, P 2.3; PH 21, RD 120, WT 3; EVE 0.19

279　　Tubular rimmed jar or ?bowl, inturned rim, edge bent out and down; 80/49, P 3.5; RD 130; EVE 0.2

280　　Jar, outbent rim, edge fire rounded; 98/12, P 4; PH 13, RD 150–160, WT 2; EVE 0.17

281　　Jar, as 280; 98/16, P 3.5, KG 25; PH 12, RD *c* 110, WT 1; EVE 0.17

282　　Jar, as 280; 98/90, P 3.3; EVE 0.17

283　　Jar, rim bent out horizontally, edge bent down and in; 90/125, P 3.3; RD 105, WT 2; EVE 0.17

284　　Jar, outbent rim, edge first rolled down then folded down and in; 98/ 40, F672, P 3.1, KG 16; RD 160, WT 1, EVE 0.17

285　　Jar, funnel mouth, rim edge rolled in; 98/51, F680, P 3.1, KG 16; PH 6, RD *c* 85, WT 1; EVE 0.17

286　　Conical jug, straight ribbon handle with central rib, broken claw lower attachment with upper part of central pinched extension trail; 98/138, P 2.3; HS 35x6; EVE 0.28

287　　Jug, lower part of pinched extension trail retaining three projections and rounded end, convex curved body with ?two diagonal ribs in shallow relief; 90/204, P 2.2; EVE 0.14

288　　Conical ?jug, lower part of pinched extension trail retaining four projections, rounded end of return trail; slightly convex-curved body; 98/28, P 3.2, KG 17; EVE 0.14

289　　Jug, lower part of scored extension trail with three projections in low relief and rounded end, side deliberately broken around edge of trail; 90/174, P 2.2; EVE 0.14

290　　Jug, angular handle with at least two prominent ribs; 90/226, P 2.1; EVE 0.14

291　　Discoid or globular jug, convex-curved body broken at tooled junction with missing/neck, lower part of angular ribbon handle with four narrow prominent ribs, simple lower attachment. Narrow close-set ribs spiralling into base of neck; 90/164, F631, P 3.2, KG 17; HS (excluding ribs) 22 x 4; EVE 0.28

292　　Jug, handle with at least one prominent rib; 80/181, P 2.1; EVE 0.14

293　　Jug, straight ribbon handle with wide central rib resembling a narrow rib superimposed on a wider one; 98/28, F638, P 3.2, KG 17; section 26 x12; EVE 0.14

294　　?Jug, two chips from ribbed handle; 98/145, P 3.1, KG 16

295　　Military 168; P 3.3

296　　Conical ?jug, side curving into slightly concave base; 90/205, P 3.1, KG 16; PH 14, WT 1.5; EVE 0.28

297　　Jar/jug, open pushed-in base ring; concave base; 98/87, P 2.3; BD 80; EVE 0.14

298–9　　Jar/jug, two fragments from the sides of open pushed-in base rings; 90/222, P 2.2; EVE 0.14; 98/52, P 2.3; EVE 0.14

300　　Jug, funnel mouth, rim edge rolled in, cylindrical neck, ribbon handle attached to underside of rim and neck with folded and looped thumb rest; 90/+, P 4 (PH; rim and neck) 23; EVE 0.14

301　　Jug, fragment of folded handle attachment; 98/101, F933, P 3.1; EVE 0.14

302　　Jug, curved rod handle with simple lower attachment at junction of neck and side; 80/7, P 3.4B; EVE 0.28

303–5　　Jugs, three fragments from edges of handles; 98/145, P 3.1, KG 16; EVE 0.14; 80/64, P 3.3; EVE 0.14; 80/+, P 4; EVE 0.14

306　　Globular jug, convex-curved side, close-packed narrow-spiral ribs, tip of lower handle attachment; 97/133, P 2.3

307–8　　Jugs, two fragments from area of lower handle attachment; 90/204, P 2.2; 98/51, P 3.1, KG 16

309–11　　Tubular unguent bottles, three lower body fragments; 80/181, P 2.1; EVE 0.2; 98/61, P 2.3; EVE 0.2; 90/ 82, P 3.3; EVE 0.2

312　　Discoid unguent bottle, base and edge of side fragment; 90/97, P 3.1, KG 16; EVE 0.2

313　　Flask, cylindrical neck fragment, expanding slightly; 80/154, P 3.1, KG 16; EVE 0.2

314　　Jug/flask, rim bent out, edge rolled in, cylindrical neck; 90/88, P 3.1, KG 16; PH 21, RD 50, neck thickness 3.5; EVE 0.4

315　　Flask, folded and flattened rim fragment; 90/222, P 2.2; EVE 0.2

316–17 Flask, two rolled rim fragments; 98/84, P 2.1; EVE 0.2; 90/+, P4; RD 30; EVE 0.2

318 Flask/jug, rim fragment, funnel mouth, rim edge rolled in, parts of four spiral trails; 80/4, P 3.4B; PH 18, RD 40, neck thickness 1.5; EVE 0.28

319–22 Flasks, nine cylindrical neck fragments; 97/142, P 2.1, EVE 0.2; 97/139, P2.2, EVE 0.2; 97/133, P2.3, EVE 0.2; 98/8, P 3.6, KG 25, EVE 0.2

323 ?Flasks, two body fragments with edges of necks; 90/164, F631 P 3.2, KG 17; 90/+, P 4

325 Base fragment, side curving into shallow concave base; 98/52, P 2.3

326 Base fragment, side curving in steeply to concave base, circular pontil scar with small amount of additional glass; 98/106, P 3.3; BD 40, WT 1.5, pontil scar diameter c 10

327 Base fragment, concave base, circular pontil scar; 98/20, P 3.4A; BD c 60, pontil scar diameter 13

328–32 Ten fragments from concave bases; 90/169, P 2.2 (contaminated); 90/87, P 2.3; 90/205, Pit F800, P 3.1, KG 16; 90/133, P 3.3; 97/121, P 3.3

333 Base fragment, tubular pushed-in base ring, concave base with central kick, side grozed; 80/41, P 3.5; BD 65

334–5 Three base ring fragments as 333; 98/145, P 3.1, KG 16; 90/56, P 3.3

336 Base fragment, lower body sloping in from carination, part of applied pad or separately blown base; 90/+, P4

337–40 Four body fragments each with part of one trail

341 Body fragment, convex-curved side, terminal of thick curving tooled-up rib; tooling mark from pointed tool on interior forming narrow void in rib; 80/48, P 3.4B

342 Discoid ?jug, wide slightly convex-curved upper body fragment, parts of c ten vertical ribs in very low relief running; 90/137, P 2.2

343–51 Ten body fragments with ribs

481 Double-handled bottle, rim folded out, up, in and flattened, cylindrical neck. Folded upper attachments of two handles on either side of rim attached to underside of rim and neck; 80/5, P 3.4 B; PH 41, RD 60; EVE 0.28

482 Bottle, rim folded out, up and in assymetrically and flattened, cylindrical neck; 97/121, P 3.3; RD 45; EVE 0.14

483–9 Bottles, seven rim and neck fragments as 482; 80/+, P 4; RD 55; EVE 0.28; 90/204, P 2.2; RD 45; EVE 0.14; 90/9, P 3.6, KG 25; RD 40; EVE 0.14; 97/121, P 3.3; RD 55; EVE 0.14; 97/121, P 3.3; EVE 0.14; 90/204, P 2.2; RD c 50; EVE 0.14; 98/77, P 3.3; EVE 0.14

490–1 Bottles, two rim and neck fragments, rim bent out, up and in with triangular profile, cylindrical neck; 98/13, P 3.4A, KG 25; EVE 0.14; 90/177, P 2.2; EVE 0.14

492–6 Bottles, five cylindrical neck fragments; 90/204, P 2.2, EVE 0.14; 80/115, P 3.1, KG 16, EVE 0.14; 97/48, P 3.3, EVE 0.14; 90/5, P 3.5, KG 25; EVE 0.14; 98/+, P 4; EVE 0.14

497 Square bottle, four edge of neck, shoulder and side fragments; 98/62, P 3.3; EVE 0.21

498–9 Prismatic bottles, two shoulder and side fragments; 98/61, P 2.3; EVE 0.14; 90/205, P 3.1, KG 16; EVE 0.14

500–2 Bottles, three shoulder fragments; 90/179, P 2.2; EVE 0.14; 90/204, P 2.2; EVE 0.14; 97/112, P 3.1, KG 16; EVE 0.14

503 Bottle, cylindrical neck fragment with part of folded upper attachment; 90/177, P 2.2; EVE 0.14

504–7 Bottle, four reeded handle fragments; 90/204, P 2.2; EVE 0.14; 98/87, P 2.3; EVE 0.14; 80/117, P 3.1, KG 16; EVE 0.14; 80/3, P 3.5; EVE 0.14

508 Prismatic bottle, ribbon handle with central indent to form narrow two ribs, simple lower attachment retaining shoulder fragment; 90/85, P 3.3; section 39x7; EVE 0.14

509 Bottle, lower part of reeded handle with simple lower attachment retaining part of shoulder; 98/28, F638, P 3.2, KG 17; width of handle 29; EVE 0.14

510 Square bottle, horizontal shoulder broken at edge of neck, lower part of reeded handle with simple lower attachment; 98/29, P 3.2; width of handle 42; EVE 0.14

511–14 Bottles, five fragments from reeded handles and attachments; 98/60, F766, P 3.1, KG 16, EVE 0.14; 98/ 49, F679, P 3.2, KG 17, EVE 0.14; 90/163, F631, P 3.2, KG 17, EVE 0.14; 90/ 56, P 3.3; EVE 0.14; 90/144, P 3.3; EVE 0.14

515–18 Bottles, five shoulder fragments; 97/133, P 2.3, KG 31; 80/71, F455, P 3.2, KG 17; 90/141, P 3.1, KG 16; 90/+, P4

519 ?Bottle, angular ribbon handle with at least two wide ribs; 97/100, F523, P 3.1, KG 16; EVE 0.14

520 Prismatic bottle, side and base fragment of prismatic bottle, base design at least one circular moulding; 90/177, P 2.2; PH 57, OCD c 65, EW 75–80; EVE 0.175

521–2 Prismatic bottles, two base fragments each retaining part of one circular outer moulding; 97/142, P 2.1; EVE 0.14; 98/88, P 3.2, KG 17; EVE 0.14

523 Square bottle, lower body and base fragment, base design at least one circular moulding; 80/178, P 2.3; PH 17; EVE 0.28

524   Prismatic bottle, base fragment, base design at least two concentric circular mouldings, one edge grozed; 98/138, P 2.3; OCD 40, EW *c* 65–70; EVE 0.28

525   Square bottle, side and base fragment, base design at least three concentric circular mouldings; 90/205, P 3.1, KG 16; PH 30, OCD *c* 48, EW 58; EVE 0.35

526   Prismatic bottle, base fragment, base design three concentric circular mouldings, fragment possibly broken at edge of central pellet; 97/142, P 2.1; OCD *c* 63, EW 80; EVE 0.28

527   Prismatic bottle, base fragment, base design at least three concentric circular mouldings and central pellet; 90/101, P 3.2, KG 17; EVE 0.28

528   Prismatic bottle, base fragment, base design at least five concentric circular moulding; 97/148, P 2.1; EVE 0.14

529   Square bottle, side and base fragment, base design diagonally placed, concave-sided square moulding with small circular moulding and central pellet in each corner. Parts of three sides of the square and two corner circles remaining; 80/+, P4; PH 70, EW *c* 65–70; EVE 0.28

530   Small hexagonal bottle, lower body and base, base design circular pellet in each corner, two remaining, fragment broken at edge of central ?circular moulding; 90/82, P 3.3; PH 22, EW *c* 40; EVE 0.28

531   Prismatic bottle, base fragment, base design one circular moulding with small regularly spaced cavities around outer edge, narrow pointed moulding radiating out from circle. Fragment possible broken at edge of central moulding; 80/117, P 3.1; OCD *c* 70, EW *c* 110–120; EVE 0.28

532   Cylindrical bottle, two base and six side fragments; straight side with vertical scratch marks, concave base, heat-affected; 98/87, P 2.3; PH 90, BD *c* 150, WT 4; EVE 0.42

533   Cylindrical bottle, two base and ten side fragments as 532 and probably from the same bottle; 98/102, P 2.1

534   Cylindrical bottle, three side and base fragments; 90/177, P 2.2; EVE 0.28

535–52 Square bottles, 20 body fragments; 90/180; 90/209; 98/68, P 2.2; 80/117; 90/205; 97/100; 98/145, P 3.1, KG 16; 80/71; 90/101; 98/48, F678, P 3.2, KG 17; 98/20, P 3.3, KG 25; 90/69; 90/95; 90/161, P 3.3; 98/20, P 3.4A, KG 25; 80/7, P /3.4B; 80/3, P 3.5; 90/14, P 3.6, KG 25

553–625 Prismatic bottles, 167 body fragments; 80/179; 80/182; 90/226; 97/148; 98/84; 98/103; 90/174; 90/177; 90/179; 90/181; 90/204; 90/209; 90/222, P 2.2; 90/191, P

2.3; 97/133, P 2.3, KG 31; 8/52; 98/61; 98/68; 98/83; 98/87; 98/138, P 2.3; 80/115; 80/117; 80/131; 90/128; 90/189; 90/189; 97/100, F532; 97/112; 98/40, F672; 98/145, P 3.1, KG 16; 98/101, P 3.1; 80/74; 98/99; 90/101; 90/163; 98/28; 98/88; 98/98, P 3.2, KG 17; 90/51, P 3.3, KG 25; 80/84; 90/56; 90/60; 90/116; 90/125; 97/121; 90/157; 90/161; 90/167; 97/48; 97/78; 97/80; 98/90; 98/106; 98/170; 98/77 P 3.3; 90/51; 98/127, P 3.4,KG 25; 97/49, P 3.4A, KG 25; 80/5; 80/7; 80/51; 90/5; 90/9; 98/8, P 3.6, KG 25; 80/+; 90/+; 97/+; 98/+, P 4

626–30 Cylindrical bottles, 14 body fragments, many with vertical scratch marks; 87/100; 98/87; 98/52; 98/87, P 2.3; 98/77, P 3.3

631   Cylindrical bottle, body fragment with abraded band; 90/100, P 3.1, KG 16

Greenish colourless bubbly

632   Hemispherical cup, curved rim, edge cracked off but not ground, side sloping out, abraded band below rim edge; 90/29, P 4; PH 27, RD *c* 115, WT 1.5; EVE 0.4

633   Hemispherical cup, vertical rim, edge cracked off smoothly but not ground, straight side; 97/121, P 3.3; PH 19, RD 100, WT 1; EVE 0.2

634   Conical beaker, curved rim, edge cracked off smoothly but not ground, straight side sloping in. One abraded band below rim edge, one on upper body and one on side; 90/14, P 3.6 KG 25; PH 33, RD 100, WT 2; EVE 0.4

635   Conical ?beaker, curved rim, edge cracked off smoothly but not ground, side sloping in, abraded band on upper body; 90/14, P 3.6, KG 25; PH 13, RD *c* 90–100, WT 1.5; EVE 0.2

636   Conical ?beaker, straight-sided body fragment with two abraded bands; 98/3, P 4; EVE 0.2

637   Beaker/cup, curved rim, edge cracked off smoothly but not ground; 90/14, P 3.6, KG 25; PH 16, RD 110, WT 2; EVE 0.2

638   Indented truncated conical ?bowl, body fragment with part of one indentation; 97/101, P 3.1; EVE 0.2

639   Hemispherical cup, out-turned rim, edge fire-thickened, convex-curved side; 90/+, P4; PH 29, RD 90; WT 1; EVE 0.4

640   Conical beaker, out-turned rim, edge fire-rounded; 90/29, P4; PH 12, RD 80, WT 1; EVE 0.2

641   ?Beaker, light green, straight side sloping into concave base, off-centre circular pontil scar; 90/56, P 3.3; PH 10, BD 18, WT 2, pontil scar 15; EVE 0.4

642   Cup/beaker, yellow/green, out-turned rim, edge fire-rounded; 97/121, P 3.2; PH 13, RD 90, WT 1; EVE 0.2

643 Jug/flask/bottle, funnel mouth, rim edge fire-rounded, thick trail below rim edge; 90/51, P 3.4, KG 25; PH 10, RD 45; EVE 0.14

644 Jug/flask/bottle, yellow/green, as 643, heat-affected and bent out of shape; 82/1, P 4; EVE 0.14

645 Jug, high tubular pushed-in base ring with hollow tube at the end; 90/+, P 4; BD 110; EVE 0.14

646 Jug, yellow/green, high tubular pushed-in base ring lacking outer end, conical base with central kick. Pontil scar with additional glass centrally, heat-affected and distorted; 90/9, P 3.6, KG 25; EVE 0.14

647 Jug, c 30 small fragments and chips from base with tubular pushed-in base ring; 90/35, P 3.6, KG 25

648 Jug/flask/bottle, neck/shoulder junction fragment; 90/35, P 3.6, KG 25; EVE 0.2

649 Flask, cylindrical neck fragment; 90/+, P4; EVE 0.2

650 Cylindrical bottle, horizontal shoulder curving over to straight side; 96/21, P 3.6; EVE 0.17

651 Ribbed barrel jug, side fragment retaining parts of three corrugations from ribbed zone; 96/21, P 3.6; EVE 0.125

652 Ribbed barrel jug, side fragment as 651; 90/7, P 2.3; EVE 0.125

653 Bottle, fragment from centre of reeded handle; 80/3, P 3.5; EVE 0.14

654 Three joining base fragments, side curving into concave base without pontil scar, base worn; 90/87, P 2.3; BD 45

655 Ribbed body fragment

West Range

Pillar Moulded Bowls
664 Military 27; WR 3.1; EVE 0.4
665 Military 33; WR 3.1; EVE 0.2
666 Military 36; WR 2.3; EVE 0.2
667 Military 34; WR 2.3 KG 6; EVE 0.2
668 Military 39; WR 2.1; EVE 0.2
669 Military 41; WR 2.1 KG 2; EVE 0.2
670 Military 41; WR 2.3 KG 7; EVE 0.2

Cast
671 Military 47; EVE 1.0

Polychrome
672 Military 86; WR 2.3

Yellow/Brown
673 Conical jug, dark yellow/brown, part of pinched extension trail from lower handle attachment with five small projections, small part of straight side; 83/501, WR 3.1; EVE 0.14

Yellow/Green
678 Jug, two joining handle and body fragments, lower attachment of handle with (probably) multiple prominent ribs, edge of handle and one rib remaining, wide convex-curved body; 86/40, WR 2.1; 92/18, C 2.1; EVE 0.14
679 Military; 91/72, WR 2.3; EVE 0.14

Pale/Light Green
682 Military 122, WR 2.3; EVE 0.4
683 Military, WR 2.3; EVE 0.4
684 Military; 129, WR 2.3; EVE 0.4
685 Military; 130, WR 2.3; EVE 0.2
686 Military; 132, WR 2.3; EVE 0.4
687 Jug, straight ribbon handle with central rib; 84/+, WR 4; section (excluding rib) 20+ x 3; EVE 0.14
688 Jug, fragment from upper part of angular ribbon handle with three central ribs, also one light green body fragment; 91/94, WR 2.3; section (excluding ribs) 25x4; EVE 0.14
689 Jar/jug, outer edge of open pushed-in base ring; 84/201, WR 2.3; EVE 0.14
690 Fifteen body fragments, convex-curved side, seven terminals ribs, the majority in low relief, two tooled and in higher relief; 91/94, WR 2.3

Colourless
700-1 Military; 140-1, WR 2.3; EVE 0.4
702 Military; 151, WR 2.3; EVE 0.2
703 ?Beaker, outbent rim, edge missing, straight side, exterior ground and wheel-polished to leave three horizontal ribs in relief; 85/127, WR 2.1; EVE 0.4
704 ?Cup, edge of side curving into shallow concave base, two wheel-cut lines parallel with edge on underside of base; 86/+, WR 4; BD c 80; EVE 0.2
705 Cylindrical beaker, curved rim, edge cracked off and ground, straight side, one wheel-cut line on upper body with group of four below; 86/3, WR 4; PH 32, RD 80, WT 1; EVE 0.4
706 Bowl, slightly green-tinged colourless, convex-curved lower body, two wheel-cut lines; 86/21, WR 4; diameter of outer wheel-cut line c 75; EVE 0.2
707 Cylindrical trailed ?cup, eight body fragments, side curving through rounded carination to wide lower body, fine trail on underside of lower body; 83/503, WR 3.1; diameter at carination c 90, WT 1; EVE 0.2
708 Cylindrical trailed cup, straight-sided body fragment with horizontal trail; 84/48, WR 3.1; EVE 0.4
709 Cylindrical cup, vertical rim, edge fire-thickened, straight side; 86/+, WR 4; PH 12, RD 95, WT 1; EVE 0.2

710   Conical beaker, slightly green-tinged colourless; many small bubbles; straight side sloping to edge of concave base; horizontal abraded band above row of diagonal rice grain facets on lower body, four now remaining; 86/21, WR 4; PH 35, BD *c* 45; EVE 0.4

711   Jug/flask, fragment from base of cylindrical neck; 86/3, WR 4

712   Beaker/cup/?bowl, side sloping in to tubular pushed-in base ring, base missing, probably domed; 84/103, WR 2.3, KG 7; PH 14, BD 40, WT 2.5; EVE 0.14

Blue/Green

721   Collared jar, small outbent rim, edge first rolled in, then bent out and down; rim slightly distorted; 84/45, WR 4; PH 12, RD 110–120; EVE 0.19

722   Collared jar, small outbent rim, edge first rolled in, then bent out and down; 84/+, WR 4; PH 14, RD 75; EVE 0.19

723   Tubular rimmed jar or ?bowl, funnel mouth, rim edge bent out and down, 84/49, WR 3.1; PH 8, RD 140, WT 1; EVE 0.17

724   Jar, funnel mouth, rim edge rolled in; 91/56, WR 4; PH 5, RD *c* 110, WT 1; EVE 0.16

725   Jug, part of handle and upper part of pinched extension trail retaining three projections. Body possibly deliberately broken around edge of extension trail, upper broken edge of body shows heavy wear and smoothing; 84/49, WR 3.1; EVE 0.14

726   Globular jar/jug, side sloping into open pushed-in base ring; concave base; 91/23, WR 3.1; PH 21, BD *c* 70, WT 2.5; EVE 0.28

727   Globular jar/jug, side sloping into open pushed-in base ring; 83/114, WR 2.3; EVE 0.14

728   Spouted jug; funnel mouth, rim edge rolled out; 87/+, WR 4; PH 19 9; EVE 0.14

729   Jug, fragment of folded handle attachment; 84/T, WR 4; EVE 0.14

730   Jug, body fragment with parts of three spiral trails on body beneath handle attachment; 86/3, WR 4; HS 7x8; EVE 0.28

731   Jug, two fragments, part of cylindrical neck curving out to body, spiral trail on body, applied at base of neck. Straight oval-sectioned rod handle, simple lower attachment applied over trails at neck/body junction; 91/93, WR 2.3; HS 10x6; EVE 0.42

732   Jug, part of ?angular handle with at least two rounded ribs; 83/111, WR 3.1; HS 10+x5; EVE 0.14

733–4 Jugs, two body fragments with the tips of claw handle attachments; 91/23, WR 3.1; 84/+, WR 4

735   Tubular or conical unguent bottle, straight - sided lower body sloping out slightly, shallow

concave base; 83/34, WR 2.2; PH 19, max body diameter 23, WT 1.5; EVE 0.4

736   ?Flask, assymetrical rim bent out, up, in and flattened; 83/516, WR 2.2; RD 28x25; EVE 0.2

737   Flask, outbent rim, edge bent down and up and up and in, cylindrical neck; 83/523, WR 2.3; PH 21, RD 35, neck thickness 1.5; EVE 0.4

738   Flasks, two cylindrical neck fragments; 93/2, WR 2.3; EVE 0.2; 85/105, WR 2.3; EVE 0.2

740–1 ?Flasks, two body fragments with edges of neck; 91/56, WR 4; 91/94, WR 2.3

742   Base fragment, side curving into slightly convex base; 86/33, WR 2.3; PH 8, BD 50, WT 1; EVE 0.33

743   Base fragment, side curving in steeply to shallow concave base, base of indent on side; 84/49, WR 2.3; PH 19, BD *c* 45, WT 3.5; EVE 0.33

744   Base fragment, concave; 91/56, WR 4; EVE 0.16

745   Bowl/jug, applied true base ring with diagonal tooling marks, slightly concave base, wide lower body grozed, base worn; 88/5, WR 4; BD 75; EVE 0.2

746   Jar/jug, convex-curved side curving out to rim or base ring; terminal of one narrow vertical rib; 83/534, WR 2.3

747–53 Ten ribbed body fragments

754   Body fragment, convex-curved side, part of large circular indent; 84/52, WR 2.3

800   Bottle, four joining rim, neck and handle fragments, rim bent out, up and in, cylindrical neck, part of folded upper handle attachment on underside of rim; 91/94, WR 2.3; PH 23, RD 40; EVE 0.14

801–2 Bottle/jar, three folded and flattened rim fragments; 83/526, WR 2.3; RD *c* 90; EVE 0.14; 83/+, WR 4; RD 65; EVE 0.14

803–4 Bottles, two cylindrical neck fragments; 91/94, WR 2.3; EVE 0.14; 91/93, WR 3.1; EVE 0.28

805   Square bottle, edge of neck, shoulder and side fragment with part of lower handle attachment; 84/49, WR 2.3; EVE 0.14

806   Square bottle, shoulder and side fragment; 91/94, WR 2.3; EVE 0.14

807–8 Prismatic bottles, two shoulder and side fragments; 85/224, WR 2.3 (contaminated); EVE 0.14; 84/+, WR 4; EVE 0.14

809–14 Bottles, six shoulder and/or reeded handle fragments; 84/48, WR 3.1, EVE 0.14; 85/137, WR 2.1, KG 5, EVE 0.14; 84/49, WR 3.1, EVE 0.14; 84/+, WR 4, EVE 0.14; 91/94, WR 2.3, EVE 0.14; 85/137, WR 2.1, KG 5, EVE 0.28

815   Square bottle, side and base fragment, base design at least two concentric circular

mouldings, faint surface line parallel with edge of base; 84/52, WR 2.3; PH 22, OCD *c* 72, EW *c* 92; EVE 0.42

816   Square bottle, side and base fragment, base design three concentric circular mouldings with central pellet; 85/137, WR 2.1, KG 4; PH 30, OCD 57, EW 65; EVE 0.42

817–8 Prismatic bottles, two base fragments, base designs at least two concentric circular mouldings; 84/137, WR 2.1, EVE 0.14; 91/56, WR 4, EVE 0.28

819–20 Prismatic bottles, two base fragment, base designs at least one circular moulding; 91/93, WR 2.3, EVE 0.14; 83/508, WR 3.1, EVE 0.14

821   Prismatic bottle, base fragment, base design one circular moulding with probably five pairs of curved mouldings radiating out from raised centre in rosette pattern, parts of four pairs remaining, base worn; 84/59, WR 2.3; OCD *c* 55, EW *c* 70; EVE 0.28

822   Prismatic bottle, side and base fragment, base design at least one circular moulding, expansion on outer edge of moulding at one point, shallow triangular pellet between edge of base and circular moulding; 91/56, WR 4; PH 16, OCD *c* 80, EW *c* 100–110; EVE 0.42

823   Prismatic bottle, side and base fragment; 84/56, WR 2.3; EVE 0.28

824   Cylindrical bottle, three side and base fragments, straight side, edge of concave base; 85/224, WR 2.3 (contaminated); PH 64, BD *c* 140, WT 2.5; EVE 0.28

825–9 Square bottles, six body fragments; 84/106; 84/137, WR 2.1; 91/46; 91/72, WR 2.3; 84/49, WR 3.1

830–61 Prismatic bottles, 75 body fragments, 84/106; 84/137, WR 2.1; 84/178; 85/137, WR 2.1, KG 5; 83/516; 83/534, WR 2.3; 83/544, WR 2.3, KG 6; 84/52; 84/63; 84/75, WR 2.3; 84/103, WR 2.3, KG 7; 85/223; 85/224; 87/100; 91/46; 91/72; 91/94, WR 2.3; 91/503, WR 2.3, KG 6; 83/111; 83/502; 83/508, WR 3.1; 84/46, WR 3.1, KG 21; 84/48; 84/49; 91/23, WR 3.1; 85/+; 86/4; 87/+; 91/56, WR 4

862–8 Cylindrical bottles, 11 body fragments; 84/48, WR 3.1; shoulder diameter *c* 170; 85/137, WR 2.1, KG 5; 83/534; 84/52; 93/1, WR 2.3; 97/133, WR 2.3, KG 31; 84/49, WR 3.1

Greenish colourless bubbly

869   Conical beaker, curved rim, edge cracked off and lightly ground with abrasions on inner face, straight side sloping in, abraded band below rim edge; 91/94, WR 2.3; PH 33, RD 85, WT 2; EVE 0.4

870   Conical beaker, upper body fragment retaining lower part of curved rim; 84/49, WR 3.1; EVE 0.4

871   Cup/beaker, light green, curved rim, edge cracked off smoothly but not ground; 91/55, WR 3.3; PH 16, RD 90, WT 2; EVE 0.4

872   Flask, lower part of cylindrical neck curving out to convex-curved upper body, tooling marks at base of neck; 85/227, WR 2.1; EVE 0.4

873   Globular flask, 16 joining body and base fragments, broken at constricted base of neck, convex-curved body, concave base; 91/56, WR 4; PH 71, BD *c* 45; body diameter *c* 80, WT 1; EVE 0.4

874   Ribbed barrel jug, corrugated side fragment; 85/112, WR 2.3; EVE 0.125

Courtyard

Pillar Moulded Bowls
876   Military 13; C 2.3; EVE 0.4
877   Military 30; C 2.1; EVE 0.2
878   Military 32; C 2.2; EVE 0.2

Cast
879   Military 58; C 2.3; EVE 0.2
880   Military 56; C 2.1; EVE 0.2

Polychrome and strongly coloured
881   Military 82; C 2.1
882   Military 88; C 3.3

Deep blue
883   Military 96; C3.2; EVE 0.14
884   Military 99; C 2.2

Yellow/Green
891   Jug, straight ribbon handle with central rib; 47/17, C 3.1, KG 14; section (excluding rib) 20x4; EVE 0.14

892   Jug, two joining fragments, lower attachment of handle with probable multiple prominent ribs, edge of handle and one rib remaining, wide convex-curved body; 86/40, WR 2.1; 92/18, C 2.1; EVE 0.14

Pale/Light Green
896   Jug, straight ribbon handle with central rib; 11/20, C 2.4, KG 13; section (excluding rib) 20x3; EVE 0.14

Colourless
897   Military 150; 43/6, C 2.3; EVE 0.2
898   Conical beaker, curved rim, edge cracked off and ground, straight side, two wheel-cut lines below rim edge, one broad wheel-cut line on upper body; 63/+, C 4; PH 28, RD 90, WT 2; EVE 0.4

899   ?Cup, out-turned rim, edge fire-thickened; 50/32, C3.1, KG 14; PH 10, RD 85, WT 1.5; EVE 0.2

900   Bottle, rim folded out, up, in and flattened, cylindrical neck, scar from handle on underside of rim; 33/+, C 4; RD 55; EVE 0.14

Blue/Green

902   Military 173; C 2.1; EVE 0.4

903   Tubular rimmed bowl, vertical rim, edge bent out and down; straight side sloping in; 63/+, C 4; EVE 0.4

904   Collared jar, slightly outbent rim, thickened edge perhaps rolled in then bent out and down and tooled centrally, side sloping out, horizontal wear scratches on inside of rim; 92/45, C 2.1; PH 20, RD 90, WT 2; EVE 0.38

905   Collared jar, slightly outbent rim, edge bent out and down, outer edge missing; side curving out, terminal of rib running up to collared rim; 84/49, C 2.3; PH 19, RD 60, WT 1.5, EVE 0.38

906   Bowl/jar, upper part of a tubular or collared rim; 92/18, C 2.1; EVE 0.19

907   Jar, rim outbent horizontally, edge rolled in; neck tapering in; 33/2, C 3.1, KG 14; PH 10, RD 120, WT 2; EVE 0.16

908   Jar, two joining fragments, rim outbent horizontally, edge fire-rounded; 47/17, C 3.1, KG 14; RD 130; EVE 0.16

909   Jug, angular ribbon handle with central rib; 47/17, C 3.1, KG 14; section (excluding rib) 30x10; EVE 0.14

910   Jug, fragment from edge of handle as 909; 47/17, C 3.1, KG 14; EVE 0.14

911   Ovoid jar/jug, convex-curved side, open pushed-in base ring, concave base, vertical rib in high relief dying out on lower body, band of horizontal wear scratches just above base ring, base worn; 67/26, C 2.1, KG 8; PH 77, BD 90, WT 2; EVE 0.61

912   Globular jar/jug, side sloping into open pushed-in base ring; base missing; 47/15, C 3.1, KG 14; PH 15, BD 70, WT 2; EVE 0.14

913   Globular jar/jug, convex-curved side sloping into open pushed-in base ring, band of horizontal wear scratches just above base ring, base missing; 66/9, C 3.2, PH 30; WT 1.5; EVE 0.2

914   Jar/jug, fragment from the side of open pushed-in base ring; 51/9, C 2.3; EVE 0.28

915   Jug, two fragments, two prongs from claw lower attachment; convex-curved side; 77/2, C 2.2; EVE 0.14

916   Military 204; C 2.1; EVE 0.2

917   Military 205; C 2.2; EVE 0.2

918   Bell-shaped or discoid unguent bottle, concave profiled upper body, expanded discoid lower body, concave base, large off-centre pontil scar; 40/ u/s, C 4; PH 26, BD 30, max body diameter *c* 40, WT 2; EVE 0.6

919   Bath flask, cylindrical neck, convex-curved upper body, dolphin handle applied to shoulder, trailed up neck to underside of (missing) rim which has left a small scar, looped back down to shoulder with return trail running back up to rim and down to shoulder again. Tooled ridge on outer edge of handle; 92/1, C 3.3, KG 23; neck diameter 23; EVE 0.16

920   ?Bath flask, rim edge bent out, up, in and flattened, cylindrical neck, part of handle attached to neck and underside of rim; 47/17, C 3.1, KG 14; PH 15, RD 40, neck thickness 3; EVE 0.32

920b   ?Bath flask, convex-curved body fragment retaining lower part of handle attachment; 47/17, C 3.1, KG 14; EVE 0.16

921   Bath flask, convex-curved body; tip of handle attachment, parts of three spiral trails; 47/15,17 C 3.1, KG 14

922   Bath flask, convex-curved side, slightly concave base with central thickening internally, circular pontil scar, spiral trail not running to centre of base, parts of four spirals remaining with lowest one forming a base ring; 47/15,17, C3.1, KG 14; PH 16, BD 40, WT 2, pontil scar diameter 18; EVE 0.48

923   Bath flask, thick convex-curved side, shallow concave base with pontil scar, trail spiralling out from centre of base, parts of three spirals remain; 47/?, C4; PH 18, BD *c* 30, WT 5; EVE 0.48

924   Flask, outbent rim, edge rolled in, cylindrical neck, 98/98, C 3.2, KG 17; PH 25, RD *c* 32, WT 3; EVE 0.4

925   Flask, cylindrical neck curving out to side; 78/6, C 2.2, KG 9; neck diameter 17, WT 1; EVE 0.2

926   Military 219; C 2.1; EVE 0.4

927   ?Jug, straight side sloping out slightly to shallow concave base; 92/4, C 2.4; EVE 0.28

945   Bottle, complete rim bent out, up, in and flattened, narrow cylindrical neck beginning to curve out to shoulder, folded upper handle attachment on underside of rim and neck; 73/+, C4, PH 40, RD 35; EVE 0.28

946   Bottle, rim bent out, up, in and flattened, narrow cylindrical neck with small fragment of handle attached, tooling marks on upper face of rim around aperture; 47/17, C 3.1, KG 14; RD 60; EVE 0.14

947–9 Bottle, five rim and neck fragments as 946; 50/32, C 3.1, KG 14, RD *c* 60, EVE 0.28; 92/18, C 2.1, RD *c* 55, EVE 0.28; 47/17, C 3.1, KG 149, RD 55, EVE 0.28

950   Bottle, rim bent out, up and in with triangular profile, cylindrical neck, horizontal wear scratches on neck; 92/4, C 2.4, PH 38, RD *c* 70; EVE 0.28

951–3 Bottle, three cylindrical neck and/or shoulder fragments; 50/12, C 2.1, EVE 0.14; 47/+, C 4, EVE 0.28; 47/17, C 3.1, KG 14, EVE 0.14

954 Prismatic bottle, complete angular reeded handle with folded upper attachment retaining part of cylindrical neck and fragments of rim, simple lower attachment retaining part of shoulder; 92/20, C 2.1, HS 58x7; EVE 0.42

955 Bottle, handle as 954 with piece missing at angle, outer edge of shoulder by lower attachment now worn very smooth by secondary use; 47/17, C 3.1, KG 14; HS 36x5 9; EVE 0.42

956–7 Bottle, two upper handle and neck fragments; 92/18, C 2.1, EVE 0.28; 47/17, C 3.1, KG 14, HS 49+x7, EVE 0.28

958 Bottles, two reeded handle and shoulder fragments; 47/17, C 3.1, KG 14, EVE 0.14; 44/+, C 4, EVE 0.28

960 Square bottle, three joining side and base fragments of square bottle, base design single circular moulding, part of large circular pontil scar; 47/18, C 2.4, KG 13; 50/25, C 3.4, PH 56, base width 54, OCD 36; EVE 0.42

961 Square bottle, side and base fragment, base design single circular moulding with small central dot, faint traces of diagonal cross from original marking-out of mould in very low relief slightly to one side of circular pellet; 50/+, C 4; PH 41, OCD *c* 45, EW *c* 66; EVE 0.42

962 Prismatic bottle, base fragment with base design at least one circular moulding; 92/15, C 3.2; OCD *c* 80, EW *c* 100; EVE 0.28

963 Square bottle, side and base fragment, base design three concentric circular mouldings with edge of small central pellet; 63/4, C 3.1, KG 14; PH 33, OCD *c* 48, EW *c* 60; EVE 0.42

964 Prismatic bottle, four base fragments with at least two concentric circular mouldings; 75/2, C 2.1; EVE 0.14

965 Prismatic bottle, base fragment with one circular moulding; 92/20, C 2.1; EVE 0.14

966 Prismatic bottle, base fragment, base design single circular moulding with two slight expansions; 63/4, C 3.1, KG 14; EVE 0.14

967 Prismatic bottle, side and base, base design single circular moulding with broken central moulding consisting of a bar with expanded terminals, possibly part of a letter; 47/17, C 3.1, KG 14; PH 22, OCD *c* 45, EW *c* 65; EVE 0.28

968 Prismatic bottle, base fragment, base design single circular moulding with central moulding of equal armed cross with expanded terminals; 47/15, C 3.1, KG 14; OCD *c* 65, EW 70–80; EVE 0.14

969 Hexagonal bottle, body fragment; 90/128, C 3.1, KG 16

970–80 Prismatic bottles, 15 body fragments; 50/39; 92/18; 92/21, C 2.1; 70/17, C 2.2, KG 9; 47/17, C 3.1, KG 14; 50/25; 51/3; 11/11; 50/70; 70/+; 92/+, C 4

981 Cylindrical bottle, body fragment; 92/20, C 2.1

Greenish colourless bubbly

982 Conical beaker, curved rim, edge cracked off and ground, straight side sloping in, wide wheel-cut groove below rim edge; 47/15R, C 3.1; PH 24, RD 130, WT 4; EVE 0.4

983 Conical beaker, curved rim, edge cracked off and ground with abrasions on outer face, straight side sloping in, abraded band below rim edge and on upper body; 41/26, C 3.3; PH 39, RD 105, WT 2; EVE 0.4

984 Bowl, two fragments, green/yellow, curved rim, edge cracked off smoothly but not ground, side sloping in and possibly broken at edge of one indentation; 51/2 and 23, C3.4; PH 16, RD 170, WT 1; EVE 0.4

985 Cup/beaker, light green, out-turned rim, edge fire-rounded; 70/2, C 4; PH 11, RD 70, WT 1; EVE 0.2

986 Cylindrical bowl, out-turned rim, edge fire-rounded, straight side, wide shallow diagonal optic blown ribs; 50/26, C4; PH 28, RD 110, WT 1; EVE 0.4

987 Jug, light green, high tubular pushed-in base ring with hollow tube at the end; 96/21, C2.1; BD 70; EVE 0.14

Baths

Yellow/green

988 Body fragment, convex-curved side, three spiral trails; 38/35; B 4

Colourless

989 Base fragment, tubular pushed in base ring, concave base, side broken away; 37/+, B 4, BD 40

990 Bottle, funnel mouth, rim edge fire-rounded, thick trail below rim; 38/44, B4; EVE 0.14

Blue/Green

991 Military 177; B 3.1; EVE 0.20

992 ?Jug, funnel-mouth with rolled-in edge; 38/49, B 4; EVE 0.14

993 Flask, cylindrical neck expanding slightly towards constricted and tooled junction with body; 38/15, B4; neck diameter 17; EVE 0.2

996 Bottle, reeded handle fragment; 69/+, B 4; EVE 0.14

Baths Precinct

Yellow/Brown

998   Jug, dark yellow/brown, cylindrical neck with small fragment of glass and scar from upper handle attachment; 22/2, BP 4; neck diameter 21; EVE 0.14

Yellow/Green

1000   Jug, upper part of angular ribbon handle broken close at attachment to neck; 22/2, BP 4; section 24x5.5; EVE 0.14

Pale/Light Green

1001   Base fragments, two, wide slightly convex-curved lower body sloping in shallowly to flat base, trailed base ring, circular trail or central blob on underside of base; 56/29, BP 3.3; PH *c* 12, BD 50, WT 2

Colourless

1002   Cup/bowl, convex-curved side, exterior ground and wheel-polished to leave horizontal rib; 22/33, BP 3.2; EVE 0.2

1003   Beaker, nine strain-cracked fragments and chips from junction of body and separately blown foot; 58/9, BP 3.2; EVE 0.2

1004   Cylindrical cup, slightly out-turned rim, edge fire-thickened, straight side, horizontal trail in low relief on upper body; 58/2, BP 3.2; PH 38, RD *c* 110, WT 1.5; EVE 0.4

1005   Cylindrical cup, vertical rim, edge fire-rounded, straight side; 22/+, BP 4; PH 29, RD 100, WT 1; EVE 0.4

1006   ?Cup, base fragment with part of thin circular trail on underside; 58/9, BP 3.2

1007   Jug, two joining fragments, slightly green-tinged colourless, curved ribbon handle with folded upper attachment and thumb rest attached to fragment of rim with fire-rounded edge; 56/6, BP 3.3; HS 12x4; EVE 0.14

1008   Base fragment, solid pushed-in base ring, concave base, side grozed; 22/3, BP 4; BD 60.

1009   Base fragment, tubular pushed-in base ring; base and side broken; 62/1, BP 4; BD 50.

1010   Bottle, *c* 50 strain-cracked fragments and chips from a reeded handle and body fragment; 16/95, BP 3.1; EVE 0.14

Blue/Green

1015   Collared jar, outbent double tubular rim, edge first rolled in, then bent out and down; 58/5, BP 3.2; PH 14, RD 75; EVE 0.19

1016   Jar, outbent rim, edge fire-rounded; 22/2, BP 4; PH 12, RD 110, WT 1.5; EVE 0.17

1017   Jar, rim fragment as 1016; 58/5, BP 3.2; PH 15, WT 2.5; EVE 0.17

1018   Jug, ribbon handle with central rib; 25/30, BP 2.2; HS (excluding rib) 28x4; EVE 0.14

1019   Conical ?jug, straight ribbon handle with central rib, broken lower attachment retaining small fragment of side; 24/+, BP 4; HS (excluding rib) 28x3; EVE 0.14

1020   Jug, upper part of pinched extension trail from lower handle attachment retaining parts of five projections; side deliberately broken away; 16/153, BP 2.3; EVE 0.14

1021   ?Jug, chip from ribbed handle; 58/4, BP 3.2

1022   Jar/?jug, convex-curved side sloping into rim or base, parts of three ribs in shallow relief; 36/22, BP 2.2; EVE 0.14

1023   Jug, part of simple lower attachment of ribbon handle retaining part of body; 60/10, P 3.3; EVE 0.14

1024–5   Jugs, two body fragments with tips of lower handle attachments; 23/9, BP 3.2; 23/29, BP 2.1

1026   Unguent bottle, outbent rim, edge rolled in, cylindrical neck; 58/9, BP 3.2; PH 17, RD 25, WT 1; EVE 0.4

1027   Bath flask, rim bent out, up, in and flattened, short wide neck, inner parts of both dolphin handles on neck and underside of rim; 64/6, BP 3.3; PH 27, RD 39x41, WT 3.5; EVE 0.5

1028   Bath flask, complete dolphin handle applied to shoulder, trailed up neck to underside of rim, looped down to shoulder with return trail running back towards rim, handle retains a small fragment of body and outer edge of rim, and scar from neck; 22/2, BP 4; height of handle 17; EVE 0.17

1029   Bath flask, convex-curved upper body, outer part of dolphin handle applied to shoulder and made in the manner of 1028; 22/57, BP 3.1; EVE 0.17

1030   ?Bath flask, three convex-curved body fragments retaining lower parts of handle attachment; 58/4, BP 3.2; EVE 0.17

1031   ?Flask, rim folded out, up, in and flattened; 82/10, BP 4; RD *c* 30; EVE 0.2

1032   Jug/flask/bottle, rim folded out, up, in with small triangular profile, cylindrical neck; 49/+, BP 4; PH 10, RD *c* 40; EVE 0.2

1033   Flask, cylindrical neck fragment; 58/5, BP 3.2; EVE 0.2

1034   Base fragment, from thickened centre with pontil scar; 58/1, BP 3.2

1047   Bottle, complete rim bent out, up, in and flattened, narrow cylindrical neck; small fragment of upper handle attachment on underside of rim; 16/18, BP 3.2; RD 55; EVE 0.14

1048   Bottle, rim folded as 104, cylindrical neck; 22/19, BP 2.1; RD 55; 0.14

1049   Bottle/jar, four rim fragments bent out, up, in and flattened; 59/2, BP 3.2, RD *c* 110; EVE 0.14; 54/31, BP 2.2, RD *c* 45, EVE 0.14; 60/23, BP 4, RD *c* 35, EVE 0.14; 49/116, BP 3.1, KG 18, EVE 0.14

1053   Prismatic bottle, three shoulder and side fragments; 49/166, BP 2.2

1054   Bottle, upper handle and neck fragment; 60/10, BP 3.3; EVE 0.14

1055–7 Bottles, three reeded handle fragments; 58/5, BP 3.2, EVE 0.14; 48/17, BP 4, EVE 0.14; 69/+, BP 4, EVE 0.14

1058   Bottle, angular ribbon handle; 58/5, BP 3.2; EVE 0.14

1059   Square bottle, side and base fragment, base design at least one circular moulding; part of L-shaped corner moulding; 48/18, BP 3.1; PH 15, OCD c 130, EW c 140; EVE 0.28

1060   Prismatic bottle, base fragment, base design at least three concentric circular mouldings, one side of fragment grozed to sharp curved edge; 36/+, BP 4; EVE 0.14

1061–2 Prismatic bottles, two melted and much distorted side and base fragments, base designs at least two concentric circular mouldings; 6/55, BP 2.3, EVE 0.14; 16/45, BP 3.1, EVE 0.14

1063   Prismatic bottle, side and base fragment, base design two concentric circular mouldings with small central moulding now chipped and obscured. Large circular pontil scar; 56/27, BP 3.3; PH 15, OCD 70, EW c 90; EVE 0.28

1064   Square bottle, body fragment; 59/5, BP 3.2; KG 20

1065–71 Prismatic bottles, 12 body fragments; 49/168, BP 2.2; 49/50; 49/116; 49/120; 69/35, BP 3.1, KG 18; 58/2; 58/9; 59/1, BP 3.2

Greenish colourless bubbly

1072   Hemispherical cup, curved rim, edge cracked off smoothly and probably not ground, convex-curved side, one abraded band below rim and one on body, distorted by heat; 82/11, BP 4; PH 44, RD c 90, WT 1.5; EVE 0.4

1073   Jug, wide funnel mouth, edge fire-rounded, thick trail below rim edge with fragment retaining overlapping ends of trail; 70/1, BP 3.4; PH 11, RD 65; EVE 0.14

1074   Flask, funnel mouth, edge cracked off with external bevel possibly re-worked, cylindrical neck; two narrow abraded lines on neck; 58/5, BP 3.2; EVE 0.20

Function and status summary

It is important to appreciate that the way in which glass vessels were used in Britain did not remain stable throughout the Roman period. In brief this may be summarised by saying that in the first and early second century, glass vessels appear to have been used for a wide range of functions. The main ones were as drinking vessels, as vessels for serving and presenting food, as vessels for serving liquid and as containers for solid and liquids. Vessels for serving food become unimportant from the mid-second century and most container forms disappear during the third century, although unguent bottles do continue to be used. By the fourth century the use of glass vessels appears to be restricted almost entirely to activities associated with serving and drinking liquids (for an extended treatment of this pattern see Cool and Price 1995, 235). Translated into the conditions at Wroxeter this means that it would be inappropriate to compare assemblages from Periods 2 and 3 directly as obviously their composition is going to be different. Periods 1 and 2, however, can be compared as any difference between the assemblages could relate to the different activities that generated the deposits, rather than the more structural differences brought about by global changes in the way in which glass vessels were used.

In this section the different period assemblages will be compared from a functional point of view. The assemblages from 1.1, P 3.2; WR 3.1; C 2.2, 3.1 and 3.2 contain a considerable amount of residual material and are excluded from consideration.. WR 2.3 will be included but the fourth-century material will be excluded. The tableware fragments will be assigned to the categories of drinking vessels, food serving vessels, and liquid serving vessels. The container fragments will be assigned to jars (suitable for storing solids), flasks and unguent bottles (suitable for storing liquids), and bottles (suitable for storing both solids and liquids). Given the presence of the baths on the site, fragments of bath flasks will be placed in a separate category. Material that is clearly residual will be excluded from consideration. In practice this means that residual tablewares will be excluded in the first and second centuries but not any residual containers. Most containers are less closely datable and so it is frequently not possible to identify whether or not they are residual in the context. The exclusions are the Claudio-Neronian material from the Period 1 and 2 assemblages, pre-mid second century material from the Period 3 Phase 1 and 2 assemblages, and third-century and earlier material from the Period 3 Phases 3–5 assemblages.

Table 4.8 shows the distribution of the functional types of glass according to period if the residual material as defined is excluded. One feature that is immediately apparent is the absence of utilitarian jars. During Periods 1 and 2 and the earlier parts of Period 3, this is not an uncommon vessel type so the absence is noteworthy. One might speculate that the glass jar is a specialised item either in the kitchen and storeroom. Apicius, for example, advises the use of a glass cask for storing the expensive spice laser (Edwards 1984, 8) and this would seem best interpreted as a jar. If this speculation is correct, the absence of jars is perhaps less informative than their presence would be.

The Period 1 assemblages are small but show the general range of functional types to be expected at the end of the first century and into the early second. The Period 2 assemblages show a similar spread but drinking vessels are perhaps under-represented. This is

Table 4.8 Vessel glass: functional types by period (EVE values)

overall period	area period	drinking vessels	food serving vessels	liquid serving vessels	bottles	jars	flasks	bath flasks
1.2		0.2	0.2	0.32	0.35	–	–	–
1.3		0.6	–	0.48	0.95	–	0.88	–
2.1	P 2.1	–	–	0.28	1.05	–	–	–
2.1	WR 2.1	0.4	0.4	0.14	1.51	–	0.4	–
2.1	C 2.1	–	1.18	0.54	1.54	–	0.2	–
2.1	BP 2.1	–	–	–	0.14	–	–	–
2.2	WR 2.2	–	–	–	0.35	–	0.2	–
2.2	P 2.2	0.6	0.07	0.63	2.03	–	0.54	–
2.4	BP 2.2	–	–	0.28	0.32	–	–	–
2.5	P 2.3	0.4	0.66	0.6	1.93	–	0.2	–
2.5	WR 2.3	1.4	1.0	0.28	3.43	–	–	–
2.5	C 2.3	0.4	0.52	0.14	–	–	–	–
2.6	C 2.4	–	–	0.14	0.7	–	–	–
2.6	BP 2.3	–	–	0.28	0.32	–	–	–
3.1	P 3.1	3.4	–	0.84	2.31	0.34	0.4	–
3.1	BP 3.1	–	–	0.14	0.7	–	–	0.96
3.2	P 3.3	0.8	–	0.14	–	–	–	–
3.4	C 3.3	0.4	–	–	–	–	–	–
3.5	P 3.4A	0.4	–	–	0.13	–	–	–
3.5	P 3.4B	–	–	–	0.14	–	–	–
3.6	P 3.5	–	–	–	0.14	–	–	–
3.6	WR 3.3	0.4	–	–	–	–	–	–
3.6	C 3.4	0.4	–	–	–	–	–	–
3.7	P 3.6	0.8	–	0.14	0.3	–	–	–

P portico, WR west range, C courtyard, BP baths precinct

especially noticeable in the Period 2 Phase 6 contexts, but those associated with the Period 2 Phase 4 and 5 dumping episodes give a fairly typical picture of the range of functional types in use during the early to mid-second century with no specialisation apparent.

The P 3.1 assemblage is also typical of an assemblage belonging to the later second to mid-third century. With the exception of obviously residual material such the cast colourless (102–3) and tubular-rimmed (231) bowls, vessels suitable for serving and presenting food are absent. The fourth-century assemblages of Period 3 Phases 3 to 7 are dominated by drinking vessels and so they also are typical of the pattern frequently seen on fourth-century sites.

One notable feature of glass assemblages from bath houses is often the presence of large numbers of bath flasks (see for example Allen 1986, 104; Charlesworth 1976, 15). This is not directly attested in Table 4.8 as their presence is only shown in the Courtyard Period 3.1 where they formed part of the material infilling the *natatio* (920–22). They were, however, relatively common finds during these excavations though often found residually in fourth century or later contexts, in the Courtyard (919, 923, EVE 0.64) and Baths Precinct (1027–30, EVE 1.01).

The glass recovered at this site at Wroxeter is also typical of much glass recovered from Roman Britain, in that to a very great extent it is composed of very common forms. Over half of the EVE value for tablewares of the later first to mid-second century are contributed by tubular-rimmed bowls, collared jars and globular and conical jugs which are very common everywhere. Over half of EVE value for later second to third-century tablewares is provided by fragments of colourless cylindrical cups with double base rings which are ubiquitous at the period. A similar picture is present in the fourth-century tablewares where conical beakers and hemispherical cups with cracked-off rims contribute half the EVEs. In the tablewares the picture is very much of supply at the utilitarian end of the range with an occasional startling exception such as the facet-cut cast plate 671. Apart from the early facet-cut beakers, which could have been residual from the military occupation, there are very few other examples of facet-cut vessels. Amongst the later second to third-century assemblage, there are no examples of snake-thread decoration or of beakers and flasks with stemmed feet. Only in the late Roman assemblage does the assemblage depart from the more utilitarian range of tablewares with the presence of geometric facet cut cups and beakers (161–2, 710), but there are no examples of the cups and beakers decorated with applied coloured blobs or curvilinear trails.

The lack of the less common varieties of second and third-century glass vessels in such a large assemblage is interesting as they were being used more widely in the town of Wroxeter and so the utilitarian nature of this assemblage is not due to a failure of supply to the town as a whole. For example, snake thread and related forms of glass were recovered during the Bushe-Fox excavations (Bushe-Fox 1913, pl XII, fig 1.5–6), and a fragment of a late second to early third-century bowl decorated with facet and free-hand cutting (see Harden *et al* 1987, 197–9) was found during the basilical hall excavations. The later first to mid second-century assemblage at this site derives in a great part from the dumped material and the source of this is unknown. The relatively limited nature of the later assemblages found here could reflect the activities being carried out on the site. A *macellum* was perhaps not the sort of place where glass vessels would often be found. If glass vessels were being sold, the debris from any breakages would probably have been collected for re-cycling as cullet (Price and Cool 1991, 27). This seems reflected by the relatively small amount of glass recovered from WR Period 3 contexts. Bath houses can be expected to produce a large glass assemblage but it will be of a very specialised nature concentrated on bath flasks and unguent bottles. Of the 50 items catalogued as coming from Drain Group 4 (dated to AD 160–230) of the legionary bath house at Caerleon (Allen 1986, 104–13), half came from bath flasks and other flasks and most of the other items were cups or plates reflecting the socialising that appears to have been part of a visit to the baths (Zienkiewicz 1986, 20). The glass assemblage from this part of the Wroxeter baths reflects the cleanliness aspect of a visit to the baths in the number of bath flasks found, but little of the socialising aspect. The rubbish from the baths cafe and bar is obviously to be found elsewhere.

Glass and frit objects
by H E M Cool

Note: numbers refer to the archive catalogue, illustrated pieces Fig 4.47

Melon beads (1–26)

The majority of the melon beads recovered from the baths and *macellum* were made of frit, with only one example (26) being made of deep blue glass. Both types of melon beads were very common from the Conquest to the Antonine period (Guido 1978, 100; Crummy 1983, 30), but thereafter went out of use. Those from Period 1 (1–3) and Period 2 (4–6, 10–12, 17–19, 22–3) contexts could, therefore, have been contemporaneous losses, whereas those from Period 3 contexts (7–9, 13, 24–5) are clearly residual. Melon beads are very common finds on military sites and the probability is high that many of the examples found in the civilian levels at Wroxeter are residual finds from the military occupation. This seems even more likely when the size of the fragments are considered. Fifteen (4–7, 9–11, 16–17, 19–24) of the 25 frit beads consisted of less than half of the bead. This may be compared to the frit melon bead assemblage (totalling 95) from the fort and *vicus* at Castleford, West Yorkshire (Cool and Price 1998, 183–9) where the beads were certainly contemporaneous

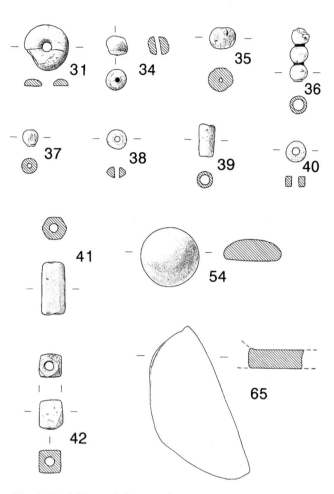

Fig 4.47 Objects of glass: scale 1:1

losses. There 73% of the beads were either complete or consisted of more than half of the bead.

Annular beads (27–31)

Four of the annular beads were made in translucent glass. Numbers 28 and 29 were made in deep blue glass and are examples of Guido Group 6iva beads (1978, 66), a long-lived type with origins as early as the third century BC and continuing to be used into the Roman period. Numbers 27 and 30 are made in naturally-tinted glasses and are examples of Guido Group 6iia (*ibid*, 66). Annular beads made in this type of glass seem to be an exclusively Roman phenomenon. The fragment 29 was found unstratified, the others were found in Period 2 contexts but again the possibility exists that they are residual from the earlier military occupation as annular beads such as this are also common on first-century military sites.

The fifth annular 'bead', 31, is most unusual and no other similar items from Roman Britain are known to the author. It was originally opaque red or orange and is now heavily weathered. Unlike the other annular beads it has a flat back and gives every impression of having been designed to be fastened against a surface rather to have been strung on a thread or wire. It seems more likely to have been a decorative fitting than a bead.

Spherical beads (32–35)

Spherical glass beads are not intrinsically dateable and only those found in stratified contexts have been catalogued here, though others were found unstratified. All were found in Period 3 contexts. Number 34 retains a fragment of copper alloy wire in the perforation and clearly came from a necklace where the beads were threaded on wire loops like the example from Gadebridge (Neal and Butcher 1974, 133, fig 133.75). Such necklaces combining copper alloy wire and glass beads seem to have been most popular in the fourth century (Cool 1983, 300).

Metal foil in glass beads (36–37)

Two examples of later second and third-century gold and silver in glass beads were recovered from unstratified contexts. These are not uncommon on Romano-British sites (Guido 1978, 93; Boon 1977), though they do not tend to occur in large numbers. Number 36 is unusual in that it retains three segments still joined together. The snapped collars at the end of most gold-in-glass beads show that they were originally made as a segmented bead but usually they were broken into individual segments for use.

Biconical bead (38)

Only one example of a biconical bead was found. This was a short biconical blue bead from a late Roman context. Such beads are relatively common in the late Roman period but are also known to have been used earlier (Guido 1978, 97; Brewer 1986a, 148).

Cylindrical beads (39–40)

Both of the cylindrical beads came from Period 3 contexts and were made in opaque green glass. Both long and short cylindrical green beads are common late Roman forms (Guido 1978, 95)

Hexagonal bead (41)

Number 41 is a heavily weathered green glass bead imitating a beryl emerald. Such beads were in use throughout the Roman period (Guido 1978, 96). This example was found unstratified.

Diamond and triangle faceted bead (42)

One example of this form was found unstratified in the Baths Precinct area. All of the examples Guido (1978, 99) quotes are fourth century but it should be noted that they were in use by the late second to early third century period as four examples were recovered from the drain deposit dated to AD 160–230 at the legionary baths at Caerleon (Brewer 1986a, 149, fig 48.67–70). In the late Roman period they were used both as parts of necklaces (Guido 1978, pl IVa) and as the heads of hairpins (Crummy 1983, 29, fig 29.486).

Glass counters (43–66)

Twenty-one of the glass counters (43–64) were custom made and of plano-convex shape. There were eight examples each of black (43–50) and white (51–8) and two emerald green counters that appear black (61–2). Two of the remaining counters are deep blue (59–60), one (63) is so heavily weathered that the original colour cannot be detected and the final plano-convex counter (64) is blue/green. The last mentioned, however, is very small and may have been the setting from a ring or a brooch. Black and white counters are very common in the first and early second century but go out of use during the second century when bone counters appear to have been preferred (Cool *et al* 1995, 1555). This pattern is reflected at Wroxeter. Three (43–4, 62) were found in Period 1 contexts and twelve (45, 47–9, 51–2, 54–8) in Period 2 contexts, but only five in Period 3 contexts. It is interesting to note that the blue counters were found in Period 3 contexts. This may be fortuitous as coloured monochrome counters were in use during the first and early second century alongside the black and white ones (Owen and Arnold 1989, 46). It could, however, suggest that coloured monochrome counters were in use again during the late Roman period.

Number 65 appears to be part of a counter though when complete it would have been rather large for this purpose. Number 66 may have come from a similar object. Both were made from re-used fragments of blue green prismatic bottles. Counters made from vessel glass fragments are not uncommon but the care taken to smooth the edges of these is unusual.

Stirring rods (67–8)

Two fragments of blue/green stirring rods were found in Period 2 contexts in the western range. Such objects are commonest during the first and second century (Isings Form 79; Crummy 1983, 57, nos 1861–2).

?Funnel (69)

Number 69 may be a fragment from the stem of a funnel (Isings Form 74). These are a relatively uncommon first-century form. It is possible that 69 is residual from the military occupation and it has already been discussed in the report on the glass connected with the military occupation (Cool and Price 1998b).

Tool (70)

Number 70 is a fragment from the side of a blue/green prismatic bottle which has been grozed along one long edge to form a sharp edge. It could have been used as a scraping tool.

Setting (71)

The small green disc 71 may have served as a setting on a brooch or ring with the indentation on one surface being part of a keying device to hold it in place.

Window glass
by H E M Cool

Both cast and blown window glass was found during the excavations of the Wroxeter baths and *macellum*, though the quantity of the former was much greater than the latter. The material is catalogued. Cast window glass was produced by pouring molten glass into frames of sand or wood and was the commonest variety during the first to third centuries. Window glass produced by blowing became much commoner in the fourth century.

Table 4.9 shows the distribution of the cast glass according to the area phasing and colour. To put this material in context, it will be useful at the outset to compare the area of glass recovered with the area of known window panes from Roman Britain. Ones where complete dimensions are recoverable are rare but a pane measuring not less than 600 by 600mm was recovered from the Flavian bathhouse at Corbridge (Charlesworth 1959, 166), and a complete pane from a second-century bath house at Garden Hill, Hartfield, Sussex, measured 255 by 235 mm (Harden 1974, 280). The former would have had an area of at least 3.6 m^2 and the latter had an area of 0.6 m^2. The total area of window glass recovered during these excavations is thus equivalent to less than two of the Garden Hill panes or less than a third of the Corbridge pane.

As may be seen from Table 4.9, the majority of the fragments consists of natural blue/green glass. There is also a small amount of glass that has been deliberately decolourised with varying degrees of success. Windows made of cast glass would not have been transparent in the manner of modern window but would have been translucent. A decolourised pane would have given a quality of internal light different from a blue/green pane. The decolourised glass was concentrated in the Portico areas and may thus have been associated with the *macellum*. Whether this is significant is difficult to say as the quantity is relatively small and approximately half came from Period 4 contexts.

Some of the fragments retained the natural rounded edges of the panes and on others there were grozed edges. On only one fragment, was there any indications of the original shape of the pane. It had two grozed edges meeting at an angle of approximately 150° suggesting it may originally have come from a polygonal rather than a square or rectangular pane.

Table 4.10 summarises the cast glass according to area of the site and overall site phasing. As may be seen no window glass was found in Period 1 contexts and relatively little was found in Period 2. Approximately half of the material was found in the Period 3 contexts of the Porticos, and overall 80% was found in the area of the Porticos and the West Range. The scarcity of window glass in the courtyard and baths area is remarkable. It is not a coincidence that the two complete panes noted above came from bath-houses. Window glass had a double role to play in such buildings for both illumination and heat conservation (Zienkiewicz 1986,122 and footnote 32). Bath-house sites generally produce larger quantities of window glass fragments than domestic sites. As an example the area of window glass from the bath-house at Catterick may be compared to the total amount of glass recovered from the much more extensive excavations at

Table 4.9 Window glass: area of cast window glass (cm²)

overall period	area period	blue/ green	light green	colourless	total
2.2	P 2.2	22	5	–	27
2.5	P 2.3	19	–	–	19
3.1	P 3.1	64	–	4	68
3.1	P 3.2	78	–	–	78
3.2	P 3.3	206	4	16	226
3.5	P 3.4A	45	–	–	45
3.5	P 3.4B	9	–	–	9
3.6	P 3.5	6	–	–	6
3.7	P 3.6	53	–	–	53
4.0	P 4	25	4	22	51
2.1	WR 2.1	10	–	–	10
2.5	WR 2.3	93	–	–	93
3.6	WR 3.3	10	–	–	10
4.0	WR 4	86	–	–	86
2.1	C 2.1	8	5	–	13
2.4	C 2.2	3	–	–	3
2.6	C 2.4	3	–	–	3
3.1	C 3.1	94	–	–	94
3.5	C 3.4	8	–	–	8
4.0	C 4	55	–	13	68
4.0	B 4	4	–	–	4
3.1	BP 3.1	18	–	–	18
3.3	BP 3.2	48	–	8	56
4.0	BP 4	11	2	–	13
total		978	20	63	1061

P portico, WR west range, C courtyard, B baths, BP baths precinct

Table 4.10 Window glass: distribution of cast window glass (cm²)

overall period	portico	west range	courtyard	baths	baths precinct	total
2.1	–	10	13	–	–	23
2.2	27	–	–	–	–	27
2.4	–	–	3	–	–	3
2.5	19	93	–	–	–	112
2.6	–	–	3	–	–	3
3.1	146	–	94	–	18	258
3.2	226	–	–	–	–	226
3.3	56	–	–	–	–	56
3.5	54	–	–	–	–	54
3.6	6	10	8	–	–	24
3.7	53	–	–	–	–	53
4.0	51	86	68	4	13	222
total	638	199	189	4	31	1061

Culver Street, Colchester, a site in the heart of the Roman colonia. At Catterick an area of 3.32 m^2 was recovered, whereas at Culver Street the area was only 1.2 m^2 (Baxter and Cool 1991, 128–30). That window glass would have been used extensively in the Wroxeter baths seems likely by analogy to other bath-houses. The scarcity of window glass from the baths area in this excavation therefore needs explanation. The deliberate removal and re-use of the panes elsewhere, either as windows or as cullet for glass working, is one possibility.

Far fewer fragments of blown window glass were found. Two fragments with a total area of approximately 60 mm^2 were recovered from Periods 3.5 and 3.6 contexts of the Insula Portico and a shattered fragment with an area of *c* 250 mm^2 came from a Period 3.1 context of the Baths Precinct.

The fragment from the Portico Period 3.6 is unusual in having purple streaks. This is a feature more frequently seen in glass of the early medieval period than Roman glass. In discussing fragments with purple streaks from Uley, Price (1993, 189) noted similar fragments occurring at northern monasteries occupied during the late seventh to late ninth centuries and elsewhere in late Saxon contexts. It should be noted, however, that at Uley the only other definitely post-Roman finds were fragments of grass-tempered pottery (Woodward and Leach 1993, 335). At Wroxeter, too, evidence of post-Roman activity is very scarce. That the window glass with purple streaks was in use in the late or sub-Roman period is therefore only a possibility. Though the number of streaks visible in the fragment from Wroxeter suggest that they were deliberately produced for their decorative effect, it should be noted that purple streaks can arise accidentally through efforts to decolourise window panes (Cole 1966). In these circumstances it would be unwise to use this very small fragment as evidence of seventh-century or later occupation.

Stone implements and other worked stone

by F W Anderson, Fiona Macalister, and David Williams

Introduction

The following text amalgamates three separate reports dealing with stone finds from the excavations and their sources. The first report dealt with a group of portable stone objects (Anderson 1980). At the same time further stone finds were incidentally commented on by Fiona Macalister in a second report looking principally at the industrial residues (Macalister 1980). The third report dealt with honestones and other worked stone, most from excavations after 1980 (Williams 1989b).

The authorship of each paragraph is identified by the author's initials in brackets.

Two pieces of statuary are dealt with in the military report (Webster forthcoming). These are the damaged sculpture of a water nymph and her accompanying water jar (Webster 1988b, fig 6.18 and 19). They were found in the P 2.3 make up levels in the south portico (Box 98) and are assumed to be from the fort. A column fragment was found in the make up layers in Room 17 (Chapter 6, para 5.7).

Wroxeter lies on Bunter sandstone with a great variety of other solid rock formations in the region, including New Red Sandstone, Carboniferous sandstones, limestones and mudstones, Triassic sandstones, Cambrian quartzites, Ordovician slates and shales, Silurian limestone, and Pre-Cambrian igneous rocks (Geol Survey 1″ Sheet 152). In addition, much of the area is covered by glacial drift and this includes erratics such as granite, basalt, greywrakes, and slates (DW).

Many of the stones identified could therefore have been obtained fairly locally. The exceptions might be five honestones, nos 2, 4, 5, 7, and 10, discussed below, of calcareous sandstone with a distinctive 'grooving' on the edges, from a source in Northamptonshire or possibly Kent (Fig 4.48), a quern from north east England, and a white marble object. This latter may have come from the Clee hills, but might also be an import from Italy, like those found at Silchester and Godmanchester (FA, DW).

Thin sectioning and study under the petrological microscope of two of the honestones of calcareous sandstone shows frequent equal-sized quartz grains, up to 0.30mm across, set in a matrix of calcite, with a scatter of brachiopod fragments and the odd grain of ?glauconite. The source originally suggested for this particular type of honestone was the Stony Stratford-Towcester area of Northamptonshire (Cantrill 1931, 96–8), based on an examination of some 100 unused examples recovered from the Forum portico gutter (Atkinson 1942, 129–30). However, more recent analysis of this material has drawn attention to the petrological similarities of this stone and Kentish Rag (Rhodes 1986a, 240–1). It is possible, therefore, that these honestones from Wroxeter may have come from a source even further away than was originally considered (DW).

A group of stones is in a dark grey micaceous flagstone. They comprise nos 34–49, 51, and 54–6, of the rounded discs/counters, and a honestone, no 16, amongst the items listed by Dr Williams, and, from their descriptions, nos 11, 20, 26, and 31 of the honestones, and one of the wall veneers listed by Dr Anderson. These may have come from the local Pre-Cambrian or Cambrian deposits or, in the case of the discs/counters, have been reused roofing tiles of micaceous flagstone which were found at the site and thought possibly to have come from Old Red Sandstone formations to the south of Wroxeter (Cantrill 1931, 95). Another possibility is that they derive from Grinshill stone, used mainly as building

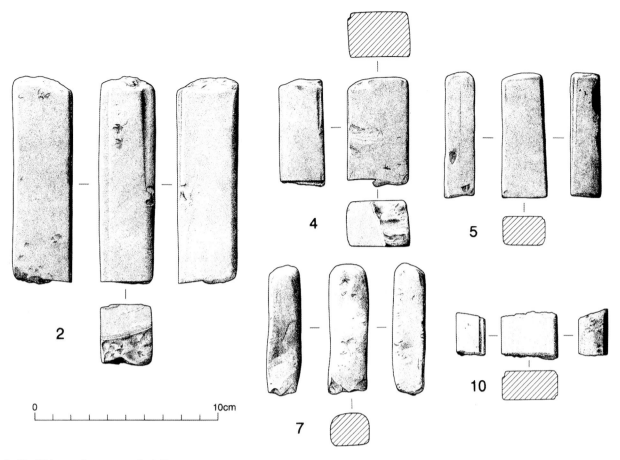

Fig 4.48 Objects of stone: scale 1:2

stone, but which also produces a micaceous sandstone known as the 'Flag Rock' in some strata (pers comm Fiona Roe). All the pieces in this stone occur in fourth-century or later contexts as do the stone roofing slates (DW).

Three fragments of wall veneer were examined. The first came from a primary building phase context in the courtyard (C 2.1). This was of porphyry, possibly a local igneous rock but perhaps an import. The second came from the make up within the *macellum* (WR 2.3). This was a grey, micaceous, fine-grained ?pre-Cambrian sandstone with black specks. The final piece came from the corridor north of the *macellum* (WR 3.1), and was of black micaceous ?Ordovician slate (FA).

Further pieces of wall veneer were examined by Fiona Macalister. She noted many different rock types including an unprovenanced slate fragment with one face smoothed and the other rough; an igneous granodiorite from a primary building level in the courtyard just east of the *macellum* (C 2.1), 13mm thick and 48mm wide with both faces smooth; and a fragment of marble from a B 4 context in Room 7. This was 19mm thick and 38mm wide and had on one side an upper polished face and a lower rough face, with the other side also polished. The upper face had patches of grey paint or slip, and a lower white layer, with a margin of 7mm left at the bottom edge. Samples of paint were removed and analysed using x-ray diffraction, and were found to be hydrocerrusite, or white lead (FM).

Thirty-three honestones were described and sourced, 19 of which derived from the porticos (FA, DW). Two were found in Period 1 levels, six from Period 2, and the remainder from Period 3 or later. A group of palettes comprised five fragments, from P 3.3 in a green ?pre-Cambrian slate; from WR 2.2 in a dark grey brown speckled ?Ordovician sandstone; from WR 4 in a dark grey ?Wenlock limestone; also from WR 4 in a dark grey spotted ?pre-Cambrian slate; and from BP 4 in a grey green spotted ?pre-Cambrian slate (FA).

Twenty-two rounded discs/counters were found. The great majority of these were in the dark grey micaceous sandstone discussed above, and the remaining items were of slate and sandstone (DW).

A handful of stone tesserae were examined. Three were of a light-grey fine-grained, ?Silurian, limestone, and two were of a dark grey Carboniferous limestone (DW).

Other items comprised a quern fragment from the south portico (Box 80), probably of Millstone Grit. A stone pot lid from a B 4 context in dark reddish brown ?Carboniferous sandstone, and a dome-shaped fragment of layered white marble, unprovenanced from the excavations were also found (FA). A rounded natural-shaped pebble was noted (DW). A group of miscellaneous items were noted by Fiona Macalister comprising a slate whetstone; a sandstone disc probably used for sharpening knives etc;

a rectangular block of worked sandstone, 46 x 21 x 11mm, with parallel striations visible on one side, again used for sharpening tools; and a fragment of a limestone bowl (FM).

A graffito was found on a quadrangular piece of mudstone with edges naturally formed (Wright 1960, 240, no 24).

Catalogue

The honestones, discs/counters, the spindle whorl, and the quernstone are listed. Descriptions of 11–13, 17–32, and 58 are by F Anderson, the remainder are by David Williams.

Honestones (Fig 4.48)

1   Light grey pebble of indurated mudstone, ?Carboniferous; roughly rectangular in section, and possibly used as a honestone on the two ends which are rounded, 144mm long; 98/178, 1.3 (AML 855531)

2   Fragment of honestone in a light grey calcareous sandstone (see petrological description above); rectangular in section 114mm long, broken at both ends and with distinctive grooves running along the corners; 98/178, 1.3 (AML 855532)

3   Small fragment of a grey sandy limestone, ?Keuper; may have come from a honestone; 80/179, P 2.1 (AML 870001)

4   Similar stone to 2; 580mm long, broken at both ends; 90/204, F951, P 2.2 (AML 844421A)

5   Similar stone to 2; 650mm long, broken at both ends, very worn and lacking the grooves of 2; 90/204, F951, P 2.2 (AML 844421B)

6   Flat darkish-grey pebble of a slightly micaceous sandstone; well-rounded edges possibly used as a honestone, 106mm long; 97/140, P 2.2 (AML 835911)

7   Similar stone to 2; 680mm long, broken at one end, worn and lacking the grooves of 2; 98/145, F1017, P 3.1, KG16 (AML 844423)

8   Elongated thin grey pebble of a slightly micaceous sandstone; possibly used as a honestone, roughly rectangular in section, 132mm long; 90/100, F602, P 3.1, KG 16 (AML 821626)

9   Grey quartzite pebble, ?Pre-Cambrian or ?Cambrian; possibly used as a honestone, roughly rectangular in section, 71mm long; 90/92, P 3.3 (AML 821625)

10   Similar stone to 2; 23mm long, broken at each end; 97/121, P 3.3 (AML 830405)

11   Dark grey very fine-grained micaceous sandstone, ?Ordovician; 90/25, P3.4A (AML 786447)

12   Pale fawn calcareous sandstone, ?Keuper; 80/5, P 3.4B (AML 786457)

13   Brown fine-grained micaceous sandstone with black spots, ?Old Red Sandstone; 80/51, P 3.4B (AML 788137)

14   Small fragment of honestone in a grey limestone; wedge-shaped in section; 80/3, P 3.5 (AML 863002)

15   Elongated grey pebble of a slightly micaceous sandstone; possibly used as a honestone, wedge-shaped in section, 146mm long; 90/20, P 3.6 (AML 821628)

16   Fragment of honestone in a dark grey strongly micaceous flagstone similar to disc/counter no 34 etc; rectangular in section, 80mm long, broken at both ends; 80/+, P 4 (AML 811179)

17   Pale brown very fine-grained calcareous sandstone, ?Keuper; 80/+, P 4 (AML 786458)

18   Dark red-brown very fine-grained quartzite, ?Pre-Cambrian; 80/+, P 4 (AML 786463)

19   Dark grey fine-grained calcareous sandstone, ?Ordovician; 80/2, P 4 (AML 788135)

20   Dark grey micaceous flagstone with irregular red-brown patches, ?Ordovician; 98/+, P 4 (AML 793571)

21   Black and grey banded slate, ?Ordovician; 90/1, P 4 (AML 801869)

22   Dark grey-brown fine-grained sandstone or flagstone, ?Ordovician; 84/154, WR 2.3 (AML 788131)

23   Brown fine-grained sandstone with black spots, ?Old Red Sandstone; 83/502, WR 3.1 (AML 793581)

24   White quartzite, ?Pre-Cambrian; 91/+, WR 4 (AML 786464)

25   Dark-grey micaceous sandstone with black spots, ?Pre-Cambrian; 50/3, C 2.4 (AML 788127)

26   Dark grey micaceous slate or flagstone, ?Ordovician; 9/6, C 3.2 (AML 786466)

27   Pale grey-green micaceous sandstone with iron patches, calcareous, ?Keuper; 81/69, F3050, C 3.3 (AML 788121)

28   Grey-brown fine-grained calcareous sandstone, ?Keuper; 67/14, C 4 (AML 786448)

29   Very dark brown fine-grained micaceous sandstone, ?Old Red Sandstone; 70/3, C 4 (AML 788138)

30   Black slate or flagstone, ?Ordovician; 38/7, B 4 (AML 786465)

31   Dark grey micaceous flagstone, ?Ordovician; 59/10, F3114, BP 3.2 (AML 788140)

32   Dark brown, micaceous, very fine-grained sandstone or flagstone, ?Cambrian; 49/+, BP 4 (AML 788139)

33   Dark brown very fine-grained flagstone; ?Cambrian; unprovenanced

Rounded discs/counters

34 Thickish disc of a dark grey very micaceous flagstone; 46mm diam; 80/7, P 3.4B (AML 788144)

35 As 34; 33mm diam; 80/51, P 3.4B (AML 786436)

36 As 34; 58mm diam; 80/4, P 3.4B (AML 786456)

37 As 34 but thinner; 16mm diam; 90/17, P 3.6 (AML 786439)

38 As 34; 19mm diam; 90/9, P 3.6 (AML 786440)

39 As 34; 61mm diam; 98/8, P 3.6 (AML 793579)

40 As 34 but thicker (18mm); 76mm diam; 96/22, P 3.6 (AML 786442)

41 As 34 but larger and thicker (12mm); 81mm diam; 96/22, P 3.6 (AML 788130)

42 As 34 but thinner, 17mm diam; 90/+, P 4 (AML 786438)

43 As 34; 54mm diam; 98/+, P 4 (AML 793570)

44 As 34; 60mm diam; 98/+, P 4 (AML 793575)

45 As 34; 35mm diam; 98/10, P 4 (AML 793582)

46 As 34; 92mm diam; 98/12, P 4 (AML 811180A)

47 As 34; 74mm diam; 98/12, P 4 (AML 811180B)

48 As 34; 56mm diam; 86/3, WR 4 (AML 788142)

49 As 34 though with a central hole; 35mm diam; 86/2, WR 4 (AML 786435)

50 Small thin disc of light grey lime-rich slate; 24mm diam; 14/34, F2255, C 2.2 (AML 788115)

51 As 34, 26mm diam; 38/+, B 4 (AML 786460)

52 Part of a thin disc of dark grey slate, ?Ordovician; 56mm diam; 22/33, BP 3.2 (AML 788122)

53 Thick disc of light grey fine-grained sandstone, ?Keuper; 22/35, BP 3.2 (AML 788133)

54 As 34; 31mm diam; 60/10, BP 3.3 (AML 788143)

55 As 34; 51mm diam; 60/+, BP 4 (AML 788123)

56 AS 34; 57mm diam; 16/+, BP 4 (AML 786462)

Spindle whorl

57 Half of a spindle whorl of mudstone, ?Carboniferous; 35mm diam; 59/10, F3114, BP 3.2 (AML 788108)

Quern stone

58 Quern fragment, coarse quartz gritstone, probably Millstone Grit; 80/+, P 4 (AML 786443)

Discussion

The stone collection is of a limited range of types and is dominated by hones and counters. The honestones seem to have been sold from the porticos. The calcareous sandstone group with grooved edges, nos 2, 4, 5, 7, and 10, are from the west and south porticos, directly on the opposite side of Watling Street from where it is known that they were stacked for sale in the second century. The earliest find (no 2) was from the upper surface of the Period 1 destruction, while two others (4 and 5) were from west portico Period 2 make up layers. These contexts predate the gutter find, but their findspots suggest that the hones were sold from either side of Watling Street. Nos 11–21 may also indicate that hones were sold from the porticos in the late market period. Those that were found in contexts other than the porticos occur in later levels with none from the second-century dumps and may have been used during building work on site.

The counters occur principally in the porticos. They are predominantly fourth-century since they probably derive from a stone not used on the site until then. They may have served some accounting function in the market stalls. Other stone types are poorly represented suggesting that discarded stones were not an important element in the make up material brought onto the site to provide fresh internal and external levels.

Analysis of plasters

by Graham Morgan, Nigel Jeffries, and Andrew Smith

The plaster collection derived predominantly from the *macellum* area and was made during the last years of the excavations. Samples from both military and post-military contexts are discussed here. All the samples supplied were examined by eye and then microscopically, to determine the thickness and number of the various layers and their initial apparent composition. Selected larger samples were then fully analysed to determine and compare their physical compositions. They were all lime-based plasters with aggregates composed mainly of the local sand and gravels or other materials such as crushed brick or tile, and, occasionally, with specialised components such as crystalline baryte. Five main types were seen, four having basically sand and gravel aggregates and the fifth having varying amounts of crushed ceramic material, referred to as brick or tile within the text. This last type is, when the aggregate is mainly ceramic material, often known as *opus signinum*.

Layer thickness and number of layers

During the preliminary analysis, 114 plasters of different construction character were noted, and of these 106 had *intonaco*, a surface layer of lime commonly associated with fresco painting. All the latter were measured and the numbers of contexts in relation to thickness counted (Table 4.11).

The plasterers clearly favoured a fine, thin layer of *intonaco* rather than the thick robust types. Only 26 of the 106 (24%) noted context types had more than one layer of plaster. The first layer ranged from 6mm to 53mm with a concentration around the 10 to 20mm area. The second layer ranged from 5 to 43.5mm, but due to the small number of context types, there are no groupings of measurements. The third layer had only one representative.

Components

The coarse components were identified through microscopic analysis once the weight had been calculated for each graded sample of the context. The predominant material was a combination of quartzite, sandstone, and sub angular quartz (becoming rounded as the sieve grades decreased in size) plus a mixture of chalcedony, mica, feldspar, coal, charcoal etc. An intrusive component to this was vitrified sand which appeared in the lower grades of sieve as translucent globules with black spots on them, these came from burning in the production of the lime. Ten contexts contained crushed ceramic material (brick or tile) with varying amounts of sand and gravel. The presence of the same sand grades in samples from different phases and plaster types points to the use of the same sand and gravel deposits over a period of time. Analysis of particle size distribution curves suggested a difference between military and post-military compositions.

There were also seven contexts containing a mineral component unusual to the normal varieties one would expect. Baryte, a mineral alien in the construction of mortar, was confirmed by X-ray diffraction in contexts 83/510 and 83/514. The *intonaco* layers also contained baryte which would give the plaster and *intonaco* a very bright white appearance, glistening where it was not overpainted. Samples with baryte came from contexts within the *macellum*, from the west and south porticos, and also from outside the baths block in Boxes 49, 70, and 81 (Fig 1.3).

Surface treatment

The paint layers provided little out of the ordinary with red and yellow produced from red and yellow ochre respectively, orange from red and yellow ochre combined, black from carbon, and green from glauconite. Some of the plain white *intonaco* contained specks of red ochre dust which had been applied by a brush to create a pale pink effect. The major decorative forms were linear arrangements probably to form panels as in the Painted House, Dover, and the Norfolk St villa, Leicester (Davey and Ling 1982, cat nos 14 and 24). Due to the small fragments and their abraded nature, little could be reconstructed. Another form of decoration appearing only on three small fragments was pseudo-marbling. This was on a thin *intonaco* with the paint applied by splashing from a distance. With a variety of colours this would have been an inexpensive way to create a marble veneer.

Conclusions

Analysis shows that the samples provided generally fit in with those found throughout Roman Britain in technology and painted style. Only two layers of plaster, the *arriccio*, and one layer of fine lime, the *intonaco*, on which the pigments were applied were seen even on the more complete pieces, against the six recommended by Vitruvius (Vitruvius 3, 7). The paint was applied in the true or *buon fresco* method to the wet lime *intonaco*. The aggregates relate to the local geology and the particle size distribution graphs show four main types and therefore possibly four phases. The lime percentages are fairly standard with the *opus signinum* having a somewhat higher lime content. The presence of *opus signinum*, mortar or plaster made with crushed brick or tile and lime, is usually indicative of damp areas, either to counteract rising damp or as a water resisting layer in bath houses etc. The find of note was of the mineral baryte, crystalline barium sulphate, in the *intonaco* of several samples. It appears to have been used in place of calcite. Vitruvius recommended that crushed coarse grained marble should be added to the final *intonaco* layer (Vitruvius 7, 6). In the absence of a suitable white marble in Britain, crushed coarse calcite was used, notably at Fishbourne Roman Palace and in sites in Fenchurch Street, London, and at Chester (Morgan 1992). The glistening white effect was however over painted, at least in part, leaving a white background.

Table 4.11 Wall plasters: thickness of *intonaco*

| | | | | | | thickness (mm) | | | | | | |
	0.25	0.5	0.75	1	1.25	1.5	1.75	2	2.5	3	4+	total
number of contexts	25	25	20	16	8	5	1	3	1	1	1	106
%	24	24	19	15	8	5	<1	3	<1	<1	<1	100

As far we are aware this use of baryte is unique in Roman Britain. Baryte often occurs as an associated mineral with some lead ores and may be a by-product of the lead extraction from mines on the nearby Welsh borders. None of the samples examined were from military contexts suggesting that it was first used for the civilian building programme.

The Roman pottery

compiled and edited by Jane Timby, with contributions by Anne Anderson, Scott Anderson, Gillian Braithwaite, Geoffrey Dannell, Margaret Darling, Brenda Dickinson, Jane Evans, Jane Faiers, Kay Hartley, Grace Simpson, Graham Webster, and David Williams

Introduction

by Jane Evans

Outline of the report

The Roman pottery collection amounts to some 78,000 sherds, weighing just under one metric tonne, and ranges in date from the first to fourth century. The assemblage provides a chronological sequence of Romano-British ceramics for Wroxeter and has been used to establish a fabric and form series upon which future work on Wroxeter and its hinterland can be based. The later Roman assemblage is perhaps slightly deficient but this is compensated for by the pottery report on the basilical hall excavations (Symonds 1997) which focused on the later occupation sequence. It should be noted however, that the two excavations had differing aims and methods for both recovery and analysis.

The present report is the culmination of several years work by a number of different researchers. The following introductory section summarises the background history to the pottery work, the aims and objectives of the current report, the methodologies employed, the nature of the archaeological deposits, and the reliability of the excavated groups. This is followed by the presentation of a form and fabric series for the complete recorded assemblage including the military material. The pottery is then discussed by period starting with a summary of the military assemblage by Margaret Darling reported in full in the military volume (Webster forthcoming), followed by sections on Period 1 pottery by Darling, on Period 2 pottery by Jane Faiers, and a discussion by Jane Timby on the Period 3 pottery. This latter material was the subject of a detailed archive report by Jane Evans. The Period 3 pottery section includes a report on material from the *natatio* infill by Graham Webster, Anne and Scott Anderson, and Grace Simpson. The decorated and stamped samian catalogue by Brenda Dickinson is then followed by a discussion of the Central Gaulish samian

supply to Wroxeter. A catalogue of mortaria stamps by Kay Hartley follows. The pottery report concludes with an overview by Jane Timby drawing the separate threads together and looking at the assemblage in its local and regional context.

Complete copies of the individual databases compiled during the preparation of this report are also housed with the pottery archive.

Background history and aims of present report

As a result of the very extended period of excavation, and the size of the assemblage, work on the pottery has had a long and complicated history. The pottery was recovered by trowel and occasionally hoe or pickaxe. Unlike the basilical hall collection no dry or wet sieving was undertaken. There was no policy of retaining post-Roman pottery, although very small quantities were in fact kept. It was not possible therefore, to identify contexts contaminated by, or relating to, post-Roman activity from the surviving pottery evidence, although some notes were made in the site notebooks.

It is known that some Romano-British pottery was also discarded. There was no consistent policy on this, however, and no record was kept of pottery thrown away. With the mortaria it is known that only rim sherds and joining body sherds were retained (pers comm Kay Hartley). In her assessment of the military pottery, Darling notes that small body sherds of coarse pottery were discarded in earlier excavation years, and possibly many body sherds of Dressel 20 amphora. During recording the later coarse wares, a very high proportion of rims to body sherds was noted in some groups suggesting that a similar policy was on occasions applied to other wares, for example, in the *natatio* group. This obviously has important implications for any quantification.

Pottery analysis has been undertaken by a number of specialists, each with a different area of involvement and often working in isolation. As a result there are a number of inconsistencies in the recording systems used and the level of analysis employed. The military and second-century groups formed the basis of two M Phil research theses by Darling (1976) and Faiers (1990) respectively. Much of the later pottery was catalogued over a period of five years successively by Sandra Garside Neville, Wendy Owen, and John Chadderton. The military and early civil samian was the subject of two reports by Geoff Dannell in 1975 and 1988, although the stamps were reported on separately by Dickinson. Additional work has been carried out by Darling (assisted by Barbara Davies) on the military period samian. Specialist advice from David Williams and Kay Hartley has been provided on the amphorae and mortaria respectively.

The various researchers involved in the analysis of the pottery, all had slightly varying aims and objectives for their original studies. Following a post-excavation assessment a number of potential aims and objectives were identified (Timby 1992) relating specifically to the latest phase of post-excavation analysis culminating in this report. Five aims were defined:

1   To isolate the distinctive pottery assemblages from the main periods of use of *insula* 5 at Wroxeter,
2   To pinpoint ceramic changes through four centuries, and
3   To explore the links between the major public buildings, the baths and *macellum* and the pottery associated with them,
4   To assess site status, economy, and sources for locally produced wares by comparing the assemblages from within the urban area to material from sites in the hinterland, and
5   To establish whether any differences exist between frontier towns and those well within the province and closer to the continent.

It was decided that for the post-military deposits attention should be focused on groups from key contexts identified from the stratigraphic sequence (Key groups: Table 1.2). By this it was hoped firstly to isolate distinctive components of the main periods of use of *insula* 5; secondly to highlight the sequence of ceramic change throughout the Roman period; and thirdly to explore the links between the major public buildings. It should be noted that not all the key contexts necessarily produced useful groups of pottery.

Methodology

The methodology employed differed slightly between workers but for obvious reasons the systems already used were adhered to. For the military and early civilian periods all the pottery was quantified by sherd counts, estimated vessel equivalents (EVEs), and weights. The recording fields for the basic pottery database in addition to the quantification fields are: fabric, form, decoration, sherd links, drawing number, and comments; individual records cover single vessels where identifiable. The same fields were used for the specialist samian database with additional fields for pottery source, potter's name and die for stamps, date, and reference to specialist reports. The basic database includes the relevant fields from the specialist samian file merged with the coarse pottery. The pottery was entered into a computer database (UNIX transferable to MS-DOS), and merged with a separate phasing database.

The entire Period 2 pottery assemblage and targeted pottery from Period 3 were also quantified by sherd count, weight, and rim EVEs. Although diameters and percentages extant had been recorded by previous workers for rims, they were not consistently recorded for bases. The data in this report is, therefore, presented by count, weight, and rim EVE, but not base EVE.

The fact that not all of the pottery was retained and that no record was kept of pottery discarded obviously has implications for the reliability of the data. As it seems to have been predominantly body sherds that were discarded it is hoped that quantification by rim EVE will be reliable, even if quantification by count and weight are not. Although this problem should not be underestimated it should perhaps be remembered that even under the best excavation circumstances biases in retrieval do occur. Sample wet sieving of contexts from the basilical hall, for example, indicated that only 26% by count of the pottery present was being collected by trowelling and dry sieving. However, the sherds missed were very fragmentary and the percentage lost by weight was therefore less marked; also rims and bases were more consistently collected so that the percentage lost by rim EVE was negligible (5.6%). A strong bias was also noted against the recovery of particular fabrics, with brightly coloured wares being recovered more frequently than dark wares (Pierpoint, unpub archive report). Although only little use was made of base EVEs in the basilical hall pottery report, care should be taken when comparing EVE data from the two sites.

The pottery was sorted macroscopically and no petrological analysis was undertaken apart from some on the amphorae by Williams. Darling and Faiers produced independent series as part of their research, while the later assemblage, prior to the current work, had been divided into broad fabric groups which were simply listed; there were no fabric descriptions or sample sherds. One of the aims of the latest pottery work was to produce a single overall fabric series, cross-referencing the various existing series including that for the basilical hall. The later key groups and the more recently catalogued pottery were recorded using the new fabric system. Fabric descriptions for wares first appearing in later contexts are based on sherds from these groups.

The data for forms has been recorded differently, each specialist using their own system. The problem is particularly marked with the pottery from later levels which was catalogued by three workers and reported on by a fourth with limited access to the original material. All specialists separated the pottery into rims, handles, bodies, and bases prior to recording. Darling recorded vessel type but not precise forms or general classes (eg jar, bowl etc). Faiers recorded vessel class and illustrated individual rims which could then be referred to by drawing numbers. The later pottery was recorded by vessel class, and free text descriptions of individual rims included in the catalogue, often combined with descriptions of decoration. These are not always consistent, for example dish, dog-dish and plain-rim dish were all used to describe the same form. An overall form series has subsequently been produced by Evans, based on the series devised by Darling and incorporating forms illustrated by the other specialists. This is described in more detail below. Forms from key groups have been recorded in more detail so that their changing proportions through time can be assessed. Vessels from the assemblage as a whole, however, can only be quantified by vessel class.

Darling devised a series of mnemonic codes for decoration which were later used by Faiers. For the later pottery, decoration was often merged with the description of form. Decoration has subsequently been recorded in more detail for later key groups, but it is not possible to quantify decorative types for the assemblage as a whole.

Darling, Faiers, and Dickinson noted cross context joins within and between areas. For the later pottery, joins within contexts were recorded but the limitations of space meant that cross context joins were not sought across larger groups. Some may, however, have been noted for more unusual wares or forms.

Comments on the condition of material, in particular the degree of abrasion, has only been noted for a few extreme cases. Other attributes relating, for example, to use (limescale, sooting) or re-use/repair (perforations/lead rivets) are recorded in the archive notes.

Condition and residuality

The condition of the pottery is obviously dependent upon the type of deposit in which it is found and the level of disturbance this deposit has been subjected to. The post-depositional history of individual contexts is described in more detail in the period discussions. As a whole, however, the pottery is in good condition with surface finish, such as burnishing, surviving well on the majority of the sherds. This is in interesting contrast with the Romano-British assemblages from Meole Brace and Duncote farm in the Wroxeter hinterland (Evans 1994). The soils in Shropshire are notoriously acidic. The PH of the 'urban' soils appears to have been balanced by the intense level of human activity on the site, in particular the presence of lime based mortar. This would have a more marked affect on more fragile categories of find, such as bone and prehistoric pottery, particularly where comparison is being made between the town and rural hinterland sites. The moderately good condition of the pottery is also a reflection of the deep stratigraphy on the site, with deposits well below the level of plough damage. Although the preservation of the fabrics was generally good, the actual sherd size and degree of fragmentation varied considerably through different deposits. This is discussed in more detail in the period discussions.

The reliability of excavated groups varied considerably. No residual material was identified in the military contexts, the fortress apparently being constructed on an unoccupied site, although there was a small degree of contamination from above. Many of the Period 1 features cut into the military deposits and were in turn heavily disturbed by the later main construction period. It is of course difficult to quantify levels of residuality with any certainty, particularly in coarseware assemblages with broadly dated forms.

In an attempt to try and assess the degree of residuality more objectively, Faiers developed a measure of calculation for the Period 2 assemblages. The fabrics were split into three groups: those sherds which could clearly be identified as residual, those sherds which appeared to be contemporary (non-residual), and those which could not be confidently assigned to either. A sherd count was made of all the residual and non-residual fabrics and the resulting totals stated as a ratio – residual:non-residual. The non-attributed material was then totalled and the balance apportioned in the same ratio.

A = overall total number of sherds.
R = total of identified residual sherds.
S = total of identified non-residual sherds.
B = total of identified residual (R) + non-residual (S) sherds.

A – B = C (balance to be apportioned).

$$\frac{C}{B} \times \frac{R}{1} = \text{residual balance (R2)}$$

$$\frac{C}{B} \times \frac{S}{1} = \text{non-residual balance (S2)}$$

R + R2 = R3 = total residual
S + S2 = S3 = total non-residual
R3 + S3 = A = overall total of sherds

$$\frac{R3}{A} \times \frac{100}{1} = \text{residual \% of total sherds}$$

$$\frac{S3}{A} \times \frac{100}{1} = \text{non-residual \% of total sherds}$$

The method is reliant on the worker being able to clearly identify residual fabrics, helped in this case by the preceding distinctive military assemblage. Using the equation presented above, Faiers estimated up to 85% residuality for some of the second-century groups. This is not at all surprising considering results from the neighbouring basilical hall excavations showed excavated layers dated post AD 367 to be composed almost entirely of residual material (Symons 1997).

Form series
compiled by Jane Evans

The form series is intended to provide a comprehensive typology for the Webster assemblage, and a basis for future work. It attempts to provide a concordance between the typologies used by the various specialists involved, but there are inevitably some inconsistencies in the approach used. It is accepted, therefore, that some refinement will be needed when new work in the area is undertaken. The system used is a development of that devised by Darling for the military assemblage.

Vessels are classified primarily on rim morphology or form depending on the completeness of available profiles. The order in which forms are presented does not necessarily reflect chronological developments. Vessels are categorised firstly by Class, arranged from closed to open form as follows:

F: Flagons/jugs; BK: Beakers; J: Jars subdivided into JHP: Honey pots, JC: Cooking-pots, JN: Narrow-mouthed jars, JM: Medium-mouthed jars, JW: Wide-mouthed jars, and JLS: Large Storage jars; C: Cups; B: Bowls; D: Dishes; P: Platters; M: Mortaria; TZ: *Tazze*; TK: Tankards; L: Lids; M: Miscellaneous, subdivided into ML: Lamps, MU: *Unguentaria*, MTV: Triple vases, CR: Crucibles, MCP: Cheese presses, and MS: Spouts.

Each class is then subdivided by Type, ie vessels sharing major features of shape. Within these, vessels sharing similar minor characteristics are classified by Form, of which any recorded example is classified as a Form variant, so for example a Flagon (F), ring-necked type (3), with an upright neck (.1) is coded F3.1, and a specific variant of this F3.11.

Each catalogue entry is structured as follows:

F1.11 – Publication form number, the number referred to in any text

WWO – Fabric code (for summary see Table 4.12)

80/201 – Box/context, followed where applicable by feature (F00) and/or KG – Key Group

Phase/internal dating – Sherds were selected for illustration as the best example of the form and may therefore be residual or intrusive in the phase in which they were found.

F FLAGONS (Figs 4.49–4.51)

Characterised by a closed body, medium to long restricted neck and handles.

F1 Collared and Hofheim type flagons (Fig 4.49)

The primary characteristic of this form is the collar around the neck which may vary considerably. The neck is usually straight and cylindrical, but may flare or taper slightly. Although examples can be single or double-handled, the majority found at Wroxeter appear to belong to the former. Vessels normally carry a footring.

The Hofheim type is a well-known Continental form (Gose 1950, forms 359–364). It occurs widely but not necessarily commonly on early military sites up to and including the Flavian period, but while it continues as a dominant type on the Rhineland, it is broadly replaced in Britain by the ring-necked type which is rare at both Wroxeter and Usk, but seemingly common at Exeter and Lake Farm. F1 types broadly equate with Hofheim types 50A and 50B (Ritterling 1913) and Usk types 1 and 2 (Greene 1993, 12) and

are the most frequent types on military sites on the continent, occurring throughout the Rhine and Danube frontiers (*ibid*).

F1.1
F1.11 WWO, 14/42, F2260, 1.3
F1.12 with slight internal lid-seating. WWOF, 41/6, military
F1.13 with slight internal lid-seating. WWOF, 87/115, military
F1.14 with shallow cupped rim. WWO, 84/328, military

F1.2 Sharp Hofheim type
F1.21 WWOC, 80/201, military
F1.22 WWO, 67/17, military

F1.3 Related to the basic Hofheim range
F1.31 with everted rim. WWOF, 78/5, military

F1.4 Related to the basic Hofheim range, with a pronounced undercutting of the rim collar
F1.41 WWOF, 98/205, military
F1.42 WWOF, 98/205, military

F2 Pulley-wheel rimmed flagons (Fig 4.49)

The commonest military flagon type with the flange rim and cordon. It is extremely difficult to parallel but it is probably contemporary with Hofheim type F1 above. It may be likened to examples from Hofheim (Ritterling 1913, Abb 62, no 1, a variant of type 50) and Neuss (Filtzinger 1972, Taf 18, no 14). Similar flagons are found on the continent but they are as infrequent as in Britain (Lorenzberg: Ulbert 1965, Taf 19, nos 3, 11; Augst: Ettlinger 1949, Taf 24, no 9; Vindonissa: Ettlinger and Simonett 1952, Taf 19, no 429; Neuss: Filtzinger 1972, Taf 18, nos 12, 13; Bad Nauheim: Simon 1960, Abb 14, no 26 from the Domitianic fort). One example was found at Fishbourne (Cunliffe 1971, type 116.1) and another at Verulamium (Frere 1972, fig 101, no 56) while some of the Eccles, Kent, flagons verge on the type (Detsicas 1977, fig 3.2). One parallel is of more interest since it occurs at Mancetter, considered to be a possible early base for the XIVth legion (Scott 1981, fig 11, no 8). This was associated with a group of amphorae on a site with exclusively pre-Flavian samian. No close parallels have been traced on other military sites, and their common occurrence at Wroxeter contrasts with other early military sites, as Usk, with its predominance of Hofheim types, and many sites where ring-necked types are more common.

Examples at Wroxeter mainly occur in local fabric WWO, with a small number in CREAM.

F2.1
F2.11 WWO, 84/393 military
F2.12 variant with slight internal lid-seating. WWO, 91/247, military

Table 4.12 Pottery: summary of fabric codes

local or regional wares

CREAM	white/cream ware
CREAMC	coarser white/cream ware
	(may include Verulamium/Oxford wares)
CREAMF	fine white/cream ware
CREAMG	white ware, grog-tempered
MICA2	coarse mica-dusted ware (?Wroxeter)
MWMID	mortaria, ?West Midlands
MWWCR	white colour-coated mortaria
MWWO	oxidized Wroxeter mortaria
MWWOC	oxidized coarse mortaria
MWWOF	oxidized fine mortaria
MWWR	reduced Wroxeter mortaria
MWWRF	reduced fine mortaria
NAT	native ware (local)
SV	Severn Valley ware
SVO	oxidized Severn Valley ware (coarser variant)
SVOF	oxidized Severn Valley ware (fine)
SVOR	reduced Severn Valley ware (fine)
SVORGO	oxidized organic Severn Valley ware
SVORGR	reduced organic Severn Valley ware
SVR	reduced Severn Valley ware (coarser variant)
SVRF	reduced Severn Valley ware (fine variant)
WWCR	colour-coated Wroxeter ware
WWMORT	Wroxeter ware mortaria
WWO	oxidized Wroxeter ware
WWOCF	= ?SVOF
WWOCC	= ?WWO
WWOC	white colour-coated oxidized Wroxeter ware
WWOF	oxidized Wroxeter ware (fine)
WWR	reduced Wroxeter ware
WWRC	white colour-coated reduced Wroxeter ware
WWRF	reduced Wroxeter ware (fine)

traded wares

BBI	Dorset black-burnished ware
BLSF	imitation Gallo-Belgic ware
MALV	Malvernian ware
MALVH	Malvernian, handmade, metamorphic rock-tempered
MALVW	Malvernian, wheelmade, metamorphic rock-tempered
MANCH	mortaria, Mancetter-Hartshill
MHOLT	mortaria, Holt
MHW	Much Hadham ware
MNVCC	mortaria, Nene Valley
MOVR	mortaria, Brockley Hill/Verulamium region
MOXFW	mortaria, Oxfordshire whiteware
MOXFRC	mortaria, Oxfordshire red colour-coated
MOXFRW	mortaria, Oxfordshire white colour-coated
NFW	New Forest ware
NVCC	Nene Valley colour-coated ware
NVCC1/2/3	Nene Valley colour-coat, fabric variants
OXFP	Oxfordshire parchment ware
OXFRCC	Oxfordshire red and brown colour-coated ware
VRW	Verulamium region whiteware

Imports

AMC189	amphorae, Carrot, Camulodunum 189 (Peacock and Williams Class 12)
AMDR2-4	amphorae, Dressel 2-4 (Peacock and Williams Class 10)

Table 4.12 continued

AMDR28	amphorae, Dressel 28 (Peacock and Williams Class 31)
AMRHOD	amphorae, Rhodian (Peacock and Williams Class 9)
AMPE47	amphorae, Gauloise 4, Pélichet 47 (Peacock and Williams Class 27)
AMGAU5	amphorae, Gauloise 5 (Peacock and Williams Class 30)
AMF148	amphorae, Fishbourne 148.3
AMC186A	amphorae, Camulodunum 186A (Peacock and Williams Class 17)
AMC186C	amphorae, Camulodunum 186C (Peacock and Williams Class 18)
AMDR20	amphorae, Dressel 20 (Peacock and Williams Class 25)
AMPW16	amphorae (Peacock and Williams Class 16)
AMRIC	amphorae, Richborough 527
AMH70	amphorae, Haltern 70
AMSPAIN	amphorae, South Spanish
BLEG	Gallo-Belgic 'eggshell' terra nigra
CGCC	Central Gaulish colour-coated ware
CGGW	Central Gaulish glazed ware
CGWH	Central Gaulish colour-coated ware (white fabric)
COLG	Cologne colour-coated ware
LYON	Lyon ware
LRCC	Lower Rhineland colour-coated ware
MICA1	mica-dusted ware
MOASTE	mortaria, Aoste/Atisii
MONG	mortaria, North Gaulish
MORHEN	mortaria, Rhineland?
MORHIN	mortaria, Rhineland
MORV	mortaria, Rhone Valley
NIEG	North Italian eggshell ware
PRW	Pompeian redware unclassified
PRW2	Pompeian redware, Peacock (1977) fabric 1
PRW3	Pompeian redware, Peacock (1977) fabric 3
SAMCG	samian, Central Gaulish
SAMCEG	samian, Central/East Gaul
SAMEG	samian, East Gaul
SAMIAN	samian (not differentiated)
SAMSG	samian, South Gaulish
TN	Terra nigra
TRR	Trier moselkeramik

wares of unknown source

CALC	late shell-tempered ware
CALGRIT	calcareous-tempered ware
CC	miscellaneous colour-coated ware
CCB	brown colour-coated ware
CREAM	miscellaneous cream wares
GBWW	Gallo-Belgic type whiteware
GREY	coarse reduced ware
GROG	grog-tempered ware
MOCRA	mortaria, fine white
MOCR	mortaria, cream
MORT3	mortaria ?West Midlands
MORTAR	miscellaneous mortaria
MUNKI	pinkish mortaria
OXID	coarse oxidized ware
PINK	miscellaneous pink ware
PRW	Pompeian red ware copies
SHEL	shell-tempered ware
WHEG	white eggshell ware

F2.2 (linked to forms F2.3, F2.4, F2.5)
F2.21 WWO, 50/52, military
F2.22 WWO, 50/31, military

F2.3 Variant of F2.2 above
F2.31 WWO, 78/57, military
F2.32 WWO, 78/57, military

F2.4 Variant of F2.2 above
F2.41 an oddity, the rim type resembles glass bottle rims (Isings 1957, type 50a). WWO, 78/57, military

F2.5 Miscellaneous, out-curving pulley rim flagons
F2.51 WWO, 84/75, WR 2.3

F2.6 Pulley-wheel rim with internal cup
F2.61 CREAM, 92/61, military
F2.62 (*cf* Gillam 1970, 6), AD 120–200. WWO, 97/137, P 2.2

F3 Ring-necked flagons (Fig 4.49)
The ring-necked flagon is characterised by a number of moulded rings on the neck. A continental form which

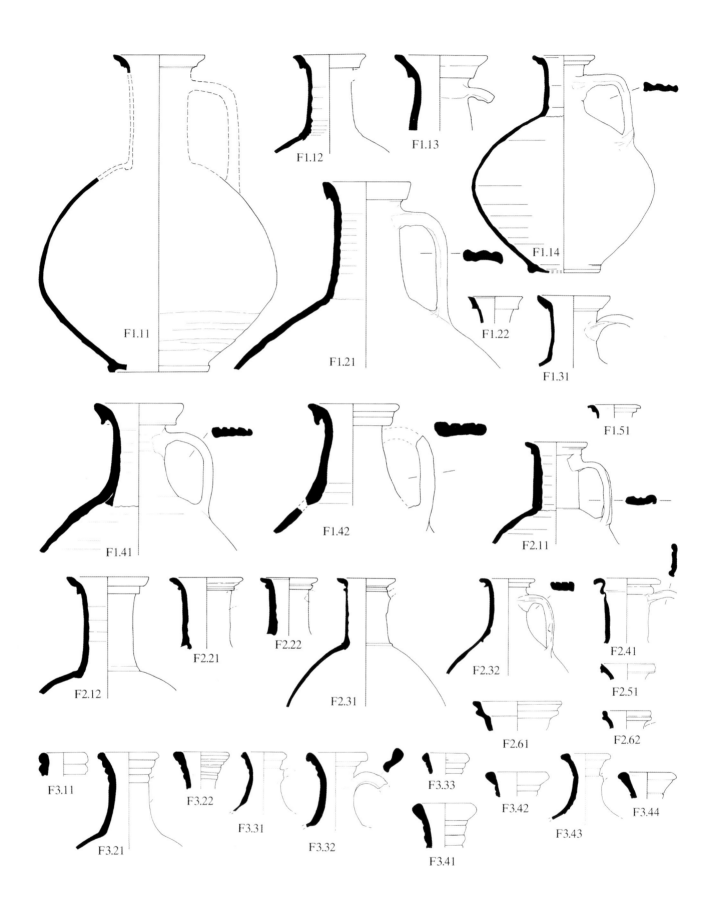

Fig 4.49 Pottery form series: flagons: scale 1:4

became popular in Britain from the Flavian period. The replacement of the Hofheim type by the ring-necked types in Britain generally, in contrast to the Rhineland, may be connected with the development of civilian as opposed to military orientated pottery production, as with the early kilns south of Verulamium (Richardson 1948, fig 6: Castle 1974, fig 3) and at Colchester (kilns 23 and 26, Hawkes and Hull 1947, 281, fig 58). Early ring-necked flagons are confined to a few examples, from pit F2807, and from the late and demolition phases, and appear to be even rarer than at Usk where they account for only 3.6% of the flagons. The ring-necked type, however, became the commonest type later, judging from the quantity occurring in Period 2 deposits, often in the local fabric with white slip (WWOC).

The typological progression starts with vertically necked forms with multiple moulding. Over time these become less well-defined and reduced in number and the neck becomes more flared. Later still the upper moulding becomes more prominent. The form has been recorded in a number of fabrics: WWOC, WWO, WWR, WWRC, OXID, CREAM and CREAMF.

F3.1 Upright neck
F3.11 WWOC, 84/137, WR 2.1

F3.2 Out-curving neck
F3.21 late first-century type (cf Holbrook and Bidwell 1991, fig 49.1.56). WWO, 86/24, WR 3.1
F3.22 thickening towards rim. WWOC, 83/526, WR 2.3

F3.3 Thickened, triangular upper ring. Mouldings on neck may be less well modelled
F3.31 SVO, 59/13, BP 3.2
F3.32 grey appearance, not same fabric as other flagons. GREY, (58)11,BP3.2
F3.33 CREAM with pinkish-brown slip, 83/523, WR 2.3

F3.4 Out-curving neck, sometimes with slight internal cupping, and pronounced upper ring
F3.41 WWO, 92/4, C 2.4
F3.42 WWO, 84/52, WR 2.3
F3.43 WWOC, 80/117, F486, P 3.1, KG 16
F3.44 with a thickened beaded rim and occasional grooves on neck, parallelled by vessels from Period 2 and may be intrusive in the military levels. OXID, 87/114, military

F4 Ring-necked, cupped mouth flagons (Fig 4.50)
Thickening of upper ring more pronounced, sometimes resulting in a near disc-shaped mouth, and a slight internal cup

F4.1 Pronounced cupped mouth and angular rim
F4.11 WWO, 51/21, F2990, 1.3; 70/16, 85, 78/11, 33, 67, military
F4.12 WWO, 78/10, 11, military

F4.2 Angular rim
F4.21 first-century type with angular rim. CREAM, 34/20, military

F4.3 Markedly thickened angular rim, poorly defined groove
F4.31 CREAMF, 49/168, BP 2.2

F4.4 Thickened triangular rim
F4.41 (cf Gillam 1970, 5 dated AD 110–150). WWO, 7/25, C 2.2
F4.42 with pronounced near triangular rim, first century. WWR, 51/10, C2.3

F4.5
F4.51 tapering neck. CREAMF, 98/60, F766, P 3.1, KG 16

F4.6 Shallow cup formed by in-turned rim, mouldings on neck less well pronounced.
F4.61 with angular, sharply in-turned rim and screw neck (possibly a waster). WWO/R, 24/21, BP 2.2
F4.62 with cream slip. CREAM, 83/104, WR3.1; 83/118, WR 2.3
F4.63 WWOC with cream slip, natatio infill, C 3.1, KG 14
F4.64 rounded in-turned bead rim, with traces of brown-yellow slip, CREAM, 83/114, WR 2.3
F4.65 with brownish-red slip. CREAMF, 83/117, WR 2.3
F4.66 with rounded in-turned, pronounced bead rim. CREAM with pale orange slip, 83/114, WR 2.3
F4.67 developed ring-necked flagon with thickened, near triangular upper ring, and shallow internal cup. Vestigial lower rings. WWOC 29/8, C 2.3
F4.68 WWOC 35/4, C 2.2
F4.69 sharply in-turned bead rim and tapering neck, orange external surface. Handle? CREAMF, 97/100, F523, P 3.1, KG 16

F4.7 Splayed cupped mouth, usually with shallow mouldings on neck. Handle?
F4.71 WWOC, 80/117, F486, P 3.1, KG 16
F4.72 slightly in-turned rim. WWOC, 98/145 F1017, P 3.1, KG 16
F4.73 sub-pulley rim. Handle? WWOC? (light brown ware with cream slip) natatio infill, C 3.1, KG 14
F4.74 WWOC? (light red-brown ware with cream slip), natatio infill, C3.1, KG14

F4.8 Double-handled flask with pronounced cupped mouth and vestigial rings on neck.
F4.81 painted whiteware, 90/97, F625, P 3.1

F5 Cupped-mouth flagons (Fig 4.50)
Flagons with a splayed, cupped rim and a single or double handle. Occurs in fabrics WWOC, WWO, WWOF and OXID

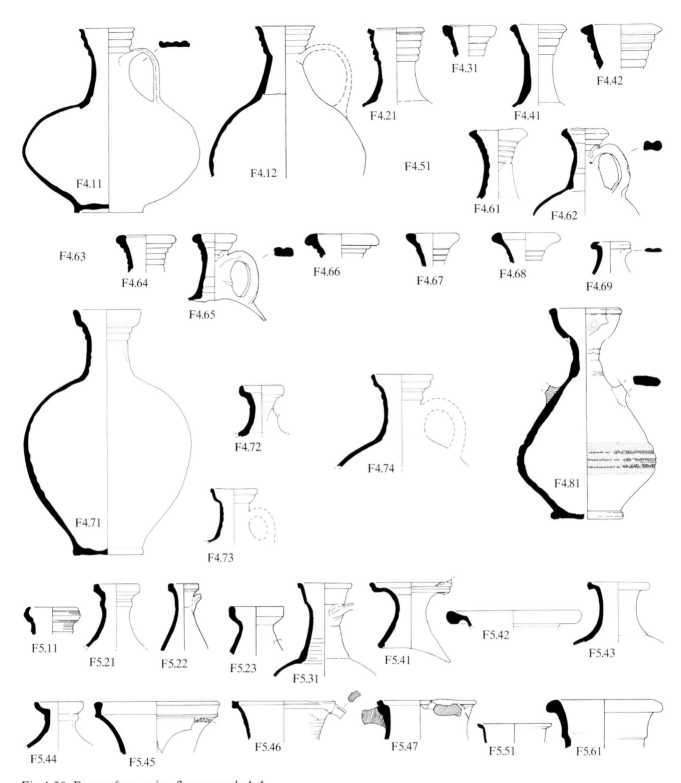

Fig 4.50 Pottery form series: flagons; scale 1:4

F5.1
F5.11 inturned rim. WWO, 78/15, military

F5.2 Squared rim and shallow cup
F5.21 slight groove on rim. WWOC, with cream slip, *natatio* infill, C 3.1, KG 14
F5.22 small cup-mouthed flask, of a type parallelled at Usk (Greene 1993,18) and having a widespread distribution. WWOF, 84/339, military

F5.23 with tapering neck. WWOC, 84/217, 125, military

F5.3 Splayed cupped-mouth with everted rim. The type is parallelled on the continent at Hofheim (Ritterling 1913, Abb 64, nos 4, 6 and 7), Haltern (Loeschcke 1909, Taf XII, no 48), and Vetera (Hagen 1912, Taf LII, no 22). The only examples with a single handle noted in Britain are from Kingsholm (Darling 1985b, fig 24.3) and Cirencester (Rigby 1982, fig 61, no 390).

The two-handled version is much commoner, and examples occur at the Neronian kiln at Sutri in Italy (Duncan 1964, fig 14, no 156ff (form 37)), Hofheim (Ritterling 1913, Abb 68, nos 4, 6, 8 and 9), and Neuss (Filtzinger 1972, Taf 22, no 6). They also appear at Camulodunum where the form is rare despite examples found associated with kiln 26 (Hawkes and Hull 1947, fig 52, no 5, a variant of form 170: Hull 1963, fig 91, nos 20–21), and it is interesting to note that it figures among the products of the kilns at both Brockley Hill (Richardson 1948, fig 7, nos 43 and 45: Castle 1974, 261) and Eccles (Detsicas 1977, figs 3.3–4).
F5.31 WWOF, 7/41, 36, military

F5.4 Markedly splayed, shallow cupped rim
F5.41 this form appears to go on until the end of the second century. Similar forms are dated AD 190 (Hull 1963, fig 56.5 type series 363–383), and first to second centuries (Sheldon 1978, fig 165, 1268). WWO with mica coating, 98/52, 68, P 2.3
F5.42 thickened beaded rim. OXID, 63/15 F2287, 1.3
F5.43 with slightly under-cut bead rim. WWO, 98/87, P2.3
F5.44 simple rim. WWO, 90/205, F800, P 3.1, KG 16
F5.45 jug/flagon with thickened sub-pulley rim. WWO, 83/534, WR 2.3
F5.46 jug/flagon with sub-pulley rim with groove on top, CREAMF, 84/48, WR 3.1
F5.47 WWO, 86/24, WR 3.1

F5.5
F5.51 WWO, 78/57, military

F5.6
F5.61 WWCR, 2/36, military

F6 Disc-rim and hooked rim flagons (Fig 4.51)
The disc-mouthed form probably has a continental origin and is found in the Rhineland in pre-Flavian contexts at Camulodunum. At Wroxeter it is found in the military deposits in fabrics WWR and OXID. The hooked rim varieties occur in later deposits and were made in the local fabric WWOC.

F6.1 Disc-rimmed flagons. Disc-rimmed flagons generally occur widely, but it is interesting that small flasks of this type are among the products of the Eccles potters in Kent (Detsicas 1977, fig 3.3, nos 65–6).
F6.11 closely resembles Ritterling (1913, Taf XXXIV) type 55, although he combines several disc-rimmed vessels under this type. WWR 14/32 F2246, 1.3
F6.12 OXID, 78/11, 57, military

F6.2 Disc-rimmed flagon of a type paralleled at Usk (Greene 1993,18) and having a widespread distribution. Probably derived from a glass type (Isings 1957, type 50).
F6.21 WWO, 98/205, military
F6.22 WWR, 34/29, military

F6.23 WWR, 7/35, military

F6.3 Hooked-rim flagons
F6.31 WWOC with cream slip, *natatio* infill C 3.1, KG 14
F6.32 WWOC with cream slip, *natatio* infill, C 3.1, KG 14

F7 Disc/flange-necked flagon (Fig 4.51)
Flagon with a tall narrow, or shorter flaring neck with a flange mid-way down and a single handle (*cf* Young 1977, form C8).
F7.1 Narrow necked flagon with mid-neck disk
F7.11 decorated with bands of red paint. WWOC with cream slip, *natatio* infill, C 3.1, KG 14
F7.12 NVCC, 98/15, P 4

F8 Two-handled flagons (Fig 4.51)
Two-handled flagons with cylindrical necks and beaded or flat-topped rims. F8.1 and 8.21/2 are types paralleled at Usk (Greene 1993, 18), and have a widespread distribution.

F8.1 is closely paralleled by a deposit of seven such flagons in a latrine at Mancetter (Scott 1981, figs 13–14), which also contained a jug type F12. Associated samian was Claudian to Neronian. Examples were produced at Brockley Hill, Herts from at least the Neronian period (Marsh and Tyers 1976, 551). The form has been recorded in fabrics WWO, SVO/WWO, WWR and WWOC.
F8.11 flattened near triangular rim. WWO, 34/45, military
F8.12 WWO, 78/57, military
8.2 Beaded rim
F8.21 WWO, 98/205, military
F8.22 bead rim, light brown slip. SVO/WWO? (light red ware with grey core), *natatio* infill, C 3.1, KG 14
8.3 With handles springing from immediately below the rim
8.31 WWR, 85/105, military

F9 Miscellaneous flagons/flasks (Fig 4.51)
F9.1 Simple flaring rim
F9.11 small flask. WWO, 84/251, military
F9.12 jug/flagon. WWO, 84/100, WR 2.2

F10 Flagons/Jugs (Fig 4.51)
Distinguished by the presence of a spout

F10.1 Trefoil or pinched-mouthed flagons. This class is characterised by the rim being pinched together to form a pouring spout. Such vessels have a widespread distribution in Britain and are paralleled at Usk (Greene 1993, 18) where, however, only two examples were found. An estimated vessel count of eight at Wroxeter simply highlights the vagaries of samples. The form is encountered in later first and early second-century contexts elsewhere. The later Roman colour-coated industries also produced a similar form (*cf* Young 1977,

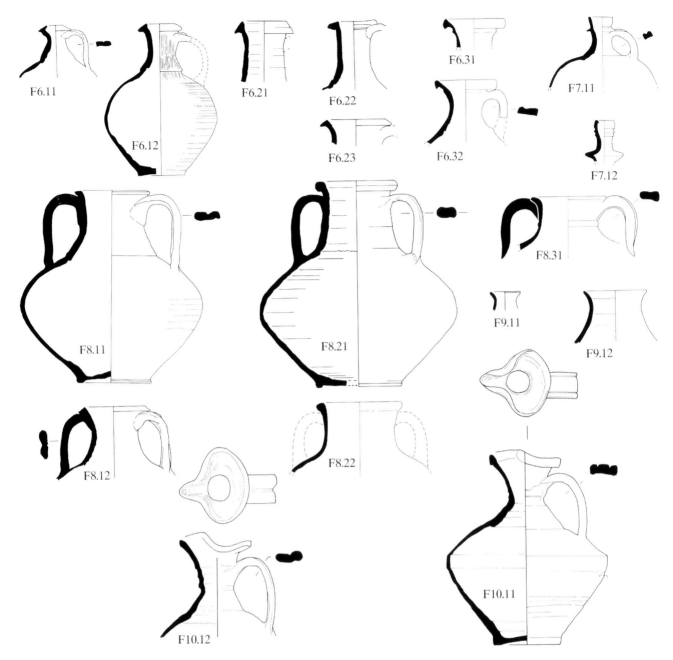

Fig 4.51 Pottery form series: flagons: scale 1:4

fig 54, C12). The Wroxeter examples are all early, associated with the military deposits and have been recorded in fabrics WWR, WWO and CREAMF.

F10.11 Hofheim type 54 (Ritterling 1913, Taf XXXIV) imitating a bronze jug. A similar jug was recovered from a latrine at Mancetter (Scott 1981, figs 13–14), associated with Claudian to Neronian samian. WWR, 80/201, military

F10.12 WWO, 90/247, military

BK BEAKERS (Figs 4.52–4.53)

Beakers are generally defined as drinking vessels of suitable size and shape to hold in the hands (Webster 1976, 17). The majority of vessels included below are covered by this definition. Although all vessels in this class have restricted mouths, not all are small and larger examples may overlap with jars.

The beakers from Wroxeter show a great diversity of form with many single examples of a particular type. Classification is difficult, and as such subjective, particularly where there are so few profiles available. Most of the forms have their origins on the Continent but are largely present in the local fabrics. The following groups are primarily based on details of rim form and vessel shape.

BK1 Butt Beakers (Fig 4.52)

Butt beakers are relatively tall vessels usually with a body divided into zones by girth grooves or cordons and frequently decorated with rouletting, combing or

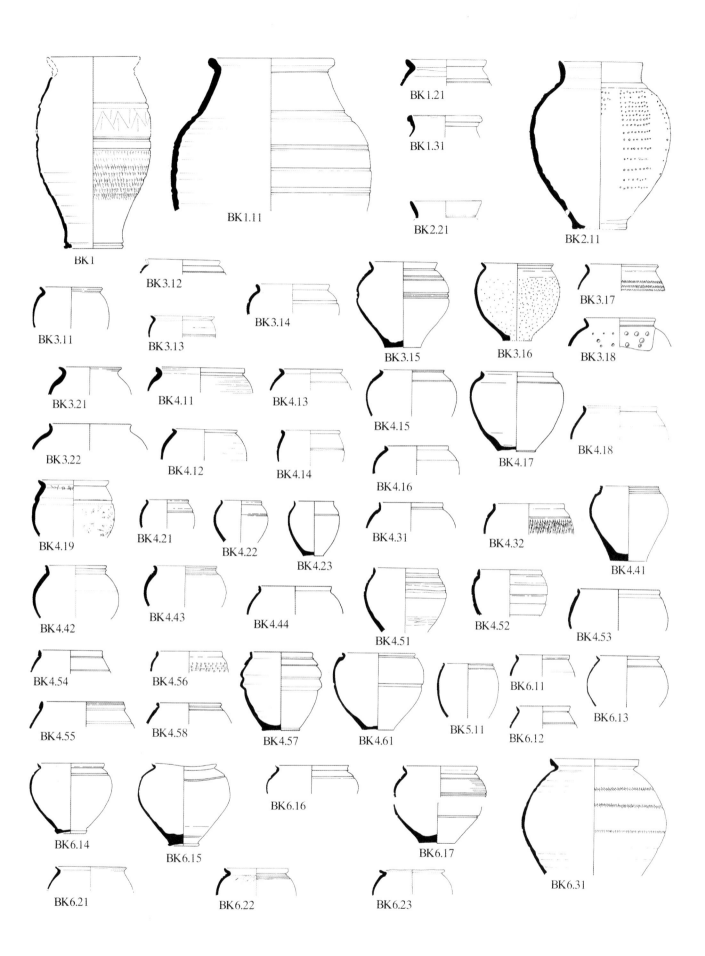

Fig 4.52 Pottery form series: beakers; scale 1:4

incised designs. The form has Gaulish origins and examples were imported into southeast Britain in the pre-conquest period. Several British kilns are known or suspected to be producing the form, in particular Chichester (Down 1978), the Abingdon area (Timby in prep a), and Verulamium. Rim forms vary from lenticular to squat bevelled to rounded, becoming less well defined with later examples. The form becomes less recognisable in British assemblages after the Flavian period.

BK1 Rim form uncertain
BK1 The lack of rim detail and undistinctive fabric make it difficult to determine whether this is an import or product of southeast England, although the latter is suspected. GBWW, 70/16,18; 72/16, 21, 25, 67, military

BK1.1 Everted rim with slight lid-seating
BK1.11 copying a Gallo-Belgic form. As a single example the significance of this form is uncertain, but it may be noted that a similar copy beaker occurred at Mancetter associated with pre-Flavian samian and fragments of *lorica segmentata* (Scott 1981, fig 11, no 7). WWR, 90/247, military

BK1.2 Simple everted rim
BK1.21 WWO, 83/526, WR 2.3

BK1.3 Slight collar below rim
BK1.31 fine light cream/buff fabric, probably imported, 98/61, P 2.3

BK2 Poppyhead beakers (Fig 4.52)
Ovoid bodied beakers with near vertical or slightly flaring rims. Often decorated with panels of barbotine dots. The type becomes common in the first half of the second century and was probably continental in origin (Tyers 1978).

BK2.1 Upright rim
BK2.11 burnished slip on outer surface with applied barbotine dots in panels, (*cf* Frere 1984a, fig 85.2048 dated AD 80–130; Tyers 1978, fig 4.3.20). WWRF, 98/68, P 2.3

BK2.2 Slightly splayed rim
BK2.21 WWRF, 86/23, WR 3.1

BK3 Ovoid or globular-bodied beakers with everted rims (Fig 4.52)
Seventy-four percent of the beakers from military contexts fit into the broad category of everted rim beakers. Many of the various sub-types distinguished in recording subsequently turned out to be single examples and slight variations are therefore, of debatable significance, particularly in the eversion or slightly vertical nature of the rim.

BK3.1 With short everted rims sharply angled from the upper shoulder. Plain bodied beakers

BK3.11 LYON? 98/154, 1.1; 98/137, 1.3
BK3.12 with girth groove on upper body. CGGW, 78/12, military
BK3.13 fine hard, pinkish-orange fabric with mica coating. MICA (*cf* Marsh 1978, type 22, fig 6.10 dated late first to early second century; Sheldon 1978, fig 202, 1631). 92/4, C 2.4
BK3.14 (*cf* Darling 1976, 139). WWR, 98/81, F804, P 3.1 KG 16
BK3.15 with girth groove(s)/constriction around centre body. WWO, 67/22, military
BK3.16 with roughcast decoration. LYON, 78/12, military
BK3.17 with rouletted decoration. WWRF, 14/43, military
BK3.18 boss decorated beaker, burnt, representing the only example of an imported mica-dusted ware in the military assemblage. It is almost certainly of the same type as those with gold mica-dusting from Usk (Greene 1979, fig 53, nos 4–7), the beakers from Lincoln stamped by CAMARO (Webster 1949, 69, fig 11, no 19 and unpublished), and beakers from Richborough (Bushe-Fox 1932, pl XXXVIII, no 286). The source of these beakers is unknown, but suspected to be northern Gaul, and a Neronian-Flavian date is probable. The continuation of this form into the Flavian period is indicated by a fine example with complex decoration from Inchtuthil (Darling 1985a, fig 100, no 65), and perhaps also the number found in London (Marsh 1978, type 20). MICA, 72/63, military; 78/+, C 4

BK3.2 Beakers with short everted S-shaped rims not sharply angled from the shoulder
BK3.21 WWOF, 98/188, F1073, 1.2
BK3.22 WWR, 7/41, military

BK4 Ovoid or globular-bodied beakers with other rims (Fig 4.52)
BK4.1 Ovoid or globular beakers with short everted thickened rims. Plain matt or burnished
BK4.11 GREY, 98/137, 1.3
BK4.12 CREAM, 90/204, F951, P 2.2
BK4.13 WWR, 10/6, C 2.2
BK4.14 hard, pale orange fabric, ?import, 92/4, C 2.4
BK4.15 WWO, 84/181, military
BK4.16 WWR, 78/57, military
BK4.17 WWOF, 95/1, 89/1, military
BK4.18 hard, fine, light grey ware, possibly local, 83/537, WR 2.3
BK4.19 (*cf* Caerleon: Greep 1986, fig 23, 13:13, early second century). WWR, 83/526, WR 2.3

BK4.2 Small ovoid beakers with short everted rims and upper body girth groove
BK4.21 WWRF, 80/191, military
BK4.22 WWRF, 84/110, military
BK4.23 WWRF, 98/234, F2005, 1.2

BK4.3 Globular beakers with short vertical rims
BK4.31 WWR, 77/9, military
BK4.32 rouletted, WWR, 50/52, military

37

BK4.4 Globular beakers with cordoned or grooved rims
BK4.41 widely parallelled on the continent at the
Magdalensberg, Hofheim (Ritterling 1913, Taf XXXI-
II, no 85B), Kempten (Fischer 1957, Taf 3, no 4; Taf
5, nos 5 and 7), Neuss (Filtzinger 1972, Taf 5, no 7)
including two from the kilns (*ibid*, Taf 61, no 10; Taf
81, no 13), Koln (Hagen 1906, Taf XXII, Grab 15)
and Nijmegen (Vermeulen 1932, pl X, no 93; Stuart
1962, pl 20, no 328). One of the earliest known examples in Britain occurs at Longthorpe, a product of the
local kilns (Frere and St Joseph 1974, fig 53, no 50).
The form, however, continues in use by military potters as an example was found at Holt (Grimes 1930, fig
64, no 78) and even later at Balmuildy (Miller 1922, pl
XLVI, no 10). WWR 77/9, military
BK4.42 WWR, 98/87, P 2.3
BK4.43 decorative band of diagonal burnishing with
cordons and grooves. SVO? (light brown ware), *natatio*
infill, C 3.1, KG 14
BK4.44 WWR, 78/57, military

BK4.5 Miscellaneous globular beakers with variously
thickened rims
BK4.51 WWR, 72/48, 114, military
BK4.52 WWR, 78/9, military
BK4.53 WWR, 72/67, military
BK4.54 WWRF, 78/26, military
BK4.55 a fragmentary example, difficult to parallel.
The form most likely derives from the continent, and
more probably from the Danubian area than further
north. WWR, 98/179, military
BK4.56 with rouletted decoration. WWRF, 75/2, C
2.1
BK4.57 WWR, 80/201, military
BK4.58 WWR, 73/27, military

BK4.6 High shouldered beaker with short everted rim
BK4.61 parallelled by examples from Hofheim
(Ritterling 1913, Taf XXXIII, no 85B), Neuss
(Filtzinger 1972, Taf 5, nos 5, 9) and Nijmegen (Stuart
1962, pl 20, no 327). No beakers of this form have
been traced in Britain. WWR?, 78/11, 33, military

BK5 Barrel-shaped beaker with beaded rim (Fig 4.52)
BK5.1
BK5.11 No close parallels from Britain, although two
distorted fragments perhaps from a similar beaker were
found at Cirencester (unpub). The best continental parallels come from the Magdalensberg, where examples
occur in two fabrics, a form of *terra nigra* current *c* AD
20–35 (Schindler-Kaudelka 1975, Taf 18, no 93), and
in a red fabric with colour coating of *c* AD 25 (*ibid*, Taf
25, no 117c; Taf 23, no 127b). WWR, 78/57, military

BK6 Beakers with cupped or lid-seated rims (Fig 4.52)
BK6.1 Very fine globular beakers
Darling notes that BK6.11–16 form a clear sub-group
within the everted rim beaker group, characterised by
thin walls, fine potting technique, delicate rims and,

where they survive, moulded bases. Some are over or
under fired, and most could be regarded at best as 'sec-
onds'. They are all in the reduced Wroxeter fabric and
none are decorated.
BK6.11 WWRF, 72/24, military
BK6.12 WWR, 73/44, military
BK6.13 WWR, 78/57, military
BK6.14 WWR, 78/57, military
BK6.15 WWR, 78/57, military
BK6.16 WWR, 78/57, military
BK6.17 a single example, burnished on the shoulder and
with a notably delicate rim. WWOF, 7/35; 7/59, military

BK6.2 Miscellaneous smaller beakers
BK6.21 CC, 9/94, WR 2.3
BK6.22 with wipe marks inside rim, WWR, 84/52, WR
2.3
BK6.23 waster. WWR, 93/2, WR 2.3

BK6.3 Larger beakers
BK6.31 rouletted. CREAM, 98/141, 1.3; 98/164, 183,
1.1; 98/222, 1.2

BK7 Globular beakers with cornice rims (Fig 4.53)
BK7.1 Small globular beakers with everted, grooved rims
BK7.11 WWR, 72/79, military
BK7.12 burnished on both the inside of the rim and
the shoulder. WWOF, 98/130, 1.2
BK7.13 WWO, 30/23, military
BK7.14 with barbotine dots below shoulder groove,
AD 80–130. WWRF, 83/111, WR 3.1
BK7.15 WWR, 86/18, WR 2.3
BK7.16 with external groove. WWRF? 84/261, military

*BK8 Bag-shaped beakers with cornice rims and roughcast
decoration* (Fig 4.53)
BK8.1
BK8.11 CGCC, probably second century, 85/223,224,
WR 2.3
BK8.12 LRCC, Hadrianic or early Antonine,
AD120/140+. 84/52, WR 2.3
BK8.13 LGCC, 39/12, military
BK8.14 probably second century. CGCC, 92/4, C 2.4
BK8.15 probably second century. CGCC, 84/75, WR 2.3
BK8.16 wipe marks inside rim, Hadrianic AD 120–40.
CGCC, 83/111 WR 3.1
BK8.17 Hadrianic AD 120–40. CGCC, 83/534,
WR 2.3
BK8.18 probably second century. CGCC, 83/114,
WR 2.3

BK9 Indented beakers with everted rims (Fig 4.53)
BK9.1
BK9.11 CGCC, 63/10, 65/15, F2287, 1.3
BK9.12 MICA2, 92/4, C 2.4

BK10 Carinated beakers copying Camulodunum type 120
(Fig 4.53)
BK 10.1 Local copies of Camulodunum type 120

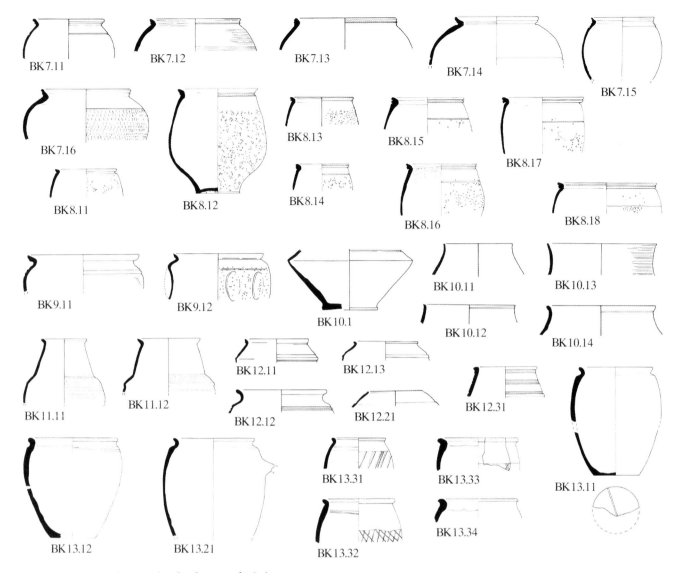

Fig 4.53 Pottery form series: beakers: scale 1:4

The copying of this form continues well into the Flavian period, and at Fishbourne copies appear more frequently in Periods 2 and 3, demonstrating the long life of this beaker.

BK10.1 Base sherd. WWR, 98/205, military
BK10.11 CREAM, 78/11, military
BK10.12 WWRF, 77/9, military
BK10.13 WWRF, 98/205, military
BK10.14 of the general form of Camulodunum type 120B, but having a relatively sandy fabric the dark grey surface of which shows considerable amounts of mica. GREY, 73/45, military

BK11 Pentice beakers (Fig 4.53)
BK11.1 Pentice beakers
BK11.11 CC, 98/12, P 4
BK11.12 CC, 98/12, P 4

BK12 Beakers with insloping necks (Fig 4.53)
BK12.1 Beakers with everted rim and straight shoulder ending in a cordoned carination. This form is

parallelled by vessels from the Neuss kilns (Filtzinger 1972, Taf 77, no 9; Taf 78, no 7).
BK12.11 WWRF, 83/536, WR 2.1
BK12.12 WWOF, 35/65, F2335, 1.3
BK12.13 WWO, 92/18, C 2.1

12.2 Beaker with incurving walls
BK12.21 BLEG, 83/530, WR 2.3

12.3 Beaker with inward tapering neck
12.31 with traces of rouletting on body under rim. WWO, 97/137, P 2.2

BK13 BB1 type barrel-shaped beakers with short everted rims (Fig 4.53)
BK13.1 Sub-cavetto type rims
BK13.11 BB1, 80/119 F466, P 3.1, KG 16
BK13.12 BB1, 84/52, WR 2.3

BK13.2 Handled beakers with sub-cavetto rims
BK13.21 BB1, 90/128, F736, P 3.1, KG 16

BK13.3 Simple everted rims
BK13.31 WWR, with black slip and burnishing, 29/8, C 2.3
BK13.32 BB1, 84/52, WR 2.3
BK13.33 BB1, 84/52, WR 2.3
BK13.34 BB1, 84/52, WR 2.3

JH JARS: HONEY POTS (Fig 4.54)

Neckless or short-necked jars, usually with two small handles near the rim.

JH1 Thickened rims
JH1.1 near triangular rim
JH1.11 WWO, 80/117, F486, P 3.1, KG 16

JH1.2 sharply angular triangular rim
JH1.21 WWO, 1/59, 9/31, military

JH2 Everted rims
JH2.1
JH2.11 possibly a honey pot but no handles found, unparalleled. CREAM, 92/65, 77, military

JH2.2
JH2.21 WWOC, cream slip externally, 98/28, F638; 98/45 F675, P 3.2

JH2.3
JH2.31 WWO, 88/3, WR 4

JH2.4
JH2.41 undercut rim. WWO, 98/199, 1.1

JH3 T-shaped rims
JH3.1
JH3.11 WWO, 41/29, military
JH3.12 burnished. WWR, 91/136, F629, WR 2.1
JH3.13 WWOC, with white slip, 58/10, BP 3.2

JH4 Pulley rims
JH4.1
JH4.11 lower bead less pronounced. WWOC, cream slip on outer surface and inner rim only, *natatio* infill, C 3.1, KG 14

JH4.2
JH4.21 both beads roughly equal size. WWOC, with white slip, 58/9, BP 3.2

JH4.3
JH4.31 lower bead more pronounced. WWOC, with cream slip, *natatio* infill, C 3.1, KG 14

JH4.4 Frilled pulley-rim
JH4.41 WWOC, 59/15, F345, BP 3.1, KG 19
JH4.5 Cupped rim
JH4.51 with pronounced shallow cup. WWO, 30/18, military

JH4.52 cupped rim. WWOC, 80/117, F486, P 3.1, KG 16

JH5 Possible honey-pot forms
JH5.1 Everted rims
JH5.11 with squared rim. WWO, 34/47, military; 63/20, F2287, 1.3
JH5.12 jar with thickened, near triangular rim. SVOF, 90/168, P 2.2

JC JARS: COOKING-POTS (Figs 4.54–4.55)

Cooking-pots are predominantly handmade in fairly coarsely tempered fabrics suitable for use over direct heat, and characterised by the regular occurrence of limescale, residue and sooting. Forms are usually derived from native traditions.

JC1 Malvernian 'tubby cooking pot' type (Fig 4.54)
JC1.1 Upright/near upright rims
Broadly Peacock types 1–8, second century on present evidence (Peacock 1967, 16–8, fig 1). The precise shape of the rim may vary greatly.
JC1.11 burnished externally, NAT variant, a fine textured, vesicular, light grey fabric with a light red-brown cortex and grey to brown surfaces, with some mica. Not certainly hand-made. 91/193, military
JC1.12 MALVH, 90/255, 1.2
JC1.13 (Peacock 1967, fig 1.5). MALVH, 98/52,68, P 2.3
JC1.14 MALVH, 29/8, C 2.3
JC1.15 WWR, 1/38, 9/30, military; 29/17 C 2.1
JC1.16 MALVH, 91/52, WR 2.3
JC1.2 Slightly in-turned rims. The precise shape of the rim may vary greatly. Broadly equates with Peacock types 1–8, second century on present evidence (Peacock 1967, 16–8, fig 1).
JC1.21 with internally thickened rim. MALVH, 90/179, P 2.2
JC1.22 with simple incurving rim. MALVH, 91/72, WR 2.3
JC1.23 with externally beaded rim. MALVH, 49/49, BP 3.1, KG 18
JC1.24 copy of Malvernian cooking pot, as Peacock 1967, fig 1.5. WWR, 85/26, WR 2.3

JC2 Miscellaneous cooking-pots (Fig 4.54)
JC2.1 In-turned rims
JC2.11 NAT, 50/52, military
JC2.12 Iron Age form, possibly from the Malvern area. ?MALVL, 90/161,P3.3; 90/169, P2.2; 90/179, P 2.2

JC3 Black-burnished ware type everted rim forms (Fig 4.55)

JC3.1 Small jars or beakers of wide girth with very slightly everted cavetto rims, usually with acute cross hatch burnish on the body of the jar.
JC3.11 BB1, 86/24, WR 3.1

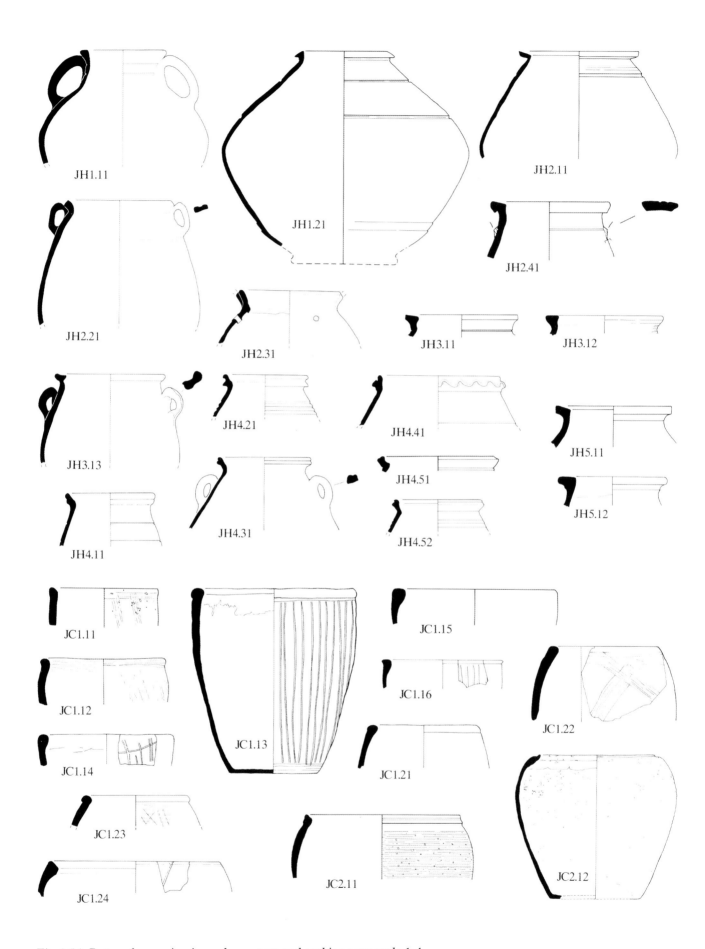

Fig 4.54 Pottery form series: jars – honey pots and cooking pots; scale 1:4

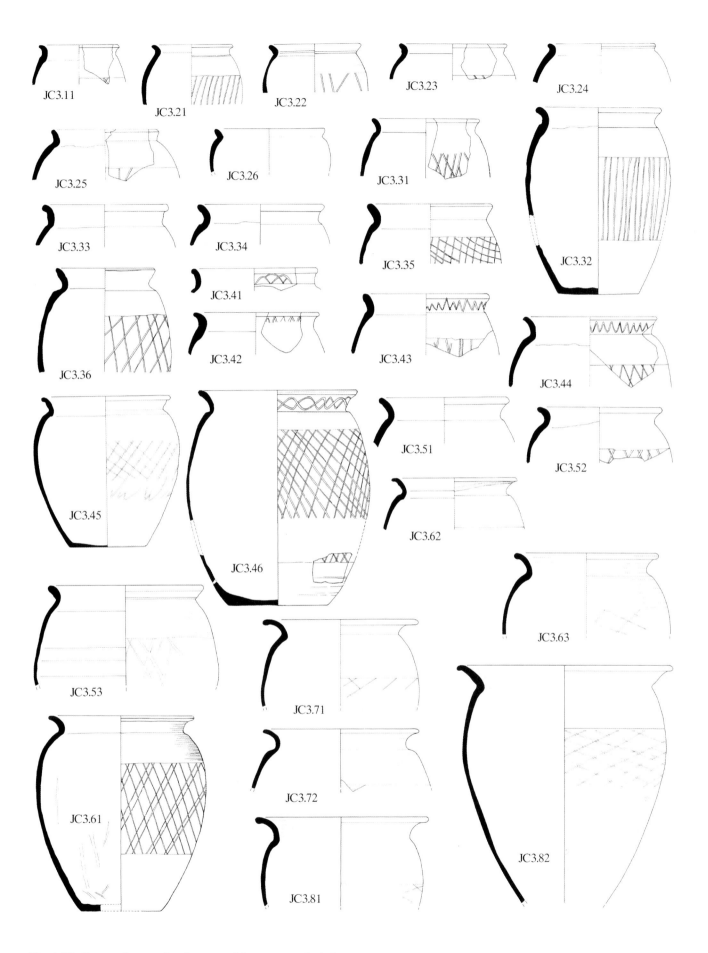

Fig 4.55 Pottery form series: jars – cooking pots; scale 1:4

JC3.2 Jars of wide girth with stubby, very slightly everted rim, usually with acute cross hatch or vertical burnished lines on body of the jar.

JC3.21 parallelled in a south-western BB1 form with vertical burnished lines, dated *c* AD 100–120 at Exeter (Holbrook and Bidwell 1991 fig 41 no 34.3b). BB1, 84/154, WR 2.3

JC3.22 WWR, 98/68, P 2.3

JC3.23 BB1, 83/114, WR 3.1

JC3.24 mid second century, or *c* AD 130–70, (Gillam 1970, no 127). BB1, 86/24, WR 2.3

JC3.25 BB1, 84/52, WR 2.3

JC3.26 BB1, 80/117, F486, P 3.1, KG 16

JC3.27 BB1, 80/117, F486, P 3.1, KG 16

JC3.3 Jars of wide girth with very slightly everted cavetto rim, usually with acute lattice on the body.

JC3.31 BB1, 83/111, WR 3.1

JC3.32 *c* AD 160–200 (Holbrook and Bidwell 1991, fig 41 34.3a). BB1,86/24, WR 3.1

JC3.33 BB1, 92/4, C 2.4

JC3.34 BB1, 86/24, WR 3.1

JC3.35 BB1, 84/52, WR 2.3

JC3.36 WWR, 29/8, C 2.3

JC3.4 Jars of wide girth with very slightly everted rims and acute burnished lattice on the body. Characterised by the presence of burnished wavy lines on the neck until the late second century, but the upright rims of these vessels suggests an early-to-mid second century date.

JC3.41 one of the earliest vessels in the cooking-pot group. BB1,84/154, WR 2.3

JC3.42 BB1, 84/52, WR 2.3

JC3.43 BB1, 92/4, C 2.4

JC3.44 AD 130–70, probably mid second century (Gillam 1970, no 127). BB1, 92/4, C 2.4

JC3.45 acute lattice burnish, late second-early third century. BB1, 90/189, 205, F800, P 3.1, KG 16

JC3.46 probably mid second century, local fabric imitation of BB1, 84/52, WR2.3 and 97/132, F747, P 2.3

JC3.5 Jars of wide girth with slightly everted rims and acute burnished lattice on the body.

JC3.51 mid second century (Gillam 1976, no 2). BB1, 92/4, C 2.4

JC3.52 mid second century. BB1, 84/52, WR 2.3

JC3.53 acute lattice burnish. SVR, 90/163, F631, P 3.2, KG 17

JC3.6 Jars of wide girth with moderately splayed everted rims and acute, right-angle or occasionally obtuse burnished lattice burnish on the body.

JC3.61 Gillam 1976, no 3, of mid-late second century date. The pattern has a parallel in a south-western BB1 type from Exeter (Holbrook and Bidwell 1991, fig 40.26.3). A very similar vessel in BB2 was found at Strageath in Antonine levels AD 160+ (Frere and Wilkes 1989, fig 121, no 117), and a similar vessel was

found at Birrens, Antonine 1 deposit, but with a wavy line under the rim (Robertson 1975, fig 67.4). BB1, 84/48, 49, WR 3.1

JC3.62 the latest jar type in Period 2, Gillam type 4 or 6, Late second/early third century (Gillam 1976) and Birrens Antonine 1 deposit (Robertson 1975, fig 71.8). BB1, 84/52, WR 2.3

JC3.63 with obtuse angled cross-hatch burnish, early to mid third century? BB1, 98/40, F672, P 3.1, KG 16

JC3.7 Jars of near equal to narrow girth, with splayed everted rims and obtuse angled cross-hatch burnish on body of vessel. The dating of these and type JC3.8 is problematical. Evidence recently published from Exeter indicates that there is little morphological development in cooking-pots from the later third century until the last quarter of the fourth century, with smaller splayed types being produced alongside less exaggerated profiles (Holbrook and Bidwell 1991 95).

JC3.71 splayed everted rim, mid-late third century (Gillam 1976, type 9/10). BB1,98/35, F651, P 3.2, KG 17

JC3.72 with obtuse lattice burnish below shoulder groove, mid third century (Gillam 1976, type 8). BB1, 98/140, F930, P 3.2, KG 17

JC3.8 Jars of narrow girth with markedly splayed everted rims and obtuse angled cross-hatch burnish on body of jar.

JC3.81 BB1, 98/20, P 3.4A, KG 25

JC3.82 a number of sherds are rivetted together. BB1, 98/2, P 4

JN JAR: NARROW MOUTHED (Figs 4.56–4.57)

Jars with a neck and mouth markedly narrower than the maximum girth of the vessel and usually having a medium to short neck. Possibly used for storing liquids.

JN1 Miscellaneous forms (Fig 4.56)

JN1.1

JN1.11 long necked, globular jar with everted, slightly thickened rim. A single vessel copying Belgic flasks as found at Nijmegen (Holwerda 1941, pl V, no 185). Similar to Camulodunum 231, but is otherwise rare in Britain. The form with rouletted decoration occurs at Usk but in a *terra nigra*-type of fabric (Greene 1979, 106ff). It is more prevalent on the continent, particularly on the Lower Rhine (as Ritterling 1913, Taf XXXVII, no 120A) but also occurs at Rheingonheim (Ulbert 1969, Taf 13, No 4). WWR, 70/16, 78/11, 33, 57, F2807, military

JN1.12 with everted lid-seat rim. This form was rare and less well defined, occurring only as fragmentary rims. It is possible that some were fragments from two-handled flagons rather than narrow-necked jars. WWO, 72/14, military

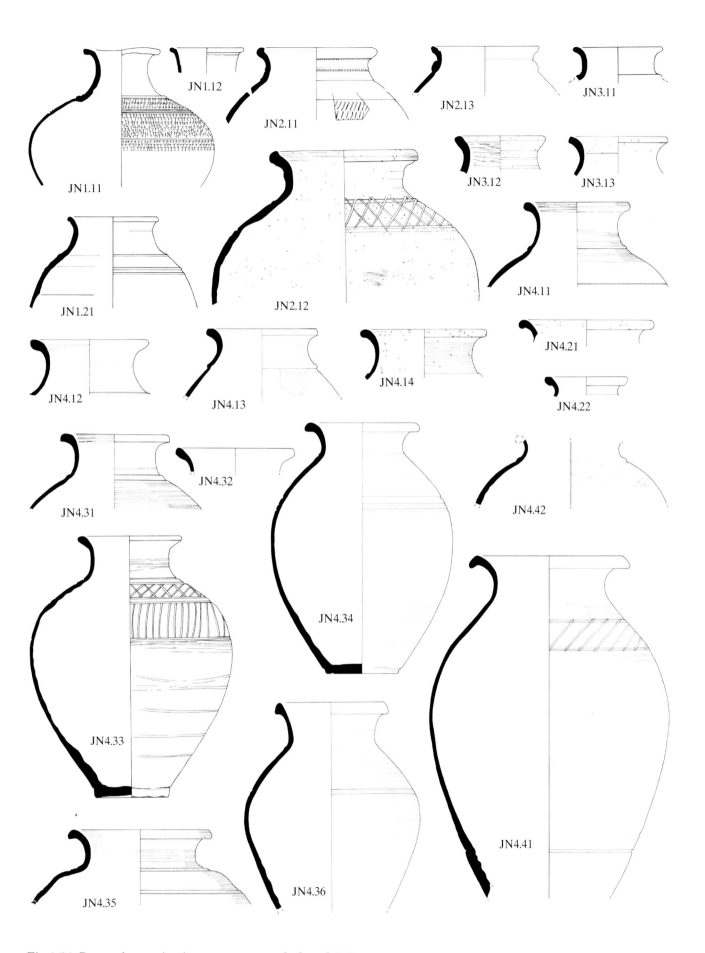

Fig 4.56 Pottery form series: jars – narrow-mouthed; scale1:4

JN1.2
JN1.21 with beaded rim. The cordoning suggests a
Gallo-Belgic derivation. CREAM, 84/244, 216, military

JN2 Jar forms in the Severn Valley ware tradition
(Fig 4.56)
JN2.1 Lid seated rims
JN2.11 Faiers notes: 'the fine workmanship and care-
ful execution of the pattern, together with the rounded
vessel form and slightly hooked inward rim may put
this vessel in the second century rather than later.'
SVO,83/530, 85/112, WR 2.3
JN2.12 larger storage jar. AD 120–70 (Gillam 1970,
No 28). SVORGO,90/179, P 2.3
JN2.13 with short neck and wide cordon. SVO, 58/3,
BP3.2; 36/10, BP 3.1

JN3 Simple out-turned rim, late first to mid
second century (Fig 4.56)
JN3.11 WWO, 12/39, F2229, 1.3
JN3.12 late first to mid second century (Webster 1976,
A2). SVOF, with wipe marks inside rim, 92/4, C 2.4
JN3.13 late first to mid second century (Webster 1976,
A2). SVOF, 35/3, C 2.4

JN4 Thickened rims (Fig 4.56)
JN4.1 Slightly beaded rims, probably late first-mid second century (Webster 1976A2).
JN4.11 groove on shoulder, burnished. SVO, *natatio*
infill, C 3.1, KG 14
JN4.12 Severn Valley ware form *cf* Webster 1976 no 3,
mid first-second century, possibly lasting into third
century. WWO, 35/4, C2.2
JN4.13 SVR, 49/50, 51, BP 3.1, KG 18
JN4.14 (*cf* Webster 1976 A5), second-early third century. SVORGO, 84/63; 83/534, WR 2.3

JN4.2 Pronounced bead rims
JN4.21 probably second-early third century (Webster
1976, A5). SVORGO, 85/221, WR 2.3
JN4.22 WWR, 10/6, C2.2

JN4.3 Out-curving, near triangular rims
JN4.31 SVO, *natatio* infill, C 3.1, KG 14
JN4.32 SVOF, 98/98, F930, P 3.2, KG 17
JN4.33 second to early third century (Webster 1976).
?SVR 84/52, WR 2.3
JN4.34 burnished rim, second to fourth century
(Webster 1976, A4/5). SVO, 59/13, BP 3.2
JN4.35 grooves on neck and shoulder, burnished.
SVO/WWO, *natatio* infill, C 3.1, KG 14
JN4.36 pronounced triangular rim, second to fourth
century (Webster 1976, A4/5). SVO, 98/60, F766, P
3.1, KG 17

JN4.4 Hooked (undercut) rims, second to third century
(Webster 1976, A6)
JN4.41 decorative band of diagonal burnish. SVO,
48/17, BP4

JN4.42 cordon and band of burnished intersecting
arcs. Distinguished by short neck. SVO, 98/12, P 4

JN4.5 Sub-pulley rims (Fig 4.57)
JN4.51 (Webster 1976, no 1). SVOF, 29/5, C 2.3
JN4.6–8 Pulley-rims with short to medium necks.
Broadly third to fourth century (Webster 1976 A9–13)

JN4.6 Two beads of near equal size
JN4.61 with decorative frilled cordon. SVO, 58/5, BP
3.2
JN4.62 SVO, 98/2, P 4
JN4.63 SVOF, 98/20, P 3.4A, KG 25

JN4.7 Lower bead more pronounced
JN4.71 third to fourth century (Webster 1976 A9).
SVO, 98/98, F930, P 3.2, KG 17
JN4.72 SVO, 98/2, P 4

JN4.8 Frilled pulley rims
JN4.81 SVO, 90/128, F736, P 3.1, KG 17
JN4.82 this vessel is included here on typological
grounds, although as a face pot it is very unusual in the
assemblage and presumably had a more specialised
function than the other jars in this category. WWO,
84/52, WR 2.3
Gillian Braithwaite writes:
The position of the face on the girth of the vessel is
normally an early feature, as the second century
face-pots in the civilian zone have the face on the
shoulder or just below the rim. Face-pots do not seem
to have been adopted into the civilian repertoire in the
west of England once the army had left.

JM JARS: MEDIUM MOUTH (Figs 4.57–4.61)

Jars with a neck and mouth neither markedly narrower
nor markedly wider than the maximum girth of the
vessel.

JM1 Neckless jars with simple everted rims, usually rusti-
cated (Fig 4.57)
JM1.1 Smaller jars/beakers
JM1.11 burnished. WWR, 84/52, WR 2.3
JM1.12 with linear rustication. WWOC, 84/48, WR
3.1
JM1.13 burnished with a black slip. WWR, 85/127,
WR 2.1

JM1.2
JM1.21 with barbotine dots under shoulder grooves,
first century (as Darling 1976, 351). WWR, 50/10, C
2.2
JM1.22 with rusticated knobs. A few examples first
appear in early military contexts, although these may
be intrusive as the form is much commoner in later
military contexts. Residual in this context. WWRF,
3/18, F2162. C 3.2, KG 22
JM1.23 with rusticated knobs, WWR, 98/84, P 2.1

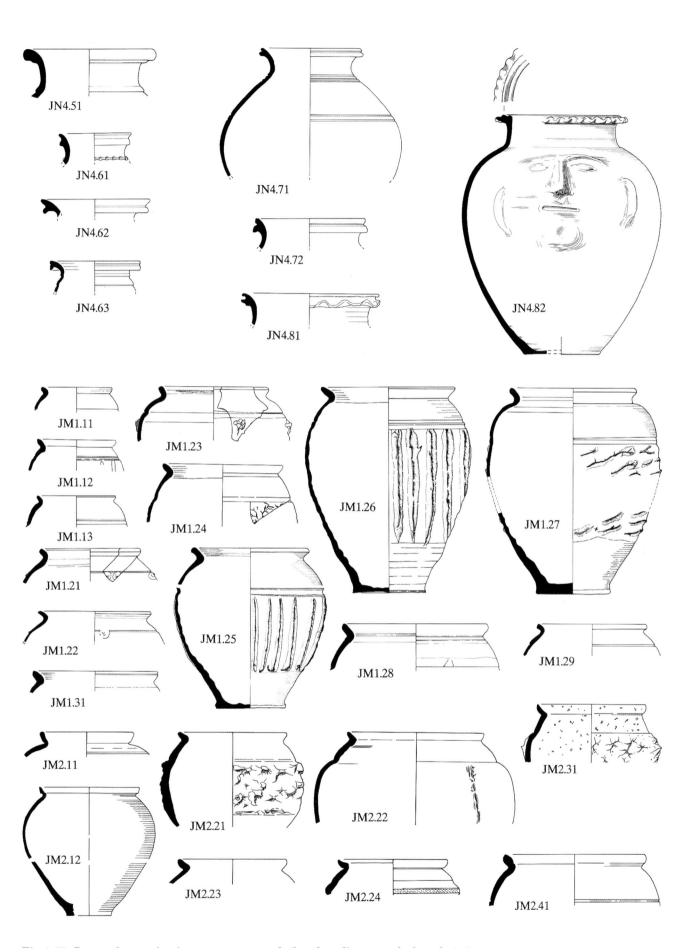

Fig 4.57 Pottery form series: jars – narrow-mouthed and medium-mouthed; scale 1:4

JM1.24 with black slip, burnished on the shoulder with spider rustication under shoulder groove. Late first to early second century. WWR,83/534, WR 2.3

JM1.25 with vertical linear rustication under groove on shoulder. Late first to early second century (*cf* Thompson 1958). WWR, 84/48, 49, WR3.1; 84/45, WR 4

JM1.26 with vertical linear rustication under groove on shoulder. Late first to early second century (*cf* Thompson 1958). WWR, 83/536, WR 2.1

JM1.27 with slanted linear rustication under double groove on shoulder. WWR, 84/48, 49, WR 3.1; 84/52, WR 2.3

JM1.28 WWR/O, 84/52, WR 2.3

JM1.29 WWR, 98/87, P 2.3

JM1.3 With slight external angle
JM1.31 WWR/O, 84/52, WR 2.3

JM2 Jars with everted cup or lid-seated rims, usually rusticated (Fig 4.57)
These are the only military forms associated with rustication. The form is burnished inside and on the rim and shoulder. Darling notes that at Lincoln burnishing associated with rustication is usually associated with later, at least Trajanic, vessels.

JM2.1
JM2.11 WWR? 35/48, military
JM2.12 WWRF, 92/61, 72, military

JM2.2
JM2.21 GREY, 81/15, military; 81/22 F3050, C 3.3
JM2.22 GREY, 63/15, 18, 19, F2287, 1.3
JM2.23 WWRF, 41/6, military
JM2.24 GREY, 84/292, military

JM2.3
JM2.31 SVR, 91/210, military

JM2.4
JM2.41 WWR, 91/94, WR 2.3

JM3 Globular jars with thickened everted rims (Fig 4.58)
JM3.1
JM3.11 GREY, 84/296, military
JM3.12 with black slip, burnished on shoulder. MALVW, 98/68, P 2.3
JM3.13 with wipe marks behind rim. WWR, 84/52, WR 2.3
JM3.14 WWR, 86/16,23, WR 3.1
JM3.15 WWR, 84/48,49, WR 3.1; 84/52, WR 2.3
JM3.16 mica-coated with pushed out bosses. Parallel at Brockley Hill dated AD 70–130 (Castle and Warbis 1973, fig 6, no 87). WWO(F?), C 2.3

JM3.2
JM3.21 with burnished horizontal lines on body below double shoulder groove. Distorted, waster or 'second'. Probably second century (*cf* Webster 1977, fig 11.2. no

33 from Balmuidy; Webster 1976, no 16). WWR, 84/52, WR 2.3
JM3.22 WWR, 29/8, C 2.3
JM3.23 WWO? (with infrequent white inclusions), 83/533, WR2.3

JM3.3
JM3.31 WWR, 75/2, C 2.1

JM3.4 Bead rim and very short neck
JM3.41 one of the main early types, similar to Camulodunum 267 (Hofheim, Ritterling 87). WWR, 91/182, 1.2

JM3.5
Darling notes that only a single rim occurs in the early military period, although the form is commoner in later military contexts.
JM3.51 WWR, 12/42, military
JM3.52 WWR, 6/73, F2208, 1.3
JM3.53 WWR, 7/58, military
JM3.54 mis-shapen rim, second or waster, WWR, 10/6, C 2.2
JM3.55 WWRF, 6/73, F2208, 1.3; 12/42, military
JM3.56 WWR, 35/3 C 2.4

JM3.6
JM3.61 WWR, 78/57, military
JM3.62 WWR, 70/51, military
JM3.63 WWR, 77/2, C 2.2
JM3.64 WWR, 50/52, military
JM3.65 WWR, 81/8, F3044, C 2.2
JM3.66 WWR, 78/57, military

JM3.7
JM3.71 WWR, 80/245, military
JM3.8 Leaf-shaped rim
JM3.81 a fairly common type a few examples of which first appear in early military contexts although these may be intrusive as the form is much commoner in later military contexts. WWRF, 92/72, military
JM3.82 with knife or straw marks on rim. WWR, 4/33, C 2.2

JM4 Globular jars with short everted rims (Fig 4.58)
JM4.1 Sharply everted rims
JM4.11 WWR, 49/166, BP 2.2
JM4.12 second century onwards (similar to Webster 1976, fig 4.15). Fine, hard, light grey, micaceous fabric. 97/137, P 2.2
JM4.13 WWR, 84/154, WR 2.3
JM4.14 WWR, 85/215, WR 2.3

JM4.2 Rim flattened at tip
JM4.21 GREY, 77/2, C 2.2
JM4.22 WWO, 84/79, military
JM4.23 WWO, 84/79, military
JM4.24 GREY, 98/141, 1.3
JM4.25 WWR, 44/14, military

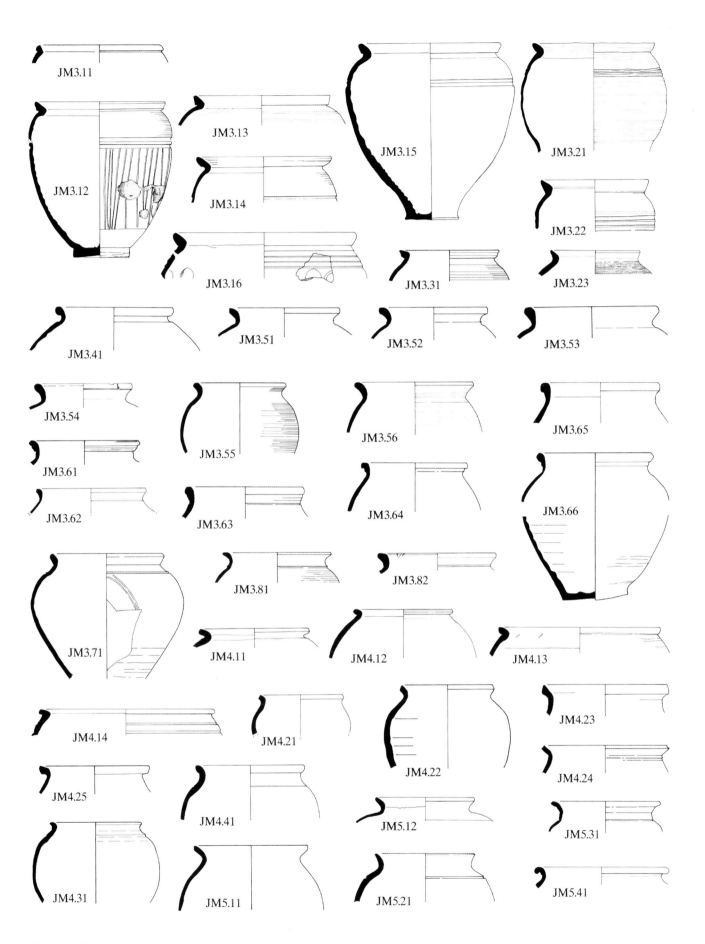

Fig 4.58 Pottery form series: jars – medium-mouthed; scale 1:4

JM4.3 Stubby rounded rim
JM4.31 WWO? 12/42, military

JM4.4
JM4.41 WWO, 90/253, 1.2

JM5 Globular jars with fine everted rims (Fig. 4.58)
JM5.1
JM5.11 WWR, 73/24, military
JM5.12 with burnished-black slip. WWR, 92/4, C 2.4

JM5.2
JM5.21 WWOF, 97/156, 1.3

JM5.3
JM5.31 WWO, 81/15, military

JM5.4
JM5.41 WWR, 4/22, C 2.2

JM6 Insloping neck (Fig 4.59)
JM6.1 Rounded rim and cordoned neck
JM6.11 WWR? 50/52, military
JM6.12 GREY, 78/5, military
JM6.13 rounded rim variant. WWR, 10/24, military
JM6.14 rounded rim variant. WWR, 35/3, C 2.4
JM6.15 rounded rim variant. WWO, 84/182, F339, WR 2.1
JM6.16 rounded rim variant. WWR, 98/68, P 2.3

JM6.2 Angular rim
JM6.21 WWO, 67/21, 28, military
JM6.22 WWO, 70/16, military
JM6.23 WWR, 6/73, F2208, 1.3
JM6.24 WWR, 90/247, military

JM6.3 Hooked rim
JM6.31 WWR, 81/15, military
JM6.32 WWR, 70/16, 72/34, military
JM6.33 WWO, 7/54, military

JM6.4
JM6.41 WWR, 35/15,19, F2260, 1.3
JM6.42 WWR, 92/62, military
JM6.43 WWO, 91/94, WR 2.3
JM6.44 WWO/R, 91/193, military
JM6.45 WWR, 35/48, military
JM6.46 WWR, 9/30,31, military
JM6.47 WWR, 85/21, WR 2.3
JM6.48 WWR, 91/240, military

JM7 Short necked jars with variously thickened rims
(Figs 4.59–4.60)
JM7.1 Near rectangular rims
JM7.11 WWR, 35/15,19, F2260, 1.3
JM7.12 WWR, 41/6, 14/31, military

JM7.2 Squat thickened rim.
JM7.21 WWR, 84/230, military.

JM7.22 blackened internally. WWO(F), 84/62, WR 2.3.
JM7.23 WWR, 50/15, military

JM7.3 Large jars with near rectangular rims
JM7.31 WWO, 73/25,45, military
JM7.32 WWO, 84/251, military
JM7.33 WWR, 75/16, military

JM7.4 Rounded bead rim
JM7.41 WWR, 9/17, C 2.2
JM7.42 WWR, 90/128, F736, P 3.1, KG 16

JM7.5 Elongated bead rims
JM7.51 WWR, 72/67, 69, 96, military
JM7.52 WWR, 78/57, military
JM7.53 WWR, 72/19, military
JM7.54 WWR, 78/57, military
JM7.55 WWR, 78/10, 11, 33, military
JM7.56 WWO, 39/20, military
JM7.57 WWR, 78/57, military
JM7.58 WWR, 78/57, military
JM7.59 WWR, 80/201, military

JM7.6 Rounded lower rim
JM7.61 WWO, 77/9, military
JM7.62 WWO, 72/19, military
JM7.63 WWR? 77/9, military
JM7.64 WWR, 77/9, military

JM7.7 Angular rim
JM7.71 WWR, 30/52, military
JM7.72 WWO, 83/516, WR 2.2
JM7.73 SVOF, 84/58, WR 2.2

JM7.8 Near triangular rims
JM7.81 WWR, 72/48,67, military
JM7.82 WWO, 44/32, military
JM7.83 WWR, 39/22, military
JM7.84 WWR, 39/20, military
JM7.85 WWR, 52/17, military
JM7.86 WWR, 92/4, C 2.4
JM7.87 WWO, 39/20, military
JM7.88 WWR, 67/22, military

JM7.9 Triangular rims
JM7.91 WWR, 72/14, 67, 114, 120, military
JM7.92 WWR, 73/45, military
JM7.93 WWR, 80/201, military
JM7.94 WWR, 72/19, military
JM7.95 WWR, 73/45, military

JM8 Hooked rims (Fig 4.61)
JM8.1
JM8.11 WWR, 14/37, military
JM8.12 WWR, 39/26, military
JM8.13 WWO, 7/54, military
JM8.14 WWO, 45/15, military
JM8.15 WWR, 70/85, military

JM8.2 Heavy rim
JM8.21 WWO, 85/215, WR 2.3

JM9 Lid-seated rims (Fig 4.61)
JM9.1
JM9.11 WWO, 7/58, military

JM9.2
JM9.21 WWR, 78/16, military

JM9.3
JM9.31 WWR, 12/42, military

JM9.32 WWOF, 92/61, military
JM9.33 WWOF, 98/137, 1.3; 98/204, 1.2
JM9.34 WWOF, 98/171, 1.2
JM9.35 WWR, 91/94, WR 2.3

JM9.4
JM9.41 WWR, 50/52, military

JM10 Miscellaneous jars (Fig 4.61)
JM10.1
JM10.11 (Hartley and Webster 1974, fig 4, No 18).
WWOC, 83/512, 83/529, WR 2.3

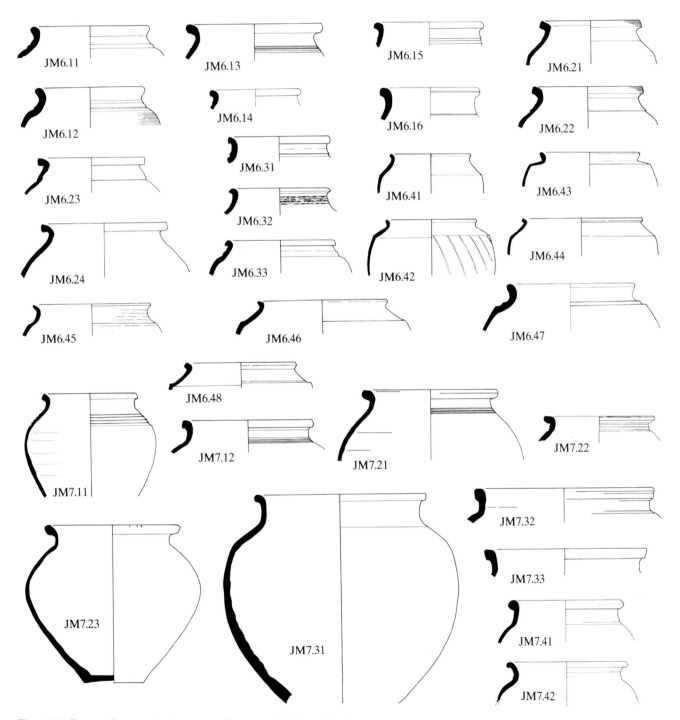

Fig 4.59 Pottery form series: jars – medium-mouthed; scale 1:4

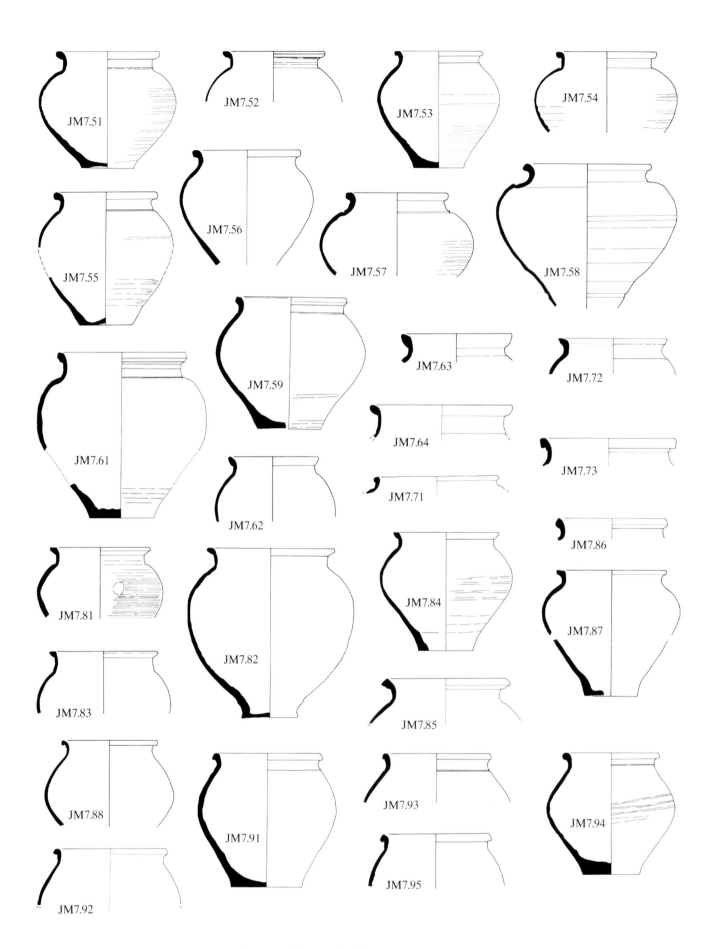

Fig 4.60 Pottery form series: jars – medium-mouthed; scale 1:4

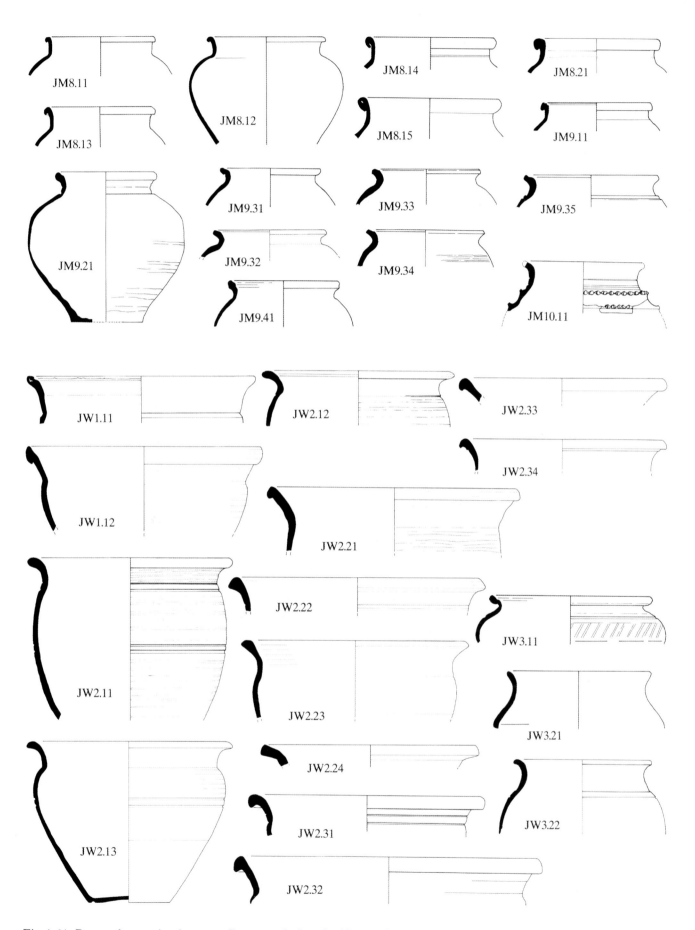

Fig 4.61 Pottery form series: jars – medium-mouthed and wide-mouthed; scale 1:4

JW JARS: WIDE MOUTHED JARS/BOWLS
(Fig 4.61)

It is often difficult to distinguish jars from bowls in this category, particularly where only short vessel profiles survive. The form is characterised by a neck or mouth near equal to, or wider than, the maximum girth of the vessel.

JW1 Jars in the Severn Valley ware tradition
JW1.1 With lid-seated rims
JW1.11 no exact parallels in Webster 1976 but C21 has a similar internal lid-seat. SVO, 83/508, WR 3.1
JW1.12 hooked lid-seated rim, burnished. Late third to fourth century (Webster 1976, C28). SVO, 98/20, P 3.4A, KG 25

JW2 Thickened rims
JW2.1 Slightly thickened rims
JW2.11 no exact parallels in Webster 1976 but probably second century. WWO with burnished horizontal lines under shoulder groove, 83/526, WR 2.3.
JW2.12 with near triangular rim. Probably second century (Webster 1977, fig 11.2 no 33 from Balmuidy, or Webster 1976, no 16). SVOF with burnished horizontal lines on body below shoulder groove, 84/52, WR 2.3
JW2.13 SVW, 58/4, 5, 10, BP 3.2

JW2.2 Pronounced thickened rim
JW2.21 bead rim jar with linear burnish, dated by Webster to the mid-to-late second century (Webster 1976, C21). The slacker profile of this example could indicate a later date. SVO? 'SV', 58/4, BP3.2
JW2.22 triangular rim, burnished. Second to third century (Webster 1976, C22). SVO, 90/154, F778, P 3.1, KG 16
JW2.23 near triangular rim. No exact parallels in Webster 1976 but probably second to third century. SVO, 98/60, F766, P 3.1, KG 16
JW2.24 no exact parallels in Webster 1976 but probably second to third century, burnished. WWO, 90/90, F602, P 3.1, KG 16

JW2.3 Hooked (undercut) rim
Late second to late third or fourth century (Webster 1976, C 23–8)
JW2.31 SVO, 90/90,100, F602, P 3.1, KG 16
JW2.32 SVO, 90/90, F602, P 3.1, KG 16
JW2.33 burnished, SVOF, 90/100, F602, P 3.1, KG 16
JW2.34 burnished, SVOF, 90/100, F602, P 3.1, KG 16

JW3 Miscellaneous wide-mouthed jars/bowls
JW3.1 High-shouldered bowl or jar with lid-seated rim
JW3.11 GREY, 78/16, military

JW3.2 Plain-rimmed bowl/jar of wide girth
JW3.21 WWO, 84/79, military
JW3.22 hard pink-cream fabric probably imported, 98/87, P 2.3

LARGER STORAGE JARS (Fig 4.62)

Characterised by larger diameters and heavier rims, but will overlap with other jar forms for example JN2.12. Darling notes that such storage jars are extremely rare in the military assemblage and are similarly sparse at Usk.

JLS1 Everted rims
JLS1.1
JLS1.11 MALVH, 47/15, *natatio* Infill, C 3.1, KG 14

JLS2 Jars with thickened rims
JLS2.1 Simple out-turned or slightly beaded rim
JLS2.11 a common Severn Valley ware type, probably late first to mid second century (Webster 1976, fig 1.2). SVR, 90/232, military

JLS2.2 Near triangular rim
JLS2.21 SVOF, 84/81, F364, WR 2.1, KG 4

JLS2.3 Thickened, triangular rim
JLS2.31 WWR, 90/220, military

JLS2.4 Shelly ware hooked rim type
JLS2.41 CALC, 98/12, P 4

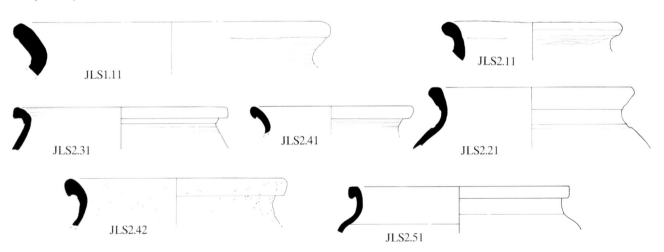

Fig 4.62 Pottery form series: larger storage jars; scale 1:4

JLS2.42 CALC, 90/47, P 3.6, KG 25

JLS2.5 Hooked rim
JLS2.51 WWO, 92/61, 65, 89, military

C CUPS (Fig 4.63)

C1 Campanulate cups, imitating samian Dr 27

Copies of this samian form are relatively common in Britain, but mainly on sites starting in the Flavian period or later. The form does not occur at Usk, Kingsholm, Gloucester or Exeter. The only other site with possible early production of this form is Fishbourne (form 50) where, out of twenty-six examples, only three are dated to the period after AD 75 (Cunliffe 1971, fig 87). There is considerable variation in form and detail in the copies of this form, the Wroxeter examples being arguably closer to the samian originals than many, as at Fishbourne, Caerleon, Colchester, Richborough, London, Holt, Templeborough, Brough-on-Humber and Silchester. The list is not exhaustive but indicates that any attempt to date these cups on typological grounds is doomed.

Copies are infrequent on the continent, and while rare examples occur at Holdeurn, in Switzerland and on the Danube, none occur in the large assemblage at Neuss. As with many samian imitations, these cups are copied in types of *terra nigra* at Aislingen and Burghofe

as well as Nijmegen. Why this form was chosen at Wroxeter rather than the form Dr 24 copied at Usk, Lincoln and Longthorpe is important to gauge for the interpretation of the assemblage from pit F2807 (military phase), and the individual pottery types, many of which are associated by fabric, technique and condition. Since the samian Dr 24 seems unlikely to have survived long after the Neronian period, the copies of Dr 27 may indicate a Flavian date for the group.

C1.1 Flat out-turned rim
C1.11 WWO, 78/57, military
C1.12 WWO, 78/57, military
C1.13 WWR, 78/57, military
C1.14 WWO, 78/57, military
C1.15 WWO, 78/57, military

C1.2 Thickened out-turned rim
C1.21 WWO, 78/33,57, military

C1.3 Cornice-type rim
C1.31 WWR, 7/57, military
C1.32 WWO, 78/57, military

C2 Sub-campanulate cups
C2.1
C2.11 imitation of a *terra nigra* cup copying the Arretine form Loeschcke 7, or perhaps the samian form

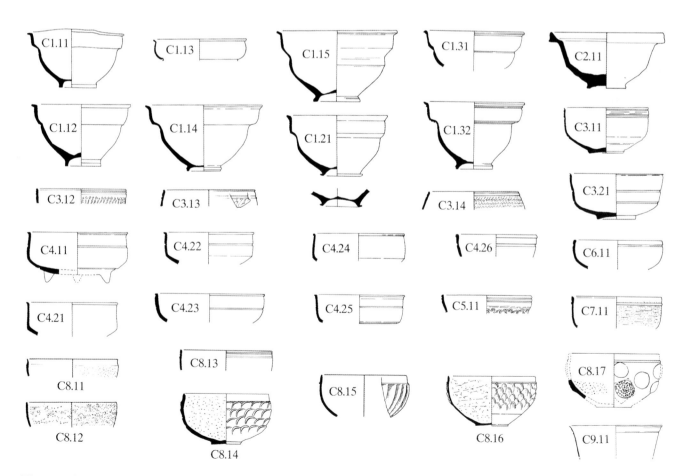

Fig 4.63 Pottery form series: cups; scale 1:4

Ritterling 14. Camulodunum 54 is similar although finer, while Camulodunum 57 is the only local copy. Fishbourne has copies of Loeschcke forms 7 and 8 in local fabric, and types 47. 1–2 are in a fine grey ware with a black micaceous surface (Cunliffe 1971). These are again much finer, thinner-walled vessels. Copies of *terra nigra* vessels are common well into the Flavian period. The source of this vessel is unknown. GREY, 77/9, military

C3–7 Local copies of fineware cups
Found in association with form C1 above suggesting a possible Flavian date.

Similar cups were made in Britain but whereas most of these appear to closely copy Lyon ware types, the more angular profile of the Wroxeter cups is more similar to Italian cups. A more detailed discussion of the form and the significance of its origins will be presented in the military volume (Darling forthcoming).

C3.1 Fineware copies but with differing details of rim moulding and decoration.
C3.11 WWR, 78/57, military
C3.12 WWRF, 98/196, military
C3.13 WWRF, 98/145, F1017, P 3.1, KG 16
C3.14 WWOF, 91/307, military

C3.2 Fineware copy with more angular profile and body grooves
C3.21 WWR, 78/57, military

C4 Tripod cups
Slightly resembling the Lyon tripod vessels, which appear to be the inspiration behind the rare copies in Britain, for example at Usk (Greene 1993, type 24, 11 examples), although these usually have a more rounded profile (but see Kingsholm, Darling 1985b, fig 26, no 520). The type in coarseware does not occur at the Magdalensberg or Sutri, although the angular wall suggests Italian influence.

C4.1
C4.11 WWRF, 72/16,21, military
C4.2/3.2 Possible tripod cups. Vessels similar to type 3.2 but which may have originally been tripod vessels.
C4.21 WWOF, 67/17, military
C4.22 CREAM, G/34, military
C4.23 WWR, G/34, military
C4.24 WWOF, 80/198, military
C4.25 WWR, 93/3, military
C4.26 WWR, 78/57, military

C5 Local copy with rouletted decoration
C5.1
C5.11 with rouletted decoration. No parallels have been traced for the single fragment of this form, but technically it aligns with the other decorated cups C3.1. WWRF, 39/18, military

C6 Squat rounded hemispherical
C6.1
C6.11 WWR, G34, military

C7 Imitation Lyon ware vessel
C7.1
C7.11 with rough-cast decoration. WWRF, 67/22, military

C8 Imported fineware cups
C8.1
C8.11 roughcast cup. CGCC, 98/172, 1.1
C8.12 roughcast cup. LYON, 4/33, C 2.2
C8.13 plain with moulded rim. LYON, 6/31, C 2.2
C8.14 scale decorated cup. LYON, 78/9, military
C8.15 ribbed cup. LYON, unstratified
C8.16 scale decorated cup. LYON, 92/65, 77, military
C8.17 with applied raspberry roundels. LYON, 12/27, C 2.2

C9 Flared-wall hemispherical? cup
C9.1
C9.11 CREAM eggshell, 92/34, C 2.3

B BOWLS (Figs 4.64–4.69)
Bowls and dishes are broadly classified using the following criteria: bowls having a height more than one-third of, but not greater than the diameter, and dishes having a height less than one-third of but greater than one-seventh of the diameter. There is inevitably some overlap between these two vessel classes, however, as there is between dishes and platters.

B1 Carinated bowls with cupped, moulded rims, copying samian form 29 (Fig 4.64)
B1.1 Squat thickened rims
B1.11 with rouletting. WWO, 6/73, F2208, 1.3; 70/16; 78/10, 15, 17, military
B1.12 with rouletting. WWO, 73/44, military

B1.2 More internally concaved with external mouldings
B1.21 late first to early second century. WWOC, 92/4, C 2.4
B1.22 undecorated. WWO, 72/9, 70/16, military
B1.23 late first to early second century with rouletting *cf* Caersws 263, 275 (Webster 1989). WWOC, 84/46, 48 WR 3.1
B1.24 slack profile. SVOF, 98/101, F855, P 3.1, KG 16
B1.25 rouletted. WWOC, with white slip, 59/8, BP 3.2

B2 Flared wall, low carinated bowls, with rims developing from simple undifferentiated through thickened slightly angular (Fig 4.64).
Darling notes that these are decorated carinated bowls rather than imitations of samian form Dr 29, many from Period 2 contexts being cream-slipped.

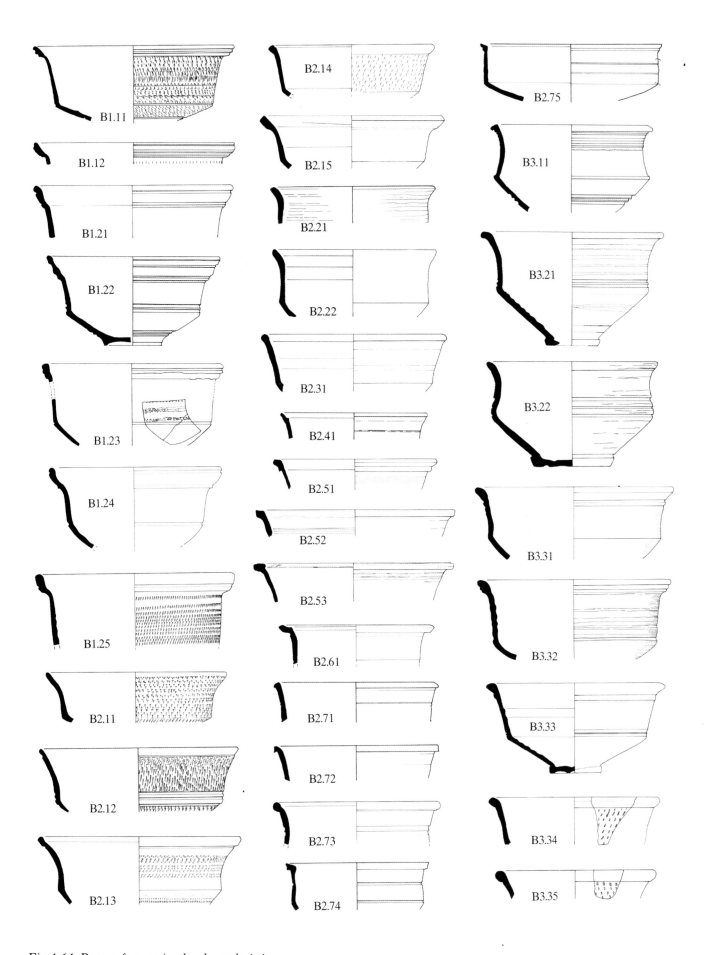

Fig 4.64 Pottery form series: bowls; scale 1:4

B2.1 Simple rims and concave walls
B2.11 rouletted. WWO, 98/131, military
B2.12 rouletted. WWRF? 12/27, C2.2; 92+, C 4; 74/6, military
B2.13 WWO, 84/78,142,206,209,217, military
B2.14 WWR, 85/105, WR 2.3
B2.15 WWO, 83/515, WR 2.3

B2.2 Simple everted rim carinated bowls
B2.21 with a burnished surface. Possibly a carinated vessel, belonging to the later pottery and a different tradition to the other military carinated bowls. Although the only example is from the military demolition phase it may be a contaminant. WWR, 80/238, military
B2.22 *c* AD 85–105, paralleled at Southwark (Williams 1978, 585, 1430). WWO, 83/111, WR 3.1

B2.3 Flared rim carinated bowl
B2.31 slightly beaded rim. WWO, 83/536, WR 2.1

B2.4 Bowl with slightly flaring upper wall and internal lid-seating
B2.41 possibly a carinated vessel. A close parallel was found at Camulodunum (Hawkes and Hull 1947, fig 48, no 16), and continental parallels appear to be confined to the Danubian area for example Aislingen (Ulbert 1959, Taf 6, no 17), Burghofe (Ulbert 1959, Taf 44, no 11) and Lorenzberg (Ulbert 1965, Taf 16, no 11). WWR, 73/27, military

B2.5 Bowls with slightly flared walls and variously thickened rims, probably carinated
B2.51 WWO, 84/58, WR 2.2
B2.52 WWO, 91/92, WR 2.3
B2.53 WWR, 97/133, P 2.3

B2.6 Bowl with flaring upper wall and flat rim with concave upper surface
B2.61 WWO, 84/122, WR 2.1

B2.7 Carinated bowls with slightly flaring upper walls marked by a groove and shaped rims.
B2.71 triangular rim. WWO, 80/201, military
B2.72 slightly hooked rim. WWO, 80/203, military
B2.73 WWO, 81/15, military; 91/68, 1.3
B2.74 WWO, 84/44, WR 2.3
B2.75 WWR, 98/131, military

B3 Bowls with a mid-way carination and slightly concave upper walls (Figs 4.64 and 4.65)
B3.1
B3.11 the only military vessel in the Wroxeter fabric for which a native British derivation might be claimed. It is closely similar to an isolated unstratified find from Camulodunum (Hawkes and Hull 1947, pl LII,A). Its angular appearance suggests the imitation of a metal form, and similar vessels occur in the Aylesford-Swarling culture, but with pedestal bases. The form may be expected to occur in late La Tène

contexts in Gaul, and the significance of the single vessel for the Wroxeter assemblage is uncertain. WWR, 70/16, 72/134, 78/17, military

B3.2 As 3.1 but with less angular carination
B3.21 burnished. WWR, 84/52, WR 2.3
B3.22 burnished lattice decoration. GREY 'RW grey', 98/81, F804, P 3.1, KG 16

B3.3 Bowls with less concave upper walls, lower carination and thickened rims
B3.31 burnished black slip on outer and inner surfaces. WWR, 88/8,84/48, 52, WR 3.3
B3.32 burnished black slip on outer surface. WWR, 35/8, C 2.2
B3.33 WWO, 83/534, WR 2.3
B3.34 WWR, 85/112, WR 2.3
B3.35 WWO, 84/20, WR 3.3

B3.4
Bowls with low carination and tall flaring walls
B3.41 WWO, with brown colour-coat, 92/15, C 3.2
B3.42 rouletted. WWOC, with cream slip externally, 49/46, BP 3.1, KG 18
B3.43 burnished black slip on outer and inner surfaces. WWR, 90/179, P 2.2

B4 Flared wall bowls with beaded rims and slack body carination (Fig 4.65)
A distinct military type with no close parallels in Britain and probably a continental form perhaps from the Danubian area.

B4.1
B4.11 WWR, 72/19, military
B4.12 WWR, 78/57, military
B4.13 WWR, 78/57, military
B4.14 WWR, 78/57, military

B5 Short flared upper rim and rounded lower body (Fig 4.65)
B5.1 Slackly carinated body
B5.11 WWR, 90/204, F951, P 2.2
B5.2 rounded body
B5.21 SVOF, 98/101, F855, P 3.1, KG 16
B5.22 WWO, 83/526, WR 2.3

B6 Shallow curved wall bowls (Fig 4.65)
B6.1 Incurving rims
B6.11 NVCC, 90/5, P 3.5, KG 25
B6.12 second century, similar vessel from Sandy, Bedfordshire (Dix and Aird 1983 fig 22.19). WWO, burnt black over half of surface. 83/111, 104, WR 3.1

B6.2 Hemispherical bowls with simple upright rims
B6.21 Grey 'RW' 49/50, 51, BP 3.1, KG 18

B6.3 Slight groove on top of rim
B6.31 WWO, 49/51, BP 3.1, KG 18

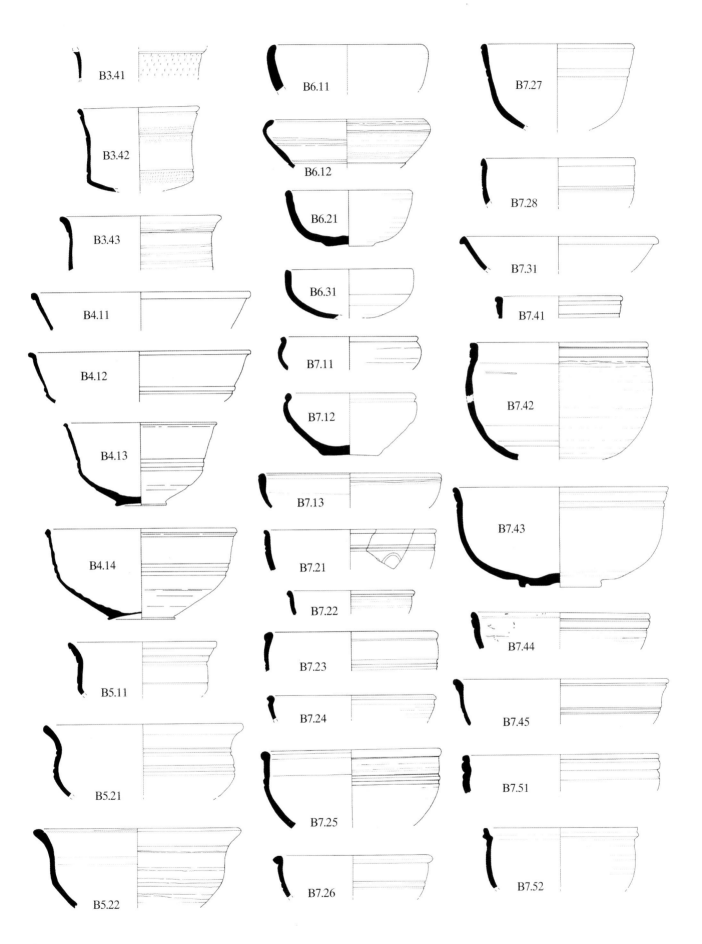

Fig 4.65 Pottery form series: bowls; scale 1:4

B7 Hemispherical bowls with bead rims (Fig 4.65)
B7.1 Shallow bowls with in-turned mouths
B7.11 WWOF, 97/212, F956, 1.1
B7.12 SVOF, 90/205, F800, P 3.1, KG 16
B7.13 possibly oval in shape, AD 80–120, (*cf* Gillam 1970, 324 and Webster 1976, fig 10.71). WWO, 83/536, WR 2.1

B7.2 Open-mouthed bowls reminiscent of samian forms Dr 37, a form current from the mid-late first to late second century, continuing to be copied after this date in colour-coated wares.
B7.21 with cream slip circles on body. SVRF, 90/161, P 3.3; 98/52, P 2.3
B7.22 Severn Valley ware form, mid first to second century possibly lasting into third century (Webster 1976, 3). SVRF
B7.23 WWR, 8/16, F2136, C 2.4
B7.24 WWO, 97/154, P 2.1
B7.25 copy of samian form Dr 37. WWO, 84/48, WR 3.1; 84/49, WR 3.1; 84/55, WR 2.3
B7.26 with multiple horizontal grooves. WWO, 90/100, F602, P 3.1, KG 16
B7.27 SVO, 48/65, BP 3.1
B7.28 SVO, 98/20, P 3.4A, KG 25

B7.3 Shallow open mouthed bowls copying samian form 31
B7.31 Young (1977) form C45 with bead rim, dated *c* AD 270–400+. OXFRCC, 98/12, P 4

B7.4 Bowls with double bead-rims
B7.41 CREAMF, 84/137, WR 2.1
B7.42 WWO, 83/534, WR 2.3
B7.43 WWO, 84/64, F203, WR 2.2
B7.44 WWR, 83/536, WR 2.1
B7.45 with mica coating. WWO, 83/111, WR 3.1

B7.5 Bowls with double bead rims and internal lid-seat
B7.51 WWO, 97/137, P 2.2
B7.52 hemispherical bowl with double bead rim copying samian Dr 37 (*cf* Young 1977 types C64–66, fig 60). Burnished. SVO? 'SV' 58/9, 10; 59/8,13, BP 3.2

B8 Bowls (or wide mouthed jars) with everted rims (Fig 4.66)
B8.1
B8.11 with a band of 'fluted' decoration and a black-burnished surface. WWRF, 47/17, *natatio* infill, C 3.1, KG 14
B8.12 waisted profile, burnished. SVOF, 90/93, F623, P 3.2, KG 17

B8.2 Short, plain rim
B8.21 similar to types produced in Severn Valley ware dated second-third century (Webster 1976, fig 7.36). Fabric not recorded, 98/101, F855, P 3.1, KG 16
B8.22 with burnished black slip. WWR, 83/534, WR 2.3

B8.3 Flatter rim
B8.31 GREY 'RW' 98/2, P 4

B8.4 Thickened, stubby rim
B8.41 SVO, 58/11, BP 3.2

B9 Flanged-rim bowls with an internal lip, second-third century (Fig 4.66; Webster 1976, type F, fig 8)
B9.1 Thickened-rim
B9.11 SVOF, 90/101, F599, P 3.2, KG 17
B9.12 brown colour-coat. SVO, 80/117, F486, P 3.1, KG 16

B9.2 Groove on rim, broadly similar to Webster 1976 fig 9.51, third century
B9.21 SVO, 98/40, F672, P 3.1, KG 16

B10 Shallow bowl with everted rim (Fig 4.66)
B10.1 Gently everted rim
B10.11 burnished lattice on rim. GREY, 90/48, P 3.4A

B10.2 Flat rim
B10.21 SVOF, 98/98, F930, P 3.2, KG 17

B10.3 Shallow bowl with everted rim up-turned at tip, probably derived from samian form Dr 36/Curle 15.
B10.31 with grey colour-coat and white painted scroll decoration on rim (equivalent of Oxford ware version Young (1977) C50 dated AD 325–400+). NVCC, 90/47, P 3.6, KG 25

B11 High flanged bowl (Fig 4.66)
B11.1
B11.11 WWO, 78/57, military

B12 Segmental bowls, including copies of samian form Dr 38 (Fig 4.66)
B12.1 High flange and in-turning rim
B12.11 WWR, 63/19, F2287, 1.3

B12.2 High flanged rim
B12.21 GREY, 59/8, BP 3.2

B12.3 Flange level with small internal bead
B12.31 WWR, 85/215, WR 2.3
B12.32 WWO, 90/168, P 2.2

B12.4 Low flanged rim
B12.41 mica-dusted internally and externally, OXID/WWO, 98/81, F804, P 3.1, KG 16
B12.42 WWO, 98/62, P 3.3

B12.5 Flange below rim
B12.51 SVO 98/60, F766, P 3.1, KG 16
B12.52 WWO? 'OW' 98/81,78, F804, P 3.1, KG 16

B12.6 Small flange and slight bead rim
B12.61 WWOF, 53/11, military

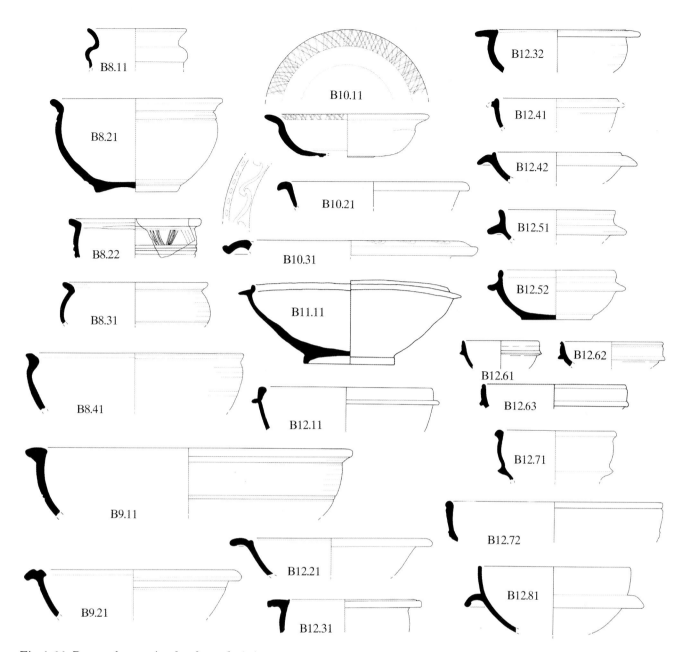

Fig 4.66 Pottery form series: bowls; scale 1:4

B12.62 WWOF, 34/29, military
B12.63 WWOF, 34/37, military

B12.7 Small flange and pronounced bead rim
B12.71 SVO, 59/13, BP 3.2
B12.72 with mica coating (dish). WWO, 83/526, WR 2.3

B12.8 Downcurving flange and plain rim
B12.81 Young type C51 flanged bowl copying Dr 38, the most common Oxfordshire colour-coated type, dated *c* AD 240–400+ (Young 1977, fig 59). OXFR-CC, 98/12, P 4

B13–B17 Reeded-rim bowls (Figs 4.67–4.68)
Darling notes: bowls of this type are extremely diverse and display most of the common variations, the flanges varying in angle, most walls being nearer the rounded than the carinated version. The angle of the wall may yet provide a dating clue to this type of bowl, but with so few stratified in the earlier contexts, there is no basis for clearly defining early and later types of these bowls. B17.2–17.3 are consistently later in their stratified appearance. Also notable is the use of the finer fabric for some of the variants, particularly 17.31–32, suggesting that the function of some of these vessels may have changed.

The general type starts in the Mediterranean, is common in the Rhineland from the Augustan period onwards, and examples still appear in third century contexts. The different development of pottery in Britain lead to its decline by the time of Trajan and it is probably commonest in the Flavian-Trajanic period. It is, however, notable that examples are scarce on early military sites in the Midlands, such as Wall, Baginton and Metchley, although one came from the pit at Mancetter which contained the group of two-handled flagons (Scott 1981, fig 13, no 30).

B13 Bowls with flat reeded-rims (Fig 4.67)
B13.1 Two grooves on rim, distinguished from B13.2 by shallow profile
B13.11 copy of Dr 17/19. WWO, 85/215, WR 2.3

B13.2 Two grooves on rim
B13.21 WWR, 9/30,31, military
B13.22 WWR, 35/48, military
B13.23 late first to early second century. WWO, 85/33, WR 2.3
B13.24 WWR, 98/178, 1.3
B13.25 WWO, 84/395, military
B13.26 WWO, 83/534, WR 2.3
B13.27 black slip externally and inside rim. SVR, 98/101, F855, P 3.1, KG16

B13.3 Two grooves, pronounced inner lip
B13.31 WWR, 52/24, military
B13.32 WWO, 81/5, C 2.2
B13.33 pronounced inner lip. WWR, 84/255, 339, 342, military
B13.34 late first to early second century (*cf* Frere 1987 fig 109.337, AD85–105). WWO, 90/181, P 2.2

B13.4 Two grooves, stubby rim
B13.41 WWR, 85/105, WR 2.3
B13.42 late first to early second century. WWO, burnt 85/112 WR2.3; 85/123, WR 2.1

B13.5 Three grooves, pronounced internal lip
B13.51 WWO, 7/35, military
B13.6 Three grooves
B13.61 WWR, 80/224, military

B14 Bowls with down-turned reeded-rims (Fig 4.67)
B14.1 One groove
B14.11 WWR, 84/244, military
B14.12 WWR/O, 92/4, C 2.4
B14.13 WWR, 51/21, F2990, 1.3

B14.2 Two grooves
B14.21 WWR, 14/37, military
B14.22 WWR, 78/57, military
B14.23 WWO, 81/15, military
B14.24 WWO, 41/6, military
B14.25 WWR, 84/403, military
B14.26 WWR, 50/87, military; 75/2, C 2.1
B14.27 WWR, 78/57, military
B14.28 blackened on rim. WWO, 90/169, P 2.2
B14.29 early second century (Gillam 1970, 215). WWR, 85/33, WR 2.3

B14.3 Three grooves
B14.31 WWO, 83/534, WR 2.3
B14.32 WWO, 70/16, military

B15 Bowls with up-turned reeded-rims (Fig 4.68)
B15.1
B15.11 WWR, 84/251, 252, 85/68, 69, military

B15.12 WWO, 90/220, military
B15.13 WWO, 85/105, WR 2.3
B15.14 WWO, 14/47, 7/61, military
B15.15 WWR, 80/130, F486, P 3.1, KG 16
B15.16 WWOC, 65/29, 30, B 3.1, KG 18

B16 Hemispherical bowls with thickened reeded-rims (Fig 4.68; Webster 1976, type G, fig 9.54–8)
B16.1 Slightly down-turned rim with two grooves
B16.11 WWO, 90/163, F631, P 3.2, KG 17
B16.2 Slightly up-turned rim with two grooves
B16.21 SVO? 'SV' 58/3, 5, BP 3.2

B17 Bowls with everted rims usually with slightly in-sloping necks (Fig 4.68)
B17.1 Down-turned rims
B17.11 WWR, 4/33, C 2.2
B17.12 Dated AD 130–40 (Frere 1984a, fig 118.659). WWR, 91/93 WR 2.3

B17.2 Up-turned rims
B17.21 WWOF, 70/16, military
B17.22 WWR, 98/186, F1073, 1.2

B17.3 Flat rims
B17.31 WWOF, 98/130, 1.2
B17.32 WWOF, 98/130, 1.2
B17.33 WWOF, 98/130, 1.2

B18 Wall-sided bowl with double-bead, lid-seated rim (Fig 4.68)
B18.1
B18.11 Young type P24, painted on the rim and exterior of the carination. The most common Oxfordshire parchment ware type, dated *c* AD 240–400+, though its popularity greatly increased in the fourth century (Young 1977, fig 27). OXFP, unstratified

B19 Bowls with flat thickened rims (Fig 4.68)
B19.1 Rectangular rim
B19.11 WWO 77/2, C 2.2

B19.2 Rim expanded at tip, neck upright or slightly in-sloping
B19.21 WWR, 84/103, F482, WR 2.3, KG 7
B19.22 WWO/R, 86/22, WR 3.1

B20 BB1 type bowls with flat rims (Fig 4.68)
B20.1 Upright walls
B20.11 burnished. WWO, 90/179, P 2.2
B20.12 BB1, 90/204, F951, P 2.2
B20.13 BB1, 90/204, F951, P 2.2
B20.14 BB1, 83/111, WR 3.1
B20.15 BB1, 84/52, WR 2.3

B20.2 Near upright walls
B20.21 BB1, 84/52, WR 2.3
B20.22 BB1, 92/4, C 2.4
B20.23 BB1, 84/52, WR 2.3

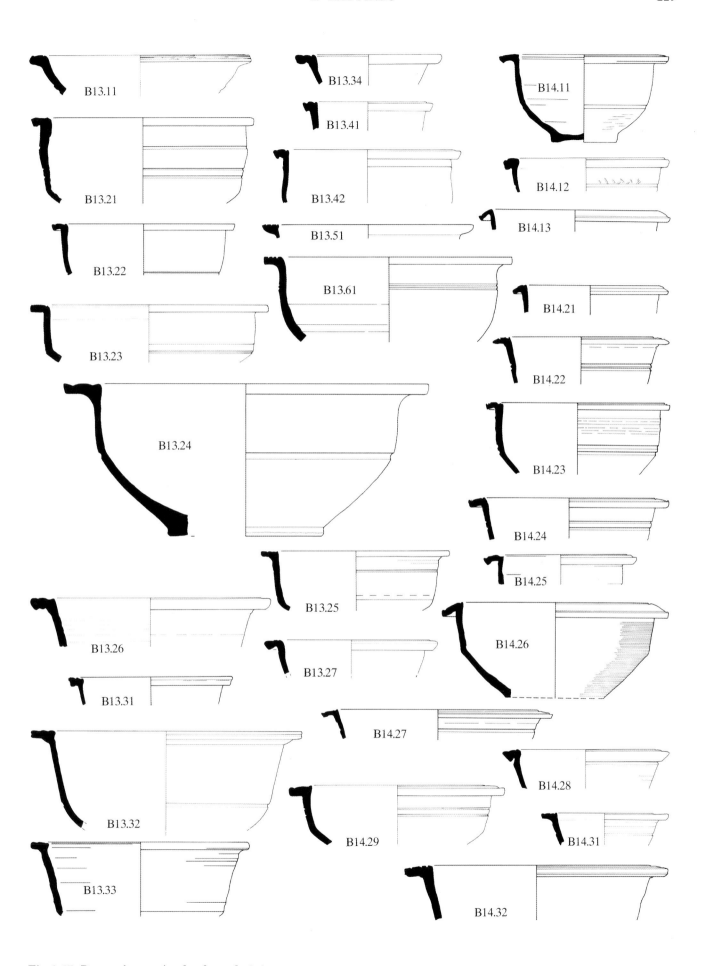

Fig 4.67 Pottery form series: bowls; scale 1:4

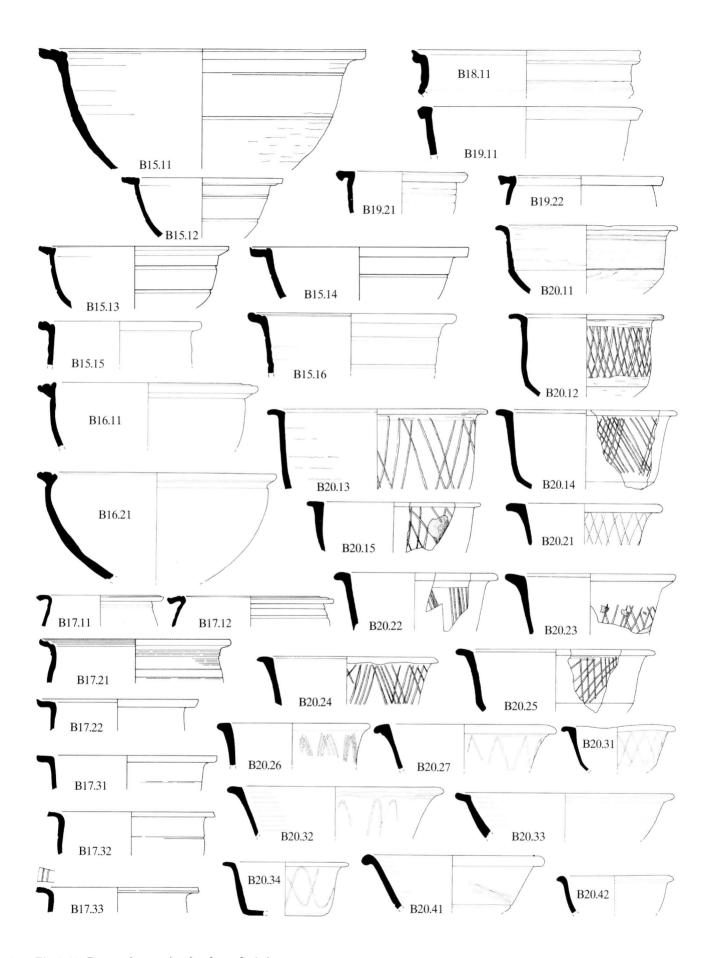

Fig 4.68 Pottery form series: bowls; scale 1:4

B20.24 BB1, 83/114, WR 2.3
B20.25 BB1, 84/52, WR 2.3
B20.26 fabric 'imitation BB1 with large grog inclusions' 98/62, P3.3
B20.27 BB1, 80/119, F466, P 3.1, KG 16

B20.3 Increasingly splayed walls, broadly parallelled at Exeter by south-east Dorset types 39–40, late Antonine to mid third century (Holbrook and Bidwell 1991 109, figs 30 and 31), and south-west Dorset type 60, late second to mid third century (*ibid*, 44, fig 44, Barker form 120).
B20.31 acute cross-hatch burnish, mid-late second century (Gillam 38). BB1, 90/189, 205, F800, P 3.1, KG 16
B20.32 burnished intersecting arcs, mid-late second century (Gillam 39). BB1, 90/141, F736, P 3.1, KG 16
B20.33 WWR, 90/163 F631, P 3.2, KG 17
B20.34 acute cross-hatch burnish, mid-late second century. BB1, 80/117, F486, P 3.1, KG 16
B20.4 Bead rimmed (Barker form 140)
B20.41 diagonal burnished lines. GREY 'RW', 98/2, P 4
B20.42 BB1, 80/115, 117, F486, P 3.1, KG 16

B21 Medium to wide-mouthed jar or bowl with heavy beaded rim (Fig 4.69)
Darling notes of forms B21.11 and 21.12 that no clear parallels have been found in Britain, but they resemble the shouldered jars found in Switzerland and the Danube area, for instance at Vindonissa (Tomasevic 1970, Taf 10, no 2), Aislingen (Ulbert 1959, Taf 4, no 15) and Kempten (Fischer 1957, Taf 5, nos 5 and 7). No parallels have been found in the Rhineland.

B21.1
B21.11 WWR, 4/17, C 2.4
B21.12 WWR, 84/278, military
B21.13 GREY, 84/122, WR 2.1
B21.14 WWR, 9/17 C 2.2
B21.15 WWR, 90/168, P 2.2

B22 Necked globular bowl (Fig 4.69)
B22.1
B22.11 WWR, 92/61, military

B23 BB1 type conical bowls with flat grooved-rims (Fig 4.69)
Although this form is here presented intermediate to flat-rimmed and flanged bowls, in the sequence proposed by Gillam (1976), it has more recently been argued that it is as likely to be an independent residual version of earlier reeded and flanged bowls (Holbrook and Bidwell 1991, 98). Its appearance is dated by Gillam between *c* AD 180 and 210 (Gillam 1976, 67–70), with production continuing until the mid-late third century. Although the form appears in secure late second-century contexts elsewhere, for example Walcot Street, Bath (Owen 1979, fig 44.21) its earliest occurrence at Vindolanda is in a mid third-century context (Bidwell 1985, 176).

B23.1 Bead lower than flange
B23.11 acute lattice cross-hatch burnish. BB1, 58/5, BP 3.2
B23.12 BB1, 97/51, F485, P 3.3
B23.13 late second to early third century. BB1, 97/107, F572, P 3.1, KG 16

B23.2 Bead and flange even height
B23.21 BB1, 98/8, P 3.6, KG 25
B23.22 BB1, 98/98, F930, P 3.2, KG 17 and 98/139, F974, P 3.1, KG 16
B23.23 early-mid third century. BB1, 90/100, F602, P 3.1, KG 16
B23.24 burnished intersecting arcs, late second-early/mid third century. BB1, 98/98, F930, P 3.2, KG 17

B24 BB1 type conical bowls with flanged rims (Fig 4.69; Barker form 160)
Evidence from Exeter confirms Gillam's dating of this form as generally appearing *c* AD 270, although its origin could be up to a quarter of a century earlier than this (Holbrook and Bidwell 1991, 99). At Vindolanda the earliest context for bowls with true flanges is dated no earlier than *c* AD 275 (Bidwell 1985, 177).

B24.1 Flange slightly lower than bead
B24.11 decorated with burnished intersecting arcs (Gillam 43). BB1,98/122, F930, P 3.2, KG 17
B24.12 BB1, 90/100, F602, P 3.1, KG 16

B24.2 Stubby flange markedly lower than bead
B24.21 BB1, 98/20, P 3.4A, KG 25
B24.22 BB1, 98/2, P 4
B24.23 BB1, 98/12, P 4

B24.3 Elongated flange markedly lower than bead
B24.31 BB1, 98/15, P 4

B25 Shelly ware type convex-walled bowls with flanged rims (Fig 4.69; Barker form 170)
B25.1
B25.11 CALC, 96/21, P 3.6, KG 25
B25.12 where flange is broken rilling can be seen to continue underneath. CALC, 98/12, P 4

B26 BB1 type bead-rimmed bowls/dishes (Fig 4.69; Barker form 110)
This form is relatively rare in Dorset but more common in the north, hinting perhaps at a Rossington Bridge source. It appears around the mid second century (pers comm Neil Holbrook).

B26.1 Near upright walls
B26.11 WWR, 84/52, WR 2.3
B26.12 BB1, 98/68, P 2.3
B26.13 BB1, 84/52, WR 2.3
B26.14 BB1, 98/53, F714, P 3.2, KG 17
B26.15 BB1, 80/117, F486, P 3.1, KG 16

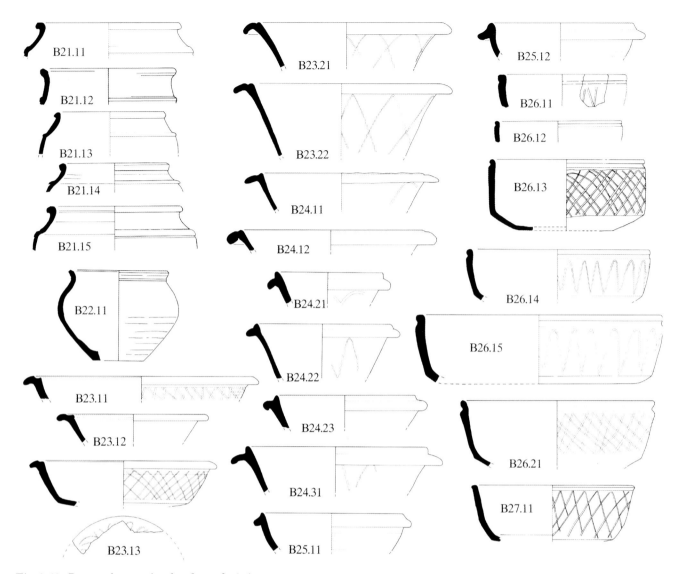

Fig 4.69 Pottery form series: bowls; scale 1:4

B26.2 Increasingly splayed walls
B26.21 acute lattice. BB1, 58/5, BP 3.2

B27 BB1 type bowls with slightly beaded rims
(Fig 4.69)
B27.1
B27.11 AD 125–60 (Gillam 1970, 316). Also parallelled at Verulamium from Antonine II period IIc (Frere 1972, fig 20.730) and Birrens, Antonine 1 (Robertson 1975, fig 70.7). BB1, 86/23, WR 3.1

DISHES (Fig 4.70)

D1 BB1 type dishes with flat out-turned rims (Fig 4.70)
D1.1 Near upright walls
D1.11 BB1, 90/204, F951, P 2.2
D1.2 Slightly spayed walls
D1.21 BB1, 80/147, F564, P 3.1, KG 16
D1.3 Increasingly splayed walls
D1.31 BB1, B/34, F4000, C 2.1, KG 27
D1.32 AD 130+ (*cf* Gillam 1970, 308). BB1, 35/4, C 2.2

D1.33 WWOF 24/21, BP 2.2
D1.4 Markedly splayed walls
D1.41 BB1, 90/204, F951, P 2.2
D1.42 increasingly splayed, decorated with burnished intersecting-arcs. Mid-late second century. BB1, 80/117, F486, P 3.1, KG 16

D2 Dish (Fig 4.70)
D2.2
D2.21 with decorated base, late second to early third century (Holbrook and Bidwell 1991, fig 32 57.4). BB1, 84/48, WR 3.1
D2.22 BB1, 98/60, F766, P 3.1, KG 16
D2.23 BB1, 90/204, F951, P 2.2
D2.24 BB1, 98/2, P 4

D3 BB1 type plain-rimmed dishes (Fig 4.70; Barker form 110)
D3.1 Slightly splayed walls
D3.11 BB1, 98/98, F930, P 3.2, KG 17
D3.12 upright sides decorated with burnished intersecting-arcs, second century. BB1, 90/154, F778, P 3.1, KG 16

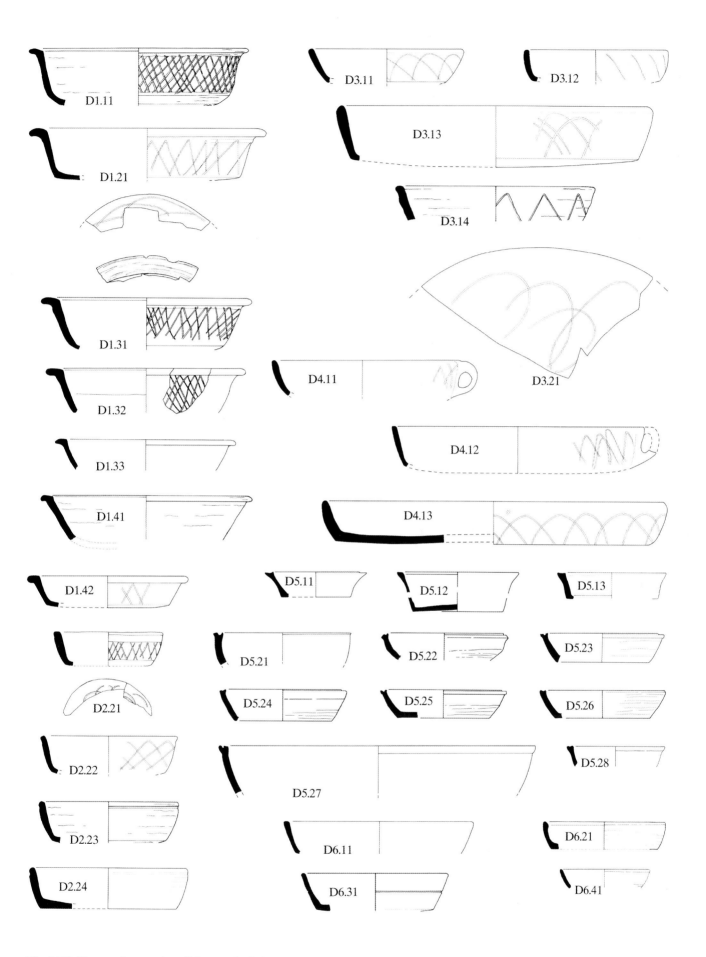

Fig 4.70 Pottery form series: dishes; scale 1:4

D3.13 BB1, 90/205, 98/69, F800, P 3.1, KG 16
D3.14 with flattened rim. BB1, 90/204, F951, P 2.2

D3.2 Increasingly splayed walls
D3.21 BB1, 90/154, F778, P 3.1, KG 16

D4 BB1 type plain-rimmed handled dishes (Fig 4.70;
Barker form 101)
Dishes with one or perhaps two handles, often oval in
shape and dating from the second century to the end
of the BB1 industry (Holbrook and Bidwell 1991,
types 62 and 63 SW/SE Dorset). Symonds (1997)
notes that in the Barker assemblage the form is rarely
decorated, but both examples illustrated here are decorated with intersecting arcs, perhaps indicative of a
chronological change. Smaller fragments without
handles will almost certainly have been categorised as
B27 above.

D4.1
D4.11 BB1, 98/40, F672, P 3.1, KG 16
D4.12 BB1, 98/28, F638, P 3.2, KG 17
D4.13 BB1, 96/21, P 3.6

D5 Dishes with 'bifurcated' or lid-seated rims (Fig 4.70)
D5.1 concave walls
D5.11 WWR, 4/17, C 2.4
D5.12 an unusual bowl or dish. WWR 80/201, military
D5.13 dish or lamp. WWR 92/9, C 2.3

D5.2 As with the copies of Pompeian red ware and
other platters/dishes, surface finish is limited to knife
trimming of the basal area and little else. The rim
diameters are small. The rim form is similar to
Camulodunum 44A but there is no evidence for
footrings on the Wroxeter dishes. The type is known on
Rhineland sites, Neuss (Filtzinger 1972, Taf 37, nos 3,
4; and from the kilns Taf 93, nos 6, 9) and continues
to the later first century as at Domitianic Bad Nauheim
(Simon 1960, Abb 15, nos 7, 8). First occurring in mil-
itary phase 7i, demolition of the rampart, but more
common in Period 1.
D5.21 WWR, 90/232, military
D5.22 WWR, 98/131, military
D5.23 WWR, 98/143, 1.2
D5.24 WWO, 98/141, 1.3
D5.25 WWR, 98/222, 1.2
D5.26 WWR, 98/131, military
D5.27 WWR, 9/29, C 2.2
D5.28 CREAM, 3/21, C 2.1

D6 Dishes/platters (Fig 4.70)
D6.1 Dishes with slightly thickened rim
D6.11 WWO, 90/168, P 2.2

D6.2 Dishes with flat thickened rims (see also Cheese
Press form MCP1.11)
D6.21 AD 80–120 (Gillam 1970, 323). SVO, 84/52,
WR 2.3

D6.3 Straight-sided dishes with very slightly beaded rims
D6.31 WWOF, 34/37, military

D6.4 Convex-sided dishes with very slightly beaded rims
D6.41 SVO, 83/534, WR 2.3

P PLATTERS (Fig 4.71)

Platters are broadly defined as having a height not
greater than one-seventh of the diameter, but overlap
with vessels classified as dishes.

P1 Bead-rimmed
P1.1
P1.11 platter copying an early samian Dr 18 or a
Ritterling 1. No parallels have been traced for the copy-
ing of this form in coarse ware. WWR, 78/57, F2807,
military
P1.12 with slight internal lid-seat. CREAM, 92/4, WR
2.4

*P2 Curved wall platter inspired by Camulodunum 16, a
type also copied at Usk.*
This form is difficult to distinguish from P5.
P2.1
P2.11 fragmentary rim from a *terra nigra* plate, a
Camulodunum 16. The type is one of the few products
of the Gallo-Belgic industry to occur on British military
sites (Rigby 1973). TN, 91/210, military
P2.12 WWOF, 9/22, military; 9/29, C 2.2; 9/30, military

P2.2
P2.21 WWO, 84/216, 248, military

P3
Platter copying Pompeian red ware platters but without
the internal slip noted on copies at Usk. Distinguished
from P5 by a more pronounced moulding at the junc-
tion of wall and base internally.
P3.1
P3.11 WWR, 78/57, military
P3.12 WWO, 98/196, military
P3.13 WWOF, 9/31, military

P4
Copying Pompeian red ware platters but without the
internal slip noted on copies at Usk. Distinguished
from P5 by a more pronounced moulding at the junction of wall and base internally.
P4.1
P4.11 WWOF, 1/59, military

P5
The commonest military platter type, copying
Pompeian red ware platters but often without the inter-
nal slip noted on copies at Usk.
P5.1 Slightly flattened rim, without internal slip
P5.11 WWR, 78/57, military
P5.12 WWR, 78/57, military

P5.13 WWO, 78/57, military
P5.14 WWR, 91/247, military
P5.15 WWO, 77/9, military

5.2 with internal slip
P5.21 PRW, cream fabric with internal slip, unlikely to be an import but source unknown. G/30, military
P5.22 PRW, coarse grey fabric with red cortex and internal slip. Unlikely to be an import but source unknown. 92/20, F154, C 2.1; 85/29, WR2.3; 98/87, P 2.3

P5.3 Local copies
P5.31 WWR? 78/57, military
P5.32 WWRF, 83/530, WR 2.3
P5.33 WWO, 72/14, 24, 34, 67; 75/14, military
P5.34 WWR, 92/18, WR2.1; 92/22 military
P5.35 WWO, 85/215, WR 2.3
P5.36 mid to late first century (Gillam 1970, 336). WWO, 84/178, F339, WR 2.1, KG 5
P5.37 mid to late first century (*ibid*). WWO, 83/536, WR 3.1

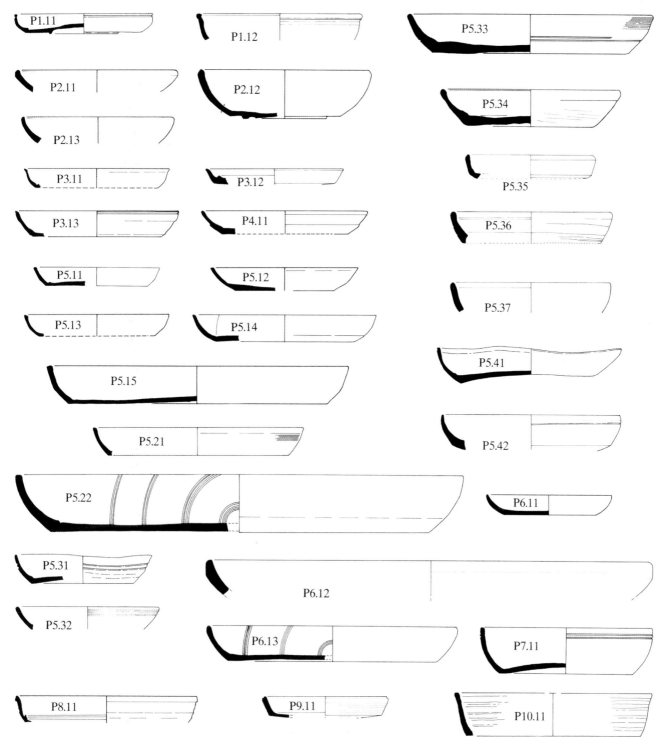

Fig 4.71 Pottery form series: platters; scale 1:4

P5.4 Beaded rim/groove below rim
P5.41 WWO? 78/11, 57, military
P5.42 burnished inside and out with badly made groove on outside under rim, mid to late first century (*ibid*). WWO, 9/17, C 2.2

P6 Imported platters
P6.1
P6.11 PRW3? 84/303, 377, military
P6.12 PRW3 (from earlier excavations)
P6.13 PRW2 92/18, C2.1; 92/61, military

P7
P7.1
P7.11 WWO, 77/9, military

P8
With a pronounced internal moulding at the junction of wall and base.

P8.1
P8.11 cannot be classified as a copy of a definite type, whether samian or otherwise, but fits into the same broad type. WWO, 72/63, military

P9 Bifid rim platter
P9.1
P9.11 WWO, 98/87, P 2.3

P10 Straight-sided dish
P10.1
P10.11 with burnishing both internally and externally. A single vessel only, either a late military form or intrusive. WWOF, 91/230, military

M MORTARIA (Figs 4.72–4.75)

The mortaria have been divided into types according to source; foreign imports, locally produced examples, regional imports and examples of unknown provenance.

Imported Mortaria

M1: Rhone Valley (Fig 4.72)
M1.1 hooked rim forms with the ledge on the top of the rim next to the bead.
M1.11 MORV, 35/61, F2299, 1.3
M1.12 MORV, 14/37, 7/36, military
M1.13 MORV, 91/97, 1.3
M1.14 MORV, 39/13, 1.3

M2: Rhenish? (Fig 4.72)
M2.1: With pronounced bead and hooked flange
M2.11 MORT2, 42/14, military

M2.2
M2.21 Rhineland?/Moselle, unstratified

M3: Gallic mortaria (Fig 4.72)
M3.1 North Gaulish mortaria with hooked flange
M3.11 MONG (Pas de Calais), stamped by the potter CASSARIUS, 51/21, F2990, 1.3

Locally made mortaria

M4 Wall-sided mortaria (Fig 4.72)
Flange turned down against side of vessel, turned out at tip.

The dating of this class of wall-sided mortaria is confined to the Claudio-Neronian period, mostly Claudian. Many of those known in fine cream fabrics without gritting are probably imports and may derive from the Rhineland, for example Neuss (Filtzinger 1972, Tafs 32–3, and 74 from the kilns), although the quantity at Colchester (Hartley 1985, figs 49–50; Camulodunum 191) suggests manufacture there. They are not usually found away from the south-east and south coast, and examples in the Midlands are very rare; one occurred at Metchley (unpublished) in a light red-brown fabric but was otherwise dissimilar to the Wroxeter examples in form and fabric, while another mended with rivets was found at Mancetter (Scott 1981, fig 13, no 35) in a dark cream fabric, probably imported from the south-east. An imported parallel occurred at Usk (Hartley 1993, fig 185, no 1). The form was made in the local fabric WWO, often without trituration grits.

M4.1
M4.11 MWWO, 98/52, P 2.3
M4.12 MWWO, 72/19, military
M4.13 MWWO, the only example to have trituration grits (fine quartz sand), 85/248, military

M5 Hooked rim down-turned at tip (Fig 4.72)
Hook rim form strongly in the Rhone Valley tradition with the ledge on the top of the rim next to the bead. Although this has trituration grits, it shares with the ungritted examples a clumsily finished base. This feature also occurs on mortaria from Kingsholm (Darling 1985b, fig 27, no 101) and mortaria of the same type from Usk (Hartley 1993, fig 190, nos 27, 28) in fabrics produced at both Kingsholm and Usk.

M5.1
M5.11 MWWCR, 84/301, 321, military
M5.12 MWWR, 92/18, C 2.1
M5.13 AD90–130. MWWCR, 86/22,24 WR 3.1

M5.2 Near straight flange (Fig 4.73)
The commonest military mortarium type. The internal finishing, particularly of M2.23 and M2.25 suggest that these were not gritted, a feature of early mortaria. These form a distinctive group, for which close parallels are very rare. One appears to be a single vessel from Usk (Hartley 1993, fig 190, no 33) in fabric 26, considered to be a locally made vessel, while another is in the interesting early fabric in London (Chadburn and

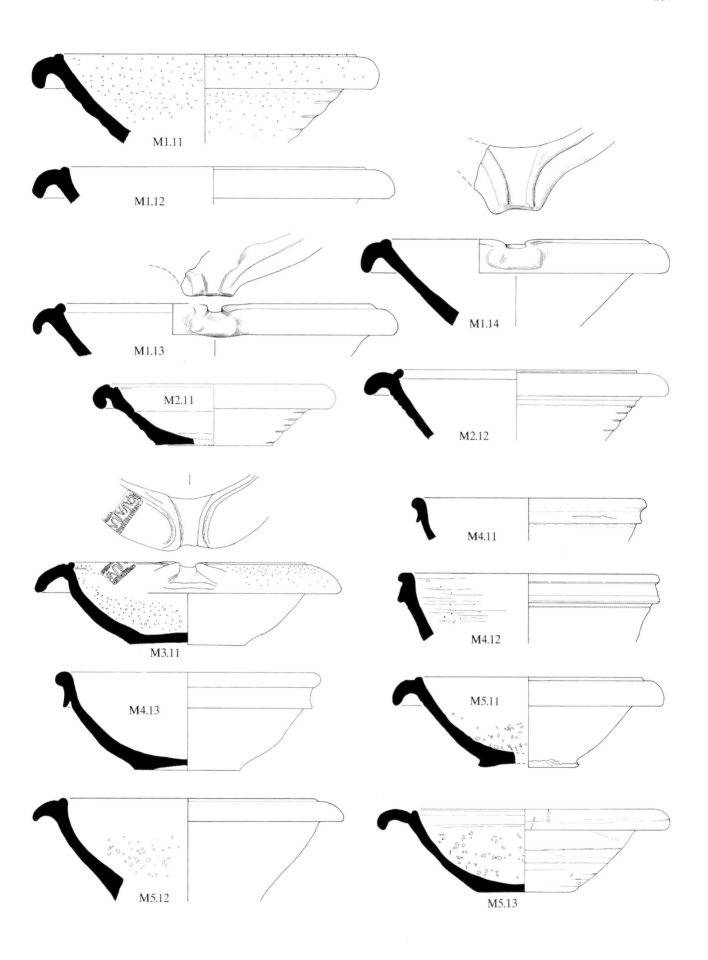

Fig 4.72 Pottery form series: mortaria; scale 1:4

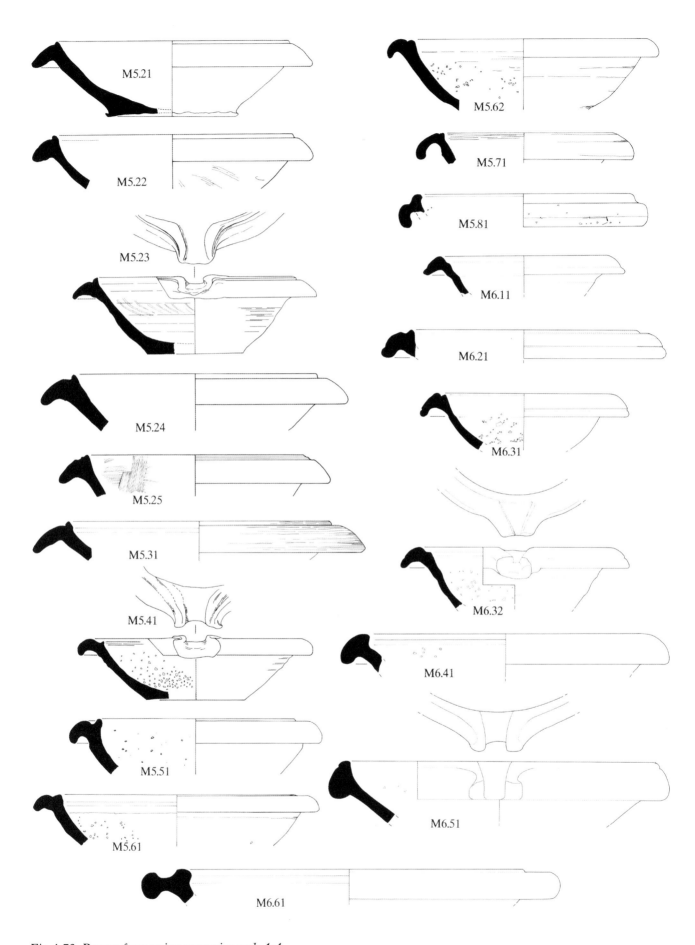

Fig 4.73 Pottery form series: mortaria; scale 1:4

Tyers 1984, no 37011). Also from London is another mortarium of broadly similar type in a fabric considered to probably derive from the early kilns at Eccles (*ibid*, no 37009; Detsicas 1977, fig 3.4–6). The Usk example is typologically dissimilar to the commoner Usk local type with a thicker hook-flange, although it has a poorly finished base, seemingly a characteristic of both Usk and Kingsholm potters, also seen on the Wroxeter bases. A continental origin seems assured but identification of its location awaits further publication and research, although south-eastern France adjacent to Switzerland is a possibility. No examples have been traced in the Rhineland or on the Danube frontier.
M5.21 MWWO, 14/32, F2246, 1.3
M5.22 with a slightly more stumpy rim. MWWO, 90/216, P 2.2
M5.23 MWWOF, 7/38, F2280, 1.3
M5.24 MWWO, 92/18, C 2.1
M5.25 MWWOF, 92/36, F167, C 2.3; 5/15, C 2.1

M5.3 Variant with angular bead
M5.31 with matt brown slip and white quartz trituration grits, AD 50–85. MWWOC, 83/516, WR 2.2

M5.4 With bead below level of rim
M5.41 this is unique amongst the military assemblage and coming from a context believed to be contaminated by later material could be a second-century vessel. It is also the only military mortarium with sandstone trituration. MWWCR, 52/22, military

M5.5
M5.51 MWWO? (the fabric is similar but atypical of the local fabric, the vessel is therefore only tentatively identified as local), 78/8, military

M5.6
M5.61 worn waster, cracked but useable ?AD 50–90. MWWOC, 92/4, C 2.4
M5.62 AD 80–100. MWWCR, 85/221, WR 2.3

M5.7 Markedly down curving flange
M5.71 AD 50–80. MWWOC, 83/534, WR 2.3

M5.8
M5.81 probably made by DOCILIS, AD 100–130. MWWOC, 84/52, WR 2.3

M6 Rhaetian mortaria (Fig 4.73)
M6.1
M6.11 A typical Wroxeter form, dated mid-late Antonine (pers comm K Hartley). MWWO, 98/60, F766, P 3.1, KG 16

M6.2 Roll-and-bead rim with a ledge on the top of the rim next to the bead, which is at the highest point of the rim
M6.21 White coating externally, possibly surface salts, early-mid Antonine (pers comm K Hartley). MWWO, 97/108, F572, P 3.1, KG 16

M6.3 Roll rim with internal bead lower than or level with peak of rim
M6.31 Early to mid Antonine (pers comm K Hartley). MWWO, 98/60, F766, KG 16, P 3.1
M6.32 Variant of above with more pronounced internal step. Sooting externally on flange near spout. MWWOC, 90/101, F599, P 3.2, KG 17

M6.4 Heavy roll-rim
M6.41 MWWOF, 98/50, F679, KG 17, P 3.2

Regional mortaria

M7 Brockley Hill/Verulamium. MOVR (Fig 4.74)
M7.1 Elongated flange, downcurving at tip
M7.11 stamped MATUGENUS, AD 80–120. MOVR, 83/536, WR 2.1
M7.12 MOVR, 14/31, 37, ?35/27, military
M7.13 MOVR, 35/27, 14/31, ?14/37, military
M7.14 stamped, MOVR, 91/106, 1.3

M8 Holt (Fig 4.74)
M8.1 Flat rim, turned down at tip
M8.11 not a typical Holt fabric but does have cracking on the surfaces which is noted on Holt wares, *c* AD 90–120 (pers comm K Hartley). HOLT (or possibly early Wroxeter), 98/60, F766, P 3.1, KG 16

M9 Mancetter-Hartshill (MANCH) (Fig 4.74)
M9.1 Hammer-head mortaria
M9.11 AD 220+ (pers comm K Hartley). MANCH, 98/98, F930, P 3.2, KG 17

M9.2 Straight flange, beaded at tip
M9.21 MANCH, 90/1, P 4

M10 Oxfordshire (Fig 4.75)
M10.1 Young (1977) form M6 with thick flange, tip turned down through a right-angle, *c* AD 100–170
M10.11 MOXFW, 50/25, C 3.4

M10.2 Young (1977) form M22 with upstanding rim and squat flange folded quite close to body, *c* AD 240–400+, the principal Oxfordshire mortarium type from *c* AD 300
M10.21 MOXFW, 78/1, C 4

M10.3 Young (1977) form WC7 copying M22, the most common white colour-coated type *c* AD 240–400+ but only popular in fourth century
M10.31 MOXFWC, 90/32, P 3.4A, KG 25

M10.4 Young (1977) form C100 with upright rim and angular flange, *c* AD 300–400+ with the form becoming more popular as the century progressed
M10.41 MOXFRC, 90/25, P 3.4A, KG 25

M10.5 Young (1977) form M13, bead rim with flange turned down against the side. Not a common form,

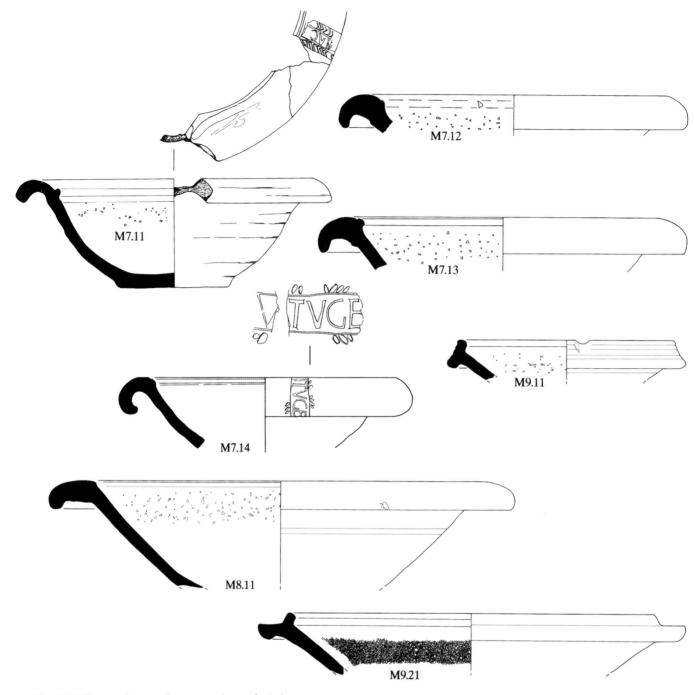

Fig 4.74 Pottery form series: mortaria; scale 1:4

typologically dated AD ?180–240 but the only dated examples are late third century or later.
M10.51 MOXFW, 83/+, WR 4

M10.6 Young (1977) form C97, wall-sided type copying samian form Dr 45, a very common type dated *c* AD 240–400+
M10.61 MOXFRC, 82/4, BP 4

Mortaria Source Unknown

M11 MOCRA (Fig 4.75)
M11.1 Bead above level of flange
M11.11 AD 90–130. MOCRA (possibly local), 86/24, WR 3.1

M11.2 Bead just below top of flange
M11.21 MOCRA, 39/28, military; 84/215, military; 92/20, F154, C 2.1

M11.3 Bead below top of flange
M11.31 AD 90–150. MOCRA (possibly local though fabric resembles Mancetter-Hartshill), 86/24, WR 3.1
M11.32/503.01 stamped DOCCAS, AD 90–120. MOCRA (possibly local) 83/534, WR 2.3

M11.4 Short flange with upstanding beaded rim
M11.41 with matt brown slip, AD 100–150. MOCRA (Wroxeter or West Midlands source), 83/534, WR 2.3

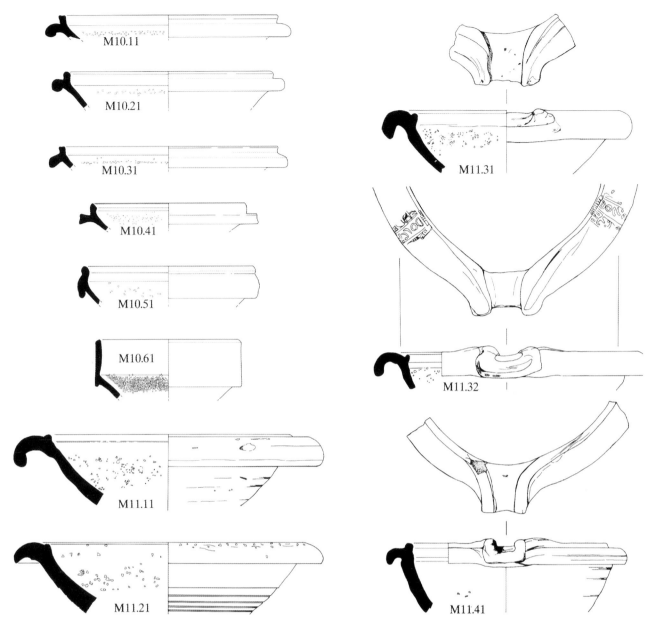

Fig 4.75 Pottery form series: mortaria; scale 1:4

TZ *TAZZE* (Fig 4.76)

Characterised by a pedestal foot and bands of frilling, may have signs of burning on the inner surface.

TZ1 Tazza with splayed walls and pinched rim
TZ1.1
TZ1.11 WWR, 50/52, 77/9, military

TZ2 Tazza with gently curving profile and frilled rim
TZ2.1
TZ2.11 WWOF, 77/9, military
TZ2.12 WWO, 78/57, military

TZ3 Tazza with splayed walls and frilled flange below the rim
TZ3.1
TZ3.11 with widely splayed walls. WWO, 3/21, C 2.1

TZ4 Tazza with gently curving walls and frilled flange below the rim
TZ4.1
TZ4.11 gently splayed/near upright walls. WWOC with cream slip, 92/15, C 3.2

TZ5 Carinated tazza with upright walls and small frilled rim
TZ5.1
TZ5.11 with pinched band at carination. WWO, 98/208, military

TZ6 Carinated tazza with frilled flange rim
TZ6.1 With sharp carination just below the rim.
TZ6.11 an example from Richborough from a pit with early pottery (although probably open until the end of the first century) is similar in fabric type and rim form, but does not have the carination (Bushe-Fox 1926, no 44). *Tazze* types 29.1–2 from Fishbourne are similar,

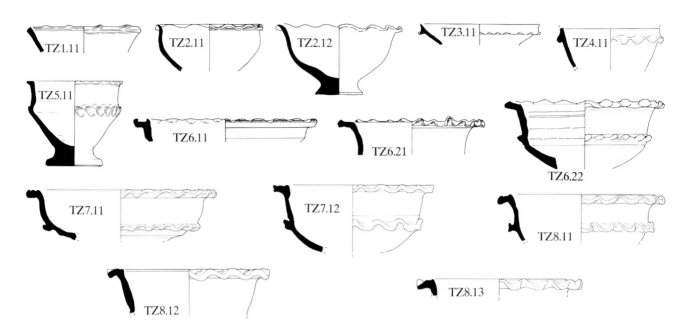

Fig 4.76 Pottery form series: tazze; scale 1:4

one having the same carination below the rim, and the other rim being very close to this example (Cunliffe 1971). A source in southern Britain is possible. CREAM, 78/15, military

TZ6.2 With slightly concave walls and carination mid way down vessel.
TZ6.21 WWR, 90/204, F951, P 2.2
TZ6.22 with frilled cordon at carination. WWR, 83/111, WR 3.1

TZ7 With flat reeded-rim
TZ7.1 Two grooves on rim and near hemispherical profile
TZ7.11 with frilled cordon half-way down vessel. WWOC with white slip, 59/8, BP 3.2
TZ7.12 with frilled cordon half-way down vessel. WWOC with cream slip, 98/45,28, F675/F638, P 3.2, KG 17

TZ8 With down-turned reeded rim
TZ8.1 Two grooves on rim and near hemispherical profile
TZ8.11 WWOC 'OF with white slip' 58/3, 4, BP 3.2
TZ8.12 blackened internally. Similar to early-mid second century forms from New Market Hall, Gloucester (Hassall and Rhodes 1974 fig 13A.95). *Tazze* were also made at Wilderspool *c* AD 90–160. WWOC, 85/224, WR 2.3; 92/4, C 2.4
TZ8.13 WWOC, 98/53, F714, P 3.2, KG 17

TK TANKARDS (Fig 4.77)

Characterised by near straight to concave sides and one or more handles.

TK1 Tankards with upright walls (broadly similar to Webster 1976 form 38, mid-late first century).
Darling notes that no handles were found associated with the military period rims, which may therefore belong to carinated cups whose presence on the site is otherwise only attested by a single carinated body sherd (not illustrated).
TK1.1
TK1.11 SVOF, 83/28, 530, 84/56, WR 2.3

TK2 Tankards with near upright walls (broadly similar to Webster 1976 forms 40/41, second-early third)
TK2.1
TK2.11 late first to second century (broadly similar to Webster 1976 forms 38/39) SVORGO? 78/5, military
TK2.12 SVORGO? 12/30, military
TK2.13 *c* AD 120–70 (Gillam 1970, 182). SVORGO, 85/21, WR 2.3
TK2.14 *c* AD 120–70 (*ibid*; Bushe-Fox 1913 fig 18,40). SVOF, 29/5, C 2.3

TK3 Tankards with moderately splayed walls (broadly similar to Webster 1976 form 42, second and third century)
TK3.1
TK3.11 handled tankard with groove below the rim. SVO, *natatio* infill, C 3.1, KG 14
TK3.12 handled tankard with groove below the rim. SVO, *natatio* infill C 3.1, KG 14
TK3.13 handled tankard with groove below the rim, burnished. SVO, *natatio* infill, C 3.1, KG 14
TK3.14 handled tankard, burnished. SVO, *natatio* infill, C3.1, KG14
TK3.15 SVO, 98/28, F638, P 3.2, KG 17
TK3.16 acute lattice burnish on body. SVO, 58/315, BP 4

TK4 Tankards with markedly splayed walls (falling between Webster 1976 form 43 and 44, third century)
TK4.1
TK4.11 handled tankard, burnished. SVO, *natatio* infill, C 3.1, KG 14

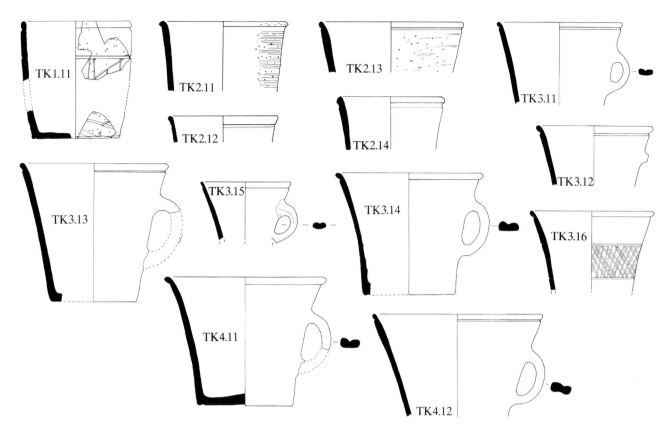

Fig 4.77 Pottery form series: tankards; scale 1:4

TK4.12 handled tankard with groove below the rim, burnished. SVO, *natatio* infill, C 3.1, KG 14

L LIDS (Figs 4.78–4.79)

L1 Lids with rims hooked upwards (Fig 4.78)
L1.1 Sub-rectangular rim
L1.11 GREY, 91/85, 1.3

L1.2 Triangular rim
L1.21 WWR, 83/530, WR 2.3
L1.22 WWO, 49/166, BP 2.2
L1.23 WWOF, 86/52, F209, WR 2.1, KG 15
L1.24 WWR, 84/52, WR 2.3
L1.25 WWR, 84/52, WR 2.3

L2 Lids with thickened triangular rims (Fig 4.78)
L2.1
L2.11 Gillam 340, AD 100–140. WWR, 84/52, WR 2.3
L2.12 WWR, 81/15, military
L2.13 burnt. WWO, 84/52, WR 2.3
L2.14 WWOF, 91/93, WR 2.3
L2.15 WWR, 92/4, C 2.4
L2.16 WWO, 12/30, military
L2.17 WWOF, 98/180, military
L2.18 PRW3, 84/404, military
L2.19 WWR, 85/507, WR 2.3

L2.2 With internal groove
L2.21 WWR, 45/15, military

L2.3 Small amphora lid or stopper
Dr D F Williams writes – The type appears similar to those used for Dressel 20 and Haltern 70 vessels recovered from the Port Vendres shipwreck (Colls *et al* 1977, fig 14) but the form seems to have been in general use.
L2.31 fine buff ware, 84/100, WR 2.2
L2.32 fine buff ware, 98/138, P 2.3

L3 Lids with splayed rims (Fig 4.78)
L3.1
L3.1 Slightly cupped and grooved externally
L3.11 WWO, 41/6, military
L3.12 WWOC (fine variant), 49/168, BP 2.2

L3.2 Flattened internally at tip
L3.21 WWR, 85/105; 85/37, F76, WR 2.3

L3.3
L3.31 WWR, 72/79, 74/3, military
L3.32 WWR, 6/73, F2208 military; 12/42, 1.3

L4 Lids with plain or slightly beaded rims (Fig 4.78 and 4.79)
L4.1 Slightly beaded
L4.11 WWR, 84/52, WR 2.3
L4.12 BB1, 84/52, WR 2.3
L4.13 BB1, 98/76, P 2.3
L4.14 BB1, 84/51, WR 2.3
L4.15 BB1, 25/24, BP 2.2

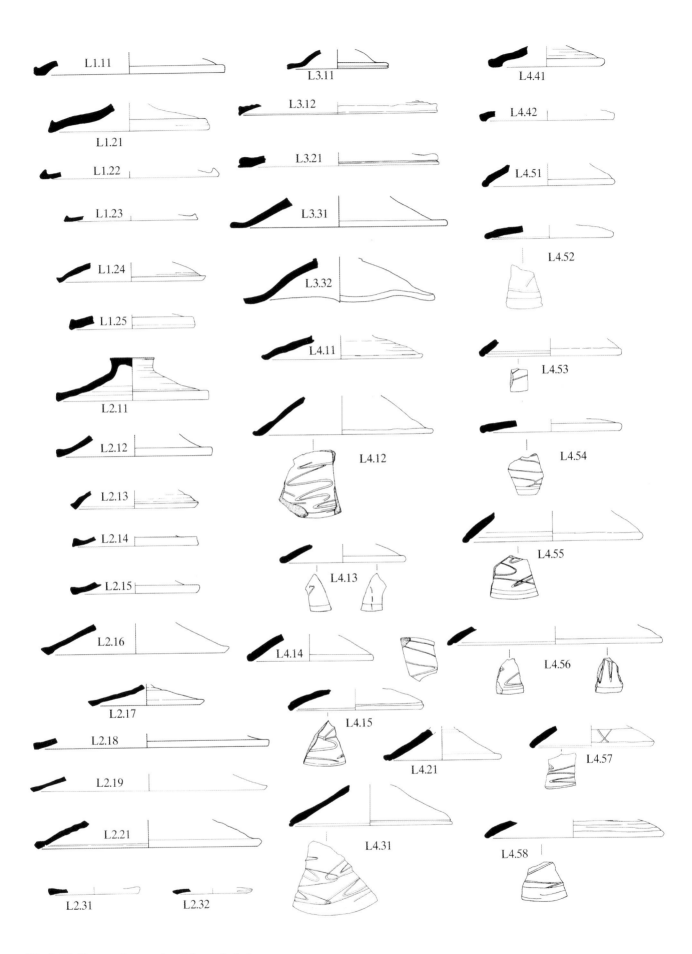

Fig 4.78 Pottery form series: lids; scale 1:4

L4.2 With double groove internally
L4.21 BB1, 80/117, F486, P 3.1, KG 16

L4.3 Pronounced groove externally and slight internal cupping
L4.31 BB1, 85/221, WR 2.3

L4.4 Marked internal cupping
L4.41 WWR, 91/93, WR 2.3
L4.42 WWO, 86/24 WR 3.1

L4.5 Slight internal cupping
L4.51 WWR, 92/4, C 2.4
L4.52 BB1, 84/52, WR 2.3
L4.53 BB1, 83/534, WR 2.3
L4.54 BB1, 83/534, WR 2.3
L4.55 BB1, 84/75, WR 2.3
L4.56 BB1, 84/52, WR 2.3
L4.57 BB1, 84/52, WR 2.3
L4.58 imitation BB1, 40/4, C 2.3
L4.59 burnished 'zig-zag' decoration. BB1, 98/101, F855, P 3.1, KG 16

L4.6 Plain rim (Fig 4.79)
L4.61 BB1, 84/52, WR 2.3
L4.62 BB1, 84/52, WR 2.3
L4.63 BB1, 92/4, C 2.4
L4.64 BB1, 84/75, WR 2.3
L4.65 WWR, 29/17, C 2.1
L4.66 WWR/O, 83/530, WR 2.3
L4.67 SVO, 83/536, WR2.1

L4.7 Rim flattened externally
L4.71 BB1, 98/101, F855, P 3.1, KG 16

L5 Lids with 'bifurcated' rims (Fig 4.79)
L5.1
L5.11 WWO, 41/6, military

L5.2 External groove
L5.21 WWR, 98/233, military

L5.3
L5.31 WWR, 84/52, WR 2.3
L5.32 WWO, 92/4, C 2.4

L5.4
L5.41 WWO, 85/112, WR 2.3
L5.42 WWR, 92/9, C 2.3

L6 Lids with in-turned rims (Fig 4.79)
L6.1 Sharply in-turned rim
L6.11 WWR, 51/21, F2990, 1.3

L6.2 In-turned near triangular rim
L6.21 WWO, 86/24, WR 3.1
L6.22 WWO, 86/24, WR 3.1
L6.23 WWR, 92/20, C 2.1

L6.24 WWR, 90/174, F154, P 2.2
L6.25 burnished. SVO, 90/142, F736, P 3.1, KG 16

L6.3 Markedly in-turned rounded rim
L6.31 SVOF, 98/98, F930, P 3.2, KG 17

L6.4 Slightly in-turned rounded rim
L6.41 WWO, 90/128, F736, P 3.1, KG 16

L6.5 Very fine in-turned rim
L6.51 WWO, 91/108, 1.3

M MISCELLANEOUS (Fig 4.80)

ML LAMPS
ML1 Covered lamps
ML1.1
ML1.11 CGCC? 77/8, military; 7/38, F2280, 1.3
ML1.12 WWOF, 72/67, military
ML1.13 CGCC? 70/17, F2712, C 2.2

ML2 Open lamps
ML2.1
ML2.11 WWR, 78/16, military

MU UNGUENTARIA
A small narrow-necked vessel, thought to have been a container for ointment or perfume.
MU1 Flaring rim, long neck and ovoid body
MU1.11 WWO, 84/48, WR 3.1

MTV TRIPLE VASES
A vessel usually with three small jars, either attached to the top of a tubular ring-base which is often hollow, or joined together at the body.
MTV1
MTV1.11 WWOF, 92/61, 63, military

MTV2
MTV2.11 CREAM, 29/7, C 2.3

CR CRUCIBLE
CR1
CR1.11 WWO, 83/111, WR 3.1. Examples also occur in WWR.

MCP CHEESE PRESS
A flat-bottomed dish with holes and concentric ridges in the bottom, presumed to have been used for cheese making.
MCP1.1 Flat-rimmed
MCP1.11 with a thickened rim. AD 140–200 at Mumrills (Gillam 1970, 350). An earlier date range is suggested by another example from Holt (Grimes 1930, 206) late first to early second century, it is probable that this form continued in use to the end of the second century and beyond. WWO, 83/534, WR 2.3
MCP1.12 WWR, 90/163, F631, P 3.2

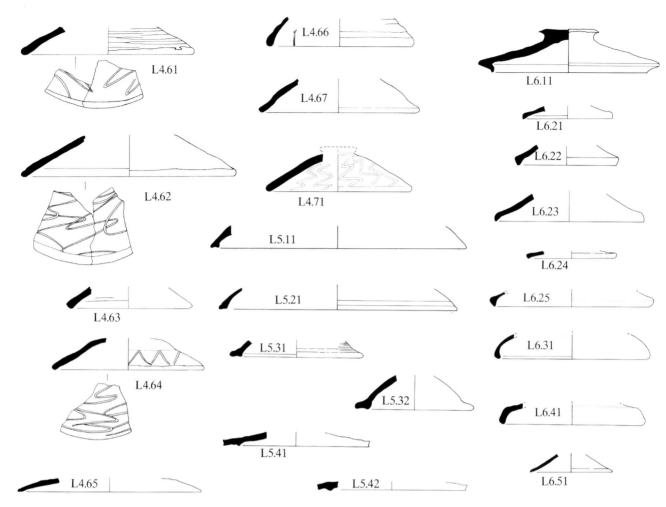

Fig 4.79 Pottery form series: lids; scale 1:4

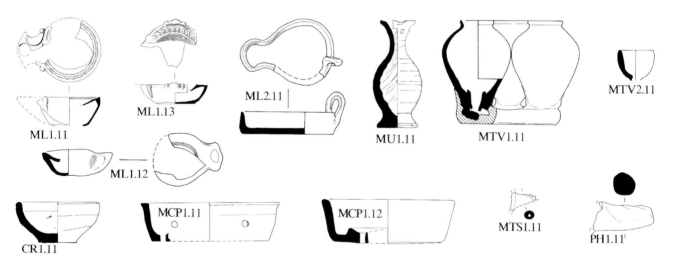

Fig 4.80 Pottery form series: lamps, unguentaria, *triple vases, crucible, cheese presses, spouts,* patera *handle; scale 1:4*

S SPOUTS
MS1 *Tettina* spout
MTS1.11 WWOC, 98/49,50, F679, P 3.2, KG 17

PH PATERA HANDLE
PH1
PH1.11 WWO, 16/31, F3177, BP 3.1, KG 19

Fabric descriptions

compiled by Jane Evans

Introduction

The following fabric descriptions encompass all the material analysed from the Webster excavations both military and civilian. A number of different systems have been used over the years and obviously there have been some difficulties in cross-matching individual identifications or descriptions, particularly with local wares. Some systems have divided wares more rigorously than others, which may have subsumed similar types into one category. It is hoped that the following distillation will provide the basis for future work in the Wroxeter region (Table 4.12). For the purposes of the report the fabrics have been divided into four groups determined by source:

1 Local or regional wares; these fabrics have been grouped together as it was not always easy to distinguish 'local' wares, produced in or near Wroxeter, from 'regional' wares, with a source generally in the Severn Valley area. Some of these wares may have been traded over a wider area.
2 Traded wares; regional wares commonly traded over a wide area and produced outside the Severn Valley area.
3 Imported wares; wares produced outside Britain.
4 Wares of unknown source; either defined fabrics whose source is as yet unknown, or fabrics represented by fragments too small to be classified.

Descriptions are based on macroscopic observation and have been kept to a minimum. Vessels are wheelmade unless stated otherwise. The following information is presented for each entry: common name; Wroxeter code; fabric description; vessels/manufacture; form types as found in type series; source, distribution, dating.

1 Local or regional wares

Problems were encountered in separating Severn Valley ware (SVW) from the finer local 'Wroxeter' ware (WW). The petrology of the Wroxeter SVWs in particular has been discussed in detail by Tomber (1981). In summary it was found that those kiln sites which were producing SVW forms in conjunction with other types, ie mortaria at Shepton Mallet, were using the same fabric for all wares. However, areas producing SVWs also produce other wares in different fabrics, for example the Malvern area with the Malvernian rock-tempered cooking wares. It would seem that the term SVW applies more to a widespread tradition, than to a clearly defined range of fabrics, causing some confusion when trying to sort unfeatured sherds or comparing a specific fabric between sites over a wider area (for further discussion see Period 2 pottery).

Native ware
NAT: Native
Fabric: A fine textured, vesicular, light grey fabric with a light red-brown cortex and grey to brown surfaces, with some mica. Also includes a coarser oxidized fabric with calcareous inclusions and a dark grey core.
Vessels: Handmade/ wheel-turned? jars (JC1.11, JC2.11)

Source, distribution and dating: Native wares are poorly represented in the assemblage overall with just 16 sherds from the military levels.

Severn Valley wares
SVOF: Oxidized Severn Valley ware (fine)
Fabric: A fine, micaceous fabric containing occasional limestone fragments, clay pellets and iron ore. This is the typical SVW fabric (Webster 1976), although perhaps slightly more hackly in fracture.
Manufacture: Wheelthrown; soft to hard fired, usually reddish orange (Munsell: 2.5YR 5/8) but may be brown (5YR 6/6) and sometimes has a reduced grey (10R 6/1) core.
Vessels: Jars, beakers, bowls, tankards and lids.
Form types: Jars (JH5.12, JM7.73, JN3.12–13, JN4.32, JN4.51, JN4.63; JW2.12–13, JW2.33– 34, JSS2.21); beakers (BK9.28); bowls (B1.24, B5.21, B7.12, B8.12, B9.11, B10.21); tankards (TK1.11, TK2.14); lids (L6.31).
Source, distribution and dating: SVWs were produced throughout the Severn Valley area from the first to fourth centuries AD. It appears to have been produced at a large number of kiln sites of which only a few have been found accounting for a number of minor variations in fabric. Kilns are known to have been operating in the Malvern area, although slight but significant differences in fabric would suggest the bulk of the Wroxeter material is coming from a more local source. Some fourth-century pottery wasters were recovered west of some possible tile works at Ismore Coppice (Houghton 1964). The overall development of the industry has been discussed in greater detail elsewhere (Peacock 1968; Webster 1976; 1993, 285ff; Tomber 1981; Rawes 1982; Timby 1990).

Small numbers of sherds of oxidized and reduced SV were recovered from the military demolition levels. Forms present from these levels include beakers, possibly tankards although these may equally be carinated cups/bowls and a large jar. An unusual vessel classified as SV is a reduced jar with rusticated decoration. From the second century onwards the fabric becomes much more popular accounting for 9% of the Period 2 assemblage, and approximately 34% of the KG14 *natatio* assemblage.

SVRF: Reduced Severn Valley ware (fine)
Fabric: As above except that reduction produces a grey finish.
Vessels: Beakers and bowls.
Form types: Beakers (BK4.31, BK6.42); bowls (B7.21–22)
Source, distribution and dating: See SVOF above.

SVO: Oxidized Severn Valley ware (coarser variant)
Fabric: As above but with moderate ill-sorted, sub-rounded quartz, up to *c* 0.6mm and visible by eye.
Vessels: Flagon, jars, beakers, dishes/platters, tankards and lids.

Form types: Flagon (F3.31); jars (JN2.11, JN2.13, JN4.11, JN4.31, JN4.34, JN4.35–36, JN4.41–42, JN4.61–62, JN4.71–72, JN4.81, JW1.11–12, JW2.21–23, JW2.31–32); beakers (BK4.43); bowls (B7.27–28, B7.52, B8.41, B9.12, B9.21, B12.51, B12.71, B16.21); dishes/platters (D6.21, D6.41); tankards (TK3.11–16, TK4.11); lids (L6.25).
Source, distribution and dating: see SVOF above.

SVR: Reduced Severn Valley ware (coarser variant)

Fabric: As above but with moderate ill-sorted, subrounded quartz, up to 0.6 mm (visible by eye) and reduced grey.
Vessels: Jars, beakers and bowls.
Form types: Jars (JH1.12; JC3.53; JM2.31, JN4.13, JN4.33, JLS2.11); beakers (BK1.31); bowls (B4.18, B13.27).
Source, distribution and dating: The earliest occurrence of this variant is two sherds in the early military period, possibly from a large jar.

SVORGO: Oxidized organic Severn Valley ware
Fabric: As above but with sparse elongated voids from burnt out organic matter appearing as black, or dark streaks in fracture, resulting in a 'corky' surface. Wheelmade and handmade/wheel-turned vessels, orange in colour.
Vessels: Jars, beakers and tankards.
Form types: Jars (JN2.12, JN4.14, JN4.21); beakers (BK4.38); tankards (TK2.11–13)
Source, distribution and dating: This variant occurs in early levels in the Gloucester area (Timby 1990; Timby forthcoming) with first-century vessels represented at Kingsholm, Frocester, and *Ariconium*.

SVORGR: Reduced organic Severn Valley ware
Fabric: As above but reduced grey.
Source, distribution and dating: See SVORGO above.

Wroxeter Ware
WWO: Oxidized 'Wroxeter' ware
Fabric: Similar to SVO but abundant quartz. Surface treatment includes mica coating, white/cream slip (10YR 7/3 to 10YR 8/4), reddish brown slip, roughcasting, rouletting (usually accompanied by a cream slip), burnishing, and rilling (infrequently).
Vessels: Flagons, beakers, jars, cups, bowls, dishes, platters, *tazze*, *unguentaria*, crucibles, cheese press, and *patera*.
Form types: Flagons (F1.11, F1.14, F1.22, F2.11, F2.12, F2.21–22, F2.31–2, F2.41, F2.51, F2.62, F3.21, F3.41–2, F4.11–12, F4.41, F5.11, F5.41, F5.43–45, F5.47, F5.51, F6.21, F8.11– 12, F8.21, F9.11–12, F10.12); beakers (BK1.21, BK3.15, BK4.15, BK7.13, BK12.13, BK12.31); jars (JH1.11, JH1.21, JH2.31, JH2.41, JH3.11, JH4.51, JH5.11; JM3.16, JM3.23, JM4.22–23, JM4.31, JM4.41, JM5.31, JM6.21–22, JM6.33, JM6.43, JM7.31–32, JM7.56, JM7.61–62, JM7.72, JM7.82, JM7.87, JM8.13–14, JM8.21, JM9.11; JN1.12, JN3.11, JN4.12; JW2.11, JW2.24, JW3.21,

JLS2.51); cups (C1.11–12, 14–15, C1.21, C1.32); bowls (B1.11–12, B1.22, B2.11, 13,15, B2.22, B2.31, B2.51–52, B2.61, B2.71–74, B3.33, 35, B3.41, B5.22, B6.12, B6.31, B7.24–26, B7.42–43, 45, B7.51, B11.11, B12.32, B12.42, B12.52, B12.72, B13.11, B13.23, 25–6, B13.32, 34, B13.42, B13.51, B14.23–24, B14.28, B14.31–32, B15.12–14, B16.11, B19.11, B20.11), dishes (D5.24, D6.11); platters (P2.21, P3.12, P5.13, P5.15, P5.33, 35–37, P5.41–42, P7.11, P8.11, P9.11); *tazze* (TZ2.12, TZ3.11, TZ5.11); lids (L1.22, L2.13, L2.16, L3.11, L4.42, L5.11, L5.32, L5.41, L6.21–22, L6.41, L6.51); *unguentaria* (MU1.1); crucible (CR1.11); cheese press (MCP1.11); *patera* handle (PH1.11).

WWR: Reduced 'Wroxeter' ware
Fabric: As WWO but reduced, sometimes with a reddish core. Surface treatment includes linear rustication (vertical or horizontal), applied spots or blobs, trailed lines 'en barbotine', black slip, plain and lattice burnishing.
Vessels: Flagons, beakers, jars, cups, bowls, dishes, platters, *tazze*, lids, lamps and cheese press.
Form types: Flagons (F4.42, F6.11, F6.22–23, F10.11); beakers (BK1.11, BK3.14, BK3.22, BK4.13, BK4.16, BK4.19, BK4.31–2, BK4.4.41, BK4.44, BK4.51–53, BK4.55, BK4.57–58, BK4.61, BK5.11, BK6.12–16, BK6.22–23, BK7.11, BK7.15, BK7.15, BK10.1, BK13.31); jars (JH3.12; JC1.15, JC1.24, JC3.22, JC3.36; JN1.11; JM1.11, JM1.13, JM1.21, 23–27, 29, JM2.11, JM2.41, JM3.13–15, JM3.21–22, JM3.31, JM3.41, JM3.51–54, 56, JM3.61–66, JM3.71, JM3.82, JM4.11, JM4.13–14, JM4.25, JM5.11–12, JM5.41, JM6.11, JM6.13–16, JM6.23–24, JM6.31–32, JM6.41–42, JM6.45–48, JM7.11–12, JM7.21, 23, JM7.33, JM7.41–43, JM7.51–55, 57–59, JM7.63–64, JM7.71, JM7.81, 83–86, 88, JM7.91–95, JM8.11–12, 15, JM9.21, JM9.31, 35, JM9.41, JLS2.31); cups (C1.13, C1.31, C3.11, C3.21 C4.23, 26, C6.11); bowls (B2.14, B2.21, B2.41, B2.53, B2.75, B3.11, B3.21, B3.31–32, 34, B3.43, B4.11–14, B5.11, B7.23, B7.44, B8.22, B12.11, B12.31, B13.21–22, 24, B13.31, B13.41, B13.61, B14.11, 13, B14.21–22, B14.25–27, B14.29, B15.11, B15.15, B17.12, B17.22, B19.21, B21.11– 12, 14–15, B22.11, B26.11); dishes (D5.11–13, D5.21–23, 25–27); platters (P1.11, P3.11, P5.11– 12, P5.14, P5.31, 34); *tazze* (TZ1.11, TZ6.21–22); lids (L1.21, L1.24–25, L2.11–12, L2.15, L2.19, L2.21, L3.21, L3.31–32, L4.11, L4.41, L4.51, L4.65, L5.21, L5.31, L5.42, L6.11, L6.23–24); lamps (ML2.11, ML2.21); cheese press (MCP1.12).

A number of minor variants of the above were also discriminated during analysis:

WWOF: Fine oxidized 'Wroxeter' ware
Vessels: Flagons, beakers, cups, bowls, dishes, platters, *tazze*, lids, lamps and triple vases.
Form Types: Flagons (F1.12, F1.13, F1.31, F1.41, F1.42, F5.22, F5.31); beakers (BK3.21, BK4.17, BK6.17, BK7.12, BK8.22, BK10.31, BK12.12); jars

(JM5.21, JM7.22, JM9.32–34); cups (C3.14, C4.21, C4.24); bowls (B7.11, B12.61–63, B17.21, B17.31–33); dishes (D1.33, D6.31); platters (P2.12, P3.13, P4.11, P10.11); *tazze* (TZ2.11); lids (L1.23, L2.14, L2.17); lamps (ML1.21); triple vases (MTV1.11).

WWR/O: Coarse reduced/oxidized 'Wroxeter' ware
Vessels: Jars, bowls and lids.
Form types: Jars (JM1.28, JM1.31); bowls (B14.12); lids (L4.66)

WWO/R: Coarse oxidized/reduced 'Wroxeter' ware
Form types: Flagons (F4.61); jars (JM6.44); bowls (B19.22)

WWRF: Fine reduced 'Wroxeter' ware
Vessels: Beakers, jars, cups, bowls and platters.
Form types: Beakers (BK2.11, BK2.21, BK3.17, BK4.21–23, BK4.54, BK4.56, BK6.11, BK7.14, BK7.16, BK10.12–13, BK12.11; BK10.52–53), jars (JM1.22, JM2.12, JM2.23, JM3.55, JM3.81); cups (C3.12–13, C4.11, C5.11, C7.11); bowls (B2.12, B8.11); platters (P5.32).

WWOC: Wroxeter, white colour-coated oxidized ware
WWRC: Wroxeter, white colour-coated reduced ware
Fabric: Distinguished by the presence of a white colour-coat. Although for the majority of the pottery this has been recorded as a single category it in fact covers the complete range of fabrics described above. For the later key groups it was subdivided into WWOCF and WWOCC.
Vessels: Flagons, jars, bowls, *tazze*, lids and spouted vessels.
Form types: Flagons (F1.21, F3.11, F3.22, F3.43, F4.63, F4.67–8, F4.71–4), F5.21, F5.23, F6.31–32, F7.11, F8.31); jars (JH2.21, JH3.13, JH4.11, JH4.21, JH4.31, JH4.41, JH4.52; JM1.12, JM10.11); bowls (B1.21, B1.23, 25, B3.42, B15.16); *tazze* (TZ4.11, TZ7.11–12, TZ8.11–13); lids (L3.12); *tettina* spout (MS1.11); spout (MS2.11).
Source, distribution and dating: Flagons with white slip appear to be common in Period 2 contexts. Given the probable high residual content of many of these contexts, it seems likely that this technique started either, in the late military period when the pottery assemblage was becoming much more diverse in both fabric and type, or in Period 1 (early civil).

Source, distribution and dating: Wroxeter ware was first produced by the army for their own requirements in the absence of any suitable local potting industries. It accounts for the bulk of the military assemblage declining slightly in the later demolition period. The cream-slipped variety (WWOC/WWRC) appears to be a slightly later development showing its main occurrence in the military demolition contexts. The ratio between oxidized and reduced versions appears to remain fairly constant throughout the military period. It is possible that the reduced version becomes marginally commoner

later on in Period 2. The fabric was used to produce a wide variety of products including flagons, copies of fine tablewares (cups, bowls and beakers), mortaria, jars, bowls, platters, lids, and lamps. All the forms find continental parallels, in particular with military sites on the Lower Rhine, but a significant number appear to derive from pottery traditions to the south, loosely located in the Upper Rhine to Rhaetia area with a westward extension into Central Gaul. Many of the fineware cups show stylistic links with North Italian wares. Continued production into the post-military period suggests that it had passed from military into civilian control.

Production of pottery in such quantity for a town of this considerable size must have occupied many kilns, few of which have been found (Houghton 1961; 1964). Material recovered in 1969 from a site near the Bell Brook, possibly the kiln site found by Jackson in 1929 (Fox and Morris 1931) has proved to be late second or early third century in date (White and Faiers forthcoming). Production sites are also noted by Evans at Meole Brace and Duncote Farm in the form of waster groups (Evans 1994). Wasters or 'seconds' occur in Period 2, but not perhaps in the numbers to be expected, although it is possible that the assemblage represents only the most saleable vessels, the 'wasters' being disposed of elsewhere.

MICA2: Coarse mica-dusted ware (Wroxeter?)
Fabric: Fabric coarser than the other mica-dusted wares, and similar to the local Wroxeter oxidized ware.
Vessels: Beakers (BK9.12).
Source, distribution and dating: mica-dusted Wroxeter wares are found in Period 2 deposits. A single body sherd found in military/Period 1 context is probably intrusive.

Local White Wares
CREAM: Cream wares
Fabric: Hard, fine fabric, usually containing varying quantities of sub-angular quartz, red granular sandstone and black ironstone fragments. Colour varies from white (2.5Y 8/2) to pinkish-cream (7.5YR 8/4), sometimes with a pale yellow external surface (2.5Y7/4). Some of the white wares were classified as one group, while others were subdivided on the basis of coarseness.

CREAMF: sparse, very fine quartz, not visible macroscopically (may include other sources, for example Mancetter-Hartshill).
Form types: Flagons (F4.31, F4.51, F4.65, F4.69, F5.46); bowls (B7.41).

CREAM: moderate fine quartz, less than *c* 0.1 mm (may include other sources)
Form types: Flagons (F2.61; F3.33, F4.21, F4.62, F4.64, F4.66); beakers (BK4.12, BK6.31, BK10.11); jars (JH2.11, JN1.21);cups (C4.22, C9.11), bowls (B12.32); dishes (D5.28), platters (P1.12); *tazze* (TZ6.11); triple vase (MTV2.11).

CREAMC: moderate to abundant fine quartz, less than 0.1 mm (may include other sources, for example Oxford and Verulamium).
Vessels: Usually occurs as flagons.
Source, distribution and dating: Identifying the source of the white wares is problematic. Analysis of the changing sources for white ware mortaria will probably indicate the major sources in any given period. Locally made mortaria certainly predominated in the military period and Wroxeter potters are known to have been producing white wares in the Antonine period (Houghton 1964, 107). They were also attempting crude and underfired copies of very fine cream ware vessels, using a pipe clay possibly from the Broseley region in Shropshire (Wright 1860, 75). Several other areas are also known to have produced white wares, however, and it seems probable that some at least of these are represented. Holt, situated on the road from Chester to Wroxeter, is a likely source and a white ware dish from Holt (Grimes 1930, no 186) is very similar to one from Wroxeter. Mancetter-Hartshill is another not too distant source. More distant sources include the Verulamium region and Brockley Hill, and Oxford.

The fabric is noted from the earliest military deposits where it occurs as beakers and flagons. Other forms in military contexts include a tazza, and a possible honey pot.

CREAMG: White ware, grog-tempered
Fabric: Very hard fabric with moderate ill-sorted, sub-angular quartz and sparse black ironstone, both less than 0.1mm, and moderate ill-sorted reddish/brown grog up to 6mm. Colour varies from white (10YR 8/2) through to pinkish-white (7.5YR 7/4) with the external surface sometimes as dark as pale brown (10YR6/3).

Mortaria, Wroxeter
Fabric: The following group of fabrics exhibit a range of fabrics similar to the Severn Valley and Wroxeter wares described above.
Manufacture: Wheelthrown. Triturition grits comprise quartz, red-brown sandstone and/or black ironstone. The group includes Rhaetian-type mortaria distinguished by the presence of a red/brown samian-like slip, restricted to the upper side of the rim, and a distinctive range of forms.

MWWRF: Mortaria, reduced fine
Fabric/manufacture: similar to SVRF.

MWWR: Mortaria, reduced
Fabric/manufacture: similar to SVR.
Form types: M5.12.

MWWOF: Mortaria, oxidized fine.
Fabric/manufacture: similar to SVOF.
Form types: M5.23, 25.

MWWO: Mortaria, oxidized
Fabric/manufacture: similar to SVO.
Form types: M4.11–13, M5.21–22, 24, M5.51, M6.11, M6.31.

MWWCR: Mortaria, white colour-coated
Fabric/manufacture: Distinguished by the presence of a white colour-coat. Although this has been recorded as a single category it in fact covers the range of fabrics described above.
Form type: M5.11, 5.13, 5.41, 5.62.

MWWOC: Mortaria, oxidized coarse
Fabric/manufacture: equivalent to WWO.
Form types: M5.31, M5.61, M5.71, M5.81, M6.42.

MWWWW: Mortaria: Wroxeter white
Fabric: A similar range of inclusions to those used for the trituration grits, ie moderate sandstone (up to 4 mm), translucent quartz/quartzite (up to 3 mm) and iron stone (up to 2 mm). Generally slightly coarser than white ware fabric CREAMC.
Manufacture: Wheelthrown. Hard fired, buff-cream, sometimes with a pink or brownish core. Trituration grits include moderate sandstone (up to 4 mm), translucent quartz/quartzite (up to 3 mm) and ironstone (up to 2 mm).
Wroxeter Mortaria: Source, distribution and dating: Wroxeter (Fox and Morris 1931, 15–16). Examples of locally manufactured mortaria (fabrics MWWO, MWWOF, MWWR, and MWWRF) occur in the military levels, forming the main supply of such vessels. The small quantity of vessels from Period 1 makes it difficult to assess whether local production continued right to the end of the military period, or beyond into the early civilian phase. A worn usable waster (MWWOC) was recovered from Period 2 deposits but believed to date to *c* AD 50–90. The occurrence of types in Period 2 dated to the broad period of late first to mid second century would suggest continuing local production. Form M5.81 (MWWOC) was probably made by DOCILIS AD 100–130.

MORT3: Mortaria: West Midlands?
Manufacture: Oxidized grey core. Trituration grits?
Source, distribution and dating: Single sherd from a Period 1 context.

2 Traded wares

Native wares
MALVH: Malvernian metamorphic, handmade
Fabric: Angular fragments of metamorphic rock, usually less than 1 mm to 3 mm in size, but larger fragments (up to 8–10 mm) are also found. The commonest inclusions are quartz, pink and white felspar and hornblende (Peacock 1968, 415–21, Group A).
Manufacture: Handmade pottery in the native Iron Age tradition. Hard fired; usually black/dark grey throughout, less commonly with a layer or patches of

orange-red/brown colour. Munsell colour range: N3 very dark grey to 7.5YR 6/8 reddish yellow. The surfaces, sometimes slightly rough to the touch where inclusions protruded, were wiped or burnished; showing either pattern burnishing or an even polish.
Vessels: Cooking-pots, both tubby and inturned, and lids. Some of those found at Wroxeter have a white limescale deposit inside.
Form types: Jars (JC1.12–14, 16, JC1.21–25; JLS1.11)
Source, distribution and dating: The ware is produced in the Malvern Hills area (Peacock 1968, 414–21. The tubby cooking-pot was dated by Peacock to the second century AD and the inturned lattice decorated form to the first or early second century AD. Those found at Astley Wall, Leintwardine, Hawford, Greensforge, Kenchester and Brecon occurred in Hadrianic/Antonine deposits, broadly contemporary with the Period 2 assemblage (Peacock 1967, 2). Only three sherds of Malvernian ware were apparently stratified in military contexts with only a further two sherds in Period 1. It appears, therefore, that the main occurrence of the ware is in Period 2 at the same period that black-burnished ware (BB1) becomes popular. There are few Malvernian copies of BB1.

MALVW: Malvernian metamorphic, wheelmade
Fabric: Moderate to abundant angular Malvernian rock fragments up to 3 mm.
Manufacture – Wheelthrown, though sometimes difficult to distinguish between handmade and wheelthrown sherds. Hard fired, grey (5YR 5/1), with occasional oxidized orange examples (5YR4/6).
Vessels: Jars (JM3.12)
Source, distribution and dating: Source in the Malvern Hills area (*ibid*, 15–28).

MALVL: Malvernian limestone, handmade
Fabric/manufacture: Handmade, reduced ware containing sparse to moderate fragments of Palaeozoic limestone.
Vessels: Jars (JC2.12).
Source, distribution and dating: Source in the Malvern area (*ibid*; Spencer 1983).

BLSF: Imitation Gallo-belgic ware
Fabric: Fine grained, slightly laminar, fabric with scatter of tiny quartz grains, up to 0.1 mm, or more rarely up to 0.3 mm.
Manufacture: Wheelmade. Very dark grey (5Y 3/1) with black surfaces (2.5Y 3/0), finely burnished externally.
Vessels: Jar, ?beakers.
Source, distribution and dating: Restricted to a small number of vessels from the military levels. Source is unknown but possibly in south-east England.

VRW: Verulamium region white ware
Fabric: Hard fired, with abundant, well-sorted, sub-angular quartz grains, typically 0.5 mm in size; and sparse iron ore and flint fragments. White core (10YR 8/2) with pale brown (10YR8/4) surfaces.
Vessels: Bowls and flagons.
Source, distribution and dating: Main period of production *c* AD 70–150. (*cf* Castle 1972; 1974; 1978; Saunders and Havercroft 1977; Tyers 1983). Sherds are first recorded in small quantities from the early military levels, and although apparently absent from the later military levels occur in more substantial quantities in the military demolition levels and Period 1.

MOVR: Mortaria: Brockley Hill/Verulamium region
Fabric: Abundant rounded and sub-angular quartz grains, typically *c* 0.5 mm in size, and sparse large (up to 3.5 mm) iron ore and flint fragments.
Manufacture: Wheelthrown. Hard fired, greyish-cream (10YR 8/2), sometimes with a pink (7.5YR 7/4) or black core. May have a self-coloured or buff (7.5YR 6/6) slip. Trituration grit mainly flint with some quartz and rare red-brown and black fragments.
Vessels: M7.11–14.
Source, distribution and dating: Main period of production *c* AD 70–150. Verulamium region, including workshops at Little Munden (Bricket Wood), Radlett and Verulamium, Herts, and Brockley Hill, Middlesex. The fabric first appears in later military contexts, increasing in Period 1, and continuing into Period 2. Its occurrence in later military phases suggests a change in supply within the military period.

BB1: Dorset Black-Burnished ware, type 1
Fabric: Williams 1977, 163–220. Unlike the basilical hall assemblage this ware has not been divided into three fabrics since they may all come from the same place of origin (*cf* Farrar 1973, 69–78; Williams 1977, 189).
Vessels: Four main classes of vessel are represented; jars, bowls, dishes and lids; with beakers and flagons just represented although with the difficulties of identification between small jars and beakers minus handle scars, there may well have been more than were recognised.
Form types: Beakers (BK13.11–12, BK13.21, BK13.32–34); jars (JC3.11, JC3.21, JC3.23–27, JC3.31–35, JC3.41–46, JC3.51–52, JC3.61–63, JC3.71–72, JC3.81–82, JM1.25); bowls (B20.12–15, B20.21–25, 27, B20.31–2, 34, B20.42, B23.11–13, B23.21–24, B24.11–12, B24.21–23, B24.31, B26.12–15, B26.21, B27.11); dishes (D1.11, D1.21, D1.31–32, D1.41–42, D2.21–24, D3.11–14, D3.21, D4.11–13); lids (4.12–15, L4.21, L4.31, L4.52–57, L4.59, L4.61–64, L4.71).
Source, distribution and dating: Black-burnished ware first occurs in Period 2. It may well have come to Wroxeter slightly before the first expansion of supplies to Hadrian's Wall ie *c* AD 120. This would not be surprising considering the evidence from other sites; Webster proposes a pre-Hadrianic date for the earliest occurrence of this ware at Caersws (Webster 1989) and Greep notes very small quantities in pre-Flavian contexts at Caerleon (Greep 1986).

Nene Valley ware
NVCC: Nene Valley colour-coated ware
Fabric: Howe *et al* 1980. NB later key groups divided by fabric colour (cf Symonds 1997).
Form types: Flagon (F7.12); bowls (B6.11, B10.31).
Source, distribution and dating: Nene Valley area, second-fourth century (Howe *et al* 1980)

NVCC1: cream/white fabric (10YR 8/3), but can be so white (5Y8/1) that it can be confused with Cologne ware (*cf* Anderson *et al* 1982).

NVCC2: Pink-buff fabric. Most common fabric in Baths basilica assemblage, predominantly beakers.

NVCC3: red fabric, somewhat earlier on typological grounds than the other variants, includes barbotine decorated beakers (Symonds 1997).

MNVCC: Mortaria, Nene Valley colour-coated
Fabric: Howe *et al* 1980.
Source, distribution and dating: Nene Valley area, second-fourth century.

New Forest ware
Fabric: Fulford Fabric 1 (1975, 24–6).
Source, distribution and dating: New Forest, Hampshire, *c* AD 280–400. Occurs in basilical hall assemblage but not recorded from the Webster excavations.

Oxfordshire industries
OXFP: Oxfordshire parchment ware
Fabric: Cream fabric with yellowish surface, may also be pinkish in colour especially at core (Young 1977, 81)
Form types: Bowls (B18.11).
Source, distribution and dating: *c* AD 240–400+ (Young 1977, 80–92).

OXFRCC: Oxfordshire red and brown colour-coated ware.
Fabric: Wheelthown, generally hard sandy fabric with sparse small black and red inclusions, and occasional lumps of chalk up to 5 mm. Pale orange (5YR 7/6) to red orange fabric (2.5YR 6/8) with an orange (2.5YR 6/8) to dark brown (5YR 4/2) slip. (Young 1977, 123)
Form types: Bowls (B7.31, B12.81).
Source, distribution and dating: Manufactured at a number of centres in Oxfordshire in the period *c* AD 240–400+ (Young 1977, 123–184).

MOXFW: Mortaria: Oxfordshire white
Fabric: Young 1977, 56–79. Kay Hartley notes that the fabric of some, especially early, Oxford mortaria is packed with transparent quartz inclusions and can appear similar to Verulamium mortaria.
Source, distribution and dating: Occurs in small quantities from Period 3.

MOXFRC: Mortaria: Oxfordshire red colour-coated
Fabric/manufacture: Young 1977, 123–184.
Form types: M7.31.
Source, distribution and dating: Occurs in small quantities from Period 3.

MOXFWC: Mortaria: Oxfordshire white colour-coated
Fabric/manufacture: Young 1977, 117–122.
Source, distribution and dating: Occurs in small quantities from Period 3.

MHW: Much Hadham ware
Fabric: Sandy brown-orange fabric with a well burnished surface, sometimes with a thin brown slip (Harden and Green 1978).
Source, distribution and dating: Much Hadham (near Braughing) Herts, major production from the third century onwards. Recorded from the basilical hall site only (Symonds 1997).

MANCH: Mortaria: Mancetter Hartshill
Fabric: Occasional large quartz grains (up to 2 mm) and re-fired pottery fragments. Kay Hartley notes that the fabric ranges from one with scarcely any inclusions to one with a fair amount of ill-sorted black slag-like inclusions.
Manufacture: Wheelthrown. Usually hard fired, creamy white (10YR 8/1), sometimes with a pink core. Outer surface may have a thin yellow (10YR 8/3) wash. Trituration grits are hard rust brown and /or black re-fired pottery fragments. Mortaria later than *c* AD 140 contain only rare quartz fragments while mortaria earlier than AD 130 usually have mixed trituration grit in which quartz and sandstone are normal components.
Form Types: M9.11, M9.21.
Source, distribution and dating: Mancetter/Hartshill (Hartley 1973, 143–47).

CALC: Fossil shell-tempered ware
Fabric: Often erroneously referred to as 'calcite-gritted' ware. Smooth soapy brown or dark grey ware made from a clay containing frequent fragments of fossil shell and other fragments frequently of calcitic composition.
Vessels: Forms include both handmade and wheelmade types, the latter frequently with a rilled surface finish. Occurs as jars, often with hooked or triangular rims and flanged bowls.
Form types: Jars (JLS2.41–42); bowls (B25.11–12).
Source: The ware is thought to have a source in the Midlands. It achieved a widespread distribution in the latter half of the fourth century.

3 Imported wares

Samian
(Divided SAMSG: South Gaulish; SAMCG: Central Gaulish; SAMCEG: Central or East Gaulish and SAMEG: East Gaulish)

PRW: Pompeian red ware
Fabric: coarse grey fabric with red cortex and internal slip (P5.15) and cream fabric with internal slip. These are unclassified Pompeian red wares, probably copies but having the internal coating not found on local Wroxeter copies.
Vessels: Platters.
Form types: P5.21–22.
Source, distribution and dating: source unknown but unlikely to be imports.

PRW2: Pompeian red ware 2
Fabric: Peacock 1977a, fabric 2, 153–4.
Vessels: Platters.
Form types: P6.13.
Source, distribution and dating: Gaul or the Mediterranean. Imported largely for military consumption in the first century. The fabric is first recorded at Wroxeter from the military demolition levels.

PRW3: Pompeian red ware 3
Fabric: Peacock 1977a, fabric 3, 154.
Vessels: Platters and lids.
Form types: P6.11–12, L2.18.
Source, distribution and dating: Central Gaul. Imported largely for military consumption. There is no evidence of pre-Conquest trade with this source, which may have captured the market by the late Flavian period. It is not known how far, if at all, production continued into the second century. Sherds are recorded from the earliest military levels.

NIEG: North Italian Eggshell ware
Fabric: Very hard with a grey-black surface and red-brown core (Greene 1979, 82).
Vessels: Cup (cf Greene 1979, fig 34, nos 1, 2).
Source, distribution and dating: The precise area of production in North Italy is not known. The ware was exported over quite large areas, though not in great quantities (ibid, fig 36). Pre-Flavian. Only a single small sherd was recovered from military pit F2807.

MICA1: Mica dusted ware
Fabric: Pink-buff fabric coated with golden mica (Greene 1979, 129).
Vessels: Beakers including one decorated with bosses.
Form types: BK3.13, BK3.18.
Source, distribution and dating: The first example of this ware occurs in the military demolition deposits. It is probably a Neronian-Flavian import, possibly from Northern Gaul (ibid).

TN: Terra Nigra
Fabric: Rigby 1973.
Vessels: Camulodunum type 16 platter.
Form type: P2.11.
Source, distribution and dating: A single rim sherd from an imported platter, probably from north-east Gaul, was found in a military context. This was one of the latest forms in the Gallo-Belgic potters repertoire and one which shows a strong connection with military sites in Britain.

LYON: Lyon ware
Fabric: Greene 1979, 13–42.
Vessels: Beakers and cups.
Form types: Beakers (BK3.11, BK3.16); cups (C8.12–17).
Source, distribution and dating: The fabric is typical of finds from the production site of La Butte, on the north bank of the Saône near its junction with the Rhone, c AD 40–70, occurring in Britain in small quantities up to c AD 75. Apart from samian this was the main imported fine ware to occur in the military levels. The proportion of earlier cups to the longer-lasting beakers appears to be fairly high reflecting the Neronian foundations of the site.

LRCC: Lower Rhineland colour-coated ware
Fabric: The fabric represented is fine, soft and white with a dark brown/grey matt colour-coating. The fabric can however, vary considerably (Greene 1979, 56–64; Anderson et al 1981).
Vessels: Beakers and hemispherical cup (Greene 1979, type 4).
Form types: Beakers BK8.12; cups C3.26,
Source, distribution and dating: A number of industries were producing colour-coated wares in the lower Rhineland in the period AD 40–70, but no kiln sites are known. Only two other vessels are known from Britain, from Colchester and Richborough. A single body sherd was recovered from a contaminated military context.

CGGW: Central Gaulish glazed ware
Fabric: Greene 1979, 86–105.
Vessels: Sherds were extremely fragmented making identification difficult, but most appeared to be from beakers, including one decorated with vertical ribs (ibid, fig 42.13). One sherd with a barbotine dot, and two tiny rim sherds probably came from a straight sided cup (ibid, fig 41.9).
Form types: BK3.12
Source, distribution and dating: Central Gaul; a number of production sites are known in the Allier region, c AD 43–70. Other glazed vessels are known from various sites at Wroxeter. All sherds come from later military or post-military contexts.

CGCC: Central Gaulish colour-coated ware
Fabric: Greene 1979, 43–9.
Vessels: Beakers (Greene type 3), and a rarer indented type, cups and two lamp fragments. Very few roughcast beakers had internal roughcasting.
Form types: Beakers (BK8.11, BK8.13–18; BK9.11); cups (C8.11); lamps (ML1.11, 13).
Source, distribution and dating: Probably produced in several centres in Central Gaul, including Lezoux, c AD 40–70. The earliest occurrence at Wroxeter is in demolition deposits though larger quantities were recovered from Period 2 deposits.

CGWH1: Central Gaulish colour-coat (white fabric)
Fabric: Fine orange fabric with rough cast decoration. Glossy blue-black coat. Diagonal wipe marks behind the rim.
Vessels: Beakers.

CGWH2: softer than fabric CGWH1. Fine micaceous pale orange-buff fabric. Pale orange-brown glossy slip. Sparser roughcasting.
Vessels: Beakers.

These fabrics may be variations of one fabric as is discussed in Symonds 1990. Symonds also notes that the fabric normally has the hard, red fabric of central Gaulish samian ware, with a dark black or greenish colour-coat (Symonds 1997).

BLEG: Gallo-Belgic 'Eggshell' *terra nigra*
Fabric: Greene Group 5 (1979, 106–27, fig 52). Hard, fine, almost grit free fabric; reddish with finely burnished grey-black surfaces.
Vessels: Beakers, Camulodunum 120A, with an unusual rim.
Form type: BK12.21.
Source, distribution and dating: Probably imported in pre-Flavian period. Found in military contexts, with the earliest occurrence from pit F2908; a single sherd from Period 1, pit F2990, and various sherds scattered through later site phases.

TRR: Trier 'Moselkeramic'
Fabric: Fine red fabric with glossy black colour-coat (Symonds 1992).
Vessels: Beakers.
Source, distribution and dating: Trier, third-century production.

COLG: Cologne colour-coated ware
Fabric: Hard, fine white, or creamish fabric with a dark black or brown slip. Inclusions consist of very fine quartz, and occasional flecks of mica and red iron ore.
Vessels: Beakers, often with roughcast or barbotine decoration.
Source, distribution and dating: Cologne bag-shaped beakers with cornice rims and roughcast or barbotine decoration were made from AD 70. The 'hunt cups' date to the Hadrianic-early Antonine period whilst later forms with a more angular profile were made from around AD 150. Sherds are recorded from the Period 2 levels.

MORV: Mortaria: Rhone Valley
Fabric: Sparse ill-sorted quartz up to 2 mm and sparse ironstone fragments up to 0.5 mm.
Manufacture: Wheelmade, hard, pale brownish cream throughout (10YR 8/4).
Forms: M1.11–14.
Source, distribution and dating: The only significant continental suppliers of mortaria in the military period. Although only a very small quantity came from stratified military contexts a much larger sample occurred residually in Period 1 deposits.

MRHEN: Mortaria: Rhenish
MORT2: Mortaria (Rhenish?).
Fabric: Fine micaceous fabric with occasional quartz up to 0.2 mm.
Manufacture: Wheelmade, hard, yellowish brown (10YR 5/4) throughout.
Source, distribution and dating: Source uncertain, but possibly an early import from the Rhineland (K Hartley pers comm).

MONG: Mortaria, North Gaulish
Fabric: Fine fabric with moderate well-sorted pinkish quartz up to 0.1 mm, and occasional chalk.
Manufacture: Wheelmade, hard, white (10YR 8/2).
Form type: M3.11.
Source, distribution and dating: A complete vessel stamped CASSARIVS, unfortunately now missing, was dated by K Hartley to *c* AD 70–100. The fabric is present in relatively small quantities, first occurring in the later military phases when it would probably have been competing with products of the Verulamium industry. The stamped vessel could have arrived in Wroxeter before the end of the military occupation, but its deposition in a pit (F2990) attributed to the early civilian occupation suggests it belongs to Period 1.

MOASTE: Mortaria: Aoste/Atisii
Fabric: Very fine-textured, micaceous fabric with sparse quartz, red-brown and sometimes black inclusions visible at x10 magnification.
Manufacture: Wheelmade. Cream to brownish-cream fabric sometimes with pinkish core. Trituration grit white and transparent quartz.
Source, distribution and dating: Workshop of the Atisii brothers at Aoste, Isere, Gallia Narbonnensis, normally dated *c* AD 50–85 (Hartley 1973, 46). Not a common fabric at Wroxeter represented by only one fragment found residually in a post-military context.

AMC189: Amphorae: Carrot (Camulodunum 189)
Fabric: Peacock and Williams Class 12 (1986, 109–10).
Source, distribution and dating: An origin in the Levant has been tentatively suggested in the past, but the dearth of finds in this region points to a source elsewhere. Often found on early military sites in Britain. They are found after AD 75 at Fishbourne, but it is at present difficult to be certain when production ceased (Cunliffe 1971).

AMRIB: as Kingsholm 117
Fabric: Broadly comparable to Camulodunum 189 above although examples from Kingsholm, Gloucester (Hurst 1985, fig 28, 117–18) demonstrate a slight digression from the standard carrot type with a more ovoid body, wider ribbing and hollow spike.
Source, distribution and dating: Source unknown. Amphorae of this type appear to be present at

Wroxeter from the military levels although the small sherd size precludes confident separation from sherds of Camulodunum 189 proper.

AMDR2–4: Amphorae: Dressel 2–4
Fabric: Peacock and Williams Class 10 (1986, 105–6). A number of different fabrics were present at Wroxeter indicating the variety of production sites for this form (Italian Dressel 2–4; Black sand Dressel 2–4, Catalan, East Mediterranean and South Spanish). The Catalan vessels are distinguished by a red granitic fabric to be equated with Williams's Fabric 1 (Peacock and Williams 1986, 96, 106). The black sand fabric is characteristic of the region of Campania, around the Bay of Naples.
Distribution and dating: Dressel 2–4 amphorae were produced from the latter half of the first century BC; its numbers decreasing considerably by the latter part of the first century AD. All the fabrics discriminated above were present in small quantities in the military levels.

AMKO: Koan or pseudo-Koan
Fabric/Source: Petrological analysis by D Williams shows a mixed range of inclusions with pieces of volcanic glass and rock and metamorphic phyllite. Also present are discrete grains of sanidine and plagioclase felspar, flecks of mica and iron oxides. The petrology points to a volcanic origin, most likely in the eastern Mediterranean region, with Kos itself a possible contender.
Form: a fragment of amphora body with a steeply arched bifid handle (cf Peacock and Williams 1986, Class 11).
Distribution: Represented by a single sherd from a Period 3 context.

AMDR28: Amphorae: Dressel 28
Fabric: Peacock and Williams, Class 31 (1986 149–50).
Source, distribution and dating: Made in Tarraconensis and possibly Baetica, and in France where a kiln is known at Velaux, Bouches-du-Rhone. Late Augustan to the first half of the second century AD. Represented by just two sherds from the military levels.

AMRHOD: Amphorae – Rhodian
Fabric: Peacock and Williams Class 9 (1986, 102–4). The majority of sherds from Period 2 belong to Peacock fabric 2, with just a single sherd of fabric 1 (Peacock 1977c).
Source, distribution and dating: Almost certainly from the Rhodian Peraea (ibid) where a number of production sites are known. They are often found on early Roman military sites in Britain, and most probably arrived as a tribute imposed by Claudius (ibid). Production continued into the early second century AD.

AMPE47: Amphorae – Gailes 4 (Pelichet 47)
Fabric: Peacock and Williams Class 27 (1986, 142–3).
Source, distribution and dating: Southern France, particularly around the mouth of the Rhone in Languedoc (Laubenheimer 1985). Importation began soon after the Boudiccan revolt (Peacock 1978). By the early second century AD this was the most common wine amphorae in the province. At Wroxeter the type forms a significant part of the military assemblage (14.7% by sherd count).

AMGAU5: Amphorae: Gailes 5
Fabric: Peacock and Williams Class 30 (1986, 148).
Source, distribution and dating: Southern France. Second half of the first century AD to the beginning of the second century AD. Possibly represented by a fragment of damaged rim from a military context.

AMF148: Amphorae: Fishbourne 148.3
Fabric: Previously published from period 1 levels at Fishbourne (Cunliffe, 1971, fig 100, Type 148.3). Petrological analysis shows the principal components to be frequent grains of sub- angular quartz up to 1.2 mm in size, though the majority are smaller sized grains than this; flecks of mica, limestone and occasional foraminifera (pers comm David Williams). In the hand specimen the fabric is very hard, rough and sandy. Colour usually light red (5YR 7/6 to 2.5YR 6/6), although one rim is more of a patchy pinky/buff red colour (not easily parallelled in Munsell). Williams has noted this form at York, Dorchester, Colchester and Leicester as well as Fishbourne
Source, distribution and dating: As yet little known type but relatively well-represented from the military levels at Wroxeter.

AMC186A: Amphorae: Camulodunum 186A/Beltran 1
Fabric: Peacock and Williams Class 17 (1986, 120–1).
Source, distribution and dating: Southern Spain, late first century BC to the early second century AD. Amphorae of Camulodunum 186 sp form the second largest category of amphorae in the military levels.

AMC186C: Amphorae: Camulodunum 186C/Beltran 11A
Fabric: Peacock and Williams Class 18 (1986, 122–3).
Source, distribution and dating: Southern Spain. Flavian or shortly before, to the early second century AD. See AMC186A above.

DR20: Amphorae: Dressel 20
Fabric: Peacock and Williams Class 25 (1986, 136–40).
Source, distribution and dating: Produced in the Southern Spanish province of Baetica along the banks of the River Guadalquivir. Small quantities were imported prior to Roman conquest, peaking in the mid second century AD (Williams and Peacock 1983). Production continued up to the late third century. Most common type found on British Roman sites and the same pattern is reflected at Wroxeter from the military levels onwards.

AMPW16: Amphorae: Peacock and Williams (1986) Class 16
Fabric: (ibid, 117–9).
Source, distribution and dating: Spanish, the form dates from the late first century BC to the first century AD.

AMRIC527: Amphorae: Richborough 527

Fabric: Peacock and Williams Class 13 (1986, 111–2).

Source, distribution and dating: A recent programme of study by Paul Arthur has suggested a likely origin in Campania, Italy (1989), in preference to the Massif Central region of France which had previously been thought to be a possible source. An Italian source has indeed recently been discovered on the island of Lipari, north of Sicily (Cavalier 1994).

The majority of the British finds date to the first century AD, although production continued much longer than this. Three Richborough 527 vessels have were found in early to mid third century AD deposits at New Fresh Wharf in London (Green 1986).

AMPH70: Amphorae: Haltern 70

Fabric: Peacock and Williams Class 15 (1986, 115–6).

Source, distribution and dating: Produced in the region of the River Guadalquivir. The sharing of a similar stamp on this form and a Dressel 20 suggests that both forms may have been produced in the same workshop. Mid first century BC to the mid first century AD. Relatively well-represented in the military amphorae assemblage.

AMSPAIN: Amphorae: Southern Spanish

Fabric: Miscellaneous Spanish fabrics insufficiently diagnostic to determine forms.

Source, distribution and dating: Coastal regions of southern Spain, late first century BC to the second century AD.

Amphorae stoppers

Several fragments of small thin stoppers used to help seal the neck of amphorae were recovered from Period 2. All are in a fairly fine-textured to sandy, off-white to buff fabric. The type appears similar to those used for Dressel 20 and Haltern 70 vessels recovered from the Port Vendres II shipwreck (Colls *et al* 1977, fig 14), but the form seems to have been in general use.

4 Wares of unknown source

WHEG: White Eggshell ware

Fabric: white fabric.

Vessel: Cup.

Form type: C5.21.

Occurrence: From a Period 2 context.

IMTN: Imitation Terra Nigra

Fabric: Finely granular with black surfaces showing specks of mica.

Vessels: A small sherd resembling platter Camulodunum type 4A (Hawkes and Hull 1947).

Occurrence: Sherd from a post-military context.

GBWW: Gallo-belgic type white ware

Fabric: cf Greene 1979, 128.

Vessels: All closed forms, probably mostly butt-beakers.

Form type: BK1.

Source, distribution and dating: The undistinctive fabric and lack of rims make it difficult to determine whether these are foreign imports or products of south-east England, although the latter is suspected. Some of the black-surfaced butt-beaker sherds present could be paralleled in the Essex area. The earliest occurrence at Wroxeter is a beaker from the military pits. A concentration of sherds probably from a single vessel came from Period 1, with fragments displaced into Period 2.

CCB: Brown colour-coated ware

Fabric: Very hard, wheelmade ware with abundant, ill-sorted sub-angular quartz. Fired yellowish red (5YR 5/6) with a dark brown grey colour-coat (5YR 4/1).

Vessels: Fabric mainly used for roughcast cornice-rimmed beakers, and a range of plain beakers with curved or cornice rims.

Source, distribution and dating: cf Symonds 1990 for range of possible sources.

SHEL: Shell-tempered ware

Fabric: Abundant ill-sorted shell up to 5 mm and occasional rounded quartz up to 0.1 mm.

Manufacture: Handmade? Core black (2.5Y 2/0) with surfaces ranging from very dark grey (5Y 3/1) or dark brown (10YR 4/3) to brown (7.5YR 5/4).

Vessels: Unknown.

Occurrence: Two sherds, one from a late military demolition context; the other from a Period 1 deposit.

OXID: Coarse oxidized ware

Fabric: Miscellaneous oxidized wares not classified elsewhere.

Vessels: Flagons (F3.44, 5.42, 6.12).

GREY: Coarse reduced ware

Fabric: Miscellaneous grey wares not classified elsewhere.

Vessels: Flagons (F3.32); beakers (BK4.11, BK10.14); jars (JM2.21–22, 24, JM3.11, JM4.21, JM4.24, JM6.12; JW3.11); cups (C2.11); bowls (B3.22, B6.21, B8.3, B10.11, B12.2, B20.41, B21.13); lids (L1.11).

CC: Miscellaneous colour-coated ware

Fabric: Miscellaneous unclassified colour-coated wares.

Vessels: Beakers.

Form type: B6.21.

MORT1: Pinkish mortaria

Fabric: Abundant, ill-sorted, sub-rounded pinkish and white quartz up to 1 mm, with occasional clay and black ?ironstone fragments less than 0.1 mm. Hard, reddish yellow (7.5YR 7/6) in colour.

Occurrence: Single body sherd from a military context.

MOCRA: Mortaria, white 1

Fabric: Fine fabric with sparse to moderate sub-angular quartz up to 0.1 mm and occasional red ?sandstone fragments of a similar size. Hard, white ware (2.5Y 8/2) with a greyish core (2.5Y 5/2).

Form types: M11.11, M11.21, M11.31–32, M11.41. Source, distribution and dating: Fabric similar to that used for the second-century mortaria produced at Wroxeter, but lacks the heavy tempering associated with these. The combination of grit and scoring inside and on top of the rim was a common first-century practice. Only occurs in demolition period deposits. If not intrusive into the military deposits this appears to be part of the diversification of supplies seen in later phases.

The military pottery

by Jane Timby (summary based on a report prepared by Margaret Darling)

Introduction

A full discussion of the military assemblage by M Darling can be found in Webster (forthcoming). The following short summary has been extracted from that report to serve as the starting point for considering the post-military pottery assemblages from Wroxeter. A detailed discussion of individual military vessels and their suggested pedigree, along with details of quantification, and comparisons with other military assemblages can be found in Darling (forthcoming). A selection of the vessel types and a description of the fabrics can be found integrated into the form and fabric series.

The military occupation, thought to span some 35 years, produced an assemblage of some 16,000 sherds, approximately 241kg. The excavated area extending from the defences into the interior of the fortress, the inner area, witnessed a number of changes of use during the military period. Most of the military pottery was recovered from discrete cut features in the inner area which were later sealed by a military demolition layer. There were few horizontal or vertical stratigraphic relationships to provide an independent framework for the interpretation of the chronology of the pottery. Later building work, and the digging of additional pits through the demolition layer, also served to disturb many of the military deposits causing some contamination.

The first phase of occupation, by *Legio XIV*, is thought to have lasted some ten years before they were withdrawn. There is then some debate as to whether the garrison was replaced, *Legio XX* being a potential candidate, or whether the fortress continued to be maintained by a reduced detail. Although the successive military phases after the withdrawal lasting up to *c* AD 90 produced commensurately more pottery, it unfortunately shows no perceptible changes to support the former proposal.

A problem that manifests itself from the late military occupation onwards is the high level of residuality which may mask small changes in the pottery development. The earliest levels, for example those associated with the first barracks, produced such small quantities of pottery that no useful discussion could be made. Pits, therefore, provide the primary assemblage although many of these had little or no pot. A notable exception is a particular unusual group from pit F2807 in the southern part of the inner area which was analysed separately.

Most of the pottery from the military deposits is of local manufacture, necessitated by the complete absence of any established local industry. The vessels produced are entirely continental in form and technique and it is likely that potters were closely attached to the legions. Analysis of the types has permitted Darling to postulate influence from North Italian traditions, seen particularly at the Magdalensberg, Austria.

Early military period

The earliest occupation was served almost exclusively by locally produced pottery and the occurrence of non-local vessels, other than finewares is rare. The main non-local fabrics are CREAM and GREY wares, Verulamium region whitewares (VRW), and Severn Valley wares (SV). The finewares comprise Lyon wares (LYON), South Gaulish samian (SAMSG), and single sherds of MICA1, and BLSF. Other imports include Pompeian redware (PRW3) and amphorae. Local, or regional oxidized (OXID) wares and a single native ware sherd also occur.

A range of vessels was present dominated by jars which accounted for over 57% by EVE. Most other vessel classes were represented including flagons, mortaria, lamps, cups and beakers. Storage jars are very rare with just one possible example recorded.

Pit F2807

This feature produced *c* 1700 sherds (18kg) of pottery, approximately 11% by weight and count of the military assemblage, and 19.5% by EVE. Many of the vessels show evidence for over or under-firing and are best viewed as poor seconds or wasters. Only four vessels, from the upper fill, were not local. Several of the vessels are unique to the site. Compared to the other military assemblages, the group shows a relatively high percentage of flagons, drinking vessels and tablewares. Beakers account for 43% by EVE of the entire military assemblage. The juxtaposition of types, notably copies of samian Dr 27 cups, unusual before the Flavian period, alongside copies of pre-Flavian cups and beakers is difficult to account for. A late military date (late Neronian or Flavian) is proposed. Many of the vessels, in particular the cups, show Italian influence and it is suggested that the vessels could be the product of a single potter, perhaps from the Upper Rhine or Danubian area where the North Italian influence is strong. Alternatively the deposit could be a dump of rejects from a store (*cf* Darling 1976 for further debate).

Later military period

Analysis of the degree of fragmentation of the pottery using a brokenness measure (Orton *et al* 1993, 169, 178) showed this to be high for the late military period. Local products continue to dominate although the assemblage begins to show increasing diversification with other products appearing. Rusticated wares emerge and there is a slight increase in CREAM, GREY and Severn Valley ware (SV) compared to the earlier levels. A single sherd of Malvernian ware first occurs (MALV). Finewares include further Lyon ware, a sherd of Central Gaulish glazed ware (CCGW) and samian (SAMSG and SAMCG). Imported mortaria from the Rhone (MORV) and further Pompeian redware (PRW3) are present.

Analysis of the vessels based on EVEs and including samian shows a marked increase in the number of flagons and a decrease in kitchen and table vessels in the later phase. There is also a slight increase in cups and beakers.

Military demolition deposits

Sherd size analysis for the military period overall showed this to be the lowest in the demolition deposits. Local products continue to dominate but other fabrics represented earlier increase (CREAM, GREY, SV and VRW) and Verulamium mortaria (MOVR) first appear. The quantity of Flavian samian broadly doubles between the late military and demolition layers but apart from the defences zone, the largest group in the demolition contexts is still pre-Flavian. A considerable quantity of amphorae was recovered from a pot and tile spread assigned to the demolition period. Other imports include Lyon ware, Central Gaulish colour-coated ware (CGCC), Central Gaulish glazed ware (CGGW) and whiteware (CGWH), Pompeian redwares (PRW2), eggshell ware (BLSF), and mortaria from the Rhone (MORV), ?Rhine (MORT2) and North Gaul (MONG). The vessel range shows a slightly higher proportion of bowls, dishes and cups which is likely to be directly related to an increased quantity of samian.

In addition to the other imports noted above, a wide range of amphorae types reached Wroxeter in the military period, from Spanish, Gallic and Italian sources. Spanish products dominate, particularly Dressel 20 vessels. It is suggested that the level of amphorae reaching Wroxeter declined significantly after the military withdrawal although sherds continue to appear residually in later periods.

Comparison of the military repertoire with that at Usk and Inchtuthil, all possibly connected through *Legio XX*, and all involved in pottery production, have shown no clear ceramic links. The continuation of pottery manufacture at Wroxeter after the end of the military period suggests that production had been transferred from military into civilian hands.

The Period 1 pottery

by Margaret Darling with contributions by David Williams and Kay Hartley

Introduction and discussion

The pottery sample from Period 1 comprised just over 52 kg or a total of 3410 sherds, representing 4221

EVEs (Table 4.13). The collection showed a high level of fragmentation and a low average sherd weight by contrast with the military pottery (Table 4.14), and this suggests that the material may be largely residual, a suggestion supported by the large quantity of much earlier samian indicating a figure of 70% residuality.

The Period 1 archaeology was represented by two distinct areas, the buildings on Watling Street and the pits to their rear. Only in a few areas was there anything like a stratified sequence, generally represented by Phase 1.3 destruction layers over the Watling Street buildings. The contexts have been divided into three groups corresponding to the later Period 2 divisions. Portico contexts comprise Buildings 2, 4, and 5, and the westernmost rooms of Buildings 1 and 3. West Range contexts cover the eastern parts of the latter, while Courtyard contexts account for the pits (Fig 4.81). Most of the pottery from the buildings, therefore, is grouped under the Portico heading with only 11–15% of all the pottery coming from the West Range. Phase 1.3 layers accounted for between 47 and 58% of the pottery and derived from the destruction layers over the buildings and from the pits. Although

Table 4.13 Pottery Period 1: quantities by phase and site area (excluding amphorae)

	1.1	1.2	1.3	total
sherd numbers				
C	5	–	741	746
P	377	1258	630	2265
WR	110	21	268	399
total	492	1279	1639	3410
EVEs				
C	10	–	1795	1805
P	370	1005	427	1802
WR	156	43	415	614
total	536	1048	2637	4221
weight				
C	54	–	11319	11373
P	3029	10267	5120	18416
WR	1056	175	2439	3670
total	4139	10442	18878	33459

P portico, WR west range, C courtyard

Table 4.14 Pottery Period 1: quantities from features and degree of brokenness by phase

	sherds/%		EVEs/%		weight/%		sherds / Wt	broken-ness
1.1	138	10	103	4	1073	6	7.8	1.34
1.2	413	30	362	15	3819	22	9.3	1.14
1.3	814	60	1904	81	12839	72	25.8	0.70
total	1365	100	2369	100	17731	100		

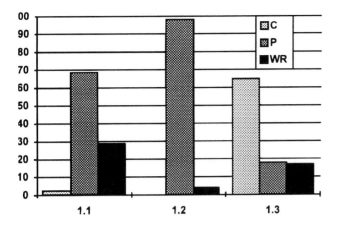

Fig 4.81 Pottery Period 1: spatial distribution (EVEs) by phase

the more diagnostic pottery from Period 1 came largely from the latter, this is also where a high level of residuality might be expected (Fig 4.82).

Trends which are apparent in the military demolition deposits (Darling 1976) continue in Period 1, namely a diversification of pottery supplies from elsewhere leading to a smaller contribution by the local potters. The local white-slipped fabric (WWCR) appears to increase in importance (Fig 4.83), and is particularly noticeable in the subsequent Period 2 in the form of slipped flagons and bowls, much of which could be residual material from Period 1. The local oxidized fabrics may be declining in favour of more reduced vessels (Table 4.15).

The high level of residual pottery from the fortress limits firm conclusions about new vessel types. The jar type JM9.3 (Fig 4.61) is recorded from the military demolition, but certainly has its main occurrence in Period 1. Everted rim jars generally increase, but it is a common Flavian type. Rusticated sherds do not substantially increase from the levels seen in the military demolition, giving little evidence to assess how many of those in Period 2 are residual from Period 1. As suggested above, it is possible that many of the slipped flagons in Period 2 belong to the earlier phase but there

are too few flagons in Period 1 to be sure. Some variations on the reeded-rim bowl theme occur only in Period 1 (eg the hemispherical bowl type B7.11: Fig 4.65), or to a greater extent than in the military collection (eg type B17.3: Fig 4.68). There is a notable trend towards the use of the finer fabric for bowls, which suggests that they may have been used as tableware rather than cooking vessels. Dishes of the type D5.2 (Fig 4.70) which occur in the military period are commoner from Period 1 deposits, but could easily all be residual. Virtually no cups occur, and the beakers decline very sharply.

Amphorae stratified in Period 1 deposits (Table 4.16) seem likely to be mostly residual from the military occupation, and the continuing decline in amphorae is apparent in Period 2. The local manufacture of mortaria seems to continue, alongside vessels coming in from the Verulamium region potters. A number of imported vessels are also present (Table 4.17) although some of these may well be residual.

Tables 4.18 and 4.19 detail the pottery by assumed function, by phase and spatially. The functions identified are as those used in the Usk report (Greene 1993). The difficulty in defining function is inevitably the 'table/kitchen' category. Here reeded rim bowls and lids have been allocated to cooking, while some other bowls have been placed in the 'table/kitchen' group on the basis of their coarser finish, together with Pompeian red ware dishes and their copies. The analysis shows a high proportion of drinking vessels in Phase 1.1, but this has to be viewed in the light of both the relatively small sample, and the high percentage of samian from the phase. Liquid holders decrease from the levels seen in the military contexts, but it is notable that otherwise the assemblage from the last phase (containing the bulk of the pottery) is otherwise relatively similar to that from the military demolition contexts. However, 66% of EVEs of Phase 1.3 came from the Courtyard area, and much of it could be residual. The higher proportion of drinking vessels from the Watling Street frontage (P areas), again reflects the abnormal quantity of samian in the Phase 1.1 assemblage, predominantly from these same areas.

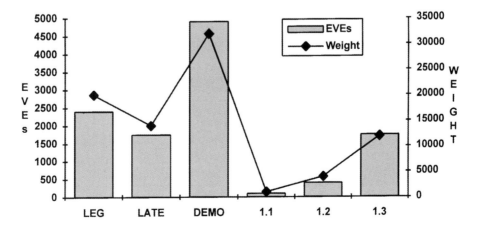

Fig 4.82 Pottery Period 1: EVEs and weight from cut features by phase

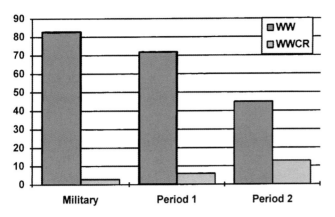

Fig 4.83 Pottery Period 1: % Wroxeter Ware (WW) and variants present by period, with variant WWCR shown as % Wroxeter Ware

Table 4.15 Pottery Period 1: fabric quantities by phase (% weight and EVE)

	% by weight			% by EVE		
	1.1	1.2	1.3	1.1	1.2	1.3
SAMSG	8	5	8	18	16	20
SAMCG	–	<1	<1	–	<1	–
MORV	–	2	8	–	–	1
MONG	1	<1	<1	–	–	<1
MORT3	–	–	<1	–	–	–
MOVR	–	1	2	–	1	<1
MWWO	–	1	–	–	–	1
MWWOF	–	–	7	–	–	2
MWWR	–	–	3	–	–	–
MWWCR	–	–	<1	–	–	<1
WWO	40	28	29	22	20	21
WWOF	3	5	2	2	7	6
WWR	25	35	30	20	39	34
WWRF	–	<1	<1	–	9	3
WWCR	9	6	3	–	–	3
LYON	<1	<1	<1	6	2	–
CGCC	<1	<1	<1	2	–	3
CGGW	–	<1	–	–	–	–
GBWW	<1	<1	<1	3	–	<1
CC	–	<1	–	–	–	–
PRW2	<1	–	–	–	–	–
PRW3	–	<1	–	–	–	–
CREAM	5	2	1	21	–	<1
VRW	<1	2	<1	–	1	–
OXID	<1	<1	<1	–	<1	1
SV	<1	5	<1	–	–	<1
SVR	2	<1	<1	2	1	–
GREY	3	5	2	4	2	2
MALV	–	<1	–	–	1	–
NAT	–	–	<1	–	–	–
SHEL	–	<1	–	–	–	–
total	100	100	100	100	100	100
sample	4139	10442	17966	536	1048	2454

Table 4.16 Pottery Period 1: occurrence of amphorae

	sherds	%	EVEs	%	weight	%
Dressel 20	103	38	113	58	19447	70
Cam 186 spp	30	11	–	–	3529	13
South Spanish	2	<1	–	–	131	<1
sub total	135	49	113	58	23107	83
Fishbourne 148 spp	15	6	–	–	572	2
Gauloise 4	43	16	–	–	1130	4
Rhodian	6	2	15	7	643	2
E Med Dr 2–4 spp	3	1	13	7	358	1
Italian Dr 2–4	6	2	–	–	75	<1
Cam 189 spp	32	12	–	–	448	2
Stoppers	8	3	54	28	21	<1
unidentified	21	8	–	–	1524	5
total	269	100	195	100	27878	100

Table 4.17 Pottery Period 1: occurrence of mortaria

	sherds	%	EVEs	%	weight	%
MWWO	5	13	28	18	1359	31
MWWO?	2	5	4	3	46	1
MWWOF	1	3	45	29	590	14
MWWCR	3	8	10	6	57	1
sub total	11	29	87	56	2052	47
MORV	6	15	35	22	1646	38
MONG	7	18	–	–	94	2
MONG?	2	5	4	3	78	2
MOVR	12	30	31	19	460	10
MORT3	1	3	–	–	57	1
total	39	100	157	100	4387	100

Table 4.18 Pottery Period 1: vessel functions by phase (% of assemblage); weight/EVEs

	phase		
	1.1	1.2	1.3
liquid holders	15/21	11/13	12/9
drinking vessels	35/7	25/3	16/4
tableware	16/7	9/4	12/7
table/kitchen	–/–	5/1	3/<1
kitchen	31/11	49/17	54/39
storage	3/7	1/4	1/<1
lighting	–/–	–/–	2/<1
unidentified	–/47	–/58	–/40
total	536/4139	1048/10442	2454/17966

Amphorae

Many of the amphorae such as the various Dressel 2–4s, Rhodians, Camulodunum 189s, and Fishbourne 148sp are probably residual from the underlying military deposits. The declining quantity of Camulodunum 186s suggests these are also residual, but the absence of rims makes it impossible to determine if any are of the later type. A total of 68% of the Dressel 20 sherds (on weight) came from a single context, 91/85, of Phase 1.3, which also produced a stamp dated *c* AD 50–100. There is no certain evidence that any of this material represented new imports in the early civilian period.

Amphorae stamps

1   POR.P(S); 91/85, 1.3 (Fig 4.85)
     It is difficult to be sure of a correct reading of the last letter, but it seems most likely to be an S. If

Table 4.19 Pottery Period 1: vessel functions spatially (% of assemblage); weight/EVEs

	C (pits)	P (Buildings 2, 4, and 5)	WR (Buildings 1 and 3)
liquid holders	17/12	11/13	6/10
drinking vessels	13/3	28/4	21/4
tableware	6/5	10/5	29/12
table/kitchen	<1/<1	5/<1	3/<1
kitchen	58/38	45/22	41/32
storage	2/<1	1/4	–/–
lighting	3/<1	–/–	–/–
unidentified	–/41	–/51	–/42
total	1805/11373	1802/18416	11373/3670

P portico, WR west range, C courtyard

so, this could be Callender (1965) no 1370 (25). The stamp PORPS is associated with the figlina of Catria, situated close by the banks of the River Guadalquivir, roughly half-way between Seville and Cordoba (Remesal 1986, no 226). At Avenches this stamp was dated c AD 50–100 (Martin-Kilcher et al 1985).

2   A further Dressel 20 stamp dated to the second half of the first century occurred residually in a Period 2 construction deposit (97/137). This can be identified as AGRICOLAE (Callender 1965, no 51, fig 3, no 23).

Mortaria

The very small quantity of mortaria stratified in Period 1 deposits makes it difficult to assess whether local production continued right to the end of the military period or beyond into the early civilian phase; while over 50% (on EVEs) of Period 1 vessels were local products, the high level of residual pottery is relevant, particularly taking into account the relatively high numbers of Rhone Valley mortaria. The fact that the types of locally made mortaria remain the same as occur in the military contexts suggests that these are residual vessels, but the occurrence of locally made mortaria in Period 2 contexts, many dated to the broad period of late first to mid second century indicates continuing local production.

The only significant continental military suppliers were the potters of the Rhone Valley, most products of which occur residually in the Period 1 deposits. A small quantity of material from North Gaul is also present. This omits a complete North Gaulish vessel stamped by CASSARIVS (no 291) from pit F2990 (Fig 4.84–4.85) which is unfortunately now missing. This could have arrived at Wroxeter before the end of the military occupation, being dated by Kay Hartley as c AD 70–100, but its deposition in a pit attributed to the early civilian occupation suggests it belongs to Period 1.

Identifiable British suppliers in Period 1 are limited to the potters working in the Verulamium region. These first appear in the later military contexts, and

mark the start of a period of trade from that area, increasing in Period 1, and continuing into Period 2. MORT3 was a single sherd, source unknown.

Catalogue of illustrated vessels (Figs 4.84–4.85)

Local wares

1   Disc-mouthed flagon F6.1, WWR, 14/32, F2246, 1.3
2   Honey pot JH2.41, WWO, 98/199, 1.1
3   Narrow-necked jar, JN3.1, WWO, 12/39, F2229, 1.3

Medium-mouthed jars

4   JM6.23, WWR; 6/73, F2208, 1.3
5   JM7.11, WWR; 35/15 and 19, F2260, 1.3
6   JM3.52, WWR; 6/73, F2208, 1.3
7   JM9.33, WWOF; 98/137, 1.3
8   JM9.34, WWOF; 98/171, 1.2
9   JM6.4, WWOF; 97/156, 1.3
10   JM3.41, WWR; 91/182, 1.2
11   Beaker with carinated shoulder, BK12.12; 35/65, F2335, 1.3
12   Flat-rim bowl, B17.22, WWR; 98/186, F1073, 1.2
13   Flat-rim bowl, B17.33, WWOF; 98/130, 1.2
14   Flat-rim bowl, B17.32, WWOF; 98/130, 1.2
15   Flat-rim bowl, B17.31, WWOF; 98/130, 1.2
16   Beaded-rim squat hemspherical bowl, B7.11; 97/212, F956, 1.1
17   Bifid rim dish, D5.23, WWO; 98/141, 1.3
18   Bifid rim dish, D5.24, WWR; 98/222, 1.2
19   Lid, L6.11, WWR; 63/15m F2287, 1.3
20   Beaker with high carinated shoulder and thickened rounded rim, BK4.5, WWOF; 63/15, F2287, 1.3
21   Beaker, BK3.21, WWOF; 98/188, F1073, 1.2
22   Beaker, BK7.12, WWOF; 98/130, 1.2
23   Flanged hemispherical bowl, B12.11, WWR; 63/19, F2287, 1.3
24   Reeded-rim bowl, B13.24, WWR; 98/178, 1.3
25   Dropped-flange bowl, B14.13, WWR; 51/21, F2990, 1.3

Non-local wares

26   Flagon, F5.42, OXID; 63/15, F2287, 1.3
27   Medium-mouthed jar, JM4.24; 98/141, 1.3
28   Medium-mouthed jar, JM2.22, GREY, JM2.22; 63/16, C2.4; 63/18, and 19, F2287, 1.3
29   Beaker with burnished finish, BK4.11, GREY; 98/137, 1.3
30   Handmade cooking pot, MALV, JC1.12; 90/255, 1.2
31   Lid, L1.11, GREY; 91/85, 1.3

Mortaria

32   MORV; 39/13, F2299, 1.3
33   MORV; 35/61, F2299, 1.3

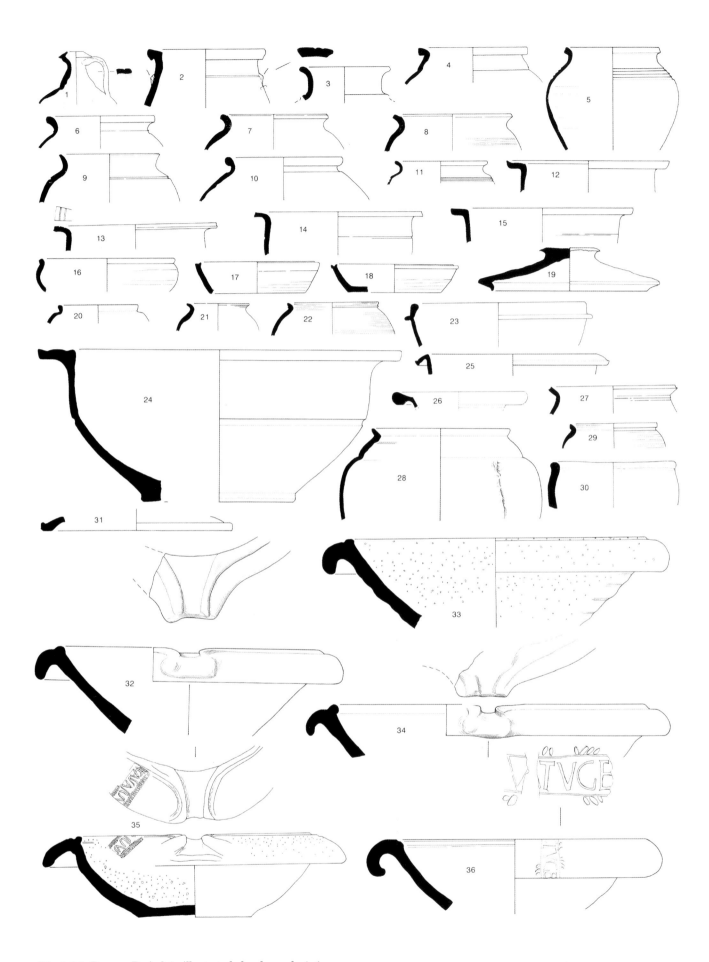

Fig 4.84 Pottery Period 1: illustrated sherds; scale 1:4

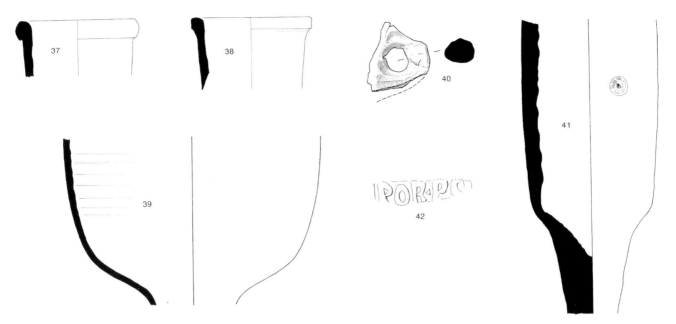

Fig 4.85 Pottery Period 1: illustrated sherds; scale 1:4

34   MORV; 91/97, 1.3
35   MONG (Pas de Calais) stamped CASSAR-
         IUS; 51/21, F2990, 1.3
36   MOVR stamped MATUGENUS; 91/106, 1.3

Amphorae
37   RHOD; 98/212, 1.2
38   Dressel 2–4, ?eastern Mediterranean;
         98/143, 1.2
39   Body sherd from Fishbourne 148; 35/61,
         F2299, 1.3
40   Handle Camulodunum 189; 98/124, 1.2
41   Body sherd/spike unclassified; 51/21, F2990,
         1.3
42   Dressel 20 stamp POR.PS?; 91/85, 1.3

The Period 2 pottery

by Jane Faiers with a contribution by David Williams

Introduction

The pottery from Period 2, amounting to some 25,130
sherds (410 EVEs, 279kg) comes from contexts which
form the make-up, construction, and consolidation of
the main stone phase of the *macellum* and the
south-west corner of the baths *insula*. These contexts
include unused construction trenches, inspection pits to
determine the strength of walls, and dumps used for
infilling and levelling the site during the building programme. The majority of the pottery is from the dumps,
some of which appear to be from the same source judging by the evidence of joining sherds of pottery from different areas and the general homogeneity of groups.

The date range of the pottery lies mainly in the
first-century to mid second-century bracket. Period 2 has
a nominal start date of *c* AD 120, as the Hadrianic period
(AD 117–38) encompassed the building of the forum on

insula 4 completed AD 129/130 (Atkinson 1942), and the
insula 5 work is presumed to be part of the same building
programme. The following sections discuss aspects of the
assemblage and specific wares, summarise the key groups,
and then discuss the pottery from the area and overall phases. The key groups relate to specific occurrences during the
building programme which may be contemporary in the
various locations, or which stand on their own. The Period
2 key groups with pottery (KG 4–9, 11–13, and 27) are
summarised in Table 1.2.

Residuality in the pottery is illustrated by the samian of which 66% is South Gaulish and predates AD
120. A study of the fabrics found in a sample of just
under half the total collection showed that only half this
figure would have been in current use at the time of the
building of the *macellum*. The wares considered to be
current included samian (SAMCG and SAMEG),
BB1, SV, 50% of the Dressel 20 and unclassified
amphorae, and 50% of the West Midlands and local
mortaria sherds. The study was undertaken to establish
a formula for assessing residuality in the various phases.
Details and the equations used are outlined above.

A quantified summary of all the fabrics found is
presented in Table 4.20. The average sherd weights
(gm) and average sherd weight less amphorae and mortaria for all locations including all phases are given in
Table 4.21. The weights may reflect the degree of disturbance and shattering of material during the construction process. If so, leaving aside the small amounts
in the Baths, the Baths Precinct shows the most
upheaval with the Porticos next followed by the West
Range. The Courtyard shows the least disturbance on
total average sherd weights and has double the average
sherd weight for amphorae and mortaria combined,
compared to the other three locations whose figures are
more or less the same, ie between 30 and 34 gm. When
the Courtyard is considered by phase, disturbance is

Table 4.20 Pottery Period 2: total quantities

fabrics	number	%	EVEs	%	weight	%
local						
WWO	4714	19	7563	19	46964	17
WWR	8032	31	12860	31	74816	27
SV	1458	6	1624	4	20746	7
traded						
BB1	2696	11	5278	13	27238	10
VRW	46	<1	69	<1	500	<1
MALV	269	1	383	1	3814	<1
imports						
SAMIAN	3978	16	7897	19	24893	9
AMP	1452	6	717	2	51593	19
CGCC	223	<1	555	1	710	<1
CGGW	7	<1	–	–	8	<1
CGWH	7	<1	–	–	15	<1
LYON	85	1	383	1	3814	1
COLG	14	<1	14	<1	34	<1
PRW	27	<1	42	<1	1309	<1
unknown						
CREAM	1164	5	1995	5	8506	3
GBWW	6	<1	–	–	15	<1
CALC	7	<1	14	<1	34	<1
OXID	213	<1	302	<1	2390	<1
GREY	111	<1	287	<1	1618	<1
MORTAR	368	1	844	2	11212	4
MISC	253	1	41	1	1815	<1
total	25130	100	40868	100	282044	100

Table 4.21 Pottery Period 2: average sherd weights by area

	overall	average excluding amphorae & mortaria	sherd weight including amphorae & mortaria	samian
porticos	10.0	8.4	31.3	4.6
west range	12.0	9.7	30.8	7.3
courtyard	12.6	10.1	61.6	6.8
baths	3.9	3.9	–	4.5
baths precinct	7.6	7.1	34.4	6.1

least in this area in C 2.1 and 2.4, especially the latter (for further discussion see below).

A quantified breakdown of the occurrence of fabrics by locations and a more detailed analysis by sub-phase and area can be found in the archive. Most of the pottery occurred in the West Range followed by the Porticos. There were several joins of pottery sherds from different layers within the same area but, more importantly, different locations, for example sherds from the West Range linked with sherds from the Porticos. These appear to show episodes of dumping where material from a single source has been spread over different areas.

The change from a military utilitarian assemblage to one geared to a civilian market saw a *floruit* in decoration. Decorated pottery from Period 2 amounted to

57% (all percentages by weight) while from the military phase the figure was 5%. On the Cream/White wares the percentage was small (16%) and comprised slips of brownish reds and yellow brown but also included darker cream and grey, the colour of which could have been due to firing rather than a different coloured slip. In the Severn Valley wares 14% are decorated rising to 54% of the Wroxeter red wares. Decoration on Severn Valley wares included lattice, white slip circles and lines en barbotine. Wroxeter red wares were the most decorated of all, including mica-gilt, slips of a variety of reddish-browns but mainly shades of cream/white. Some vessels have a burnished black slip present possibly to try and imitate BB1. Other decoration includes rustication, rough-casting using small particles of clay crushed and applied in slip, rouletting, and rilling. The decoration on Wroxeter grey ware (WWR) is of the same type as WWO but also includes applied barbotine spots and burnished lattice on jars, imitating black-burnished vessels. Of the Malvernian wares 13% are decorated. Burnished linear vertical stripes are the most common decoration, but one vessel has an unusual combed line decoration which could not be paralleled elsewhere. Finally 30% of the samian is decorated.

Fabrics

Thirty-two fabrics were originally distinguished but for the purposes of data presentation these have been reduced to eighteen, with three miscellaneous categories (Table 4.20). Fabric descriptions are given in the fabric series for all the pottery below. The miscellaneous category includes a small number of fabrics, possibly imported, plus two sherds of Nene Valley presumably intrusive in P 2.3 and WR 2.3. The following section discusses some of the main wares and forms encountered. Samian, mortaria, and amphorae are additionally discussed separately for each location, with details of average sherd weight.

Fine wares (imported and traded)
Samian ware amounted to 16% of the total sherd count and 9% of total weight. South Gaulish samian accounted for 2767 sherds weighing 14675gm, Central Gaulish 1207 sherds weighing 10201gm, and East Gaulish samian four sherds (Table 4.20). The proportions of samian in relation to the whole collection are much in excess of the basilical hall count of 5% by sherd count and 3% by weight (Symonds 1997). It is, however, much nearer the Meole Brace figures (Evans 1994) of 10% by sherd count and 7% by weight. Whether the quantity of samian reflects the use of the buildings at Wroxeter and perhaps the date of the deposits examined, is open to speculation, but the evidence with regard to Wroxeter and Meole Brace seems to differ from the data from the south west where both rural and urban sites appear to have the same proportion of samian (Millett 1990, 126). In comparison to

sites in the south west, Wroxeter is in the range of the largest consumer.

The only other fine ware groups represented in any numbers were Central Gaulish colour-coated ware with rough-cast decoration, Lyon ware rough-cast beakers, Pompeian redware, and Cologne colour-coated ware. There were a few sherds of other finewares, ie Central Gaulish grey ware and whiteware and mica-slipped ware. The latter included a cup BK3.13 (Fig 4.52), dated late first to early second century (Marsh 1978, type 22, fig 6.10), part of a flanged bowl dated late first to early second century (Greep 1986, fig 36, no 3.90), and a foot from a tripod bowl similar to another example from Wroxeter (Bushe-Fox 1914, fig 18.55), and from Gloucester (Rawes 1972, fig 4, 38–39) dated AD 80–120. Other mica-slipped sherds in the local fabric were also found (see regional wares below). There were also six sherds of Gallo-Belgic type white-wares.

Imported wares: amphorae

The amount of amphorae present (Table 4.22) seems low and may reflect the function of the earlier fortress. By comparison with early military sites the amount of amphorae by weight from the fortress is itself low (Wroxeter 36%, Kingsholm and Lake Farm 60%, Exeter 75%). This may reflect that Kingsholm and Lake Farm were supply bases. However the Wroxeter second-century data compare well with Lincoln where the figure for the first colonia rampart which has rubbish of AD 90–120 is 17%, and that for the later addition to the rampart is 15%. Data from later sites shows 39% from stratified deposits at Vindolanda (Bidwell 1985, 173), and 24% at East Bight, Lincoln (Darling 1984).

The most common amphorae types were the southern Spanish globular olive oil vessel Dressel 20, Fishbourne 148.3, again thought to contain olive oil, and the southern French wine vessel Gauloise 4. Many of the other types present, are likely to be residual sherds derived from military period imports.

Table 4.22 Pottery Period 2: occurrence of amphorae

type	number	%	weight	%
Dressel 20	288	20	18747	36
Gauloise 4	21	1	583	1
Dressel 2–4	14	1	368	<1
Camulodunum 186	11	<1	732	1
Camulodunum 189	56	4	437	<1
Fishbourne 148.3	437	30	8969	17
Richborough 527	1	<1	185	<1
Rhodian	4	<1	303	<1
South Spanish	13	1	1541	3
Peacock and				
Williams Class 16	2	<1	192	<1
undesignated	605	42	19536	38
total	1452	100	51593	100

Amphorae catalogue

by David Williams

Dressel 20 (AMPDR20)

Five Dressel 20 rims were found in Period 2. These can be roughly paralleled with examples illustrated by Martin-Kilcher (1983) in her scheme for the development of Dressel 20 at Augst:

1   Dated at Augst late first-mid second century (*ibid*, no 30); 78/3, C 2.1
2   Dated at Augst *c* AD 75–125 (*ibid*, no 23); 35/8, C 2.2
3   (*ibid*, no 25); 35/8, C 2.2
4   Dated at Augst *c* AD 75–125 (*ibid*, no 17); 92/4, C 2.4
5   Dated at Augst *c* AD 75–125 (*ibid*, no 23); 90/193, P 2.1

Stamps

1   Almost a complete handle with two stamps *in ansa* on either side of the central ridge approaching the summit. It is about clear that they read the same name. The one on the left side is very faint, and it would appear that the potter was dissatisfied with this effort and had pushed more firmly into the wet clay. Unfortunately the handle is slightly damaged on the right side and the stamp is incomplete. However, a combined reading from both stamps downwards from the summit of the handle produces the letters C N O V I I. This stamp is listed by Callender (1965, no 408) who suggests that it may be connected with the much more common series of stamps belonging to G. Antonius Quietus, dating to the Flavian-Trajanic period (cf also Martin-Kilcher *et al* 1985, Abb 5). Stamps of G. Antonius Quietus are connected with the Dressel 20 production site at Alcolea del Rio on the River Guadalquivir, near Villanueva (Ponsich 1974, 139–41); 80/123, P 2.3.
2   AGRICOLAE (Callender 1965), dated second half first century; 97/137, P 2.3
3   SAXOFERRO (Callender 1965) dated *c* AD 150; 97/52, P 2.3

Fishbourne 148.3 (AMF148)

An unusual type of amphorae represented at Wroxeter was the Fishbourne 148.3. The rim-form is quite distinctive, and appears as a small bead-rim sitting on top of a larger one. The shape of the remainder of the vessel is unknown, as is the source and contents carried. Three separate rims occur at Wroxeter, and although there are some nuances of variation on this rim theme, the fabrics are very similar and they can almost certainly be grouped under one heading. Two rims from 84/100, WR 2.2, are quite similar to the Fishbourne type specimen, while the other rim from 86/42, WR 2.1, and 86/62, 1.3, is somewhat fatter, though still retaining a vestige of the small top bead.

Mortaria (local, traded, and imported)
Non-local sources represented included North Gaul (MONG) (2); Rhone Valley (MORV) (4); Rhineland (MORHIN) (3); Aoste, Atisii (MOASTE) (1); Verulamium (MOVR) (96), and West Midlands (MORT3) (65). A total of 38% of the mortaria was local fabrics and if the west Midlands group is added the total rises to 55%. It is probable, given the high incidence of vessels in local fabric, that workshops making mortaria were situated near to Wroxeter. One making Rhaetian types in Wroxeter fabric has been noted near the Bell Brook (Fox and Morris 1931). The site has been relocated, and the mortaria appear to be similar to those found at Whitchurch (Jones and Webster 1968, fig 15, 222) and dated AD 140–200 there. The sub-Rhaetian mortaria sherds from the excavations may well be of the same fabric as the Bell Brook sherds.

The second largest number of mortaria derive from the Verulamium region. Verulamium mortaria are usually accompanied by imported wares from London (Rhodes 1986b, 203) and a supply route from London in the later second century is indicated by the forum gutter find (Atkinson 1942, 127). However, during the period AD 118–140 there were problems in the supply of samian entering the country (Marsh 1981, figs 11.6, 11.7), and if mortaria supplies from Verulamium were linked with samian supplies from London, then the period may have seen a decrease in Verulamium mortaria at Wroxeter. It seems from the Wroxeter data that an expansion in favour of the local potters is apparent in the second century and this may reflect a fall off in Verulamium supplies. Mancetter-Hartshill products appear not to increase and mortaria potters moved closer to the army in this period thus undercutting the prices of mortaria from the South East. At least one of the potters working at Brockley Hill, Matugenus, is known to have moved to the West Midlands, and Decanius with 201 stamps extant from sites almost all of which are in the west Midlands and Wales, could well have worked locally (pers comm Kay Hartley).

Traded wares
Dorset black-burnished ware (BB1)
Black-burnished ware may well have come to Wroxeter *c* AD 120 as part of the first expansion of supplies to Hadrian's Wall. However earlier dates are possible. A pre-Flavian date for the appearance of BB1 in very small quantities (5%) is suggested at Caerleon (Greep 1986) and a pre-Hadrianic date at Caersws (Webster 1989).

Four main vessel forms are represented, jars, bowls, dishes, and lids, with beakers and flagons also represented, although some of the jars may have been beakers given the difficulties of identification between small jars and beakers without handle scars. Cooking-pots were represented in the greatest numbers in this assemblage with 2770.5 EVEs, to which jars could be added (545 EVEs). Bowls were the next largest numbers (EVE 936) with dishes including oval fish dishes (27 EVEs) not far behind at 827 EVEs. Lids were next with 598.5 EVEs, a large number considering they are not usually represented in very large amounts, or perhaps not recognised or illustrated. Flagons accounted for 21 EVEs and beakers just 7 EVE. A comparison of the rim diameters of BB1 and local Wroxeter grey ware (WWR) jars (Fig 4.86) show that both were manufactured in a broadly similar range of sizes with those with diameters between 120–140mm being the most popular.

The small numbers of BB1 sherds recorded in Period 2.1 (35) in all locations support the suggestion that most of the BB1 vessels at Wroxeter date from around AD 120 and are associated with expanded marketing northwards to Hadrian's Wall. One bowl (type B20), however, is rare in the Dorset range of black-burnished and may well come from Rossington Bridge (pers comm Neil Holbrook). This bowl, dated to the mid-second century, was found in a P 2.3 context (Fig 4.87,1).

Bowls and dishes in BB1 are mainly of early to mid-second century date except for one (B20.13 and Fig 4.87, 2) which is very similar to a vessel at Exeter (Holbrook and Bidwell 1991, 38.36, fig 30). The Exeter vessel comes from south-east Dorset and was dated to the Hadrianic/Antonine period. Both the Wroxeter and Exeter vessels have the multi-lattice form of decoration which is less common. A dish with chevron decoration (D3.14 and Fig 4.87, 3) is probably the latest in this

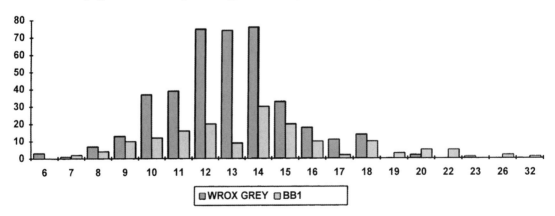

Fig 4.86 Pottery Period 2: comparison of rim diameters of BB1 and WWR jars

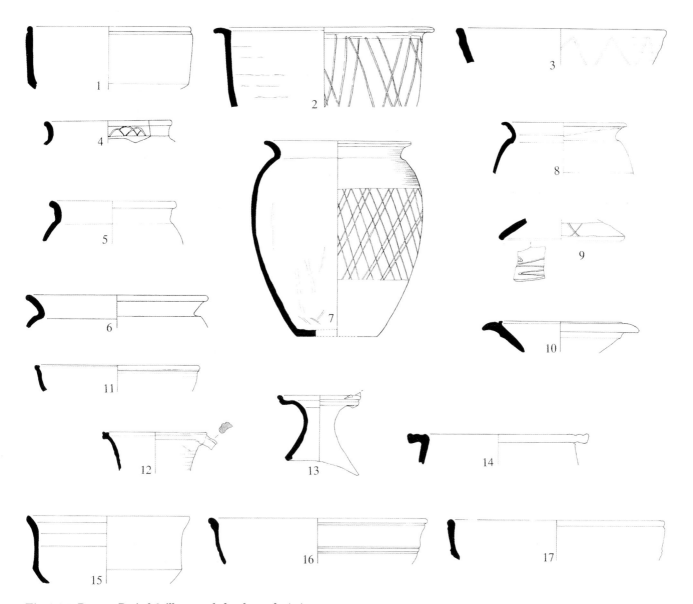

Fig 4.87 Pottery Period 2 illustrated sherds; scale 1:4

group. Cross hatching or latticing had given way to the inverted, overlapping, chevron design by *c* AD 160, and to intersecting arcs by *c* AD 180 (Gillam 1976, 68). The dish is probably *c* AD 150+ in date.

The earliest vessels in the cooking-pot group were found in WR 2.3, and C 2.4 (JC3.41 and JC3.33, Fig 4.87, 4 and 5). The wavy line decoration under the rim appears on BB1 cooking-pots and jars until the late second century, but the upright rims of these vessels suggest an early to mid-second century date. At the other end of the date range, jars which could well be Antonine in date were found in C 2.4 and WR 2.3 (Fig 4.87, 6 and 7; Gillam 1976 no 3), and the latest jar dated late second/early third century (Fig 4.87, 8) was found in WR 2.3 (Gillam 1976, 4 or 6; Robertson 1975, fig 71.8).

Dating evidence for lids is at present limited and ranges from the Conquest period or before (Brailsford 1958, 101–19) to the third century. One lid (Fig 4.87, 9) from WR 2.3 resembles one dated AD 160–200 from Exeter (Holbrook and Bidwell, 1991, fig 33).

Lids appear to be most common in the first and second centuries. All the lids at Sidbury, Worcester, were in the local Malvernian ware (Darlington and Evans 1992, 50), suggesting that BB1 was more successful in cornering the market in a large town where large amounts of pottery could be sold to the detriment of the smaller more local suppliers.

The jug or flagon form dates from the first to the fourth century. The form is a rare one at Wroxeter in this phase, and the only sherds found, five in number, came from P 2.2 contexts.

Malvernian wares
This pottery with its distinctive Iron Age forms may have been residual by the mid second century. The sample agrees with Peacocks's findings (1967, 2) that the handmade cooking-pot, or jar, is the most popular form of Malvernian ware found in 22 sites out of the 23 known to include this ware in their assemblages. The Wroxeter group is parallelled by Malvernian wares found in Hadrianic/Antonine deposits at

Astley Wall, Leintwardine, Hawford, Greensforge, Kenchester, and Brecon. There is little sign of this pottery in the military or Period 1 assemblages and the few sherds found are usually attributable to disturbance from later deposits. This ware is therefore possibly coming to Wroxeter at the same period as BB1 becomes popular. Apart from a dish base and a bowl, there are no parallels with black-burnished forms. The jars have crude bead rims and continue in this form whereas the BB1 cooking-pot rim gradually evolves into an everted rim. Black-burnished wares were probably of better, more standardised quality, and competitively priced beside the lesser transport costs of Malvernian wares. Malvern wares are heavy and fairly crudely made compared to BB1 and might well have been a cheaper local alternative.

It is probable that these vessels were primarily intended as cooking-pots and for boiling water as some of those found at Wroxeter have a white limescale deposit inside.

Coarse mica-dusted ware (MICA2)

There were 34 sherds in the Wroxeter red ware fabric (WWO) with this distinctive finish. Forms included a flagon (F5.41, Fig 4.87, 13) from P 2.3 (Hull 1963, fig 56.5, type series 363–83 dated AD 190; Sheldon 1978, fig 165, 1268, dated first to second century; a reed-rimmed bowl (B13, Fig 4.87, 14) from WR 2.3 (Darling 1976, no 118, late first century but with no mica-gilt coating); a bowl (B12.72, Fig 4.87, 17) from WR 2.3; a bowl (B2.22: Fig 4.87, 15); a bowl (B7.45: Fig 4.87, 16); and a folded beaker (not illustrated) from WR 2.3 and C 2.4 (Bushe-Fox 1914, fig 18.55, dated AD 80–120).

Although mica-gilded pottery was in competition with samian wares (Marsh 1978, 207) and could have filled the shortfall in supply in the Hadrianic period, at Wroxeter, given the small numbers of sherds and previous dating by Bushe-Fox (1914), it is unlikely that this form of decoration on vessels extends far into the Hadrianic period, although mica-dusted wares are known later in the century in the Staines area (Crouch and Shanks 1984, 67) and at Colchester (Hull 1963, kilns 17, 16 and 99).

Cream and whitewares (CREAM)

Although other forms are represented, the flagon is the form which most often occurs in this fabric, some of which can be parallelled in the military assemblage. There are several known places of manufacture including the Verulamium region, and Brockley Hill is known to have made triple vases to the end of the second century (Sheldon *et al* 1978, 229). A sandy white fabric was being produced at Wroxeter in the Antonine period (Houghton 1964, 107), as well as a clumsy, white, underfired, pipe clay possibly from the Broseley region in Shropshire (Wright 1860, 75), presumably trying to copy a very fine, thin, hard fired, creamy ware without much success. Small white clay vases found in a pit

dated AD 90–130, may have been this ware (Bushe-Fox 1916, 64). Other forms include a bowl (Fig 4.87, 10) from C 2.3, a dish (Fig 4.87, 11) from C 2.4, and a jug (Fig 4.87, 12) from WR 2.3. Holt is thought to have made fine whitewares and a dish from there (Grimes 1930, no 186) resembles the one from Wroxeter.

Severn valley wares (SV), Wroxeter red wares (WWO), and Wroxeter grey wares (WWR)

These wares are discussed together here although separated in the tables, because of the difficulty in distinguishing between the finer local products and so-called SVW (Webster 1972; 1976; 1977; Tomber 1981; Timby 1990). The small amount of SVW recognised, 1458 sherds (5.8%), belies the actual amount of vessel forms attributable to the SV tradition of potting. Many of the Wroxeter red-buff wares (WWO) occur in the same Severn Valley forms and have a grey core. It has been suggested that SVWs cannot be petrologically defined per se but instead must be defined typologically (Tomber 1981, 119); atomic absorption spectrophotometry tests on samples from a number of sites concurred with this premise and showed that the majority of the fabrics were so similar as to be indefinable (Faiers 1990).

Wroxeter red wares (WWO) and Wroxeter grey wares (WWR)

Eight wasters were noted. Copies of BB1, SV, and Malvernian vessels are apparent in local fabrics, indicating an already proven sale for the original. Local potters also appear to have been making rough-cast beakers, as several sherds with rough-casting occur in the local red fabric. The comparison of WWR jar diameters with BB1 (Fig 4.86) showed that the 130mm size was poorly represented in BB1, but the third highest amount found in WWR. This may indicate that the BB1 potters were not making this size or that their products were eclipsed by the WWR version. BB1 jars were made in larger sizes and it is possible that the local potters were reluctant to supply the small amounts which would be required at this size, preferring to concentrate on bulk production of the smaller form.

Previous work on the local fabrics at Wroxeter (Faiers 1990, 207) has shown that forms found in WWO and WWR differ, with certain forms appearing more often in one fabric than the other. Bowls were more prolific in WWO than WWR, and jars more prevalent in WWR than WWO. Flagons in red-ware with a cream slip (WWOC) far outnumbered greyware flagons. This appears to indicate a fashion for a particular vessel to be manufactured in a certain fabric or a marked preference on the part of the consumer. Minimum vessel numbers for the two main fabrics, WWO and WWR are shown graphically in Fig 4.88. Jars feature as the largest group followed by flagons, bowls and dishes. The minimum vessel numbers for the whole collection are shown in Fig 4.89.

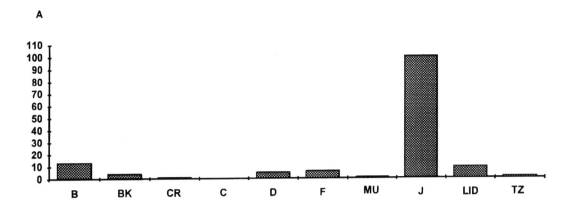

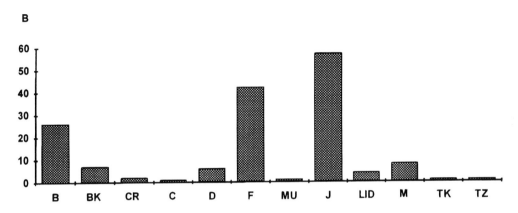

Fig 4.88 Pottery Period 2: forms present (by minimum vessel number) in WWO and WWR

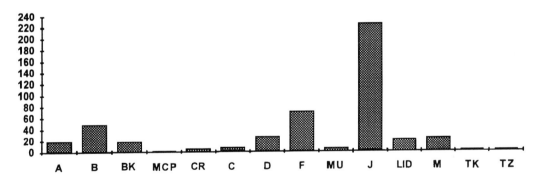

Fig 4.89 Pottery Period 2: forms present (by minimum vessel number) in the collection

Area phases

Porticos

P 2.1
A total of 86.7% of the pottery was calculated as residual. The latest South Gaulish samian ware was
Flavian-Trajanic, but other wares, Central Gaulish
samian of Hadrianic/Antonine date, BB1, and
Malvernian, together with a local beaker copy, indicate
a date of AD 120+ and more probably AD 130+ since
an average sherd weight of 5.5 gm indicates high fragmentation.

P 2.2
Samian wares from South Gaul decreased in compari-
son to P 2.1, while Central Gaulish slightly increased.
The Central Gaulish samian includes 15 sherds of
Hadrianic/early Antonine date and 10 sherds of
Antonine date from 5 vessels. The average sherd
weight was 9.9 gm, nearly double that of P 2.1 suggesting a dump of material during this period with further shattering of earlier pottery sherds (Fig 4.90).
There were four mortaria stamps from F951 (nos 35,
36, 62, and 71). Residuality was calculated at 31%.
The range of vessels present include certain types only
found in small numbers on the site, ie flasks, tankard,

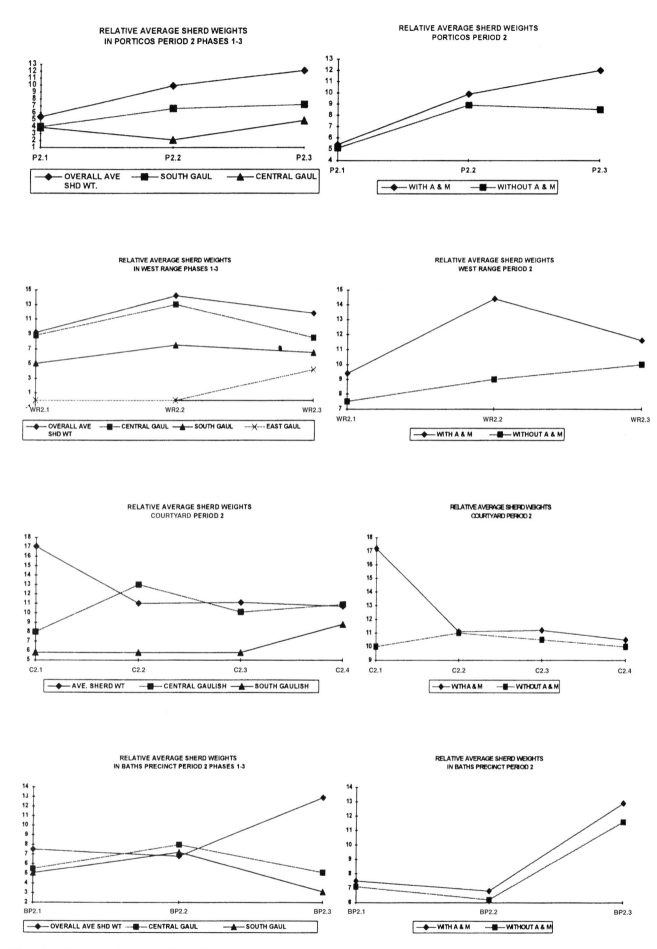

Fig 4.90 Pottery Period 2: indices of brokenness (sherd weights) by phase

triple vase, *tazze*, and three crucibles. The earliest pot is a Hofheim type flagon of the first century and the latest, a BB1 dish (Fig 4.70, D3.14) with what appears to be a pointed looped pattern, could be *c* AD 150. Central Gaulish samian of Antonine and Hadrianic/early Antonine date with the BB1 dish, indicate a date of at least AD 150.

P 2.3

Wroxeter red ware exceeded Wroxeter grey ware, while the proportion of South Gaulish samian increased and black-burnished decreased by comparison with P 2.2. Samian sherds were heavier and larger (Fig 4.90). The overall average sherd weight was 12 gm. Joining sherds were found with P 2.1. The level of residuality was 46%. The range of vessels contained only one unusual form, a *patera*. There were five stamped mortaria (nos 16, 31, 88, 89, and 90).

The latest coarse-wares are two sherds of Rhaetian mortaria with red-brown slip generally dated to the Antonine period at Wroxeter. There was also an amphora stamp of SAXOFERRO dated by Callender (1965) to *c* AD 150 (no 3 above). Third-century pottery was present and is presumably intrusive. A Nene Valley sherd in Box 80 may be from the Period 3 rebuild of the stylobate wall. An Oxfordshire white ware sherd in the west portico came from a posthole. Apart from an Antonine mortaria and the stamped amphora, there were 28 Central Gaulish Antonine sherds from 19 vessels, together with two stamps dated AD 160–200 (nos 18 and 125). A form 37 in the style of Paternus v or an associate was dated AD 160–95, and a form 45 was dated AD 170–200. A date of AD 160 at the earliest is suggested and perhaps later unless the latest sherds are contamination from third-century pit digging.

West Range

WR 2.1

There were no unusual vessels in this group. The latest samian ware sherd was a Central Gaulish dish Curle 15/23 dated to the Hadrianic-early Antonine period. The latest samian stamp was dated AD 110–25 (no 99). A stamped mortarium was dated AD 80–125 (no 50). The residual content of this phase and the small numbers of black-burnished sherds suggest a *terminus post quem* of *c* AD 130.

WR 2.2

The high sherd weight of 14.3 gm falls to 9 gm when the amphorae and mortaria sherds are excluded. There were few fabrics but a relatively large amount of amphorae, more than in WR 2.1. Of the amphora total 94% were Fishbourne type 148.3. There were 64 sherds which could be dated to the first century or late first/early second century and were thus residual confirming the residuality calculation. There were no unusual vessels in this group. The latest samian was

Trajanic in date and a locally made mortaria dates to AD 120–60. The small numbers of BB1 equate with the WR 2.1 although the residuality level is higher (77.5%), perhaps indicating an earlier assemblage. A *terminus post quem* of the same date as WR 2.1 is suggested.

WR 2.3

There were more sherds in WR 2.3 than in all the Period 2 portico phases. There was a wide range of vessel forms including a *patera* handle, cheese press, colander, lamp, *tazze*, small unguent flasks, and crucibles. Also a Severn Valley tankard in the earlier vesicular fabric (?early second century) and the only face pot (first century) to be found in Period 2 (Fig 4.57, JN 4.82). The vessel range was very similar to those found in P 2.2, but there were joining sherds with P 2.3, and a similar residuality figure (43%), indicating a similar source. There was one stamped mortarium (no 37).

Central Gaulish samian wares included 29 Antonine sherds from 10 vessels, 76 Hadrianic/early Antonine Central Gaulish (Fig 4.97, D13; stamp no 195), and two sherds of East Gaulish samian ware. The large amount of BB1, together with the high levels of Hadrianic/early Antonine, and Antonine samian suggest a *terminus post quem* of AD 160–70. Three third-century East Gaulish and Nene Valley sherds are likely to be intrusive.

Courtyard

C 2.1

There were only four sherds of BB1 in this group and 64% of the total were either Wroxeter grey wares or South Gaulish samian wares. Residuality was high. The latest of the Central Gaulish sherds was Trajanic, and this is probably the earliest group in Period 2 with a high level of first to early second-century pottery. A *terminus post quem* of AD 120 is suggested.

C 2.2

Featured sherds from this phase include a tripod bowl foot in a non-local fabric with mica-gilt, and two wasters in local grey ware of late first-century to early second-century date. Residuality was high. There were three Central Gaulish sherds dated later than AD 130: two Dr 37 bowls dated AD 130–40, and a sherd given a Hadrianic-early Antonine date (Fig 4.97, D24). Together with four Hadrianic-Antonine sherds a date in the Hadrianic period rather than the Antonine is suggested with a *terminus post quem* of AD 130. However, a stamp dated AD 160–290 was found (no 146), and a sherd of Oxfordshire white-ware, the latter and perhaps the former presumably intrusive.

C 2.3

The sherd count was lower that for C 2.2, with a drop in samian wares and a rise in BB1. The only unusual vessel was a cup from a Cream-white ware triple vase.

There were joins both within this phase and with P 2.3. The low level of residuality coinciding with the same levels in P 2.3 and WR 2.3, makes it likely that the dumps in the three areas came from the same source. The higher level of BB1 sherds together with a sherd of Antonine samian and Hadrianic-early Antonine sherds gives a date of *c* AD 140–50 (Fig 4.97, D25).

C 2.4

A clear increase occurred in BB1 and there were five Antonine sherds, three Hadrianic/early Antonine (stamp no 193), and one Hadrianic/Antonine. There was a join with a C 2.3 context. There was a mica-gilt bossed beaker and two stamped mortaria (nos 61 and 68). Residuality was calculated at 48%. The five sherds of Antonine samian from five vessels plus the high levels of BB1 suggest a later *terminus post quem* than C 2.3 at *c* AD 150.

Baths

B 2.1

There were 39 sherds weighing 151 gm including two sherds of South Gaulish samian Ritt 9 of Neronian date. The only datable sherd in the coarsewares was a carinated bowl with cream slip and rouletting of Flavian/Trajanic date. There was no B 2.2 pottery.

Baths Precinct

BP 2.1

The average sherd weight was 7.5 gm and the pottery was of medium size and not shattered. Residuality was high. Samian wares made up nearly 50% of the pottery in this phase. There were no amphorae sherds and the four mortaria sherds were residual Verulamium wares. There were no black-burnished wares. The coarse pottery was of late first to early second-century date. A later date was suggested by three samian sherds in Box 49, two Hadrianic/early Antonine and one of AD 125–50. A *terminus post quem* of AD 130 is therefore suggested.

BP 2.2

Central Gaulish wares increased from BP 2.1. Residuality was similar. Seventeen sherds of Antonine Central Gaulish samian from fourteen vessels included a stamp dated AD 150–80 (no 39), and these, together with early to mid-second century BB1 would make this phase likely to date to *c* AD 160.

BP 2.3

There were no amphorae sherds and only four sherds of mortaria. Residuality was high as was reflected by the dateable coarsewares which were first and early second century. Three sherds from the same number of Antonine Central Gaulish samian vessels were found. A burnt form 37 was possibly dated AD 155–95 suggesting an overall *terminus post quem* of AD 160+.

Table 4.23 Pottery Period 2: residuality and dates of sub–phases

location	residuality	date of phase
P 2.1	87%	AD 130+
P 2.2	32%	AD 150+
P 2.3	47%	AD 160/170+
WR 2.1	66.5%	*c* AD 130
WR 2.2	77.5%	*c* AD 130
WR 2.3	43%	AD 160/170+
B 2.1	100%	AD 100–125
C 2.1	86%	*c* AD 120+
C 2.2	73%	AD 130+
C 2.3	46%	AD 140/150
C 2.4	48%	AD 150+
BP 2.1	85%	*c* AD 130
BP 2.2	41.5%	*c* AD 160+
BP 2.3	75%	AD 160+

P portico, WR west range, C courtyard, B baths, BP baths precinct

Overall phases
The levels of residuality proposed, together with associated sherd weights should demonstrate any periods of dumping. The dates given by the pottery should also indicate whether the sub-phases in the various locations could be happening within a similar time scale (Tables 1.3 and 4.23).

Phase 2.1 (P 2.1, WR 2.1, C 2.1, BP 2.1, B 2.1)
The overall residuality for all five groups is high, with the WR 2.1 group the lowest at 66%. The average is 85%. All groups show a similar range of pottery and a similar *terminus post quem* of *c* AD 120/130. The Baths show a greater degree of fragmentation and thus disturbance than any other. The phase has the second largest selection of fabrics present. Black-burnished sherd numbers were low as in the next phase. There were no amphorae sherds in the Baths Precinct.

Phase 2.2 (WR 2.2)
See WR 2.2 above – the only area with pottery in this phase.

Phase 2.4 (P 2.2, C 2.2, BP 2.2)
The increased amount of pottery comes mainly from the west portico Boxes 90 and 97 (5298 sherds, EVEs 7003.5, weight 52525gm) and this is far greater than the quantities for the Courtyard and Baths Precinct. The west portico assemblage had *tazze*, unguent flask, tankard, triple vase, honey pot, and three crucibles, vessels whose numbers were scarce in the collection as a whole. The group equated more with WR 2.3 in Phase 2.5 which dates to *c* AD 160/170+. There were also seven sherds of Central Gaulish Antonine samian and nine sherds of Central Gaulish samian of Hadrianic/early Antonine period and ten of Hadrianic-Antonine.

It has been suggested (Webster 1993) that dump F951 in P 2.2 cannot be as late as AD 140 partly due to the absence from it of vessels which can be parallelled by those in the Antonine 1 assemblage at Newstead (Richmond 1950, 31, fig 7.5–18). This absence may simply be due to the small numbers present at Newstead. In F951, the decoration and form of a BB1 dish (Fig 4.87, 3) was quite different to any other BB1 found in the Period 2 assemblage, and may show the changeover from lattice decoration to over-lapping inverted chevron decoration, occurring c AD 160 (Gillam 1976, 68). A similar vessel occurred at Exeter (Holbrook and Bidwell 1991, fig 32, 59.2) with plain dishes of similar form attributed to the Antonine period. Two black-burnished jars with unusual multi-lattice in the group 90/204 can also be paralleled in the Exeter group but the absence of a rim makes dating difficult as the form goes from first to third century. The eight Hadrianic/Antonine samian sherds present together with the different vessel forms and the Antonine BB1 vessel, would make the date of F951 likely to be in the AD 140s at least, and more likely AD 150. The low level of residuality in P 2.2 would also point to a dump of contemporary material.

While the average sherd weights for P 2.2 and C 2.2 continued to rise in tandem in this phase, the Portico weights continued to increase while those in the Courtyard dropped in the next phase. This might indicate a cessation in dumping activity after C 2.2 with more disturbance and shattering of sherds. In fact the level of residuality and average sherd weight of C 2.2 is more comparable with Phase 2.2. The figures may reflect the disturbance of the building process and an inversion of stratigraphy due to digging out and dumping. In BP 2.2 the sherd weight reduced indicating more disturbance but with a lower level of residuality. There were pottery joins between P 2.2 and P 2.3.

Phase 2.5 (P 2.3, WR 2.3, C 2.3)
Most pottery was found in this phase with 26 fabrics represented and the highest number of unusual forms. In addition to those present in 2.4, were a cheese press, lamp, *patera*, and colander. Proportionately amphorae and mortaria were overtaken by the Central Gaulish samian sherds. The overall date of this phase is likely to be AD 150+ for the Courtyard and AD 160/170 for the completion of the West Range and Portico areas with latter last. There are joins between P 2.3 and WR 2.3, and between WR 2.3 and C 2.4 in phase 2.6, indicating a homogeneity of material and reinforcing the similar suggested dates.

Phase 2.6 (C 2.4, BP 2.3)
The residuality calculation includes a very small sample for the Baths Precinct, although the sherd weights of the two locations are similar. Dating the final Period 2 surfaces is problematic since later repair work may not have been clear, and material could easily be intrusive from later features.

Catalogue of illustrated sherds from Key Groups
(Fig 4.91)
1   Body sherd in fine, hard, light orange fabric with rouletted decoration, probably from a beaker; 84/81, KG 4
2   Dish, WWO; 84/178, KG 5
3   Wide-mouthed jar, WWO; 84/182, KG 5
4   Lid, WWOF; 86/52, KG 5
5   Wide-mouthed flat-topped jar, WWR; 91/136, KG 5
6   Flanged bowl, WWR; 91/502, KG 6
7   Tripod bowl foot, hard, fine, fawn buff fabric with a mica coating, late 1st to early 2nd century (*cf* Rawes 1972, fig 4, 38–39); D/7, KG 9
8   Jar, WWR; 50/11, KG 12
9   Dish, WWO; 11/7, KG 13
10   Flat-rim dish with burnished decoration, BB1; B/34, KG 27

The Period 3 pottery
by Jane Evans and Jane Timby with contributions by Brenda Dickinson, Grace Simpson, and Graham Webster

Introduction

A total of 11,810 sherds of pottery was catalogued, weighing 224kg, and with a total rim EVE of 252.66. Of these 7,842 sherds, weighing 104.2kg, came from key stratigraphic contexts (Key Groups). The material had originally been catalogued by Graham Webster with John Chadderton and others but it was felt that a more detailed record was required using the new fabric and form series. Rather than amending the original records this material was therefore re-analysed.

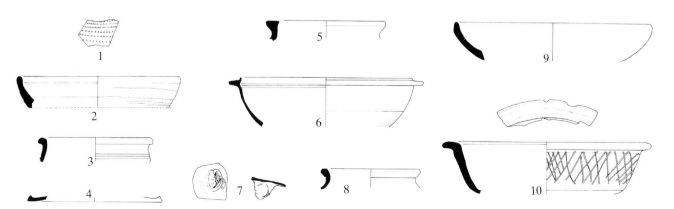

Fig 4.91 Period 2 pottery key groups; scale 1:4

A report on the pottery from the Period 3 Key Groups (Table 1.2) is in the archive, with the exception of KG14. A sample of the pottery from the *natatio* infill (KG 14) was reported on by Graham Webster with contributions by Anne and Scott Anderson, and Grace Simpson, and a summary of the coarsewares is included here along with the samian report. Previously uncatalogued pottery was recorded in less detail than for the key groups in order to complete the archive. This included about 60kg of pottery from KG 14 which had not been included in the report by Graham Webster. A selection of pottery from key group 14 is illustrated (Figs 4.92–4.94). Other vessel forms from Period 3 contexts have been incorporated into the overall form series.

Key group 14: the infilling of the *natatio*

based on a report by Graham Webster with a report on the samian by Grace Simpson

The coarsewares

A very large quantity of pottery (3926 sherds, *c* 130kg) was recovered from the primary backfilling of the *natatio* along with other finds of animal bone and small-finds. The deposit was considered to be a contemporary one covering a relatively short period of time. Just over half the pottery was studied in the late 1970s, the remainder, by Jane Evans, in the 1990s. The pottery offers a rare opportunity to study a closely datable range of wares. The time between the date of manufacture, breakage, and disposal will obviously depend on the type of vessel. There is no such thing as a contemporary collection of domestic pottery, unless it is all completely new. Most households have vessels spanning a considerable range of production dates covering perhaps a generation, and in special cases of inherited pieces even longer. Tablewares are normally more expensive than those for the kitchen and would have been treated more carefully and used selectively, whereas cooking-pots would have a more rapid breakage rate and consequently a much shorter life. The vessels with the longest life would have been those used very occasionally, or in a fixed position such as large storage jars in a pantry.

The samian, reported on below by G Simpson with some additional pieces by B Dickinson, mainly comprised Central Gaulish wares dating to the Antonine period. The latest recorded material appears to date to the period AD 170–90. A number of colour-coated wares were reported on by Scott and Ann Anderson. These included several sherds of Nene Valley colour-coat, and imported beakers from the Lower Rhineland, Trier, or Rheinzabern, and north-east France.

The coarsewares broadly reflect the date span accorded to the samian but would also appear to continue later. The mortaria include examples of the Rhaetian type made at Wroxeter in the later second century along with products from Mancetter-Hartshill dated AD 130–60. Severn Valley wares and BB1 are particularly well represented, the majority of forms having a currency in the mid-late second century. Of the total 2033 sherds recorded in the 1970s, 34% were identified as SVW, 48% as BB1. The presence of the BB1 grooved-rim bowl form suggests a date after *c* AD 180 (Holbrook and Bidwell 1991, 98). Similarly the flange-necked flagon may date to the very late second or early third century. A provisional date range for the pottery *natatio* infill is thus suggested to be AD 210–30.

The disparity with the samian dating may well be more a reflection of a fall-off in samian supplies in the later second and early third centuries.

Catalogue of illustrated sherds (Figs 4.92–4.94)
1   Cup-mouthed flagon with vestigially ringed neck in a light red-brown ware with cream slip.
2   A single handled flagon with a flanged neck in light red ware with cream slip decorated with bands of red paint.
3   Narrow necked everted rim jar with a cordon at the neck. Zone of burnished lattice decoration on the upper body. Buff burnished ware, ?SVW.
4   Narrow necked jar in a partly burnished red-brown ware decorated with vertical lines. ?SVW.
5   Narrow-necked jar in buff burnished ware. ?SVW
6   Bifid rim jar in light brown buff ware.
7   Narrow-necked jar with pie-crust decoration below the rim in buff ware.
8–12 BB1 jars
13 Wide-mouthed jar in light red buff ware partly burnished, SVW.
14 Handled beaker in a black-grey burnished ware.
15–16   Handled tankards, SVW.
17 Bag-shaped beaker (Anderson 1981, rim type 3). Dark red, hard, sandy fabric with glossy dark brown colour-coat with fine particles of clay roughcasting. Identified by A Anderson as coming from Trier or Rheinzabern.
18 Beaker in buff ware.
19 Beaker with short everted rim in brown ware.
20 Bowl in buff burnished ware, ?SVW.
21 Bowl with flanged rim in buff ware, partly burnished, ?SVW.
22–4 Bowls with flanged rims in buff burnished ware, ?SVW.
25 Bowl with flanged rim in light red ware.
26 Bowl with flanged and beaded rim in buff/light red ware, the flange burnished and decorated with white paint.
27 Bowl with incurved sides in grey ware with black-brown surface in the central fluted zone.
28 BB1 dish with flat rim, decorated on the body and base.
29 Deep flat-rimmed BB1 bowl, decorated on the body and base.
30 Dish with flat rim imitating BB1 form, in grey ware with grey-brown burnished surface.
31 Decorated BB1 dish with beaded rim.

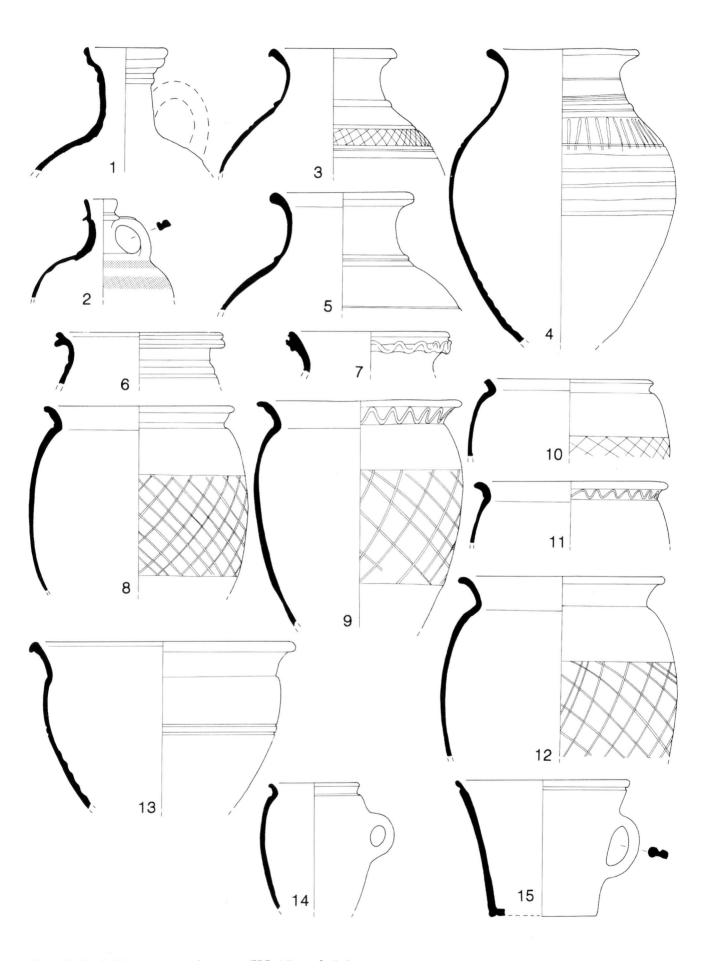

Fig 4.92 Period 3 pottery natatio *group (KG 14); scale 1:4*

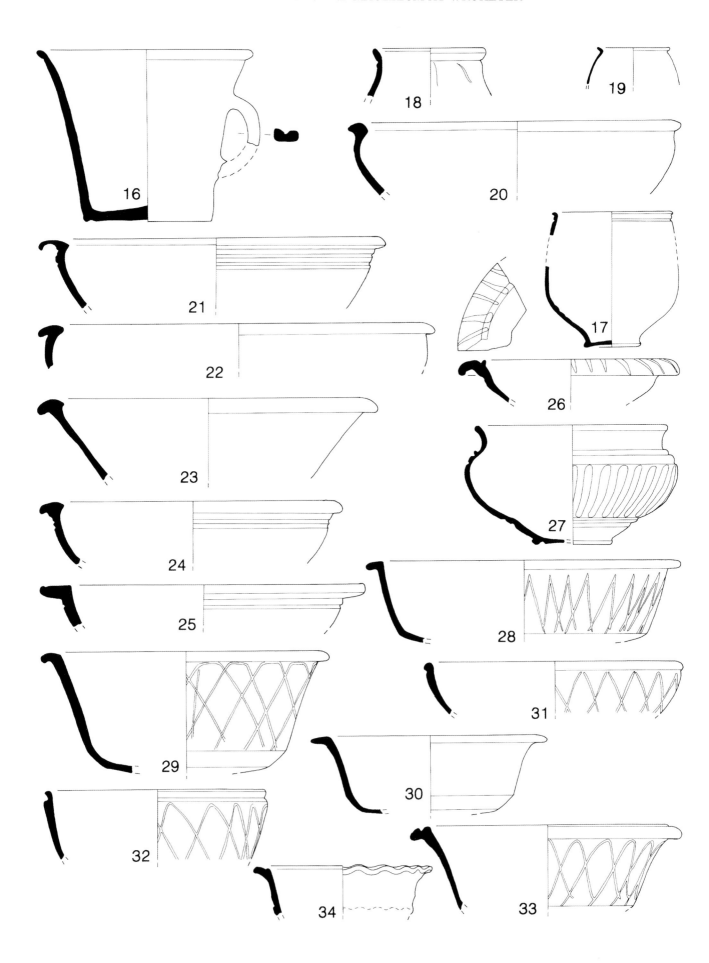

Fig 4.93 Period 3 pottery natatio *group (KG 14); scale 1:4*

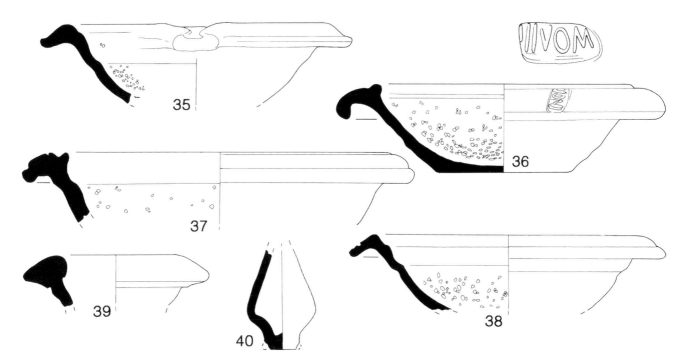

Fig 4.94 Period 3 pottery natatio *group (KG 14); scale 1:4*

32 Decorated BB1 bowl with beaded rim.
33 BB1 bowl with flat grooved rim.
34 Bowl with pie-crust rim in brown ware with cream slip.
35 Mortarium with hook rim in brown red ware with red slightly burnished surface, and dark red pebble grits and a few white quartz grits, ?MWWO
36 Mortarium with a flanged and beaded rim in cream ware. The stamp]INOM is from one of the five dies of Minomelus, who worked at Mancetter-Hartshill. AD 130–60.
37 Rhaetian-type mortarium with bead and grooved flange in light red-brown ware with red burnished surfaces and white quartz grits (MWWO).
38 Rhaetian-type mortarium with grooved hook rim in light red-brown ware with grey core, red burnished surface and dark red grits (MWWO)
39 Dressel 20 amphora.
40 Unguent flask in buff ware.

The samian

by Grace Simpson

The full report on the 276 plain and decorated vessels found in the low deposit in the *natatio* was written with the guidance of Dr Webster. Plain vessels numbered 198 and made an interesting study; the full report, including drawings by Marion Cox of the potters' stamps, is in the Midland Region Archive and Objects Store at Atcham, near Wroxeter.

Most of the vessels were made at Lezoux, during the Antonine period unless otherwise described. A few came from Rheinzabern, and three South Gaulish sherds are rubbish survivors. There are Pudding Pan Rock types *c* AD 179; four of the name-stamps are matched in the Wroxeter forum gutter find (Atkinson 1942, 137–8) and the large numbers of Dr 31 and 33 are mostly like those in the stacks which had been set out for sale in the gutter *c* AD 160–70.

The latest forms are stamp no 13, the Casurius bowls (Fig 4.95, 19), the Dr 45 in layer 47/15, and the Walters 81 in layers 47/17 and 18 (Walters 1908). There are Casurius bowls in the Wroxeter gutter find.

A total of 276 vessels were represented. Two occurred in Curle 11, fifty in form 18/31, three in Curle 21, six in form 27, fifty seven in form 31, sixty in form 33, six in form 36, seventy one in form 37, thirteen in form 38, one each in forms 45 and 72, three in form 79, one in form 80, and two in form 81.

Illustrated pieces (Fig 4.95)
1 Dr 37 ovolo and five smaller sherds, one with the tripod Rogers Q16
2 Dr 37 with 'feathers' of the early Cinnamus style and another sherd with his leaf-tips style
3 Dr 37, ovolo of Potter X-2, Les Martres-de-Veyre, Trajanic
4 Dr 37, style of Acaissa (Stanfield and Simpson 1958, pl 79.11)
5 Dr 37 in Cinnamus style. The ovolo is 3a or Rogers B143. Eight small sherds of Lezoux Dr 37, early Antonine
6 Casurius style with man to right O.638 and Diana and hind (not in Oswald). Two other sherds in his style, from different mould, *c* AD 160–90
7 Dr 37 in Banuus style, with his ovolo, Rogers B24
8 Dr 37 in Reginus I of Rheinzabern style, identified by Dr Hans-Günther Simon, who kindly informs me that the ovolo is Ludowici, VI, E54,

Fig 4.95 Pottery: decorated samian from the natatio (KG 14); scale 1:1

eight-petalled rosette O49, man M243a, and ornament O214. Dated by Dr Simon to between 150–70 at Hesselbach (Simon 1973, 96)

9 Sun chariot, see O101, possibly style of Butrio or Paternus

10 Style of Potter X-6

11 Typical style of Divixtus, and his ovolo on two different bowls

12 Large ovolo, see Rogers B145, sea-horse below

13 Style of Censorinus (Stanfield and Simpson 1958, pl 101.4 and 8)

14 ALBVCI in the decoration in layer 47/17 is probably from the same bowl as a sherd with his ovolo

15 Rim from a Dr 37, glossy slip, AD 65–75

16 Dr 30 rim and lower wall, with a tiny portion of the decoration, from a worn mould, AD 75–90

17 Advocisus style with his large ovolo and his special dolphins. Also a sherd from his small ovolo and sea-horse, mended with a lead rivet

18 Censorinus-style (see 13). The sea horses are O48 and 31, Triton wielding a club O21, Luna in her two-horse chariot O117A, and small siren O862A

19 Two Dr 37 in the style of Casurius. Both have been very large bowls

20 Three sherds join to show a free-style animal design

21 A scroll design, the drawings being conflated from eight overlapping sherds. Figure seated on rocks is O111, and the Pan mask is smaller than O1214. The ovolo is Rogers B1

22 Cinnamus style with O783 but here Hercules is strangling only one snake and that has lost its head

23 A Divixtus name stamp, and another in very worn condition is not illustrated, nor are two of four sherds in his style

24 Divixtus style

Potters' stamps
by Grace Simpson

1 DRAVCIM with damaged D, on a large sized Dr 33. Elegant serifs on the letters. Not micaceous Lezoux fabric – there are yellow specks in a slightly purple-red fabric. Antonine as on a Dr 79 from Richborough (Bushe Fox 1928, 76; Oswald 1931, 383).

2 A long palm leaf stamp on a large Dr 33, the wall is straight and lacks an outer girth groove.

3 RVF[with serifs, probably RVFFI.M, on a large-sized Dr 33. For the stamp see Hofmann (1971, 24, no 161).

4 DIVICATVS on a small Dr 33 base, with a good gloss, see Atkinson (1942, 248), Lezoux, Hadrianic-Antonine.

5 GIPPI.M on the base of a Dr 18/31. Gippus of Lezoux, see Atkinson (1942, 259), Antonine.

6 MAXIMI on a medium sized Dr 33 with a glossy red slip. Early Antonine, as at Birrens (Robertson 1975, 146, no 24).

7 MOXI[on the base of a Dr 31R. Lezoux, see Hofmann (1971, 26, no 248).

8 REBVRRI.OFF on the base of a large Dr 33. The second R is damaged and looks like an O. Lezoux (Hofmann 1971, 24, no 154.1).

9 SEVE[Sever(with the reversed S on a small Dr 33 base with the walls chipped off (Knorr 1907, Taf xxxi.94).

10 SIIVIIRI on a large Dr 33 with outward-flaring wall. The lettering is like Hofmann (1971, 27, no 181.5), from Lezoux. Graffiti LV and XX under base.

11 TITVRONIS in very small letters, with possibly a final tiny O. On the base of a Dr 31. Tituro of Lezoux, like the Wroxeter Gutter find (Atkinson 1942, 275). AD 160–90.

12 AETERNIM, retrograde on the base of a small Dr 33, with the walls chipped off. Lezoux. A Wroxeter Gutter find (Atkinson 1942, 138). Found with a large sized Dr 31.

13 Dr 18/31 clearly stamped for half of the very long stamp of Augustalis of Rheinzabern as AVCVST[......] with the reversed S. The second half of the stamp is present but illegible. The length of the stamp indicates that it is probably not by Augustinus (Simon 1984, 525). The even longer stamp of Augustalis is Ludowici V (1927, 209, no 1), which corresponds with Hofmann (1971, pl IX, 34.5). Dr Simon kindly sends the following dating evidence: in a cellar in Zugmantel, destroyed shortly after AD 187; also a stamp on a Dr 18/31 at Neuberg, tomb 28. Last third of the second century.

Additional Notes
by Brenda Dickinson

14 Aeternus 2a 33 AETERNIM retr: Lezoux. The stamp occurs in the Aquincum Hoard (thought to have been destroyed in the Marcomannic Wars) and the Wroxeter Gutter. The die was used on forms 31, 33 and 80. Aeternus used a different die on forms 27 (rarely) and 79. c AD 155–85.

15 Cleus 1a 33 CLIIVSMM: Lezoux (c). Only four other examples of this stamp have been noted by the present writer. Antonine, on form, fabric and gloss.

16 Divicatus 3f 33 DIVICATVS Lezoux (b). Divicatus's output includes many dishes of forms 18/31 and 18/31R and cups of form 27, which will be before c AD 160. At the end of his career he was stamping form 79. His stamps have been noted in a group of burnt samian of c AD 140–50 at Castleford (forthcoming). c AD 140–70.

17 Draucus ii 1b 33 DRAVCIM Lezoux (b). The range of forms associated with this stamp includes 27 and Ludowici Tg/Tx. The latter suggests activity continuing beyond c AD 160, and his record in general shows a bias toward the latter half of the second century. This particular stamp

does not occur in Scotland, unlike one of his others, and so is likely to be from one of his later dies. *c* AD 160–80.

18   Priscus iii 9a 33 PRIƧCVƧ (Walke 1965, no 300) Lezoux (a). Priscus iii was associated with the mid- to late-Antonine potter, Clemens iii, in the production of moulds. This stamp, used only on plain forms, occurs in a group of burnt samian of *c* AD 170 at Tác (Hungary). *c* AD 160–90.

19   Severus vi 7c 33·SIIVIIRI·Lezoux (b). This Severus stamped forms which did not evolve before *c* AD 160, such as 31R, 79 and 80. His stamps reached forts in northern Britain which were recommissioned *c* AD 160. *c* AD 160–90.

20   Tituro 5b 31 TITVRONIS (Hartley and Dickinson 1991, fig 104) Lezoux (b). A stamp used on forms current in the later second century, such as 79, 80 and Ludowici Tx. *c* AD 160–90.

21   ]SF on form 18/31R, Central Gaulish. Hadrianic or early-Antonine.

22   M[on form 18/31R, Central Gaulish. Hadrianic or early-Antonine.

23   ]A[on form 18/31R or 31R, Central Gaulish. Hadrianic or early-Antonine.

24   ]S·F on form 31R, Central Gaulish. Mid to late-Antonine.

Summary discussion by area

by Jane Timby

The greatest amount of pottery by far was recovered from the Porticos, in total some 18,600 sherds (191 kg) representing 52% (by weight) of the overall Period 3 assemblage. The Baths Precinct produced the next largest quantity by sherd count some 7284 sherds, 20% by weight, followed by the Courtyard with 3481 sherds, but 23% by weight. In contrast, negligible quantities were recovered from the West Range and Baths. A tabulated breakdown of pottery by area and sub-phase can be found in the archive.

Looking at the range of fabrics present across the Portico sub-phases some slight differences are apparent (tables in archive). Black-burnished ware (BB1) is one of the commonest fabrics present and this remains consistent throughout P 3.1 and P 3.2 at 40–43% by sherd count. In P 3.3 this falls to just 25% with a corresponding higher percentage of miscellaneous grey ware. In P 3.4A–P 3.6 the percentage of BB1 continues to decrease. Severn Valley ware, the second most common fabric remains fairly consistent throughout at *c* 23–6% with a slight fall in P 3.4B. The amount of Oxfordshire ware recorded, although low, shows a marked increase in P 3.5 and P 3.6 compared to earlier portico sub-phases reflecting perhaps a slightly later market penetration. Fossil shell-tempered ware (CALC) also appears for the first time in P 3.3 suggesting the presence of contexts dating to the second half of the fourth century. The largest number of sherds of this late ware were recovered from P 3.5 where it represented 9% (weight) of the group. Mancetter-Hartshill and Nene Valley products similarly show a very marked increase in the later sub-phases, the latter accounting for 13% (weight) of P 3.5 and P 3.6.

Average sherd size is very similar in P 3.1 and P 3.2 at 12–13gm but this decreases to just 9–10gm in P 3.3 and P 3.4A suggesting a greater level of disturbance and reflecting the fact that the pottery from P 3.3 was largely from layers subjected to trample, rather than feature fills. The sherd size rises again in P 3.4B to 19gm to decrease again in P 3.5 and P 3.6 to 12–13gm.

A consideration of the form composition from the Porticos (Table 4.24) shows flagons to be particularly marked in P 3.1 at 19.5% (EVEs), whereas in P 3.2 jars (28%) and bowls (18.5%) dominate. For the later Portico phases jars shows a progressive increase accounting for over half of the P 3.6 assemblage (54%) and flagons are less frequent. In P 3.3 flagons do show a slight increase (11.5%), an interesting correspondence with the underlying P 3.1. It may be just possible that some of the P 3.3 layers had sunk into the pits and were excavated as fills, or conversely some of the pit fills may have been incorporated into the later surface deposits. Beakers and tankards remain fairly consistent through each sub-phase. Cups decline from 6% (EVE) and 7% in P 3.1 and P 3.3 down to 1% in P 3.5 and none in P 3.6. Bowls tend to fluctuate being particularly marked in P 3.4 at 30.5%. The same sub-phase produced the highest incidence of mortaria. It could be speculated that the preponderance of flagons and cups in P 3.1 may suggest a drinking facility in the area for customers using the market. Glass cups were similarly well represented in P 3.1.

The West Range produced a total of just 807 sherds (12609gm). Most of this (97% by weight) came from WR 3.1 with the rest from WR 3.3 apart from a single sherd of samian from WR 3.2. The general composition of the wares shows some differences compared to the Porticos. Black-burnished ware (BB1) is less well-represented at only 3% (sherd count and weight). The figures are however, greatly distorted by a large quantity of recorded samian accounting for 66% by number and 44% by weight from WR 3.1. The moderately large sherd size for this material could suggest a dump of discarded stock from a nearby source being incorporated into the deposits. Severn Valley wares remain common accounting for 20% of WR 3.1. By contrast the material from WR 3.3, although only ten sherds, contains no samian or BB1 but is dominated by Oxfordshire and Mancetter-Hartshill products reflecting a later date of activity, suggested by the coins to be at least in the second half of the fourth century. The overall average sherd size for the West Range material is high compared to the Porticos at 15gm despite the possibly high residual component hinted at from the analysis of KG 21. In terms of form composition WR 3.1 shows a high percentage of tablewares, with cups at 24.5% (EVE) and bowls (21%) again reflecting the samian presence. This was also the only area to record an inkwell.

The Courtyard produced 3481 sherds of pottery (84.4kg), most of which came from C 3.1 (77.5% by weight). In contrast to the Porticos and West Range the material is in an even better state of preservation, with an average sherd size of 31gm. The group is dominated by BB1 (34%) and SVW (46%) with only small quantities of the finer colour-coated wares. The high sherd size reflects in part the particularly good group of material from the *natatio* infill (KG14). In C 3.2 the material coming mainly from layers and post-holes appears to be more fragmented with the sherd size decreasing to 9gm. This rises again in C 3.3 to 13 gm and in C 3.4 reaches 43 gm. The pottery from C 3.3 shows a slight increase in Oxfordshire colour-coats and a single sherd of CALC supports the later fourth century date indicated by the coins. Flagons are moderately well-represented in the Courtyard assemblages C 3.1–3.3 although they are absent from C 3.4 where, by contrast, mortaria are more marked. Bowls and jars remain the commonest vessel classes present.

The Baths produced a very small assemblage of just 311 sherds (3629gm), 95% of which came from B3.1. The average sherd size from B 3.1 is relatively low at 9.5 gm, comparable with material from C 3.2 and P 3.3. The same dominance of BB1 (25%) and SVW (28.5% by count) continues. Later wares are completely absent, emphasising the greater residual element to the Baths material much of which possibly derived from the constructional work.

In contrast to the Baths, the Baths Precinct produced slightly more pottery (7284 sherds, 7460gm). The average sherd size was greatest for the BP 3.1 material at 16.5gm compared to 9gm for BP 3.2 and 12gm for BP 3.3. As with the other areas BB1 and SVW dominate; for BP3.1 representing 15% (count) and 26% respectively. Mortaria was better represented in the Baths Precinct area compared to other areas at 14% (BP 3.1 EVE) and 13% (BP 3.3), but overall the forms reflect the usual dominance of bowls and jars.

Period 3 on the whole showed a low proportion of material residual from first-century contexts. This mirrors a similar conclusion from the basilical hall excavations which also showed little disturbance of military levels. The deposits are dominated by two main fabrics, BB1 and SVW (both oxidized and reduced) which tend to mask the more chronologically sensitive wares present in smaller amounts. The basilical hall assemblage is similarly dominated by these two wares, SVW accounted for over 30% (red wares only) and BB1 for 20–26% (Symonds 1997). There is, however, a major difference apparent between the two adjacent assemblages seen in the much greater emphasis on later wares from the basilical hall where fossil shell-tempered wares account for 7–11% and both Oxfordshire and Nene Valley colour-coated wares show a marked increase. Types made before AD 200 were considered to account for *c* 5% of the total basilical hall assemblage. By contrast the baths and *macellum* assemblage appears to contain a higher percentage of residual late second and third-century material, and the later wares although present, are in insufficient quantities to allow any patterning, chronological or otherwise, to

Table 4.24 Pottery Period 3: occurrence of forms by phase (% EVE)

FORM	P 3.1	P 3.2	P 3.3	P 3.4	P 3.5	P 3.6	WR 3.1	WR 3.3	C 3.1	C 3.2	C 3.3	C 3.4	B 3.1	B 3.2	B 3.4	BP 3.1	BP 3.2	BP 3.3
flagon	19.5	7.5	11.5	3.5	4	4	5	–	9	15	18	–	12.5	–	–	8.5	7	8.5
beaker	3.5	5	2	5	2	3	<1	–	4.5	–	1	–	12.5	–	–	8	7	8.5
cup	6	4	7	1.5	1	–	24.5	–	3	11	5	6	7.5	–	–	14	4	4
cup/beaker	<1	<1	<1	–	–	–	<1	–	<1	<1	–	–	–	–	–	–	–	–
tankard	1	1	<1	1	<1	<1	–	–	4	<1	1	–	–	–	–	–	3.5	3
bowl	18.5	20.5	16.5	30.5	21.5	18.5	21.5	26	12.5	16	8.5	34	14	30	23	11.5	13	21
dish	7	12	5.5	3.5	6.5	6.5	9	–	8	7.5	1.5	2	2.5	–	–	5	3	2.5
bowl/dish	7.5	6	6.5	3.5	2	1	22.5	–	11	2.5	–	–	7	70	–	5.5	6.5	4
platter	–	–	–	–	–	–	<1	–	–	–	–	–	–	–	–	–	–	–
jar (JC)	15	20	9	15.5	7	5	1	–	15	5	21	–	–	–	–	15.5	12.5	7
mortar	4	4.5	4	8	4.5	6	7	74	4	5	12.5	57	<1	–	77	13.5	2	13
jar	13	14	30.5	20	45	49	4.5	–	23	32.5	28.5	1	23	–	–	17	39.5	31.5
jar (JH)	<1	1.5	–	<1	<1	–	–	–	1	–	–	–	–	–	–	<1	1	–
lid	3	1	1	<1	<1	1	1.5	–	2	1	<1	–	–	–	–	–	<1	–
inkwell	–	–	–	–	–	–	1	–	–	–	–	–	–	–	–	–	<1	–
tazza	<1	<1	<1	–	–	<1	–	–	<1	–	–	–	–	–	–	–	<1	–
box	–	–	–	<1	<1	<1	–	–	–	–	–	–	–	–	–	–	–	–
beaker/jar	–	–	<1	<1	<1	1	–	–	–	–	–	–	–	–	–	–	–	–
jar/flagon	<1	<1	<1	–	2	<1	–	–	–	–	–	–	–	–	–	–	<1	1
bowl/jar	<1	<1	2	1	–	<1	<1	–	<1	–	–	–	–	–	–	<1	2.5	<1
unid	<1	<1	2.5	4.5	1.5	3.5	<1	–	2	3.5	2	–	–	–	–	<1	1	2.5
EVE total	9004	5085	6837	2428	2391	5805	1889	46	7932	877	822	595	717	20	22	1663	9115	1477

P portico, WR west range, C courtyard, B baths, BP baths precinct

be made. This is clear, too, when considering the forms present in the Period 3 pottery (Table 4.24). It is apparent from the basilical hall pottery that Nene Valley, Oxfordshire and shell-tempered wares all increase very rapidly in the third quarter of the fourth century. These differences, although they may in part reflect different excavation and recovery techniques, could well suggest different usage of the two areas, the baths area perhaps still being considered a public space throughout the fourth century and beyond where little contemporary rubbish was allowed to accumulate.

The samian

by Brenda Dickinson, with South Gaulish decorated ware
by Geoffrey Dannell

The samian recovered from second-century or later contexts is characterised by its consistently high residual content. Most of the first-century sherds are small and battered, and were almost certainly redeposited more than once. The second-century ware is generally less fragmented.

The South Gaulish ware from the early civil settlement (Period 1) and the Hadrianic construction onwards is largely composed of sherds from vessels which must have been in use in the fortress. Indeed, the samian recovered from Period 1 is, with one exception, entirely South Gaulish. Only a few pieces could have reached the site as late as *c* AD 110, when export to Britain from La Graufesenque ceased. Apart from one vessel, samian belonging to the second half of the Trajanic period is missing for this phase, but it is found as residual material in later contexts, perhaps due to building activity or changes in the pattern of rubbish disposal.

The samian from the Hadrianic construction onwards has been examined first by sherd count and then by minimum vessel count and the results are remarkably consistent. The percentages are as follows:

	sherds	vessels
South Gaul	31.0	32.0
Central Gaul		
(Les Martres-de-Veyre)	16.0	15.0
Central Gaul (Lezoux etc)	52.0	52.0
East Gaul	1.0	1.0

Samian assemblages from British sites occupied from the first century down to *c* AD 260, when import ceased, tend to display more-or-less standard variations in supply (Table 4.25). The lowest points are normally in the first two decades of the second century, when much of the samian came from the Central Gaulish factory at Les Martres-de-Veyre, and towards the end of the second century, when dwindling imports from Lezoux were supplemented by relatively modest quantities of East Gaulish ware. The baths site partly conforms to this pattern, but has produced more early second-century samian than the norm and very little East Gaulish ware. Les Martres was certainly a smaller concern than La Graufesenque and Lezoux, whose wares form the bulk of this collection, and its distribution, unlike theirs, varies in different areas of Britain. The point is well illustrated by finds from Richborough, where the fluctuations in the numbers of discarded stamped plainware vessels represent a familiar pattern for Britain, with a clear drop in the Trajanic period, and from Verulamium, where there is very little variation in loss at any time during the first and second-century occupations (Dickinson *et al* 1968, 146).

Les Martres ware would usually account on average for about 10% of the samian supplied to British sites occupied continuously during the second and early third centuries. On this site the proportion is in the order of 20%. About 10%, or higher at sites in the vicinity of the east coast, would be a normal proportion for East Gaulish ware. Away from the east coast the distribution of East Gaulish samian varies considerably, but, in general it is not very common in the west except in the northern sector. The percentage from this part of Wroxeter (1.7%) is comparable with the meagre East Gaulish finds from sites such as Exeter, Usk, Gloucester and Chester, though no precise figures are available. In contrast, Carlisle, Old Penrith and Stanwix, all of which had easy access from the east along the line of Hadrian's Wall, have produced quantities of East Gaulish samian which are proportionately not vastly different from those recovered at Lincoln, York and Corbridge. The implication is that East Gaulish ware was landed on the east coast and the comparatively small supplies were usually monopolised by eastern markets and by forts in the Hadrian's Wall system.

Most of the East Gaulish ware, as normally in Britain, comes from Rheinzabern. There is a smaller, though significant, quantity from La Madeleine, which carried on a modest, but regular, trade with the province in the Hadrianic-Antonine period, mainly in plain samian. Lesser contributions are made by Trier, which certainly traded with Britain, and Chémery-Faulquemont, which probably did so, on a very small scale.

The South Gaulish factory at Montans is another source of supply of particular interest for the study of samian trade to Britain. The first-century wares from these kilns are extremely rare here, except in the south-east, where the two sites which have produced the greatest number of examples, London and Richborough, are both possible points of entry. However, a small consignment reached Mancetter, on Watling Street, and now we have six sherds from Wroxeter. This raises the interesting question of whether they were brought there by troops who had previously served at Mancetter.

Table 4.25 Pottery: occurrence of samian forms by factory

forms	SGLG	SGM	SGE?	CGMV	CGLZ	CGV?	EG		forms	SGLG	SGM	SGE?	CGMV	CGLZ	CGV?	EG
Ritt.1	3	–	–	–	–	–	–		40	–	–	–	–	1	–	–
Ritt.8	2	–	–	–	–	–	–		42	3	–	–	6	9	–	–
Ritt.9	3	–	–	–	–	–	–		44	–	–	–	–	1	–	–
Ritt.12	22	–	–	–	–	–	–		45	–	–	–	–	8	–	4
Ritt.12 or Cu.11	33	–	–	–	–	–	–		46	–	–	–	3	7	–	–
15/17	73	–	–	3	–	–	–		64	–	–	–	–	1	–	–
15/17 or 18/31	–	–	–	1	–	–	–		67	18	–	–	–	–	–	–
15/17R	13	–	–	2	–	–	–		68	–	–	–	–	1	–	–
15/17 or 18/31R	–	–	–	2	–	–	–		72	–	–	–	–	3	–	–
15/17 or 18	74	–	–	1	–	–	–		78	2	–	–	–	–	–	–
15/17 or 18R	27	–	–	–	–	–	–		79	–	–	–	–	6	–	–
15/31	–	–	–	–	4	–	–		79 or Tg	–	–	–	–	4	–	–
15/31R	–	–	–	–	1	–	–		79/80	–	–	–	–	1	–	–
16	1	–	–	–	–	–	–		79R or TgR	–	–	–	–	4	–	–
17	1	–	–	–	–	–	–		80	–	–	–	–	5	–	–
18	305	–	–	–	–	–	–		80 variant	–	–	–	–	1	–	–
18R	33	–	–	–	–	–	–		80 or Tx	–	–	–	–	–	–	1
18R or 18/31R	1	–	–	–	–	–	–		81	–	–	–	3	6	–	–
18/31	1	1	–	262	141	–	–		Cu.11	31	–	–	25	24	–	–
18/31 or 31	–	–	–	5	237	–	–		Cu.15	1	–	–	3	9	–	–
18/31–31	–	–	–	2	7	–	1		Cu.15 or 23	–	1	–	3	13	–	–
18/31R	1	–	–	24	163	–	1		Cu.21	–	–	–	–	6	–	–
18/31R or 31R	–	–	–	–	21	–	–		Cu.23	–	–	–	–	4	–	–
18/31R–31R	–	–	–	–	6	–	–		Tx	–	–	–	–	1	–	–
24	36	–	–	–	–	–	–		dish	49	1	1	13	64	–	6
27	339	3	–	160	159	–	–		rouletted dish	9	1	–	1	12	–	–
29	152	–	–	–	–	–	–		dish or bowl	28	1	–	7	130	–	8
30	26	–	–	6	12	–	–		cup	124	1	–	51	73	–	–
30 or 37	50	–	–	23	185	–	–		cup or bowl	4	–	–	5	2	–	–
31	–	–	–	–	384	–	11		bowl	9	–	–	6	25	–	2
31R	–	–	–	–	63	–	7		decorated bowl	31	–	–	1	4	–	–
32	–	–	–	–	–	–	4		jar	12	–	–	6	57	–	–
33a	10	–	–	9	11	–	–		inkwell	1	–	–	1	3	–	–
33	7	1	–	27	397	1	8		barrel beaker	–	–	–	–	3	–	–
35	37	–	–	20	19	–	1		enclosed vessel	2	–	–	2	3	–	1
35/36	3	–	–	1	1	–	–		pedestal vessel	1	–	–	–	–	–	–
35 or 36	9	–	–	6	4	–	–		GSM	–	–	–	–	7	–	2
36	41	–	–	27	63	–	1		flagon	–	–	–	–	1	–	–
37	227	4	–	144	585	–	3									
38	–	–	–	–	54	–	7		total	1852	11	1	861	3046	1	68
38 or 44	–	–	–	–	30	–	–									

number of vessels (excluding scraps and flakes): 5840

SGLG South Gaul (La Graufesenque); SGM South Gaul (Montans); SGE? South Gaul (Espalion?); CGMV Central Gaul (Les Martres–de–Veyre); CGLZ Central Gaul (Lezoux); CGV Central Gaul (Vichy, Terre–Franche); EG East Gaul; GSM gritted samian mortarium.

Second-century Montans wares found a fruitful and widespread, though mostly small-scale, market in Britain in the Trajanic to early-Antonine period. Areas with the largest concentrations are the south-east, particularly London and Richborough, and also Lowland Scotland and the Antonine Wall (Hartley 1972b, 42–5). In the west, scattered instances have been noted from sites south of Wroxeter and as far west as Carmarthen and, more regularly, from Wroxeter to Carlisle. It is certain, therefore, that some of the Montans samian was landed, and distributed, from west-coast ports. This would be logical, since Montans ware would have been shipped to Bordeaux down the Tarn and Garonne and must have passed through the Bay of Biscay en route to Britain. Two western sites in particular have produced substantial quantities of late Montans ware. From the baths site there are ten sherds and there are at least twenty-one more stamped and/or

decorated sherds from Wroxeter as a whole, conserved in Rowley's House Museum in Shrewsbury and in the site museum. A collection of similar size comes from Wilderspool.

One stamped piece, no 124, is perhaps from Espalion, where it is thought that a few potters from La Graufesenque established a satellite workshop (pers comm M Tilhard). A few vessels apparently from there reached Britain, though probably not through trade.

The Central Gaulish samian includes one sherd of distinctive first-century Lezoux ware. A small-scale trade with Britain went on in the Neronian and early-Flavian periods, tailing off in the later first century and not picking up until the Hadrianic period, when serious export began. No very clear distribution pattern for the first-century material has yet emerged for Britain, but a few vessels have turned up in the western half of the province as far west as Caerleon. It would be unwise to explain a single vessel as an object of trade, and there is no reason why it should not have reached Wroxeter as a legionary's personal possession.

The fabrics of two Central Gaulish vessels suggest possible origin at the Terre-Franche kilns at Vichy. Samian from this source, though not unknown in Britain, has never occurred in such quantities as to suggest regular trade with the factory. There is no obvious explanation for their presence at Wroxeter.

Of possible significance are three, or perhaps four, decorated bowls in the style of the Central Gaulish potter, Tetturo. Mr G B Rogers (pers comm) believes that this potter's decorated ware comes exclusively from Toulon-sur-Allier, whose products rarely appear in Britain. However, in view of the known trade of samian moulds between potteries, there is no reason why the Tetturo moulds used at Toulon-sur-Allier should not have been made at Lezoux. Indeed, this is highly likely, since the bulk of his output, both of plain and decorated samian, seems to have been sent to Britain.

Wroxeter drew its samian from a comparatively large number of sources, but the range of plainware vessel forms on this site is unremarkable. Decorated samian accounts for about 20–25% of the South and Central Gaulish assemblages, which is an acceptable figure for a major romanised site in Britain. This contrasts with the East Gaulish material, in which the proportion of decorated ware is only seven per cent, but this does not appear to be unusually low for sites in some parts of Britain (pers comm B Hartley).

Comparison of the number of examples of form 27 (319) with form 33 (444) and of form 18/31R (178) with 31R (80) from the post-military phases suggests that the dumping of samian on this site in the second century had reached its peak *c* AD 150–60. Forms 27 and 18/31R had virtually disappeared from the Lezoux repertoire by AD 160 and the standard form 31R had not fully evolved before then. It is less easy to distinguish between early- and late-Antonine form 33s from single sherds, but sites with heavy concentrations of samian going down to the end of the second century and beyond might be expected to produce a higher ratio of form 33 to form 27 than this one. The decorated ware tells the same story. Potters who were at work before AD 160, notably the Sacer i-Attianus ii and Cerialis ii-Cinnamus ii groups, Cinnamus in his developed style, Secundus v and Divixtus i, are much more heavily represented than those whose careers did not begin until then. In particular, Cinnamus's total of 40 bowls from the Wroxeter baths stands out against a maximum of 18 by the Paternus v group, whose decorated wares are so common in Britain in the late second century. Other contemporaries of Paternus whose work appears at Wroxeter, such as Advocisus (eight), Banuus, Censorinus ii (two?), Doeccus (two), Iullinus ii (four) and Servus iv, only increase the later second-century total of decorated ware by a maximum of 18 bowls.

The drop in the quantities of discarded samian of the later Antonine period seems to apply not only to the baths site, but to Wroxeter as a whole, as far as the evidence for the potters' stamps goes. This implies that there really was a reduction in supply, rather than that the pattern of rubbish disposal changed after *c* AD 160. However, there is no doubt that this particular site, and other areas of Wroxeter, had access to substantial quantities of samian after that. In the first half of the third century the supply had been reduced to a trickle, but there would still have been some samian vessels made in the late second-century surviving in use.

Catalogue of decorated ware (Figs 4.96–4.98)

Porticos

D1   Form 37, Central Gaulish. Style of Paternus v (Rogers's Paternus II), with ring-tongued ovolo (Rogers B105), horse and rider (D.157 = 0.246), leopardess (D.971 = 0.1533/4) and striated spindles. All the details are on a stamped bowl from Albens (Musée d'Annecy). The leopardess is a rare figure-type for Paternus. *c* AD 160–95; 80/115, F486, P 3.1, KG 16

D2   Form 37, Central Gaulish. Style of Advocisus, with ovolo (Rogers B102), sea-horses to left (D.33 = 0.33) and right (D.35 = 0.52A), trifid motifs (Rogers G70), six-petalled rosette (Rogers C122) and his twist motif (Rogers U103). The trifid motifs stem-to-stem are on a stamped bowl from the first destruction of the forum at Wroxeter (Atkinson 1942, pl 33, H3) and the twist is on one from Colchester (Stanfield and Simpson 1958, pl 112, 13). The ovolo, beads (Rogers A2) and rosettes were also regularly used by Advocisus, but the choice of fiqure-types and the composition of the vertical motif are unusual for him. *c* AD 160–90; 80/119, F466, P 3.1, KG 16

D3   Form 37, Central Gaulish. Style of Casurius ii, with ovolo (Rogers B208), large beads (Rogers A2), Cupid (D.230 = 0.382), hare (D.950a = 0.2116), polygonal leaf (Rogers J5) and cogged festoon (Rogers F38). His stamped bowls show the ovolo (Stanfield and Simpson 1958, pl 133, 17: Leicester), the hare (*ibid*, 19: Naples) and the Cupid and leaf (Karnitsch 1959, Taf 63, 1: Wels). The Cupid is also on a bowl in his style in the Wroxeter Gutter deposit (Atkinson 1942, pl 36, G9). *c* AD 160–90; 80/84, P 3.3; 80/119, F466, P 3.1, KG 16; 80/140, F564, P 3.1

D4   Form 37, East Gaulish. Style of Satto ii-Saturninus i at Chémery-Faulquemont. *Cf* Delort 1935, Taf 61 for bowls of Satto with

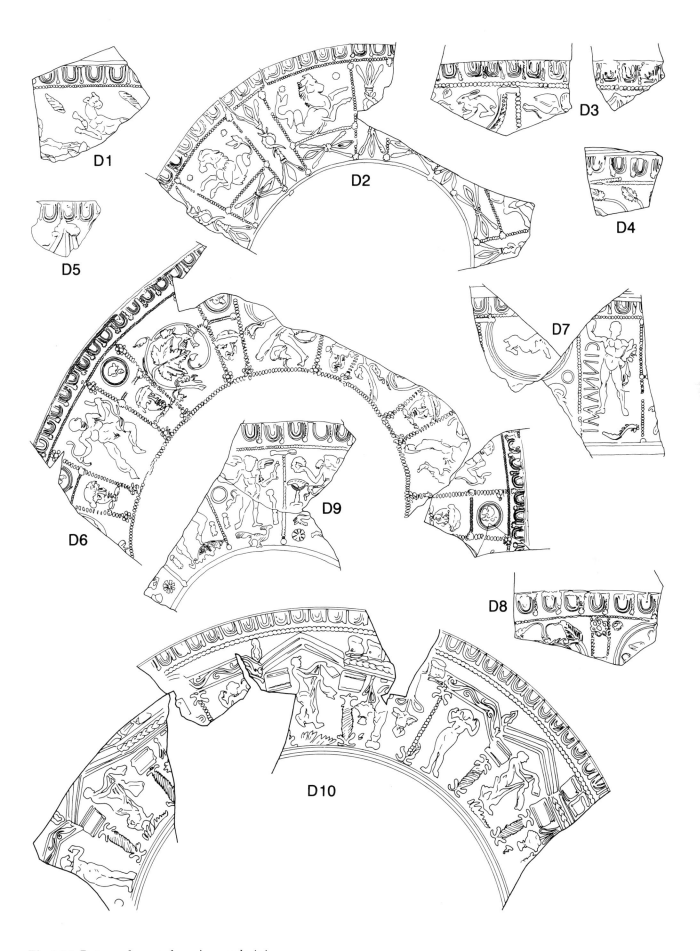

Fig 4.96 Pottery: decorated samian; scale 1:1

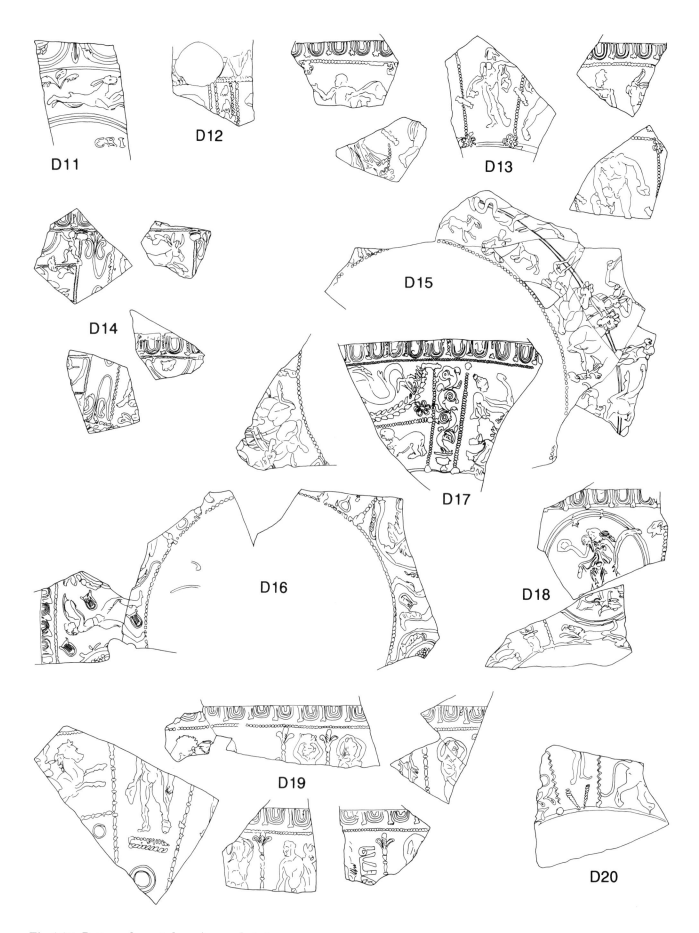

Fig 4.97 Pottery: decorated samian; scale 1:1

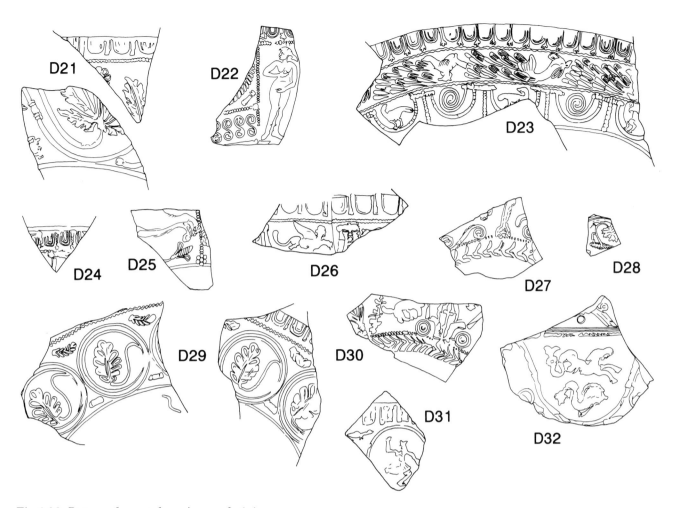

Fig 4.98 Pottery: decorated samian; scale 1:1

the ovolo and leaf and Knorr 1910, Taf IX, 8 (Rottenburg) for both motifs on an unsigned bowl. The leaf is on a stamped bowl of Saturninus from Straubing (Walke 1965, Taf 16, 10). Moulds of both potters were used at more than one East Gaulish factory, but most of their bowls which reached Britain seem to be in Chémery fabrics. They are not very common in the province, but their site record includes forts on Hadrian's Wall and others in northern Britain which were evacuated when the Antonine Wall was built. Hadrianic or, less probably, early-Antonine; 90/109, F643, P 3.2, KG 17

D5   Form 30, East Gaulish, with one of the commonest Rheinzabern ovolos (almost certainly Ricken and Fischer 1963, E26). The scheme of decoration is far from clear, but two panels are probably involved, each containing a festoon (*ibid*, KB62?) suspended from a single inverted acanthus (*ibid*, P145). All the potters using the ovolo worked in the later second century or the first half of the third century. *c* AD 180–240; 97/72, F523, P 3.1, KG 16

D6   Form 37, Central Gaulish, in the fabric of Les Martres-de-Veyre. An almost complete bowl, with the rim mended in four places with lead rivets. The style is that of an anonymous potter (Rogers's X-13) who supplied moulds to Donnaucus and others. The ovolo (Rogers B6), small and large beads (Rogers Al, A2), scarf-dancer (0.361A?), seven-beaded rosette and vine-scroll (Rogers M10) are all on bowls in a group of samian from Regis House, London, which were destroyed in the early second-century fire. One of the potters who used the ovolo was Sacirius, and it occurs on a signed bowl from recent excavations at Alchester (forthcoming). The Hercules (D.464 = 0.783), medallion and the use of animal heads, as in the medallion, all feature on bowls in the Donnaucus/X-13 style (Stanfield and Simpson 1958, pl 46, 534; 43f 491 and 44 505, respectively). The mask is almost certainly the same as the one on a bowl from Cirencester (*ibid*, pl 46, 539), but has been consistently impressed so that only one side of the face registers. *c* AD 100–20; 90/161, P 3.3

D7/S44   Form 37, Central Gaulish, with mould-stamp CINNAMI retr: Cinnamus ii, Die 5b. The details, all previously attested for Cinnamus, include the ovolo (*ibid*, B143), Perseus (D.146 = 0.234), kneeling stag (0.1704) and a cornucopia (*ibid*, U247). *c* AD 150–80; 80/58, P 3.3

D8   Form 37, Central Gaulish. The ovolo (Rogers B231) originated at Les Martres-de-Veyre, but was later transferred to Lezoux, where it was still in use in the second half of the second century. The idiosyncratic decoration does not suggest the work of any of the better known Lezoux potters and Rogers does not record either the leaf or the rosette. The absence of junction-masks and the continuation of the bead-row into the ovolo zone are reminiscent of Secundus v, an associate of Cinnamus, who is chiefly associated with the ovolo. The figure-type in the medallion is perhaps the sphinx, D.496 = 0.853, which is known for Secundus. The rosette is on a bowl from Great Chesterford (Museum of Archaeology and Ethnography, Cambridge), in the style of Iullinus ii and with a rim-stamp of Muxtullus. The leaf may be on a bowl from Saltney, also in the style of Iullinus (Newstead 1935, pl 3, 2). *c* AD 150–80; 80/5, P 3.4B, KG 25

D9   Form 37, Central Gaulish, with the same ovolo as the last. The details comprise a Hercules with snakes (D.464 = 0.783), Cupid with torches (D.265 = 0.450), Victory (D.474 = 0.809), peacock (D.1027 = 0.2365), acanthus (Rogers K7), seven-petalled rosette (Rogers C171), cup (Rogers T36), horizontal astragalus (probably a reduced version of Rogers R70), large ring and space-fillers of upright astragali. Small bowls, such as this one, tend to be in hybrid styles, often combining details used by both main groups of Antonine Lezoux potters, those headed by Cinnamus ii and Paternus v; the Cupid and peacock belong in this category. There are also parallels with Iullinus ii, whose characteristic hollow bead appears at the base of the bead-rows (Stanfield and Simpson 1958, pl 126, 11, from Leicester). The Cupid, Victory and cup are on a bowl in his style from Great Chesterford (Museum of Archaeology and Ethnography, Cambridge), with a rim-stamp of Muxtullus. In view of the parallels, a date *c* AD 160–90 is likely; 80/7, P 3.4B, KG 25

D10   Form 37, Central Gaulish. The complicated design includes elements which appear principally in the work of Servus iv (Rogers's Servus II) and Iullinus ii. The ovolo (Rogers B155) occurs on a bowl from Lezoux in the style of Servus (pers comm B Hartley), and this, on the whole, tips the balance in his favour, though the connections with Iullinus are almost equally strong. Servus used the Venus (D.173 = 0.278), cup (Rogers T29) and, probably, the caryatid (a variant of D.656 = 0.1199) on a signed bowl from Lezoux (Sauvaget 1969, pl IV, 21). The grass beneath the dancer is the edge of a leaf, almost certainly Rogers H93, which is known for Servus. I am indebted to Mr Rogers for information on his use of the beads (Rogers A3) and, probably, the dancer (D.216 = 0.353) and arrow-heads on bowls from Lezoux. Iullinus used the caryatid, balustrade (Rogers U263) and chest (Rogers U214, in double impression) on a stamped bowl from Great Chesterford (Stanfield and Simpson 1958, pl 125, 1), the Venus on one from South Shields (*ibid*, 2, not from Newcastle, as noted on p 222) and the arrow-heads on a mould from Lezoux. The basket of fruit is on a mould in his style from Lezoux (Musée des Antiquités Nationales, Saint Germain-en-Laye). Bowls in this distinctive style, from Colchester and La Plaiderie (Guernsey), show the spindles used as columns, with the same ends, and the (freehand) trifid motifs. Only the *bucranium* seems to be unknown. *c* AD 160–200; 80/7, P 3.4B, KG 25

Dll/Sl45   Form 37, Central Gaulish, with mould-stamp of Sacer i, [OFI]SACRI below the decoration. The zonal arrangement of the decoration is typical of this potter's style, and the upper zone is parallelled on a bowl from London (Stanfield and Simpson 1958, pl 82, 6). For the goat (0.1842 variant?) and tree (Rogers N16, partly impressed), see Stanfield and Simpson 1958, pl 82, 3 (Augst) and 1 (Silchester), respectively. All the parallels quoted have the same stamp as the Wroxeter piece. *c* AD 125–45; 90/48, P 3.4A, KG 25

West Range

D12   Form 37, South Gaulish. A second-century Montans bowl, with an ovolo replacement of solid triangles, as on bowls from Leicester, York and Camelon. See also Déchelette 1904.1, 116, fig 78 for a bowl with the same ovolo, much truncated, thought by the author to be late-Italian, but with details known for Montans. *c* AD 115–40; 86/3, WR 4

D13   Form 37, Central Gaulish. A bowl in the later style of Geminus iv, with ovolo (probably Rogers B17), Minerva (D.77 = 0.126), Venus at an altar (D.184 = 0.322), Bacchus (0.566), warrior (D.111 = 0.193), Vulcan (a larger version of 0.67), standing figure and goat(?) to left. The beads, rosettes (Rogers C29) and double astragali stamped diagonally across the borders (Rogers R91) are on a signed bowl from Le Mans and, on this analogy, a bowl from Scole, which also has the ovolo, has been ascribed to Geminus (Hartley and Dickinson 1977, fig 71, D19). The Minerva is on a signed bowl from York (Stanfield and Simpson 1958, pl 65, 1) and on one almost certainly by him from Brecon (Wheeler 1926, fig 78, S 140): both bowls are in his earlier style. The Wroxeter bowl adds considerably to Geminus's repertoire of figure-types. c AD 130–45; 86/2, WR 4; 86/22, 24, WR 3.1; 86/33, WR 2.3

D14   Form 37, Central Gaulish, in the fabric of Les Martres-de-Veyre. Style of the potter X-13, who supplied moulds to Donnaucus. The ovolo (Rogers B16) and leaf (Rogers G137 variant) are on a bowl from Nether Denton (photographed by the late Mr Donald Atkinson). The festoon (Rogers F78) with dog's-head is on a bowl from Ilkley (Stanfield and Simpson 1958, pl 47, 551). The Cupid and festoon are on bowls from Vichy (ibid, pl 45, 517) and London, the latter from a group of burnt samian in Second Fire groups. The cup (Rogers U64) and partly impressed acanthus (from Rogers K2) are on bowls from London (Stanfield and Simpson 1958, pl 43, 491 and 46, 529, respectively). The finely beaded borders are Rogers Al and the stag is a variant of 0.1822EE. c AD 100–20; 86/24, WR 3.1; 86/25, WR 4

D15   Form 37, Central Gaulish. Style of Butrio, with Cupids on sea-bulls to right and left (one D.28 = 0.43), as on a stamped bowl from Jort (Stanfield and Simpson 1958, pl 57, 651); goat (0.1834) and sheep (D.895 = 0.1868), as on one from London (ibid, pl 58, 661). Also depicted are a Diana with chariot (D.73 = 0.117), triton (D.20 = 0.25), Pan (0.728) and Neptune on dolphin, carrying a mask (a smaller variant of 0.731). The beads (Rogers A4) and guide-line are common features of Butrio's style (Stanfield and Simpson 1958, pl 60, 678, from Lisieux). c AD 125–45; 86/3, WR 4; 86/24, WR 3.1

D16   Form 37, Central Gaulish. There are traces of a mould-signature..... n..s retr below the decoration, which almost certainly belongs to one of the Lezoux Secundini. There are several broadly contemporary homonyms who worked at Lezoux in the Hadrianic-Antonine period; this man's production was connected with that of Rentus. The candelabrum (Rogers Q40), the base of which can be seen here, is on a Lezoux mould with a stamp of Rentus in the decoration and a signature of Secundinus on the plain band above the footring. The same mould almost certainly features the ovolo, which is also on bowls in Rentus's style from Heilbronn (FBB-W 2 (1975), Taf 261, 9, 10). The other details are a lyre (Rogers U230), used by Rentus, athlete (D.385 = 0.677), vine-scrolls (Rogers Ml-2) and beaded borders (Rogers A4). c AD 125–50; 83/111, WR 3.1; 86/+, WR 4; 86/24, WR 3.1

D17   Form 37, Central Gaulish, with figure-types and motifs used at Lezoux by Attianus ii and Drusus ii. Attianus on stamped bowls and Drusus on signed bowls used the following details: the ovolo (Rogers B61): Attianus at Friedberg (Stanfield and Simpson 1958, pl 87, 26) and Drusus at Doncaster; the Diana with hind (D.64 = 0.106): both Attianus and Drusus at London (Stanfield and Simpson 1958, pl 85, 9 and 89, 16); the panther (0. 1566): Attianus at Colchester (Stanfield and Simpson 1958, pl 85, 3) and Drusus at Lancaster (ibid, pl 88, 5). Attianus also used the vine-scroll (Rogers M50), on a bowl probably from York, and the festoon (Rogers F8), on a bowl from London (Stanfield and Simpson 1958, pl 85, 9). The dolphin to left (probably a reduced version of D.1052 = 0.2392) is on signed bowls of Drusus from Corbridge and Worcester. The six-petalled rosette is not illustrated by Rogers and does not seem to be known for either potter. On the whole, the beads (Rogers Al) are more reminiscent of Drusus than Attianus, but that does not affect the date of this bowl. c AD 125–45; 86/24, WR 3.1

D18   Form 37, Central Gaulish. The ovolo (Rogers B52) is chiefly associated with Divixtus i, but appears in association with a straight line, as here, on bowls in the style of Secundus v. The dog (D.934 = 0.1980), and probably the medallion, are on a stamped Secundus bowl from Gloucester and the small dolphin in the upper corner of one panel is probably the same as on a stamped bowl from Great Chesterford (Simpson and Rogers 1969, fig 2, 4). The caryatid (D.657 = 0.1206) and Victory (D.474 = 0.809) are on bowls in his style from Dymock, Gloucestershire, and in the Department of Archaeology, Durham (unprovenanced). Secundus v was clearly connected with Cinnamus in some way, and used his ovolo 3 (Rogers B143), or a version of it, and many of Cinnamus's figure-types and motifs. *c* AD 150–80; 98/60, F766, P 3.1, KG 16

D19/S102 Form 37, Central Gaulish, with the large label-stamp of Paternus v. The motifs and figure-types comprise a T-tongued ovolo (Rogers B206), beaded and astragalus borders (Rogers A2 and A10, respectively), a Cupid on a sea-bull (as on Stanfield and Simpson 1958, pl 57, 651), Mercury (D.289 = 0.529 variant, with a purse), tambourine dancer (D.210 = 0.368), caryatid (D.655a = 01201), chevron divider (Rogers P70), trifid motif (Rogers G159), small, double medallion, plain ring and an unidentified, draped figure. While this is easily recognisable as a bowl of Paternus from the decoration as a whole, it includes elements which he is not known to have used, or only used rarely, such as the caryatid, the dancer and the trifid motif. *c* AD 160–95; 98/60, F766, P 3.1, KG 16

D20   Form 37, Central Gaulish. Style of Tetturo, with a Venus (D.176 = 0.286), lion (D.737 = 0.1379), zig-zag border (Rogers A26) and large and small chevrons (perhaps Rogers G390 and 284). A bowl from Lezoux, apparently from the same mould, adds an ovolo (Rogers B144), a vine-scroll (Rogers M2?), warrior (D.614 = 0.1059), and mask in a double medallion (Stanfield and Simpson 1958, pl 131, 1). *c* AD 130–60; 91/56, F87, WR 4

D21   Form 37, Central Gaulish. The ovolo (Rogers B144) is mainly associated with the Cerialis ii-Cinnamus ii group. It occurs with the goat (Rogers D 889 = 0.1836), leaf (Rogers H24), and astragalus (Rogers R14) on a bowl from Alcester by one of the potters in the group. The leaf is on a bowl from Heronbridge with a mould-signature of Cinnamus (Stanfield and Simpson 1958, pl 162, 57) and on an anonymous bowl from Chesters, together with the rosette, Rogers C53 (Simpson and Rogers 1969, fig 8, 23). *c* AD 135–70; 91/56, F87, WR 4

D22   Form 37, Central Gaulish. Style of the Large S Potter, with his rosette-tongued ovolo (Rogers B24), Venus (D.176 = 0.286), chevron festoon (Rogers F13), astragalus (Rogers R21) and characteristic S-motifs. See Stanfield and Simpson 1958, pl 76 for the ovolo, festoon and S-motifs. The Venus and astragalus are on unpublished bowls of this potter from York and Carlisle, respectively. *c* AD 125–40. 83/+, WR 4

Courtyard

D23/S12 Form 37, South Gaulish. The trident-tongued ovolo occurs at La Graufesenque on bowls with signatures of Albanus iii, G. At-Pas-, Bassinus i, and Litugenus i. It is also on bowls with mould-stamps of Amandus iii, and one of these is almost certainly below the decoration here, though only O and D are visible. The figure-types are a dolphin (D.1049 = 0.2389) and birds to left (0.2259B, upper zone; 0.2290(?), lower zone) and right (D.1009 = 0.2247?). The 'waves' are partial impressions of a four-bladed plant (Hermet 1934, pl 14, 49). This motif occurs on an unstamped bowl from Malton, with the same ovolo and beaded festoons. For the larger bird to left, see a bowl from Holt (Grimes 1930, fig 35, 19). *c* AD 85–110; 92/4 C 2.4

D24   Form 37, Central Gaulish. The ovolo, with diagonally-beaded tongue ending in hollow rosettes, occurs on bowls at Lezoux in late Hadrianic contexts, containing decorated ware of Sacer i and Attianus. It is also, significantly, on plainware of Cinnamus ii, which is in the same overfired condition as the bowls with this particular ovolo. *c* AD 130–40; 63/13, F2288, C 2.2

D25   Form 37, Central Gaulish, with lion (D.766 = 0.1450), trifid motif (Rogers G168) and seven-beaded rosette (Rogers 280). The elements of the decoration on this piece, and their composition, originated at Les Martres-de-Veyre, with an anonymous mould-maker, Rogers's X-13, a supplier to Donnaucus. However, they also appear at Lezoux, where the Wroxeter bowl seems to have been made, and they are all on a bowl from Holt in the style of Drusus ii (Grimes 1930, fig 49, 150). *c* AD 125–45; 92/34, C 2.3

D26   Form 37, Central Gaulish. Style of the Cerialis ii-Cinnamus ii group, with its commonest ovolo (Rogers B144). Signed bowls of Cerialis feature the dog (D.934 = 0.1980: Oldbury-uponSevern), leopard (D.798 = 0.1521: Stanfield and Simpson 1958, pl 164, 4: Silchester) and Neptune (D.14 = 0.13: Stanfield and Simpson 1958, pl 164, 3: Aquincum). The sphinx (D.496 = 0.853) and dolphins on a basket (Rogers Q58) are on bowls of Cinnamus from Romula-Reşca (Popilian 1973, pl VI, 4) and Besançon, respectively. Both are from moulds stamped with plainware stamps, and therefore, some of his earlier Antonine products. The festoon (Rogers F26) is on a mould in his style from

Lezoux. Paullus iv used the leopard on bowls from York and Leicester (Stanfield and Simpson 1958, pl 165, 3–4). *c* AD 135–70; 65/3 and 69/2, both B 3.1, KG 18 (Part only illustrated).

D27 Form 37, South Gaulish. The chevron wreath, spiral and column are on an unpublished bowl in second-century Montans fabric from Wilderspool, which, like Wroxeter, has produced significant quantities of this ware. *c* AD 115–40; 3/13, F2159, C 3.2, KG 22

Baths Precinct

D28 Form 37, Central Gaulish, in the fabric of Les Martres-de-Veyre. The vine-scroll (Rogers M27) was used by the mould-makers X-11 and X-13 on bowls from Leicester, Holt and Caerleon (Stanfield and Simpson 1958, pl 37, 430) and London and Cirencester (*ibid*, pl 43, 491). The added spindle seems unparalleled in the work of either potter. *c* AD 100–120; 49/58, BP 2.1

D29 Form 37, Central Gaulish. The S in relief below the decoration is the last letter of a mould-signature of Sissus ii and the wavy line (Rogers A3), leaf (Rogers J13), astragalus (Rogers R60) and double medallions are already recorded on signed bowls (pers comm G B Rogers). This bowl confirms his use of the single-bordered ovolo (Rogers B166) and leafy spray (Rogers J16O). *c* AD 130–60; 16/78, 16/31 F3177, BP 3.1, KG 19

D30 Form 37, South Gaulish. Second-century Montans ware, probably by Felicio iii. The pointed leaf spray is on a bowl from a stamped mould in the Second Fire deposits at London. The basal wreath is on a bowl from Camelon with an internal stamp, applied after firing. The roundel motif is on an unstamped bowl from Wilderspool which is almost certainly from the same mould as a stamped bowl from Montans. The donkey, trilobed motif and the elements of the composite motif are unparalleled so far. *c* AD 115–40; 58/5, BP 3.2

D31 Form 37, Central Gaulish. The ovolo, a variant of Rogers B247, and bird are on signed bowls of Tetturo from Alcester and Le Lary, respectively. The single scroll with kilted figure (D,103 = O.177) is on a bowl in his style with the same ovolo, from Camelon (Hartley and Dickinson forthcoming). *c* AD 130–60; 60/23, BP 4

D32 Form 37, Central Gaulish. The scroll is unusual in having figure-types and a motif in its upper concavities, instead of the more usual vine leaves. There are perhaps more figures in the lower concavities. All the elements of the decoration, with the exception of the small rings, are known for Cinnamus ii. The sea-horse (D.36 = O.52) is on a stamped bowl from Chesters (Stanfield and Simpson 1958, pl 158, 22); the dolphin (D.1050 = O.2382) is on form 30 from Balmuildy (*ibid*, pl 159, 24); the pediment (Rogers U266) is on a bowl from Corbridge (*ibid*, pl 160, 39). However, this bowl is unlikely to be by Cinnamus, whose style is particularly consistent. Iullinus ii used the pediment (Stanfield and Simpson 1958, pl 125, 7, from Leicester) and the dolphin, but he hardly ever made scroll bowls. This bowl, therefore, though undoubtedly Antonine, cannot be attributed to any of the known Lezoux potters of that period; unstratified

D33/S6 Form 37, Central Gaulish, with a mould-stamp of Advocisus. The twist motif (Rogers U103) and six-petalled rosette (Rogers C122) are common elements of his style; the figure-types, a seated Apollo (O.83), triton (D.20 = O.25) and philosopher (D.524 = O.907) are on a stamped bowl from Richborough in the same arrangement as here (Bushe-Fox 1949, pl LXXXIII, 62), but are far from being the commonest in his repertoire. *c* AD 160–190; unstratified (Not illustrated).

Catalogue of potters' stamps

Each entry gives: potter (i, ii, etc, where homonyms are involved), die number, form, reading of the stamp, published example (if any), pottery of origin, date, and excavation context

(a), (b) and (c) indicate:
(a) Stamp attested at the pottery in question
(b) Potter, but not the particular stamp, attested at the pottery in question
(c) Assigned to the pottery on the evidence of fabric, distribution and, or, form

1 Acaperrus 1a 33 ACAPER RI Lezoux (a). Only one die has been attested so far for this potter and all the pots known for him are cups of form 33, all of Antonine date; unstratified

2 Acutus i 19a 27 OAC La Graufesenque (a). A stamp nearly always found on form 24, though one example has been noted on form Ritt 8. Other stamps of this potter occur at Velsen (before AD 47), in a Claudio-Neronian group at Narbonne and on Tiberian form 29s. *c* AD 35–60; 98/186, F1073, 1.2

3–5   Advocisus 1a 31; 33 (2)]VOCIS[; [A]DVOCIS[IOᴱ];]DVOCISIOᴱ Lezoux (a). A stamp used on some of the later second-century forms, such as 31R, 79 and 80. *c* AD 160–90; 90/101, F599, P 3.2, KG 17; 80/117, F486, P 3.1, KG 16; 80/74, F455, P 3.2, KG 17

6   Advocisus 8a 37 ADVOCISI (Stanfield and Simpson 1958, pl 169) Lezoux (a). Decorated bowls with this stamp occur at several forts on Hadrian's Wall and some of its hinterland forts which were recommissioned *c* AD 160. There are also three from the Wroxeter forum destruction deposits. *c* AD 160–90; unstratified

7   Aelianus i 1a 18/31 or 31⚹AELIANI· ᴧᴧ (Juhász 1935, no 3). Aelianus is known to have worked at Les Martres-de-Veyre, but he may have moved to Lezoux in the early-Antonine period. This particular vessel looks to have been made at Les Martres, however. The stamp occurs on form 15/17, which should be Trajanic, but some of the dishes in the 18/31 range look rather later. *c* AD 130–45; 73/+, C 4

8   Aestivus 3c 31R AESTIᴧM (Walke 1965, no 53) Lezoux (a). A stamp known from Haltonchesters and Wallsend. It comes from one of his later dies, to judge by many examples on form 31R and a few on form 79, though his occasional use of other stamps on form 27 suggests that he started work in the 150s. *c* AD 160–85; 80/3, P 3.5, KG 25

9   Amabilis ii 4r (probably) 27 AM[ᴧBILᴋIS] La Madeleine (b). There is a heavy concentration of Amabilis ii's stamps in the Rhineland. There are also many from Saalburg, some of them from the Erdkastell, which was evacuated *c* AD 139. This is only the third of his stamps to have been recorded from Britain, and the only one from the western side of the province. *c* AD 130–60; unstratified

10–11   Amandus ii 4a 27g; 27 OFᴧᴧN La Graufesenque (a). A stamp recorded from the Cirencester Fort Ditch deposit of *c* AD 55–65 (Hartley and Dickinson 1982, 120, no 1). It is usually on form 27, but occasionally appears on the pre-Flavian cups, forms 24 and Ritt 8. The site record includes Camulodunum, Fishbourne (Period 1B) and Hofheim, and there is another example from Wroxeter (Site Museum A677 T.T). *c* AD 50–65; 91/55, WR 3.3; 92/18, C 2.1

12   (Probably) Amandus iii 1a 37, from a mould stamped below the decoration, O(FAMAN)D(I) retr (Laubenheimer 1979, 106, fig 3) La Graufesenque (a). The die for this was used on Flavian-Trajanic decorated

bowls and on dishes of forms 18/31 and 18/31R, rather than 18 and 18R. This makes him one of the latest potters of La Graufesenque to have exported to Britain. *c* AD 85–110; 92/4, C 2.4

13   Andegenus 1c 31 [ᴧND]EGENIM Lezoux (b). Andegenus is one of the Lezoux potters whose wares reached the Danube provinces in the early- to mid-Antonine period. One of his stamps is in a group of burnt samian of *c* AD 170 from Tác (Hungary) and another occurs in the Second Fire deposits at Verulamium (after AD 150). His range of forms includes 18/31, 18/31R, 27 and 79. *c* AD 150–80; 92/15, C 3.2

14   Anniano 1a 27 [ANNI]ᴧOF, retr Les Martres-de-Veyre (a). The fabrics and glazes associated with this stamp are in the Trajanic range for Les Martres. There is an example from Ilkley. *c* AD 100–20; unstratified

15   Apolinaris 1a 33 [ᴧPOᴋIᴧᴧR]IS Les Martres-de-Veyre (c). One of Apolinaris's dies was used at Vichy (Terre-Franche), but 1a seems always to be associated with fabrics in the Les Martres range. The stamp is known from the Saalburg Erdkastell (evacuated *c* AD 139). A stamp from the Vichy die comes from Camelon. *c* AD 130–50; 61/+, BP 4

16   Aquitanus Incomplete 2 15/17 or 18 OFAQ[La Graufesenque (b). Aquitanus was basically a Claudio-Neronian potter, who may have started work by AD 40. His stamps occur at Velsen (before AD 47), in the pottery shops at Colchester destroyed in the Boudiccan burning and on decorated ware which does not look later than the middle of the Neronian period. *c* AD 45–60; 80/172, P 2.3

17   Arncus 1a 33 ARNᴄIMA Lezoux (c). There are several vessels with this stamp in the group of late-Antonine samian recovered off Pudding Pan Rock, Kent. Further evidence of late second-century use is its occurrence on form 80. *c* AD 160–200; 37/+, B 4

18   Atilianus i 2c 33 ATILIᴧ·O Lezoux (a). The record for this potter is consistently late-Antonine and he is represented in the group of samian recovered off Pudding Pan Rock. His forms include some which were not made before *c* AD 160. This particular stamp was used on forms 31R and Ludowici Tg. *c* AD 160–200; 97/55, P 2.3

19   Attianus ii 37 4a OF·A[TT], retr (Stanfield and Simpson 1958, pl 169) Lezoux (a). This large label stamp was used at Lezoux from the Trajanic to the early-Antonine period. The fabric of this piece is not one of the earliest ones in the range. *c* AD 125–45; unstratified

20–22 Balbinus 2a 18/31 (3) IIИIBI[NI·Ⓜ];]Ⓜ (Terrisse 1968, pl LII) Les Martres-de-Veyre (a). This stamp has sometimes been attributed to non-existent potters, such as Ainibinus and Enibinus, because of damage to a die which originally gave BⴷLBINI·Ⓜ. It is a common stamp, but very few examples are known from the undamaged die. The second version occurs in the London Second Fire deposits and occasionally on form 15/17, which was not normally made at Les Martres after the Trajanic period. There are eight other examples from Wroxeter. *c* AD 100–20; 41/26, C 3.3; 98/77, P 3.3 and unstratified

23 Bassus iii 2b 15/17 or 18/31 OF.BAS[SI] La Graufesenque (a). A stamp of the later South Gaulish Bassus, who worked at La Graufesenque in the Flavian-Trajanic period. His stamps occur at Butzbach (3), Saalburg and the main site at Corbridge. *c* AD 90–110. 84/45, WR 4

24 Beliniccus i 11a 33 BEⱧINICIⱰ retr (Curle 1911, no 12) Lezoux (a). This potter worked first at Les Martres-de-Veyre, under Trajan, and later at Lezoux. Die 11a, probably his latest, was used only at Lezoux. Stamps from it occur in Scotland, at Haltonchesters and in the Wroxeter forum destruction deposits. *c* AD 135–65; 50/25, F2497, C 3.4

25–6 Caletinus 1c 33 (2) CALETIⱯIↆ·;]IⱯIↆ Lezoux (c). The forms recorded for Caletinus are 31, 33 and 38. Stamps from two of his other dies occur in a group of predominantly late-Antonine samian from London, St Magnus. The proportions of his dishes are close to those from the Pudding Pan Rock wreck. *c* AD 160–200. 47/17, C3.1, KG 14; 97/72, F523, P 3.1

27 Caletus 2a 33 CAⱧ·[ETIⱲ] (Dickinson 1986, no. 3.24) Vichy, Terre-Franche (b), Lezoux (a). A stamp noted in groups of late-Antonine samian from Pudding Pan Rock, Kent, and London. It occurs also at Haltonchesters and South Shields. *c* AD 160–200; 80/21, P 3.5, KG 25

28 Calvus i 2a 33? [O]FIꝹALVI La Graufesenque (a). The earliest vessel on which this stamp has been recorded is from Risstissen (before *c* AD 75) and the latest comes from Newstead. *c* AD 70–95; 91/94, WR 2.3

29 Carus i 11a 18 KARV[Ꙅ·F] La Graufesenque (a). Decorated ware stamped by this potter is Neronian-Flavian, but this particular stamp is more likely to be entirely Flavian. It is known from Brecon, Caerleon, and the main site at Corbridge. *c* AD 70–90; 80/22, P 4 joining 81/69, F3050, C 3.3

30 Catullinus i 1a dish or bowl CⴷTVLLIⱯVS Lezoux (c). A concave base with a bevelled footring, not from a standard Central Gaulish form. Some of the stamps from this die are in fabrics in the Les Martres-de-Veyre range and one of them is in Period IIA at Verulamium (*c* AD 75–105: Hartley 1972a, S33). The Wroxeter vessel, however, and a few others, are in Lezoux fabric and should be Hadrianic, almost certainly before AD 130; 90/116, P 3.3

31 Caupirra 2a 18/31R CⴷV[·PIRI·ⴷM] Lezoux (b). A stamp noted in the burnt material from the Period IID fire (after AD 150) at Verulamium (Hartley 1972a, S132). It is also known from Benwell. The range for the die should be *c* AD 155–85, but the date of this dish will be *c* AD 155–65, in view of its form; 90/101, F599, P 3.2, KG 17

32 Celsianus 1a 33 (2 or 1) CELSIAⱯI·OF Lezoux (a). The die was used to stamp mid- to late-Antonine forms, such as 31R, 79 and 80. A stamp from Bainbridge will therefore belong to the reoccupation of *c* AD 160. *c* AD 160–90; 49/68, BP 4 joining 80/5, P 3.4B, KG 25

33 Celsus ii 8b 27 CELSI (Hermet 1934, pl.110, 32) La Graufesenque (a). The lettering of South Gaulish Celsus stamps divides into two distinct styles, one pre-Flavian, the other almost certainly after AD 70 and certainly in use until the 90s, at least. This belongs stylistically to the later group, and there are two examples from the Ulpia Noviomagus site at Nijmegen. *c* AD 75–95; 85/536, WR 2.1

34 Cenna 1a 18/31R, burnt, [CENN]ⴷE·Ⱳ Les Martres-de-Veyre (c). The die for this may have been used at some time at Lezoux, but this dish is in the fabric of Les Martres. An example from Malton suggests Trajanic date, since the pieces which are apparently from Lezoux are stylistically Hadrianic or very early Antonine; 98/75, F855, P 3.1, KG 16

35 Censor i 2a 15/17 or 18 OFCENS (Laubenheimer 1979, no 38) La Graufesenque (b). Censor i may have started work *c* AD 65, but there is no evidence that this stamp was used in the pre-Flavian period. Examples have been noted from the fortress and Ulpia Noviomagus sites at Nijmegen, and at Ilkley and Chester. *c* AD 70–95; 92/17, C 2.3

36 Cerialis i 1a 33 CERIALISFEC, in guide-lines, Les Martres-de-Veyre (c). There are two mouldings on the base of this cup, but no external grooves at the junction of

base and wall. It is rather messily finished, which would be consistent with early second-century Les Martres ware. Two burnt vessels from London with the same stamp may well come from the Second Fire deposits. Trajanic or early-Hadrianic; 90/62, P 3.3; 90/152, P 2.3

37–38a Cinnamus ii 5b 30, 37 CINNAMI retr CINNA[MI] retr CI[retr (Walke and Walke 1968, Taf 57, 6) Lezoux (a). This very common label stamp occurs repeatedly in Scotland and at forts on Hadrian's Wall, but is more common in Scotland. It has also been noted several times in the Danube area, where there was a considerable market for Lezoux ware in the early- to mid-Antonine period. *c* AD 150–80; 80/58, P 3.3; 80/59, F477, P 3.2, KG 17; 91/55, WR 3.3

39 Cintugenus 3a flat base CIA/[T·VGENI] (Popilian 1973, 213) Lezoux (a). A stamp used on forms 31, 33, 38 and (once) 79. The site record includes Newstead and South Shields. *c* AD 150–80; 22/45, BP 2.2

40 Cintusmus i 2b 33 (burnt) [CINTVSM]IM (Durand-Lefebvre 1963, no 226) Lezoux (a). Much of Cintusmus i's output is later than AD 160, though some of it must go back to the 140s. This stamp turns up at Birdoswald and Chesterholm and was used on form 31R. *c* AD 155–85; 80/7, P 3.4B, KG25

41–42a Cintusmus i 2c 31 CINTVSMIM Lezoux (b). A stamp noted from South Shields. The die was used to stamp form 31R. *c* AD 155–85; unstratified

43 Coccillus 6a 18/31R or 31R COCIhh[·MA] Coccillus was a wandering potter, who is already known to have worked at both Lezoux and Banassac. This particular stamp seems to have come from neither, but is more likely to have originated at Les Martres-de-Veyre or Vichy, to judge by its fabric and glaze. At Lezoux he stamped form 79, which will be after AD 160, but also form 18/31R, which will be earlier in the Antonine period. The whole of his career is likely to have been Antonine. *c* AD 150–65; 73/, C 4

44 Comprinnus la 33 COMPRINNIM Lezoux (b). There is no close dating for Comprinnus, but his use of forms 18/31, 18/31R and 27 suggests that he was no longer at work by the later Antonine period. Nevertheless, this cup seems to be Antonine, rather than earlier. *c* AD 140–65; 73/+, C 4

45 Condollus 2a 31 [CONDO]LLVSF Lezoux (b). This die, and others belonging to this potter, were used to stamp form 18/31R. His decorated ware is Hadrianic-Antonine, and

this date agrees with the form of his rouletted dishes. *c* AD 130–60; 80/117, F486, P 3.1, KG 16

46 (A.?) Cosius Iucundus 1a' <O>FCO·IV<C> (Vanderhoeven 1975, 51, no.182) La Graufesenque (a). All the dating evidence for this potter points to Flavian-Trajanic activity. The stamp, from a broken die, occurs at Catterick, while the complete version is attested at Newstead. *c* AD 80–110; 85/127, WR 2.1

47 Cosius Rufinus 5a 18 COSIR[VFI] La Graufesenque (a). The whole of this potter's output is Flavian and his latest stamps, from other dies, are known from Camelon and Newstead. This is from an earlier die, used on form 29. *c* AD 75–90; 85/105, WR 2.3

48 Crestio? 5a? 15/17 or 18 [OF>CREST]IO (Dickinson 1984, 83) La Graufesenque (a). This appears as an internal stamp on form 29s from La Graufesenque and the Gloucester Kingsholm site, both from moulds signed Mod (presumably by Modestus i). It is also in Period I at Verulamium. However, it is not unknown at Flavian foundations, such as Chester (2), the Nijmegen fortress (3) and York (2). *c* AD 55–70. 83/+, WR 4

49 Dagomarus 3b 18/31 DAGOMARVSF (Terrisse 1968, pl LII, third column, eighth from bottom) Les Martres-de-Veyre (a). There are nine examples of this stamp in the London Second Fire deposits. The potter moved from Les Martres to Lezoux in the Hadrianic period, taking some of his dies with him, but there is no evidence that 3b was among them. *c* AD 110–25; 86/24, WR 3.1

50 Dagomarus 4c 18/31 DAGO[MR'S·F], (Hartley 1972a, S72). The fabrics associated with this stamp suggest that the die may have been used for a short time at Lezoux, though most of the examples noted by us, including this one, seem to have been made at Les Martres, where he is known to have worked. It occurs in Period IIB at Verulamium (*c* AD 110–40: Hartley 1972a, 243, S72). *c* AD 110–25; 83/114, WR 2.3

51 Doccalus 5c 18/31R [DOC]CALI (Dannell 1971, no 36) Lezoux (b). There are eleven examples of this stamp from a pottery shop at Castleford which was burnt down in the 140s (Hartley and Dickinson forthcoming). It also occurs in the Rhineland, which received very little Central Gaulish samian after *c* AD 150. However, it is also in a pit of the 150s at Alcester. *c* AD 130–60; unstratified

52 Donatus ii 2c 18/31 DO(NATI·)M (Durand-Lefebvre 1963, no. 279) Lezoux (b). A stamp used on forms 18/31, 27 and 31, which in itself suggests Hadrianic-Antonine date. His wares reached Rhineland forts, where Lezoux ware is scarce after the middle of the second century. c AD 130–50; 22/2, BP 4

53 Donnaucus 2a 27 DOMV[NCI] Les Martres-de-Veyre (a). This common stamp was used almost exclusively on cups. It is noted in the London Second Fire groups. c AD 100–20; 98/140, F930, P 3.2, KG 17

54 Ego la 27g EGOFE, in a frame with swallow-tail ends, La Graufesenque (c). This stamp was presumably meant as a joke, ego fe(ci), or just possibly an abbreviated name in Ego-. Some examples, including one from Newstead, seem almost to have lost the swallow-tail ends, but here they are pronounced. Flavian; 84/100, WR 2.2

55 Elvillus 1a 31 [EL]VILLI Lezoux (a). There are many examples of this stamp from the Wroxeter Gutter hoard. It is also known from Birdoswald and occurs on forms 31R and 80. c AD 160–90; 80/7, P 3.4B, KG 25

56 Fabus 5a' 15/17 or 18 <F>ABVSFE (Hartley 1972a, S117) La Graufesenque (a). A stamp from a broken die, used on the pre-Flavian cups, forms Ritt 8 and 9. This version occurs in the Cirencester Fort Ditch of c AD 55–65 (Hartley and Dickinson 1982, 121, S10), while a stamp from the complete die turns up in Period IA (c AD 40–47) at Valkenburg ZH. c AD 55–65; 98/52, P 2.3

57 Felicio iii 5a 46? CEFΓICIO retr Montans (a). This stamp, though misspelt, is certainly from a die of the Felicio who worked at Montans in the second century. His stamps are quite common in Antonine Scotland, and this particular one is known from Balmuildy and Old Kilpatrick. Others appear in a group of burnt samian from St Catherine Coleman, London, which was probably part of the debris of the Second Fire. c AD 125–145/50; 69/26, B 3.1, KG 18

58 Firmo iii 3a or a' cup [OFIR]MON[IS] or [OFIR]MON La Graufesenque (a). A stamp from the original die occurs in a group of burnt samian from a pottery shop at Oberwinterthur, Switzerland, which burnt down in the early 60s (Ebnöther forthcoming). Stamps which cannot be assigned to one version or the other, but which are more likely to be from the broken die, occur at Newstead and Malton. c AD 60–85; 98/83, P 2.3

59 Flavius Germanus 9t 18/31 OF·F·GER (Dannell 1971, no 33) La Graufesenque (b). One of the potter's less-common stamps. His wares occur repeatedly at Domitianic foundations, both in Britain and Upper Germany, and examples have been noted from sites such as Chesterholm, Malton, Butzbach and Saalburg. He should have been at work by the early 80s, in view of his occasional use of form 29, but this particular stamp is only on plain ware. c AD 85–110; 98/20, P 3.4A, KG 25

60 Florus ii 3a' (possibly), 27g FЛ[O<RI>]l La Graufesenque (b). If correctly identified, this stamp is from a broken die, the original of which was used to stamp a pre-Flavian form 29. A vessel stamped with the broken die (3a') occurs in an early-Flavian context at the Caerleon fortress. c AD 50–65; 98/61, P 2.3

61 Gentilis iii 6a 18/31 or 31 GENT[ILISII] Lezoux (a). The best dating evidence for this stamp comes from Lezoux, where it occurs in Hadrianic-Antonine groups. c AD 130–50; 53/+, C 4

62–3 Gippus 2a 31 (2) GIPPI·M (Dickinson 1986, no 3.58) Lezoux (a). This stamp occurs in a group of burnt samian of c AD 170 at Tác (Hungary), but was also used on form 18/31R-31R, which will be mid-Antonine. A range c AD 155–85 is likely, therefore; 47/17, C 3.1, KG 14; 98/+, P 4

64 Habilis 1b 31 [H]ABILIS·M Lezoux (b). Habilis's stamps sometimes occur on forms 18/31R and 27, but his later forms outnumber the earlier ones. This particular stamp is known on form 18/31R. c AD 150–80; 90/128, F7736, P 3.1, KG 16

65 Indercillus 1a 18/31 [(I)NDERCILL]VSF(M) Les Martres-de-Veyre (a). The forms and fabrics associated with this stamp are Trajanic and there are two examples from the London Second Fire groups. Two of his other dies, by the same criteria and if they belong to the same potter, seem to have been in use at Lezoux in the early-Antonine period. c AD 100–20; 90/171, P 3.3

66 Ioenalis 2a 18/31 IOENAЛIS (Vanvinckenroye 1968, no 28) Les Martres-de-Veyre (b). The forms and fabrics associated with this stamp suggest Trajanic date and origin at Les Martres, though the potter is also known to have worked at Lezoux. c AD 100–20; 98/88, F852, P 3.2, KG 17

67 Iullinus ii 3a 37 IVLLINI[M], retr (Dickinson 1986, 190, 3.371) Lezoux (a). A stamp used on moulds with decoration typical of the mid- to late-Antonine period and on contemporary plain forms, such as 31R and 79. Two examples are noted on form 38 in

the late second-century samian found off Pudding Pan Rock, Kent. *c* AD 160–90; 98/20, P 3.4A, KG 25

68 Lalianus 1a 31R LΛ⊦IΛ[NIΛ] Lezoux (b). The form of this dish is sufficient to indicate mid- to late-Antonine date, in the absence of other evidence. *c* AD 160–90; 90/105, F602, P 3.1, KG 16

69 Lentiscus 2a 18/31R LEΛ[TI*SCVS*] (Terrisse 1968, pl LIII) Les Martres-de-Veyre (a). There are three examples of this in the London Second Fire groups and it was used on the Trajanic type of form 33. *c* AD 100–20; 98/138, P 2.3

70 Licinus 7b 29 LICI[NIΛΛO] (Fiches *et al* 1978, no 61) La Graufesenque (a). The decoration of the bowls with this stamp is typical of the period *c* AD 40–60; 17/41, BP 3.1

71 Lupus ii 3a' 15/17 or 18 LVPIΛ (Dannell 1971, no 59) La Graufesenque (a). 3a has a frame with swallow-tail ends; the frame of 3a' has had the ends rounded off. Lupus ii's output seems to be entirely pre-Flavian and, although this particular version of the stamp occurs at the Nijmegen fortress, an even later version is known from Risstissen, a site which seems to have been evacuated in the early 70s. *c* AD 50–65; 46/+, C 4

72 Lupus ii 6a 18 LVPVS (Glasbergen 1955, nos 224–5) La Graufesenque (a). There is no site dating for this stamp, but it was used on the pre-Flavian cups, forms 24, Ritt 8 and Ritt 9. A graffito,]an[or]nu[is inscribed on the lower wall, after firing. *c* AD 45–65; 3/13, F2159, C 3.2, KG 22

73 Malledo 3a 33 [Μ]·Α⊦·⊦EDO Lezoux (a). Malledo's stamps turn up at forts in northern Britain which were recommissioned *c* AD 160. His output includes the later second century forms, 31R, 79, 80 and Ludowici Tx. *c* AD 160–90; 49/+, BP 4

74 Malluro i 3b 27 ΛLL[VRO·F] Lezoux (a). Much of this potter's output consists of forms not made much after *c* AD 150, but Oswald (1931, 181) notes form 79 from Cirencester and there are (unconfirmed) reports of single examples of forms 80 and Ludowici Tg. This presumably means that he was still at work in the 160s, though Die 3b, used mainly on forms 18/31 and 27 and occasionally on form 42, is unlikely to have survived so long. *c* AD 136–60; 60/7, BP 4

75 Mammius 8a 33 ΜΛΜΜI (Walke 1965, no 223) Lezoux (a). The stamp has been noted several times in Antonine Scotland (Camelon, Carzield and Newstead), but also in a group of burnt samian of *c* AD 170 at Tác (Hungary). *c* AD 150–80; 50/25, F2497, C 3.4

76 Manius? i la 38 or 44 MλNII? Lezoux (c). This stamp has been noted before by the present writer, in a group of late second century samian from London, when it was thought to be East Gaulish (Dickinson 1986, no 3.91). The Wroxeter piece, however, looks Central Gaulish, and is certainly late-Antonine; 23/+, BP 4

77 Mansuetus ii 4b 33 [ΜA·]SV·ETI (Hartley 1972a, S119) Lezoux (b). One of the earlier stamps of a potter whose output was mainly late-Antonine. Its date comes from its use on forms 18/31R and 27, which will not be later than *c* AD 165. Its site record includes Verulamium (Period IID, after AD 150) and Malton, where it will belong to the period of reoccupation *c* AD 160. *c* AD 150–70; 61/4, BP 3.3

78 Martius iv 1c 33 MARTIM Lezoux (b). This is the only example of this stamp known to the present writer. Martius iv's output includes forms 18/31R, 27, 80 and Ludowici Tx, giving him a range *c* AD 155–85. His wares have been noted from Brancaster, Malton and South Shields; unstratified

79 Modestus 9a' 27g OFMOI (from a die originally giving OFMOD) (Laubenheimer 1979, no 135) La Graufesenque (a). Both versions of the die were used in the pre-Flavian period, but the later one, 9a', must have continued in use into the 70s or even later, on the evidence of sites such as Ebchester and Broomholm. By this time the die must surely have passed from Modestus to another potter. *c* AD 60–75/80; 98/141, 1.3

80 Modestus i 9b 27g OFMOD (Ulbert 1969, no 44) La Graufesenque (a). There is no site dating for this stamp, but its use on form 24 and, probably, Ritt 9 confirms its pre-Flavian date. *c* AD 45–65; 3/20, C 2.1

81 Mommo 9c'' (almost certainly) ƆFΜOΛ (from a die originally giving OFMOM) La Graufesenque (a). Stamps from the original die occur on form 24, but also at Rottweil and the main site at Corbridge, the last certainly a survival. The two subsequent versions of the die are not precisely dated, but the final version probably falls within the range *c* AD 75–85; 98/194, 1.2

82 Mommo 9i 15/17 or 18 [OIᴵΜ]OΜ La Graufesenque (a). An earlier stamp than the last, noted on pre-Flavian forms (24 and Ritt 1) and in a group of burnt samian from a pottery shop at Oberwinterthur, Switzerland, destroyed by fire in the early 60s (Ebnöther forthcoming). *c* AD 60–80; 98/52, P 2.3

83 Montanus i 7c or c' 15/17 or 18 MOИT[ΛNI] or MOИT[ΛN] (Glasbergen 1955, no 277 or 278) La Graufesenque (a). The original die was used to stamp the pre-Flavian dish, form 16. The broken version was also used in the pre-Flavian period, on the evidence of a stamp from the Gloucester Kingsholm site, and it was still in use in the early 70s, with stamps occurring at Caerleon and Chester. *c* AD 55–75; 85/32, WR 2.3

84 Mox(s)ius ii 2a 18/31R MOXI[VS·F] Lezoux (a), Les Martres-de-Veyre (c). Moxius ii seems to have been one of the later group of potters working at Les Martres. This stamp turns up in the Wroxeter Gutter deposit, where it will be residual, and at Carzield. *c* AD 130–60; 47/17, C 3.1, KG 14

85 Murranus 10d' 27g OF/ИⱤR/ (from a die originally giving OF/ИⱤRΛ) La Graufesenque (a). Both versions of the die were used on the pre-Flavian cup, form Ritt 8. The broken version, as here, occurs in a group of samian from a pottery store at Oberwinterthur, Switzerland, destroyed by fire in the early 60s (Ebnöther, forthcoming). *c* AD 50–65; 98/49, F679, P 3.2, KG 17

86 C. N- Celsus 3a 27 [OF·C·]N·CE La Graufesenque (b). All the examples noted so far have been on form 27. Stamps from other dies of this potter come from Chesterholm, Wilderspool and Nijmegen (in a burial with an *as* of Nerva of AD 97). *c* AD 80–110; 98/133, P 3.3

87–8 Natonus la 27 (2) ИΛTO[И VSF], ИΛTO[И VSF] Les Martres-de-Veyre (c). All the examples of this stamp known to this writer are on form 27. The site record includes Corbridge and Maryport. Trajanic or early-Hadrianic; 90/+, P 4; 97/25, P 3.3

89 Nicephor ii 2a 33 NICEPHOR·F (*ORL* B16, 30, no 19) Lezoux (a). The use of this stamp on forms 18/31, 27 and 42 and its occurrence in the Rhineland suggest that the potter's career was mainly early-Antonine, but a single example on form 80 extends its life to AD 160 or later, and a stamped dish from Wallsend will belong to the period of reoccupation. *c* AD 140–65; 58/5, BP 3.2

90–2 Niger ii 3a 27?; 27g (2) OFNGRI;]GRI; OFNGRI (Hermet 1934, no 113) La Graufesenque (a). The die was reserved for cups, including the pre-Flavian forms 24 and Ritt 8 and 9. There is one example from Chester. *c* AD 55–70; 3/14, C 2.2; 14/32, F2246, 1.3; 85/105, WR 2.3

93 Osbimanus-Cadgatis la 31 OS·BIMCΛ[DG] Lezoux (c). This stamp presumably represents an association, though not necessarily a partnership, of two potters. Both men are known to have stamped separately in the Antonine period. The stamp occurs on form 18/31R, which is unlikely to be after *c* AD 160, and 79 and Ludowici Tx, which will be after that date. *c* AD 150–80; 58/4, BP 3.2

94 Pass(i)enus 5a 29 OFP(Λ𐤔𐤔)ENI (Durand-Lefebvre 1963, no 547) La Graufesenque (a). This stamp, used only on form 29, is one of Pass(i)enus's latest. All the bowls concerned are early-Flavian, and there are examples from Caerleon (2), Carlisle (2) and the main site at Corbridge. *c* AD70–80; 97/133, P 2.3

95 Paterclinus la 31 PΛT[ER(CLIN)IOF] Lezoux (a). Some of Paterclinus's stamps occur on Hadrian's Wall and at Pennine forts which were reoccupied *c* AD 160. This particular stamp, however, is from a noticeably early die, used on forms 18/31, 18/31R and 27, rather than on his later forms, such as 31R and 79/80. *c* AD 150–65; 54/22, F3127, BP 3.3

96 Paterclinus lb 33 PΛTERCLINIOF (*ORL* B2a, 16, no 21) Lezoux (b). There is no internal dating for this stamp. For other evidence of Paterclinus's range, see the last. *c* AD 150–80; 72/+, C 4

97 Paterclus ii 10a, a' or a'' 18/31 [PΛ] TERC[LOSFE], or from the die in one of its altered forms, Les Martres-de-Veyre (a). The final version of this stamp occurs in the London Second Fire groups, at Chesterholm and at Nether Denton, thus indicating a life *c* AD 100–125 for the die as a whole; 69/13, BP 3.1, KG 18

98–9 Paterclus ii 12a 18/31 (2) [PATER]CLVSF; PATE[(Terrisse 1968, pl LIII). The potter is known to have worked at both Les Martres-de-Veyre and Lezoux; this is from a die attested at Les Martres, but there is no suggestion that it was ever used at Lezoux. It was broken at some stage and both complete and broken versions of the stamp occur in the London Second Fire groups. *c* AD 110–25; 87/4, WR 4; 85/127, WR 2.1

100 Paternus ii 2a 18/31 PATERNVSF (Durand-Lefebvre 1963, no 563) Lezoux (a). The fabrics and glazes associated with this stamp suggest that the die was used at both Les Martres-de-Veyre (in the Trajanic period) and Lezoux; this piece seems to have been made at Lezoux and the fabric belongs to the Hadrianic range. *c* AD 125–40; 98/101, F855, P 3.1, KG 16

101–2 Paternus v 7a 37 (2) PΛ[TERNFE], retr PΛTER[retr (Stanfield and Simpson 1958, pl 169) Lezoux (a). This common label stamp is very familiar in Hadrian's Wall assemblages, but is completely absent from Scottish sites with normal Antonine occupations. *c* AD

160–95; 80/50, P 3.4B, KG 25; 98/60, F766, P 3.1, KG 16

103   Patricius i 3h 15/17 or 18 [OFP]ARIC(I) (Laubenheimer 1979, no 170) La Graufesenque (a). The earliest example of this stamp noted by this writer is from the Burghöfe Geschirrdepot of AD 69. The latest ones come from Camelon and Oakwood. *c* AD 65–95; 84/100, WR 2.2

104–5   Patricius i 4c 15/17 or 18 (2) [OF]PARIC,]ARIC (Laubenheimer 1979, no 171) La Graufesenque (b). Most of this potter's output is Flavian, and there is no evidence that this stamp was in use before *c* AD 70. It has been noted once on an early-Flavian bowl of form 29. *c* AD 70–90; 92/18, C 2.1; 98/100, F933, P 3.1, KG 16

106   Patricius i 13j 24? [PATR]ICI La Graufesenque (b). If the form is correctly identified, this must be from one of Patricius's earlier dies, which would have first been used in the pre-Flavian period. *c* AD 65–75; 84/137, WR 2.1

107   Patricius ii 9a 33 PATRI[CIVSF] (Hartley 1972a, S147) Lezoux (b). A stamp recorded from Scottish forts and in the Antonine fire deposit at Verulamium (after AD 150). The potter's wares are not common on Hadrian's Wall or in the Pennines and this particular stamp does nor occur there at all. *c* AD 140–70; 59/1, BP 3.2

108   Potitianus ii 1b 79? POT[ITIΛΙ·M] (Tilhard 1976, E4) Lezoux (a).The use of this stamp on forms 31R and 79R is clear evidence of mid-to late-Antonine date. A stamp from another die at Chesters will belong to the period of its reoccupation. *c* AD 160–90; 58/+, BP 4

109   Primus iii 12r 15/17 or 18 [OFPR]IΛΙ (Nieto *et al* 1989, no 39.1) La Graufesenque (a). The lettering of this stamp leaves no doubt that it comes from a die of Primus iii, in spite of the vertical stroke in the first part of the M, which could be taken to represent ΛM ligatured. The site record includes Colchester (unburnt, but with burnt material from the Boudiccan destruction), Verulamium (Period II, in a pit filled by *c* AD 75), Caerleon and a wreck of *c* AD 75 or slightly later, recovered off Cala Culip, southern Spain. *c* AD 60– 75/80; 16/153, BP 2.3

110   Primus iii 12v 18 OFPRIM(I) La Graufesenque (a). The style of the letters on this stamp suggests Neronian date, though one example comes from the Nijmegen fortress. It also occurs in one of the Colchester pottery shops destroyed in AD 60/61. *c* AD 50–65; 98/83, P 2.3

111   Primus iii 18b 18 OFPRIM (Hartley 1972a, S4) La Graufesenque (a). Footring slightly worn. This stamp is known both from Period I at Verulamium and from the two pottery shops at Colchester destroyed in AD 60/61. It was used on the pre-Flavian cups, forms 24 and Ritt 8. *c* AD 55–65; 63/15, F2287, 1.3

112   Quintilianus i 4a' 33 V■NTIL■A (from a die originally giving QVINTILIΛNI Lezoux (b). Quintilianus's record in general, and his decorated ware in particular, suggest Hadrianic-Antonine date. A complete version of this stamp is known from Camelon. *c* AD 140–50; 3/5, C 3.2

113   Quintus iv 2a 33 [QVI]NTI Lezoux (a). A stamp of the earlier Lezoux Quintus, used mostly on forms 27 and 33. Examples have been noted from Corbridge (2) and Newstead (Curle 1911, 239, no 77). One of his other stamps, probably slightly later than this, occurs in Antonine fire deposits at Worcester. *c* AD 140–60; 98/77, P 3.3

114   Reginus ii 2a 18/31 [REGIN]VS·F (Fabricus 1894 et seq, 8, Taf 12, 51. B16) Les Martres-de-Veyre (a). Reginus ii began work under Trajan and seems to have continued into the early-Antonine period. This particular stamp occurs in the London Second Fire groups, on Hadrian's Wall (Chesters Museum) and at Corbridge and Malton. A stamp from another die is known from Antonine Scotland. *c* AD 115–35; unstratified

115   Roppus ii 1a 18/31 ROP[PVSFE] (Hartley 1970, 24, no 56) Les Martres-de-Veyre (b). The stamp occurs on forms 18/31, 18/31R, 27 and 33. It also appears occasionally on form 15/17, which was rarely, if ever, made at Les Martres after the Trajanic period. Two stamps from another die are in the samian from a pottery shop at Castleford destroyed by fire in the 140s, but they are unburnt and almost certainly residual. A range *c* AD 105–30 is likely for the potter; unstratified

116   Roppus ii 2a 15/17R or 18/31R ROP·VSιFE Les Martres-de-Veyre (a). This stamp occurs on form 15/17, which at Les Martres was normally Trajanic, and also on forms 18/31, 18/31R and 27. Another stamp of Roppus ii is known from the Saalburg Erdkastell (before *c* AD 139). *c* AD 105–30; 98/101, F855, P 3.1, KG 16

117   Roppus ii-Rut(us?) 1a, a' or a'' 18/31 ROPPI·RV[T·M], ROPPI·RV■ or ROPPI·RV (Dickinson 1984, S44) Les Martres-de-Veyre (a). This stamp presumably represents the names of two potters, one of whom is almost certainly the Roppus discussed above. The only dating is for the complete die, with

stamps on three vessels from the London Second Fire deposits. As far as can be seen, there is no difference in date between stamps of Roppus and Roppus-Rut-. *c* AD 105–30; 83/+, WR 4

118 Ruttus la' 33 <RV>T+OFFIC (Curle 1911, no 101) Lezoux (a). The distribution of stamps from both versions of the die seems to have been confined to Britain. Most of the vessels are dishes of form 18/31R and cups of form 33, though form 18/31 has been recorded once. Stamps from the broken die occur at Benwell and Newstead. *c* AD 140–65; 73/+, C 4

119 Sabinianus iii la 31R SABINIA[NI] Lezoux (c). There is no site dating for this, or any other of Sabinianus's stamps, but its use on forms 31R and 79 suggests a mid- to late-Antonine range. *c* AD 160–90; 80/3, P 3.5, KG 25

120 Sacer i 1a 37 (below the decoration) [OFI]S ACRI (Stanfield and Simpson 1958, pl 169) Lezoux (a). Bowls with this stamp are known from Corbridge, Maryport and Piercebridge. Sacer i's decorated ware is commoner on Hadrian's Wall than in Antonine Scotland. *c* AD 125–45; 90/48, P 3.4A, KG 25

121–2 Sacer i 4a 27 (2) SACRI·OF·,]RI·OF Lezoux (a). This stamp is particularly common on form 27 and occurs in the Rhineland, where imports of Lezoux samian had virtually ceased by AD 150. *c* AD 125–45; 90/163, F631, P 3.2, KG 17; 90/169, P 2.2

123 Sacer-Vasil- la' 18/31 [SAC]ER·\ASILF (Terrisse 1968, pl LIV, col 1, sixth from bottom) Les Martres-de-Veyre (a). The die for this stamp was made, by *surmoulage*, from an impression on a pot and is therefore somewhat shorter than the original die. There is not necessarily any chronological difference between the two dies, however. Two stamps from the longer die occur in the London Second Fire deposits. *c* AD 100–120; 98/77, P 3.3

124 Saciro i 2a dish, slightly burnt, S$\wedge$CIROF Espalion (c). A large dish, with base and footring like 15/17R and 18R, but without rouletting. There is a central ring on the base, perhaps round a stamp, and a wide ring above the footring, across which the stamp is placed, at about 45 degrees to it. Stamps of Primulus and Primus are similarly placed on dishes from Espalion, which are thought to have originated there, rather than at La Graufesenque (M Tilhard 1976). Saciro used a different die to stamp form 29. Neronian-Flavian?; 91/72, WR 2.3, 91/85, 1.3

125 Sacrillus 3a flat base [SACRI]$\hbar\hbar$·I·[M] (Dickinson 1986, 3.180) Lezoux (a). One of the stamps which occurs in the group of late-Antonine samian recovered off Pudding Pan Rock. It is also known from Carrawburgh and was used to stamp the rim of a bowl from a stamped mould of Do(v)eccus, whose wares are some of the latest to be exported to Britain from Lezoux. *c* AD 160–200; 97/55, P 2.3

126 G. Salarius Aptus la 29 OF·G·SAL·AP+ (Hermet 1934, no 148) La Graufesenque (a). Footring scarcely worn. The die was used exclusively on bowls of form 29, one of which, at La Graufesenque, is from the same mould as a bowl stamped by the Claudio-Neronian potter, Lucceius i. *c* AD 50–65; unstratified

127 Sanciro la 33 S\/CIRO Lezoux (a). The reading of this stamp is not entirely certain. Sanciro, Sauciro, Suauciro or Saciro are all possible, since both the diagonal strokes flanking the A are less prominent than the letters and could have come from scratches on the die. However, we have settled for Sanciro, as the second diagonal is reasonably bold. The stamp was used on forms 79 and 80 and is known from Chesters and South Shields, where it will have been in use after *c* AD 160. No other dating evidence has come to light for the potter, and only one die is known for him. *c* AD 150–80; 80/147, F564, P 3.1, KG 16

128 Secundinus i la 18/31R [SECVNDI]NIΛ La Graufesenque (a). This occurs in a predominantly Flavian-Trajanic group at La Graufesenque (Vernhet 1981, 34, no 19). Other examples come from Dambach, Ober Florstadt and Saalburg (3). Graffito X inscribed under the base, after firing. *c* AD 85–110; 84/49, WR 3.1

129 Secundus ii 11b 27 OFSEC[V] La Graufesenque (a). Most of Secundus ii's output is early-Flavian. Some of his dies, though not this one, were used to stamp pre-Flavian cups, such as forms 24 and Ritt 8. *c* AD 70–90; 86/21, WR 4

130 Sedatus iv 2b 27 [SIID]ATIΛ Lezoux (a). This stamp reached sites in the Rhineland, presumably before AD 150, by which time imports from Lezoux had virtually ceased. It was used mainly on forms 18/31 and 27. *c* AD 130–50; 58/5, BP 3.2

131 Sedatus iv 2c 33 [S$\exists$D]ATI·[M] (Walke 1965, no 341) Lezoux (a). For dating evidence, see the last. *c* AD 130–50; 90/+, P 4

132 Senicio 6a' 29 <S>ENIC(I)<O> (Nieto *et al* 1989, no 15.1) La Graufesenque (a). The original version of this stamp occurs in the Cirencester Fort Ditch group of *c* AD 55–65 and on forms 24 and Ritt 9. Stamps from 6a', the broken die, while noted once on forms 24 and, probably, Ritt 8, are much commoner on form 27. Examples are recorded from a

wreck of the early 70s off Cala Culip (Spain). *c* AD 65–80; 98/178, 1.3

133 Severus iii 9d 27 OFSEVER Lezoux (a). One cup of form Ritt 8 was probably stamped with this die, which would make it one of the potter's earlier ones. The stamps are mainly Flavian, however, with examples from the Nijmegen fortress, Rottweil and, probably, Saalburg. *c* AD 65–95; 98/146, F1012, P 3.1, KG 16

134 Sextus v 2c 31R SEXTI·[MN] Lezoux (b). Stamps of the later Lezoux Sextus occur on Hadrian's Wall and in the group of late-Antonine samian recovered off Pudding Pan Rock. This particular stamp is known from Benwell. *c* AD 160–200. 80/2, P 4

135 Silvanus ii 4a 27 ƆIᛗVᗡNVS retr Les Martres-de-Veyre (c). Silvanus ii seems to have migrated from Les Martres to Lezoux, but this die apparently did not travel with him. Much of his output consists of forms 18/31 and 27, which will largely belong to the second quarter of the second century. His latest stamps are on form 80 (after *c* AD 160) and on a cup in Period IID at Verulamium (after AD 150). His main period of activity will have been AD 130–50, but this stamp might be Trajanic and will certainly not be later than the Hadrianic period; 69/35, B 3.1, KG 18

136 Silvius ii 1a (probably) 18/31 SILVI·OF Lezoux (a). This stamp was confined to forms 18/31, 18/31R and 27, giving it a Hadrianic or early-Antonine range. His dishes stamped with other dies tend also to be 18/31, rather than 31. *c* AD 125–45; 90/71, P 3.3; 90/66, P 3.3

137 Silvius ii 1c 27 SIL(VI·O)F Lezoux (a). All the known examples of this stamp are on form 27. Some of them come from the Rhineland, and should therefore be before *c* AD 150, since Lezoux was had almost certainly ceased to be imported into the area by then. *c* AD 125–45; 90/+, P 4

138–9 Suobnus 5a 18/31, 33 SVOB[NI·ᐱ],]OBNI·ᐱ (Terrisse 1968, pl LIV) Les Martres-de- Veyre (a). Suobnus belongs to the later group of potters at Les Martres. His stamps are common in Antonine Scotland, and this one is known from Mumrills. *c* AD 130–55; 47/15, C 3.1, KG 14; 98/77, P 3.3

140 Surdillus 5a 18/31(R?) [SVRD]ILLVSF Les Martres-de-Veyre (b). The only dating for this particular vessel comes from its fabric and glaze, which both belong to the Trajanic range at Les Martres. By the same criteria, the die was also used later at Lezoux. *c* AD 100–20; 2/5, C 3.3

141 Tiberius ii la' 27 TIBERI·M Lezoux (a). The die from which this comes originally had ansate ends, and was used on forms 27 and 42. The broken die was mainly used on form 27 and possibly on form 80, though we have not been able to verify this. If the form was identified correctly, this would extend his career at least to AD 155, and probably to 160. *c* AD 140–60; B/6, C 4

142 Tintirio 1a 31 TINT[IRIOᛗ] Lezoux (a). Tintirio was at work in the early- to mid-Antonine period and stamped forms 18/31, 18/31R, 27, 31R and 80. This stamp is likely to be from one of his later dies, since it was used on form 80. *c* AD 155–75; 90/105, F602, P 3.1, KG 16

143–6 Tituro la 31 (2), 38, 80]VRONISƆᴲ, TITVRONI(SƆᴲ),]ITVRONIS[, TITVRO-NISƆᴲ (Dickinson 1986, 3.209) Lezoux (a). A common stamp at forts on Hadrian's Wall and in the Pennines. There are also five examples from the Wroxeter Gutter hoard. *c* AD 160–90; 80/7, P 3.4B, KG 25; E/3, B 4; 49/32, BP 3.1, KG 18; 53/4, C 2.2

147 Q.V-C- le 33 [Q.]VC Montans (b). This stamp is in a group of burnt samian from St Catherine Coleman, London, which is almost certainly from a Second Fire deposit. It occurs also under the original floor of the Wroxeter forum, where it must have been deposited before the end of AD 130. *c* AD 115–30; 22/54, BP 3.1

148 Vanderio 1a 29 Vᴺ[DERIo] (Knorr 1919, Taf 80A) La Graufesenque (a). A stamp used in the Neronian-Flavian period, mainly on bowls of form 29. It occurs in a group of samian of the 70s at Nijmegen, probably from a pottery shop (Morren 1966, 229, 7, 8). There is also an example on form 18 from Binchester. *c* AD 65–80; 88/6, WR 4

149 Vespo 2b 33 VES[POF] Lezoux (b). The stamp was used on forms 27 and 42 and so will have been current in the Hadrianic-Antonine period. His range of forms in general contains nothing which need necessarily have been made after AD 150. Stamps from other dies occur at Camelon and Newstead and in a group of burnt samian of *c* AD 140–50 from Castleford (forthcoming). *c* AD 130–60; 90/128, P 3.1, KG 16

150 Vitalis i lc 18 OFVIᴀIS La Graufesenque (a). This stamp of the earlier South Gaulish Vitalis occurs in a burial at Mainz with other stamped samian belonging to the period *c* AD 50–65 (Mainzer Zeitschrift 73/74 (1979), 252, no 19); unstratified

151 Vitalis ii 4b or b' 29 [OF]VIT[ALIS] or [OF]VIT[AL] La Graufesenque (a). Graffito IV [?] inscribed under the base, after firing. Both the original die and the broken version were used mainly on early-Flavian form 29s.

Stamps from the broken die, which are much commoner, occur at Caerleon, Rottweil and the Nijmegen fortress. *c* AD 70–85; 92/20, F154, C 2.1

152 Vitalis ii 8h'' 33 (burnt) OF.VITA La Graufesenque (a). This is from the final version of a die which was modified when it was damaged. The original die was in use before AD 75, on the evidence of a stamp from Risstissen. Stamps from the earlier modification come from Ribchester and the Domitianic fort at Butzbach. There is no internal dating yet for the latest die, but it will almost certainly fall within the period *c* AD 80–95; 84/158, WR 2.3

153 Vitalis iii 7a 27 VITAⱢIS Les Martres-de-Veyre (b). No other stamps have been noted from this die, but the general appearance of the vessel suggests that it is by a Les Martres potter whose wares occur in the London Second Fire groups and who occasionally stamped form 15/17, which was rarely made at Les Martres after the Trajanic period. *c* AD 100–20; 90/161, P 3.3

154 Vogenus 2a 33 VOGENE Lezoux (c). A stamp used on forms 33 and 27. It occurs in the Rhineland, suggesting currency before the middle of the second century. *c* AD 125–50; 86/3, WR 4

Unidentified

155 O[or]O on form 15/17 or 18, South Gaulish. Neronian; 83/+, WR 4

156]/CI? on form 24, South Gaulish. Neronian; 9/17, 2.2

157 MVR ... ?? on form 27, burnt, South Gaulish. Neronian; 51/21, F2990, 1.3

158 ..V..M? on form 29, South Gaulish. Neronian; 83/530, WR 2.3

159 Illegible stamp on form 27g, South Gaulish. Neronian; 98/84. P 2.1

160]ⱮIO on form 24, South Gaulish. Neronian; 63/+, C 4

161 IICⱯ or IICV retrograde on form 24, marbled, South Gaulish. Neronian; 91/93, WR 2.3

162 GERM[?? on form 15/17 or 18, South Gaulish. Neronian or early-Flavian; 29/17, C 2.1

163 Ɱ:IꞀXI on form 15/17 or 18, South Gaulish. One of the commoner illiterate stamps, already known from Wroxeter (Rowley's House Museum E1285). Examples are noted from Flavian foundations, such as Carlisle and Castleford, but the die may have been made slightly earlier. This is Neronian or early-Flavian, to judge by the fabric and glaze; 91/93, WR 2.3

164]OƧ? on form 15/17 or 18, South Gaulish. Neronian or early-Flavian; 98/33, P 3.3

165 D[on form 15/17R or 18R, South Gaulish. Neronian or early-Flavian; 97/132, F747, P 2.3

166 ⱯVⱮ on form 27g, South Gaulish. Neronian or early-Flavian; 93/2, WR 2.3

167 VIⱯC on form 27g, South Gaulish. Neronian or early Flavian; 92/20, F154, C 2.1

168 OFI/I on form 27g, South Gaulish. Neronian or early Flavian; 92/20, F154, C 2.1

169 ..NIAS·I ... (?) on form 27g, South Gaulish. Neronian or early-Flavian; 98/52, P 2.3

170 C[on form 27g, South Gaulish. Neronian or early-Flavian; 98/61, P 2.3

171 OF.VII or OⱢⱯTI retr, on form 27, South Gaulish. Neronian or early-Flavian; 92/+, C 4

172]XI on form 27, South Gaulish. Neronian or early-Flavian; 92/4, C 2.4

173 Illegible, on form 27g, South Gaulish. Neronian or early-Flavian; 98/52, P 2.3

174 [O]IIIⱮXI on a cup, South Gaulish. An illiterate stamp, previously noted at the Gloucester Kingsholm site and on forms 27 and Ritt 8. Pre-Flavian; 85/61, WR 1.3

175 ..EN.C.. on form 29, South Gaulish. Pre-Flavian; 98/178, P 1.3

176 OF..[? on form 15/17 or 18, South Gaulish. Probably pre-Flavian; 84/182, F339, WR 2.1, KG 25

177 IV or Ⱨ[on form 27, South Gaulish. Early-Flavian; 98/4, P 3.4A, KG 25

178 Vⱨ[or]VⱨI on form 15/17 or 18, South Gaulish. Flavian; 98/33, P 3.3

179 OXI .... X[on form 27g, South Gaulish. Flavian; 85/227, WR 2.1

180 IⱮIII[on form 27g, South Gaulish. Flavian; 88/3, WR 4

181 NII on form 27g, South Gaulish. Flavian; 93/2, WR 2.3

182 OF·[on form 27, South Gaulish. Flavian; 90/101, F599, P 3.2, KG 17

183 OFF[(?) on form 18, South Gaulish. Flavian or Flavian-Trajanic; 86/3, WR 4

184 ..IⱮ... on form 27, slightly burnt, South Gaulish. Flavian or Flavian-Trajanic; 51/21, F2990, 1.3

185]OD? on form 27, South Gaulish. Flavian or Flavian-Trajanic; 85/224, WR 2.3

186 I\[or]\I on form 27 South Gaulish. Flavian or Flavian-Trajanic; 22/46, BP 2.2

187]ASC? on form 27, South Gaulish. Perhaps a stamp of L.Tr–Masculus, for whom the date would fit. Flavian-Trajanic; 83/530, WR 2.3

188]HIVI on form 27, South Gaulish. Flavian-Trajanic; 86/21, WR 4

189 C[, O[or]O on form 15/17 or 18, South Gaulish. First-century; 88/7, WR 4

190 R[? on form 18/31, from Les Martres-de-Veyre. Trajanic; 90/164, F631, P 3.2, KG 17

191]Ƨ ? on form 27, from Les Martres-de-Veyre. Trajanic; 49/119, BP 3.1, KG 18

192 C[on form 18/31 or 31, Central Gaulish. Hadrianic or early-Antonine; 58/4, BP 3.2

193]\F on form 18/31, Central Gaulish. Hadrianic or early-Antonine; 92/4, C 2.4

194]S·[? on form 18/31, Central Gaulish. Hadrianic or early-Antonine; 98/100, F855, P 3.1, KG 16

195]IM on form 18/31R, Central Gaulish. Hadrianic or early-Antonine; 91/46. WR 2.3

196]NIΛ on form 18/31R?, Central Gaulish. Hadrianic or early-Antonine; 84/49, WR 3.1

197 V[or]Λ on form 27, Central Gaulish. Hadrianic or early-Antonine; 59/13, BP 3.2

198 ΛΛ[on form 27, Central Gaulish. Hadrianic or early-Antonine; unstratified

199 SE[on a flat base, Central Gaulish. Hadrianic or Antonine; 65/30 BP 3.1, KG 18

200]·M on form 18/31R or 31R, Central Gaulish. Antonine; 80/87, F462, P 3.2, KG 17

201]VLLII[on form 33, Central Gaulish. Antonine; 80/+, P 4

202]MA on form 18/31R or 31R, Central Gaulish. Antonine; 80/+, P 4

203]N..[on form 31, Central Gaulish. Antonine; 86/3, WR 4

204]ΛVI[on form 31, Central Gaulish. Antonine; 86/21, WR 4

205]/TIΛ[on form 31, Central Gaulish. Antonine; 22/2, BP 4

206]IΛ on form 33, Central Gaulish. Antonine; unstratified

207 ΛV/[on form 33, Central Gaulish. Antonine; 59/1, BP 3.2

208]FE on form 33, Central Gaulish. Antonine; 59/13, BP 3.2

209]M on form 33, Central Gaulish. Antonine; 72/+, C 4

210]IO·[? on form 33, Central Gaulish. Antonine; 80/58, P 3.3

211]ISF on form 38 or 44, Central Gaulish. Antonine; 60/11, BP 3.2

212 ΛΛ[on form 38 or 44, Central Gaulish. Antonine; 98/20, P 3.4A, KG 25

213 D[on form 31, Central Gaulish. Mid- to late-Antonine; 90/88, F597, P 3.1, KG 16

214]M on form 31R, Central Gaulish. Mid- to late-Antonine; 80/55, P 3.3

215]IΛ on form 31R, Central Gaulish. Mid- to late-Antonine; 98+, P 4

216]VILVI? on form 31R, Central Gaulish. Mid- to late-Antonine; 90/102, F602, P 3.1, KG 16

217 Rosette with eight(?) petals, on form Curle 15 or 23, Central Gaulish. Antonine; 80/7, P 3.4B, KG 25

Cursive signatures

218 CI[retr on form 37, from a mould signed below the decoration, before firing: Cerialis ii of Lezoux. The decorated ware of this potter and his associates is very common in Antonine Scotland, but comparatively rare on Hadrian's Wall and at its associated forts (Hartley 1972b, 33). *c* AD 135–70; 90/90, F602, P 3.1, KG 16

219 GII/[retr on form 37, inscribed upside-down below the decoration before firing: Geminus iv of Central Gaul. There is no site dating for the signed decorated ware of this potter, but his stylistic connections with Arcanus, for whom there is better evidence, suggest a range *c* AD 125–45; 80/66, P 3.3

220 S ... N ... retr on form 37, from a mould signed upside-down below the decoration, before firing. Almost certainly a signature of a Secundinus of Lezoux. This man's signature occurs on a stamped mould of the Hadrianic-Antonine potter, Rentus (pers comm G Rogers). Another of this Secundinus's bowls is known from Newstead. His range will be *c* AD 125–50, therefore; 86/+, WR 4

221]S retr on form 37, below the decoration, from a mould signed before firing: Sissus ii of Lezoux, who is known only for decorated ware. There is no site dating for it, but stylistically it falls within the range *c* AD 130–60; 16/31, F3177, BP 3.1, KG 19

Stamped mortaria
by Kay Hartley

All stamps are on different vessels except where stated otherwise

Legible names (Fig 4.99)

1 AXCH retr, Wroxeter, AD 100–150, now missing; 59/13, BP 3.2

2 AXCH retr, Wroxeter, AD 100–150; 83/+, WR 4

3 BIIL[...], probably for Bellus, Wroxeter, AD 100–150; 44/25, F3142, C 3.4

4 [...]ILVS retr Wroxeter, probably AD 100–150, probably Bellus; 47/17, C 3.1, KG 14

5 BVTRIO, two stamps from the same vessel, Mancetter-Hartshill, AD 135–65; 63/+, C 4

6 CASSARIVS, Northern France (MONG), complete vessel now missing, AD 65–100; 51/21, F2990, 1.3

7 DC.VER, Wroxeter, AD 100–150; 78/1, C 4

8 Decanivs or illiterate, Wroxeter, AD 100–150; 12/1, C 3.2

9 DECANIVS, Wroxeter, AD 100–150; 44/25, F3142, C 3.4

10 DECANIVS, Wroxeter, AD 100–150; 50/70, C 4

11   DECANIVS, Wroxeter, AD 100–150; 53/+, C 4

12   DECANIVS, Wroxeter, AD 100–150; 67/14, C 4

13   Decanivs, or illiterate, Wroxeter, AD 100–150; 83/+, WR 4

14   DECANIVS, Wroxeter, AD 100–150; 84/+, WR 4

15   DECANIVS, Wroxeter, AD 100–150; 88/3, WR 4

16   DECANIUS, Wroxeter, AD 100–150; 98/52, P 2.3

17   Decanius or illiterate, Wroxeter, AD 100–150; 86/+, WR 4

18   Possibly Decanius, Wroxeter, AD 100–150; 83/+, WR 4

      For the potter Decanius *cf* Manning 1993, 420, no 2, and James (forthcoming).

19   DOCCAS, Mancetter-Hartshill, AD 90–120. Doccas is believed to have worked in the Mancetter-Hartshill potteries for part of his life but this and no 20 could have been made at Wroxeter; type M2.41; 83/534, WR 2.3

20   DOCCAS, Mancetter-Hartshill or Wroxeter, AD 90–120; 98/101, F855, P 3.1, KG 16

21   DOCI[..], Wroxeter, AD 100–150; 8+/, C 4

22   DOCI[..], Wroxeter, AD 100–150; 48/65, BP 3.1

23   DOCI[..], Wroxeter, AD 100–150; 49/122, BP 3.1, KG 18

24   DOCI[..], Wroxeter, AD 100–150; 52/22, M (intrusive)

25   DOCI[..], Wroxeter, AD 100–150; 78/1, C 4

26   DOCI[..], Wroxeter, AD 100–150; 83/+, WR 4

27   DOCI[..], Wroxeter, AD 100–150; 85/49, F75, WR 2.1

28   DOCI[..], Wroxeter, AD 100–150; 86/+, WR 4

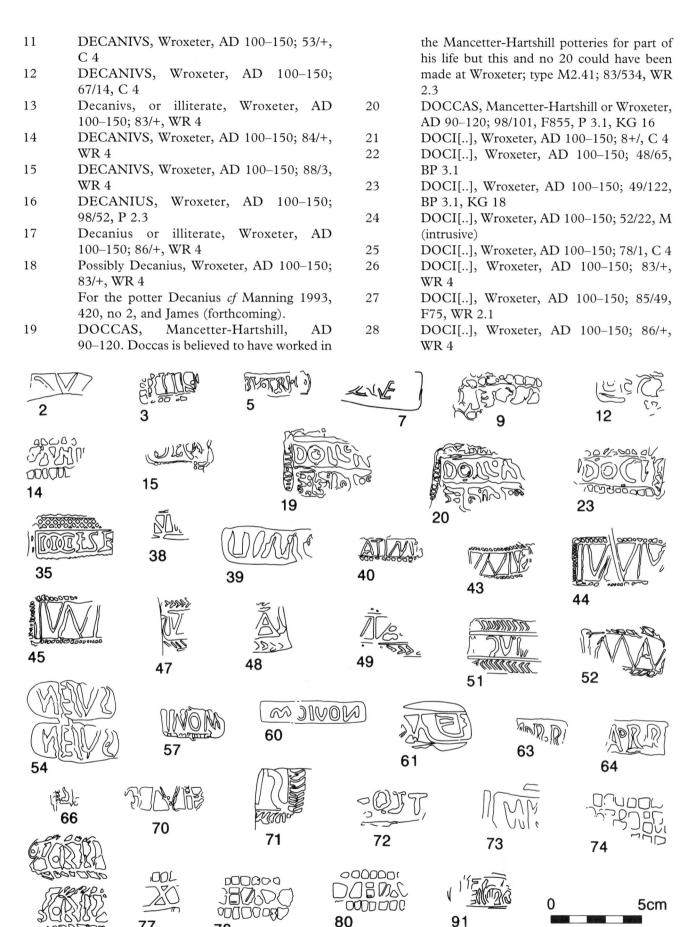

Fig 4.99 Pottery: mortaria stamps; scale 1:2

29   DOCI[..], Wroxeter, now missing, AD 100–150; 86/16, WR 3.1

30   DOCI[..], Wroxeter, AD 100–150; 86/16, WR 3.1

31   DOCI[..], Wroxeter, AD 100–150; 98/138, P 2.3

32   Probably Docilis, Wroxeter, AD 90–130; 83/+, WR 4

33   DOCILIS, Wroxeter, AD 90–130; 98/95, F890, P 3.1, KG 16

34   DOCILIS, Wroxeter, AD 90–130; 84/49, WR 3.1

35   DOCILIS, Wroxeter, AD 90–130; 90/204, F951, P 2.2

36   DOCILIS, Wroxeter, AD 90–130; 90/204, F951, P 2.2

37   Probably DOCILIS, Wroxeter, AD 90–130; 84/52, WR 2.3

Doci (…), Docilis etc

Doci (…): The name of this potter may be Docilis though it is not certain (he is erroneously referred to as Docilis 2 in some reports eg J Britnell 1989, 123, 466). There is an outside possibility that he was the same man who stamped DOCILIS, but the stamps, the style, the forms, and the gritting are so different that it cannot be assumed. The question is further complicated by there being a potter working in the north at Wilderspool and then Carlisle who stamped DOCI and DOCCIE etc, whose name was Docelis or Docilis (Hartley 1991, 365). The Wilderspool/Carlisle potter has something in common with the Wroxeter potter who stamped DOCI but there is no die link to prove it; he has nothing in common with the Wroxeter potter who stamped DOCILIS. It is, therefore, best to treat these three as different potters until there is good reason to suggest otherwise.

38   DOINVS, Verulamium region, probably Brockley Hill (Castle 1972, fig 5, A), AD 70–110; 83/+, WR 4

39   [Gio]MILI retr, for Giomilis or the genitive of Giomilus, Wroxeter, AD 90–120, fabric unusually fine; the only two known stamps are from Wroxeter; 78/1, C 4

40   GRATINVS, Mancetter-Hartshill, AD 130–50+; 63/+, C 4

41   IVNIVS, Mancetter-Hartshill, AD 150–75; 47/15, C 3.1, KG 14

42   IVNIVS, Mancetter-Hartshill, AD 150–75; 47/17, C 3.1, KG 14

43   IVNIVS, Mancetter-Hartshill, AD 150–75; 47/17, C 3.1, KG 14

44   IVNIVS, Mancetter-Hartshill, AD 100–175, possibly from same vessel as no 46; 62/1, BP 4

45   IVNIVS, two fragments from one vessel, same die as nos 44 and 46, Mancetter-Hartshill, AD 150–75; 63/4, C 3.1, KG 14

46   IVNIVS, *cf* nos 44 and 45, Mancetter-Hartshill, AD 150–75; 63/4, C 3.1, KG 14

47   LALLAIVS retr, Verulamium region, AD 80–125; 90/138, F708, P 3.1, KG 16

48   LALLAIVS retr, Verulamium region, AD 80–125; 90/164, F631, P 3.2, KG 17

49   LALLAIVS retr, Verulamium region, AD 80–125; 98/138, F708, P 3.1, KG 16

50   MATVGENVS retr, Brockley Hill, AD 80–125; 83/536, WR 2.1

51   MATVGENVS retr, Brockley Hill, AD 80–125, almost a complete vessel; 84/45, WR 4; 84/46, WR 3.1, KG 21; 84/49, WR 3.1
      For discussion of Matugenus *cf* Verulamium, Frere 1984a, 286, nos 83–7.

52   MAVR[us], Mancetter-Hartshill, AD 150–75; 59/2, BP 3.2

53   MAVR[us], Mancetter-Hartshill, AD 150–75; 47/15, C 3.1, KG 14 (now missing)

54   MELVS 2, Wroxeter, AD 100–150; 47/17, C 3.1, KG 14

55   MELVS 2, Wroxeter, AD 100–150; 24/10, BP 3.2

56   MELVS 2, Wroxeter, AD 100–150; 98/139, F974, P 3.1, KG 16

57   MINOMELVS, Mancetter-Hartshill, AD 130–60; 47/17, C3.1, KG14

58   MINOMELVS, same die as no 57, Mancetter-Hartshill, AD 130–60; 50/25, F2497, C 3.4

59   MINOMELVS, Mancetter-Hartshill, AD 130–60; 83/+, WR 4

60   NOVIOM[A?..] retr, possibly to be interpreted as Noviomagus, Verulamium region, Flavian; 84/249, M

61   Q.D.VALENS, possible but exact reading uncertain, Wroxeter, AD 90–130; 92/4, C 2.4

62   RAMSER, Wroxeter, AD 90–130; 90/204, F951, P 2.2

63   SARRIVS, Mancetter-Hartshill, AD 140–70; 50/70, C 4

64   SARRIVS, Mancetter-Hartshill, AD 140–70; 90/90, 90/100, 90/105, F602, P 3.1, KG 16

65   SENNIVS, Mancetter-Hartshill, AD 150–75; 2/24, C 3.3, KG 23

66   SENNIVS, Mancetter-Hartshill, AD 150–75; 83/+ WR 4

67   SIMILIS 1, retro. Mancetter-Hartshill, AD 130–50+; 83/+, WR 4

68   VITALIS 3, Wroxeter, AD 90–140; 92/4, C 2.4

69   ?Vitalis 3, Wroxeter, AD 90–130; 90/163, F631, P 3.2, KG 17

Incomplete stamps, reading uncertain

70   [...]DINI or [...]OINI, Mancetter-Hartshill, AD 120–60; 90/128, F736, P 3.1, KG 16

71   [...]IS retro? Verulamium region, AD 80–125?; 90/204, F951, P 2.2

Illegible or semi-literate stamps

72   Illegible, Verulamium region, probably Brockley Hill (Castle, 1972, fig 6 M68–70 for the namestamp; M71 for the *fecit* counterstamp, the same as the Wroxeter example.): AD 80–110; 40/4, C 2.3

73   Illegible or Decanius, Wroxeter, AD100–150; 80/+, P 4

74   Illegible, Wroxeter, AD 100–150; 48/36, BP 4

75   Illegible, Wroxeter, AD 100–150; unstratified from *insula* 5

76   Illegible, two stamps from the same mortarium, Mancetter-Hartshill, AD 140–70; unstratified from *insula* 5

77   Illegible, Wroxeter, AD 100–150; 83/+, WR 4

78   Illegible, Wroxeter, AD 100–150; 90/92, P 3.3

79   Illegible, Wroxeter, AD 100–150; 98/+, P 4

80   Illegible, Wroxeter, AD 100–150; 98/139, F974, P 3.1, KG 16

Nos 74–5, 77–80 are stamps on mortaria made at Wroxeter. Nos 78–80 are from one die, nos 74–5 and 77 are from three other, different, dies all used in the same potteries. See Sidbury (Hartley 1992) for further details.

Unidentified stamps

81   Unidentified, Mancetter-Hartshill, AD 150–75; 83/+, WR 4

82   Unidentified, Wroxeter or Mancetter-Hartshill, AD 100/130–170; 83/+, WR 4

83   Unidentified, ?Mancetter, ?mid 2nd century; 83/+, WR 4

84   Unidentified, Wroxeter, probably AD 90–130; 83/+, WR 4

85   Unidentified, Wroxeter, AD 90–150; 85/+, WR 4

86   Unidentified, ?Wroxeter, ?AD 90–130; 86/22, WR 3.1; 86/24, WR 3.1

87   Unidentified, Wroxeter, AD 100–150; 91/56, F87, WR 4

88   Edge of stamp, not identifiable, Verulamium region, AD 70–110; 98/52, 98/61, P 2.3

89   Unidentified, Verulamium region, AD 80–130; 98/138, P 2.3

90   Unidentified, Wroxeter, AD 100–50; 98/138, P 2.3

91   Perhaps a trademark, Wroxeter, AD 130–70. Form and, to some extent, slip point to manufacture in a pottery making Rhaetian-type mortaria; exceptional since their mortaria were never stamped; thick brown slip all over; 83/+, WR 4

Overview of the pottery
by Jane Timby

Introduction

Excavations in *insula* 5 produced just under a tonne of recorded Roman pottery, which together with the material from the adjacent Barker excavations provides one of the largest groups collected from systematic excavation in Britain this century. Spanning the first to fourth centuries, the Webster assemblage provides one of the first opportunities to study pottery from the earliest occupation of the site through to its later history. Having been collected over a period of some thirty years, and analysed by different individual specialists in selected portions of the whole assemblage for over ten years, there is naturally a degree of disfunction in the way the whole can be viewed. This stems from two primary problems. First is a practical one resulting from selective retention polices, methods of retrieval, the level of site recording and the degree of analysis applied. It would have been an extremely time consuming process to have attempted to reanalyse the complete extant raw assemblage, and it might not, at the end of the day, have greatly assisted in our interpretation of either the site history or the pottery. The approach adopted for the preceding reports was considered the best way of making use of the existing work and for attempting to get the maximum out of the pottery, both from the pottery specialist's point of view and for the stratigraphic interpretation, namely the use of targeted key groups.

The second problem is the evolution of theoretical perspectives and shifts in the orientation of pottery studies. Our increased recognition of different fabrics and sources, the mechanisms of trade, the application of more sophisticated techniques for analysing data, the widespread use of quantification, and a greater understanding of site formation processes extends the potential of the pottery assemblage. Inevitably some of the questions we may like to pose now cannot be addressed by the type of data collected in the past. The techniques used cannot be criticised, they were simply a reflection of their time. A considerable bias has also been introduced by the level of work put into the different periods. The military and Hadrianic material has been intensively studied as part of two separate research theses (Darling 1976; Faiers 1990). Further the level of information that can be extracted from the military phase, in even a relatively short time span with very distinctive vessels, is quite different to that which can be obtained from the subsequent three centuries. Recording was more minimal for the later Roman levels and greater reliance had to be placed on work carried out by earlier workers. In this respect the pottery report is perhaps a little deficient. Fortunately, this is compensated to some extent by concurrent work carried out by Robin Symonds on the adjacent Barker excavations which focused on the later Roman and sub-Roman development. These factors need to be kept in mind when viewing the assemblage as a whole.

Generally speaking, with the exception of the recent work on the Webster and Barker assemblages little work has been carried out on studying pottery from either the town or immediate locality. For this reason the foregoing report is intended as a first step to setting up a form and fabric framework on which subsequent pottery work can focus. Despite the shortcomings in the quality of the data and the nature of the deposits from which the material was recovered (see below) the pottery does provide a useful indicator as direct evidence for trade, and for assessing the economic and social status of the town and some of its occupants. Many of the conclusions reached must remain somewhat tentative but it is hoped that the work has established a firm base for future work in the region.

The following overview will focus on two main aspects; firstly the assemblage will be considered from the point of view of the site itself, looking at changes through time and the usefulness, or otherwise, of the pottery for examining chronological and functional aspects of the site. Secondly the assemblage will be looked at in terms of Wroxeter as a military base and its subsequent development into a civilian town and will consider aspects of trade and supply, comparing it with other towns within the province.

Pottery use and discard in *insula* 5

The materials generally available for dating include coins, pottery, and to a lesser extent small finds. The reliability of the former varies considerably. Ideally the different components of the material culture need to be studied in relation to one another and set against the archaeology of the site and its stratigraphy. Unfortunately, circumstances are often far from ideal, and to produce a chronology for the first century material from Wroxeter much reliance has been put on the pottery, in particular the samian and imported finewares. The bulk of the military assemblage comes from discrete pit fills. It represents the first pottery assemblage deposited on the site and, as such, together with the fact it mainly came from fills which presumably once deposited were subject to little further disturbance, should represent a moderately prime assemblage with negligible problems of residuality.

One aspect of pottery work that has received much attention over recent years is the problem of redeposition. This phenomenon is particularly acute at Wroxeter, which is perhaps not surprising considering the massive amount of earth-moving that must have taken place for the public building programme. Not only has material been disturbed and recycled, perhaps several times, within the area of the site but also it would appear that earth containing rubbish was brought in from elsewhere. For the pottery this presents serious problems, both in the recognition of how much material might be residual and the validity of

attempting to look at things like vessel composition which are unlikely to bear much relation to the uses of the public buildings. Primary refuse, ie refuse which remains where it was first discarded, is the only type of assemblage that can be used as dating evidence and to trace the arrangement of different activities. The most likely groups that might fall into this category are from the fills of negative features in the military period, and from Period 3. It has also been argued that small fragments tend to remain *in situ* in regularly maintained activity areas (Schiffer 1972) whereas larger pieces are removed to a midden. Determining the chronology of such fragments, if indeed they were recovered, very much depends on the distinctiveness of styles current in that period. The residual problem is also reflected in other datable finds, such as the glass and coins. In a number of cases cross-joins have been identified by the different workers between areas and in the case of the samian both horizontally and vertically across periods. These can be interpreted in three ways: the fragments may have been deposited in different places at the same time, or several deposits containing sherds within a discrete area may be subsequently mixed with later, or earlier, material and redeposited, or the material was deposited in a single place, ie a midden or municipal rubbish dump, and subsequently redeposited in a completely different area.

The short time span of the military occupation, some 35 years, resulted in the accumulation of approximately 241 kg (16,000 sherds) of pottery from contexts identified as relating to this period. In reality this figure is much greater since pottery relating to the military occupation continues to feature residually in later levels, probably accounting for approximately between 66 and 100 percent of the Period 2.1 assemblage.

One feature of the military pottery is the preponderance of locally produced wares accounting for approximately 87% by weight (excluding amphorae) of the total assemblage. The earliest features identified on the site thought to be of pre-legionary origin, contained examples of this locally made legionary ware along with sherds of samian dating to AD 70–85/90. Three possible scenarios could account for this: the fills may have been contaminated from above; the features existed after the establishment of the legionary fortress; or the 'legionary' ware production was established by an earlier military unit and continued when the legion arrived. The occurrence of non-local vessels other than finewares is extremely rare in the earliest military period but begins to increase slightly in the later military and demolition periods.

A consideration of the average sherd size from each of the early, later, and demolition phases for three selected wares: samian, Wroxeter oxidized ware (WWO) and Wroxeter reduced ware (WWR) (Table 4.26) shows that the material is already surprisingly fragmented from these early features. This begs the question as to whether most of the material is already secondary rubbish moved from elsewhere prior to its incorporation in these features. The degree of fragmentation is particularly high for the later military and demolition material although this might be expected.

Despite a postulated change of garrison around AD 65, when Legio XIV Gemina was withdrawn to the continent and replaced by Legio XX Valeria (Webster 1988b), there does not appear to be a recognisable change in the local pottery repertoire (Darling 1977; forthcoming), perhaps indicating that the potters remained. This might suggest that they were civilians employed by the army rather than military personnel.

The early civilian period, a time when great changes might be expected in the assemblage is disappointing from the evidence of the pottery. The lack of diagnostic potsherds and a high level of residuality from the military levels are particular problems, although the glass finds include types in use in the later first and early to mid second century. It is estimated that 60% of the samian occurring in civilian Period 1 is derived from the military levels although there could be a possibility of unused stores being available, or the finer wares having a lifespan of more than thirty five years. Apart from one sherd, samian belonging to the second half of the Trajanic period is missing, although found as residual material in later contexts. Newly introduced pottery vessels are unlikely to appear in the archaeological record until some time later, ie when they become broken and disposed of, and it is thus likely that many of the trends perceived in Period 2 reflect the changed status of Wroxeter from military to civilian Period 1. For example, rusticated wares begin to appear along with cream-slipped local wares and there is an increased use of decoration, the potters perhaps actively trying to capture the market by diversifying their products.

In the second century both samian and glass provide useful sources of dating evidence although after c AD 120 black-burnished ware (BB1) types dated by their occurrence on northern military sites provide some assistance. Although samian formed the largest fineware group and accounted for 16% overall from Period 2, 69.5% of this was South Gaulish. Period 2, lasting approximately forty years produced a similar

quantity of pottery to the military occupation. In terms of distribution, 48% of this came from the West Range, 31% from the Porticos, 19% from the Baths Precinct and a negligible amount from the Baths. If the material was essentially *in situ* it might be expected to bear some relationship to the function of the different areas, but this is unlikely to be the case. The glass ware recovered reinforces this view. Baths often show a distinctive glass assemblage in which baths flasks are common, but these are not apparent from Wroxeter except from the *natatio* infill, Period 3.1 (see Cool, this volume).

A comparison of the average sherd size across the Period 2 deposits shows this to be greatest for the Courtyard area (Table 4.27), that is, the material appeared to be less fragmented in comparison with the Baths Precinct area for example. Singling out specific wares for comparison across the periods shows that samian sherds appear to be better preserved in the West Range and Courtyard areas in Period 2 and that the sherds were on average larger than those recovered from the military deposits. Sherds recovered from the Porticos, Baths Precinct, and Baths were of more comparable size to the legionary, late military, and demolition material. Comparing other fabrics (Table 4.26) shows both oxidized Wroxeter ware (WWO) and reduced Wroxeter ware (WWR) to have the greatest average size in the Courtyard area and smallest in the Baths Precinct. Comparing the same fabrics in the military groups showed WWO to average around 10–11gms for the legionary, late military, and demolition assemblages comparable to material from the West Range in Period 2 but more fragmented than the Courtyard. WWR appears to be more fragmented overall except in the legionary groups but compares well with that from Period 2.

Joins of pottery were made from different layers from both within and between areas, for example between the West Range and the Porticos thought to indicate a common source for the dumped material and that the dumping took place as a single episode of activity. A consideration of the vessel forms found in Period 2 shows an appreciable decline in the numbers of drinking vessels, tableware and lamps compared to the military period (Faiers 1990, 124). This is also evident in the glass repertoire. This could be explained in a number of ways; firstly such forms are distinctly linked to Romanized habits and may not have necessarily been in much demand from a local populace who

Table 4.26 Pottery: average sherd size for selected fabrics by area and period

	Samian	WWO	WWR	BB1	SV
early military	4.4	11.0	12.4	–	–
later military	6.0	10.0	8.6	–	–
military demolition	5.6	10.0	9.6	–	–
period 2: porticos	4.5	7.8	8.4	8.1	16.0
period 2: west range	7.3	10.4	9.4	11.9	12.8
period 2: courtyard	6.8	13.0	10.0	10.0	15.0
period 2: baths precinct	6.0	5.6	8.8	6.7	9.5
period 3.1: P3.1, P3.2	–	11.0	–	10.5	13.7
period 3.1: C3.1	22.0	22.4	–	23.3	35.5
period 3.1: B3.1	8.4	18.5	–	13.7	15.9
period 3.1: BP3.1	7.4	13.8	–	11.2	15.7
period 3.3: WR3.1	10.4	8.8	–	12.0	23.0

Table 4.27 Pottery: average sherd size by area and period

		period		
area	military	1	2	3
porticos	10.0	8.0	10.0	14.5
west range	8.0	9.0	11.5	15.5
courtyard	12.0	15.0	12.5	24.0
baths	–	–	4.0	11.5
baths precinct	–	–	7.5	10.0

only a few decades earlier had essentially been aceramic. Alternatively the pottery may have been derived from a domestic source where kitchen wares were used, or from an area of lower social status. Thirdly it could be suggested that such vessels reflect a healthy economy which may not have been the case immediately following the withdrawal of the army and the concomitant decline in population. The decline in tableware is also accompanied by a decline in the range of imported amphora which from the second century, mainly comprise Dressel 20 olive oil types. This suggests also that wine and other imported food commodities were not being traded perhaps through lack of demand; the lack of an established mechanism for obtaining such items, or an established market to make it worthwhile to bring in such trade. Such a phenomenon is not unique to Wroxeter and the amphorae trade in general shows a decline in the later first and early second centuries. Specialised vessels first occurring in Period 2 include small crucibles for metal-working, possibly connected with the building works.

For Period 3, starting in the later second century, the samian dating becomes a little less precise and by the third century it ceases to be imported and dating becomes more reliant on coarsewares. This is helped in the later third and fourth centuries by the appearance of products of the regional colour-coated industries. Diagnostic material for the later second and early third centuries is difficult to pinpoint and is not assisted by the continued occurrence of redeposited material. Much reliance has been put on the presence of new BB1 forms and the angle of latticing on BB1 jars, in the absence of other means, for assessing the date of the Period 3 features. On products of the South-east Dorset industry there was a transition from acute- to right-angled lattice in the late second century, followed in the next two to three decades by the introduction of obtuse-angled lattice (Holbrook and Bidwell 1991, 96). The level of redeposited material, however, appears to have dropped and generally speaking the pottery from Period 3 is better preserved with a larger overall sherd size, particularly from the Courtyard area (Table 4.27). A comparison of selected fabrics from Period 3.1 against Period 2 (Table 4.26) shows an increase in sherd size in all cases.

Of all the key groups in Period 3 that from the *natatio* infill is perhaps one of the more interesting from the point of view of both the glass and pottery. It appears to contain a large assemblage of relatively well-preserved sherds representing the substantial parts of single vessels, along with glass bath flasks suggesting the deposit may reflect activities from the immediate locality. The vessel repertoire does not appear unusual in its composition containing examples of most of the forms to be expected at this time, including kitchen wares (jars, mortaria, bowls), serving vessels (flagons, dishes, bowls), drinking vessels (tankards, handled beakers), and tazze. The main drain at the Fortress baths at Caerleon produced a high proportion of beakers which are assumed to directly reflect vessels in use in the baths (Greep 1986, 50). A typical baths assemblage might also be expected to contain unguent flasks and the several narrow-necked large jars, possibly of use for pouring, seen in the *natatio* group here. Serving and food preparation vessels in both glass and pottery could be anticipated if eating and drinking facilities were available to the users of the complex.

Although the bulk of the Period 3 material is difficult to date precisely, a problem often encountered elsewhere at this period, a useful ceramic horizon is marked by products of the Oxfordshire colour-coated industries. Manufacture of these began in the mid third century but it is unlikely that they would make much of an impact at places like Wroxeter until the later third and fourth centuries. Their occurrence at Wroxeter is first documented in phases BP 3.2, C 3.2 and W 3.3 although in very small quantities. Another useful ceramic indicator is the appearance of Midlands fossil shell-tempered ware (CALC) which is unlikely to have been made before AD 350/60, possibly even a little later. Six sherds of this occur in phase C 3.1, with single sherds in C 3.3 and C 3.4 accompanied by commensurately more sherds of the Oxfordshire industries. The highest incidence of fossil shell-tempered sherds came from P 3.3 and BP 3.2, accompanied by several Oxfordshire products suggesting late fourth century activity in these two areas. Further examples of both wares occur in the post-Roman levels.

The average sherd size for Period 3 varies considerably through the different contexts but is noticeably much greater than the preceding periods. This is a reflection both of the nature of the deposits and the reduced amount of construction work causing soil disturbance.

The overall impression of the Period 3 assemblage is that it has a very domestic bias, the commonest vessels, with the exception of the portico pits (P 3.1) being associated with cooking and food preparation. This is similarly reflected in the glass which appears to be very utilitarian and not necessarily typical of the town as a whole (see Cool, this volume). The pits show a heavy bias towards flagons and drinking vessels in both glass and pottery perhaps indicating debris from a bar or tavern serving the market area.

Pottery supply to Wroxeter

Pre-Roman occupation

Despite indications of a pre-Roman focus in the immediate locality, based on both aerial photographic evidence and the known occupation of the Wrekin, a hillfort overlooking Wroxeter, remarkably little is known about local potting traditions in the pre-Roman and early Roman periods. Excavations at the Wrekin (Kenyon 1942; Stanford 1984) produced very little ceramic material and it has to be concluded that pottery did not feature strongly in the material culture of the area. This is supported by the results of work at other sites in the Upper Severn Valley and Welsh Marches, for example Collfryn, an Iron Age enclosure occupied into the Roman period in Powys (W Britnell 1989). Petrological analysis of the small number of sherds from the Wrekin suggested that most pieces were made from locally available clays (Morris 1984). Despite the poor pottery assemblage, several of the pre-Roman sites of the area produced pieces of briquetage, salt-containers originating from Droitwich indicating that some level of trade was in operation. A very small quantity of handmade Malvernian ware from Wroxeter (A Woodward pers comm) might suggest this was coming with the salt, but suggests that there was no great demand for outside pottery in this period. It would also seem that Roman wares were not reaching inland sites such as Collfryn until the early second century and were not in common use in the region until the end of the second century (W Britnell 1989, 119).

The legionary fortress
The legionary fortress appears to have been set on a previously unoccupied site, strategically placed to block the main natural access routes into Wales and to control the main north-south routes. Thus situated, it had direct access to the fortresses at Gloucester and Usk to the south, Chester to the north, and London via Watling Street to the south-east.

The absence of a locally available source of pottery has been seen as the main reason for the army to establish kilns (Darling 1976; forthcoming). Similar situations are documented at Inchtuthil, where locally made wares account for over 80% of the pottery (Darling 1985a), and Usk (Greene 1993). However, such a practice was not that unusual even where native products were available, the local pre-Roman repertoire did not include the range of everyday vessels required by the Romans who had differing cooking, eating and drinking habits. Vessels such as flagons, fine tableware, and mortaria are all new forms present only as imports prior to the Roman conquest and then largely confined to the southern half of Britain. It is clear that many of the earlier military sites provided their immediate pottery requirements on-site, supplemented by smaller amounts of imported wares. Production is attested at Kingsholm and slightly later in Gloucester (Timby 1991), Exeter (Holbrook and Bidwell 1991), Longthorpe (Dannell and Wild 1987), and possibly Chichester (Down 1978). It might be expected that places such as Wroxeter, Usk, and Inchtuthil produced commensurately more kitchen wares to compensate for the lack locally but this is not evident from the current data. Storage jars are noticeable by their low numbers at both Usk and Wroxeter and cooking wares are not prominent.

Most of the military sites superficially appear to share the same range of imported products suggesting certain civilian potteries had military supply contracts. Prominent amongst these are products from Lyon (beakers and cups), Pompeian red wares, particularly Peacock (1977b) fabric 3, Gallo-Belgic *terra nigra* cups and platters (Camulodunum types 16 and 58), South Gaulish samian, mortaria from South, Central and Northern Gaul, and amphorae from a range of sources. A variety of other wares from Spain, Central, and Northern Gaul have also been documented but often in very small amounts. Wroxeter clearly had a share of these supplies despite its inland location although the diversity in the fineware range is perhaps not as great as, for example, Usk or Exeter. Mortaria are also moderately limited, the only identified imports from the early military levels being from the Rhone Valley. The Wroxeter fortress also got its fair share of amphorae with a wide diversity of types matching that found, for example, at Kingsholm, although overall the quantities recorded are less than those for sites such as Kingsholm, Lake Farm, or Exeter. This may simply be a reflection of the sample, or may suggest a genuine lower figure, perhaps due to the difficulties of overland access for such a bulky commodity. The only curiosity at Wroxeter which makes it differ from these other sites is the apparent large numbers of the type Fishbourne 183 present. This might suggest a slightly different supply route compared to sites located on the western seaboard.

Analysis of the first-century samian assemblages shows a peak at Wroxeter around AD 55–65 followed by a gradually fall-off and a further slight peak at AD 75–80. A comparison with Usk using the same methodology also shows a peak at AD 55–65 followed by a gradual fall-off, whereas at Exeter it has been shown that the highest percentage of stamps occur in the period AD 60–65, with a second minor peak at AD 70–80 (Holbrook and Bidwell 1991, 3). Both Usk and Exeter were considered to have a good measure of similarity reflecting perhaps the fact that the two fortresses were established within a few years of one another. Manning suggests AD 55 for the founding of Usk whereas Exeter is dated to around AD 55–60 (*ibid*). The Exeter range also shows good parallels with Wroxeter both in the spread of dates and the overall relative incidence. It has been pointed out, however, that the degree of similarity seen across a number of sites in terms of the occurrence of samian may be more reflective of samian production and marketing than site chronology (Marsh 1981).

Another product that seems to appear consistently in military levels in moderately small amounts are wares from the Verulamium region, either mortaria or flagons and other whitewares. This is true of both Wroxeter and the Flavian auxiliary fort at Whitchurch (Jones and Webster 1968) to the north. Brockley Hill mortaria also occur at other military outposts such as Inchtuthil, Kingsholm, and Usk. At Wroxeter these products show an increase in the later military layers and Period 1. The quantities involved do not suggest that the army formed a significant market for the Verulamium potters who were clearly supplying most of their wares to the London area, but might suggest small consignments being despatched with other goods.

The Wroxeter potters, were either army personnel, or potters attached to the army when it transferred to Britain. A study of the possible pedigree of individual vessels by Darling (1976; forthcoming) has suggested that potters may have originated from the area of the Upper Danube or somewhere, such as the Magdelensburg, Austria, where Italian influence was strong. The Wroxeter cups in particular have some affinities with Italian designs. Unfortunately most of the other vessel forms can be found on any of the Middle and Lower Rhineland sites. Research by Tyers (pers comm) has demonstrated that the same combination of types also extends westwards into the Rhone-Saône valley widening up the potential recruitment area for the potters brought to Britain. The only other British production site making comparable wares is in the London area, referred to as Sugar Loaf Court ware after a deposit of wasters found there (Chadburn and Tyers 1984). The repertoire is very similar to the Wroxeter range with collared flagons, necked jars, carinated shoulder jars, honey pots, beakers, cups, reeded rim bowls, mortaria, platters, and lamps.

A number of potential routes exist for supplies to reach Wroxeter, from the south, north, or east. The very minute quantities of Malvernian ware until the second century might suggest that this route was not very active in the first century. The strongest links appear to be to the east and it may be that Wroxeter was receiving its supplies via London and Watling Street. It has been clearly demonstrated from recent work that London was receiving large consignments of samian stored in waterfront warehouses, some of which was presumably destined for redistribution (Miller *et al* 1986b). It is suggested that in the first century much of the Midlands and north was supplied by London and that Verulamium mortaria was retailed alongside less bulky products such as samian (Rhodes 1986b, 203). The presence of the rarer South Gaulish samian from Montans at Wroxeter and Mancetter also emphasizes the use of Watling Street. To date the greatest occurrence of this ware has been London and Richborough (Dickinson, this volume). A comparison with the military occupation phase at Gloucester itself at this time (based on the Berkeley Street assemblage) shows very similar figures for local, traded and imported wares (Table 4.28) emphasising perhaps the fact that most military sites from this period, irrespective of their location are likely to be mirror images. The absence of Roman wares at this time from sites in the hinterland suggests Wroxeter was not acting as a redistribution centre itself for products until later.

Period 1
The transition of Wroxeter from a military base to a civilian town would have had a dramatic effect on the economy and trading links. Initially it is likely that there was a minor economic decline, with a decrease in population and services. To a certain extent this may be reflected in the pottery where there is a greater emphasis on utilitarian wares and a decline in the finer eating and drinking vessels. The Wroxeter potteries continued to produce wares although they had presumably transferred at some point from military to civilian control. Perhaps it had become a small family concern run by the apprentices or successors to the original potter(s). Although there seems to be a general adherence to the same basic forms, particularly bowls and flagons in the post-Flavian period, changes are seen in the increased used of decoration and slipping. Not only did the potters have to maintain their livelihood in the absence of a military contract and smaller market, but they had to compete with other larger regional industries which were beginning to make an impact.

A similar situation prevailed in Gloucester where kilns dating to the military occupation continued to supply the new *colonia* into the second century (Rawes 1972; 1978; Timby 1991), and at Exeter (pers comm Paul Bidwell). Here there seems to have been an increased emphasis on the greywares as opposed to the oxidized ware and forms become much more standardised with less variety.

The eastern trade connection appears to be still functioning, as Verulamium wares continue to feature. The quantity of samian dateable to the first two decades of the second century is slightly higher than the norm (cf Dickinson, this volume). In many other areas a slight decline in samian at this point is seen as the reason for a proliferation of small workshops producing finer wares, including mica-slipped beakers, dishes and platters, and barbotine decorated beakers. A number of new industries appear in the Trajanic and Hadrianic periods, for example, at Holt (Grimes 1930), York (Perrin 1990), and Caerleon (Boon 1966) at this time, whilst other extant industries such as Gloucester evidently extended their repertoire to produce mica-slipped wares (Rawes 1972). Although some diversification can be seen at Wroxeter there do not seem to be many of the finer tableware being made, so possibly samian was still fulfilling this role here.

There is a possibility that there might be a hiatus between Periods 1 and 2. This may explain the apparent paucity of early second-century pottery from Period 1, particularly noticeable in the absence of late Trajanic samian, and perhaps the absence of other wares such as BB1. Alternatively the building works in Period 2 may have effectively truncated any surviving contemporary Period 1 deposits since these wares appear residually in later contexts.

Period 2
From around AD 120 two new wares begin to appear in quantity: black-burnished ware from Dorset and Severn Valley wares (Table 4.29). A nominal starting date of AD 120 for the appearance of BB1 at Wroxeter, and indeed elsewhere, is based on evidence from the northern frontier. BB1 vessels have been found on a number of sites in north Somerset and south Wales

from the early Flavian period and thus a pre-Hadrianic date at Wroxeter might theoretically be possible. Unfortunately the nature of the deposits at Wroxeter does not allow this possibility to be pursued. The presence of these two wares, however, would suggest a demand was being created as the town began to establish itself. Located as it was on major route ways and acting essentially as a frontier post it is likely to have acted as a market and collecting point for the surrounding area for agricultural produce, goods and services. By around the mid second century the Wroxeter potteries seem to have gone out of business although it is possible that mortaria continued to be produced until the later second century. The slight but significant differences in fabric between the Malvern Severn Valley wares and that found at Wroxeter suggests one or more fairly major production centres near the town. Some fourth-century pottery wasters were found at Ismore Coppice on the north bank of the Severn (Houghton 1964) suggesting the likelihood of a Severn Valley production site nearby.

The growing economy of the town is reflected in the large building works started in the early second century. Although it is difficult to attribute any features of the assemblages to the use of the buildings the increased range of wares coming into the town are testament to its changing status.

Faiers (1990) has considered the route options for the BB1 trade, including direct overland routes or carriage by sea either via Gloucester or Chester. In the light of the quantities of BB1 found along the Severn this may well have been the route used, with material perhaps being off-loaded at Gloucester for further distribution. This would also explain why Malvernian wares also begin to appear in greater quantities in Wroxeter from this period.

It is suggested that some samian was also being traded through west-coast ports in the second century coming from the Bay of Biscay (Dickinson, this volume). Other products that continue to show an increase at this time are products of the Verulamium kilns and mortaria from the Continent. It is possible that many of the former are residual since it clear from elsewhere that with the rise of the Mancetter-Hartshill kilns in Warwickshire the Verulamium region mortaria become less common outside the London region (Rhodes 1986b, 203). Mancetter-Hartshill mortaria start to appear in the ceramic record. Little ware has been identified as coming from the Holt legionary kilns (Grimes 1930) to the north which was known to have been producing a range of finewares from the early second century. Like most other larger Roman settlements, Wroxeter was also receiving small quantities of imported beakers from North Gaul and the Rhineland along with samian from the Central Gaulish factories. Thus by the mid second century Wroxeter had strong trading links established to the south-west but perhaps slightly less so with the south-east. The drop in the samian supply may have also caused a fall-off in wares

from the London region. From this point sites in the hinterland and in mid Wales, eg Collfryn (W Britnell 1989) and sites such as Meole Brace and Duncote Farm, near Shrewsbury (Ellis *et al* 1994) are beginning to receive Roman wares much of which probably came via Wroxeter.

The trends seen at Wroxeter reflect those seen elsewhere, Gloucester being a good case in point. The second century here also sees an increased diversification of wares from different sources along with the appearance of new imported finewares, although locally produced wares are still dominant. The essentially locally based industries are beginning to be challenged by the commencement of sporadic long distance provincial trade. A comparison of the quantities of BB1 in Gloucester in the second century show that it accounted for 7% by weight of the early *colonia* assemblage on the Berkeley Street site (Timby, unpub) compared to 12% from Wroxeter Period 2. The lower figure at Gloucester may be a reflection of the much greater diversity of wares present. Severn Valley wares on the other hand account for 20% of the Gloucester assemblage compared to 9% at Wroxeter. As noted above there does seem to be a greater diversity of wares present in Gloucester in the second century. This could be explained by its location on the navigable portion of the river Severn perhaps encouraging more waterborne trade; the existence of native ceramic traditions; the proliferation of small suppliers in the southwest in the early second century producing Roman wares; the fact that it was a *colonia* and therefore, had an already established Roman population as well as a local population already using pottery and perhaps already conversant with some Roman wares through pre-Roman trade. A comparison of the four main sources of ware between Wroxeter and Gloucester (Table 4.28) suggest that the latter was receiving a higher proportion of its wares more locally although the inclusion of Severn Valley wares may be skewing this figure a little. Wroxeter appears to show a higher proportion of imports although again the figure may be distorted by the large number of military wares present.

Period 3
Period 3, marking the maintenance and refurbishment and final disuse of the public buildings, sees a continuation of the trends seen earlier. Dorset BB1 and SVW dominate the market accounting for approximately 20% and 33% respectively overall. Typologically most of the pottery still belongs mainly with the Severn basin and the south rather than with the Cheshire plain to the north. There seems to be an appreciable decline in the amount of samian reaching Wroxeter from the later Antonine period, suggesting it was no longer economically viable to bring it such a distance. However, it may have still been arriving from the London region, because although the Verulamium industries had ceased to exist from around AD 160, other products from the South-east were apparently coming to

Wroxeter. A re-examination of the hone hoard from the Wroxeter forum gutter showed them to belong to a large-scale Kentish Rag industry (Rhodes 1986b, 203). The gutter produced a large collection of unused sami-an dated AD 160–90, interpreted as coming from stalls in the portico (Atkinson 1942, 137ff). Much of this was comparable with material from the infilling of the *nata-tio* (Simpson, this volume). Finer wares are represent-ed in the third century by products of Nene Valley industries and a small amount of East Gaulish samian. The occurrence of the latter is limited but comparable with that found from other western sites (Dickinson, this volume). Much of the mortaria present comes from Mancetter-Hartshill.

The fourth century sees the arrival of products from the Oxfordshire potters, including colour-coated wares and mortaria. Domestic wares are mainly from the Severn Valley and BB1 kilns. Like most other towns by the late Roman period, Wroxeter was dependent on the large regional industries for its pottery supplies. Traded wares account for 60% of the overall Period 3 assem-blage compared to 62% of the later Roman material from Berkeley Street, Gloucester (Table 4.28). Towns in the east of the country, for example Chelmsford and Colchester (Going 1987), show a very similar pattern of development with a noticeable decline of the small-er producers in deference to the larger suppliers.

In summary, it would appear that much of the pot-tery from *insula* 5 comprises rubbish material that has either accumulated *in situ* and been continuously moved around, or a mixture of *in situ* rubbish and material brought in from elsewhere. This may have been part of the building operations to raise the ground level, or to fill in pits and depressions dug for other purposes. The fact that it is rubbish raises some interesting questions about why and where it was deposited in the first place. If material was being brought in from elsewhere, where did it come from? If it came from a midden the date given to the deposit might depend on whether that material came from the top, or bottom of the midden, and how long ago it had been deposited. The content of the midden might also reflect the source and social context of the pottery. Did towns operate a communal rubbish tip or did individual households create their own? If a public space accumulated rubbish then had the use of that

public space changed either temporarily or perma-nently? This might account for the presence of the Period 3 pits in the portico areas. Whilst this might have some drawbacks in determining detailed chronol-ogy and has failed to identify any characteristics of composition that could be linked to the use of the pub-lic buildings, it does make a suitable basis for examin-ing the sources of the pottery in the broader context. An accumulated dump of rubbish is perhaps more likely to give a reasonable cross-section of pottery sup-ply than some other types of more specialised deposits. Discrete pit groups for example may reflect a single activity or the rubbish of a single household.

By looking at the different wares and their occur-rence through time it has been possible to map Wroxeter's history and identify changes in the pattern of supply. The military occupation period is the most distinctive and shows the most diverse range of imports (Fig 4.100). Following the withdrawal of the army there appears to be a brief decline reflected in the quality of the pottery from this *insula*. This could be attributed both to the sudden decrease in population and the fact that there may have been little desire ini-tially for the widespread use of pottery. By the mid second century it would appear that Wroxeter had

Table 4.29 Pottery: occurrence of main fabrics (excluding amphorae) by weight (%)

fabrics	M	period 1	2	3
import				
fineware	<1	<1	1	<1
samian	6	7	11	6
mortaria	1	4	nd	<1
total	7	11	12	6
local				
WWO/WWCR	47	37	21	6
WWR	37	33	33	nd
WW MORT	3	4	nd	13
total	87	74	54	19
regional				
Verulamium	<1	4	<1	<1
SV Severn Valley wares	<1	3	9	33
MALV Malvernian wares	<1	<1	2	<1
BBI Dorset black burnished ware	<1	–	12	20
Nene Valley	–	–	<1	<1
Oxfordshire	–	–	–	<1
Holt	–	–	<1	<1
Caerleon	–	–	–	<1
Mancetter Hartshill	–	–	nd	6
CALC late shell-tempered ware	–	–	–	<1
total	<1	7	23	59
miscellaneous				
OXID	2	<1	<1	2
GREY	<1	3	<1	4
CREAM	2	3	4	–
other	<1	<1	<1	7
mortaria	–	–	6	–
total	4	6	10	13
grand total	100	100	100	100

nd not distinguished

Table 4.28 Pottery: pottery sources serving Wroxeter and Gloucester (% of weight with figures in brackets including amphorae; Gloucester = Berkeley Street)

	local	traded	import	misc
Wroxeter military	87 (53)	4 (3)	8 (43)	1 (1)
Gloucester military	(47)	(4)	(49)	(1)
Wroxeter period 2	54 (40)	23 (14)	12 (30)	11 (16)
Gloucester second-century	(72)	(10)	(18)	–
Wroxeter period 3	20	60	6	14
Gloucester third/fourth-century	(31)	(62)	(6)	(1)

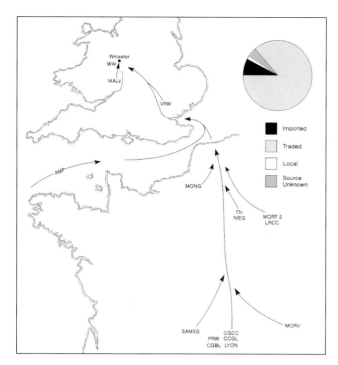

Fig 4.100 Pottery: military period sources

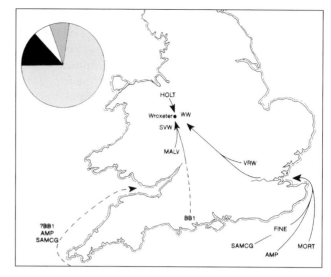

Fig 4.101 Pottery: mid second-century sources

sufficient status to have established itself as a major frontier market attracting products from the major industries (Fig 4.101). One of the more striking features perhaps is the quantities of samian that continued to reach the site. The increased appearance of Roman wares in the wider region suggests Wroxeter was acting as a redistribution centre from the second century onwards. Its subsequent development appears to mirror that found elsewhere in Britain with a gradual decline of imports and products from small producers and a greater reliance on the larger regional industries (Fig 4.102).

Pigments in ceramic bowls

by Michael Heyworth, Helen Hughes,
Barry Knight and Fiona Macalister

The following report is based on three Ancient Monuments Laboratory reports (Macalister 1980; Knight 1981; Hughes and Heyworth 1990).

A number of pottery bowls with a variety of coloured staining were found (AML 780034 and 90006). Scientific analysis suggests that the bowls contained paint and it is therefore likely that they were used for mixing a variety of pigments, possibly associated with the painting of plaster walls. No tests were undertaken specifically to ascertain whether the pigments were organic. However no crystalline phases were detected by x-ray diffraction, and no elements were detected by x-ray fluorescence which could have accounted for the colours. Two groups were found, one in and near the *macellum* (Macalister 1980, Knight 1981), and the other in Period 4 backfill in Room 11A on the east side of the baths (Hughes and Heyworth 1990).

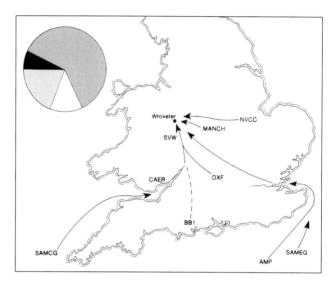

Fig 4.102 Pottery: later Roman sources

Macellum

A potsherd from a WR 3.1 layer in the *macellum* with a dark red deposit inside was examined by x-ray diffraction. The deposit was found to be haematite. From a similar layer a sherd with an Egyptian Blue pigment was found. A sherd from a WR 2.3 layer in Room 22.7 with a blue colouring inside was examined by x-ray fluorescence. It seemed likely that the colour noted was from a natural blue dye such as an extract of blue flowers absorbed onto chalk. Two further sherds with coloured deposits came from the west portico of the courtyard directly east of the *macellum*. In one sherd, from posthole F105, C 2.3, the pigment was identifiable by diffraction as Egyptian Blue, and the second, from a C 2.4 layer, contained a pink powder, thought to be of haematite mixed with chalk. A lump of kaolin was also found which may have been used in the production of pottery or paints.

Baths

Several ceramic sherds containing pigments were examined to identify the pigments involved. The sherds were from bowl-shaped vessels of Severn Valley ware found in layer 38/33, Phase B 3.1, in Room 11A (S16, layer 10: Fig 2.12).

The sherds bore heavy traces of red paint, with small traces of green and a light pink paint apparent on closer examination. The red pigment was examined by x-ray fluorescence and under the polarising microscope, and both methods suggested that it was a natural red iron oxide. Under examination the green pigment was characteristic of *terre verte*, an iron oxide. The light pink paint appeared to be a complex mixture of pigments. One is likely to be some type of lake pigment made by precipitating a dye onto an inert substrate. Other pigments are probably Egyptian Blue and yellow ochre.

The earliest red dye used in antiquity was madder which is a natural dyestuff obtained from the root of the plant *Rubia tinctorum*, grown in Europe and Asia Minor, and known to have been used since classical times. Egyptian Blue was an artificial pigment made from copper, calcium, silica, and sodium sesquicarbonate (natron). It was made from about 1500 BC, but the secret of its manufacture was lost between AD 200 and 700. Whilst the use of pigments such as Egyptian Blue and haematite are well known in Romano-British contexts (Biek 1981), no previous identification of a lake pigment (possibly with madder) are known from Romano-British contexts.

Crucible fragments

by Michael Heyworth

A number of fragments of ceramic crucibles were submitted for examination to attempt to identify the metals melted in them. Because of the fragility of the crucible material it may be assumed that most of the pieces were found in their initial place of deposition. One crucible reported on here is from a military context. Of the remainder one came from a BP 2.1 layer, three from a dump, F951, forming part of the P 2.2 and make up layers in the porticos, one from a P 2.3 layer, three from WR 2.3 make up layers in the *macellum*, three from Period P 3.1 pits in the portico outside the *macellum*, one from a late layer in the *frigidarium*, and three from late portico layers. The contexts of two are unknown. They are therefore present throughout the excavated sequence though with most examples from Period 2, and with a concentration in the porticos.

The crucibles were mostly fragments of thick, rough, hand-made thumb pots, some of which showed evidence of pinched spouts. All the fragments showed evidence of heating and vitrification on the surface. The most complete crucible, no 17, was approximately 60mm deep and with a 50mm internal diameter; the broken off base of a similar crucible was associated with it. Another crucible fragment, no 7, may represent a much wider, shallow crucible with an estimated diameter of about 200mm. However, this size might not be strong enough to be usable, and a more likely interpretation is that the fragment represents part of a triangular crucible, although no corner of a triangle survives. These latter crucibles are usually Iron Age in date so it is a late example of its type if this interpretation is correct. A couple of the fragments, nos 9 and 13, represent much finer, thinner walled crucibles, made of a more refractory clay.

All the fragments were examined at low magnification (x 10) and were qualitatively analysed using x-ray fluorescence to attempt to identify any traces of metal remaining on them. A number had obvious metal droplets on the surface which could be analysed to give an accurate indication of the metals melted. Others had traces of metal which were analytically detectable though not visible, which could also be used to identify the metal. However, some fragments had no traces of metal and it was not possible to link them with the melting of any specific metal.

The crucibles, where it was possible to detect metal traces, can be divided into two groups, one associated with silver melting and one associated with copper alloy, probably bronze, melting. Three crucible fragments, nos 10, 11, and 18, had traces of silver with minor impurity levels of copper and zinc. Two of these fragments, nos 10 and 11, came from third-century pits, F572 and F523, in the portico and may indicate a silver working area nearby. The rest of the fragments with metal traces were all associated with copper alloy melting, particularly bronze (copper and tin). The components of a metal melted in the crucible behave differently depending on their chemical nature. Both zinc and lead can act as glass-forming elements and so are chemically bound into the crucible slag. This tends to enhance the concentrations of these elements in any analysis of the deposits on the crucible. It is therefore likely that although zinc and lead were often detected in the analyses, their concentrations in the original melt were quite small, and that copper and tin were therefore the major elements in the metal melted. The only exceptions to this were no 12 which had no traces of tin and may have been associated with melting pure copper with minor levels of zinc, and no 14 which had no traces of tin, but a much higher concentration of zinc and would have been used for brass melting.

Three of the crucibles associated with bronze working came from the dump F951 (P 2.2) from the south end of the west portico; the dump also contained iron smithing slag.

The fragment from the military levels (no 1) is a piece of hearth lining with a layer of copper alloy metal and vitrification on the inside. The alloy contained significant levels of copper, zinc, lead, and tin, and is a leaded gunmetal.

Of the fragments which had no traces of metal when analysed, the majority were vitrified and appeared to have been used as crucibles, though nos 5 and 15 show no indication of heating and are unlikely to have been associated with metalworking. The fragments of no 5 contained a layer of a calcium-rich deposit.

Industrial residues
by Fiona Macalister

Technological processes are attested by finds of industrial residues, suggesting iron smithing and possibly lead working. Copper working is dealt with separately by Heyworth.

There was evidence of iron smithing on a small scale. The slags examined (10kg in total) are of two principal types, smithing and fuel ash slag, but there is a complete gradation between the two and much iron-rich fuel ash slag. Some of the smithing slag is magnetic, due to the presence of hammer-scale. The smithing slag, produced by secondary working of iron in a smithing hearth, is in the form of plano-convex hearth bottoms, which collected at the bottom of the hearth, dribbles, puddles, and irregular lumps. There are also a few pieces of hearth lining, that is the clay lining of the hearth which becomes vitrified on one side and grades into fuel ash slag. All the evidence from the hearth lining comes from a WR 3.1 context, 83/111, which produced 6 kg of slag. This context formed part of the make up for the herringbone floor of the *macellum*. The lining varies in thickness from 3 to 15mm. Evidence of the fuel used is found as wood and charcoal within both forms of slag. Various corroded iron oxide lumps, pieces of magnetic iron, and corroded iron objects, such as nails, give further evidence for iron working.

Lead was found on the site, in addition to objects, in the form of dribbles and puddles of solidified molten lead and also as fragments of lead sheeting. A particular group was found in the west portico. This may be the result of building debris, such as pipes, tank lining, etc, which has fallen into a fire. It may also, however, be the product of lead working. A few of the pieces have cut marks which might be expected to disappear if the lead had been subjected to heat, and there are also pieces of lead cuttings, one group from layer 84/48 probably the same WR 3.1 context as the hearth linings above, which are further evidence of lead working. Much of the lead has the characteristic white/cream lead oxide surface.

Miscellaneous items

In addition to the industrial residues a number of other items indicative of industrial processes were examined. Some of the data has been added to reports on stone, bone, mortar, and pigments.

A mould fragment with a lowered recess and a curved outer edge was perhaps part of a mirror mould, although this was not certain. The fragment was analysed using XRF and zinc was detected. The end of a clay pipe with an outer diameter of 69mm and an inner diameter of 27mm was decorated with ribbing and had an extra outer layer. This was probably a water spout.

Fragmentary remains of two infant burials
by Simon Mays

Human bone from two individual infants was examined in 1989 and the following is a summary of the report (Mays 1989). An infant burial from outside Room 9C was noted in the site records but was not submitted for analysis. An infant burial was found north of 12A by Thomas Wright (Chapter 6, para 8.1).

1   Approximately a quarter of the skeleton was present mainly comprising parts of the skull, ribs, and long bones. The material was fragmentary but moderately well preserved. The tibia length of *c* 70mm suggested a neonatal individual (Stloukhal and Hanakova 1978). The gender could not be determined.

The left tibia shows a deposition of woven bone upon its lateral surface. This lesion represents periostitis, the sub-periosteal deposition of new bone upon the normal cortex. Periostitis is a not uncommon finding in skeletal remains of infants and young children from archaeological sites. It may be a response to a variety of insults, particularly infectious disease (Mensforth *et al* 1978).

The bones were found in the Period 2 phase 3 dump in the south portico; 98/52, P 2.3

2   Only the right half of the mandible (with teeth missing) and a cranial fragment were present. The right half of the mandible has not fused with the left suggesting an age of less than one year (Workshop of European Anthropologists 1980) while the size of the tooth crypts suggests an age of over 6 months. The gender could not be determined.

The bones were found in a Period 3 phase 1 pit F933 in the south portico; 98/101, F933, P 3.1, KG 16

The animal bone
by Beverley Meddens with a contribution by Barbara Noddle

Introduction

The animal bones retrieved from the excavations form a huge collection, filling over 900 boxes. Initially it was hoped that a basic archive could be prepared for all the bone, but as the collection accumulated it became clear that only samples could be dealt with. In the event four groups of bone have been examined. The first comprises bone from the infilling of the *natatio*, and the report on this, by Barbara Noddle, is presented below. The second group comprises about 80 boxes of bone mainly from Period 1 levels in the west and south porticos, catalogued by Frank Meddens, and the third group material from the Period 2 dumps. The fourth group is represented by a large sample of material from third-century pits in the west and south portico, recorded by the author following an assessment of the entire collection (Meddens 1987). The selection of material for groups 2–4 was based on an initial phasing which was subsequently refined. Apart from the *natatio* collection, the majority of the bone derived from the south and west porticos of the public buildings abutting the *macellum* (Boxes 90, 97, and 98), with some from Box 80 to the east, and some from Box 91 in the corridor to the north of the *macellum* (Fig 1.3).

The following report represents a recasting of this earlier work based on the detailed phasing of the contexts. It combines a previous interim report by this author on the portico pits in 1989, with archive data on the Period 1 bone. No new material has been examined, but the statistical data have been re-examined and regrouped in the light of the detailed phasing. The total number of bones reported on amounts to 23798 fragments.

The Period 1 (AD 90–130) sample comes from 77 of the 107 contexts containing bone from Boxes 90, 91, 97, and 98. A total of 2513 animal bones were recorded. The bone from the Period 2 dumps comes from material dumped in the *insula* porticos during the second-century building campaign dated AD 130–70. The total of 3834 fragments is from 31 of the 140 contexts containing bone from layers in the west and south portico (Boxes 90, 97, and 98), and from the corridor (Box 91). The bone from Period 3 is material from 16 of the portico pits from Key groups 16 and 17, most dated to the first half of the third century, but with one, pit F930, dating to the fourth century. The pits contained large collections of animal bones which may derive from activities in the *macellum* or from stalls set up under the porticos. The bone from the *natatio* fill dated to AD 210–30 is likely also to be *macellum* rubbish. A total of 33 pits contained bone. The total number of 17451 fragments would thus represent about half the Period 3 total.

The assessment of all the animal bone from Wroxeter (Meddens 1987) identified the major groups of bone bearing layers, and presented an assessment of the value of further work. For Period 2, apart from the material reported on here, a large group of bone, comprising over 30 boxes, was collected from the *macellum* construction and dump layers, and over 100 boxes of material were noted for similar horizons in the porticos, the latter suggesting that the Period 2 material reported on here was a fraction of the total. Bone was not collected from the courtyard (C) or from the baths precinct (BP), areas excavated early in the excavation

campaign. For Period 3 there remains a further large quantity of material from the portico pits aside from the material reported on here. About 100 boxes of bone came from the late levels in the porticos (P 3.3 onward) and a further 30 boxes from the robber trench for the main drain beneath the *macellum*. At the time of the assessment there was no information on the contexts of over 200 further boxes from the excavations. Although the present report might have been more complete if bone from the P 3.3 and later levels in the porticos had been examined, the work undertaken in the basilical hall on similar late levels provides an excellent substitute (Armour-Chelu 1997).

Validity of the samples

It is possible to assess the validity of the groups examined, in the light of information from other categories of finds and from the structural analysis. For Period 1, the areas examined represent the location of the great majority of the Period 1 archaeology, and the sample may be regarded as representative. The pottery evidence suggests that residuality was high. There was, however, little ground disturbance for the Period 1 buildings, and it is possible that the animal bone is predominantly contemporary, with little material disturbed from the military horizon. Bone from the Period 1 pits in the courtyard area would have provided a more definite Period 1 group, but this material has not been located and may not have been retained.

The Period 2 dumps may derive in part from redeposited material from foundation trenches, but in the portico area seem to have been brought in from elsewhere. Pottery analysis suggested that residual material in the portico dumps was around 30–40%. In terms of pottery finds the porticos accounted for 30% of the total Period 2 assemblage, while in terms of volume the dumps represented less than 10% of the total. This evidence suggests that the animal bone, although a useful group, cannot be taken as representative of the Period 2 dumps as a whole.

The portico pits are dated to the first half of the third-century. The two groups, P 3.1 and P 3.2, were assigned on the basis of stratigraphic relationships and pit types. However, the pottery suggested three groups of pits, the first dated no later than AD 225, the second no later than AD 270 and probably mid second-century, and the third later still, comprising pits containing later third and early fourth century material, in some cases perhaps intrusive. Of the pits discussed here F462, F486, F561, F597, F643, F675, F804, F852, and F855 belong to the first category, and F455, F471, F547, F638, and F736, to the second, while F930 was identified as of early fourth-century date. F801 contained too little pottery to provide a date.

Aims

This report is focused on the animal bone from the pits outside the *macellum* dating from the third century.

The initial question asked was whether the bone could be defined as deriving from the *macellum* or from a streetside market as its specialised appearance suggested. Next the animals represented, their sex, age, and size, and the types of butchery used were analysed. Leading on from this the intention has been to look at the wider picture of supply and consumption at the market, and the kinds of food represented by the butchery. The *natatio* collection, analysed by Noddle provided a useful comparable group. In addition the data already gathered from the Period 1 and 2 animal bone was interrogated in the same way as that from Period 3 to establish any differences in function and types of animal exploited through time. For Period 1 it was of particular interest to note whether the animal bone collections differed between the military and early civil periods. As a background to these detailed studies, other questions were considered such as the nature of the data on diet, animal husbandry, and slaughter in the context of the town and its hinterland, by comparison with other Romano-British towns. Wider questions of where Wroxeter stands in relationship with the economic indicators of other towns, whether *macellum* assemblages differ from other urban collections and what might define a *macellum* or market assemblage were also addressed. In the event the report has only touched on the implications of the data, which must form part of the ongoing programme of data collection from urban sites to be analysed with increasing sophistication as the database expands.

Methods

The bones were recorded using the Ancient Monuments Laboratory osteometry data capture programme (Jones *et al* 1981). The recording was carried out between 1986 and 1988 first by Frank Meddens and then by the author. The animal bones were identified to species and anatomical part wherever possible. Ribs and vertebrae however were not generally identified to species, but placed in one of two categories – large ungulate (ie, cattle, red deer and horse), and small ungulate (ie sheep, goat, pig, and roe deer).

The largest component of this sample is the cattle bones, and this is reflected by the proportion of bone, particularly vertebrae and ribs, that was allocated to the large ungulate category. Only 25 of the 4252 bones identified to cow, horse, and deer belonged to horse and deer, and it therefore seems likely that the large ungulate group can be considered as cattle.

Using the criteria described by Boessneck (1969) and Payne (1985), 104 bones were identified as sheep and only 1 as goat. Measurements recommended by Payne (1969) for separating sheep and goat metacarpals were plotted in order to determine the approximate ratio of sheep to goat, and again sheep were seen to be dominant. Further details are given below. The method described by Grant (1982) was used for ageing mandibles and isolated teeth were also recorded and are

given in the tables. Tooth eruption and epiphysial fusion ages were calculated following the data provided by Sissons and Grossman (1975), Silver (1969), Noddle (1984b), and O'Connor (1982; 1984).

Application to study the faunal material should be made to the Ancient Monuments Laboratory of English Heritage. The laboratory also holds the archive records on floppy discs. All contexts with bone are listed, as are the box contents. The recorded data from separate campaigns of work has been merged and is sorted by context, by species, and by anatomy. Full details of the archive are given in Meddens (1987). In addition there is an archive of tables, photographs, figures and detailed text from this programme of work.

Recovery and condition

In common with many other British excavations, no sieving was undertaken in the excavations and recovery was by hand. Material not recovered is therefore most likely to be in the categories of small mammals, birds, fish and amphibians, and it is noticeable that these categories form only a small part of the sample examined.

Preservation of the bone was generally good, although in some contexts, in particular in the pits from Box 80, many of the bones were brittle and broke easily with the surface tending to flake off. For the three groups examined here the percentage of freshly broken bone is around 3–5% excluding cattle ribs. Including the latter, freshly broken bone amounts to 9% of the Period 2 group, and 18% of the third-century group where the frequency of fresh breakages generally corresponds to the condition of the bone. However, in some of the pits, the level of breakage was highest for ribs and scapulae, and in this case, the high breakage might be explained by the large fragment size making them more vulnerable to breakage on excavation or during transportation and storage.

The number of loose teeth has been used to assess the degree of fragmentation, and preservation of bone assemblages (Maltby 1985). In this sample the percentage of loose teeth throughout is 3%. This can be compared to the 10% recorded for the military bone which is described as fragmentary (Noddle forthcoming), and that from the baths basilica report where loose teeth comprise between 8% and 26% (median 19%) of the assemblages (Armour-Chelu 1997). The differences reflect the primary nature of the bone from the third-century pits, although the more stringent recovery methods used on the baths basilica site may also be a factor.

The proportion of damaged or eroded bone was generally low. This contrasts with the baths basilica site. However the late levels there were heavily used, with one instance of high damage being consistent with use of the area as a thoroughfare (Armour-Chelu 1997).

On average 2% of the sample was gnawed. By species the figure for cattle/large ungulate was 1%, while for sheep the figure was 10%, for pig 6%, and for small ungulate, 3%. This might suggest that the processes leading to the small ungulate bones being deposited were different to those for the cattle. A few bones were altered in a way which may indicate that they had been digested. Small amounts of the bone were burned, charred, and calcined. This is probably the result of different activities to those that produced the main bulk of the assemblage. A few fragments were stained green, presumably as a result of close proximity to copper-alloy objects.

Species present and their frequencies

Details of the fragment numbers and identifications from the three groups are given in Table 4.30. The species represented comprise 10 mammalian: cattle, sheep, goat, pig, horse, red deer, roe deer, dog, hare, hedgehog, and six bird: domestic fowl, mallard, brent goose, woodcock, pigeon, and raven. In addition fallow deer was identified from a tibia midshaft fragment (AML 857545, 91/503); this should be treated with caution in the absence of an epiphysial portion.

The majority of the bone from all three periods belongs to cattle, sheep/goat, and pig. Of the total of 1240 sheep/goat bones and teeth, 104 were identified as sheep and, only one was identified as goat, a deciduous lower fourth premolar in the Period 1 group. Plotting the distal metacarpal measurements indicates that all the metacarpals in the Period 1 and the third-century samples are sheep. Six bones from the Period 2 group and 83 from the third-century group were identified as definite sheep, but no goat bones were found. All bones recorded as sheep/goat are therefore referred to as sheep throughout the rest of this section.

Goats appear to be more abundant in the military phase as do deer and horse and this may have some significance. The only goat specimen definitely identified in this sample was the deciduous premolar noted above; a pelvis in the Period 1 group may also be goat. Nevertheless, goat may be underestimated in bone assemblages (Levitan 1993).

The range of species represented varies little through time. As sieving was not carried out on site, low numbers of bones from smaller animals and low numbers of small bones may be due to their not having been collected rather than their actual absence, so no great significance can be placed on their low numbers.

Of the three main species represented cattle bones are by far the most abundant. Table 4.31 gives the relative percentages of the identified fragments of cattle, sheep, and pig for the three groups reported on here, together with comparable data from other Wroxeter sites. The table suggests that the relative proportions of the three species remain similar throughout the first two centuries of occupation, with a possible slight increase in sheep in Period 1 at the expense of cattle in comparison to the military proportions. In the third century an increase is shown in the cattle bones, with the proportion of cattle going up to 63%-71% from

46%-52%. This increase is present in the samples from the *natatio*, the portico pits, and the baths basilica site (Armour-Chelu 1997). The later material from the baths basilica from the fourth-century and later, shows a slight decrease in cattle in favour of pig.

The data for the pits suggests that there are differences between the types of deposit in different pits, and, in some cases, within a pit. Table 4.32 shows the relative frequency of pig, cattle, and sheep identified to species within all 16 pits. Pits F455, F471, F852, and F855, have a considerably smaller percentage of identified cattle than the other pits. However in the case of pit F852 this is due to the presence of a large number of butchered ribs recorded as from large ungulates but presumably cattle. Pits F455 and F471 contained some butchery waste and some domestic refuse, and the latter seems to have a higher proportion of sheep and pig than the cattle butchery deposits. Pit F855 differs from the others in that it not only contained a larger proportion of sheep and a probable butchery deposit, but also a human baby jaw and skull fragment, a dog skeleton, and possible domestic rubbish.

Other species such as horse, deer, and hare, are represented by very few specimens. Comparison of the pig measurements with those from the military phase (Noddle forthcoming), where there were two wild specimens, shows one possible wild pig specimen in the third-century sample. However, wild animal carcasses do not form a significant proportion of the sample, and hunting seems to have played a greater part in the military period than in any of the later phases. Dog bones occur throughout but not in large numbers, and the majority are accounted for by two dog skeletons in pit F561 and pit F855.

The proportion of birds in the pits is much lower in comparison to the earlier phases, 0.6% in the pits compared to 2% in the Period 2 sample, and 3.5% in the Period 1 sample. However, the types of birds represented are the same and they occur in similar proportions to each other. The majority are domestic fowl but with some wild birds indicating some hunting, mainly woodcock, ducks, and wild geese, all presumably caught for food. Additionally raven, which was probably scavenging on site, and pigeon were found. This is very much the same type of fauna as observed from the military deposits (O'Connor forthcoming) and from the baths basilica site (Armour-Chelu 1997).

The cattle assemblage

Sex and measurements

Sexing data for cattle have been derived from three different bones, horncores, pelves, and distal metapodials. Horncores occurred in all three groups, one from Period 1, 13 from Period 2, and 27 from the third-century pits, and were recorded with reference to Armitage and Clutton-Brock (1976, 329–48). Of the 41 described horncores, 28 could be sexed as males, females, and

Table 4.30 Animal bone: species present (fragment numbers)

species	period 1 n	period 1 %	period 2 n	period 2 %	third-century pits n	third-century pits %
cattle	325	13	474	12	3428	20
probable cattle	1057	42	1728	45	10049	58
horse	1	<1	1	<1	5	<1
red deer	1	<1	3	<1	5	<1
fallow deer	–	–	1	<1	–	–
red/fallow deer	–	–	1	<1	1	<1
large ungulate	41	2	99	3	72	<1
sheep	15	<1	6	<1	83	<1
goat	1	<1	–	–	–	–
sheep/goat	202	8	218	6	715	4
pig	159	6	221	6	706	4
roe deer	–	–	2	<1	4	<1
small ungulate	524	21	607	16	1220	7
dog	5	<1	33	<1	211	1
dog/fox	–	–	3	<1	–	–
hare	13	<1	1	<1	6	<1
hedgehog	–	–	1	<1	–	–
cf domestic fowl	52	2	43	1	60	<1
domestic duck/mallard	2	<1	–	–	2	<1
brent goose	–	–	–	–	2	<1
geese/ducks	4	<1	3	<1	5	<1
duck	1	<1	–	–	–	–
woodcock	4	<1	11	<1	7	<1
pigeons	–	–	–	–	2	<1
raven	3	<1	–	–	11	<1
unidentified bird	23	1	21	1	27	<1
unidentified mammal	77	3	352	9	726	4
unidentified species	2	<1	5	<1	2	<1
total	2512	100	3834	100	17349	100

Table 4.31 Animal bone: relative frequency of main species on insula 5 (% of fragments)

period	pig	cattle	sheep/goat
baths and macellum			
military	24	49	27
period 1	23	46	31
period 2	24	52	24
natatio	12	69	19
P 3.1 pits	14	67	19
P 3.2 pits	15	71	14
third-century pits	14	70	16
basilical hall			
second/third-century	19	63	18
fourth to sixth-century	25	60	15

Table 4.32 Animal bone: relative frequency of main species in portico pits (% of identified bone)

pits	pig	cattle	sheep/goats
P 3.1			
F597	12	80	8
F736	18	65	17
F804	21	55	24
F801	23	69	8
F855	22	44	34
F486	11	73	16
F561	10	60	30
F547	14	67	19
P 3.2			
F643	7	81	12
F852	46	34	20
F638	9	77	14
F675	21	68	11
F930	12	80	8
F471	25	39	36
F462	22	67	11
F455	26	47	27

century pits. One possible female horncore from the latter was a small horn core type typical of the Iron Age. Three specimens were possibly of 'medium' length.

In bulls the medial wall of the acetabulum is thicker than in cows (Grigson 1982). In the third-century sample there were 59 pelves on which observations and in some cases measurements could be made. These showed that 49 were female, three male, with seven indeterminate. Only female pelves were recorded from Period 1 and Period 2 with one and five examples respectively. Plots of the distal widths of cattle metapodials from Wroxeter are comparable with other sites in Britain, and, assuming the distribution of these measurements do show sexual dimorphism, most of these bones were from cows (data in archive). Comparison of the distal width cattle metapodial measurements for Period 1 and for the military collection shows an increase in size.

Age

The age data are summarised in Table 4.33. Judging by the fusion data for the proximal femur, only 10% of the animals represented in the third-century pits were younger than 36–42 months (Sissons and Grossman 1975). Using eruption data from Sissons and Grossman (1975) and Silver (1969), absolute ages can be equated with ranges of wear stages. In all except one perinatal specimen of the Period 3 mandibles, the permanent second molar was erupted, so the animals can be assumed to have been older than 18 months at death. A minimum of eight mandibles out of 112 (8%) had the permanent fourth premolar unerupted, and since this tooth erupts at 30–36 months then only c 7% of animals were younger than 30–36 months at death. The remainder are all older than three years but none achieved a wear stage greater than no 49.

Although the precise age at which the teeth erupt or the epiphyses fuse is problematic (Payne 1984; Noddle

castrates in equal proportions. This contrasts with other sexing data discussed below. Short, small, and medium-horned cattle were represented. A major category was a short-horned variety, curved and oval in cross-section, one of which occurred in Period 1, nine in Period 2, and ten in the third-century pits. Another type was a twisted horncore. Like the first category, this was also short-horned, oval in cross-section, and curved, but it was twisted upwards, forwards, and outwards. Two were noted in Period 2, and nine in the third-century pits. Most of the small-horned specimens were thought to be male with one in Period 2 and five in the third-

Table 4.33 Animal bone: summary of cattle age data

	fusion state	porous	unfused		fused	
		n	n	%	n	%
period 1	*age group*	2				
	1 0–10 months		–	–	56	100
	2 10–20 (24) months		–	–	42	100
	3 24–30 months		–	–	15	100
	4 36–42 months		5	33	10	67
	5 42–48 months		6	30	14	70
	6 very late		43	53	38	47
period 2	*age group*	1				
	1 0–10 months		–	–	97	100
	2 10–20 (24) months		1	1	82	99
	3 24–30 months		5	15	29	85
	4 36–42 months		5	15	29	85
	5 42–48 months		15	32	32	68
	6 very late		25	26	70	74
third–century pits	*age group*	11				
	1 0–10 months		5	1	657	99
	2 10–20 (24) months		6	2	283	98
	3 24–30 months		13	8	141	92
	4 36–42 months		40	11	326	89
	5 42–48 months		21	18	98	82
	6 very late		349	44	436	56

n number of examples

1984b), in general the two sets of data appear to correlate very well with tooth wear data suggesting 7% and femur fusion data suggesting 10% of cattle slaughtered up to three to four years. At the other end of the range, 44% of the vertebrae are unfused indicating that 56% of the animals were fully mature at death. Of the 28 horncores in the aged group, one was very porous, seven were porous, two were porous/compact, and 18 were compact, suggesting a majority of mature animals in line with the other data.

Comparison of the different phases and sites at Wroxeter indicates some differences. The military sample suggests a 30% cull at three to four years and 48% of the animals being fully mature at death. There were many more juvenile specimens than in later phases, with 13% of the early fusing bone still unfused. In Period 1, with the exception of two vertebrae recorded as porous, none of the very early fusing bones was unfused. About 30% of the animals represented by the later fusing bones were younger than three or four years at death, and 47% of the animals were fully mature at death. For Period 2, the picture is rather more like the third-century pits. Very few juveniles were present, 15% of the animals represented by the early fusing bones had died before two to three years of age, and there seems to have been a cull at about four years of 32%. A total of 67% of the animals represented by vertebrae were fully mature at death. The sample from the third-century pits has a low percentage (2%) of the very early maturing bones unfused. Eighteen per cent of the animals represented by the later fusing bones (those fusing between three to four years) were under 42–48 months at death, and 56% of the animals were fully mature at death. On the baths basilica site,

9% of the early maturing bones were unfused, there was a cull of 25% at three years, and 60% of the remainder fully mature at death. The differences suggest that more animals were older in the later phases.

Pathology and anomalies

The most common anomalies in the cattle mandible are the absence or reduction of the second premolar and the absence or reduction of the third cusp (the hypoconulid) of the third molar (Andrews and Noddle 1975). There were three pairs of jaws with complete tooth rows, two of these pairs had identical conditions, but the third pair had both PM2 missing but one third cusp M3 missing and the other only reduced. These kinds of data may prove useful in determining populations (Baker and Brothwell 1980; Armour Chelu 1997).

Other traits that have been described as non-pathological are depressions and grooves in articular surfaces (Baker and Brothwell 1980, 110–11). These were recorded on mandibular condyle, all three phalanges, proximal metacarpal, carpals, tarsals, and proximal tibia. Also presumably of congenital origin (*ibid*, 37), are holes in the parietal bone. Frequencies for these observations are available in the archive.

One scapula from Period 2 and 15 from the third-century pits had extra bony growth around the caudal and medial edges of the glenoid causing a slight lip to form. No eburnation was recorded on the scapula articulation. Slight distortion (?spreading) of the metacarpal proximal articulation was seen in two bones, and six of the distal condyles, usually the medial condyle, all from the third-century pits. In the hindlimb the pelvis and femur were affected with more severe conditions. Extra bony growth around the medial margin of the acetabulum, and eburnation on the pubic part of the articular surface was recorded on one pelvis from Period 1, one from Period 2, and seven from the third-century pits. Eburnation, pitting and sometimes grooving on the medial and posterior surfaces of the caput femoris, often with bony growth around the articulation as well, was observed on one bone from Period 1, one from Period 2, and 45 from the third-century pits. Some distortions, extra bony growths, and spreading of articular surfaces were also noted on one distal metatarsal and a first phalanx from Period 1, one distal metatarsal and two first phalanges from Period 2, and, from a proximal tibia, calcaneum, astragalus, four centroquartal distal articular surfaces, 11 proximal and seven distal metatarsals, three first phalanges, and four second phalanges from the third-century pits.

The diagnosis of osteoarthritis and evidence for traction in cattle as shown by pathology in the skeletal remains has been discussed (Armour-Chelu and Clutton-Brock 1985). The situation they present is very similar to that found at Wroxeter, though the ageing evidence at Wroxeter suggests that many of the animals there were much older than those at Etton. This could mean that the pathological conditions observed at Wroxeter are age related, although osteoarthritis is rare in modern dairy cattle (Baker 1984). But it would seem more likely that the data can be used to give more weight to the interpretation that these pathologies are evidence of cattle being used for traction.

The only observed breaks in cattle bones were in the ribs, five bones with healing breaks were found in Period 2, six in the third-century pits where there were also ten with healed breaks. One of the proximal metatarsals (above) in the third-century pits had a condition which may have resulted from an infection.

Cattle vertebrae exhibited some pathologies. From Period 1, one thoracic vertebra had a hole or enlarged foramen at the base of the spine on the dorsal caudal side, although this may not have been pathological. A lumbar vertebra had exostosis/bony growth and pitting on a transverse process. From the third-century pits only three thoracic vertebrae fragments showed pathologies. One had an enlarged foramen above the articular processes, another had a swelling at the most dorsal part of the spine with a large foramen, consistent with an abscess, and the third had pitting and eburnation on the cranial joint surface.

Butchery and body-parts

Period 1

All parts of the skull are represented, the fragility of the bone perhaps causing over representation by fragment numbers. Only a sawn horncore evidenced butchery. All parts of the mandible are more or less equally represented. Butchery to the mandible is standard: through the diastema medio/laterally; through the tooth row from the lateral medio/laterally and from the medial medio/laterally; and through the ascending ramus lateral medio/laterally. Two jaws were chopped twice giving a section of teeth, and butchery to the mandibular condyle was seen both as knife cuts and as chops to the medial and lateral dorso-ventrally. The great number of scapula fragments would suggest that all parts of the bone are represented. Butchery is almost exclusively to the articular end and is systematic and severe, often with many blows around the glenoid, spine, and neck, which would have produced numerous fragments though these were not recovered.

The humerus is under-represented compared to the scapula, but the MNI is comparable with the mandible. There are many broken long bone fragments as was noted in the military collection. The humerus is differentially represented by the distal end and the radius by the proximal end, and this may be significant in terms of butchery and the preparation of meat joints. Only the intermediate and radial carpals were recovered. Three out of nine were burnt, and one was eroded. The smaller carpals were probably not recovered. The metacarpal is differentially represented by the distal end. Only one

bone was butchered with the lateral side of the proximal part of the bone split off. In contrast to the metacarpal all parts of the metatarsal are equally represented, but again with very little butchery. One was chopped through the midshaft, and one chopped repeatedly on the back of the shaft. The metapodials are generally present as larger fragments than the other long bones, commonly a third or half of the bone. Phalanges were almost entirely complete and generally under-represented in terms of MNI, probably due to non-recovery rather than a depositional difference.

The ilium and acetabulum occur more frequently than the pubis and ischium. The pelvis is difficult to quantify but is present in comparable numbers to other parts of the body. The pelvis was chopped through the acetabulum, the ischium shaft, the ilium shaft, and the pubis. Fragmentation of the femur is very high. The caput femoris is more highly represented than the other parts of the bone, and is similar in frequency to the acetabulum. The shaft of the bone is probably present in the longbone fragments, and the proximal and distal parts are more vulnerable to decay than more robust bones. Butchery to the caput was almost exclusively from the ventral, disarticulating the femur from the pelvis. Other chops to the proximal and distal ends split the bone axially, and also chopped off medial and lateral parts of the articular ends. The shafts are habitually chopped, battered, and split into fragments. Patellae are few but complete. One was chopped indicating disarticulation of the femur from the tibia at the joint. This can be seen on the tibia where the raised parts of the proximal articulation are shaved off by the chops going through the joint rather than through the main part of the bone. Tibia representation accords with the average. The bone is generally chopped up and split like the other longbones. The proximal end was typically butchered with blows from the ventral upwards through the crista tibia and up through the anterior parts of the articular end. The midshaft was chopped through medio/laterally and chopped superficially dorso/ventrally presumably removing meat from the bone. One of the two calcanea and one of the three astragali were butchered. This joint was butchered to remove the feet in a pattern typical of later phases. The calcaneum was chopped through the lateral side of the proximal medio/laterally, while butchery of the astragalus was more random.

Although ribs form an apparently very large proportion of the sample, they represent a MNI of only one when counting proximal articulations, and two or three if all fragments are included. These calculations are based on length of fragment. The ribs were chopped up into different sizes. Where chops at both ends of the fragment were visible there were three each between 30 and 50mm and 60 and 70mm, and two each at 80mm, between 150 and 170mm, and between 200 and 230mm. Knife cuts were also observed.

The atlas was chopped both axially and medio/laterally. Three axis bones were randomly butchered.

One fragment of the cervical vertebrae was chopped through medio/laterally. Butchery of the thoracic vertebrae showed a pattern, with the dorsal spine removed by a chop medio/laterally, one central body chopped through medio/laterally, and the transverse processes removed with axial chops. For the lumbar vertebrae the transverse processes were removed and one central body was chopped through medio/laterally. Sacrum and caudal vertebrae are almost certainly under-represented. The sacrum was highly butchered. The lateral flanges were removed probably as part of the disarticulation of the pelvis.

Period 2

Skull bones were fragmented with all parts represented. The mandible is very fragmented with all parts equally represented. Many of the small scapula fragments are broken blade pieces, the articular ends all butchered in a very specific way. The humerus too is very fragmented and butchered with the occasional larger fragment. Radius and ulna again are quite fragmented and heavily butchered, but whole bones are present. The proximal part of the articulation in the ulna is slightly more abundant than other parts of the bone.

The pelvis is again highly fragmented and butchered, but all parts of the bone are represented in more or less equal numbers. The femur is represented almost entirely by fragments of less than 25% of the whole bone. The MNI of the shaft and distal ends (both of which are represented by 11 fragments) are around two for shaft and three for the distal end. The proximal end is around two for the lateral and ten for the proximal medial. All of the femur is represented in approximately similar proportions except the caput femoris which is over-represented. The tibia is represented by mostly small fragments of less than 25% of the bone. The whole bone is represented with a slight bias towards the proximal end, the bone is heavily butchered and heavily fragmented.

The metacarpal is represented by either whole bones or proximal articulation with various degrees of shaft, but with a bias to the lateral part and the distal end. The midshaft sections are less well represented than their articular ends. Very little butchery was observed. For the metatarsal whole bones are also present but proximal fragments are more abundant than distal fragments and there are more midshaft sections and butchery marks than for the metacarpal. Phalanges are mostly complete with no butchery at all. The carpals, tarsals, and patella are poorly represented and not butchered. The centroquartal gave a MNI of four. The astragalus is poorly represented but is heavily butchered. The calcaneum is also heavily butchered.

Cervical vertebrae are poorly represented. Thoracic vertebrae occur in about the same numbers as lumbar vertebrae, with dorsal and central body fragments, and whole bones represented, but bones were less heavily butchered. Lumbar vertebrae were represented mostly by the central bodies, with most transverse processes

and dorsal fragments butchered. Sacrum was represented mostly by the cranial and lateral flanges which articulate with the pelvis. These were chopped in various directions. Caudal vertebrae are represented only by fragments. The ribs are over-represented compared to the rest of the body. All proximal ends are butchered and the rest of the ribs are highly butchered into lengths from 50 to 300mm. Out of 167 fragments of longbones, 22 were butchered, split, chopped, and knife cut.

Third-century pits

The fragmentation and butchery patterns indicate that the bones from the pits are not primary but secondary butchery waste. The resulting deposits are heavily biased in certain bones. Scapulae are a significant component of the group, as well as mandible, femur pelvis and metapodials. Caution must be exercised in the interpretation of apparently numerous bones, such as the femur.

All parts of the skull are represented and four very young animals could be identified. Five main types of butchery were noted: heavy oblique chops to horncores and frontal to remove the horncores; chops to the zygomatic arch (usually removing a slice of bone from the lateral side); chops through the occipital condyles and sphenoid during removal of the head (the chops were normally directed to the back of the neck but in some cases from the underside, here the sphenoid was often found chopped too); chops to the temporal facet; and chopping through of the incisive/maxilla. There were two cases (both from F638) of possible poleaxing.

The mandible was heavily butchered and fragmented. Large numbers of tooth row fragments were recovered, often with the basal edge chopped off. Some were nearly complete jaws, but the majority were butchered at the distal and proximal end. There were also chops breaking the jaw into fragments. Two individuals were very young. The MNI from the teeth is mostly from the M3. The premolars are slightly less well represented. Five main types of butchery were noted: through the diastema generally dorso/ventrally, but in some cases through the buccal side; splitting of the horizontal ramus to remove the basal part; chops through the ascending ramus with many variations but usually from the lateral side or with the mandibles held open; chops through the lateral part of the articulation from the ventral side; and gouges to the buccal side of the horizontal ramus.

The scapula is characterised by very systematic butchery and high fragmentation. The glenoid is the most commonly occurring part. High numbers of other parts of the bone were recovered suggesting that whole bones are represented. The spine is frequently chopped off and many spines were recovered. Four main types of butchery were noted: chopping through the spinous process; chopping through the supraglenoid tuber; chops through the glenoid cavity, perhaps as a result of the above; and superficial chops along the caudal, medial, and cranial margins of the neck of the scapula.

Longbone fragments occur in large numbers and are chopped, split, and battered. The sizes of the fragments vary but the majority fall between 20 and 60mm. The humerus is also highly fragmented although the distal end sometimes occurs in larger sections. This end, however, is mostly broken and chopped into medial and lateral pieces. The shaft is fractured into front and back fragments rather than medial and lateral fragments as for other longbones. This is probably due to the shape of the bone but may have been to extract marrow. The proximal articulation again is heavily butchered. Whole bones are represented, although in certain pits, F638 for example, only fragments of proximal articulation were present. This corresponds closely to the situation observed for the femur suggesting that the humerus fragments were removed when the scapula was disarticulated from the humerus. Four main types of butchery were noted: chops to the proximal articulation from distal to proximal often removing parts of the articular surface (both fragments of articulation and larger fragments with part of the articular surface chopped off were recovered); superficial chops to the shaft from distal to proximal typically to the anterior side of the shaft; heavy chops through the distal articulation; and chops to the shaft, often only seem as impact notches.

The radius is consistently split axially and the distal part is less represented than the proximal part. One foetal bone was found. Four main types of butchery were noted: chops through the lateral part of the proximal articulation; chops generally through the anterior part of the proximal articulation and sometimes through the posterior part shaving off parts of the articulation, usually ventro/dorsally; splitting of the bone axially, rather than battering as in the case of the humerus; and chopping through the distal end, mostly dorso/ventrally through the lateral side of the articulation. Most of the ulna fragments were part of the proximal articulation. Three main types of butchery were noted: chops through the olecranon medio/laterally; chops through the articular notch medio/laterally with lateral chops slightly more common than medial (corresponding with chops to the distal humerus); and chops through the posterior side of the ulna.

The metacarpals are less fragmented than other long bones and whole bones are represented. The proximal end was very often chopped axially, or split, giving small medial and lateral fragments. There were also proximal and distal sections of varying size chopped through the shaft. The midshaft fragments were battered, chopped, and split. Both proximal and distal section of varying size chopped through the shaft were also found. Two main types of butchery were noted: chopping right through the midshaft most often from the posterior, but occurring from every direction; and splitting and chopping through the proximal part of the bone.

The pelvis is common and most parts of the bone and whole bones are represented. Of the MNI of 60, 31 are large fragments heavily butchered and defleshed suggesting that very little of the pelvis bone was sold with the meat. Six main types of butchery were noted: chops to the ilium blade and hence the articulation with the sacrum; chops through the ilium shaft, from all directions; chops through the acetabulum, usually medio/laterally, slicing of the most lateral parts of the articulation of the acetabulum; chops through the ischium axially and medio/laterally; chops through the dorsal part of the ischium and acetabular flange; and chops through the pubic parts usually axially and dorso/ventrally.

For the femur the identified distal and midshaft parts of the bone are equally represented. However, the trochanter minor and the lateral proximal parts of the bone have MNIs of eight and four respectively. The MNI of bones may be too low and many more bones are indicated by the presence of large numbers of unidentified longbone fragments, most battered, chopped, and split, presumably for marrow removal. The caput femoris occurs in very large numbers, with 310 fragments. Eight foetal or neonatal bones were recovered. Four main types of butchery were noted: chopping through the caput femoris; chops through the proximal lateral ventro/dorsally; superficial chops to the midshaft, splitting and battering the shaft; and chops through the distal articulation both dorso/ventrally and medio/laterally. None of the five patellae recovered were butchered.

Most of the tibia fragments are small butchered pieces. Shafts were chopped and split with the proximal end heavily butchered. The tibia is less well represented compared to the femur by comparison with the earlier periods. Three foetal or neonatal animals were represented. Four main types of butchery were noted: chops through the proximal articulation, the majority of which redirected ventro/dorsally; chops through the distal articulation mostly directed dorso/ventrally; chops through the shaft with splitting and battering to break up the bone; and superficial chops to the shaft which could be the result of defleshing.

Metatarsal and metacarpal fragmentation was almost entirely due to butchery. Many of the proximal ends were split axially giving lateral and medial fragments, and the small midshaft fragments were chopped, split and battered. Distal ends were complete with varying lengths of shaft attached. The proximal lateral is more highly represented than the medial. Four main types of butchery were noted: chopping to the proximal part of the bone, mostly to the posterior, sometimes with shallow chops posterior/anteriorly, and sometimes dorsoventrally; chops through the shaft both medio/laterally and latero/medially, and posterior/ anteriorly but rarely anterior/posteriorly; battering and chopping of the shaft; and splitting the proximal part of the metatarsals.

Calcaneum fragmentation resulted from systematic butchery. Whole bones and portions of proximal, midshaft, and distal bones were present. Proximal fragments occur more often than distal ones in a ratio of 2:1. The astragalus was represented by whole bones and by butchered proximal lateral fragments, and small distal fragments chopped off the main bone. One main type of butchery was noted: chops through the proximal part, from the medial and lateral. This chopping almost certainly corresponds with the butchery of the distal tibia. The navicular-cuboid was chopped either through the bone dorso/ventrally or superficially on the posterior side. The other tarsals were mostly complete with some butchery and four articulated groups. Carpals were mostly complete but again under-represented. There were three articulated groups. The phalanges were well represented.

The ribs form a large proportion of the assemblage. They were heavily butchered into sections of varying length from 30mm to 290mm and with chopping at both ends of the fragment. The length measurements clustered at 50–80mm, 150mm, and 170–200mm.

Atlas representation was similar to the skull but under-represented compared to the mandible. Two articulated groups were recovered, one with an axis and the other with an axis and three cervical vertebrae. The axis is less well represented with two complete bones butchered in the same way as the cervical vertebrae. Other fragments were cranial articulations. Cervical vertebrae were very under-represented. The most common butchery noted was chopping along the transverse processes. On dismemberment the atlas and axis may have remained with the skull or the cervical vertebrae. There was one observed bifurcated spine on a cervical vertebra and on two lumbar vertebrae. The thoracic vertebrae are better represented by the dorsal spine than the central body. The four most common butchery types were: chopping through the transverse processes, usually ventro/dorsally; chopping through the centrum or articulations transversely, either from the side or dorso/ventrally; chopping through the ventral part of the central body, a method more common to lumbar vertebra; and chopping through the spinous process horizontally, both towards the most dorsal part of the spine and severing the spine from the central body. Lumbar vertebrae are well represented and heavily butchered. The majority of the bones were central body fragments, and the counts for the dorsal and lateral processes were low. The four main butchery types were: chopping off the transverse processes, usually from the ventral side ventro/dorsally, but also caudo/cranially; chopping through the ventral part of the centrum; chopping through the neural arch to separate the dorsal part from the centrum; and chopping through the centrum axially through the medial plane.

Sacrum too are under-represented and butchered in a systematic way. The two main butchery types were: chopping off the transverse processes, possibly during butchery of the ilium; and chopping through the centrum axially. The caudal vertebrae are mostly complete with one group of 14 articulated caudal vertebrae from F638.

The sheep/goat assemblage

Sex and measurements

Sexing of sheep was undertaken using the pelvis and horncores. Atlas and astragalus were also sexed using criteria described by Boessneck (1969). The sexing data were sparse but what there is indicates a majority of females. A pelvis in Period 1 recorded as a male, may well be goat (the MRDA is very large), and an atlas was female. In Period 2 there were two male pelves and one female astagalus. The third-century pits gave the largest sample with four female horncores, ten female pelves with two indeterminate, possibly male or castrate, three female astragali and five male.

Data for assessing the type of sheep at Wroxeter are few in this sample. However, comparing the data with those from the *natatio*, the military phase, and the baths basilica sites, begins to reveal a pattern. Very few horn cores were recorded but those that were invariably oval in cross section. The scapula neck proportions are at the low end of the range given by Noddle (1978) and typical of the Welsh mountain sheep as Noddle observed for her sample from the *natatio*.

Comparing the tibia distal width measurements of the sheep from different phases at Wroxeter there appears to be an increase in the size of the sheep through time. This is also seen when comparing metapodial lengths and withers heights. Sheep size appears to stabilise by the fourth century. Two withers heights of 69.9 and 68.7 stand out as exceptionally large for this assemblage. O'Connor (1982; 1985) has suggested that some Roman samples are made up of a mixture of different sized sheep. Comparison with material from other sites (see references in Luff 1982 and Armour-Chelu 1997) shows, as might be expected, that the picture country-wide is more complicated. Sheep from London and Chelmsford for example are larger than their equivalents at Wroxeter. Maltby (1993, 324) discusses regional variation of sheep in the Roman period, and showed at Exeter (1979) that although the size of sheep increased from the Roman period to the medieval, this was not reflected in withers height but in the widths of the bone.

Information from all the Wroxeter material indicates that the sheep at Wroxeter were of a similar size to many other Romano-British assemblages. They showed some increase in size from the first to fourth centuries AD. The scapula neck proportions indicate a type representative of a fairly primitive long-tailed sheep such as the Welsh Mountain, and Noddle identifies a variety of types from the military and *natatio* samples. Noddle also found a variety of types of horncores of sheep, although the sample reported on here had only one type, oval in cross section and looking very similar to a modern Soay.

Age

Epiphysial fusion data show that there is little change between the three phased samples (Table 4.34). In all phases there is a higher percentage of neonatal or 'porous' bone than is present for either cattle or pigs, and probably some animals were slaughtered at less than one year. However over 80% of sheep survived their first year. The sheep were slaughtered fairly consistently in their second, third, and fourth years (ie between 18 and 42 months), but over 40% of the sheep were older than 42 months at death. This is a higher figure than those from the baths basilica site where only 25% were older than 42 months.

The mandible tooth eruption and wear stage data support the epiphysial fusion data but serve to clarify some differences between the phases. In the Period 1 and Period 2 samples approximately 60% of the mandibles represent sheep less than 30 months at death. However, in the third-century pits about 50% of the mandibles represent sheep older than 36 months at death, ie PM4 was in wear, and about 15% of the mandibles were relatively old with wear stages of 36+. These results should be treated with caution. The sample sizes are different and the two earlier phases are quite small in comparison with the third-century pits sample.

Generally the age profile for the samples from all phases suggests that the sheep represented here were reared and slaughtered mainly for meat. They would have provided one or two fleeces, but following the argument suggested by Maltby at Exeter (1979, 46) most of the breeding stock or those kept for wool-growing purposes, and most of the infant mortalities, would not have found their way to market in Wroxeter.

Table 4.34 Animal bone: summary of sheep age data

	fusion state	porous	unfused		fused	
		n	n	%	n	%
period 1	age group	10 (+20 small ungulate)				
	1 birth		2	10	19	90
	2 0-10 months		5	14	32	86
	3 15-24 months		6	33	12	67
	4 36-42 months		9	60	6	40
	5 42-48 months		4	40	6	60
	6 very late		9	56	7	44
	6 very late small ungulate		25	69	11	31
period 2	age group	21				
	1 birth		1	4	22	96
	2 0-10 months		4	19	17	81
	3 15-24 months		10	34	19	66
	4 36-42 months		5	56	4	44
	5 42-48 months		6	67	3	33
	6 very late		13	81	3	19
third-century pits	age group	34				
	1 birth		7	7	90	93
	2 0-10 months		16	19	70	81
	3 15-24 months		26	27	71	63
	4 36-42 months		23	47	26	53
	5 42-48 months		27	56	21	44
	6 very late		31	56	24	44

n number of examples

Pathology and anomalies

Not many sheep bones with pathological conditions were recorded. One sheep radius from Period 1 had marginal osteophytes on the lateral edge of the proximal articular surface. A jaw from Period 2 had porous bone on the buccal side of the horizontal ramus, and another jaw had calculus.

There were more specimens from the third-century pits. One jaw had the permanent second premolar missing. Four exhibited malocclusion: one with interdental wear between PM4, M1, and M2 irregular wear, lingual side higher; on a second the anterior cusp of M1 is higher than the rest of the tooth row, interdental wear between PM4/M1; a third jaw has an extra foramen on the buccal side below the permanent third premolar, and interdental wear between PM3, PM4, M1, and M2, the fourth permanent premolar looks misshapen, and there is irregular wear on M1. Two mandibles and two maxillae had calculus.

Five mandibles all exhibited a similar condition. One had an extra foramen on the buccal side of the diastema, two jaws had an extra foramen below the permanent third premolar on the buccal side (one of these had irregular tooth wear described above), and one had extra foramen below the deciduous third premolar on the buccal side although this may be an epigenetic trait.

Other bones with pathologies were a first phalanx which had extra bony growth around the distal joint surface, a small ungulate rib was fractured, and another had changes to the proximal articulation consistent with a dislocation which had developed an alternative articular surface.

Butchery and body parts

The representation of different anatomical parts of sheep is very similar from all three periods. All parts of the body are present, but small bones tend to be under-represented relative to the whole body. The proportion of skull and mandible is low compared to many assemblages where they dominate the figures, and the proportion of the longbones, particularly the tibia, in the whole sample is high. All parts of the bones are equally represented, with some under-representation of the more vulnerable and therefore less well preserved unfused articular ends. Only 5% of the sheep bones from Period 1, and 9% from Period 2 were butchered. This contrasts with the 28% from the third-century pits.

In Period 1, one skull was split by chopping through it axially, as was a cervical vertebra which was chopped from caudal to cranial. A thoracic vertebra was chopped medio-laterally. Chops were also recorded on the scapula, and to the shafts of metacarpal, femur, and tibia. A pelvis was also chopped through the acetabulum with repeated blows. Only one record of knife cuts was made and this was to the anterior of a tibia shaft.

The bones from Period 2 showed more butchery marks in a more consistent manner. One mandible had a superficial chop on the lateral side of the ascending ramus. The radius was chopped through the midshaft, as was the femur. The femur was also chopped through the proximal lateral medio-laterally. The pelvis was chopped through the pubic part of the bone and through the acetabulum. The tibia was the most commonly butchered and the most commonly occurring bone. It was chopped either through the medial, or the lateral, or the posterior side of the midshaft. In three cases the bone was chopped through both the proximal and distal parts of the shaft giving a portion or joint of the bone. In one other tibia the anterior part of the proximal articulation was chopped dorso-ventrally removing the anterior section of the bone. One calcaneum was butchered, this was chopped repeatedly on the posterior side. Knife cuts were observed on one metatarsal on the anterior of the proximal articulation, and one other metatarsal was chopped through the medial midshaft medio-laterally. An axis was butchered in such a way as to suggest that the head was removed here rather than chopping through the occipital condyles as in cattle. The caudal end was chopped through medio-laterally and the cranial articulation were chopped or cut repeatedly but superficially, suggesting disarticulation. Butchery to cervical vertebrae include splitting axially and removal of the transverse processes.

The third-century sample is larger, but the proportion of the sample butchered is also larger. This suggests that the sheep bones in the pits were subjected to a higher degree of processing than those from the earlier periods, and may suggest that these bones too were part of the specialised activity taking place around or in the *macellum*.

Horncores were removed by chopping through the basal part close to the frontal bones, both frontals and horncores were recovered butchered in this way. Skulls were split axially by chopping through the top of the skull presumably to remove the brains. No clear pattern of butchery to the mandibles was observed, although all parts of the bone were observed to be chopped in similar ways to that of the cattle mandible. The fragmentation of this bone suggests that all parts of the bone were recovered in the same quantities, the extreme distal and proximal parts being slightly less well represented probably due to their greater fragility. Only five mandibles were observed to have butchery marks; one was chopped through the lateral diastema medio-laterally and the ventral edge of the horizontal ramus was chopped off also, a second mandible was chopped through the ventral part of the horizontal ramus also, another was chopped through the tooth row from the lateral medio-laterally, and another through the medial medio-laterally, one mandible was chopped through the proximal part.

The scapula was generally chopped through the medial side of the neck medio-laterally, and in one case the spine was also chopped of as with the cattle scapulae. Other chop marks were noted to the articulation.

Butchery to the humerus exhibited a pattern. Typically the bones were chopped through the midshaft and either knife cuts or chop marks were also noted to the distal joint. Some superficial chops to the shaft possibly as a result of deboning were observed. General chopping-up of the bone, splitting and battering of the bone into smaller fragments was also noted. The fragmentation shows that the distal part of the bone is more highly represented than the proximal and this is also seen in the epiphysial fusion data. This may be the result of differential preservation or of the proximal part being removed as a joint along with the scapula.

Butchery to the radius and ulna was of three basic types, very like the cattle butchery; chopping through the shaft either from the lateral medio-laterally, or through the medial medio-laterally, or indeterminate. The latter was generally midshaft but sometimes slightly to the proximal. The bones were also split, chopped, or, as in one case, chopped through the posterior of the proximal end axially splitting the bone. The last type of butchery observed was dorso-ventral chopping at the articulations, very much like that described for the cattle, in one case to the ventral part of the posterior and medial edges of the proximal articulation, and in other cases around the distal articulation shaving off slices of bone from the lateral, anterior and posterior edges. The fragmentation shows that all parts of the bone are represented equally. Metapodials were mainly split axially, in three cases chops were observed for this, or battered to fragment the bone.

The pelvis was commonly chopped through the ilium shaft medio-laterally, most commonly from the medial side, also through the ischium shaft either through the medial or dorso-ventrally, and one ischium was chopped axially. The acetabulum was also chopped through the pubic part, and chopped through dorso-ventrally, and medio-laterally. Again all parts of the bone are represented more or less equally. So too was the femur although there was some under-representation of the more vulnerable unfused articular ends. Chops were typically through the shaft medio-laterally, from lateral medio-laterally and through the medial medio-laterally, and from the posterior anterior-posteriorly. The bone was also chopped up by splitting axially and battering. In one case the caput femoris was chopped through from the ventral dorso-ventrally and the shaft was chopped superficially possibly for deboning.

The tibia was the most commonly occurring element, with nearly 60% of all tibia fragments butchered in a consistent manner. As with other elements the more vulnerable unfused articular ends were under-represented, otherwise all parts of the bone were present. Two main types of butchery were observed on the tibia. Chopping through the shaft either once or twice, giving joints of different sizes with the articular end or a portion of shaft only, usually from the lateral medio-laterally or from the medial medio-laterally, but also from the posterior. The second type of chop was to the articular ends, at the proximal usually dorso-ventrally from the ventral up the tibia crista, also to the lateral, medial, and posterior also dorso-ventrally. Similarly to the distal articulation chops from the dorsal were downwards through the lateral edge, the anterior face, and the posterior face. Chopping and battering of the shaft into fragments was also observed.

The atlas was split axially, and the axis was mostly chopped through medio-laterally, but in one case was split axially. Six cervical vertebrae were butchered. They were chopped through medio-laterally, and split axially, and the transverse processes were chopped off. Thoracic vertebrae had the transverse processes chopped off, and one example was split axially. Lumbar vertebrae too had their transverse processes chopped off, split, and chopped through medio-laterally.

The pig assemblage

Age and sex

The number of mandibles that could be aged by tooth eruption and wear stage was few. In all phases there were porous bones but very few mandibles under one year (ie with second molar erupting). It is likely that the bones of neonatal and juvenile pigs are under-represented due to recovery and preservation bias, but very young pigs are present. All the mandibles in Periods 1 and 2, and 13 out of 16 mandibles in the third-century pits have unerupted or unworn M3s. The animals must therefore have been slaughtered before reaching 20 months (Sissons and Grossman, 1975). The epiphysial fusion data (Table 4.35) indicated for all phases that pigs were being killed at around one year

Table 4.35 Animal bone: summary of pig age data

	fusion state	porous n	unfused n	unfused %	fused n	fused %
period 1	age group	1				
	1 birth		1	5	19	95
	2 12 months		4	21	15	79
	3 24 months		19	86	3	14
	4 24–30 months		5	100	–	–
	5 36–42 months		2	100	–	–
	6 very late		12	92	1	8
period 2	age group	4				
	1 birth		–	–	19	100
	2 12 months		7	37	12	63
	3 24 months		23	72	9	28
	4 24–30 months		11	100	–	–
	5 36–42 months		3	75	1	25
	6 very late		16	94	1	6
third–century pits	age group	23				
	1 birth		–	–	56	100
	2 12 months		9	23	30	77
	3 24 months		65	80	16	20
	4 24–30 months		29	94	4	6
	5 36–42 months		11	92	1	8
	6 very late		24	96	1	4

n number of examples

followed by a major cull at around two years (or the equivalent age associated with the fusing of the bones in age group three to four). This is consistent with the exploitation of pigs for meat, skin, and lard etc, and is observed on many sites. Some older pigs are present represented by the later fusing bones and a few mandibles with third molar in wear.

Sexing was undertaken using the upper and lower canines. This showed a mixed sample with a majority of males. However, the sample size is very small and the aged mandibles were mostly unsexed.

Pathology and anomalies

From Period 2, one scapula was recorded as having a pit in the glenoid articular surface, probably similar to those described by Baker and Brothwell as non-pathological (1980), and also described as osteodystrophic lesions by Noddle. One maxilla had a rotated fourth premolar.

From the third-century pits a jaw had crowding of the tooth row with the first permanent molar pushed buccally and the second permanent molar pushed lingually. One maxilla had lost the first permanent molar antemortem, had deformed roots to the second permanent molar, and had deformed roots and an antemortem break of the third permanent molar with bone resorbed around the affected areas. In another maxilla the second and third permanent premolars were joined together.

Other pathologies noted were all from the feet and lower limb. From Period 1, one metapodial had a bony growth on the shaft, and from Period 2 a fibula had a healed fracture. In the third-century pits sample, a fourth metacarpal had extra bony growth around the proximal articulation, a third metatarsal had swelling and distortion of the proximal articulation which could have been the result of an infection or other bone disease, and a calcaneum had extra bony growth on the anterior and lateral sides at the distal end.

Butchery and body-parts

The bias caused by the effects of differential preservation is difficult to assess. Gnawing probably had some effect on the survival of some bones and the collection bias to larger fragments will also have affected the sample. The proportion of bones gnawed was higher in the third-century pits, and so was the proportion of bones butchered, which suggests differential preservation between the phases if not different use and disposal. There seems to be a higher proportion of limb bones in both Period 2 and third-century pits, despite the fact that these bones are the most commonly gnawed and therefore subject to loss. This also suggests that there is some difference between the phases in the way pigs are being utilised and their bones disposed of.

The occipital condyles and atlas were chopped through to remove the head. The zygomatic arch and ascending ramus of the mandibles were chopped through to remove the mandibles as with the cattle.

The mandibles were then split through the front. The scapula was chopped through the symphisis between the incisors from the lingual to buccal, and the pelvis through the ischium, ilium, and acetabulum. The humerus was commonly chopped and battered into fragments, and the forelimb was disjointed at the elbow. The ulna and radius were chopped through the shaft, and the radius was also broken up into fragments. In Period 2, the femur and tibia were more often chopped through the shaft but in the third-century pits, the femur was battered like the humerus and the tibia split axially. The hindlimb was disjointed at the astragalus and calcaneum.

The Period 1 butchery mainly dismembered the carcass. The scapula was chopped through the neck and the humerus through the shaft. The pelvis was chopped through and the astragalus through the distal end. Knife cuts were also noted on the astragalus. Cervical and thoracic vertebrae were chopped through axially and split, the axis was chopped through transversally to chop off the head. The transverse processes were chopped off the lumbar vertebrae. Superficial defleshing chops were seen on the shaft of the radius.

Similarly in Period 2, butchery was also for dismembering the carcass and chopping it up into usable portions. The skull was split axially, by chopping through the top dorso-ventrally, repeated chops were noted to the occipital condyles presumably for removing the head. The front of the mandibles were split by chopping from the lingual side, sometimes with repeated blows. Scapulae were chopped through the neck either through the lateral side or the medial side, some knife cuts were observed either for defleshing or dismembering. The humerus was chopped all over, and the shafts broken up. Radius and ulna were chopped through the shaft and knife cuts found around the proximal end of the ulna were probably the result of disjointing the carcass. The femur was chopped through the shaft from the lateral side, and the tibia was chopped through the distal part of the shaft from the medial rather obliquely. Knife cuts were observed on the astragalus and metatarsal. The atlas was chopped through transversally, and the axis was split axially. Lumbar vertebrae had transverse processes removed by chopping, they were also chopped through the caudal transversally.

The larger sample from the third-century pits showed a pattern consistent with the previous phases. The occipital condyles were chopped to remove the head. The frontals and temporals were chopped and the zygomatic arch was chopped mediolaterally in a similar way to that observed for cattle to remove the mandibles. The mandibles were split through the front, and chopped through the ascending ramus from the lateral side, as in the cattle, presumably to remove them from the skull. The scapula was typically chopped through the neck either from the lateral or the medial side. The humerus was often split or battered. In these cases percussion marks could be seen but no

chop marks, sometimes chopmarks were also associated with the breaking up of the bone, other more superficial chops gave the appearance of filletting.

Another typical butchery method to the humerus was chopping through the distal part of the shaft or the distal articulation usually from the medial side but also from the lateral, anterior, and the posterior. Butchery to the proximal end was less common. The radius was also split and battered, and also split axially with observed chop marks at the distal and proximal ends. The radius was also chopped through the medial side of the shaft mediolaterally. The ulna was mostly chopped through the proximal joint latero-medially and anterior-posteriorly, and chopped through the shaft. The pelvis was chopped through the ilium, the ischium from the lateral medio-laterally, and through the acetabulum. The femur was again battered and split, also with associated chops chopped through the proximal medial obliquely, and chopped through the midshaft. The tibia again was often battered and split, and chopped at the proximal to split the bone axially, one tibia was chopped through the distal part of the midshaft medio-laterally, common in sheep tibia but not on pigs. The fibula was chopped through the shaft, the calcaneum was chopped, and both the astragali were chopped on the medial side medio-laterally. One rib was chopped at the proximal end. The atlas was commonly butchered, and lumbar vertebrae were either chopped and split axially or had their transverse processes chopped off.

Other mammals

Nine bones were identified as red deer. A mature butchered ulna was found in Period 1, and, from Period 2, a large mature butchered ulna, two complete first phalanges, and a piece of antler not identified to species, which was sawn. From the third-century pits, a scapula which was butchered in a very similar way to the cattle scapulae, was measured and is rather smaller than that found in the military phase (Noddle forthcoming). The fragment of metatarsal was possibly worked, and one piece of antler was sawn. One other piece of antler not identified to species, was recorded as shaved.

Only one bone was tentatively identified as fallow deer as noted in the introduction. This was a tibia from Period 2 and it was butchered. Two roe deer bones were also identified from Period 2, a radius and a metacarpal, both butchered. Four roe deer bones from the third-century pits were recovered, a jaw, a butchered scapula, a humerus, and a femur.

Only seven bones were identified as horse, of these three were complete and measured. A radius from Period 2 gave a withers height of 12 hands and is similar in size to ponies commonly found in the Iron Age. A metatarsal from the third-century pits also gave a withers height of 12 hands. This bone had knife cuts around the proximal end, and was porous and pitted on the posterior edge of the proximal end and on the proximal joint surface, consistent with the effects of an infection. The metacarpal also from the third-century pits is much larger, around 15 hands, and is of a similar size to the metatarsal reported on from the military phase described as a large pony (Noddle forthcoming).

Most of the dog bones (79%) came from two skeletons, 1 and 2, deposited in the third-century pits. The remainder were either individual bones or partial skeletons. There was evidence on the baths basilica site that dogs had been left to decompose with the bone subsequently dispersed (Armour-Chelu 1997), and the same may have been true for these examples. The incompleteness of the skeletons may be the result of disturbance of burials but is more likely to reflect the level of recovery.

The number of specimens giving withers heights is small but other measurements and comparison with known breeds, shows that a range of different sized dogs were kept. The largest seems to be in the middle of the range given by Harcourt (1974) for the Roman period.

Of the five dog bones from Period 1, four were found together (pelvis, femur, and two tibia), and probably come from one animal. The dog appears to be rather small judging from the pelvis measurements. It was smaller than Skeleton 1, somewhere between a fox terrier and a miniature poodle.

Nineteen of the 33 dog bones from Period 2 were found together and were probably from one animal (skull, maxilla, temporal, mandible, humerus, pelvis, femur, fibula, atlas, six vertebrae, sacrum, two teeth). This animal is larger than Skeleton 1. A pair of immature femurs were also found, and three bones from the same context may also be from the same individual. The other specimens are all single bones from layers and gave few measurements. Two mandibles from the same context were measured and compared to Skeletons 1 and 2. Of these one is very big, and the other rather small. Another specimen, a humerus, was smaller than a fox. Only two bones were pathological. A mandible had broken pieces of the first permanent molar present and the bone was resorbing around them, and a lumbar vertebra had marginal osteophytes around the articulations, possibly the start of some more serious condition, but one not affecting the articular surfaces.

Skeletons 1 and 2 found in the third-century pits account for 196 of the 211 dog bones from this phase. None of the other bones gave withers heights but morphological comparisons with known breeds of dog, suggest breeds similar in size and robustness to a Jack Russell (scapula), a small and gracile breed slightly larger than the miniature poodle (humerus), and a breed similar in shape and size to the fox terrier (pelvis). One specimen, though immature, was seen to be similar in size to the greyhound (humerus). The two skeletons themselves have withers heights ranging from 48.7–51.2 (average 49.7) and 46.6–48.0 (average 47.2), which is in the middle of the range found by Harcourt (1974).

Skeleton 1, the larger of the two skeletons an adult male (baculum present), was found in pit F561. Almost all the skeleton was present, except the lumbar vertebrae and nearly all the smaller bones, ie metapodials, carpals, tarsals, and phalanges. This most probably reflects the level of recovery although why the whole lumbar section except the first should be missing is unclear. Four caudal vertebrae were recovered. The left humerus had slight swelling on the posterior lateral shaft near the foramen and the right humerus had a swelling on the posterior lateral shaft just below the foramen, this pathology is present in all the other forelimb bones except the scapula. The right radius had swelling and distortion in the shaft possibly due to either breakage or some type of osteomyelitis, the left radius had swelling and distortion on the shaft similar to the other radius. The right ulna had swelling and distortion to the proximal part of the shaft, also a small amount of bony growth near the distal end possibly periostial infection. The left ulna had a small bony growth osteophyte near the distal end on the posterior side.

Skeleton 2 was found in F855. It was almost complete except for part of the pelvis, sacrum and caudal vertebrae, part of the right leg, and nearly all the carpals and tarsals. No baculum was found. This individual was also adult, and had three abnormal bones; a rib, 11 or 12, had a healed fracture, the eleventh thoracic vertebra had holes in and extra bony growth around the facets for the ribs, and the twelfth thoracic vertebra also had pitted rib facets.

The bird assemblage

A total of 283 fragments of bird bones was recorded from the samples reported on here. Of these over half were domestic fowl. Measurements of the tarsometatarsus are comparable with those from the military phase. Of the tarsometatarsi from all phases four had fused spurs, four had spur scars, and nine were definitely unspurred, indicating that neither sex was reared preferentially. Only two immature bones were recovered, both domestic fowl from Period 1, but this may reflect bone survival and the recovery methods. Only two bones were butchered, one goose scapula from Period 1, and a fowl coracoid from the third-century pits, both had knife cuts around the proximal articulation.

Woodcock is the next most abundant species. This was also common in both the military material and the bones from the baths basilica. Ducks and geese were also caught locally. Secure identification to species was in most cases not possible here. Two of the bones listed as unidentified, were probably crane. It is quite possible that the pigeons and ravens were living within the city, but there was no indication as to whether they were eaten or not.

All the abnormalities observed on the bird bones came from the bones assumed to be domestic fowl, and only the humerus and tarsometatarsus were affected. Single examples of humeri from Periods 1 and 2 had a healed fracture midshaft, and a humerus from the third-century pits had a massively distorted and swollen shaft. A tarsometatarsus with an unfused spur was broken below the spur scar and showed signs that healing had started to take place before the bird had died.

Discussion

The exploitation of animals

A variety of cattle were exploited judging by the number of different horncore types observed. The two main types were both short horned, but others were noted including a horncore very like those from the small cattle typical of the Iron Age. There is also some evidence for an increase in the size of the cattle over the period studied. From all periods the cattle were mainly female, and generally about half the animals were fully mature at death. A variable proportion of the animals were immature, and about a third of the animals were aged between three and four years old at death. A predominance of beef in the diet is entirely to be expected in a Roman town (King 1984).

The sheep seem to have been from a homogeneous stock with only one type identified, and there appears to have been some improvement between Periods 1 and 3. There was little evidence of pathologies. In Periods 1 and 2 the majority (60%) of animals were younger than 30 months at death, suggesting that these animals were reared for meat. In Period 3, however, over half of the animals were older than three years at death, suggesting a possible change in husbandry. Sheep butchery, as illustrated by bone in one of the pits, appeared to be quite different to the pattern for cattle.

Pigs were slaughtered mostly between the ages of 1 and 2 years. This is commonly observed on other sites and is consistent with the keeping of an animal with a high reproductive rate, exploited for postmortem products only. Evidence for the keeping of pigs in the city is inconclusive although porous and neonatal/juvenile pigs were found. Sexing implies a majority of males but the data are too few to reconstruct a definite picture of husbandry methods. Butchery patterns were slightly different to those for cattle and sheep.

Wild pig, birds, and two or possibly three species of deer were present, suggesting hunting and catching, presumably locally, for prized produce. Hunting does not appear to have provided much meat for Wroxeter in the later phases, but the incidence of butchery and working on the bones recovered indicates that the animals represented here were probably eaten and the antler and bone used for making objects. As has been noted elsewhere, woodcock was the most favoured wild bird, with ducks and geese not so commonly found. The most common bird was domestic fowl, and this may well have been kept for both eggs and meat. A range of dogs were kept from small to large (up to *c* 500mm withers height). Dog skeletons were buried in

pits and also seem to have been left lying in the open as was observed in the basilical hall. Horses ranged from 12–15 hands or small Iron Age pony to large pony size. Some knife cuts around the metapodial could indicate skinning of ponies.

Periods 1 and 2

The bone samples from Periods 1 and 2 are much less clearly defined than that from the third-century pits. The Period 1 bones may have been redeposited material from the fortress, although there are sufficient differences to suggest that this was not the case. The Period 2 bones may have derived from redeposited fortress material disturbed by the building work or from dumped material brought in from outside. However the deposition pattern of other finds suggests that an appreciable quantity of the artefacts were deposited along the Watling St frontage suggesting that items were sold there during the long construction period. The presence of a significant quantity of butchered bone, much of it showing the same pattern as that from the *macellum*, may indicate that food products were sold along Watling Sreet during the second-century building campaign. Unfortunately bone was not collected from the Period 2 dumps to the east of the site so any concentration of bone waste on Watling St cannot be confirmed.

The macellum *assemblage*

The assemblage from the *natatio* and from the portico pits is the first collection to be published in detail in Britain that can be linked with a *macellum*. The great majority of the bone from the pits in the west and south porticos came from adult female cattle that had been systematically butchered. The butchery waste was, for the most part, deposited directly into the pits with little evidence, such as weathering and chewing, that it had been initially dumped elsewhere. The porticos around the *insula* of a major public building would not have been the site of slaughtering of animals or of waste left exposed for long, and the bone must have derived from the *macellum* or from stalls selling meat from around its entrance. The latter are assumed from the fourth-century evidence, which includes both structural remains and quantities of animal bone, and from the use of the forum porticos in the second century (Atkinson 1942). The pits also contained a significant number of iron hooks perhaps used to hang meat from. The cattle present would represent a good sample of the type of animal brought to the *macellum* area, presumably as carcasses.

The most striking feature of the bone content of the pits, particularly well illustrated in pit F638, was that certain anatomical parts were highly represented whilst others were largely absent. The most commonly occurring cattle bones were scapula, mandible, ribs, pelvis, and caput femoris. Ribs, pelvis, and femur have the highest meat value (Binford 1978), and it would seem likely that these bones were waste after meat had been filleted from them. Mandible and scapula, also of high meat value were similarly filleted out, along with the central body of the lumbar vertebrae. Other meat-bearing bones of medium value such as thoracic and cervical vertebrae, humerus, skull, and tibia, occur in far lower quantities; perhaps a higher proportion of these bones were sold with the meat to end up in the household. Other bones present in the pits represent a mixture of low value meat bones such as metapodials and phalanges deposited as waste. These low value meat bones are even more poorly represented than the medium value meat bones, and they may have been deposited elsewhere before the carcasses came to the market. Sheep tibia and pig humerus were also particularly abundant.

The cattle bones from the baths and *macellum* site, omitting the *natatio* collection, can be grouped according to Binford's (1978) criteria into four categories ranging from high quality meat bone to lowest quality meat bone (Table 4.36). Category 1 was represented by ribs, pelvis, and femur; Category 2 by mandible, scapula, and lumbar vertebrae; Category 3 by thoracic and cervical vertebrae, humerus, radius, ulna, skull, and tibia; and Category 4 by metapodials, phalanges, carpals, and tarsals etc. The results underline the suggestion that the bone waste from the Period 3 pits was from good quality meat cuts, but also indicates a similar picture for Periods 1 and 2.

Other methods for gauging the significance of this kind of data have been discussed and suggested by O'Connor (1982; 1984) and Levitan (pers comm). Table 4.37 gives the number of fragments expected for the different parts of the skeleton, the numbers actually present, and the minimum number of individuals represented from the third-century pits. These give an idea of how many of the bones have remained in the assemblage, whether all parts of the body are represented equally, or whether certain bones are exceptionally abundant. The data suggest that the pit bone is a very specialised assemblage in contrast to Periods 1 and 2 where the whole skeleton appears to be more evenly represented (data in archive).

Not all the bones in these pits was butchery waste. The pits combined, to various degrees, bones from different activities; there was throughout a component of household rubbish and one pit contained the semi-complete skeleton of an adult male dog. This material seems likely to have arrived in the pits as a result of levelling up over the sunken primary fills.

Table 4.36 Animal bone: types of cattle butchery waste (after Binford 1978)

| | category | | | |
	1	*2*	*3*	*4*
period 1	43.1	20.0	27.1	9.8
period 2	59.8	14.5	16.1	9.6
third-century pits	62.5	15.7	14.0	7.8

Table 4.37 Animal bone: representation of anatomical parts from third-century pits (no of fragments/%)

	F455	*F471*	*F486*	*F547*	*F638*	*F675*	*F462/F561/ F801/F855*
mandible	32/13	12/14	123/9	15/14	186/18	24/13	409/13
maxilla	3/1	2/2	22/2	1/1	21/2	4/2	55/2
skull	51/20	18/23	110/8	22/20	231/22	36/19	488/16
loose teeth	30/12	3/4	68/5	7/7	64/6	20/11	204/7
scapula	11/4	18/23	245/19	7/7	135/13	34/18	467/15
humerus	7/3	3/4	94/7	9/8	18/2	3/2	141/5
radius	3/1	1/1	52/4	2/2	6/1	2/<1	69/2
ulna	6/2	1/1	44/3	3/3	14/1	-	76/2
os coxae	30/12	6/7	105/8	10/9	82/8	18/10	265/9
femur	12/5	6/7	160/12	6/6	124/12	19/10	340/11
tibia	3/1	1/1	68/5	6/6	11/1	2/<1	98/3
carpals	1/<1	-	9/1	2/2	6/1	3/2	23/<1
astragalus	1/<1	1/1	15/1	1/<1	4/<1	1/<1	23/<1
calcaneum	1/<1	-	23/2	1/<1	15/1	1/<1	44/<1
tarsals	2/1	-	8/1	2/2	2/<1	1/<1	15/<1
metacarpal	9/4	2/2	34/3	1/<1	26/3	7/4	83/3
metatarsal	24/10	4/5	51/4	5/5	35/3	4/2	131/4
metapodial	2/1	-	5/<1	-	2/<1	-	9/<1
phalanx 1	8/3	2/2	24/2	2/2	27/3	2/<1	71/2
phalanx 2	6/2	2/2	22/2	1/<1	13/1	2/<1	48/2
phalanx 3	9/4	1/1	18/1	3/3	15/1	3/2	51/2
vertebrae	(41)	(21)	(182)	(14)	(240)	(28)	(564)
ribs	(141)	(61)	(1271)	(115)	(1668)	(555)	(3975)
total	251	83	1300	106	1037	186	3110

totals exclude ribs and vertebrae, skull includes horn cores

The bone collection from the infilled *natatio* reported on by Barbara Noddle below is directly comparable with the butchery waste in the pits. Although it is possible that the *natatio* infilling included general rubbish, it seems highly likely that the bone deposited there can be closely linked with the *macellum*. While the similarities between the portico pit and the *natatio* contents could suggest that the portico pits contained only *macellum* waste, they seem more to suggest that butchers' waste from the *macellum* and from portico booths was similar.

Any reconstruction of the pattern of meat sales and consumption from the bone waste has to accept that some meat may have been sold on the bone and would therefore be absent from the record. Certain meat joints from cattle, pig, and sheep, and categories of meat such as poultry and game may well have been sold to be either cooked on the bone or filletted in the home. Fish bones were entirely absent. This seems unlikely to reflect a recovery bias, and if fish was sold from the *macellum* it must also have been prepared by the purchaser rather than the vendor. Some of the more exotic animals and birds sold in the *macellum* as attested from literary records may also have been prepared in the purchaser's kitchen (de Ruyt 1983). The bone waste from the pits does however suggest the types of meat that were sold ready filleted. Generally in urban assemblages it is difficult to be sure whether waste bone was of high meat value and had been filleted out, or of little meat value and thus disposed of in the first stages of preparing the carcass. The Wroxeter deposit, however, must be presumed to exclude waste

from carcass preparation and to have resulted from waste at the point of sale to the consumer. The recognition that bone from high value meat was filleted out means that the absence of those bones in domestic rubbish deposits need not imply poor households. There is evidence for the cooking of filleted meat in the Roman period with beef and veal often sliced and served in an elaborate sauce.

Studies of animal bone from Romano-British urban sites suggest that the slaughtering of animals and the processing of their carcasses was frequently undertaken on central sites. At Dorchester, the *insula* adjacent to the forum and baths was the site of processing of animal carcasses (Maltby 1993, 315). Bone there was heavily gnawed suggesting that bone waste was initially deposited in middens. At Wroxeter, *insula* 2 may have served the same function. It is also possible that slaughtering occurred on the farm and carcasses were brought to town as may have happened at Gatcombe (Branigan 1977, 201).

In a discussion of the Romano-British economy, Maltby (1984) highlighted a number of urban butchery assemblages. Table 4.38 repeats data from his paper with some of the Wroxeter material expressed in the same way. Primary butchery waste is seen as the material resulting from the initial preparation of carcasses to remove parts such as hides and horns to be processed separately. At Silchester a large number of scapulae and pelves were interpreted as indicating that some disjointing of the carcasses took place as well. At Gloucester, where scapula and pelvis with caput

Table 4.38 Animal bone: butchery assemblages from Romano-British sites after Maltby 1984 (no of fragments/%)

	Exeter	Silchester	London St John	Cirencester	London AC7	London AC9	Gloucester 1 Westgate St
mandible	258/37	35/15	198/17	605/23	24/16	54/10	9/4
maxilla	30/4	6/3	48/4	140/5	2/1	10/2	1/0
skull	87/12	48/21	604/51	552/21	11/7c	123/22d	6/3
loose teeth	148/21	18/8	134/12	330/13	17/12	38/7	6/3
scapula	9/1	23/10	1/<1	143/5	5/3	32/6	81/39
humerus	1/<1	6/3	4/<1	89/3	10/7	26/5	9/4
radius	6/1	1/<1	8/1	71/3	4/3	26/5	6/3
ulna	-	2/<1	2/<1	21/<1	-	8/1	3/1
os coxae	15/2	11/5	8/1	65/2	-	4/<1	33/16
femur	11/2	2/<1	1/<1	119/5	2/1	6/1	20/10
tibia	7/1	5/2	1/<1	108/4	-	18/3	6/3
carpals	1/<1	-	-	7/<1	-	-	1/<1
astragalus	-	2/<1	-	14/<1	-	-	-
calcaneum	2/<1	3/1	-	24/<1	-	-	3/1
tarsals	-	-	6/1a	19/<1	9/6a	11/2a	1/<1
metacarpal	26/4	21/9	-	71/3	24/16	71/13	3/1
metatarsal	86/12	27/12	-	190/7	38/27	115/21	12/6
metapodial	-	2/<1	84/7b	-	-	-	-
phalanx 1	10/1	11/5	27/2	27/1	1/<1	3/<1	8/4
phalanx 2	1/<1	6/3	14/1	16/<1	-	2/<1	2/1
phalanx 3	1/<1	-	24/2	12/<1	-	3/<1	-
vertebrae	(128)	(19)	(165)	(230)	(5)	(34)	(29)
ribs	(102)	(77)	(45)	(536)	large no	(42)	(68)
total	699	229	1164	2623	147	550	210

totals exclude ribs and vertebrae
a all carpals and tarsals; b metacarpals and metatarsals; c all horn cores; d includes 98 horn cores

femoris were dominant features, the collection was again described as carcass trimmings. At Cirencester, primary butchery waste and the waste from disjointing, filleting, and marrow extraction from the whole carcass, were all present together. The Wroxeter assemblage differs from these collections in the numbers of ribs and vertebrae present. While it is difficult to distinguish primary and secondary butchery in some collections, the Wroxeter pit and *natatio* groups may be taken to represent secondary specialist butchery waste.

Understanding the bone assemblage from the portico pits is hampered by the absence of detailed reports on animal bone from other *macellum* sites. At Leicester a number of cattle skulls were found predating the *macellum* when the site was not in use, while at Cirencester, pits containing butchery waste were found both within and outside the *macellum*; but at neither site are there further details. On the continent, animal bone assemblages are reported from *macellum* sites by de Ruyt (1983). These comprise Alba Fucens where mainly cattle bones were found, Geneva, Ordona in Apulia, Morgantina, Sicily, the Republican *macellum* at Pompeii, and Baelo, Spain.

The literary evidence might lead to the expectation of a *macellum* assemblage of predominantly immature bones. However the age profile at slaughter of the cattle sold at the Wroxeter *macellum* was not significantly different to that from other Romano-British urban animal bone collections. This could be an indication that *macella* in the Province were not as specialised as their Mediterranean counterparts. It might also reflect that farming in the Wroxeter hinterland did not respond to the demands of the *macellum* for high quality meat from younger animals, through a desire to maintain the breeding stock, although it may simply have been the Romano-British practice that cattle were not generally slaughtered before maturity and that this practice remained uninfluenced by specialised demand.

Animal bone from the *natatio*

by Barbara Noddle

Introduction

The following report on the natatio animal bone collection was written in 1982 (Noddle 1982).

The animal bone assemblage from the *natatio* is of unusual interest, since it is such a large group perhaps accumulated during a relatively short period. It may be assumed in these circumstances that once the material was buried there was little intrinsic loss due to fragmentation as a result of surface activity. However it should not be assumed that this group is representative of all Wroxeter bone at this time, since there may have been specialisations of the catchment area which affected the assemblage.

Though the bone is in an excellent state of preservation, the majority of the long bones are very fragmented. Consequently there was some difficulty in distinguishing between some of the bones of the larger species, cattle, horse, and red deer, and between the small ruminants, sheep and goat (roe deer was not identified); as a result of this, cattle and sheep are probably overestimated at the expense of the less frequently occurring animals (Table 4.39).

Methodology

Following identification an attempt was made to establish the minimum number of individuals, not only for the whole group, but also for each bone, as a means of determining the relative frequency of the anatomical parts. The numbers were established in as much detail as possible, using measurements and age structure as well as the most frequently occurring element. Bourdillon and Coy (1980) consider that the animal individual concept is not valid for an urban site where retail butchery can be assumed to have been practised, but they were dealing with smaller groups of bone within a very large assemblage.

Measurements of whole bones and frequently occurring parts of mature bones were carried out according to the methods of von den Driesch (1976), except that distal measurements of the metapodials were taken at the epiphysial line. Weighing was not carried out as the bone had already been sorted by other workers, and in any case was heavily contaminated by soil..

The minimum number of animals was aged whenever possible (Table 4.40). Chronological ages were not employed, as the commonly accepted data (Silver 1969) may not apply to animals of some 2000 years

Table 4.39 Animal bone: *natatio*, species present

animal	fragments		MNI	
	number	%	number	%
cattle	1767	65	75	47
sheep	448	17	47	37
goat	28	1	6	4
pig	306	11	14	9
horse	38	1	5	4
dog	9	<1	3	2
cat	3	<1	1	<1
red deer	81	3	4	3
fallow deer	2	<1	1	<1
total	2683		155	

Table 4.40 Animal bone: *natatio*, age range of commonest species

animal	neonatal		juvenile		immature		mature		total
	no	%	no	%	no	%	no	%	
cattle	3	6	2	4	10	19	37	71	52
sheep	4	8	4	8	26	54	14	30	48
pig	2	14	3	21	4	28	5	36	14

ago. Also their validity has not been fully established in some cases. Instead, stages of maturity were employed as follows:

Neonatal: from birth up to the maturation of the first fusing epiphysis and the appearance of the first permanent molar

Juvenile: up to the appearance of the third permanent molar and first permanent incisor, and the maturation of the earliest group of epiphyses (phalanges, distal humerus, and proximal radius)

Immature: until all cusps of the lower third molar are in wear and all epiphyses are mature with the exception of the vertebrae and the pelvic bones

Mature: after all these events are complete.

In modern terms these ages would be about four months, about 18 months, and about four years, but tends to be considerably later in male cattle castrated at birth (Figdor 1927).

Species represented

Table 4.39 presents the relative numbers of species, as fragment counts and as individuals. The total identified bone count was 2683 of which 65% originated from cattle, sheep came second in frequency and pig third. Goat, horse, dog, and cat were present in small quantities, red deer were slightly more numerous and there were two bones considered to have come from the same fallow deer. There were also a few bird bones; these have been evaluated separately. When these findings are compared with the previous military period at Wroxeter, it can be seen that the proportion of cattle has increased at the expense of cattle and sheep (Noddle forthcoming).

Age

The age range of the individuals of the three major species is presented in Table 4.40. Percentages have been calculated for the sake of comparison, but this apparent precision is not justified by the small numbers available in some instances. The majority of the animals were mature at death. This mature proportion was highest amongst cattle and lowest among sheep; the proportion of newborn and juvenile animals was the opposite of this. However the majority of sheep were immature. In all cases there were more mature animals than in the military period, the greatest increase being amongst cattle.

Economy

Assuming that the *natatio* assemblage is a true representation of all the animals killed at Wroxeter at this time a number of economic inferences can be made. The bulk of the meat consumed was beef with mutton in second place and pork third. Hunting played a limited part in the meat supply and was probably not a commercial enterprise. The high proportion of mature cattle in particular suggests less than opulent circumstances as the best carcasses from the slow maturing animals likely at this period would come from immature animals, and juvenile animals would be killed from necessity rather than choice; however, horn and hide would be of greater relative value than they are today. Mature animals are likely to have provided other economic returns beside the carcass in the form of offspring, labour, or wool according to species.

The cattle bone measurements, and in particular the horn cores, suggest that the majority of the bones came from females. The only bone where there appears to be a diphasic peak which might indicate two sexes is the lower third molar, and here the situation is complicated by the number of teeth which have a reduced posterior cusp (those where it was absent have not been included). About half the vertebrae were immature indicating an age of greater than 6 years in the case of females. The proportion of mature animals is higher than at other Roman sites including the military period at Wroxeter (48%). It is of course possible that male horn cores were not found because they were preferentially removed to a workshop for manufacture. It is also possible that there was a particular reason for cows to be slaughtered in the catchment area of this rubbish dump such as the presence of a tannery, but if this were so one would have expected a greater proportion of phalanges than found. Otherwise the inference is that meat consumption in Wroxeter at this time was so low that it could be supplied by local agricultural surplus, and there was little demand for specially reared beef animals. The same argument cannot be made for the pig because this animal has no economic function other than to supply meat or offspring; there is a possibility that animals were kept for a long time to accumulate fat as happened in the eighteenth and nineteenth centuries (Noddle 1981). However, the numbers involved are so small that they may be fortuitous. Only the sheep shows signs of having been reared deliberately for meat, and here again the skin may be of considerable value.

Types and size of animals

Some evidence of animal size and type is also supplied by the bone measurements (details in archive). The cattle were of a normal size for Romano-British settlements. An estimate of live weight made from the dimensions of the astragalus (Noddle 1973) is as follows: 158, 162, 173, 178, 207, 209, 223 (2), and 257 kg. For comparison a modern Friesian cow weights about 550 kg. The horn cores were all of one type and oval in cross section, though not quite as markedly so as the Celtic shorthorn typical of many Iron Age sites. The size and curvature are reminiscent of the modern Friesian, although no direct relationship is suggested. Another non-metrical characteristic which may go with breed is the position of the nutrient foramen of the femur. This is either above the supracondylar fossa or medial to it. Of 13 examples 9 were in the supracondyle position, or 70%, a much higher proportion than that found in modern British animals including breeds of supposed ancient origin.

The sheep were a less uniform group. This is indicated both by the horn cores and the shape of the scapula neck; the other measurements indicate a fairly uniform group of normal Romano-British size. The horn cores were all oval in cross section at the base with one exception, but the larger horns were less oval, and perhaps the two groups were females and male castrates. However, one specimen was perfectly circular and there were also two polycerate (four-horned) skull fragments, two rudimentary horns or scars and two polled frontal bones. The direction at which the horn core projected from the head was also variable, being either lateral or backwards. The scapula neck proportions also suggest divergent types. Though the majority have a length-width ratio of unity, typical of a fairly primitive long-tailed sheep such as the Welsh Mountain, there is also one short thick mutton type and three specimens with the long thin neck typical of the short-tailed primitive Soay (Noddle 1978). The sheep of the military period were also variable; they were characterised by prominent orbits, which could not be detected in the more fragmentary *natatio* material. The military sheep group contained a higher proportion of primitive scapulae.

As usual there is little to say about the type of pig. There are some larger bones; these are thought to have originated from wild boar. Otherwise the animals were again of typical Romano-British type, though they are a little larger on average than those of the military group.

Bone measurements from horse indicate large ponies. The red deer are typical of the period, considerably larger than the present day Scottish animal.

Pathology

As might be expected, there were a number of congenitally abnormal and pathological specimens although no unusual conditions were observed. Apart from one spavined horse hock, and a sheep calcaneum with osteomylitis, all abnormalities were bovine. Out of 43 mandibles with complete adult tooth rows, 32 had the normal complement of six teeth, ten lacked the second premolar, and one lacked both this and the third molar. The five tooth condition has been discussed by Andrews and Noddle (1975), and the skeleton of a Chillingham bull with only four teeth is exhibited at the Oxford University Natural History Museum. A total of 107 lower third molars had the normal posterior fifth cusp present, but in 12 it was absent, ie 10% – a normal proportion.

Amongst 105 first phalanges, one had arthritis of the proximal joint, another one had distal exostoses and osteomylitis and there were two cases of low kingbone. There were four small osteodystrophic lesions, two proximal and two distal. Out of 37 second phalanges there was one case of proximal joint arthritis, and two small osteodystrophic lesions, one proximal and one distal. These conditions are discussed by Baker and Brothwell (1980). There was a further case of osteodystophy in a mandibular condyle. There was also a lesion present on a metatarsal shaft, thought to be the result of a haematoma. It is perhaps worthy of note that none of the sheep mandibles exhibited periodontal disease.

Bones present and butchery

The anatomical analysis of the bones is of considerable interest, particularly that of the cattle bones. Except in the case of immediate burial of a carcass, it is rare for all the available bones to survive burial and excavation. A high proportion of all bone is lost from surface material, 83% within 6 months in the trial conducted by Brain (1976). Not all bones disappear at the same rate which is influenced by their basic composition (cancellous or compact) and also by the ultimate treatment of the bone after the flesh has been removed (tertiary butchery). Guilday (1977) who had some idea of the input of bones to his eighteenth century colonial military camp in Canada recovered only about 0.004% of possible bones. However the anatomical composition of the surviving sample tends to be fairly constant under natural conditions (eg Brain 1976; Voorhies 1969) and any deviation from this may be evidence for the use made of the bone and its taphonomy. The anatomical details of the three principle species show nothing notable about sheep and pig, but a number of hypotheses are suggested by the cattle bone. The numbers of individual animals represented by each bone are very varied, from 72 for the scapula, 65 for metacarpals, 50 by mandibles and loose teeth, down to very small numbers for the small carpal and tarsal bones. It appears that heavy bones such as skull and scapula were defleshed in the catchment area of this deposit. The majority of scapulae exhibited a characteristic butchery which is not peculiar to this site; 60% of these bones had the base of the spine removed, 15% had the spine completely removed, and in 25% it was untouched. Despite the name of this bone being taken from the Latin for shovel, there was no sign of these bones being used as tools (Curwen 1926). The large number of complete metapodial bones, the preferred raw material for the manufacture of bone needles, also indicates that bone was in excess of need for this purpose. The relative paucity of the other limb bones was probably because they had been chopped into unrecognisable pieces for the purpose of soup manufacture (von Mensch 1974) or for the extraction of fat from the marrow, a process that is graphically described for the Caribou Eskimo by Binford (1978). The latter explanation seems the most likely; this would also explain the large quantities of scapulae, a solid bone useless for this purpose.

5 Discussion
by Peter Ellis

The early town

The Period 1 buildings may represent similar structures to the late first-century/early second-century shops at Verulamium (Frere 1972, figs 10 and 11). There the street frontages were occupied by successive commonly-roofed blocks (*ibid*, 15). A single unit was argued on the basis of the presence of internal party walls which would not have allowed drainage between separate elements and thus indicated a single roof. The structures at Wroxeter are similar, although whether one or two units are represented is not clear.

A timber building, successively Rooms 1.10 and 3.7, set on the surviving footings of a demolished legionary mess hall, formed the core of the Period 1 buildings. Other similar military stone buildings are known at Wroxeter from aerial photography in the same position between the *via sagularis* of the fortress and the rampart. They, too, may have been reused in the early town, perhaps in some cases as standing buildings, and their survival as cropmarks suggests retention through the lifespan of the town, unlike the excavated example. Similar re-use of military buildings is attested elsewhere, as at Colchester and Gloucester (Crummy 1988, 42; Hurst 1988, 56).

The street frontage was formed by adding timber-framed buildings to the west of Room 1.10/3.7. It was not clear if a single range was represented in the excavated area. A two-storey structure was suggested at Verulamium and is possible at Wroxeter. There was no evidence of buildings directly to the rear of Room 1.10/3.7 although timber structures added to north and south expanded eastward beyond the line of its rear wall, and a garden may have been maintained here judging by the presence of layers resembling buried soil.

Arrangements to the east of the excavated buildings saw rubbish pits lying on, or east of, the line of a former military store building from the last military phase (Webster forthcoming). It might be that the area of the former store building was retained for some purpose that prohibited the excavation of pits. Within its former confines only the latrine pit and the truncated features to its west were found; there was also evidence for mortared surfaces. All these features and surfaces were, however, sealed beneath an overall soil and demolition horizon which was easily identified across the eastern excavated areas. This layer would then represent a change in use before the public buildings when the whole area east of the Period 1 buildings was perhaps cultivated.

A standard pattern suggested for late first- and second-century buildings is for a shop on the street frontage with workshops behind and private accommodation further to the rear with increasing prosperity bringing additional private rooms (Perring 1987, 150).

At Wroxeter many of the rooms to the rear of the street frontage have hearths and floors such as would be expected in private accommodation, and there is also a bias in the distribution of finds away from the street frontage. There was, however, no evidence for the function of Room 1.10/3.7 itself.

Evidence of buildings using similar construction methods has been found elsewhere in the town, and their date and context can now be reviewed in the light of the *insula* 5 evidence (Fig 5.1). On the opposite side of Watling Street in *insula* 4 were the remains of beam trench and post structures on the street frontage beneath the later forum (Atkinson 1942, fig 5), while on the opposite side of the road in *insula* 9 to the south of Buildings 2 and 4, a single frontage trench 20m long was all that could be planned of what may have been three phases of occupation (Kenyon 1981). Other parallels came from *insula* 8, south of *insula* 4, where first and early second-century structures with party walls were replaced by individual timber-framed units (Bushe-Fox 1913, 21; 1916, 1 and 4). These lacked front wall trenches, suggesting that they were shops with open fronts presumably closed off with wooden shutters out of business hours (Frayn 1993, 108).

The date of these buildings, summarised by Atkinson (1942, 123), is earlier than those suggested for the *insula* 5 buildings. The *insula* 4 buildings were suggested to occur in two phases between AD 60 and AD 90, while the sequence on Sites I-IV in *insula* 8 commenced AD 80, and at Site VI AD 75. The buildings were presumed to have been from the fortress *canabae* and thus based on a road running north south in front of the west face of the fortress.

The *insula* 4 dating evidence was based on the assumption that the timber-framed buildings were sealed beneath the *palaestra* of the early baths, and this evidence served to date the baths to *c* AD 90 with a suggested abandonment date in the first decade of the second century (Atkinson 1942, 23, 123). Atkinson's *palaestra* is supported by Mackreth (1987, fig 58). A later date *c* AD 120 has also been suggested (Webster 1993, 49). Webster's argument also involves *insula* 5 and is discussed further below.

However, the evidence for a *palaestra* for the early baths can be interpreted as relating instead to the later forum in which case the dating evidence falls (Bidwell 1982, 87; see Mackreth 1987, fig 58). The context of the early baths can then be seen as military, as its design suggests. It may have been intended for a projected new fortress for *Legio XX*, abandoned *c* AD 90 when the legion was transferred to Chester (Frere 1987, 104, n 20). A bath house as the first civilian building initiative is not parallelled elsewhere in the Province (Wacher 1995).

338

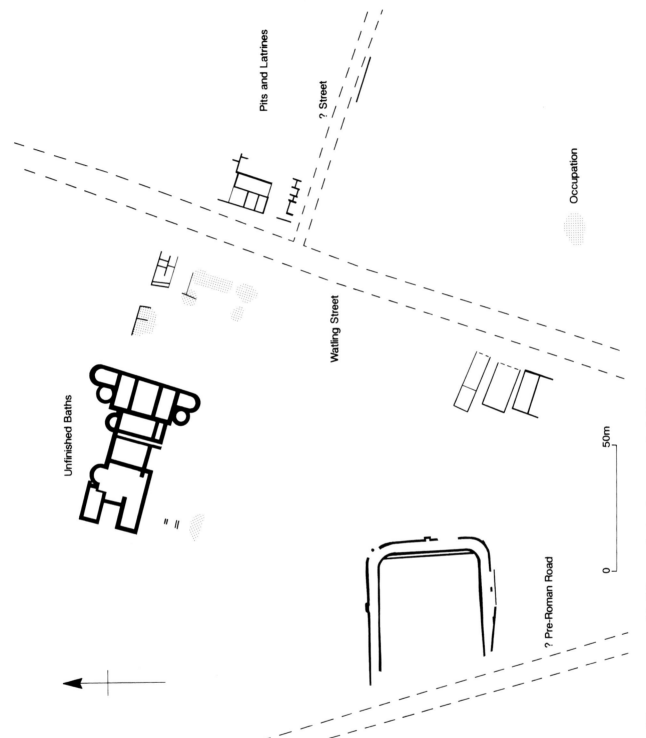

Pits and Latrines

? Street

Occupation

Watling Street

Unfinished Baths

50m

0

? Pre-Roman Road

Fig 5.1 Late first-century Wroxeter, excavated buildings and other features; scale 1:1500

If the evidence for a baths *palaestra* is brought into question, then the timber-framed buildings can be seen as postdating the baths. Their position suggests that they must also postdate the fortress. A road and buildings fronting its defences would not have been possible until the fortress ditch had been infilled. The pre-AD 90 pottery recorded by Bushe-Fox must be seen as residual.

In summary, the presumption must be that the early baths were begun in the 80s and left unfinished *c* AD 90 possibly within a western annexe of the fortress, itself also left unfinished. The early town layout after the final abandonment of the fortress commenced with the establishment of a street grid, with Watling Street representing a relocation westward of the former main route through the centre of the fortress. Shops and houses in *insulae* 4, 5, and 8 were established along this route.

A comparison of these buildings suggests that the room sizes on *insula* 5 were smaller than those on *insula* 4 and 8. These latter were large and seemed to form individual structures, underlining the interpretation of the *insula* 5 layout as that of a single building. This might be taken to indicate that the more complex buildings lay within the former fortress area, as might be expected if it formed the core area of the early town, and that simpler individual shops-cum-workshops lay outside.

The initial plan

Graham Webster has suggested a different solution to the problem of the early baths by arguing that just as the forum on *insula* 4 was preceded by baths, so the baths on *insula* 5 were preceded by a forum (Webster 1988b, 142; 1991, 67; 1993). However this theory is not supported by the excavation evidence. The origins of the argument lie in the analysis of the *insula* 5 site by Kenyon, herself following George Fox. Faults in the analysis by Kenyon have been highlighted above. In addition to the view that the north side of the Old Work was an exterior wall, Kenyon introduced the argument that the east and west walls of the main baths were reused from a preceding building. She suggested the quarters of an officer while Dr Webster favours these being part of a forum range.

Other elements of the *insula* 5 forum plan are suggested to be the disused walls butting the baths walls, evidence for a proposed monumental entrance from the south, the double sleeper wall at the west end of the south portico, and the unused trenches beneath the *macellum* (Webster 1993). Each of these elements has been differently explained in this text. The main argument in favour of the baths building being intended as a baths *ab initio* is that its side walls indicate a span which can only be matched in Roman architecture by other baths buildings.

The lines of the walls of baths, basilical hall, and west range seem to have been marked out by slight trenches backfilled with small stones and light-coloured sand. This was the case in the basilical hall where such a trench was seen at the east end marking a preliminary layout before it was realised that access was necessary from the hall to the baths precinct (Barker *et al* 1997). One of those beneath the *macellum* may represent the east wall of a proposed layout which would have seen rooms the depth of 17 and 18 continuing down the west frontage. This argument would place both the *macellum* and the latrines as a secondary element in the plan.

The construction process

The excavations allow insights into the construction process. The initial plan, as has been seen above, was laid out on the ground in the form of trenches. In the examples found under the *macellum*, the spoil from these was left on either side of the trench which was backfilled with small stones. All previous buildings and any undergrowth must have been cleared beforehand.

The drainage system was primary with drain sides integrated into the walls of buildings. The construction process involved the initial building of walls to about waist height. The sequence as seen at the *macellum* was logical and carefully prepared. Both here and on the *insula* as a whole, access was from the south. As the first wall rises were completed the ground level was brought up by dumping, and access was maintained to the new levels by subsidiary areas filled with dumps as in the west portico. These were presumably approached by ramps although none was found. Some but not all of the levelling material derived from the construction trenches.

Plans were modified during the building work. Some unused trenches may have been cut by mistake, others may have been abandoned in changes of plan, as at the east end of the basilical hall. Built items, such as the walls in Rooms 8 and 10 may have been removed soon after they were constructed, while the treatment of the wall between Rooms 3 and 4A/4B was changed radically. The flexibility of approach is particularly marked by the decision to double the width of the main load-bearing walls to provide additional support for the vaults over the *tepidarium* and *caldarium*.

Evidence for the testing of the depth of foundations occurred across the site. Sixteen examples of 'inspection pits' were found. These were cut to the full depth of existing footings against the face of the foundation and rapidly backfilled. Occasional examples of pits dug against walls are found elsewhere, but no examples match the scale of the inspection pits at Wroxeter.

The stone used changed during the building campaign. One reason may have been that the Keele Beds red sandstone quarry source became exhausted, another that a newly opened Hoar Edge Grit quarry was cheaper, or the stone more easily won, and a third that a quarry simply ceased production for a while, perhaps for a reason unconnected with demand (Adam 1994, 24).

Evidence from the construction of the third century *thermae* in Rome suggests short time spans dictated by the nature of the buildings whose vaults would have needed to be rapidly erected (Yegül 1992, 152).

Although vaulted buildings at Wroxeter may have been rapidly erected, it is clear that the *insula* 5 programme took much longer than the 10 years or so to build the forum on *insula* 4. This would presumably have been because the building work was undertaken *pari passu* with the receipt of income for the town. While the baths buildings may have been completed, perhaps only as a shell, their fitting out, completion, and the provision of *palaestra* and porticos may have taken 20–30 years; donations perhaps acting as a spur. The inspection pits may therefore reflect the return to a building campaign of fresh teams with no memory of the extent of earlier work. Long building campaigns in Roman towns have been paralleled with those attested for the medieval cathedrals (Todd 1989, 88).

The parallels between the building periods for the forum and baths at Wroxeter, and those suggested by Duncan-Jones (1990, 177) for a city's annual income to fund public buildings (11 years for a forum, 33 years for baths) is of interest. For much of the time the *insula* would have resembled the large scale building projects which Pliny the Younger found abandoned unfinished in Bithynia (Duncan-Jones 1990, 67).

The forum was dedicated to Hadrian, and Dr Webster has suggested that Hadrian himself would have taken an interest in the urban programme at Wroxeter and might have funded it perhaps by remission of taxes (Webster 1990, 2). Hadrian's interest in encouraging urban public building projects is well attested and can be shown in other parts of the Empire (Duncan-Jones 1990, 66). His travels brought him to the region in AD 122 (*Scriptores Historiae Augustae, Vita Hadriani*). However, the architectural evidence from the Province does not support the suggestion that the *civitas* capitals were built with direct grants from central government (Blagg 1980). Further, the Wroxeter evidence suggests a continuing and high level of financial commitment to public buildings over a long period starting with the forum, and the progress of construction does not reflect that it was resourced by one major grant from outside. The long building timescale and the costs of maintenance and repair over the succeeding centuries, suggests that the wealthy inhabitants of the town must have played the major part in funding its buildings, whether through the *summa honoraria* or through private donations – although these are rarer in the northern Provinces than elsewhere on the evidence of inscriptions (Duncan-Jones 1990, 184; Millett 1990, 82). The dynamic of urbanisation in the province seems not to have been affected by outside grants, and seems to owe more to competition between towns than between individuals and families.

The baths

The parallels between the Wroxeter baths and the Flavian baths at Chester have been noted (Fig 5.2; Mackreth, Chapter 3). Similar Corinthian column capitals from the two sites have suggested a regional architectural style (Blagg 1980, 33). Motifs in the *caldarium* roof painting design have parallels with sites to the south and have suggested workshops with shared stylistic traits based on the Severn valley (Davey and Ling 1982, 201). That ambitions for expensive architectural details may have outstripped resources is illustrated by the undecorated capitals in the basilical hall which may originally have been left until funds were raised.

The similarity between the contemporary baths at Colonia Ulpia Traiana (Xanten) and those at Wroxeter is also striking (Fig 5.2; Nielsen 1993, cat no 153; pers comm Roger White). Analysis of the two different Corinthian column capitals used in the Chester area suggests that Chester's masons were not felt to be adequate for the ambitious building programme, and that masons were therefore imported from Trier (Blagg 1980, 39). These continental links support the suggestion that the civilian settlement had a large military element (Webster 1991, 48), and hint at the possibility of some military involvement in the Wroxeter building programme.

The additional *caldarium* and the alterations in the west *laconica* do not seem to be paralleled in the plans of other baths. Essentially the alterations in the late third/early fourth century were to the *praefurnia* of the two *laconica*, shifting these from the north to the south sides of the outer rooms. In addition, on the west side the opportunity was taken to add a *caldarium*, Room 12, with the additional *praefurnium*, Room 13. A similar arrangement would not have been possible on the east side because of the higher ground level. Additional *praefurnia* are well attested, and it is therefore Room 12 which requires explanation rather than Rooms 13, 9B, 9C and 11C. It seems unlikely that this was a replacement for Room 6. The arguments for the abandonment of the latter are based on the door blockings between 3 and 4A and B. If these did take place in the third or fourth century, they could have been intended to retain heat. The added *caldarium* may have been built for exclusive use for a high status group, or for the use of women, and may have been a reaction to the widening of citizenship in the later third century. Alternatively the evidence may be taken simply to suggest that use of the baths required more *caldarium* space in the early fourth century implying an increased population or increased social or geographical access. The use of public buildings and baths at different times of the day allowed class and gender separation to be maintained (Laurence 1994, fig 8.3). Whatever the explanation the rather *ad hoc* and idiosyncratic arrangements witnessed at Wroxeter reflect a practical approach to the building, apparently uninfluenced by the classical standards of the core of the Empire which might have ruled out such a development.

The function of baths has been recently discussed (Yegül 1992). Two points made there may be underlined. The first is that bathing acted as a social bond between peoples of different origin. The common experience, widely spread through different social strata and shared, although at different times of the day, by

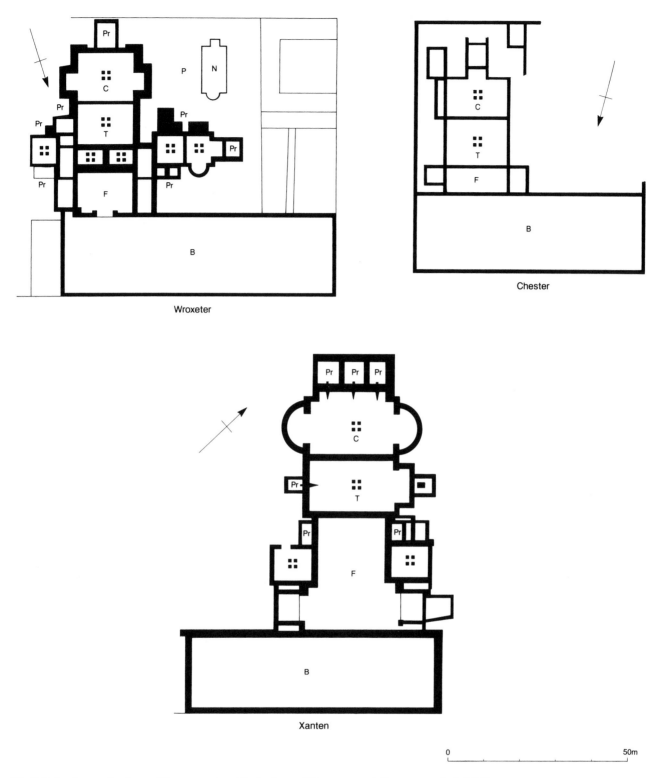

Fig 5.2 Legionary baths at Chester and public baths at Wroxeter and Xanten; scale 1:1000

men, women, and children, could be seen as under-scoring the commonalty of the participants (Yegül 1992, 2). The second point is that the basilical hall acted as the heart of urban social and educational life; more so than the forum perhaps because this was a public space without a clearly defined function (*ibid*, 400). In this respect it is of interest that the forum was apparently not rebuilt after its destruction in the third century, while excavation has demonstrated the inten-

sity of continuing use in the basilical hall. Both points suggest that the baths and basilical hall at Wroxeter were genuinely popular.

The *macellum*

The *macellum* was a feature of Italy and other Mediterranean and Danubian areas of the Empire rather than the northern provinces (de Ruyt 1983, passim and foldout 1). Its distinguishing mark, according to de Ruyt, is the presence of an enclosed area with the booths looking inward to a central court, where access by way of a major entrance way on one side of the enclosure was easily controlled. This would have provided security and may too have underlined the fact that this was a market place with restricted social access.

The exteriors of the buildings were nondescript, while the interiors were highly decorated. The principal decorative element was some kind of central focus in the inner courtyard or in a recess in the wall facing the entrance: a *tholos*, fountain, or statue). Drainage systems were elaborate and often linked with main drains nearby. *Macella* were also generally raised above surrounding levels, and the interior walkways above the courtyard. *Opus spicatum* walkway floors are known at the Hadrianic Esquiline *macellum* at Rome and, later, at Timgad.

The *macellum* would have been open every day (de Ruyt 1983, 365; Frayn 1993, 4). It sold best quality meat, poultry, and game, sea and fresh fish, crustacea, and vegetables, and may also have sold good quality grain, bread, and perhaps dairy products and spices. Ham and sausages are also suggested. Meat would have been from animals freshly slaughtered and butchered elsewhere in the town and provided ready for purchase (Frayn 1993).

Although supplies to the *macellum* may have involved middlemen, direct supply by the producers would have been the general case (de Ruyt 1983, 364; Finley 1973). Sources would have been the better off estates and market gardens (Frayn 1993, 19, 30). Cash crop agriculture is frequently noted near towns with *macella* (*ibid*, 54), and this may have been the case at Wroxeter where market garden layouts are suggested nearby (Ellis *et al* 1994, 67). These may have been contemporary with the construction of the *macellum* (*ibid*, 68).The booths may have been let on a long-term, semi-permanent basis, and run by the nominees of the lessees (Frayn 1993, 104). The *macellum* would have been used principally by the chief families of the town. The exchange of gifts and entertainment was important in Roman society (Duncan-Jones 1974, 139) and dining was an important finale to the bathing ritual (Yegül 1992, 39). Although a high status function would have accounted for much of the daily sales, the *macellum* was not exclusively for the rich, and the poor may also have used it from time to time (de Ruyt 1983, 370). In addition, it would have furnished provisions for dinners on special occasions such as weddings and funerals, or for the *curia*, for public feasts, for *collegia*, for cult observances, for magistrates, or as gifts (Duncan-Jones 1974, 29, 136, 139, 149, 182, 202, 269, 281, 283; de Ruyt 1983, 369, 370).

How much of this can be applied to *macella* in towns on the periphery of the Empire is difficult to gauge. The Wroxeter building itself does not suggest any deviation from the norm. The drain beneath the building and the very solid foundation covering the

whole courtyard area, suggest that a fountain was placed within the central court. The space is restricted by comparison with other sites, but a similarly sized courtyard at Geneva was provided with a drain, and a lead spout was found suggesting a central fountain there (*ibid*, 74). A higher level in the interior of the building was indicated early in the levelling process within the *insula*. In none of the other *insula* 5 buildings examined in modern excavations is there the two-stage infilling apparent in the *macellum* courtyard. The walls were plastered with good quality materials for which minerals were sought which would enhance the whiteness of the plaster, and were painted to resemble marble. The walkway around the courtyard was carefully floored in the second phase of the building and a latrine was provided. The north-east corner room would have served as a stairwell to an upper storey, with access from a corridor room to its west. Finally, Wright located a number of weights in the courtyard (Chapter 6, para 6.4).

Despite widespread excavation in towns in the province, only at Cirencester, Verulamium, and Leicester have similar sites been identified (Fig 5.3). The Wroxeter *macellum* is smaller than these and has smaller booths. At Cirencester pits filled with animal bones were found both around and, unlike Wroxeter, within the building (Wacher 1962). At Verulamium, a second-century building was partially rebuilt repeating some of the earlier walls in the late second century (Richardson 1944). At Leicester, a *macellum* with aisled hall was built in the late second or early third century on the site of a domestic courtyard house (Wacher 1959; 1995, figs 2 and 160). The painted plaster decoration of a ceiling from this building has been restored (Davey and Ling 1982, cat no 23). The buildings at Verulamium and Leicester are rejected by de Ruyt as true *macella* (de Ruyt 1983, 268, 338), although the second building at Verulamium falls within her definition of a type 2 *macellum* with the apsidal structure presumably containing some kind of focus (de Ruyt 1983, pullout 4). The first Verulamium building and the Leicester building may not fit exactly into de Ruyt's categories but it is hard to see what function they had other than as *macella*.

It could be argued that although the social context of the *macellum* in Roman Italy need not have been repeated at these sites, the choice of building one would have been thought to bring credit to the city. The success of the Wroxeter building, marked by its refurbishment and evidence for its use late in the fourth century if not in the fifth, might mean that the habits and wealth of an elite amongst its inhabitants maintained the building in something reasonably similar to its specialised function nearer the centre of the Empire. However it is also possible that the building was adapted to the special needs of the inhabitants over time. A possibility is that initial market buildings may have found a later use simply as lock up stores. Indeed the two building forms may not have differed very much.

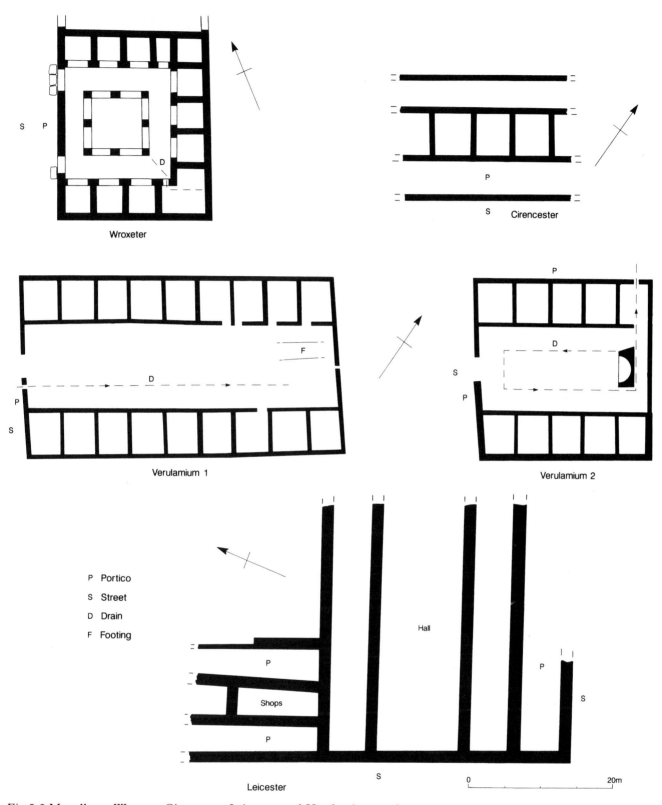

Fig 5.3 Macella *at Wroxeter Cirencester, Leicester, and Verulamium; scale 1:500*

At Ostia store buildings with lock up rooms have *opus spicatum* courtyards and are very similar to the town's *macella* (Meiggs 1960, 277). The main difference is suggested to be the presence of a front wall and door in the store building rooms.

The role of *macella* as the focal point of market systems may indicate that they were thought essential in imposing Romanised customs on existing and flourishing markets in addition to the provision of fora, and this may well have been the case at Wroxeter where a market may have preceded the *macellum*, as argued below. If the argument below is correct that at Wroxeter *insulae* 4 and 5 were the focal point of a weekly market throughout the Roman period, then the building of a *macellum* may have been thought of as a way of Romanising the process and distinguishing the different status of inhabitants.

Insulae 4 and 5 at Wroxeter therefore seem the epitome of Romanisation. In the streets and under the covered walkways the important citizens could make their way from home to forum. When business there was finished they could themselves order their dinner at the *macellum*, and then spend the afternoon at the baths before returning home to entertain guests at the evening meal (Laurence 1994). The rites of public life involved ceremonies, shows, and handouts (Duncan-Jones 1990, 159) and these would have taken place in the public buildings at the heart of the town. The buildings, although public, would also have represented an individual's home as much as a private residence. Ulpian (quoted in Duncan-Jones 1990, 159) defined domicile as the place where a man makes his purchases, sales, and contracts, and where he goes to the forum, the baths, and the shows.

Portico market

If the identification of the Period 1 post-military structures as shops is accepted, then these may have provided the impetus for the location of markets. A market here may have been a *nundinae* market held weekly (MacMullen 1970; Frayn 1993, 3). It seems certainly to have been taking place in the second century on the other side of the street since market stalls selling honestones and pottery were caught up in the fire on the forum *insula* (Atkinson 1942, 127).

The excavations in the *insula* 5 porticos uncovered market evidence from the third century onward, and indicate that other items may have been both made and sold, including metal objects as witnessed by the crucibles. Food, attested by the animal bone assemblages, was also sold, and would have represented the main part of the items which changed hands. The later fourth-century areas of worn cobbles may indicate the upper surfaces of a generally levelled surface partly made up of stone rubble. However it is possible that the areas represented the position of individual market pitches; two separate structures were indicated in the south portico by trenches for sill beams. The surfaces succeeding the concreted gravel surfaces of P 3.3 were all strewn with animal bones.

The contents of the pits in the baths *insula* porticos seem unlikely to represent waste from permanent market stalls. Waste disposal from the latter would have been organised and would not have taken place beneath the stall placements. The pits may indicate the waste at the end of the market day, from market vendors who did not belong in the town and who were making use of whatever waste disposal method was to hand. Frayn suggests that the market may have ended as early as eight or nine o'clock in the morning (1993, 22). Other explanations are possible, as for instance that the pits were themselves rubbish containers which

were regularly cleaned out, or that the pits were dug for some other reason and only used secondarily for waste.

The archaeological evidence suggests that a market flourished here from the first century and was not a product of the public buildings or Romanisation. The longstanding nature of regular places of exchange is underlined by MacMullen (1970). Although there is no evidence on *insula* 5 of market activity, other than the pits, until the late fourth century, it must be seen as highly likely that the porticos were regularly used on market day, as were those outside the forum opposite. The surfaces laid and relaid indicated general use by pedestrian traffic as would have been the daily case, and this traffic must have increased again on market day.

Insula 5 in the late- and post-Roman period

Proving the existence of fifth-century structures depends on demonstrating stratified sequences starting from a securely dated base in the later fourth century (Esmonde Cleary 1989, 148). The potentially fifth-century portico sequence in the porticos starts from whenever the final concreted gravel surface of phase P 3.3 went out of use. This surface was laid soon after AD 346 on the basis of an unworn coin incorporated in it. An earlier similar surface lasted with heavy patching and repairing from almost a century before.

The south portico was subsequently reinstated at a higher level, and the west portico and the west end of the south portico were re-floored with large stones which survived for a long period judging by their heavy wear. When the portico roofs were demolished and the drain running down the outside of the portico sleeper wall had been lifted, stone paths and surfaces spread out toward the street located 10m from the *insula* buildings. The paths led from the street to the two *macellum* entrances and to the baths corridor. Evidence of market activities was recorded in the basilical hall excavations in the porticos outside the basilical hall and, definitely in the fifth century, inside it.

The late paths and spreads outside the *macellum* can be dated to the fifth century, since they seal a robbing trench with coins giving a *terminus post quem* of AD 395. A very large number of late fourth-century coins were found on these later levels, but still later coins were found in the robbing trench; therefore none of the fourth-century coins is the same date as the paths. Furthermore the coin evidence indicates that Wroxeter was not receiving a similar proportion of late fourth-century coins by comparison with the core urban sites in the diocese, suggesting that the coin evidence will not reflect the true date of any late Roman sequences (Brickstock and Casey, this volume).

De Ruyt points out the longevity of *macella* in the Empire (1983, 270); the continuation of the Wroxeter example into the fifth century is thus a strong possibility judging by the maintenance of its entrance. The same is unlikely to be true of the baths. Servicing a baths complex must include a stable supply network; the baths would need to have been maintained 24 hours a day with constant fuel supplies, and a paid workforce in charge of the daily running. From the evidence in the diocese generally it must be assumed far more likely that public baths would cease to be in use at the end of the Roman period in AD 410, although domestic hypocausts still in use in the fifth century are known. Nevertheless managed programmes of structural alterations were undertaken in the basilical hall in the mid-fifth century, and it is just possible that the baths continued in use until then.

The excavations in the basilical hall area suggested that the portico to its west was standing until the end of the fifth century. Without this data it would probably be acceptable to date the Period 3 Phase 5 robbing to the last decades of the fourth century and to suggest a date into the early fifth century for the final use of the *macellum*, although this would compress the Phase 3 and Phase 4 portico evidence. Again, without this data there would be no acceptance for any suggestion that the baths continued to be run after the fourth century.

The evidence from the basilical hall suggests a major demolition campaign, when the hall roof and walls were carefully reduced, a process of re-flooring paralleled in the *frigidarium*, and lastly the incorporation of roof plaster possibly from the added baths in a floor make up, all three events dating to the fifth century. The portico evidence is likely to be similar on the north, west, and south sides of the *insula*. The P 3.3 evidence is paralleled in the north portico, although the gravel surfaces are separated by rather more substantial dumps. There too stone flagging had been removed from outside major entrances prior to the final surface. This latter was laid in the fourth century and used for a long period. Subsequently there were stone platforms and divisions of the portico areas, and from a hearth in this phase came a remanent magnetic date probably in the first half of the sixth century. The porticos were then removed and two further phases of use were identified. The similarities between the two sequences are: i) gravel surface, ii) worn surface, iii) robbing, iv) post-portico use, although only one phase of the latter was recognised.

Of interest from the southern portico excavations is the evidence from the latest phase of the well worn entrance paths leading to both *macellum* entrances and to the corridor through to the baths courtyard. Even if this data were not to hand, continuing use of the *insula* 5 buildings, for whatever purpose, would be attested by the maintenance of the walls marking the west range and bounding the courtyard. The activity continuing after the porticos had been demolished still respected an existing enclosure. However the overlying dark soil layers may, as elsewhere (Esmonde Cleary 1989, 147), mark the end of use of the area.

It is possible that the sequence could have continued longer; although Cool cautions against giving the evidence too much weight, the fragment of window glass from a Phase 3.6 context introduces the possibility that it is the remains of a seventh-century or later glazing, perhaps of a church. Yegül has pointed out the continuing use of Baths sites as Christian buildings (1992, 314), and the possible conversion of the Wroxeter *frigidarium* to a church and the burials nearby are evidence of this (Chapter 6, section 8; Barker *et al* 1997).

Whatever the function of the areas and buildings within the *insula*, it would seem likely that a market continued in the fifth century in and near the porticos and in the *macellum*. This may perhaps have been a periodic fair (Frayn 1993, 133), and comparisons could be made with religious sites with fifth-century structural evidence where fairs are possible such as Uley, Gloucestershire (Woodward and Leach 1993) and Nettleton Scrubb, Wiltshire (Wedlake 1982). An agreed venue where exchanges could be adjudicated on, perhaps the neutral ground of a religious site, would be both a continuing necessity in the farming cycle, and something that would be unlikely to be easily abandoned.

Wider implications of the excavations

Changes on the *insula* may be linked with the changing fortunes of the town, marked at the outset by the Period 2 buildings which are part of an impulse to urbanisation clear throughout the Province (Wacher 1995; Millett 1990, 69). The completion date on *insula* 5 might have been fairly close to the fire which affected the forum *c* AD 170.

The complete resurfacing of the porticos in a distinctive compacted gravelling around the mid-third century might have been part of a programme of works on other street side porticos and pavements across the town. Atkinson (1942) suggested that later in the third century, the rebuilt forum, following the first fire, was again burnt down and then abandoned since the destruction material was not cleared away but sealed in beneath new surfaces or exposed to the elements. However, towards the end of the third century or the beginning of the fourth the city administration instigated a major programme of building and re-flooring including herringbone floors and the additional *caldarium* built across the *palaestra*. If the forum was no longer a cost factor, then resources could have been concentrated on the baths *insula*. Throughout the later third and the first half of the fourth century the portico surfaces were relaid and levelled up as they sank into the earlier pits beneath.

The levelling undertaken in the south portico represents a major re-establishment of the porticos perhaps in the late fourth or early fifth centuries which may have occurred on other *insula*. Although the street evidence from the excavations was limited to very slight exposures of the latest surfaces, renovations of the streets around the *insula*, known from excavations by Bushe-Fox (1913, 2), Atkinson (1942, 3) and Webster and Daniels (1972), would also have been town-wide.

Although the architecture of *insulae* 4 and 5 would appear to set them apart from their surroundings, both would have articulated with their surroundings. Meat supplies to the *macellum* would require a nearby area for slaughtering and butchering, perhaps *insula* 2. A parallel might be Dorchester where an *insula* bounding the baths *insula* and the presumed forum *insula* had few shops and little evidence of town houses, and may have been devoted to livestock processing (Woodward *et al* 1993, 375).

The excavations provided some evidence of the nature of the population of the town. A link with the military following the abandonment of the fortress and continuing until the later Roman period was suggested by finds of military equipment, noted above, and may also be suggested by the influences apparent in the construction of the baths. The *macellum* mortar and plaster analysis showed the presence of material which could only have been quarried, supporting the suggestion that there was a connection between the town and mining (Wacher 1995, 373). The size of the population itself may be indicated by the similar size of the baths to legionary examples, suggesting an ability to service a population of *c* 5000 (pers comm Donald Mackreth).

Evidence from the hinterland of the town suggests the abandonment of farmsteads occurring in the second century, the establishment of new roadside settlements *c* AD 150, and a change in field layouts near the town also in the second century (Ellis *et al* 1994). This may represent the impact of Wroxeter as a centre of consumption, making demands on the surrounding countryside in terms of tax and obligations, and bringing about social and economic change by virtue of its patterns of supply needs (Finley 1973; Hopkins 1983, xiii). However, it is interesting to note that the *macellum* animal bone studies showed little evidence of a response by meat suppliers to the demand for younger animals that might be expected from a *macellum*.

In the hinterland of the town, third and fourth-century changes witnessed the decline of the roadside settlement at Meole Brace together with the development of a more independent settlement at Duncote Farm north of the town with pottery production part of its economic base (Ellis *et al* 1994). The impression is of an increase in population but less dependence on the town. However, there is no evidence in the hinterland of the changes identified by Millett elsewhere (1990, table 6.3). This may be an indication of the continuing commitment of the Wroxeter elite to the town and perhaps that the economic predominance of the town had an adverse affect on the development of its hinterland (Ellis *et al* 1994, 111).

Looking further afield it is clear that Wroxeter shares its geomorphological and political border position with towns to the south not to the north and east. Cornovian territory in the Iron Age shares affinities with areas to its south reflected in settlement types and the dominance of hillforts (Cunliffe 1991, figs 20.2 and 20.6). Millett suggests that the pre-Roman pattern is a major factor in the structure of the Roman province, and it may be significant that later Roman administrative organisation of the province continues to link Cornovian territory with the Dobunni and the south (1990, figs 55 and 56). A Severn Valley cultural connection is attested by the shared Corinium school mosaics (White and Cosh forthcoming), by motifs used in the painted roof of the *caldarium* (Davey and Ling 1982, 201), by similar architectural traits (Blagg 1980, 33), and by the pottery (Figs 4.100–4.102).

6 The nineteenth-century excavations in the baths *insula* by Thomas Wright and others

edited and with a commentary by Donald Mackreth

Introduction

The accounts written and published on the excavations at Wroxeter during the last century tend, as a collection, to be repetitious. As they appeared in a variety of outlets and tended to be reports on successive seasons of work, they do not make for easy understanding of what was actually found. Wherever possible, only the words derived from the original accounts are used. The basic text is that of Wright's *Uriconium* (1872). Occasionally, supplementary words in square brackets are used in order to provide a convenient elision, but they never change the sense of the account being abstracted at the time. The figure numbers are shown similarly. The Harvard references in round brackets are placed at the end of any passage or word where the source changes. The only major departure from Wright's own account is the insertion of Johnson's account of his work on the area between the basilical hall and the southern public office and the south half of the latrine. The latest account incorporated in this cannibalised report is of the small scale excavations carried out in 1894 and 1896 and summarised by Fox in 1897. There has been no attempt to prune all the specifically non-archaeological detail; to have done so would have been to destroy one of the essential characteristics of the style of the period.

The plan of the baths *insula* is based upon the recent survey carried out by the Birmingham University Field Archaeology Unit (Fig 6.1). Since this closely conforms to the plan prepared by Hillary Davies (Fox 1897, 138) who, it seems, was responsible for the base plans used by Wright, that one has had preference here where others are less convincing. The plan shows different lettering mostly in some form of container to conform with the different texts. Where possible, arrows mark the various viewpoints of the published illustrations. The only major plan element which Wright never included was the northern of the two public offices as well as the north half of the latrine. This area has been drawn in from Johnson's account published in the first place in the *Proceedings of the Society of Antiquaries* (Johnson 1868) and secondly in an appendix to Wright's *Uriconium*. It is on the basis of that plan that the west wall of the *insula* has been drawn as a single line and not with a step in it as was customary until current excavations demonstrated that Johnson was right.

Other cases which deserve special mention are the following: Rooms 9D and 9C are shown on the plan in *Uriconium* and one may assume that they were also on the original used by Fox. The hypocaust *pilae* in Rooms 12 and 9 are taken from Fox, the rest from Wright. The stone slabs, F, have been resited and fitted into the known area of the *natatio*. Door 5, the easternmost between 1 and 15N, is clearly incorrectly sited on all plans except for Johnson's who may be a little out in his placing of it, but his is the one chosen here as it represents very closely the position which can be observed on the site today. The flooring in the *caldarium* is derived from *Uriconium*. The drain, y, in the *frigidarium/tepidarium* is incorrectly shown in Wright (1859, 210). There is a difficulty in reconciling the only view of 9D (Wright 1867, pl opp 156) with the plan as drawn by both Wright and Fox (presumably both following Davies) and the plan position of the door into 9D has been adopted here. The only feature which is shown only on modern plans which has been inserted is the wall separating the praefurnium 13 from 12 as it fits between the internal and external features recorded by Wright and Fox and which do not really survive any more. Any temptation to fill out details such as the full plan of the *macellum* or the various butt joints has been resisted.

A commentary follows the text and is numbered according to the paragraphs of the main text.

Although I have benefited greatly from discussion with Dr Webster and Mr Barker, the views expressed in the notes are not always theirs and in dealing with Room 4A and 4B there are mentions of an interpretation which, as far as I know, has not been published and which has not been subjected to critical attention by others.

In the following amalgamation of the information contained in these various papers, the material has been arranged in sections according to the structural elements of the baths *insula*.

The text

1 The basilical hall, its eastern room, and the yard to the east of that [1, 2, and 16]

1.1 In the year 1841, a wagoner's lad, in grubbing about the Old Wall, pulled out a piece of the mortar, or rather concrete, from the interior of the wall, in which was imbedded a coin of the emperor Trajan. This coin, which is now in the possession of my friend Mr Samuel Wood, is of large, or as it is called by numismatists, first brass, having the inscription SPQR OPTIMO PRINCIPI, with a figure of the emperor on horseback darting a javelin at a prostrate foe, who appears by his bonnet and trousers to be a Dacian. It is in a perfect state of preservation (Wright 1872, 332–3).

1.2 In [the] plan, the mass marked A, B, is the portion of building remaining above ground, which is known by the name of the Old Wall. The figures 1, 2, 3, 4, mark the different parts of the building to the north, now covered up (Wright 1860a, 158). On the 3rd of February, 1859, a pit was sunken against the northern side of the Old Wall, a little to the left of the aperture; and it was not without some surprise that the men found themselves obliged to dig to a depth of fourteen feet below the present surface of the ground before they came to the bottom of it. For about two-thirds (Wright 1872, 110) (it sank seven feet into the sand which forms the under stratum of the soil (Wright and Johnson 1859a, 208)) of this depth it was built in the under stratum of sand which forms a geological feature of the locality, so that the wall must have had a very deep foundation. A large capital of a column, ornamented by a plain band (Wright 1872, 110) (ornamented only with plain bands (Wright 1859, 213)), lay on the original level of the ground, in a reversed position, as though it had fallen from above. But we have continually found architectural fragments of this sort scattered about in such a manner, as to leave little doubt that they had been removed from their original places (Wright 1872, 110–11). The reader will have noticed a number of small holes in the face of the 'old wall' (Fig 6.2). It is not easy to make out for what purpose these were left. Many of them go right through the thickness of the wall. That some of them had supported the builders' scaffold is evident from the complete impress of circular poles left in the mortar, but this can hardly have been the case with all the holes in the old wall, some of which are regularly built square apertures (Anderson 1867, 52).

1.3 [In the Old Wall] there is a large breach, it is very probable that there was originally a doorway here, and that the large stones of which it was formed held out a temptation to the depredators (Wright 1859, 213), [and] on digging out the earth from the whole space of the opening (6), traces of a mortar face could be seen on each side against which the large stone jambs of the doorways, perhaps monoliths, had been set. The bed of the sill also was uncovered, the holes in the wall at the foot of each jamb showing that it must have been made of stones having a thickness of 15 or 18 inches (Fox 1897, 147). On looking up under the great breach an impression in the plaster can be discerned, as if caused by some large stones (Anderson 1867, 29).

1.4 From this point, trenches were carried to the northwards of the line of the Old Wall, which ran nearly east and west, and these brought successively to light a series of parallel walls marked *bb*, *cc* (Wright and Johnson 1859a, 208–9), each 4 feet thick (Roach Smith 1859c, 450), and *dd* (Wright and Johnson 1859a, 209), 3 ft 8 in thickness (Roach Smith 1859a, 450). These walls were traced during

their whole extent, with interruptions, caused no doubt by the tearing up of masonry for building materials in comparatively modern times (Wright and Johnson 1859a, 209). The first of these was at a uniform distance of fourteen feet; the space between this and the next parallel wall was exactly thirty feet; and the last wall was fourteen feet from the previous wall at its western end, and sixteen at its eastern end, so that these walls were not accurately parallel, and consequently the whole building was a little out of square (Wright 1872, 111). The wall *dd* terminated to the west in a wall running at right angles to it (Wright and Johnson 1859a, 209), and running parallel to the hedge (Roach Smith 1859a, 450), which has now been traced to a considerable distance southwards, and there can be no doubt that it also bordered upon a street, the site of which is occupied by the modern Watling Street Road (Wright and Johnson 1859a, 209).

1.5 1 in the plan, appeared to have been an open alley; and there were some traces of it having been paved with flagstones. There can be no doubt, indeed, that the northern face of the Old Wall, which formed one side of this alley, was the outside of a building (Wright 1872, 111–12). The continuation of the Old Wall, *aa*, was traced westward, after a short interruption, to the whole extent of the exterior area forming one side of a long narrow inclosure, uniformly 14 feet wide. Herring-bone pavement was found here and there in this passage (Wright and Johnson 1859a, 211–12). I have been led to think that it was a public passage, and I believe that some traces were found of its having been paved with flagstones. Moreover, it was at a lower level than the floors of the central and northern slip. It appears that about its centre some fragments of tessellated pavement were found by the men employed in excavating (Wright 1872, 198–9), about half way along (Roach Smith 1859a, 450), but, as the site of this building, the Basilica, had been greatly broken up in excavating for building materials, for large breaches were found in the long central walls almost if not quite to their foundations, and as only very small fragments of the northern tessellated pavement remained, I suspect that the fragments of pavement first mentioned as found in the southern passage were merely bits of the northern pavement dropped there by the excavators while carrying away materials (Wright 1872, 199).

1.6 The two walls *bb* and *cc* inclose a rectangular area, 226 feet long by 30 feet wide, which appears to have had in its whole extent a uniform pavement (Wright and Johnson 1859a, 205), and lying here about four feet under the surface of the ground, formed of small bricks, three inches long by one wide, set in what is technically called herring-bone pattern (Wright 1872, 111). A few pieces of

Fig 6.2 North side of Old Work (Wright 1859, pl 15)

broken roof-tiles were found scattered about (Roach Smith 1859a, 450). In the wall which formed the western end of this central area were two original openings, within which were found, evidently in their original position, on one a large squared stone, and in the other two similarly squared stones placed one upon another. One of these was bevelled off at the upper edge into a plain moulding, and their general appearance lead to the belief that they had formed the bases of something – perhaps of large columns. Several capitals, bases, and portions of shafts of columns, all of a very plain and rather late character were found scattered about [the interior of the building] (Wright and Johnson 1859a, 209–11).

1.7 In the northernmost of [the elements of the basilical plan] were found several fragments of tessellated pavement (Wright 1872, 198) distributed throughout the north-east half of the corridor (Maw 1861, 100) at sufficiently distant spots to leave no doubt that a pavement extended continuously along its whole length. These fragments of the northern pavement have now all been covered up; but before this was done, they were carefully examined and drawn by my friend Mr George Maw, of Benthall Hall, near Broseley. At the Congress of the British Archaeological Association at Shrewsbury in 1860, Mr Maw exhibited a drawing of a restoration of this pavement accompanied by a paper, both of which

were published in the Transactions for 1861. As the workmen dug below the level of the pavement, Mr Maw had an opportunity of examining the construction of the foundation on which it was laid (Wright 1872, 198–201).

1.8 Before the ground was filled in, I took careful drawings of each fragment of pavement; also exact measurements as to their relative position in the building, and have endeavoured to embody the information I collected in (Fig 6.3).

1.9 It represents the eastern half of the north corridor, which having a concrete foundation, similar to

Fig 6.3 Part of tesselated pavement in basilical hall (Maw 1861, pl 9)

that on which the fragments of pavements rested, extending throughout its whole length, there appears good reason to suppose that two pavements originally existed at *Uriconium*.

1.10 The fully coloured portions of (Fig 6.3) represent the pieces of pavement found perfect during the excavations, and the parts tinted of a lighter shade, such as are necessarily implied by the existing remains. The annexed wood-cut represents the remaining portion of panel E, drawn to a scale of an inch to a foot (Fig 6.4). Very fortunately these fragments, although small in relation to the space originally covered, were so situated as to enable the plan of the pavement to be made out with but little doubt or difficulty. You will see by my drawing (Fig 6.3) that it consisted of a series of oblong panels of simple patterns, composed of dark grey and cream-coloured tesserae, and was surrounded with a broad field, next the wall, of uniform colour of a greenish grey tint. Narrow bands, about five inches wide, branching from this, divided the pattern into panels of about 8 feet by 11 feet.

1.11 The end panel marked A, being complete from side to side, gave a key to the width of the panels across the pavement, and as small portions of the dividing dark bands were perfect next to the four adjacent panels of pavement marked D, E, F, G, I have been able to decide with exactness as to the recurring intervals of the panels in the corridor lengthwise.

1.12 There being nothing to show how the spaces intervening between the panels B E and C F were filled in, I have left them vacant; but as the space they occupy exactly corresponds with the size of the existing panels, I have felt justified in supposing that the whole length of pavement was made up of compartments of nearly equal size, and have, therefore, inserted the partitional bands in my drawing.

1.13 I think, from the nature of the pattern, and the space occupied by it, that panel A at each end of the pavement was square, and all the others of about the average size shown on the drawing. They may have varied a few inches in width to adapt them to the several patterns with which they were filled. This I found to be the case in taking the measurements; but on the whole, for Roman work, they appear to have been planned with considerable accuracy and uniformity. The exact formation of the centre of the panel is a little obscure, and I have had some difficulty in deciding whether or not the fret border along the two sides of panel B ran into the plain ground beyond the line of the panels; but I think it did as shown on the drawing, and probably defined the position of two opposite door entrances in the corridor. There is also no clue to the filling in of the three small compartments into which panel E was divided, so I have left them blank. Beyond these points, I have carefully avoided inserting anything in the plan that is not distinctly implied by some remaining portions, and have no hesitation in considering it, as far as it goes, an exact representation of the pavement as it originally existed.

1.14 With respect to the division of the pavement into equal panels, it has struck me that these may have been proportioned in relation to some other members of the building. Possibly the sides of the corridor next the central pavement may have been some kind of open arcade, the piers of which corresponded with the partitional bands of the design.

1.15 The foundations on which tessellated pavements were laid were of two distinct kinds, – one formed in connection with the hypocausts, where it consisted of a thick and uniform layer of coarse concrete resting on the large tiles that formed the tops of the flue-pillars, and termed by classical writers the *suspensura*. The other formed for the pavements of apartments such as those now under consideration, where they rested on the solid ground without the intervening subterranean air-flues, and termed the *ruderatis* by Vitruvius.

1.16 This appears to have been an elaborate and rather careful construction, and agrees in its formation in nearly all Roman remains that have been described. At Wroxeter it consisted of four distinct layers of materials, forming in the aggregate a substratum nearly three feet thick. Its principal bulk consisting of a bed, two feet thick, of lumps of red sandstone, the surface of which was levelled by a layer of a kind of mortar rather soft and fine in texture, of about eight inches in thickness. It

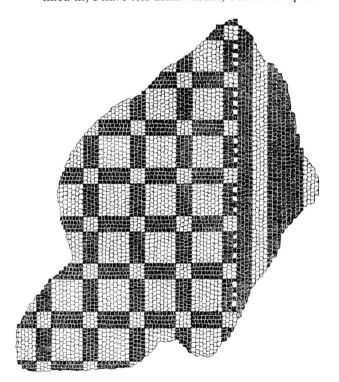

Fig 6.4 Detail of tesselated pavement in basilical hall (Maw 1861, 102)

appears to have served merely to fill up the irregular cavities of the stone. The bed resting on this, and forming the immediate foundation of the mosaic, was a level layer of singular hardness, about two inches and a half thick, composed of a mixture of lime and coarsely powdered burnt earth, or brick rubbish; and from its uniform thickness and even surface, appears to have been very carefully prepared for receiving the tesserae.

1.17 The fourth layer, in which the tesserae were immediately bedded, consisted of quite white and very hard cement, which was also used for filling in the joints.

1.18 It is a rather interesting fact, these remains of pavements afford confirmatory evidence of the supposed destruction of the building by fire. Nearly all the fragments of pavement are more or less discoloured, (especially panel E), the grey tints graduating in patches, from its darkest shades to the natural colour of the stone, in such a manner as to render it certain that they would not be produced by selection in the arrangement of the tesserae; and I think there is little doubt, that they are the effect of the burning timbers of the building that fell upon the floors on the destruction of the city. Here and there, also, we find corresponding patches of the pavement, where the concrete foundation is entirely decomposed, and has the character of slacked lime. I am more inclined to think, that this was also the result of the partial application of heat, than that it was due to mere exposure to the weather, as a large portion of the foundation remains in its original state (Maw 1861, 101–109).

1.19 About the middle of the outer wall, *dd*, the traces of the wall were lost through a considerable space; but the broken condition of the masonry at each end of this breach seemed to show that it had been caused by the carrying away of the materials for the use of the builders. It is probable that here was an entrance (Wright and Johnson 1859a, 209).

1.20 The sort of brick pavement which formed the floor of the great central inclosure 2 [Room 1 nave] is generally found in courts and places open to the sky, and the very extent of the inclosure, in this case, would lead us to suppose that it also was not roofed. The narrow inclosure to the north 3 [also 1] has had, in its whole length, a rather elegant tessellated pavement, arranged in a series of compartments, and this would seem to indicate that it at least had a roof. No doorway was found communicating between these several places; but as the walls of separation were in several places entirely broken away down to the foundations, we cannot positively decide whether there were doors or not (Wright 1872, 112). There may have been a doorway at the eastern end of the wall *bb*, as it was not traced up to the eastern wall (Wright and Johnson 1859a, 209).

1.21 The central area is just the width of the side aisles taken together. The walls of these which remain probably supported columns, and were, in fact, only the base upon which they rested. I have heard that rows of columns were found in this field, and that these were dug up to form the coping stones of the enclosure walls; a labourer mentioned to me some years since the fact of their lying in rows (Scarth 1859, 266).

1.22 The only articles found in the course of excavating these inclosures, calculated to throw any light upon the object for which they were designed, were a portion (two or three links) of a rather ponderous iron chain, the steel head of an axe (Wright 1872, 112), and a candlestick, [found] on the floor of the Basilica (*ibid*, 264), about five inches and a half long. Portions of several padlocks, apparently intended for fetters, were also picked up in this part of the excavations. Many fragments of the stucco, painted in fresco, were found in digging these buildings, among which was part of an inscription in large letters, two of which were perfect, and sufficient remained of the first and last, when first picked up, to show that the four letters were ARCA (*ibid*, 112–13).

1.23 At the eastern extremity of the large central area, at *g* in the plan, there was a step, formed of one large squared stone, and above it a decided passage (Wright and Johnson 1859a, 211) or bottom (Roach Smith 1859a, 450) of a doorway through the wall, leading (Wright and Johnson 1859a, 211) into a smaller inclosure 4 [2] (Wright 1872, 113), which had no pavement (Wright and Johnson1859a, 211), which, from the set-off on the walls, was supposed to have been a quadrangular yard or court, built a little out of square, and measuring about sixty-six feet from north to south, and about thirty from east to west. Beyond this was a much larger inclosed space [16] (Wright 1872, 113), bounded by the continuation of the wall *ddd*, and by a wall rising at right angles to it at the point where the hedge and modern road prevented this wall from being traced any further (Wright and Johnson 1859a, 211). [The enclosed space] was trenched across in several directions, but no floor or transverse walls were found, and it was conjectured that it may have been a garden (Wright 1872, 113).

1.24 I have already remarked that the northern face of the Old Wall presents all the appearance of having been the exterior of a building; and this had evidently been the case with its continuation westward, in which (*ibid*), after a small interval, where it has probably been dug up for materials, its continuation was met with (Roach Smith 1859a, 450), and at a considerable interval from each other, were found two openings for doors, each approached from the narrow passage by a step (Wright 1872, 113), similar to that at *gg* (Wright and Johnson 1859a, 212), composed of one large squared stone. The step to the westward (6 on the plan) was very much worn by the action of people's feet, and must, therefore, have been much fragmented; but this was not the case with the other (5) (Wright 1872, 113–14).

2   The baths [Rooms 3–13]

2.1   The excavators were directed to cross the southern wall [of the Basilican Hall] at the step at *l*, and to carry a trench southward at right angles to it. They seem to have come into some open courts, which have not yet been carefully explored, because the trench brought them to the semicircular end of the hypocaust marked *m* in the plan. The northern end of this hypocaust, the wall of which remained to the height of several feet, presents an imposing mass of masonry (Wright and Johnson 1859a, 212) and was partly covered with plaster or stucco, which had been worked to a smooth surface (Wright 1872, 114), and was painted red, with stripes of yellow. Near it lay an immense stone, hewn into the shape to fit the semicircular wall (Wright and Johnson 1859a, 212–3). It is of the sandstone of the country, and measures 7 ft 2 in by 5ft 9 in; it is one foot in thickness. Mortar adheres to the upper surface (Scarth 1859, 268), and a piece of iron remains soldered into it with lead. It is now placed on top of the wall (Wright 1872, 114). Unfortunately [large] stones have, for the most part, been carried away for building purposes. Large steps and corner stones are removed, which if kept *in situ*, would prove of great service in forming a correct idea of the buildings, but unfortunately the excavations are not allowed to be kept open, and, as the foundations must be covered up, these stones are thought too valuable to be buried again (Scarth 1859, 268).

2.2   The hypocaust, 37 feet long (Wright and Johnson 1859a, 212), including the semicircular end (Roach Smith 1859a, 452), by 25 feet wide. The pillars, of which 120 were counted (Wright and Johnson 1859a, 212), were formed of square flat bricks, placed one upon the another without mortar (Wright 1872, 115), [and] were from 2 to 3 feet 10 inches high (Wright and Johnson 1859a, 212). The tiles of the piers which supported the floor appeared to experience very little damage from exposure to the air, and, but for external violence, would have been in perfect condition at the present time (Wright 1872, 191). The floor of the interior of this large room, which appeared to have presented merely a smoothed surface of cement, was all destroyed, with the exception of a small fragment, of hard concrete (*ibid*, 115), perfectly smooth on its upper surface (*ibid* 195), eight inches thick, on its supports in the

north-east corner. In this corner were found the ashes from the fires (*ibid*, 115) some of which had been alimented with mineral coal (*ibid*, 195). Our plate (Fig 6.5) represents a portion of the hypocaust, viewed from the SSW, that is looking towards the semicircular end, as it appeared when it was first opened. It is taken from a photograph. The floor had all been broken up, but pieces of the concrete which composed it were found scattered about (*ibid*, 115).

2.3   About the middle of this hypocaust, there was a sort of passage across, from west to east (*ibid*), considerably wider than the spaces between the pillars of brick (Wright and Johnson 1859a, 213), which communicated to the west with a building formed of cross walls and hypocaust columns, 10 [13], which is not easily described, but which appeared to have been a repository for fuel, for a quantity of unburnt coal, both charcoal and mineral, was found in it when opened (Wright 1872, 115).

2.4   On the eastern side, the passage alluded to brought us to a doorway in the wall, through which we entered the similar hypocaust of another large room, 8 [9]. The columns in this second hypocaust were much more dilapidated than in the first (*ibid*, 116) [and] absolutely fell into heaps of powder, not long after they were uncovered (*ibid*, 191), but some of them were found entire, supporting a portion of the floor in the south-east corner, where also were found the ashes from the fire and soot on the walls, the latter appearing quite fresh when first uncovered. The floor appeared here to have been at the same height as in the other room, and it was similarly formed of a bed of smooth concrete. In the northern side of this room, where the wall remained to the height of nine or ten feet, there was a doorway, with an arch turned with large flat Roman tiles (*ibid*, 116) [which] remained perfect for some months, and then fell into absolute decay (*ibid*, 191).

Fig 6.5 Hypocaust Room 12A (Wright 1859, pl 16)

2.5 This [9B] was found to be approached from without by a staircase, 9, of three large steps, each composed of (*ibid*, 116) one large well-squared stone, descending from a square platform, which was apparently on a level with the original floors of the rooms (Wright and Johnson 1859a, 213), which was approached from the north (Wright 1872, 116). The masonry here has been given in the accompanying engraving from a drawing by a talented young artist of Shrewsbury, Mr Hillary Davies (Fig 6.6). When the steps were first opened, a broken shaft of a large column was found lying across them, which was removed, and raised upright on the platform above, as it appears in our engraving (Fig 6.7), and a squared block of stone lay by the side of the staircase in what seemed to have been its original position. The north-eastern corner of the space at the foot of the staircase, that is, the corner which was opposite the stairs and the archway, and therefore out of the way of those who had to pass up and down the one and through the other, presented an appearance which would lead us to suppose that, at the close of the Roman period, it had been used as a receptacle for refuse, such as the sweepings of the floors, for the earth (Wright 1872, 116), for about a foot deep on the floor, was literally filled with articles such as coins, hair-pins, fibulae (Wright and Johnson 1859a, 213), buttons, nails, broken pottery and glass, bones of birds and other edible animals, and a variety of other objects, which were carefully collected, and have been placed in the Museum, at Shrewsbury (Wright 1872, 117).

2.6 Immediately to the east of this staircase is a rectangular chamber, 14 [9A] (*ibid*, 118), a small room only eight feet square (Wright and Johnson 1859a, 213), with a herring-bone pavement formed of small bricks, exactly like that of the large inclosure to the north of the Old Wall. The eastern side of this room, which is in line with the eastern wall of the second room with a hypocaust,

appears to have been originally open in nearly its whole width, although it has been, at some later period, built up (Wright 1872, 118).

2.7 The great court [15] appears to have extended originally up to the southern wall of Rooms 10, 7, 8, 11 [13, 12, 9, 8], but at a later period new buildings were erected, adjoining to this wall, and encroaching upon the court to the southward, but to what extent is not known, as this part of the site has been very imperfectly explored (*ibid*, 139–40) as a small portion only has been uncovered, but this operation has brought to light the lower part of the walls of four small rooms [12B, 9C, 9D], as represented in the accompanying engraving (Fig 6.8). These walls are of very inferior masonry, and are merely built up to the wall of the older building without being in any way united with it. There is nothing to be observed to lead us to conjecture the purpose for which they were intended. In the middle of one of them lay some architectural fragments, including a part of a rather elegant stone cornice (Wright 1867, 157), some other materials from the ruin of the building, and a large mass of iron (Wright 1872, 140), probably weighing about one cwt (Scarth 1864, 131), wrought into a square at one end (Anderson 1867, 26), which presents some appearance of having been exposed to a powerful fire. This room was entered by two steps from a little recess in the court, at F, between the wall of this latter building and the original wall of the great court (Wright 1872, 140).

2.8 The annexed cut (Fig 6.9) represent[s] a portion of two adjoining walls, built at right angles to each other [in the recess]. In the wall to the left, close to the ground, runs a narrow slightly projecting string-course, composed of a double layer of long flat tiles. Then follows three rows of squared stones, then the string-course of tiles is repeated, then follow four courses of stone, then another double row of tiles, next four more courses of stone, then a fourth bonding course; and finally, the remains of five rows of stones can be counted ere the broken-off top is reached. On the contrary, fourteen rows of squared stones can be counted in the right-hand wall without the occurrence of a single string-course. Of the four string-courses of tiles visible, it is only the upper one that goes through the thickness of the wall the three lower rows of tiles are not seen. The side of the wall not seen is formed of very rough masonry. Material used in the wall to the right, light coloured sandstone; the stone used in the wall with the tiles is red sandstone. Both walls are rather over three feet in width [and] are not built into, but merely up to each other. It may also be observed that the stones and tiles used in these walls are set in very thick layers of mortar, the marks of the trowel being still visible in several places (Anderson 1867, 37–8).

Fig 6.6 Room 9B looking west (Wright and Johnson 1859b, 258)

Fig 6.7 Room 9B looking south (Roach Smith 1859c, facing 219)

Fig 6.8 Rooms 9D and 9C looking north (Wright 1867, facing 157)

Fig 6.9 Junction of Walls 5/15 (right) and 8/15 (Anderson 1867, 37)

2.9 This recess in the court, when the ground was uncovered in the course of the excavations, was extremely interesting in several points of view. The view in our engraving [but not in the copy of the source seen by DFM] represents the eastern wall, the original boundary wall of the great court on this side – to the left we have part of the Old Wall, to the right the mound of earth thrown out from the excavations, and in the distance the Wrekin. It will be seen that, at some period, a great breach has been made in this piece of wall, and it had been built up with masonry very inferior to that of the rest of the wall. But, which is still more interesting, further building operations were evidently in progress at the time of the attack in which the town was destroyed. On the ground were found three (Wright 1872, 140) large dark unfinished (Anderson 1867, 26) blocks of stone, one of which has since been raised to the top of the wall where it is seen in the engraving. These blocks had been in the hands of the stone-cutters, who, when they were interrupted, had begun to form them roughly into shape, and in this very unfinished condition they are now found. They appear to have been designed to form the top of the arches of doorways or windows (Wright 1872, 140).

2.10 Other materials for building also lay scattered about the ground, a heap of which, as they were piled up against the wall by the excavators, are seen to the right in our view. Among them are rather numerous blocks of a sort of artificial tufa, made chiefly of vegetable materials, and cut into the form of modern bricks. It appears to have been employed indiscriminately with the squared stones in the facing of the walls. In course of time this Roman artificial tufa has attained the hardness of stone. But the leaves, in this state of petrifaction, have preserved their forms so perfectly, that, when broken, they actually offer studies for the modern botanist. It may be remarked, that there were portions of the branches mixed up with the leaves, which, decaying and leaving holes, made this artificial tufa lighter than it would otherwise have been (*ibid*, 141–2).

2.11 A rather wide passage through the eastern wall of [9A] led into another room with a hypocaust [8], the floor of which is also gone. The pillars of this hypocaust were rather more neatly constructed, but they seem to have been considerably lower than those of the hypocausts previously opened (Wright and Johnson 1859a, 213–14). In the southern wall of this hypocaust, there is a breach, which has no doubt been a small entrance from a court outside (Wright 1872, 118).

2.12 The space to the northward of these hypocausts has as yet only been slightly excavated, but one wall, which was partly uncovered, near the hypocaust last mentioned [8], represented a mode of ornamentation which we think is unique in this country; the inner surface was tessellated, the tesserae, alternately of dark and light stones, one-half by three-fifths of an inch square, being set into the cement. A fragment of this tessellated wall is represented in the annexed wood-cut (Fig 6.10). Immediately beyond this spot we come upon the rooms which joined up to the south side of the Old Wall (Wright and Johnson 1859a, 216). Between the range of hypocausts and the Old Wall there were five apartments, 16, 17, 18, 19 and 20 [3, 3A and 3B], the southern parts only of which will be at present excavated, in the fear of endangering the stability of the Old Wall itself (Wright 1860a, 159). The surface of the Old Wall presents unmistakable evidence of having been the interior of a building; the startings of three distinct rooms, being perfectly visible (Wright 1872, 120). At the same time that [the] breach [in the Old Wall] was examined (in 1896), the digging was carried further on each side-inside-and revealed the remains of two square piers (11) – (11), each about a foot from the broken edge of the doorway. Very little remained of the western, but the eastern one was standing to a height of about 4 feet six inches. It was bonded into the wall to that height, but there seemed no traces of bonding any higher. Possibly this die of masonry may have served, with its companion, as a pedestal to solid stone pilasters supporting the springing of the vaulting, which was in line with them above. It was perfectly clear that those masses of masonry, which were each 3 feet on face and something over 3 feet in projection from the wall to which they were attached, could not be the offsets of walls dividing the hall (D) into three parallel compartments, for on the southern face and on the sides of the more perfect one pieces of finished wall plastering of pink cement were distinctly to be seen.

2.13 The problem remains to be solved with what kind of vaulting this hall was covered. In 1894, shortly before the visit of the Archaeological Institute to Shrewsbury, a search was made in the much-encumbered area, by Mr Herbert Jones, by means of a small grant from the Council of the Archaeological Institute; but although two trenches were carried from the south wall in line

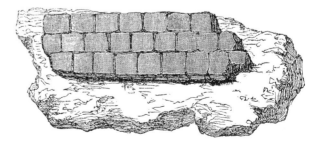

Fig 6.10 Wall mosaic, Room 3A (Wright and Johnson 1859b, 216)

with the piers uncovered last year, for more than half the distance across the hall, only the western trench showed any trace of such supports as must have existed to carry the vaulting. There were, however, in this trench some indications of what might have been the footings of a pier, but the spot required more examination than could be given to it at the time. Incomplete though this examination was, it led to the conclusion that supports, probably in the shape of square or oblong piers, had existed at central points between the south wall and each of the piers to the right and left of the great doorway, and that the hall had been covered by an intersecting vault in six compartments.

2.14 From fragments of the vaulting dug up in 1894, it would seem to have been constructed partly with box, partly with flanged, tiles, the latter, with their flanges upwards, lining the rubble concrete like a skin and forming a surface on their undersides for the plastering of the vaults. The box tiles are 11 inches by 8 3/4 inches, and six inches thick; the flanged tiles are 6 inches by 7 inches (Fig 6.11) (Fox 1897, 147–9).

2.15 A series of rooms, therefore, which were five in number, have not yet been explored, with the exception of a very partial excavations to trace the walls, and of the southern part of Room 20 [3] (Wright 1872, 120), and transverse walls have been discovered answering to all these arches (Roach Smith 1859a, 453). Here [in 3B] was found, on a level with the floors of the hypocausts, a perfect tessellated pavement, formed, very laboriously, of small cream-coloured tesserae, laid in a uniform field, without any attempt to introduce a pattern (Wright 1872, 120). The tesserae of this floor are made of the same material as the cream-coloured tesserae of the pavements of the corridor of the Basilica (*ibid*, 204). It was evidently the floor of a bath, and there were extensive remains of a raised step around it, forming a rectangular basin to contain water. A little higher on the side of the wall are indications of the former existence of something like a platform, or wooden floor, too low, however, to admit of people standing beneath it. The surface of the southern wall of this room, which forms the separation between it and the Room 13 [10], was ornamented with tessellated work instead of fresco-painting, and the lower edge of it, consisting of a guilloche border (*ibid*, 120) formed of red, white, and bluish-grey tesserae, less than an inch square (Fig 6.12) (Anderson 1867, 20), which no doubt had enclosed a large central pattern, or possibly a picture (Wright 1872, 207), still remains (*ibid*, 120). It has nearly all fallen since it has been exposed to the atmosphere, but a piece of it is preserved in the Museum at Shrewsbury (*ibid*, 207). On uncovering the corresponding wall of the room marked 16 [3A], similar tessellated work was found

upon it, so that when the two rooms are completely excavated, they will be found to correspond to each other. The three intervening walls have not been examined, with the exception of a trench run into that marked 17, where a quantity of charred wheat was found (*ibid*, 120–21) and contains a hypocaust still supporting its floor of cement, though this is considerably damaged (*ibid*, 133).

2.16 The floor of this hall (D) [3], as far as it could be examined in 1894 and 1896, showed many traces of repair. Originally it appeared to have been laid with tesserae, for in the corner behind the western pier beside the great doorway (11) a very small fragment of the tessellation remained, consisting of some few cubes of cream-coloured stone with others of a larger size of the dull green kind so frequently used as a ground or bordering in the mosaics on this site. Lining the foot of the pier at the same spot could be traced the quarter-round plaster moulding, which is the usual edging of floors in Roman buildings in this country.

2.17 Another detail also merits notice. Against the southern wall, at about 6 feet from the eastern doorway, was a stone foundation (12) running at right angles to the wall, and showing a returning angle at 5 feet from it. A row of tiles lay close along the wall, the last one being partly laid in a chase of the stonework. Whatever the construction had been of which these faint traces formed part, it had evidently been destroyed at some period and floored over with *opus signinum* (Fox 1897, 149).

2.18 Other rooms, and what appeared to be a passage (Wright 1872, 118) between two walls (Roach Smith 1859a, 452) followed to the eastward of [8].The first of these was the large room, or perhaps two rooms, 12 [4A and 4B], also with a hypocaust (Wright 1872, 118) which is partly formed of flues, instead of rows of columns (Roach Smith 1859c, 220). The *supensurae* of this hypocaust received a pavement of mosaic, a fragment of which may still be seen at the foot of the wall near the eastern doorway, showing that the bath, if bath it was, had been completely covered over and obliterated by the later alterations. A trace of this floor is shown on [the plan], just above the letter (H). Even this floor was covered at a later time by a layer of *opus signinum* (Fox 1897, 154).

2.19 From the appearances presented in the course of excavating, a passage seemed to have run along the southern side of the northern wall of the Room 12, which was interrupted by (Wright 1872, 130) a square pit in very good masonry (Wright and Johnson 1859a, 217) occupying the whole breadth of it (Roach Smith 1859a, 453). A substantial dwarf wall of brick was built to form, it would seem, a narrow enclosure at least 15 feet long by 6 feet wide. The western end of this brick wall remains, and a conduit 2 foot wide runs in at

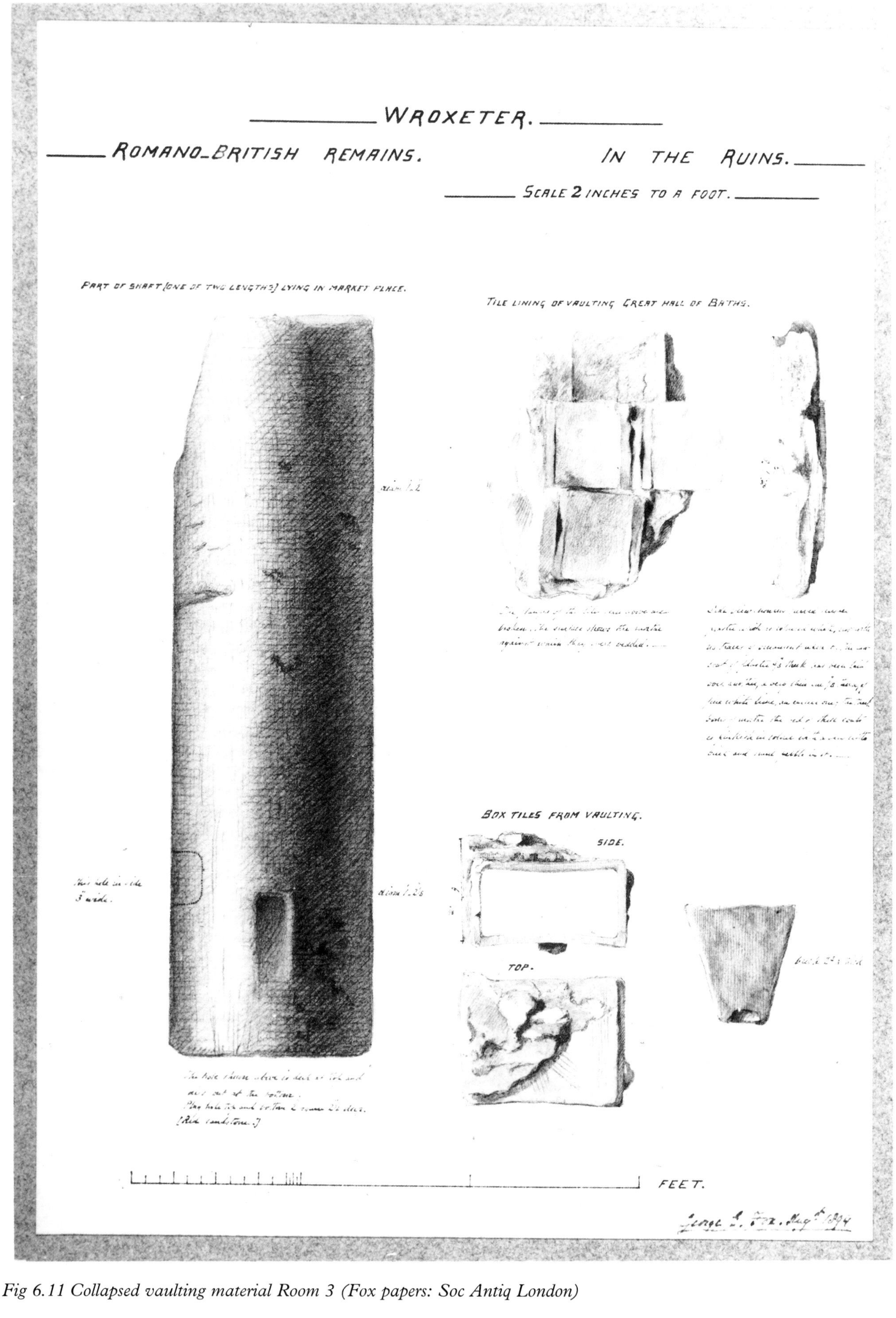

Fig 6.11 Collapsed vaulting material Room 3 (Fox papers: Soc Antiq London)

the north-west corner, at (15) (Fox 1897, 153), which is represented in the accompanying cut, from a drawing by Mr Hillary Davies (Fig 6.13). The masonry of this drain, and all the buildings adjacent, is extremely good, with a profusion of the large Roman tiles. These form the sides of the drain, which was opened only to a very inconsiderable distance towards the north. It is covered by a large block of stone, belonging to a course of similar stones which run horizontally along the wall. The floor of the drain is formed of a course of roof-tiles, the flanged edges turned upwards. When first uncovered, the square pit and drain were in a remarkably good state of preservation, and are accurately represented in the cut (Fig 6.13), but they have since suffered by exposure to the air (Wright 1872, 216). At two places there were wide openings through the wall from this passage to the northern side of it; and at the more easterly of these openings, a large stone scooped out in a singular manner, and joining on the other side to other similar stones which run round the end of the wall. The first of these stones is shewn in our view from the east (Fig 6.14) and the whole group appear in (Fig 6.15), taken from the opposite side, as they appeared lying on the ground when this passage was first opened (*ibid*, 130).

2.20 The surface of the southern side of the wall of the passage described above was covered with plaster or stucco, and a little to the eastward of the pit an inscription was found, scrawled in large straggling characters with some sharp pointed instrument. When this part of the wall was uncovered, two lines of this inscription remained, which appeared to have been its conclusion, and seem to have been perfectly well preserved, but, before anyone had the opportunity of examining it, two casual visitors amused themselves by employing their walking sticks or umbrellas to break off the plaster and they were not observed by the workmen until the first line had been completely destroyed,

and the second, which had been a shorter one, was very much broken into. When I visited the excavations next morning, I could only trace distinctly the letters N T, which had formed the termination of the second line, but I was satisfied by what remained that the letter which had preceded them was an A, and that these letters had formed the termination of a verb in the plural number at the end of the sentence. I gave directions for making a careful facsimile of what remained on the wall, but before this could be done, we were temporarily excluded from the field, and what had been left of the inscription was further damaged by the weather, and perhaps by other meddling visitors, so that all that remained of this inscription when I was at length enabled to have it copied, was reduced to a few mere scratches (Fig 6.16) (Wright 1872, 130–31). A strigil found in the last century, in one of the rooms of the baths at *Uriconium*, [is] now preserved in the library of Shrewsbury School. It is of bronze, about nine inches long (*ibid*, 127).

2.21 Beyond the Room 12 [4], is another room [10] with a hypocaust, resembling exactly in shape and dimensions the Room 11 [8] (*ibid*, 119), [with] in all twelve rows of pillars in depth, and six rows in breadth (Anderson 1867, 44), and adjoining to it a small square chamber with a floor of bricks set in herring-bone 15 [11A], exactly resembling that marked 14 [9A] on the plan, (Wright 1872, 119), and has a wide opening westward into (Wright and Johnson 1859b, 257) the Room 13 [10], just as the Room 14 [9A] was originally open to that marked 11 [8]. Adjoining the Room 13 [10], to the south, was a smaller room with a hypocaust [5A]. Our engraving (Fig 6.14), taken from a drawing by Mr Fairholt, represents them looking westward, at a

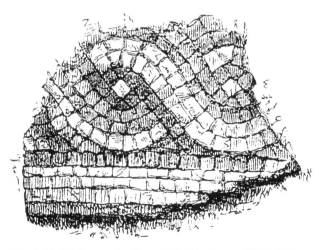

Fig 6.12 Wall mosaic, Room 3B (Anderson 1867, 20)

Fig 6.13 Drain Room 4A (Wright and Johnson 1859a, 217)

Fig 6.14 Rooms 11, 4A, 4B, and 8, looking west (Wright and Johnson 1859b, facing 257)

time when they were only partially excavated, and shows the northern ends of the rooms just described. The foreground is formed by the herring-bone pavement of the small room, 15 [11A] (Wright 1872, 119), [and] there is a large stone scooped out in a singular manner [see commentary note 21]. The floor was here again formed of smoothed cement, a large piece of which remains in its original position, and is seen in the engraving (Wright and Johnson 1859b, 257).

2.22 In the hypocaust of the room marked 13 [10], the bases of the columns alone remained when it was opened, the columns themselves having been cleared away (Wright 1872, 132), but their height is marked on the stucco of the wall (*ibid*, 119). The floor has been of smoothed concrete, which also appears to have been the material of the floors of the passages leading to it. Passages at the north-western corner of the Room 13 [10] appear to have communicated directly with the three rooms 12, 19 and 20 [4B, 3 and 3B] (*ibid*, 132–3). The western end of [the north] wall is squared off to the passages, forming apparently the side of a cross passage, and at the foot it has a kind of base formed of large stones hollowed or scooped out in a very remarkable manner [see commentary note 21], which appears to have joined in with the concrete of the floor. In the

eastern wall of the room marked 13 [10], there is a neatly-built recess, which has either been a fire-place for the hypocaust, or more probably a passage through the wall, which here appears to have been the eastern boundary of these buildings (*ibid*, 119).

2.23 The northern wall of 13 [10] was, when first opened, covered with the remains (*ibid*) and impressions of the flue-tiles which carried up upwards the hot air from the hypocaust through the room. They had run up in rows close together, as will be seen in our engraving (Fig 6.15), which represents a view looking towards the north. A few of the backs of the broken flue-tiles are found still attached to the wall, the surface of which is, as will be seen, covered with the impressions of the surfaces of others, which were usually striated with lines in various patterns, to give them a firmer hold on the mortar (*ibid*, 132).

2.24 The [east-west] trench, after passing the reservoir E [14], brought the excavators to a very substantial wall at *o*, which was traced in its whole extent, and was clearly the exterior of a building (*ibid*, 121–2), having a large square projecting room. The cement floor continued inside this wall until it sank (Wright 1859, 222–3) about three feet below the level of the cement floor of the very

Fig 6.15 North wall of Room 12 (Wright 1859, pl 17)

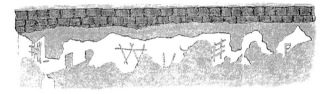

Fig 6.16 Inscription on north wall of Room 4B (Wright and Johnson 1859a, 221)

large apartment [6] enclosed by the wall *o*, *p*, *p*, and the others parallel to them (Wright 1872, 122). This floor, formed very neatly of flat Roman tiles eighteen inches long by twelve inches broad, is ten feet wide from east to west, by thirty feet long, has been entirely uncovered (Wright 1859, 223). When first opened, the middle of this pavement was broken and indented in such a manner as to lead to the supposition that it was hollow underneath; but on excavating, this was found not to be the case (Roach Smith 1859c, 223). The cement floor was continued eastwardly until it reached the continuation of the wall, which I have already mentioned as forming apparently the eastward boundary of this building (Wright 1859, 223). It has been traced continuously from the spot where this trench reached it to the hypocaust and small room with herring-bone pavement (Roach Smith 1859c, 223). There were two

entrances to this building from the south, at *p*, *p*, of one of which the walls are well preserved and defined (Wright 1872, 122).

2.25 On the northern end of the interior of the building a numerous series of pillars of a hypocaust were found, but whether they formed a continuation of the Room 12 [4], or belonged to a room adjoining it, is at present uncertain. Internally, the building has [at the south end] evidently undergone considerable alterations at different times, as even the elevation of the floor has been changed. The western wall, which is well preserved in its whole extent to the height of five or six feet, has been covered with stucco outwardly towards the great court, much of which was perfect when uncovered (*ibid*, 139), and I believe presented similar indications of painting [to that on the apse], but it perished on exposure to the atmosphere (*ibid*, 197).

2.26 We have, no doubt, ascertained quite satisfactorily, the limits of the site of the public baths of *Uriconium* towards the north, west, south, but they are less certain on the eastern side. At first I imagined that they were bounded on this side by a line drawn G to K in the plan, but one or two hot and dry summers have furnished evidence that this is not the case. We can distinctly trace, looking down from the summit of the mound of earth raised from the excavations, lines of walls which exist underground, to a little distance eastward, which appear to have formed part of the building of the Balnea (*ibid*, 142).

3 The palaestral area and its porticos [14, 15]

3.1 Opposite E in the plan, a wide trench was carried from west to east, in the course of which was discovered first a wall, H, I; and next at a distance of about 12 feet (*ibid*, 121), a strong parallel wall running north and south. Within this wall was, first, a low narrow passage parallel to it; and then a raised floor of concrete, extending four or five feet, when it suddenly sank, with a ledge on one side, to a (Wright 1859, 222) depth of upward of four feet from the floor of cement, to a floor of large flagstones (Wright 1872, 122), of considerable extent (Wright 1859, 222). The floor of flags, covered with black earth, marked by the letter E in the plan, appears to have been a reservoir of water; for the bottom was found covered with black earth filled with broken pottery and other objects, such as may be supposed to have been thrown into a pond (Wright 1872, 121). At the further side the ground again rose abruptly to a floor of cement similar to the former (Wright 1859, 222). From the height of the original surface of the ground on the other side, the water appears to have been about three feet deep (Wright 1872, 121).

3.2 The floor of cement was continued eastwards till it was bounded by massive walls, having a large square projecting room (Wright 1859, 222). More recent excavations have brought to light a strong wall running north and south [15W], a little way to the west of [13], and parallel to the eastern boundary wall, which seems to be the west boundary of this building; and, considerably to the south, a wall running east and west, or parallel to the Old Wall, which was no doubt the southern boundary of what thus formed a very extensive rectangular parallelogram (Wright and Johnson 1859b, 258). A further exploration of the two parallel walls first brought to light by [the first] trench, showed that they belonged to a gallery, which extended along two sides of a rectangular inclosure [15], about two hundred feet square, H, T, K, and that these galleries formed the boundary of the building towards the west and south (Wright 1872, 121). A portion of a stone column, 1 foot 10 inches in diameter, has been found in the line of the south wall of the ambulatory of the Baths (Scarth 1860, 244).

3.3 The doorway 5 by which we first crossed the line of the Old Wall leads into a court. The ground here has been imperfectly explored, but parallel

walls have been traced from which we might be induced to suppose that there was a flight of steps ascending eastwards to the level of the floors of the various rooms (Wright 1872, 138).

3.4 Before making the recent excavations no doorway to the latrine HH was known, but now a good wide one, with two well-made steps, much worn, has been uncovered JJ. By this doorway the apartment in question communicates easily with the basilica at K and with the bath buildings by the corridor LL. The external surface of the wall facing the corridor has still some traces of having been covered with stucco and coloured in panels. Other walls besides those which I have alluded to have been laid open, especially about MM, but nothing definite has been made out (Johnson 1868, 58).

4 The latrine [20]

4.1 The building which I am going to describe, presented arrangements evidently calculated for the interior of a town, where good drainage was required, rather than for the open ground outside. The excavations have been carried on extensively on the ground immediately to the south [of the west end of the basilica], and have exposed to view the buildings represented in the accompanying plate (Fig 6.17). Our view, from the pencil of Mr Hillary Davies, of Shrewsbury, is taken from the ground which covers the foundations of the Old Wall, looking southward. It will be seen that the building in front is formed of four parallel walls running south from the line of the Old Wall (Wright 1867, 159–60).

4.2 The distance between the two walls on the left is only two feet and three inches, and the passage between them is three feet eleven inches deep from the level of the floor in the middle of the building. The appearance of the floor of this passage, when opened, left no room for doubt that it had been a drain into which refuse had been dropped, and which had carried off apparently by a continuation of the drain under the buildings to the north (*ibid*, 160), in the same direction, and no doubt in the same manner, as the drain we discovered more to the east running under the rooms marked 12 and 19 [4 and 3] on the plan. The earth at the bottom presented similar characteristics to that found in the pits at Richborough, and in it were found fragments of pottery and other objects, among which was a small earthen vessel containing almost unbroken the shell of a hen's egg. This is preserved in the Wroxeter Museum at Shrewsbury. From some indications on these walls, we are led to believe that it was originally covered with wood-work (Wright 1872, 148): that there was a row of seats of a latrine.

THE PUBLIC LATRINÆ OF URICONIUM.

Fig 6.17 Rooms 17 and 18 (right), 19 (centre), and 20A (Wright 1867, facing 160)

4.3 The similar space between the two walls on the other side (to the right in the engraving) is five feet two inches wide, and six feet nine inches deep. It presents also some indications of having been covered with some description of wooden frame or floor; but, if designed for the same purpose as the other, it was arranged, no doubt, somewhat differently (Wright 1867, 160–1). It will be seen that there is a slight set-off in the wall to the right at the same elevation at which there is a row of holes on the wall opposite, which seems to have been intended for the support of a wooden structure, but of what kind I will not venture to conjecture. It appears with the drain on the other side, to have formed part of the arrangements of one and the same building (Wright 1872 148).

4.4 The middle compartment [20], which is about fifteen feet and half wide, has been filled up with earth so as to form a floor, which was covered with a pavement of small bricks set in herring-bone pattern. A portion of the pavement still remains as shewn by the shading in the engraving (*ibid*, 148–9). There is a close chamber marked GG in the plan, it is 71 feet long and five feet broad at one end, and six at the other. It is, like all the other Roman works, very substantially built. It was cleared out to a considerable depth,

without finding any bottom or floor (Johnson 1868, 55–7).

4.5 The subjoined (Fig 6.18) represents a small portion of [the] wall. Six courses of red sandstone are first seen above ground, then three courses of white sandstone are laid upon them; next follows

Fig 6.18 Drain in west wall of Room 20A (Anderson 1867, 40)

a string-course of long thin tiles, above which there remain six more courses of white sandstone. Now the other side of this identical wall presents two string-courses of tiles; the one represented which goes right through the thickness of the three feet wall, and another string-course lower down, not appearing on the side of the wall sketched (Anderson 1867, 46).

4.6 About fifteen feet from the narrowest end, and 2 feet 6 inches below the level of the adjoining chamber, there is a singular opening in the wall, 10 inches high, 6 inches wide. The contents of this chamber or pit were very peculiar, and unlike common soil. On analysis they yielded distinct traces of ammonia, and a considerable quantity of alkaline phosphates. Traces of ammonia and phosphates might be expected in garden soil or in that of the surface of a well-manured field. But I think the abundant presence of these matters in earth taken from a depth of several feet, is almost a proof of my conjecture, that this was a cesspool. And it is another confirmation of this conclusion that it would receive the over-flowings of the adjacent latrine, by the opening which I have described. In this pit, or cesspool, if I may so designate it, many curious things were picked up. Among these was a bronze head of a lion, very well made, which had probably been the hilt of a sword or dagger; and the beautiful red carnelian signet ring, with engraved device in intaglio. The gem, I am sorry to say, was abstracted from the Museum by a visitor before it had been deposited in the proper case (Johnson 1868, 57).

4.7 If the former was a *cloaca*, or cesspool, the structure which I am next to describe must certainly have been a *latrina*. The [southern] part of the plan was discovered and described at the time of our former excavations. What has recently been done has tended greatly to confirm what was then stated, as to the probable nature and use of this building. It is an oblong chamber HH of some 71 feet in length by 20 in breadth. In the middle there still remains at H a patch of brick pavement of the herring-bone pattern (*ibid*).

4.8 On the one side of this paved floor, and at a lower level, there is a very well-formed and deep narrow drain *ii*, part of which was discovered and laid open in our former excavations. After it was made, there appears to have been some alteration or repair necessary, and a cross-wall has been built right across it at *j*, and it is not easy to discover how or where it empties itself. But, to our great surprise, we found, on digging down towards the foundations of the wall of the basilica at *bb*, at about a depth of 9 feet, that instead of a solid wall we got into a regular drain or sewer, so large that one might creep up it for some distance each way. There is no doubt that the drain *ii* just mentioned, and one which was discovered and still remains open near the public baths, have both terminated in this grand trunk (*ibid*, 57–8).

4.9 On the other side of the herring-bone pavement, deep in the ground, we traced a small wall running near the outer wall of this apartment. There is no doubt, therefore, that there was a drain on this side as on the other (*ibid*, 58) eight or ten feet below the central pavement (Anderson 1867, 31); and I have already stated there is a free passage from this drain into the great cess-pool *bb* (Johnson 1868, 58).

4.10 Before making the recent excavations no doorway to the *latrina* HH was known, but now a good wide one, with two well-made steps, much worn, has been uncovered JJ. By this doorway the apartment in question communicates easily with the basilica at K and with the bath buildings by the corridor LL (*ibid*) [see commentary note 36].

5 The public offices [17, 18]

5.1 Building N presents some rather singular features, which I will proceed to describe. This room is nearly a square, and is about thirty feet in its longest dimension. The side towards the street seems to have been open, or at least the masonry of the wall presents the appearance of having had wide folding doors, or a framework of wood of some kind, in two compartments cc (Wright 1860a, 161), separated by a pier of masonry, and no doubt capable of being closed with wood-work, the sides being grooved for this purpose (Wright 1872, 161) as if to receive a beam (Anderson 1867, 31). On this side of the room, internally, there was a smooth floor of cement, nearly level with the sill of the entrance openings, and extending not quite to the middle of the room. Beyond this, there is a floor at a much lower level, formed entirely of very fine sand, which has been brought from a distance, and placed to a considerable depth upon the natural soil of the spot. The occupants appear to have left it hastily, when the town was taken by the barbarians; for one of them, as he passed over the cill of the front opening into the street, dropped his money, which had been placed in a small earthen vessel. The latter was found on the sill, near its northern end, at the spot shewn in our cuts, broken into fragments, and the money lying a little scattered about it. Among it was found a small circular disc resembling a button, represented in the accompanying cut. There were, also with it, the remains of some other ornament made of metal, which had been of a globular form, and of delicate workmanship, much broken to pieces (Wright 1872, 161–3). These coins were:

CARACALLA
  (a silver denarius)   1
SEVERUS ALEXANDER
  (a plated denarius)   1
MAXIMUS
  (second brass)   1
GALLIENUS   2
SALONINA
  (copper, washed with silver)   1
POSTUMUS   1
VICTORINUS   8
TETRICUS   3
CLAUDIUS GOTHICUS   2
CARAUSIUS   1
THE CONSTANTINE FAMILY   12
VALENTINIAN   1
GRATIAN
  (AD 375–83)   1
a *MINIMUS*   1
DECOMPOSED   2

total number 38
(Wright 1872, 169)

5.2 Towards the north-western corner of the room, at a spot marked 2, stood a (*ibid*, 159) sort of furnace or forge (Wright 1860a, 161), in the form of a sugar loaf, about six feet high, built very roughly of (Wright 1872, 159) red (Wright 1860a, 161) clay, mixed with stones and other unprepared materials, among which were several pieces of unburnt mineral coal, a sufficient proof that substance was plentiful in Roman *Uriconium*. On the eastern side of this structure (Wright 1872, 159), was a hole or cavity in the upper part sufficiently large for a man to thrust his head in (Wright 1860a, 161) which had contained a fire so intensely hot that the whole internal surface was vitrified to some depth. From the form and position of this little furnace, it is quite evident that it must have been heated by a powerful blast, no doubt of bellows, but which, with their machinery, have long disappeared. Remains of burnt charcoal were found in it, and on the ground near it (Wright 1872, 159).

5.3 Upon the low wall *a*, *a*, a little behind the forge at 3 (Wright 1860a, 161) by the side of this sugar loaf, and just opposite the furnace, stands upright a rudely formed cylindrical stone 3 resembling the stump of a column, which was evidently used, in one way or another, for working metals which were melted, or rendered malleable, in it. These objects will be better understood by the accompanying sketch, taken from the south-east (Fig 6.19). The cylindrical block of stone is strongly bevelled round the top, perhaps to receive a wooden case on which the anvil was placed. A considerable quantity or the scoriae from molten metals were found scattered about, both within and room and outside (*ibid*, 161).

Fig 6.19 Room 18 (Wright 1872, 159)

5.4 Among other things found in this room were (Wright 1860a, 162) many fragments of worked metal (Wright 1872, 161), nearly a dozen hair-pins, two of which were much more ornamental than any we had found before; a much greater quantity of fragments of Samian ware, and of higher artistic merit, than had previously been met with in one spot; a portion of a large bronze fibula; a number of coins, and other things. One of the vessels of Samian ware is a fine bowl, with figures in high relief, representing a stag-hunt (Wright 1860a, 162).

5.5 The floor of sand had been supported on the northern side by a low wall *a*, *a*, from which another low wall *b*, *b*, crossed to the northern wall of the room, and between these low walls and the latter there had been a sort of pit, in which were found many pieces of scoria, and other apparent articles of refuse. On one side of the room, upon the floor of sand, was found a quantity of pounded granite, which, I am told, might be used for the purpose of enamelling; and many fragments of fine glass were also scattered about. On this same floor of sand, near the middle of the room, lay a large piece of a shaft of a column (Fig 6.20), of dark grey stone (Anderson 1867, 31). This, however, had probably found its way here by accident, and did not, apparently, belong to this room. Its appearance and position may be seen in the fore-going cut, which represents the interior of this room, as seen from the floor of the *latrinae*. In addition to the furnace already described, there are on the higher floor of cement near the south-western corner of the room, the remains of another furnace, which was built of masonry, and heated by means of a flue; and that, in the middle of the room, there is a square mass [or] pier (Wright 1860b, 106) of rather rough masonry, with a level surface about the height of the floor, which has been intended to support some heavy object, or possibly to serve as a work table. This mass of masonry is shown in the front of our first cut (Fig 6.19), with the higher floor to the left, and the lower floor of sand before it and to the right (Wright 1872, 162–4).

Fig 6.20 Room 18 (Wright 1872, 162)

5.6   There is another room [17], adjoining to this workshop, and lying between it and the wall of the basilica, which was, perhaps, also a shop, but it has not yet been opened. The excavators began to work upon it at the commencement of winter, when, as it was found that the walls were covered with stucco, and perhaps with fresco-painting, which would have been entirely destroyed by a sudden frost, they were ordered to desist, after filling up as much as they had already opened (*ibid*, 164).

5.7   Mr Wright was anxious to know the nature of the buildings between what we have always called the enameller's workshop AA, and the oblong square building supposed to have been a basilica, of which BB is the boundary wall. Between these two, therefore, the excavations were made. I am indebted to Mr Davies for the accompanying plan of the ground, and of the Roman works formerly and more recently brought to light. Here was found, in the first place, a large building about 40 feet square CC exactly like AA the enameller's shop. Like the latter it also faced the old Watling Street Road DD, and was entered by a large folding (or sliding) doors, for the reception of which the stone sockets still remain. In the centre of this apartment there is a small platform of masonry, about 5 feet square E, with a step going up to it all round [see note 5.5]. In one corner there is a low and imperfect flight of steps, and near it (at F) an irregular block of building which had certainly been a furnace. Many fragments of vitrified earthy and metallic substance or slag, and bits of charcoal and coal were found strewed about. There was also found the bowl end of an iron ladle, such as plumbers' men use for melting lead. The present floor of this chamber consists of pure red sand. Above the present floor of sand there

was formerly another of concrete, about 8 inches thick, which has been removed. In this were found several large bronze coins of Trajan, Hadrian, and his wife Sabina, with fragments of pottery, etc. There is, I think, no doubt that this had been the workshop of an artificer in metals. Although the walls are not correctly square, they are beautifully built, and look as perfect as when the builders first left them (Johnson 1868, 55).

6   The *macellum* [22]

6.1   It was soon found that a line of wall extended continuously southward from the end of the basilica and in continuation of its southern face (Wright 1872, 150). The front portion of the [*macellum*] now under excavation runs flush with the front of the basilica (Scarth 1859, 275). In tracing this wall to the south, the excavators came to two openings, at some distance apart, which induced us immediately to explore the ground on the other side of the wall. The first of these openings was twelve feet wide, at an elevation of two or three feet from the level of the street, and had been approached by an inclined plane (Wright 1872, 150–1), for the floor of the court was about 3 feet higher than the level of the street (Wright and Johnson 1859b, 259), the central part of which was formed by three great blocks of squared stone, and the rest apparently of smoothed concrete. These stones which are represented in the engraving as they now lie (Fig 6.21), were, when first uncovered, in their original position, as forming part of the inclined plane (Wright 1872, 151).

6.2   The other opening through the wall was at the same elevation (*ibid*), it was only five feet wide (Wright 1859, 221), but it was approached by two steps (Fig 6.22). Both entrances were found to lead into the same inclosure, a quadrangular court (Wright 1872, 151) between 40 and 50 feet square (Wright and Johnson 1859b, 259), paved with the same herring-bone brickwork which we have met with in other parts of these ruins (Wright 1872, 151). A large portion of the pavement still remains, the effect is very good, all crumbled and broken although the tiles are (Anderson 1867, 32). This extended over the whole space, except apparently in the centre, where, over a small extent, there were no traces of the former existence of pavement, and the appearance of the ground, when examined, led us to suppose that it might have been occupied by some structure, the remains of which had all been cleared away for building materials (Wright 1872, 151).

6.3   On the northern and southern side of this court we found a series of square rooms, marked *g, g, g*, on the plan, four on the northern side [22.1–4], and three on the southern [22.10–12], each about

Fig 6.21 North entrance to macellum *(Wright 1859, pl 18)*

twelve feet square. Our view of the larger entrance
(Fig 6.21) represents these rooms on the northern
side when three of them had been partly opened.
The one nearest the street [22.1], shewn in front
of our view, which is the only one yet cleared out,
was found to be no less than ten feet deep, with a
low cross wall at the bottom. In it was found a
quantity of unburnt charcoal, with some remains
of mineral coal. In two of the rooms, one on the
north side, the other on the south, great quantities
of bones of various animals and horns of stags
were found; and, as many of these had been cut
and sawed, the notion suggested itself that they
may have been stores of the materials used by the
manufacturers of the objects made of bone which
are found so numerously among the ruins of
Uriconium, and, in fact, that all these square cham-
bers were depôts of materials for sale (*ibid*, 151–2).

6.4   This conjecture appears to receive some confirmation from the circumstances that a number of
undoubted weights were picked up in the court,
which would seem to show that articles of some
kind had been delivered out by weighing (*ibid*,
152). The weights [are] of different sizes, made of
metal and of stone, some with Roman numerals,
thus leaving no doubt of their true character.
Four of these are represented in [a] cut. Three are
made of lead, and the larger one of stone. The
latter weights, according to our modern reckon-
ing, 11½ ounces; the larger one of the leaden

weights 20½ ozs, the one marked II, 2½ ounces,
and the other 2¼ ounces (*ibid*, 165). Among
other objects found in this part of the excavations
was a handle several inches long, perhaps of some
culinary vessel, made of block tin, a very unusual
metal to find in Roman remains: a fragment of the

Fig 6.22 South entrance to macellum *(Wright 1859, pl 19
top)*

vessel to which it had been attached remains with it (Roach Smith 1859c, 222).

6.5 The larger entrance is supposed to have been intended for horses, and perhaps for carts; and this supposition seems confirmed by the circumstances that the pavement on this side of the court had evidently been much damaged and repaired in Roman times, and that a portion of an iron horseshoe was found upon it (Wright 1872, 152).

6.6 The appearance of the southern, or smaller, entrance to the court was still more remarkable. The appearance of the two steps by which it was approached will be best understood by the view on our plate, and the stone of the upper step has been so much worn and hollowed by the same cause – the feet of those who had walked over it – that it broke into three pieces when the excavators attempted to raise it (Fig 6.22). There is also, on the most worn side of this upper stone, corresponding exactly to the worn corner of the lower stone, a deep hollow, in the form of a man's foot, which looks as though it had been scooped out intentionally, for we can hardly suppose it to have been worn into this form merely by people treading upon it. The condition of these steps proves that this quadrangular court must have been frequented by a great number of people on foot, and that the concourse of visitors came up from the street from the south (ibid).

6.7 We may suppose that [the quadrangular court's] architecture was more or less ornamental, especially if we might assume that the sculptured fragments found among its ruin belonged to it. When it was excavated, the portion of a capital of a column, represented in (Fig 6.23), was found lying on the floor. It is rather classical in style, and of large dimensions, for in its present state it is more that two feet high, and this is little more than two-thirds of its original height, for an upper part of a capital, corresponding with it, was also found, and is placed over it in the Museum at Shrewsbury. As, however, this upper part evidently belonged to another capital, and not to the one represented here, there must have been at least two of them (ibid, 156–7).

6.8 Among other objects found on the floor of this court were the remains of (ibid, 157) six dogs, which appeared also to have been massacred by the merciless invaders of the town (ibid, 323), the skull of one of which, now preserved in the Museum, bespoke an animal of the mastiff kind, of an unknown species, perhaps the British dog spoken of so much by Roman writers (ibid, 157).

6.9 It will be seen in the plan, that the series of rooms does not extend along the whole of the southern side of the court; but leaves an opening at the south-eastern corner, at H [22.9], where there was a descent, apparently by steps, to a level about two feet lower than the floor of the court, which also was paved with the small bricks in herring-bone pattern.

There appeared to have been here a descent to an opening into the bottom of the easternmost of the rooms marked g, but the ground has been so much broken that it was not possible to decide on its true character. From this lower floor, ran, along the eastern side of the court, what we supposed at first to have been a sort of long gallery, or cryptoporticus, which had for its eastern side the outer wall of the ambulatory of the Baths but, on being cleared out, it presented an unexpected appearance. It extends the whole length of the court and its side rooms, and is divided into compartments by transverse walls running from the wall forming the side of the court, about half-way across the space between it and the opposite wall [22.5–9]. A passage is thus left (ibid), which seems to have been paved only with concrete (Wright 1859, 221), which runs along the whole extent of this building, and appears to have communicated at both extremities with openings of some kind which ran along the northern and southern sides of the buildings of the court, but which have not yet been fully explored. The present appearance of these walls at the back of the quadrangular court, or market, will be better understood by the view given in our engraving (Fig 6.24) (Wright 1872, 157–8). In the eastern wall, opposite the first compartment from the south (ibid, 221), there appears to have been a door in the wall leading from the passage or gallery in front of [it] into the ambulatorium of the baths (ibid, 158).

6.10 On the floor of one of [the recesses], the northernmost, the excavators found a small cylindrical coffer, or box, in diameter about the size of an ordinary tumbler glass, and supported upon three short legs (ibid). An accidental blow of the excavator's pick has made a little breach in the upper rim,

Fig 6.23 Column capital found in macellum *(Wright 1872, 157)*

Fig 6.24 Rooms 22.5-9 (Wright 1859, pl 19 bottom)

which exposes in the interior a mass of decomposed wood, apparently of an uncommon and delicate kind; in the middle of which there is evidently some metal instrument which has almost the appearance of burnished silver (Wright 1859, 222). The lid was upon it, and the decomposition of the metal had caused it to be in a manner hermetically sealed. It has, however, been sawed off since it was deposited in the Museum, and the state in which its contents were found seemed to indicate that it was in an untouched condition, as if for sale, rather than having been in use (Wright 1872, 158). It appeared to have contained some description of unguent, but it was no longer possible to discover of what it was composed (*ibid*, 312–3).

6.11 The walls of the rooms mentioned above as bordering [the court] on each side, and which are probably all of the same depth as that which was excavated to the bottom, as high as they now remain, that is, about two feet above the floor of the court, present no traces of entrances, which, must, therefore, have been higher in the wall, and they were perhaps entered by a ladder, or by wooden steps (*ibid*, 158).

6.12 Walls of other buildings have been traced to the south of this supposed market, until, at a very short distance, the excavators came upon another transverse street (Wright and Johnson, 1859b, 260).

7   The streets to north and south

7.1 The wall which formed the northern side of the Basilica, ran at right angles from the face of the buildings fronting the Forum, and was traced in a direct line without any variation up to the edge of the field, where we were stopped. There could be no doubt, from various appearances which were noticed, that this wall formed the southern side of a street (Wright 1872, 184), the central pavement of which (CC, in the plan), composed of small round stones, was found at a distance of a few feet

to the north of the wall (*ibid*, 112) running nearly east and west (Wright 1860a 158), and that it was wide, paved in the middle in the same manner as that subsequently found to the south. The part of it immediately adjoining the wall appeared to have been formed of concrete (Wright 1872, 184).

7.2 The baths, again, were bounded to the south, by a line of buildings which ran at right angles to the Forum, and parallel to the street on the north, and it has been traced as far as the land allotted for excavation will permit. Here the roadway of the street has been uncovered, and the foundations traced of the houses on the opposite side. The paved part of this street, marked L, L, L, in the plan of the buildings excavated, which was bounded by kirb-stones, and did not reach quite to the walls of the houses, was somewhat more than twenty feet (*ibid*).

7.3 The remains of a chariot have been found at Wroxeter in the middle of the ancient town (*ibid*, 185) [in the form of] a wheel. It has been thus described by Dr Henry Johnson – 'In the centre of the hoop, as it lay in the ground, we found two smaller rings, one 7 inches and the other 5 inches in diameter. I have no doubt that they formed the nave of a wheel; the outer ring was to give strength, the inner one lined it with iron; traces of wood were found between the two; the axle-tree had been 5 inches in diameter, and worked within the inner ring. The outer iron hoop, or tire, is 3 feet 4 inches in diameter, 1½ inch wide, and it is still so sound that it rings when struck. There are traces of wood inside it, but it cannot be ascertained whether the wheel had fellies and spokes, or merely a piece of board to fill up the circle. It might serve for a light cart or chariot, but it is less substantial than any of our cart-wheels.' Similar hoops of iron have been found, which had probably likewise belonged to wheels (Scarth 1860, 244).

7.4 At Wroxeter the pavement of the street is formed of small stones, such as might be gathered from gravel, well put together, and hard beaten in, and presenting an appearance not much unlike that we call macadamizing. A row of kirb-stones was placed on each side. At the western end of the street of *Uriconium* just described, another street leaves it towards the south, also at right angles, and probably broad, because, from its position, it was evidently one of the principal streets of the town, but it lies under the modern road (Wright 1872, 185).

7.5 [Water pipes] were made of plates of lead, bent round into the form of a tube, not perfectly cylindrical, but having a sort of ridge at the juncture of the edges. Fragments of leaden tubes, answering exactly to this description, were found to the north-east of the Baths and Basilica, in the direction towards rather higher ground in which springs are said to be plentiful. They are preserved in the Museum at Shrewsbury (*ibid*, 218).

8   The Burials

8.1   From the number of human remains found in it, it is evident that, at the time of the destruction of the Roman city, many of the inhabitants had sought shelter [in the baths] and had been pursued and massacred (*ibid*, 114). In trenching across what were perhaps open courts to the south and the south-east of the door through the wall at *l* [south of 15N], remains of (Wright and Johnson 1859a, 214) human bones belonging to at least three or four individuals [were] gathered up (Roach Smith 1859a, 455), and in what appears to have been a corner of a yard at *n*, outside the semicircular end of the hypocaust, lay the skull and some of the bones of a very young child (Wright and Johnson 1859a, 214), believed, from the appearance of the skull, to have been an infant in the arms, which had perhaps been murdered and thrown down from a room above (Wright 1872, 114). Other scattered bones were subsequently met with (Roach Smith 1859a, 455).

8.2   In [8], three skeletons were found, that of a person who appears to have died in a crouching position in one of the corners, an examination of the skull (Wright and Johnson 1859a, 214) and jaw (Roach Smith 1859a, 456) leaves no room for doubting that he was a very old man (Wright and Johnson 1859a, 214). The others were lying down at the foot of the north wall (Wright 1872, 118). One at least was a female. Near the old man lay a little heap of Roman coins, in such a manner as to show that they must have been contained in a confined receptacle, and a number of small iron nails lying among them, with traces of decomposed wood, prove that this was a little box, or coffer. The remains of the wood are found attached to two or three of the coins (Wright and Johnson 1859a, 214). These coins, all copper but one, and in number a hundred and thirty-two, belonged to the following emperors:

TETRICUS	1
CLAUDIUS GOTHICUS	1
CONSTANTINE THE GREAT	13
CONSTANS	1
CONSTANTINE II	36
CONSTANTIUS II	5
JULIAN	1
HELENA	2
THEODORA	1
URBS ROMA	24
CONSTANTINOPOLIS	34
VALENS	1
MINIMI	6
DECOMPOSED	6

total number 132
(Wright 1872, 68)

8.3   In another hypocaust, to the eastward of that containing these three skeletons, another skeleton was found, which shows that in the midst of the terror with which the population of *Uriconium* was overwhelmed in this terrible moment, there was an impulse to seek concealment in the hypocausts (*ibid*, 323). Adjoining the room 13 [10], to the south, was a smaller room with a hypocaust, in which were found two skeletons, one that of a young person, but the other wanted the head (*ibid*, 119).

8.4   Among other things found in the [*macellum*] are one or two nice finger-rings, and human remains have again been met with (Roach Smith 1859b, 625).

Commentary

1.1   'perfect state of preservation' Wright appears to be distinguishing between free-built foundation, which is faced, and trench-built foundation which is not. In which case, the 'about two thirds' depth should refer to free-built walling lying both in a construction trench and in make up for the finished floor levels of the building, and this provides the context for his comment concerning the very deep foundation the wall must have.

1.2   'fallen from above' While the reversed capital may have been that found in the basilical hall (Barker *et al* 1997), it is tempting to take the comment to imply that it was part of a similar porch associated with the doors through the Old Work and that the *frigidarium* of the baths at least remained roofed during the later occupation of the *insula*. As Wright tells us that large stones exposed in his foundations were removed as they were thought to be too valuable, it does look as though there may have been such a porch on the grounds that had the stone been that uncovered in the modern excavations, it should not have been left behind.

1.4   'with interruptions' The excavations probably did not follow each sleeper wall continuously from end to end: the technique used in looking for structural remains was trenching, coupled with following wall tops at times. Some continuous lengths were probably exposed, but Wright's comments on the walls being interrupted or broken down to the foundations does not allow an interpretation of what he saw.

1.5   'after a short interruption' The break is still visible and, when viewed from the south, the lowest exposed part on the west consists of part of a very large stone of the same type as those used for major architectural features and the slabbing drain tops as well as the walling of drains where excessive water wear was expected. It is possible that the great drain found by Johnson (see 4.8) ran through the south wall of the basilical hall at this point.

'carrying away materials' Wright had difficulty in visualising the building north of the Old Work and its relationship to that. The south aisle was converted into an open alley as that removed structural difficulties – a solution adopted by Dame Kathleen Kenyon for the same reason. Wright found what seemed to be three kinds of flooring in this 'alley'. Firstly, mosaic which he discounted for two reasons: there were two other types to choose from, and he had decided that the aisle had been open to the skies. He found herringbone and enough large stone to think that there had been flagstones. Excavation has shown that there had been flagging by the Old Work and tessellation elsewhere, the latter being replaced by the herringbone floor at a later date (Barker *et al* 1997).

1.6 'two original openings' It is now known that there was only one door in the west wall of the nave (Barker *et al* 1997).

1.19 'here was an entrance' The doorway has now been found (Barker *et al* 1997). It is a pity that Wright and his colleagues tend to give very few details of some of the indications which led them to their conclusions.

1.20 'up to the eastern wall' Excavation has shown that the south sleeper wall in the hall had once been dressed with large blocks of stone (Barker *et al* 1997). At approximately 15 Roman feet intervals there had been special settings which would, if analogies in other large aisled halls may be relied on, have supported columns whose base diameters would have been about three Roman feet. There is, therefore, little chance that Wright's door existed. What he found was a section of robbed-out sleeper wall, and although the walling was not bottomed, the indications are that the construction sequence is the same as that in the east range of the *macellum*. There, the sequence was related to the building of one of the major drains of the *insula* and the same may have applied here as well.

2.1 'too valuable to be buried again' A useful indication of why some features will not be found as Wright described them: note also Scarth 1859, 266.

2.7 'a powerful fire' Wright thought that this probably came from the 'enameller's workshop' and had been an anvil. It was more likely to have been a fire-bar from a *praefurnium*.

2.9 'the rest of the wall' The 'very inferior' masonry has now gone. It may have been a rebuilding of the same date as the later third-century rebuilding in the *macellum* and the south portico.

2.10 'facing of the walls' Wright's 'artificial stone' is clearly ordinary tufa. His description of it as having been 'employed indiscriminately with the squared stones in the facing of the walls' strongly suggests that, in the vicinity of the heap of building materials, F, he saw work which could only be late and possibly part of the repairs at present dated to late third or early fourth century. The walling of 9C and 9D has been much reduced since Wright's workmen first uncovered it and it is possible that it was this structural element of the west lateral suite that he was thinking of, as the walling of the earlier periods in the same area will not serve.

2.11 'hypocausts previously opened' Wright's comment on their being more neatly built may reflect a different period, or that they were less affected by heat from the *praefurnium*.

'a small entrance' Obviously never a door, the gap is reminiscent of the one in the east wall of the *macellum* (see 6.9). Wright evidently tried to make sense of the structure and, having found several doorways, hoped to find enough to give some idea of access. What was not appreciated, and cannot be when only a plan is looked at, is the topographical fall from east to west and also, to a less marked extent, from north to south. This, coupled with the gradually less well preserved quality of the remains away from the Old Work, made Wright look for doors at a depth under the field surface to match those around the *frigidarium*.

2.12 'being perfectly visible' The contradiction here between what Wright surmised and the thoughts of Fox has been retained as it was difficult to construct an elision between such opposed views. Fox was right in supposing that there had been only one room south of the Old Work, but Wright's interpretation conditioned his thinking on how the baths operated just as Kenyon's denial that there had ever been an entrance in the middle of the Old Work was a fundamental feature of her interpretation.

2.15 'all these arches' Although there cannot be any guarantee that the fragment of vaulting found by Fox (Fig 6.11) did indeed come from the roof of the *frigidarium*, there is no particular reason for thinking that it could not have, as the scale of the structural remains shows that such a vault would not have been out of the question. However, the curve of the vault is less than would be expected and it is just possible that the fragment came from the nineteenth-century spoil heap (Fig 6.14). What is not clear is what walls Wright thought answered the two piers in the middle of the Old Work. He may have been interpolating two on the basis that his work had found the sleeper walls separating the cold plunges from the main area of the *frigidarium*. Fox's pier in the middle of room is equally mystifying. It should be noted that the only trace was in the west trench and, therefore, part of the east side of the drain y under the floor was found and misinterpreted.

'floors of the hypocausts' The meaning is that the tessellation was level with the floor of the hypocaust basement.

2.18 'rows of columns' Kenyon thought that the hypocaust in 4 was a later insertion. The major problem is that if it and the drain with the associated feature are all primary, how did they all fit together to form a coherent scheme? To have a hypocaust in 4 *ab initio* would provide the main suite with two *tepidaria*. This is no particular objection, but the best interpretation is for the hypocaust to be late and the best evidence for that is the remains of a dividing wall visible in the north wall: this would have had good foundations and, as Wright shows the *pilae* running through the line of the wall, that had gone when they were inserted to serve a new *tepidarium* when the old one was converted to a *caldarium*.

2.19 'exposure to the air' What this feature looked like when first uncovered is obscure. Both the text and what survives show that much has been lost and the remains presumably began to disintegrate. The earliest published plan (Wright and Johnson 1859a, 210) shows a wall with a central break running parallel withthe north wall of 4. To the east of the break is a square lying between the two walls and through which runs the drain still to be seen. There is an inaccuracy here as it is clear from the site that the drain lies west of the break. Another plan (Wright 1860a, pl 16) which seems to be the basis for the one published in *Uriconium* (Wright 1872) rearranges the features. The drain has been moved to its correct position, but the walling within Room 4 has been changed to show only the western part which now returns to meet the north wall of 4. It is possible that both show partial truth.

'in a singular manner' The scooped out stone is the worn threshold of a door.

2.21 'room with a hypocaust' Presumably the hypocaust was dismantled when either the west lateral suite was extended, or when the main suite was redesigned, if these activities are not part of one and the same event.

2.22 'having been cleared away' The small room with a hypocaust lying south of Room 10 is a puzzle. Kenyon in excavating this area found a room, her 15, for which she could suggest no real function except that it may have been a fuel store. There is no suggestion in her report that it ever had a hypocaust. It is possible that Wright was wrong in his description of the site and that he located part of the *caldarium* of the east lateral suite (11), and he meant south of 11A.

'of these buildings' The recess was the flue between the *tepidarium* and the *caldarium* which Wright never deduced as having existed despite his comments on the symmetry of the baths' plan.

2.24 'until it sank' The description of the behaviour of the cement floor within the great *caldarium* is difficult to reconcile with its condition when excavated this century let alone with the site as it is to

be seen today: it sounds as though Wright is describing the mass concrete floor of the suspensura still in position. He can hardly have been describing the remains of the inner wall of the *caldarium* as this seems not to have survived even as high as the basement floor of the hypocaust and, if it had, would have been described by Wright most probably as a ledge (see 3.1).

'well preserved and defined' The doors mentioned are not as easy to interpret as it may appear at first sight: Wright followed the revetment wall of the main suite which clearly ended at the points shown on the plan and did not run across the main *praefurnium* area. On re-excavation, the only structure found here was the mass of a much repaired and ruined *praefurnium* and its condition would not have allowed Wright to say that one door had its walls 'well preserved and defined'. Most probably he mistook the ends of the revetment wall which stopped short of the east and west walls of the *praefurnium*.

2.25 'is at present uncertain' The 'numerous series of pillars' clearly belong to the area occupied by the early *tepidarium* even if the *pilae* had been rebuilt to suit the final arrangements in this area.

2.26 'building of the Balnea' Presumably the remains of the rest of the east lateral suite and *caldarium exedra* as well as the later modifications between the two.

3.1 'running north and south' The 'strong wall' should be the sleeper wall for the west portico of the palaestral area, while the 'low passage', on the analogy of his description of the lower wall offset to the south in Room 4, should be the very wide lower wall along the east side of his 'strong wall' and which is almost certainly the bedding for a line of gutter blocks to take the rain water from the porticos overlooking the palaestral area.

'a ledge on one side' The 'ledge' was perhaps the unrecognised retaining wall for the *natatio*.

'of considerable extent' Clearly the floor of the *natatio*, 14, it would seem that he only saw it in a few places as, on re-excavation, the rubbish fill seems to have been largely intact.

'similar to the former' The 'raised floor of cement' should be the walkway round the *natatio*.

3.2 'wall running east and west' The rear wall of the south portico.

'towards the west and south' T-K is the south portico (23S). Some of the confusion in the interpretation in this area is due to the fact that Wright, following the tops of the walls, failed to find the junction of the rear wall of the south portico with the south-east corner of the *macellum*. This, coupled with his misinterpretation of the east range of the *macellum* and the east wall of the main drain across the south portico, which is shown on his plan, created the impression of an ambulatory around the baths, rather than two porticos only in the palaestral area and the existence of street-side porticos.

'ambulatory of the baths' The column diameter is appropriate for a portico and the wall line described shows that the fragment was found in the street-side colonnade, although no trace has so far been found of any original elements of a colonnade, and the rebuilding of the stylobate support wall at approximately (L) on the plan suggests strongly that the column fragment was an adventitious survival.

3.3 'of the various rooms' These parallel walls, or wall, were, or was, almost certainly the sleeper wall of the north portico of the palaestra (15N). Wright's mention of walls may be because he found a dual construction like that in the west portico of the same area (see 3.1). On the other hand, his suggestion of a flight of steps rising eastwards was almost certainly because he failed to clear the ground properly. His plan shows the north palaestral portico running up to the west cold plunge bath of the *frigidarium*, the wall of which might have led him to suppose that the portico sleeper wall returned north short of the bath buildings and that the wall of the plunge bath, of which he only dug the south end, runs right up to the south wall of the basilical hall.

3.4 'has been uncovered JJ' All evidence for the door and its steps has now vanished.

4.2 'buildings to the north' This is the built latrine trench now on the east side of the latrine building.

4.3 'nine inches deep' This is, in fact, the space (19) between the latrines and the public offices: a cordon sanitaire and light well.

'venture to conjecture' The holes in the wall are for putlogs and show that the wall, which forms the west side of the main drain running through the latrines and *macellum*, was built like the east wall of the *macellum* from or below the top of the military and Period 1 town demolition deposits. The offset on the other side may mark the level at which the wall was finished when the working or construction level was the top of the demolished buildings lying under the baths *insula*; the rest of the wall being continued from a new level formed when some or all of the make-up material, which had been brought in for the planned floor levels, was spread out.

4.6 '6 inches wide' One of the discoveries made when the *macellum* was first re-opened was that Wright's cryptoporticus was the result of robbing out a major drain. In the light of the 1955–85 excavations it is now possible to interpret the plan published by Johnson as showing, as he said it did, that the drain turned to run along the west side of the latrines. The thin wall which he shows towards the north end and describes in 4.9 is not the drain wall as such, but rather, as it is in the *macellum*, the

backing for a tile or stone-and-tile face. The south face of the south wall of the basilical hall in this area showed, before the ground was brought up to the level of the palaestral area, fairly convincingly that there had once been a drain set at a low level. What cannot be explained is the walling and other features found by Johnson inside the north end of the latrines because of attrition.

The 'singular opening' is certainly not an overflow channel from the latrines into a closed cess-pit but may have been to allow rain water to get into the main drains. If the latrine trenches were not cleaned out regularly, there could have been a build-up in them with the result that urine could have run out into this narrow area to create the conditions Wright so convincingly described (but see below).

'which I have described' The earth taken from a depth of several feet should have been from the military destruction deposits which have a greenish tinge and the objects he describes as having been found here may well have come from those or the thinner ones belonging to demolished Period 1 buildings. The phosphates and ammonia could have derived from a military latrine pit.

4.8 'where it empties itself' Johnson was puzzled by the complexity of the arrangements at the north end of the latrines. The 1955–85 excavations showed that the east drain ran from north to south, and that a room at a lower level lay to the north of the cross wall at the north end of the latrine.

'grand trunk' Johnson saves up his comments on the drain to form a kind of climax to his account. The letters bb, where he located the drain, are placed on the plan just south of the basilical hall and running from the north-west corner for a short distance to the east, and completely within the width of the latrine block. This is the location of the 1955–85 re-excavation. What is not clear is how far to the east Johnson dug. He certainly went east of the colonnade wall of the west portico of the palaestra as his comments on wall <M> show.

As the plan he published was the first which showed door 5 in approximately its correct position, it is possible that he excavated that far and perhaps as far as the break in the south wall of the basilical hall just to the west of the *frigidarium* and its west adjunct. That this was probably so is indicated by the plan published by Johnson (1868, 56) on which the offset which could until recently only be seen at the north end of the latrines in the south wall of the basilical hall is shown running well to the east of door 5 and it seems probable that Johnson found the drain running into the south aisle of the basilical hall (see 1.5).

4.9 'great cess-pool' Johnson describes the west latrine trench as having its bottom some eight or ten feet below the central pavement in the latrine.

The great drain at bb was found at a depth of nine feet, but nine feet below what, or what part of it was so deep, is not given. If the west drain was about nine feet below the floor, the main drain should be measured from the same level and it may be presumed that it was the top which was found at that depth. Although these measurements were confirmed in the 1955–85 excavations, there is a general slackness in giving measurements and it is possible that many were estimated in walking-stick or umbrella lengths rather than by using a proper measure.

5.1 'middle of the room' The floor of smoothed cement is clearly the floor of the chamber in the public building.

'soil of the spot' The lower 'floor' is obviously much lower than the cill of the entrance when Figs 6.19 and 6.20 are looked at. The walls, therefore, are almost certainly rampart buildings in the fortress (Webster 1996). Some faith may be placed in the siting of the west and south walls of these, but there is some ambiguity in the location of the east wall as this changes according to which plan is looked at: Wright 1872; Wright 1860a, pl 16; Johnson 1868, 56. All three are based on Hillary Davies' work. The only two plans which seem to agree are Wright 1872, the worst drawn of all, and Fox 1897, pl IV, and that is specifically based on an updated corrected master prepared by Davies (Fox 1897, 138). The position selected for Fig 6.1 is based on Wright 1869, pl 16.

A problem with interpreting the building as military is that its south wall runs on east from the east wall, whatever position that had been in, and this might have encroached on the *via sagularis*. The wall might be a military or early civilian timber addition, although it might be thought that Wright and his accomplices would only have recognised stone walling. Confirmation is needed that the whole of this low walling is indeed military.

'small earthen vessel' The hoard was presumably buried after the street-side portico had been adapted to purposes other than that of a plain public walkway.

'the accompanying cut' Wright 1872, 163. The button looks very much like a fragment of first-century military equipment.

5.5 'pounded granite' The description suggests that there is a misinterpretation here. Experience in excavating the construction deposits of the baths *insula* has shown that the mason's debris derived from building the grey sandstone secondary walling rots down to a loose coarse granular sand which might be thought to be a foreign material as it becomes much whiter than the stone from which it comes. If this supposition is acceptable, then Wright and Johnson excavated their way through the floor make-up deposits finding on

their way intermediate layers without knowing what it was that their workmen were throwing up from the excavations.

'built of masonry' The higher floor is the one belonging to the public building. The description of the furnace suggests that it was the same kind of feature found by Atkinson in the deposits he recognized as belonging to the late occupation of the forum and of which he found three (Atkinson 1942, 108, 111). Similar features have been found at the west end of the basilical hall (Barker *et al* 1997).

'the height of the floor' The square mass of rather rough masonry lies below the floor of the room and was intended to be the lower part of a pier supporting the ceiling or roof of the structure. Each of the public offices is over thirty feet across in either direction and it may be doubted whether if it had ever been intended to cover this in one span. There may well have been an upper floor and loadings on an unsupported span of this sort of size would hardly have been contemplated. The basilical hall has a span of this size, but that was a public space of altogether greater magnificence and would have been covered with trusses supporting only the stone roofing. The ledge found round the base of the central pier was only an offset, possibly at the top of trench-built foundations.

5.7 'enameller's workshop AA' It should be clear from the text, the figures, and the notes above that there is no justification for retaining Wright's interpretation of these two rooms as workshops. The length of monolithic column found under the floor of the public building raises important questions of where it may have come from. A similar question is posed by the weathered and battered statue of a nymph found under the finished floor levels of the *macellum* (Webster forthcoming). Both statue and column may have been reserved buildings materials from the Early Baths not needed in the new forum built over them. The column may have derived from the suggested east portico of the baths (Mackreth 1987, 141, fig 58).

'been a furnace' A view showing the relative levels of the imperfect flight of steps and the furnace would be useful: on the precedent of the remains found in 18, it may be supposed that the furnace lay at a higher level than the steps as the latter look, on plan, like one of Wright's 'low walls'. The steps may be the robbed out end of a wall belonging to a military rampart building. The furnace should have been either a military oven like those found in the rampart buildings to the south or, perhaps, an industrial feature belonging to the Period 1 town. The text makes no mention of the feature shown in plan in the north-east corner of the room.

Here again are two floors. Although there is little sense of level given in the text, the tenor of the comments made suggests that the relationship of the floors was precisely like those in 18 with the possible exception that Johnson dug to a greater depth than Wright. It is just possible that the 'coins of Trajan, Hadrian, and his wife Sabina' provide a date for the completion of this part of the baths *insula*, but much would depend, presumably, on their state of wear.

'builders first left them' The description could mean that they were plastered and painted as Wright thought they were going to be (Wright 1872, 164). However, it is more likely that they looked like well-laid masonry with freshly mortared joints. Johnson does not mention any plaster, let alone paint, although he tells us that this was found in the west portico of the palaestra. A feature of walling newly exposed when the make-up deposits were removed in the *macellum* was that it was free-built with struck joints and all, quite naturally, looked very fresh as it was the first time they had been exposed since the floor make-up was put in position.

6.1 'in continuation of its southern face' This should be its western face. Johnson's plan and this comment are enough to show that the dog-leg in the main west facade wall of the *insula* so often reproduced in past plans could have been corrected long ago, had it been customary to read through the fragmented accounts of the nineteenth-century excavations.

'inclined plane' The description of the inclined plane was incomprehensible until the area was re-excavated. The slope occurs in what seems to be the construction mortar deposits under the formal flooring of the west portico and may have been caused by the consolidation of make-up deposits lower down and lying over the front of the rampart and the inner edge of the back-filled fortress ditch.

6.2 'building materials' Fig 6.22 shows that the five feet was measured from the broken edge of the original entrance to the south side of the rebuilt central section. The presence of only one of the original bottom steps influenced Wright in his assessment and he failed to notice the north edge of the entrance with the remains of a large block of stone set in it. The stone belonged to a major framing like those in the baths doors, best seen in the west lateral suite.

6.3 'at the bottom' The low wall proved, on re-excavation, to be the rear wall of a rampart building, itself an extension in stone of the first rampart building, also of stone, north of the *porta principalis* of the fortress (Webster forthcoming). The deposits of charcoal, etc. were almost certainly inside the timber and clay rampart building sealed under the stone extension. Wright only dug down deep in the north-east corner of the room.

6.4 'in a cut' Wright 1872, 165.

6.7 'original height' The illustration (Wright 1872, 157) has been used to locate the fragment of capital and the stone survives in care of English Heritage. The upper stone Wright mentions has not been identified.

6.9 'rooms marked *g*' The apparent descent was almost certainly Wright's workmen digging their way into the robber trench of the drain from the court of the *macellum* to the main drain in the east range. When re-excavated, a stretch of absent facing was found in the north wall precisely where the robber trench butted it. Wright possibly saw this and interpreted it as some kind of doorway. In reality, the recess in the wall may well have been created by building the wall around the already existing structure of the drain, which, when robbed out, left the recess: in other words, there may never have been any facing here.

'paved only with concrete' Wright's passage is the upper part of the robber trench for the north-south drain. Fig 6.24 seems to show in the furthest cross-wall a large stone bedded in its east end. This should have been part of a lintel block carrying the wall over the drain. The only visible evidence today for these lintels is the end of one built into the main east wall of the *macellum*. Details of this kind emphasise the importance of locating Davies' original drawings and any early photographs.

'ambulatorium of the baths' The 'door' is a robbed out section of the main east wall. On re-excavation, no evidence was found to suggest that there had been any special feature here.

6.11 'by wooden steps' Wright was led astray by the depth to which he dug in the north-western room of the *macellum* as to where the floor levels of the ranges would have been, and his 'cryptoporticus' in the east range may well have flowed from that as well as from the aberration of the low-level herringbone flooring in the south-east corner room. Re-excavation has established that the top of the construction debris over the make-up for the *macellum* is well below the floor level of the walkway round the central court. It is also clear that there had been no formal deposits over the construction rubbish. Therefore, the floors of the rooms may be assumed to have been of wood and what is missing is the level of the joists and the steps up into the rooms from the walkway round the court.

6.12 'another transverse street' The walls of 'other buildings' can only be the sleeper wall of the south portico, coupled possibly with the drain in the street next to that. The existence of the south portico (23S) and its return up the west side of the *insula* was not established until the recent excavations, even though Wright's workmen had run out at least one trench to the west and uncovered the sleeper wall for the colonnade of the west portico.

7.1 'where we were stopped' Two points of interest arise from the published plan of this wall. The first is at the west end. Wright shows the west wall of the basilical hall continuing north. What this may signify is not yet known. Kenyon, on her plan, omits the continuation. Wright shows the east end of the north wall going beyond the line of the north-south wall at that end of the *insula*. Kenyon shows a clean corner, but has an addition on the east side of the corner which she describes as a buttress.

'formed of concrete' The emptying of one of Kenyon's trenches across the north portico (23N) has shown that there is at least one thick concrete, or coarse *opus signinum*, floor inside the portico. Such floors are known in the west portico, but not in the southern one.

7.2 'kirb-stones' The term is obscure. No kerbs as such have been seen marking the edge of any of the three streets recently exposed. It is possible that the sleeper walls for the porticos might have given Wright this impression, but the description of the street as not quite reaching the walls of the houses and the showing of a gap between the street metalling and the south portico sleeper wall suggests that this interpretation will not do. At present there is no answer.

A note, however, may be made of the gap between the metalled street and the south portico wall. It could be argued that there had been a row of gutter blocks which had been robbed out. While that is possible, it is known that the robber trench of the drain running through the *macellum* runs on through the south portico. The north-south wall across that and lying on the east side of the drain has been re-excavated and can be seen to be the retaining wall of the drain which once carried the portico floor over the drain on stone cover slabs. It seems highly likely that the drain turned west down the street and ran on towards the river. But there is the possibility that in the street there was a T-junction and that the other arm of the drain is represented by the gap running east along the road-side.

8.4 'been met with' There would appear to be sufficient burials present on the site for their occurrence to be deliberate rather than adventitious. As yet there is little evidence to suggest a large and well-organised cemetery, but the ruins may have inhibited a regular layout even though they may have been the reason why the site was selected. The reason why the Old Work survived at all could have been because it had formed part of a church or chapel. The burials would then have a context. The one piece of apparently adventitious damage the wall has suffered, the hole east of the original entrance, may have been a window. The *frigidarium* is aligned east-west and its major entrance opened into an area full of late buildings (Barker *et al* 1997). Is it too fanciful to see such a complex having been furnished with a church? If not, then such a building would predate the Middle Saxon work in the present parish church.

Bibliography

Adam, J-P, 1994 *Roman building: materials and techniques*, London

Adams, B, and Jackson, D, 1989 The Anglo-Saxon cemetery at Wakerley, Northamptonshire, excavations by Mr D Jackson, 1968-9, *Northamptonshire Archaeol*, **22**, 69-178

Allason-Jones, L, 1984 A lead shrine from Wallsend, *Britannia*, **15**, 231-2

—, 1989a *Ear-rings in Roman Britain*, BAR, **201**, Oxford

—, 1989b *Women in Roman Britain*, London

—, 1993 The small finds, in Casey and Davies 1993

Allason-Jones, L, and Miket, R, 1984 *The catalogue of small finds from South Shields Roman Fort*, Soc Antiq of Newcastle upon Tyne monograph 2, Newcastle upon Tyne

Allason-Jones, L, and MacKay, B, 1985 *Coventina's Well: a shrine on Hadrian's Wall*, Chesters

Allen, D, 1986 The glass vessels, in Zienkiewicz 1986, II, 98-116

Anderson, A C, 1981 Some continental beakers of the first and second centuries AD, in Anderson and Anderson 1981, 321-48

Anderson, A C, and Anderson, A S, 1981 *Roman pottery research in Britain and north-west Europe*, BAR Int Series, **123**, Oxford

Anderson, A, Fulford, M A, Hatcher, H, and Pollard, A, 1982 Chemical analysis of hunt cups and allied wares from Britain, *Britannia*, **13**, 229-38

Anderson, F W, 1980 *Wroxeter, Shropshire: Roman stone finds*, Ancient Monuments Lab Rep 3212

Anderson, J C, 1867 *The Roman city of Uriconium at Wroxeter, Salop*, London

Andrews, A, and Noddle, B A, 1975 Absence of premolar teeth from ruminant mandibles found at archaeological sites, *J Archaeol Science*, **2**, 137-44

Apted, M R, Gilyard-Beer, R, and Saunders, A D (eds), 1977 *Ancient Monuments and their interpretation, essays presented to A J Taylor*, Chichester

Archer, S, 1979 Late Roman gold and silver hoards in Britain: a gazetteer, in *The end of Roman Britain* (ed P J Casey), 29-64, Oxford

Armitage, P, and Clutton-Brock, J, 1976 A system for classification and description of the horn cores of cattle from archaeological sites, *J Archaeol Science*, **3.4**, 329-48

Armour-Chelu, M, 1997 The animal bones, in Barker *et al* 1997

Armour-Chelu, M, and Clutton-Brock, J, 1985 Notes on the evidence for the use of cattle as draught animals at Etton, *Antiq J*, **65**, part 2, 297-302

Arthur, P, 1989 On the origins of Richborough form 527, in *Anfore Roman e storia economica: un recennio di recherche*, Collection de l'ecole française de Rome, **114**, 249-56

Arthur, P, and Marsh, G (eds), 1978 *Early fine wares in Roman Britain*, BAR, **57**, Oxford

Atkinson, D, 1942 *Report on excavations at Wroxeter (the Roman city of Viroconium) in the County of Salop, 1923-1927*, Oxford

Baker, J R, 1984 The study of animal diseases with regard to agricultural practices and man's attitude to his animals, in Grigson and Clutton-Brock 1984, 253-7

Baker, J R, and Brothwell, D, 1980 *Animal diseases in archaeology*, London

Barb, A A, 1969 Review, *Gnomon*, **41**, 298-307

Barker, P A, 1990 *From Roman Viroconium to medieval Wroxeter*, Worcester

Barker, P A, White, R H, Pretty, K B, Bird, H, Corbishley, M H, 1997 *Wroxeter, Shropshire: Excavations on the site of the baths basilica, 1966-90*, London

Bassett, S R, 1990 The Roman and medieval landscape of Wroxeter, in Barker 1990, 10-12

Bastien, P, 1967 *Le monnayage de bronze de Postume*, Wettern

Baxter, M J, and Cool, H E M, 1991 An approach to quantifying window glass, in *Computer applications and quantitative methods in archaeology 1990* (eds K Lockyear and S Rahtz), BAR Int Ser, **565**, 127-132

Bidwell, P T, 1979 *The legionary bath-house and basilica and forum at Exeter*, Exeter

—, 1982 *Legionary baths and their place in the development of bath-house architecture*, unpub MA thesis, Univ Exeter

—, 1985 *The Roman fort of Vindolanda at Chesterholm, Northumberland*, HBMC Archaeol Rep, **1**, London

Biek, L, 1981 Analyses of pigments, in Davey and Ling 1982, 220-22

Binford, L, 1978 *The Nuniamit Eskimo*, New York

Bishop, M C, 1989 Soldiers and military equipment in the towns of Roman Britain, in *Roman frontier studies* (eds V Maxfield and M Dobson), 21-7, Exeter

Bishop, M C, and Coulston, J C N, 1993 *Roman military equipment from the Punic Wars to the fall of Rome*, London

Bishop, M C, and Dore, J N, 1988 *Corbridge, excavations of the Roman fort and town*, London

Blagg, T F C, 1980 Roman civil and military architecture in the province of Britain, *World Archaeol*, **12**, 27-42

Bland, R, and Johns, C, 1993 *The Hoxne treasure*, London

Blockley, K, 1989 *Prestatyn 1984-5: An Iron Age farmstead and Romano-British industrial settlement in North Wales*, BAR, **210**, Oxford

Blockley, K, Blockley, M, Frere, S S, and Trow, S, 1995 *Excavations in the Marlowe car park and surrounding areas*, The Archaeology of Canterbury, **5**

Boessneck, J, 1969 Osteological differences between sheep and goat, in *Science and archaeology* (eds D Brothwell and E Higgs), 2nd edn, 331-58, London

Böhme, A, 1970 *Saalburg Jahrbüch*, Bericht des Saalburg Museums, **27**

—, 1972 Die fibeln der Kastelle Saalburg und Zugmantel, *Saalburg Jahrbüch*, **29**, 5-112

Boon, G C, 1961 Roman antiquities at Welshpool, *Archaeol J*, **88**, 13-31

—, 1965 Lightwights and limesfalsa, *Numismatic Chron*, 7 ser, **5**, 161-76

—, 1966 Legionary ware at Caerleon?, *Archaeol Cambrensis*, **113**, 45-66

—, 1969 Belgic and Roman Silchester: the excavations of 1954-8, with an excursus on the early history of Calleva, *Archaeologia*, **102**, 1-81

—, 1977 Gold-in-glass beads from the ancient world, *Britannia*, **8**, 193-207

—, 1982 The coins, in *Report on the excavations at Usk, 1965-1976: The coins, inscriptions and graffiti* (ed W Manning), 3-15, Cardiff

—, 1983 Potters, oculists and eye-troubles, *Britannia*, **14**, 1-12

—, 1988 Counterfeit coins in Roman Britain II, *Coins and the archaeologist*, (eds P Casey and R Reece), 2nd edn, 102–88, London

Boon, G C, and Savory, H N, 1975 A silver trumpet-brooch with relief decoration, parcel-gilt, from Carmarthen, and a note on the development of the type, *Antiq J*, **55**, 41–61

Bourdillon, J, and Coy, J, 1980 The animal bones, in *Excavations at Melbourne Street, Southampton, 1971–76* (P Holdsworth), 79–121, London

Brailsford, J W, 1958 Early Iron Age 'C' in Wessex, *Proc Prehist Soc*, **24**, 101–9

—, 1962 *Hod Hill I, antiquities from Hod Hill in the Durden Collection*, London

Brain, C K, 1976 Some principles in the interpretation of bone accumulations associated with man, in *Human origins, perspectives in human evolution*, **3** (eds G Isaac and A McCown), 97–116, London

Branigan, K, 1977 *Gatcombe: The excavation and study of a Romano-British villa estate 1967–76*, BAR, **44**, Oxford

Brassington, M, 1980 Derby racecourse kiln excavations 1972–3, *Antiq J*, **60**, 41–61

Breeze, D J, 1977 The fort at Bearsden and the supply of pottery to the Roman army, in Dore and Greene 1977, 133–45

Brewer, R J, 1986 The beads and glass counters, in Zienkiewicz 1986, II, 146–56

Brewer, R J, 1986 The bronze brooches, in Zienkiewicz 1986, II, 168–172

Brickstock, R J, 1987 *Copies of the Fel Temp Reparatio coinage in Britain*, BAR, **176,** Oxford

—, 1992 Wroxeter, Shropshire, in *Coin hoards in Roman Britain:* **9**, The Chalfont hoard and other coin hoards (ed R Bland), London

Brickstock, R J, and Casey, P J, 1997 The coins, in Barker *et al* 1997, 264–8

Britnell, J, 1989 *Caersws vicus, Powys*, BAR, **205**, Oxford

Britnell, W, 1989 The Collfryn hillslope enclosure, Llansantffraid Deuddwr, Powys: excavations 1980–1982, *Proc Prehist Soc*, **55**, 89–134

Brodribb, A C, Hands, A R, and Walker, D R, 1968 *Excavations at Shakenoak Farm, near Wilcote, Oxfordshire, I: Sites A and D*, Oxford

—, 1971 *Excavations at Shakenoak Farm, Wilcote, Oxfordshire, II: Sites B and H*, Oxford

—, 1973 *Excavations at Shakenoak Farm, near Wilcote, Oxfordshire, IV: Site C*, Oxford

Brown, R A, 1986 The Iron Age and Romano-British settlement at Woodcock Hall, Saham Toney, Norfolk, *Britannia*, **17**, 1–58

Brown, A E, and Woodfield, C, 1983 Excavations at Towcester, Northamptonshire: The Alchester road suburb, *Northamptonshire Archaeol*, **18**, 43–140

Buckland, P C, and Magilton, J R 1986 *The archaeology of Doncaster I, The Roman civil settlement*, BAR, **148**, Oxford

Bushe-Fox, J P, 1913 *Excavations on the site of the Roman town at Wroxeter, Shropshire, in 1912*, Soc Antiq Res Rep, **1**, London

—, 1914 *Second report on the excavations on the site of the Roman town at Wroxeter, Shropshire, 1913*, Soc Antiq Res Rep, **2**, London

—, 1916 *Third report on the excavations on the site of the Roman town at Wroxeter, Shropshire, 1914*, Soc Antiq Res Rep, **4**, London

—, 1926 *First report on the excavations of the Roman fort at Richborough, Kent*, Soc Antiq Res Rep, **6**, London

—, 1928 *Second report on the excavations of the Roman fort at Richborough, Kent*, Soc Antiq Res Rep, **7**, London

—, 1932 *Third report on the excavation of the Roman fort at Richborough, Kent*, Soc Antiq Res Rep, **10**, London

—, 1949 *Fourth report on the excavations of the Roman fort at Richborough, Kent*, Soc Antiq Res Rep, **16**, London

Butcher, S A, 1977 Enamels in Roman Britain, in Apted *et al*, 1977, 41–70

Callender, M H, 1965 *Roman amphorae*, Oxford

Calvi, M C, 1968 *I vetri Romani del Museo di Aquileia*, Pubblicazioni dell'Associazone Nazionale per Aquileia 7, Aquileia

Canti, M, 1988 *Wroxeter baths site: soil report*, Ancient Monuments Lab Rep 1/88

Cantrill, T C, 1931 Geological report on Uriconium, *Archaeol Cambrensis*, **86**, 87–98

Carson, R A G, and Kent, J P C, 1960 *Late Roman bronze coinage, 2*, London

Casey, P J, 1974 A coin of Valentinian III from Wroxeter, *Britannia*, **5**, 374–5

—, 1991 Coin evidence and the end of Roman Wales, *Archaeol J*, **146**, 320–9

—, 1994 *Roman coinage in Britain*, 2nd edn, Aylesbury

Casey, P J, and Davies, J L, with Evans, J, 1993 *Excavations at Segontium (Caernarfon) Roman fort, 1975–1979*, CBA Res Rep, **90**, London

Castle, S A, 1972 A kiln of the potter Doinus, *Archaeol J*, **129**, 69–88

—, 1974 Excavations at Brockley Hill, Middlesex, March-May 1972, *Trans London Middlesex Archaeol Soc*, **25**, 251–63

Castle, S A, and Warbis, J H, 1973 Excavations on Field No 157, Brockley Hill (Sulloniacae?), Middlesex, 1968, *Trans London and Middlesex Archaeol Soc*, **24**, 85–110

Cavalier, M, 1994 Les Amphores Richborough 527 decouverte d'un atelier a Portinenti (Lipari, Italie), *Soc Francaise d'Etude ceramique antique Gaule, Actes du Congrés de Millau*, 189–92

Chadburn, A, and Tyers, P, 1984 *The Roman ceramics from Fenchurch Street*, DUA Early Roman Pottery from the City of London, **5**, London

Champion, S, 1995 Jewellery and adornment, in Green 1995, 411–19

Charlesworth, D, 1959a Roman glass from northern Britain, *Archaeol Aeliana*, ser 4, **37**, 33–58

—, 1959b The glass, in The Roman bath house at Red House, Beaufront, nr Corbridge (C Daniels), *Archaeol Aeliana*, ser 4, **37**, 164–6

—, 1966 Roman square bottles, *J Glass Studies*, **8**, 26–40

—, 1976 Glass vessels, in *Finds from a Roman sewer system and an adjacent building in Church Street* (A MacGregor), The Archaeology of York, **17/1**, 15–18

—, 1979 Glass (including material from all other Exeter sites excavated between 1971 and 1976), in Bidwell 1979, 223–31

—, 1981 Glass from the burials, in Partridge 1981, 268–71

—, 1984 The glass, in Excavations at Dorchester on Thames 1962 (S Frere), *Archaeol J*, **141**, 152–5

Christison, D, 1901 Account of the excavation of the Roman station of Camelon, near Falkirk, Stirlingshire, undertaken by the Society in 1900, *Proc Soc Antiq Scotland*, **35**, 329–417

Clay, P, and Mellor, J E, 1985 *Excavations in Bath Lane*, Leicestershire Museums, Art Galleries and Record Service Archaeol Rep, **19**, Leicester

Clifford, E, 1961 *Bagendon: a Belgic oppidum, a record of the excavations of 1954–56*, Cambridge

Cole, H, 1966 Analyses and discussion of the Caerleon window glass, *J Glass Studies*, **8**, 46–7

Coles, F R, 1904/5 Report on stone circles in Aberdeenshire, *Proc Society Antiq London*, **39**, 206–18

Collingwood, R G, 1930 Romano-Celtic art in Northumbria, *Archaeologia*, **80**, 37–58

Collingwood, R G and Wright, R P, 1991 Weights, gold vessels, silver vessels, bronze vessels, lead vessels, pewter vessels, shale vessels, glass vessels, spoons, in *The Roman inscriptions of Britain, 2, instrumentum domesticum* (ed S Frere and R Tomlin), Stroud

Colls, D, Étienne, R, Lequément, B, Liou, B, and Mayet, F, 1977 L'épave Port-Vendres II et le commerce de la Bétique just a l'époque de Claude, *Archeonautica*, **1**

Cool, H E M, 1979 A newly found inscription on a pair of silver bracelets from Castlethorpe, Buckinghamshire, *Britannia*, **10**, 165–8

—, 1983 A study of the Roman personal ornaments made of metal, excluding brooches, from southern Britain, unpub PhD thesis, Univ Wales

—, 1990 Roman metal hair pins from Southern Britain, *Archaeol J*, **147**, 148–82

—, 1993 Copper alloy, in Darling and Gurney 1993, 72–140

Cool, H E M, Lloyd-Morgan, G, and Hooley, D, 1995 *Finds from the Fortress*, Archaeology of York, **17/10**, York

Cool, H E M, and Price, J, 1995 *Roman vessel glass from excavations in Colchester 1971–85*, Colchester

Cool, H E M, and Price, J, 1998 The vessels and objects of glass, in *Roman Castleford excavations 1974–5. I: the small finds* (eds H Cool and C Philo) Yorkshire Archaeology, **4**, 141–94, Wakefield

Cool, H E M, and Price, J, forthcoming Report on the vessel glass associated with the military occupation at Wroxeter, in Webster forthcoming

Crawford, M, 1974 *Roman republican coinage*, Cambridge

Cree, J E, 1922 Account of the excavations on Traprain Law during the summer of 1921, *Proc Soc Antiq Scotland*, **56**, 189–259

Crouch, K R, and Shanks, S A, 1984 *Excavations at Staines, 1975–76, the Friends burial ground Site*, London and Middlesex Archaeol Soc and Surrey Archaeol Soc joint publication, **2**

Crummy, N, 1983 *The Roman small finds from excavations in Colchester, 1971–9*, Colchester Archaeol Rep, **2**

Crummy, P, 1988 Colchester, in Webster 1988a, 24–47

—, 1992 *Excavations at Culver Street, the Gilberd School, and other sites in Colchester 1971–85*, Colchester

Cunliffe, B W (ed), 1968 *Fifth report on the excavations of the Roman fort at Richborough, Kent*, Soc Antiq Res Rep, **23**, Oxford

—, 1971 *Excavations at Fishbourne, 1961–1969, II: The finds*, Soc Antiq Res Rep, **27**, London

—, 1975 *Excavations at Portchester Castle, I: Roman*, Soc Antiq Res Rep, **32**, London

—, (ed), 1988 *The Temple of Sulis Minerva at Bath, 2: The finds from the Sacred Spring*, Oxford Univ Comm Archaeol Monograph, **16**, Oxford

—, 1991 *Iron Age communities in Britain*, 3rd edn, London

Curle, J, 1911 *A Roman frontier post and its people, the fort of Newstead in the parish of Melrose*, Glasgow

—, 1933 An inventory of objects of Roman and provincial Roman origin found on sites in Scotland not definitely associated with Roman constructions, *Proc Soc Antiq Scotland*, **66**, 277–397

Curwen, E C, 1926 On the use of scapula as shovels, *Sussex Archaeol Colln*, **67**, 139–45

Daniels, C (ed), 1978 *Handbook to the Roman Wall with the Cumbrian coast and outpost Forts*, Newcastle

Dannell, G B, 1971 The samian pottery, in Cunliffe 1971, 260–318

—, 1987 Coarse pottery, in Dannell and Wild 1987, 133–68

Dannell, G B, and Wild, J P, 1987 *Longthorpe II, the military works-depot: an episode in landscape history*, Britannia Monograph, **8**, London

Darling, M J, 1976 The pottery from the legionary fortress at Wroxeter and associated military sites, unpubl MPhil Thesis, Univ Nottingham

—, 1977 Pottery from early military sites in Western Britain, in Dore and Greene 1977, 57–100

—, 1984 *Roman pottery from the upper defences*, Archaeology of Lincoln, **16/2**

—, 1985a The other Roman pottery, in *Inchtuthil: the Roman legionary fortress*, (L F Pitts and J K St Joseph), Britannia Monograph, **6**, London, 323–38

—, 1985b Roman pottery, in *Kingsholm: Excavations at Kingsholm Close and other sites with a discussion of the archaeology of the area* (H Hurst), 67–93, Gloucester

—, forthcoming The pottery, in Webster forthcoming

—, forthcoming The pottery from the military site at Lake Farm, Wimborne, Dorset

Darling, M J, and Gurney, D, 1993 *Caister-on-Sea excavations by Charles Green, 1951–55*, East Anglian Archaeology Rep, **60**

Darlington, J, and Evans, J, 1992 Roman Sidbury, Worcester: excavations 1959–1989, *Trans Worcs Archaeol Soc*, **13**, 5–104

Davey, N, and Ling, R, 1982 *Wall-painting in Roman Britain*, London

Déchelette, J, 1904 *Les Vases céramiques ornés de la Gaule romaine*, Paris

Delaine, J, 1988 Recent research on Roman baths, *J Roman Archaeol*, **1**, 11–32

Delort, E, 1935 La céramique de Satto et Saturninus, *1 Annuaire de la Société d'Histoire et d'Archéologie de Lorraine*, 1–52

de Ruyt, C, 1983 *Macellum marché alimentaire des Romains*, Louvain

Detsicas, A (ed), 1973 *Recent research in Romano-British coarse pottery*, CBA Res Rep, **10**, London

—, 1977 First-century pottery manufacture at Eccles, Kent, in Dore and Greene 1977, 19–36

Dickinson, B M, 1984 The Samian ware, in Frere 1984, 175–97

—, 1986 Potters' stamps and signatures on samian, in Miller *et al* 1986, 186–98

Dickinson, B, Hartley, B R, and Pearce, F, 1968 Makers' stamps on plain samian, in Cunliffe 1968, 125–48

Dickinson, T M, 1982 Fowler's type G penannular brooches reconsidered, *Med Archaeol*, **26**, 41–68

Dimitrova-Milcheva, A, 1981 *Antique engraved gems and cameos in the National Archaeological Museum in Sofia*, Sofia

Dix, B, and Aird, P, 1983 Second century pottery from Sandy, Bedfordshire, *Bedfordshire Archaeol*, **16**, 2–7

Dix, B, and Taylor, S, 1988 Excavations at Bannaventa (Whilton Lodge, Northants), 1970–71, *Britannia*, **19**, 299–356

Dollfus, M A, 1975 Catalogue des Fibules de Bronze Gallo-Romaines de Haute Normandie, *Mémoires présentés par divers Savants à l'Académie des Inscriptions et Belles-Lettres de l'Institut de France*, **16**, 9–261

Dool, J, and Wheeler, H, 1985 Roman Derby: excavations, 1968–1983, *Derbyshire Archaeol J*, **105**

Dore, J, and Greene, K, (eds) 1977 *Roman pottery studies in Britain and beyond*, BAR, **30**, Oxford

Down, A, 1978 *Chichester excavations*, **3**, Chichester

—, 1989 *Chichester excavations*, **6**, Chichester

Down, A, and Rule, M, 1971 *Chichester excavations*, **1**, Chichester

Dudley, D, 1967 Excavations on Nor'Nour in the Isles of Scilly, 1962–6, *Archaeol J*, **124**, 1–64

Duncan, G C, 1964 A Roman pottery near Sutri, *Papers of the British School at Rome*, **32**, 38–88

Duncan-Jones, R, 1974 *The economy of the Roman Empire, quantitative studies*, Cambridge

—, 1990 *Structure and scale in the Roman economy*, Cambridge

Durand-Lefebvre, M, 1963 *Marques de potiers Gallo-Romains trouvées a Paris*, Paris

Edwards, J, 1984 *The Roman cookery of Apicius*, London

Ellis, P, 1991 Wroxeter, the 1955–85 excavations, a post-excavation and publication assessment, BUFAU typescript rep, **174**

—, 1992 Revised research design, BUFAU typescript rep

—, (ed) forthcoming *Wroxeter archaeology: excavation and fieldwork on the defences and in the town, 1975–92*

Ellis, P, Evans, J, Hannaford, H, Hughes, G, and Jones, A, 1994 Excavations in the Wroxeter hinterland 1988–1990: the archaeology of the A5/A49 Shrewsbury bypass, *Trans Shrops Archaeol Hist Soc*, **69**, 1–119

Elmer, G, 1941 Die munzpagung der Gallischen Kaiser in Koln, Trier und Mailand, *Bonner Jahrbücher*, **146**, 1–106

English Heritage 1991 *Management of archaeological pojects*, London

Esmonde Cleary, S, 1989 *The ending of Roman Britain*, London

Ettlinger, E, 1949 *Die Keramik der Augster Thermen, Ausgrabungen 1937–8*, Basel

—, 1978 Stempel auf römischer Keramik von der Engehalbinsel Bern, *Jahrbuch des Bernischen Historischen Museums*, 55–58 (1975–1978), 115–128

Ettlinger, E, and Simonett, C, 1952 Römische Keramik aus dem Schutthugel von Vindonissa, *Veroff Ges Vindonissa*, **3**, Basel

Evans, J, 1994 The Roman pottery, in Ellis *et al* 1994, 76–91

Exner, K, 1939 Die provinzialrömischen Emailfibeln der Rheinlande, *Bericht des Römische-Germannische Kommission*, **29**, 33–121

Fabricus, E (ed), 1894 *et seq. Der obergermansiche-raetische Limes des Romerreiches*

Faiers, J E, 1990 The socio-economic aspects of the Roman pottery industry in Britain in the early second century, arising from a detailed study of a large assemblage from construction deposits found during the excavation of the south-west corner of the Baths Insula at Viroconium, unpubl M Phil Thesis, Univ of London

Farrar, R A H, 1973 The techniques and sources of Romano-British black-burnished ware, in Detsicas 1973, 67–103

Feachem, R W, 1951 Dragonesque fibulae, *Antiq J*, **31**, 32–44

Feugère, M, 1985 Les fibules en Gaule Méridionale de la conquête à la fin du Ve siècle après J-C, *Revue Archeologique de Narbonnaise Supplement*, **12**, Paris

Figdor, H, 1927 Uber den einfluss der kastration auf das knochenwachstum des hausrindes Z tierzucht, *Zuchtungsbiol*, **9**

Finley, M I, 1973 *The ancient economy*, Harmondsworth

Fiches, J-L, Guy, M, and Poncin, L 1978 Un lot de vases sigillées des premières années du règne de Néron dans l'un des Ports de Narbonne, *Archeonautica II*, 185–219

Filtzinger, P, 1972 Novaesium V: Die Römische Keramik aus dem Militarbereich von Novaesium, *Limesforschungen*, **11**

Fischer, U, 1957 *Cambodunumsforchungen, 1953, die keramik aus der Holzhäusern zwischen der 1 und 2 Querstrasse*, Kallmünz

Fox, G E, 1897 Uriconium, *Archaeol J*, **54**, 123–73

Fox, G E, and Morris, J A, 1931 *A guide to the Roman city of Uriconium and Wroxeter, Shropshire*, Shrops Archaeol Soc, Shrewsbury

Frayn, J M, 1993 *Markets and fairs in Roman Italy*, Oxford

Frere, S S, 1972 *Verulamium Excavations, I*, Soc Antiq Res Rep, **28**

—, 1984a *Verulamium Excavations: III*, Oxford Univ. Comm Archaeol Monograph **1**, Oxford

—, 1984b Roman Britain in 1983, I sites explored, *Britannia*, **15**, 266–332

—, Roman Britain in 1984, I sites explored, *Britannia*, **16**, 252–316

—, 1987 *Britannia, a history of Roman Britain*, 3rd edn, London

Frere, S S, and St Joseph, J K, 1974 The Roman fortress at Longthorpe, *Britannia*, **5**, 1–129

Frere, S S, and Wilkes, J J, 1989 *Strageath, excavations within the Roman fort 1973–86*, Britannia monograph, **9**, London

Friendship-Taylor, R M, 1979 The excavation of the Belgic and Romano-British settlement at Quinton, Northamptonshire, Site `B', 1973–7, *J Northampton Museums and Art Gallery*, **13**, 2–176

Frisch, T G, and Toll, N P, 1949 *The excavations at Dura-Europos, final report*, New Haven

Fulford, M G 1975 *New Forest Roman Pottery*, BAR, **17**, Oxford

Fürtwangler, A, 1986 *Konigliche Museen zu berlin Beschreibung der Geschnittenen Steine im Antiquarium*, Berlin

Gaitzsch, W, 1980 *Eiserne Römische werkzeuge*, BAR Int Series, **78**, Oxford

Gillam, J P, 1970 *Types of Roman coarse pottery vessels in northern Britain*, 3rd edn, Newcastle upon Tyne

—, 1976 Coarse fumed ware in North Britain and beyond, *Glasgow Archaeol J*, **4**, 57–80

Glasbergen, W, 1955 Pottenbakkersstempels op Terra Sigillata van Valkenburg Z H (1942), *33e–37e Jaarverslag van de Vereniging voor Terpenonderzoek*, 127–48

Going, C J, 1987 *The mansio and other sites in the south-eastern sector of Caesaromagus: the Roman pottery*, CBA Res Rep, **62**, Chelmsford Archaeol Trust Rep, **32**, London

Gose, E 1950 *Gefässtypen der Römischen Keramik im Rhineland*, Bonner Jahrbuch Beiheft, **1**

Gould, J, 1964 Excavations at Wall, Staffs, 1961–3 on the site of the early Roman forts and the late Roman defences, *Trans Lichfield South Staffs Archaeol Hist Soc*, **5**, 1–47

—, 1967 Excavations at Wall, Staffs, 1964–6, on the site of the Roman Forts, *Trans Lichfield South Staffs Archaeol Hist Soc*, **8**, 1–40

Grant, A, 1982 The use of tooth wear as a guide to the age of domestic ungulates, in Wilson *et al* 1982, 92–108

—, 1986 The waterfront group: amphorae and analagous vessels, in Miller *et al* 1986, 100–6

Green, B, Rogerson, A, and White, S G, 1987 The Anglo-Saxon Cemetery at Morning Thorpe, Norfolk, *East Anglian Archaeol*, **36**

Greene, K T, 1979 *Report on the excavations at Usk, 1965–1976: the pre-Flavian fine wares*, Cardiff

—, 1993 The fortress coarse ware, in Manning 1993, 3–124

Greep, S, 1986 The coarse pottery, in Zienkiewicz 1986, 2, 50–96

Grigson, C, 1982 Sex and age determination of some bones and teeth of domestic cattle: a review of the literature, in Wilson *et al* 1982, 7–24

Grigson, C, and Clutton-Brock, J (eds), 1984 *Animals and Archaeology: 4 Husbandry in Europe*, BAR Int Set 227, Oxford

Grimes, W F, 1930 Holt, Denbighshire: the works-depot of the twentieth legion at Castle Lyons, *Y Cymmrodor*, **41**

Grose, D F, 1991 Early Imperial Roman cast glass: the translucent coloured and colourless fine wares, in *Roman glass: two centuries of art and invention* (eds M Newby and K Painter), 1–18, London

Guido, M, 1978 *The glass beads of the prehistoric and Roman periods in Britain and Ireland*, London

Guilday, J E, 1977 Animal remains from archaeological excavations at Fort Ligonia, in *Experimental Archaeology* (eds D Ingersoll *et al*), 121–32, New York

Guiraud, H, 1988 *Intailles et camées de l'epôque romaine en Gaule*, 48 supplement to *Gallia*, Paris

Gurney, D, 1986 Settlement, religion and industry on the Roman Fen-Edge, Norfolk, *East Anglian Archaeol*, **31**

Guyon, J, Aupert, P, Dieulafait, C, Fabre, G, Gallagher, J, Janon, M, Pailler, J M, Paillet, J L, Petit, C, Sablarolles, Schaad, D, Schenk, J L, and Tassaux, F, 1991 From Lugdunum to Convenae: recent work on Saint-Bertrand-de-Comminges (Haute-Garonne), *J Roman Archaeol*, **4**, 89–122

Haalebos, J K, 1986 Fibulae uit Maurik, *Oudheid Kundige Mede Delingen*, Supplement 65, Leiden

Hagen, J, 1906 Ausgewahlte römische Graber aus Koln, *Bonner Jahrbücher*, **114–15**, 379–441

—, 1912 Augusteische Topferei auf dem Furstenberg, *Bonner Jahrbücher*, **112**, 343–62

Harcourt, R A, 1974 The dog in prehistoric and early historic Britain, *J Archaeol Science*, **1**, 151–175

Harden, D B, 1962 Glass in Roman York, in *An inventory of the historical monuments in the city of York, 1: Eburacum Roman York*, 136–141, London

—, 1974 Window-glass from the Romano-British bath-house at Garden Hill, Hartfield, Sussex, *Antiq J*, **54**, 280–1

Harden, D B, Hellenkemper, H, Painter, K, and Whitehouse, D, 1987 *Glass of the Caesars*, London

Harden, D and Green, C, 1978 A late Roman grave-group from The Minories, Aldgate, *Collecteana Londiniensia*, London and Middlesex Archaeol Soc Special Paper, **2**, 163–175

Hartley, B R, 1970 The dating evidence for the end of the Saalburg Erdkastell, in H Schönberger, Die Namenstempel auf glatter Sigillata aus dem Erdkastell der Saalburg, *Saalburg Jahrbüch*, **27**, 28–30

—, 1972a The Samian Ware, in Frere 1972, 216–62

—, 1972b The Roman occupations of Scotland: the evidence of samian ware, *Britannia*, **3**, 1–55

Hartley, B R, and Dickinson, B, 1977 The samian ware, in Rogerson 1973, 155–72

—, 1982 The samian, in *Cirencester Excavations, 1: early Roman occupation at Cirencester*, (J Wacher and A McWhirr), 119–47, Cirencester

—, forthcoming, Samian ware from Camelon (V Maxfield)

Hartley, K F, 1973 The marketing and distribution of mortaria, in Detsicas 1973, 39–51

—, 1985 The mortaria, in R Niblett, *Sheepen: an early Roman industrial site at Camulodunum*, CBA Res Rep, **57**, 92–3

—, 1992 The stamped mortaria, in Darlington and Evans 1992, 64–5

—, 1993 The mortaria, in Manning 1993, 390–437

—, forthcoming The stamped mortaria (Old Grapes Lane, Trench A), nos 3–5 in McCarthy, forthcoming, fasc 3

Hartley, K F, and Webster, P V, 1974 Romano-British pottery kilns near Wilderspool, *Archaeol J*, **130**, 77–103

Haselgrove, C, forthcoming Kingsholm and Celtic coinage circulation in the Western (Dobunnic) region, in *Kingsholm excavations, 2* (P Garrod)

Hassall, M, and Rhodes, J, 1974 Excavations at the new Market Hall, Gloucester, 1966–7, *Trans Bristol Gloucs Archaeol Soc*, **93**, 15–100

Hassall, M W, and Tomlin, R S O, 1982, Roman Britain in 1981, II, inscriptions, *Britannia*, **13**, 396–422

Hattatt, R, 1985 *Iron Age and Roman brooches, a second selection of brooches from the author's collection*, Oxford

—, 1987 *Brooches of antiquity, a third selection of brooches from the author's collection*, Oxford

Haverfield, F, 1911 The Corbridge excavations of 1910, *Proc Soc Antiq*, **23**, 478–90

Hawkes, C F C, 1947 Britons, Romans and Saxons round Salisbury and in Cranborne Chase, *Archaeol J*, **104**, 27–81

Hawkes, C F C, and Hull, M R, 1947 *Camulodunum, first report on the excavations at Colchester, 1930–1939*, Soc Antiq Res Rep, **14**, Oxford

Henig, M, 1974 *A corpus of Roman engraved gemstones from British sites*, BAR, **8**, Oxford

—, 1977 Death and the maiden: funerary symbolism in daily life, in Munby and Henig 1977, 347–66

—, 1978 *A corpus of Roman engraved gemstones from British sites*, BAR, **8**, 2nd edn, Oxford

—, 1980 An intaglio and sealing from Blackfriar's, London, *Antiq J*, **60**, 331–2

—, 1991 Antique gems in Roman Britain, *Jewellery studies*, **5**, 49–54

Hermet, F, 1934 *La Graufesenque (Condatomago)*, Paris

Hill, P V, and Kent, J P C, 1960 *Late Roman bronze coinage, Pt 1*, London

Hinchliffe, J, and Green, C S, 1985 Excavations at Brancaster, 1974 and 1977, *East Anglian Archaeology*, **23**

Hirst, S M, 1985 *An Anglo-Saxon inhumation cemetery at Sewerby, East Yorkshire*, York Univ Archaeol Publications, **4**

Hofmann, B, 1971/1972 *Catalogue des estampilles sur vaisselle sigillée. Notice Technique* 21, 22, Paris

Holbrook, N, and Bidwell, P T, 1991 *Roman finds from Exeter*, Exeter Archaeol Rep, **4**, Exeter

Hopkins, K, 1983 Introduction, in *Trade in the ancient economy* (eds P Garnsey, K Hopkins, C Whittaker), London, ix–xxv

Holwerda, H H, 1941 *De Belgische waar in Nijmegen*, The Hague

Houghton, A W J, 1961 A Roman tilery and brickfield at Ismore Coppice, Wroxeter, *Trans Shropshire Archaeol Soc*, **57**, 7

Houghton, A W J, 1964 A Roman pottery factory near Wroxeter, Salop, *Trans Shropshire Archaeol Soc*, **57**, part ii, 101–111

Howe, M D, Perrin, J R, and Mackreth, D F, 1980 *Roman pottery from the Nene Valley: a guide*, Peterborough City Mus Occas Paper, **2**

Hull, M R, 1958 *Roman Colchester*, Soc Antiq Res Rep, **20**, London

—, 1963 *The Roman potters' kilns at Colchester*, Soc Antiq Res Rep, **21**, London

—, 1967 The Nor'Nour brooches, in Dudley 1967, 28–64

Hull, M R, and Hawkes, C F C, 1987 *Pre-Roman bow brooches*, BAR, **168**, Oxford

Hughes, H, and Heyworth, M, 1990 *Examination of pigments from Wroxeter, Shropshire*, Ancient Monuments Lab Rep, 91/90

Humphrey, J, 1976 et seq *Excavations at Carthage conducted by the University of Michigan*, Tunis

Hurst, H R, 1985 *Kingsholm: excavations at Kingsholm Close and other sites with a discussion of the archaeology of the area*, Gloucester

—, 1988 Gloucester, in Webster 1988, 48–73

Isings, C, 1957 *Roman glass from dated finds*, Groningen Djarkarta

Jackson, D A, and Ambrose, T M, 1978 Excavations at Wakerley, Northants, 1972–75, *Britannia*, **9**, 115–242

Jackson, D, and Dix, B, 1987 Late Iron Age and Roman settlement at Weekley, Northants, *Northamptonshire Archaeol*, **21**, 41–93

James, H, forthcoming *Excavations in Roman Carmarthen*

Jarrett, M G, and Wrathmell, S, 1981 *Whitton, an Iron Age and Roman farmstead in South Glamorgan*, Cardiff

Jobst, W, 1975 Die römischen fibeln aus Lauriacum, *Forschungen in Lauriacum*, **10**, Linz

Johns, C, 1997 *The Snettisham Roman Jeweller's Hoard*, London

Johnson, H, 1868 Excavations undertaken at Wroxeter in 1867, *Proc Society Antiq London*, ser 2, **4**, 54–9

Jones, G D B, and Webster, P V, 1968 Mediolanum: Excavations at Whitchurch 1965–6, *Archaeol J*, **125**, 163–254

Jones, M W, 1989 Designing the Roman Corinthian order, *J Roman Archaeol*, **2**, 35–69

Jones, R T, Wall S M, Locker, A M, Coy, J, and Maltby, M, 1981 *Computer based osteometry data capture user manual, 1*, Ancient Monuments Lab Rep, 3342, and 1st supplement to 2333

Juhász, G, 1935 Die Sigillaten von Brigetio, *Dissertationes Pannonicae*, ser 2, no 3, Budapest

Karnitsch, P 1959 *Die Reliefsigillata von Ovilava*, Linz

Kenyon, K M, 1938 Excavations at Viroconium 1936–37, *Archaeologia*, **88**, 176–228

—, 1942 Excavations at the Wrekin, Shropshire, *Archaeol J*, **99**, 99–109

—, 1948 *Excavations at the Jewry Wall site, Leicester*, Soc Antiq Res Rep, **15**, Oxford

—, 1981 Excavations at Viroconium in Insula 9, 1952–3, *Trans Shropshire Archaeol Soc*, **60**, 5–73

Kenyon, R, 1987 The Claudian coinage, in N Crummy (ed) *The coins from the excavations in Colchester, 1971–9*, Colchester Archaeol Rep, **4**, 24–41, Colchester

Kilbride-Jones, H E, 1980 *Zoomorphic penannular brooches*, Soc Antiq Res Rep, **39**, London

King, A, 1984 Animal bones and the dietary identity of military and civilian groups in Roman Britain, Germany and Gaul, in *Military and Civilian in Roman Britain* (eds T Blagg and A King), BAR, **136**, 187–217, Oxford

Kirk, J R, 1949 Bronzes from Woodeaton, *Oxoniensia*, **14**, 1–45

Knight, B, 1981 *Identification of pigments from Wroxeter baths*, Ancient Monuments Lab Rep, 3306

Knorr, R, 1907 *Die verzierten Terra-sigillata Gefässe von Rottweil*, Stuttgart

—, 1910 *Die verzierten Terra-Sigillata-Gefässe von Rottenburg Sumelocenna*, Stuttgart

—, 1919 *Töpfer und Fabriken verzierter Terra-Sigillata des ersten Jahrhunderts*, Stuttgart

Kovrig, I, 1937 Die haupttypen der Kaiserzeitlichen Fibeln in Pannonien, *Dissertationes Pannonicae*, ser 2, no 4, Budapest

Krug, A, 1981 *Antike gemmen im Römisch-Germanischen Museum, Koln*, Bericht der Römische-Germanischen Kommission, **61**, 151–260

La Baume, P, 1964 *Römisches Kuntsgewerbe*, Braunschweig

Laubenheimer, F, 1979 La collection de céramiques sigillées gallo-romaines estampillées du Musée de Rabat, *Antiquités africaines*, **13**, 99–225

—, 1985 La production des amphores en Gaule Narbonnaise, *Centre de Recherches d'Histoire Ancienne*, **66**, Paris

Laurence, R, 1994 *Roman Pompeii, space and society*, London

Leach, P, 1982 *Ilchester, 1: excavations 1974–1975*, Bristol

Lee, J E, 1862 *Isca Silurum*, London

Lerat, L, 1956 Catalogue des collections archéologiques de Besançon, II: les fibules Gallo-Romaines, Annales Littéraire de l'Université de Besançon, *Archéologie*, **3**, iii–vi, 1–51

—, 1957 Catalogue des collections archéologique de Montbeliard, Annales littéraire de l'Université de Besançon, *Archéologie*, **4**, 2–26

Lethbridge, T C, 1952 Excavations at Kilpheder, South Uist, and the problem of brochs and wheelhouses, *Proc Prehist Soc*, **18**, 176–93

Levitan, B, 1993 Vertebrate remains, in Woodward and Leach 1993, 257–301

Loeschcke, S, 1909 Keramische Funde in Haltern, *Mitteilungen der Altertums Kommission fur Westfalen*, **5**, 103–322

Lowther, A W G, 1937 Report on excavations at Verulamium in 1934, *Antiq J*, **17**, 28–55

Ludovici, W, 1927 *Katalog V: Stempel Namen und Bilder römischer Töpfer aus meinen Ausgrabungen in Rheinzabern, 1901–14*, Munich

Luff, R, 1982 *A zooarchaeological study of the Roman north-west provinces*, BAR Int Ser, **137**, Oxford

Maaskant-Kleibrink, M, 1978 *Catalogue of the engraved gems in the royal coin cabinet, The Hague: the Greek, Etruscan, and Roman collections*, The Hague

—, 1992 Three gem engravers at work in a jeweller's workshop in Norfolk, *Bulletin Antieke Beschaving*, **67**, 151–67

McCarthy, M R, forthcoming *Excavations at The Lanes, Carlisle*, **1**

Macdonald, G, and Curle, A, 1929 The Roman fort at Mumrills, near Falkirk, *Proc Soc Antiq Scotland*, **63**, 396–575

Mack, R P, 1973 *The coinage of ancient Britain*, 3rd edn, London

Mackreth, D F, 1978 The Roman brooches, in Down 1978, 277–87

—, 1981 The brooches, in Partridge 1981, 130–151

—, 1985 Brooches from Roman Derby, in Dool and Wheeler 1985, 281–99

—, 1986 Brooches, in McWhirr 1986, 104–6

—, 1987 Roman public buildings, in Schofield and Leech 1987, 133–46

—, 1988 The brooches, in Trow 1988, 43–51

—, 1989a Brooches, in Blockley 1989, 87–99

—, 1989b The Roman brooches from Chichester, in Down 1989, 182–94

—, 1991 Brooches, in Holbrook and Bidwell 1991, 232–41

—, 1992 The brooches, in Darlington and Evans 1992, 73–7

—, 1996 The brooches, in *Excavations at Stonea, Cambridgeshire, 1980–85* (D Jackson and T Potter), London, 300

—, 1997 The brooches, in Barker *et al* 1997

—, forthcoming The brooches, in *Excavations in Gloucester* (A Garrod and M Atkins)

Mackreth, D F, and Butcher, S A, 1981 The Roman brooches, in Down 1981, 254–61

Macalister, F, 1980 *Wroxeter, Shropshire: technology*, Ancient Monuments Lab Rep, 3182

MacGregor, A, 1985 *Bone, antler, ivory and horn*, London

MacMullen, R, 1970 Market-days in the Roman Empire, *Phoenix*, 24, 333–41

McWhirr, A D, 1986 *Houses in Roman Cirencester, Cirencester excavations*, **3**, Cirencester

McWhirr, A D, Viner, L, Wells, C, 1982 *Romano-British Cemeteries at Cirencester, Cirencester Excavations*, **2**, Cirencester

Maltby, M, 1979 *Faunal studies on urban sites: the animal bones from Exeter 1971–1975*, Sheffield

—, 1984 Animal bones and the Romano-British economy, in Grigson and Clutton-Brock, 1984, 125–38

—, 1985 Patterns in faunal assemblage variability, in *Beyond Domestication in Prehistoric Europe* (eds G Barker and C Gamble), 33–74, New York

—, 1993 Animal Bones, in Woodward *et al* 1993, 315–40

Manning, W H, 1981 *Report on the excavations at Usk 1965–76: the fortress excavations 1968–71*, Cardiff

—, 1985 *Catalogue of the Romano-British iron tools, fittings and weapons in the British Museum*, London

—, (ed) 1993 *Report on the excavations at Usk 1965–1976: the Roman pottery*, Cardiff

Margary, I D, 1973 *Roman roads in Britain*, 3rd edn, London

Marney, P T, and Mackreth, D F, 1987 Brooches, in Mynard *et al* 1987, 128–33

Marsh, G, 1978 Early second century fine wares in the London area, in Arthur and Marsh (eds) 1978, 119–223

—, 1981 London's samian supply and its relationship to the development of the Gallic samian industry, in Anderson and Anderson (eds) 1981, 173–238

Marsh, G, and Tyers, P, 1976 Roman Pottery from the City of London, *Trans London Middlesex Archaeol Soc*, **27**, 228–44

Martin-Kilcher, S, 1983 Les amphores romaines a huile de Betique (Dressel 20 et 23) d'Augst (Colonia Augusta Rauricorum) et Kaiseraugst (Castrum Rauracense). Un rapport preliminaire, in *Prod y com del aceite en la antiguedad. II congresso* (eds J Blazquez and J Remesal), 337–47, Madrid

Martin-Kilcher, S, Schupbach, S, Stern, W B, and Ballie, J, 1985 Keramikanalysen an römischen olamphoren aus Augst, Kaiseraugst, Avenchesund Lausanne-Vidy naturwissenschaftliche und archaologische aspekte, *Jahrbüch Der Schweiserischen Gesellschaft fur Ur-Und Fruhgeschichte*, **68**, 173–204

Mattingly, H, 1965–68 *Coins of the Roman Empire in the British Museum*, **1–6**, London

Mattingly, H, Sydenham, E A, Sutherland, C H V, Carson, R A G (eds), 1926–84 *The Roman Imperial coinage*, **1–9**, London

Maw, G, 1861 The pavements of Uriconium, *J British Archaeol Assoc*, **17**, 100–10

Maxwell, G, 1974 Objects of glass, in Rae and Rae 1974, 177–9

May, T, 1930 *Catalogue of the Roman pottery in the Colchester and Essex Museum*, Cambridge

Mays, S A, 1989 *Human bone from Wroxeter, Salop, excavated 1955–85*, Ancient Monuments Lab Rep, 26/89

Meates, G W, 1987 *The Roman villa at Lullingstone, Kent, II: the wall paintings and finds*, Kent Archaeol Soc Monograph 3, Maidstone

Meddens, B, 1987 *Assessment of the animal bone work for Wroxeter Roman city, Shropshire*, Ancient Monuments Lab Rep, 171/87

Meiggs, R, 1960 *Roman Ostia*, Oxford

Mensforth, R P, Lovejoy, C O, Lallo, J W, and Armelagos, G J, 1978 The role of constitutional factors, diet and infectious disease in the etiology of porotic hyperostosis and periosteal reactions in prehistoric infanct and children, *Medical Anthropology*, **2**, 1–59

Merrifield, R, 1965 *Roman London*, London

Miller, L, Schofield, J, and Rhodes, M, 1986 *The Roman quay at St Magnus House, London*, London Middlesex Archeol Soc special paper, **8**, London

Miller, S N, 1922 *The Roman fort at Balmuildy*, Glasgow

Millett, M, 1990 *The romanization of Britain*, Cambridge

Morgan, G C, 1992 Romano-British mortars and plasters, unpubl PhD thesis, Univ Leicester

Morgan M H, 1960 *Vitruvius; the ten books on architecture*, Dover

Morren, C G A, 1966 Een Terra-sigillata-handelaar te Nijmegen? *Numaga*, **13**, 223–32

Morris, E L 1981 Petrological report on the Beaker and Iron Age ceramics from Midsummer Hill, in Stanford, S, *Midsummer Hill: an Iron Age hillfort on the Malverns*, Hereford

—, 1983 Salt and ceramic exchange in western Britain during The first millennium BC, unpub PhD thesis, University of Southampton

Morris, J A, 1932 Wroxeter excavations, *Trans Shropshire Archaeol Soc*, **46**, viii–ix

—, 1934 Wroxeter excavations, *Trans Shropshire Archaeol Soc*, **47**, 214–16

Morris, E 1984 Petrological report for the ceramic material from the Wrekin, in Stanford 1984, 76–80

Mould, Q, 1991 The metalwork, in *Bewcastle and Old Penrith: a Roman outpost fort and a frontier vicus, excavations, 1977–78* (P Austen), Cumb Westm Antiq Archaeol Soc Res Ser, **6**

Munby, J, and Henig, M, 1977 *Roman life and art in Britain*, BAR, **41**, Oxford

Musty, J, Rogerson, A, with Lloyd-Morgan, G, 1973 A mirror from the Romano British cemetery at Whitchurch, Salop, *Antiq J*, **53**, 278–81

Mynard, D C, Zeepvat, R J, and Williams, R J, 1987 *Roman Milton Keynes, excavations and fieldwork, 1971–1982*, Bucks Archaeol Soc Monograph, **1**

Mynard, D C, and Zeepvat, R J, 1992 *Excavations at Great Linford, 1974–80, The Village*, Bucks Archaeol Soc Monograph, **3**

Nash-Williams, V E, 1930 Further excavations at Caerwent, Monmouthshire, 1923–5, *Archaeologia*, **80**, 229–88

Neal, D S, 1974 *The excavation of the Roman villa in Gadebridge park, Hemel Hempstead, 1963–8*, Soc Antiq Res Rep, **31**, London

Neal, D S, and Butcher, S A, 1974 Miscellaneous objects of bronze, in Neal 1974, 128–49

Neal, D S, Wardle, A, and Hunn, J, 1990 *Excavation of the Iron Age, Roman and medieval settlement at Gorhambury, St Albans*, English Heritage Archaeol Rep, **14**, London

Newman, C, 1989 Fowler's type F3 early medieval penannular brooches, *Med Archaeol*, **33**, 7–20

Newstead, R, 1935 Roman Chester: the extra-mural settlement at Saltney, *Annals of Archaeology and Anthropology*, **22**, 3–18

Nielsen, I, 1990 *Thermae et Balnea*, Aarhus

—, 1993 *Thermae et Balnea*, 2nd edn, Aarhus

Noddle, B A, 1973 Determination of the body weight of cattle from bone measurements, in J Matolcsi (ed) *Domestikationsforschung und geschichte der haustiere*, Budapest, 311

—, 1978 Some minor skeletal differences in sheep, in D Brothwell, K Thomas, and J Clutton-Brock (eds) *Research problems in zooarchaeology*, 133, London

—, 1981 Notes on the history of the domestic pig, *The Ark*, **8**, 390–5

—, 1982 *Animal bones from the* piscina, *Wroxeter*, Ancient Monuments Lab Rep, 3690

—, 1984a A comparison of the bones of cattle, sheep, and pigs from ten Iron Age and Romano-British sites, in Grigson and Clutton-Brock 1984, 105–24

—, 1984b Exact chronology of epiphyseal closure in domestic mammals of the past: an impossible proposition, *Circaea*, **2**, 21–7

—, forthcoming The animal bones, in Webster forthcoming

O'Connor, T P, 1982 Animal bones from Flaxengate, Lincoln, *c* 870–1500, in *The Archaeology of Lincoln*, **18/1**, Lincoln

—, 1984 Selected groups of bones from Skeldergate and Walmgate, *The Archaeology of York: the animal bones*, **15/1**, York

—, 1985 On quantifying vertebrates – some sceptical observations, *Circaea*, **3**, 27–30

—, forthcoming Bird bones, in Webster forthcoming

Oldenstein, J, 1976 Zur ausrustung Römischer auxiliareinheiten, in *Bericht der Römisch-Germanischen kommission*, **57**, 49–285

Oliver, A, 1984 Early Roman faceted glass, *J Glass Studies*, **26**, 35–58

Oswald, F, 1931 *Index of potters' stamps on Terra Sigillata ('samian ware')*, East Bridgford

—, 1936 *Index of figure-types on terra sigillata ('samian ware')*, Liverpool

ORL 1894 – *Der Obergermanisch-raetische Limes des Römerreiches* (ed E Fabricus)

Orton, C, Tyers, P, and Vince, A, 1993 *Pottery in archaeology*, Cambridge

Owen, M, 1979 Walcot St, 1971, in *Excavations in Bath 1950–75* (ed B Cunliffe), 102–11, Bristol

Owen, W J, and Arnold, J, 1989 Beads, glass counters and other glass objects, in Britnell 1989, 44–9

Partridge, C, 1981 *Skeleton Green, a late Iron Age and Romano-British site*, Britannia Monograph, **2**, London

Payne, G, 1893 *Collectanea Cantiana or archaeological researches in the neighbourhood of Sittingbourne and other parts of Kent*, London

Payne, S, 1969 A metrical distinction between sheep and goat metacarpals, in *The domestication and exploitation of plants and animals* (eds P Ucko and G Dimbleby), 295–306, London

—, 1984 The use of early 19th century data in ageing cattle mandibles from archaeological sites, and the relationship between the eruption of M3 and P4, *Circaea*, **2**, 77–82

—, 1985 Morphological distinctions between the mandibular teeth of young sheep, *Ovis*, and goats, *Capra*, *J Archaeol Science*, **12**, 139–47

Peacock, D P S, 1967 Romano-British pottery production in the Malvern district of Worcestershire, *Trans Worcs Archaeol Soc*, **1**, 15–28

—, 1968 A petrological study of certain Iron Age pottery from Western Britain, *Proc Prehist Soc*, **34**, 414–27

—, (ed) 1977a *Pottery and early commerce, characterisation and trade in Roman and later ceramics*, London

—, 1977b Pompeian red ware, in Peacock 1977a, 147–62

—, 1977c Roman amphorae: typology, fabric and origin, *Coll de L'Ecole Francaise de Rome*, **32**, 261–78

—, 1978 The Rhine and the problem of Gaulish wine in Roman Britain, in *Roman shipping and trade: Britain and the Rhine provinces* (eds J du Plat Taylor and H Cleere), CBA Res Rep, 24, 49–51

Peacock, D P S, and Williams, D F, 1986 *Amphorae and the Roman Economy*, London

Penn, W S, 1960 Springhead Temples III and IV, *Archaeol Cantiana*, 74, 113–40

Perrin, J R, 1990 *Roman Pottery from the Colonia 2: General Accident and Rougier Street*, The Archaeology of York, **16**

Perring, D, 1987 Domestic buildings in Romano-British towns, in Schofield and Leech 1987, 147–55

Petch, D F, 1978 The major buildings of the fortress, in Strickland and Davey 1978, 17–24

Peter M, 1990 *Eine Werkstätte zur Herstellung von subaeraten Denaren in Augusta Raurica*, Studien zu Fundmünzen der Antike, 7, Berlin

Phaar, C (ed), 1952 *Codex Theodosianus*, New York

Philp, B, 1981 *Excavation of the Roman forts of the Classis Britannica at Dover, 1970–1977*, Kent Monograph Series, Res Rep, **3**, Dover

Pirling, R, 1968 Neue Funde Römischer Glaser aus Krefeld-Gellep, *Kölner Jahrbuch fur Vor- und Frigeschichte*, **9**, 34–42

Plommer, H, 1973 *Vitruvius and later Roman building manuals*, Cambridge

Ponsich, M, 1974 *Implantation rurale antique sur le Bas-Guadalquivir*, Madrid

Popilian, G, 1973 La céramique sigillée d'importation découverte en Olténie, *Dacia NS*, **17**, 179–216

Potter, T W, 1979 *Romans in north-west England, excavations at the Roman forts of Ravenglass, Watercrook and Bowness-on-Solway*, Cumberland Westmorland Antiq Archaeol Soc, Res Ser, **1**, Kendal

Pretty, K B, 1997 The finds, in Barker *et al* 1997, 192–220

Price, J, 1987 Glass from Felmongers, Harlow in Essex; a dated deposit of vessel glass found in an Antonine pit, *Annales du 10e Congrés de l'Association Internationale pour l'Histoire du Verre*, 185–206

Price, J, 1993 Window glass, in Woodward and Leach 1993, 189

Price, J, and Cool, H E M, 1991 The evidence for the production of glass in Roman Britain, in *Ateliers de Veriers de l'antiquite a la period pre-industrielle* (D Foy and G Sennequier), Actes du 4e Rencontres d'Association Francaise pour l'archeologie du Verre, 23–9

Prieto, J, *et al* 1989 *Excavacions arqueologiques subaquatiques a Cala Culip,1*, Girona

Rae, A, and Rae, V, 1974 The Roman fort at Cramond, Edinburgh, excavations 1954–1966, *Britannia*, **5**, 163–224

Rahtz, P A, and Greenfield, E, 1977 *Excavations at Chew Valley Lake*, DOE Archaeol Rep, **8**, London

Ravetz, A, 1964 The fourth-century inflation and Romano-British coin finds, *Numismatic Chron*, 201–32

Rawes, B, 1972 Roman pottery kilns at Gloucester, *Trans Bristol Glos Archaeol Soc*, **91**, 18–59

—, 1978 Roman pottery kilns at Gloucester: a supplementary note, *Trans Bristol Glos Archaeol Soc*, **96**, 77–8

—, 1980 The Romano-British site at Wycomb, Andoversford, excavations 1969–1970, *Trans Bristol Glos Archaeol Soc*, **98**, 11–55

—, 1981 The Romano-British site at Brockworth, Glos, *Britannia*, **12**, 45–77

—, 1982 Gloucester Severn valley ware, *Trans Bristol Glos Archaeol Soc*, **100**, 33–46

Rees, S, 1981 *Ancient agricultural implements*, Oxford

Remesal, J, 1986 *La Annona Militaris y la Exportacion de Aceite a Germania*, Madrid

Rhodes, M, 1986a Discussion, in Miller *et al* 1986, 88–95

—, 1986b Dumps of unused pottery near London Bridge, in Miller *et al* 1986, 199–203

—, 1986c Stone objects, in Miller *et al* 1986, 240–3

Richardson, K M, 1944 Report on excavations at Verulamium: Insula XVII, 1938, *Archaeologia*, **90**, 81–126

—, 1948 Report on the excavations at Brockley Hill, Middlesex, August and September 1947, *Trans London Middlesex Archaeol Soc*, **101**, 1–23

Richmond, I A, 1950 Excavations at the Roman fort at Newstead, 1947, *Proc Soc Antiq Scot*, **84**, 1–37

—, 1968 *Hod Hill*, II, London

Ricken, H, and Fischer, C, 1963 *Die Bilderschüsseln der römischen Töpfer von Rheinzabern, Textband*, Bonn

Rigby, V, 1973 Potters' stamps on Terra Nigra and Terra Rubra found in Britain, in Detsicas 1973, 7–24

—, 1982 The coarse pottery, in, *Early Roman occupation at Cirencester* (J Wacher and A McWhirr), Cirencester, 153–200

Riha, E, 1979 Die Römischen Fibeln aus Augst und Kaiseraugst, *Forschungen in Augst*, **3**, Augst

Ritterling, E, 1913 Das frührömische Lager bei Hofheim im Taunus, *Annalen des Vereins fur Nassauische Altertumskunde und Geschichtsforschung*, **40**, 1–416

Roach Smith, C, 1859a *The Gentleman's Magazine*, 1859, 449–458

—, 1859b *The Gentleman's Magazine*, 1859, 625

—, 1859c *The Gentleman's Magazine*, 1859, 219–25

Robertson, A S, 1970 Roman finds from non-Roman sites in Scotland, *Britannia*, **1**, 198–226

—, 1975 *Birrens (Blatobulgium)*, Edinburgh

Rogers, G B, 1974 Poteries sigillées de la Gaule centrale, *Gallia Suppl*, **28**, Paris

Rogerson, A, 1977 Excavations at Scole, 1973, *East Anglian Archaeol Rep*, **5**, 97–224

Ross, A, 1995 Ritual and the Druids, in Green 1995, 423–44

Rouvier-Jeanlin, M, 1972 *Les figurines Gallo-Romaines en terre cuite au Musée des Antiquités Nationales*, Gallia Suppl, **24**, Paris

St George Gray, H, 1930 Excavations at Kingsdown Camp, Mells, Somerset, 1927–9, *Archaeologia*, **80**, 59–98

Saunders, C, and Havercroft, A B, 1977 A kiln of the potter Oastrius and related excavations at Little Munden Farm, Bricket Wood, *Herts Archaeol*, **5**, 109–56

Sauvaget, R, 1970 Le potier Servus II de Lezoux, *Revue Archaeol du Centre*, **34**, 127–42

Scarth, H M, 1859 The recent discoveries at Wroxeter, *Archaeol J*, **16**, 264–79

—, 1860 Report on the progress of the excavations at Wroxeter, the Roman Uriconium, *Archaeol J*, **17**, 240–9

—, 1864 Report on the progress of the excavations at Wroxeter, the Roman Uriconium, since July, 1860, *Archaeol J*, **21**, 130–7

Schiffer, M B, 1972 Archaeological context and systematic context, *Amer Antiq*, **37**, 156–65

Schindler-Kaudelka, E, 1975 *Die Dunnwandige Gebrauchskeramik vom Magdalensberg*, Klagenfurt

Schofield, J, and Leech, R (eds) 1987 *Urban archaeology in Britain*, CBA Res Rep, **61**, London

Scott, K, 1981 Mancetter village: a first century fort, *Trans Birmingham Warwickshire Archaeol Soc*, **91**, 1–24

Sellwood, D, 1976 Minting, in *Roman crafts* (D Strong and D Brown), 63–73, London

Sena Chiesa, G, 1966 *Gemme del Museo Nazionale di Aquileia*, Aquileia

—, 1978 *Gemme di Luni*, Rome

Sennequier, G, 1985 *Verrerie d'Epôque Romaine*, Rouen

Sheldon, H L, 1978 *Southwark excavations 1972–74*, London Middlesex Archaeol Soc and Surrey Archaeol Soc publication, **1**

Sheppard, T, 1907 *Notes on a collection of Roman antiquities from South Ferriby, in North Lincolnshire*, Hull Museum Publications, **39**, Hull

Silvester, R J, and Bidwell, P T, 1984 A Roman site at Woodbury, Axminster, *Proc Devon Archaeol Soc*, **42**, 33–57

Silver, I A, 1969 The ageing of domestic animals, in *Science in archaeology* (D Brothwell and E Higgs), 283–302

Simon, H-G, 1960 Römische Funde aus Bad Nauheim, *Saalburg Jahrbücher*, **18**, 5–34

—, 1973 Bilderschüsseln und Töpferstempel auf glatter Ware, *Limesforchung*, **12**, 76

—, 1984 Terra Sigillata aus Waiblingen, *Fundberichte aus Baden-Württemberg*, **8**, 471

Simpson, G, and Rogers, G, 1969 Cinnamus de Lezoux et quelques potiers contemporains, *Gallia*, **27**, 3–14

Sissons, S, and Grossman J D, 1975 *The anatomy of the domestic animals*, 5th edn, London

Spencer, B, 1983 Limestone-tempered pottery from South Wales in the late Iron Age and early Roman periods, *Bull Board Celtic Studies*, **30**, 405–19

Spier, J, 1992 *The J Paul Getty Museum, catalogue of the collections: ancient gems and finger rings*, Malibu

Stanfield, J A, and Simpson, G, 1958, 1990, *Central Gaulish Potters*, OUP, Oxford; Gonfaron, France

Stanford, S C, 1974 *Croft Ambrey*, Hereford

—, 1984 The Wrekin hillfort, excavations 1973, *Archaeol J*, **141**, 61–90

Stead, I M, 1976 *Excavations at Winterton Roman villa, and other Roman sites in north Lincolnshire, 1958–1969*, DOE Archaeol Rep, **9**, London

—, 1980 *Rudston Roman villa*, Leeds

Stead, I M, and Rigby, V, 1986 *Baldock, the excavation of a Roman and pre-Roman settlement, 1968–72*, Britannia Monograph, **7**, London

Stead, I M, and Rigby, V, 1989 *Verulamium: the King Harry Lane site*, English Heritage Archaeol Rep, **12**, London

Stevenson, G H, and Miller, S N, 1912 Report on the excavation of the Roman fort of Cappuck, Roxbrughshire, *Proc Soc Antiq Scotland*, **46**, 446–83

Stloukhal, M, and Hanakova, H, 1978 Die lange der langsknochen altslawischer Bevolkerungen – unter besonderer Berucksichtigung von Wachstumfragen, *Homo*, **29**, 53–69

Stuart, P J J, 1962 Gewoon aardewerk uit de Romeinse Lagerplaats en de Bijbehorende Grafvelden te Nijmegen, *Oudhkde Meded Rijks mus Oudh Leiden*, **43**, Suppl, Leiden

Sutherland, C V H, 1935 *Romano-British imitations of bronze coins of Claudius I*, ANS Numismatic Notes and Monographs, **65**, New York

Symonds, R P, 1990 The problems of roughcast beakers, and related colour-coated wares, *J Roman Pottery Studies*, **3**, 1–17

—, 1992 *Rhenish wares, fine dark-coloured pottery from Gaul and Germany*, Oxford Univ Comm Archaeol Monog, **23**

—, 1997 The Roman pottery, in Barker *et al* 1997, 269–318

Taylor, H M, and Taylor, J, 1965 *Anglo-Saxon architecture*, Cambridge

Terrisse, J-R, 1968 Les céramiques sigillées gallo-romaines des Martres de-Veyre (Puy-de-Dôme), *Gallia Suppl*, **19**, Paris

Thomas, C, 1981 *A provisonal list of imported pottery in post-Roman western Britain and Ireland*, Redruth

Thomas, G D, 1988 Excavations at the Roman civil settlement at Inveresk, 1976–77, *Proc Soc Antiq Scotland*, **118**, 139–76

Thompson, F H, 1958 A Romano-British pottery kiln at North Hykeham, Lincolnshire, *Antiq J*, **38**, 15–51

—, 1963 Two Romano-British trumpet brooches with silver inlay, *Antiq J*, **43**, 289–90

Tilhard, J-L, 1976 *La céramique sigillée I, Les estampilles.* Musée Archéologique de Saintes

—, 1988 Céramiques a vernis noir et sigillées des fouilles de 'Ma Maison' a Saintes, *Revue Aquitania*, Suppl, **3**, 85–197

—, 1991 Récherches en céramique sigillée. Etude d'un nouvel atelier de Gaule Méridionale, unpub thesis, Univ Bordeaux

Timby, J R, 1990 Severn Valley wares: a re-assessment, *Britannia*, **21**, 243–251

—, 1991 The Berkeley Street pottery kiln, Gloucester, *J Roman Pottery Studies*, **4**, 19–31

—, 1992 *Wroxeter Roman pottery: post-excavation assessment*, unpublished rep

—, The pottery from Abingdon Vineyard, Oxon

—, The pottery from Coppice Corner and adjacent sites, Kingsholm, Gloucs

—, unpub The pottery from Berkeley Street, Gloucester

Todd, M, 1989 The early cities, in *Research on Roman Britain: 1960–1989* (ed M Todd), 75–89, London

Tomasevic, T, 1970 Die Keramik der XIII Legion aus Vindonissa, Ausgrabungen Konigsfelder 1962–3, *Veroffentlichungen der Kessellschaft pro Vindonissa*, **7**, Brugg

Tomber, R S, 1981 *A petrological assessment of Severn Valley ware kilns and selected distribution*, unpubl M Sc Thesis, Univ Southampton

Toynbee, J M C, 1964 *Art in Britain under the Romans*, Oxford

Tyers, P A, 1978 Poppyhead beakers of Britain and their relationship to the barbotine-decorated vessels of the Rhineland and Switzerland, in Arthur and Marsh 1978, 61–108

—, 1983 *Verulamium region white ware*, DUA pottery archive rep, **4**

Ulbert, G, 1959 Die römischen Donau-Kastelle Aislingen und Burghöfe, *Limesforschungen*, **1**, Berlin

—, 1965 *Der Lorenzberg bei Epfach*, Munich

—, 1969 Das frührömische Kastell Rheingönheim, die funde aus den Jahren 1912 und 1913, *Limesforschungen*, **9**, Berlin

van Arsdell, R D, 1989 *Celtic coinage of Britain*, London

Vanderhoeven, M, 1975 *De Terra Sigillata te Tongeren*, Tongeren

Vanvinckenroye, W, 1968 Naamstempels op Terra Sigillata van Heerlen, *Publications de la societé historique et archéologique dans le Limbourg*, CIII–CIV

Vermeulen, W, 1932 *Een Romeinsch Grafveld op den Hunnerberg te Nijmegen*, Amsterdam

Vernhet, A, 1981 Un four de La Graufesenque (Aveyron): la cuisson des vases sigillées, *Gallia*, **39**, 25–43

von den Driesch, 1976 The measurement of animal bones from archeological sites, *Peabody Museum Bulletin*, 1

von Mensch, E, 1974 A Roman soup kitchen at Zwammerdam, B*erichte van dr Rijksdienst voor het Oudeidkundig Bodemondetzock Jaargang*, **24**, 159

Voorhies, M, 1969 *Taphonomy and population dinamics of an early Pliocene vertebrate fauna, Knox County, Nebraska*, Geology Special Paper, 1, Univ Wyoming

Walke, N, 1965 Das römische Donaukastell Straubing-Sorviodurum, Limesforschungen 3, Berlin Relief Sigillata von Gauting, *Bericht der Römisch-Germanischen Kommission*, 46–47, Berlin, 77–132

Walke, N, and Walke, I, 1968 Reliefsigillata von Gauting, *Bericht der Römisch-Germanischen Kommission 1965–1966*, 77–132, tfn 28–57

Waugh, H, 1966 The hoard of Roman silver from Great Horwood, Buckinghamshire, *Antiq J*, **46**, 60–71

Wacher, J S, 1959 Leicester, *J Roman Stud*, **49**, 113–4

—, 1962 Cirencester 1961, second interim report, *Antiq J*, **42**, 1–14

—, 1995 *The towns of Roman Britain*, 2nd edn, London

Walters, H B, 1908 *Catalogue of the Roman pottery in the Department of Antiquities, British Museum*, London

Walthew, C V, 1978 Property boundaries and the sizes of building plots in Roman towns, *Britannia*, **9**, 335–50

Webster, G, 1949 The legionary fortress at Lincoln, *J Roman Stud*, **39**, 57–80

—, 1969 *The Roman Imperial army*, London

—, 1975 *The Cornovii*, London

—, 1981 Final report on the excavations of the Roman fort at Waddon Hill, Stoke Abbott, 1963–69, *Proc Dorset Nat Hist and Archaeol Society*, **101**, 51–90

—, 1985 *The Roman Imperial army*, 2nd edn, London

—, (ed), 1988a *Fortress into city*, London

—, 1988b Wroxeter (Viroconium), in Webster 1988a, 120–44

—, 1990 Wroxeter – the military and Hadrianic phases, in Barker 1990, 1–2

—, 1991 *The Cornovii*, 2nd edn, Stroud

—, 1993 Wroxeter, in *Roman Towns; the Wheeler inheritance* (ed S Greep), CBA Res Rep, **93**, London

—, forthcoming *The legionary fortress at Wroxeter*, London

Webster, G, and Daniels, C, 1972 A street section at Wroxeter, *Trans Shropshire Archaeol Soc*, **59**, 15–23

Webster, G, and Smith, L, 1982 The excavation of a Romano-British rural establishment at Barnsley Park, Gloucestershire 1961–1979, II, *Trans Bristol Glos Archaeol Soc*, **100**, 65–189

Webster, G, and Woodfield, P, 1966 The Old Work at the Roman public baths at Wroxeter, *Antiq J*, **46**, 229–39

Webster, P V, 1972 Severn Valley ware on Hadrian's Wall, *Archaeol Aeliana*, ser 4, **50**, 191–203

—, 1976 Severn Valley ware: a preliminary study, *Trans Bristol Glos Archaeol Soc*, **94**, 18–46

—, 1977 Severn Valley ware on the Antonine frontier, in Dore and Greene, 1977, 163–76

—, 1989 The coarse ware, in J Britnell 1989, 89–121

Wedlake, W J, 1958 *Excavations at Camerton, Somerset*, Bath

—, 1982 *The excavation of the shrine of Apollo at Nettleton, Wiltshire, 1956–1971*, Soc Antiq Res Rep, **40**, London

Wheeler, R E M, 1924 *Segontium and the Roman occupation of Wales*, London

—, 1926 The Roman fort near Brecon, *Y Cymmrodor*, **37**, London

—, 1943 *Maiden Castle, Dorset*, Soc Antiq Res Rep, **12**, London

Wheeler, R E, and Wheeler, T V, 1928 The Roman amphitheatre at Caerleon, Monmouthshire, *Archaeologia*, **78**, 111–218

—, 1932 *Report on the excavation of the Prehistoric, Roman, and post-Roman sites in Lydney Park, Gloucestershire*, Soc Antiq Res Rep, **9**, London

—, 1936 *Verulamium, a Belgic and two Roman cities*, Soc Antiq Res Rep, **11**, London

Whimster, R, 1989 *The emerging past: air photography and the buried landscape*, London

White, R H, and Cosh S J, forthcoming The mosaic pavement, in Ellis forthcoming

White, R H, and Faiers, J, forthcoming The Bell brook kiln, in Ellis forthcoming

White, R H, and Ixer, R, 1997 The architectural fragments, in Barker *et al* 1997, 259–63

White, R H, and Webster, G, 1994 Two Roman javelin heads from the Wrekin hillfort, Shropshire, *Trans Shrops Archaeol Hist Soc*, **69**, 126–8

Wild, J P, 1970 *Textile manufacture in the northern Roman provinces*, Cambridge

Williams, D F, 1977 The Romano-British Black-burnished Industry, an essay on characterisation by heavy mineral analysis, in Peacock 1977a, 163–220

—, 1989a Amphorae, in Stead and Rigby 1989, 115–16

—, 1989b *Roman honestones and other worked stone from Wroxeter Shropshire*, Ancient Monuments Lab Rep, 88/89

Williams, D F, and Peacock, D P S, 1983 The importation of olive-oil into Roman Britain, in *Prod y Com del Aceite an la Antigüedad, II Congr* (eds J Blazquez and J Remesal), Madrid, 263–80

Wilson, B, Grigson, C, Payne, S (eds) 1982 *Ageing and sexing animal bones from archaeological sites*, BAR, **109**, Oxford

Wilson, R J A, 1983 *Piazza Armerina*, St Albans

Woodward, A, and Leach, P, 1993 *The Uley shrines, excavations of a ritual complex at West Hill, Uley, Gloucestershire 1977–9*, London

Woodward, P J, Davies, S M, Graham, A H, 1993 *Excavations at the Old Methodist Chapel and Greyhound Yard, Dorchester, 1981–1984*, Dorchester

Workshop of European Anthropologists, 1980 Recommendations for age and sex diagnoses of skeletons, *J Human Evolution*, **9**, 517–49

Wright, R P. 1960 Roman Britain in 1959, inscriptions, *J Roman Studies*, **50**, 236–42

—, 1964 Roman Britain in 1963, inscriptions, *J Roman Studies*, **54**, 177–85

—, 1966 Roman Britain in 1965, inscriptions, *J Roman Studies*, **56**, 217–25

—, 1968 Roman Britain in 1967, inscriptions, *J Roman Studies*, **58**, 206–14

Wright, T, 1859 Uriconium, *J British Archaeol Assoc*, **15**, 205–24

—, 1860a Uriconium, 3rd article, *J British Archaeol Assoc*, **16**, 158–62

—, 1860b On the recent discoveries in excavating the remains of the ancient Roman town of Uriconium, (Wroxeter) near Shrewsbury, *Proc Geological Soc West Yorks*, **4**, 102–9

—, 1867 Notes of the more recent discoveries at Wroxeter, *Archaeol Camb*, ser 3, **13**, 157–63

—, 1872 *Uriconium; an historical account of the ancient Roman city and of the excavations made upon its site at Wroxeter in Shropshire*, London

Wright, T, and Johnson, H, 1859a Report of the excavations at Wroxeter, *Archaeol Camb*, ser 3, **5**, 207–18

—, 1859b Excavations at Wroxeter, official report, no II, *Archaeol Camb*, ser 3, **5**, 257–68

Yegül, F, 1992 *Baths and bathing in classical antiquity*, Cambridge, Mass

Young, C J, 1977 *Oxfordshire Roman pottery*, Oxford

Zienkiewicz, J D, 1986 *The legionary fortress baths at Caerleon, I: the buildings, II: the finds*, Cardiff

Zwierlein-Diehl, E, 1979 *Die antiken gemmen des Kunsthistorischen Museums in Wien*, **2**, Munich

Zwierlein-Diehl, E, 1991 *Die antiken gemmen des Kunsthistorischen Museums in Wien*, **3**, Munich

Index

by Susan Vaughan